GOING TO SCHOOL IN
EAST ASIA

Recent Titles in
The Global School Room
Alan Sadovnik and Susan Semel, Series Editors

Going to School in South Asia
Amita Gupta, Editor

GOING TO SCHOOL IN EAST ASIA

EDITED BY
GERARD A. POSTIGLIONE AND
JASON TAN

The Global School Room
Alan Sadovnik and Susan Semel, Series Editors

GREENWOOD PRESS
Westport, Connecticut • London

Library of Congress Cataloging-in-Publication Data

Postiglione, Gerard A., 1951–
    Going to school in East Asia/Gerard A. Postiglione and Jason Tan.
      p. cm.—(Global school room, ISSN 1933–6101)
    Includes bibliographical references and index.
    ISBN 978–0–313–33633–1 (alk. paper)
    1. Education—East Asia. I. Tan, Jason, 1962– II. Title.
    LA1141.P67   2007
    370.95—dc22   2007008801

British Library Cataloguing in Publication Data is available.

Library of Congress Catalog Card Number: 2007008801
ISBN-10: 0–313–33633–4
ISBN-13: 978–0–313–33633–1
ISSN: 1933–6101

First published in 2007

Greenwood Press, 88 Post Road West, Westport, CT 06881
An imprint of Greenwood Publishing Group, Inc.
www.greenwood.com

Printed in the United States of America

The paper used in this book complies with the
Permanent Paper Standard issued by the National
Information Standards Organization (Z39.48–1984).

10 9 8 7 6 5 4 3 2 1

CONTENTS

SERIES FOREWORD

Over the past three decades, with globalization becoming a dominant force, the worldwide emphasis on schooling has accelerated. However, a historical perspective teaches us that global trends in schooling are by no means a recent phenomenon. The work of neo-institutional sociologists such as John Meyer and his colleagues has demonstrated that the development of mass public educational systems became a world wide trend in the 19th century and most nations' schools systems go back significantly further. *The Global School Room* series is intended to provide students with an understanding of the similarities and differences among educational systems throughout the world from a historical perspective.

Although comparative and international educational research has provided an understanding of the many similarities in school systems across nations and cultures, it has also indicated the significant differences. Schools reflect societies and their cultures and therefore there are significant differences among different nations' school systems and educational practices. Another purpose of this series is to examine these similarities and differences.

The series is organized into nine volumes, each looking at the history of the school systems in countries on one continent or subcontinent. The series consists of volumes covering schooling in the following regions:

North America
Latin America
Europe
Sub-Saharan Africa
North Africa and the Middle East
South Asia
Central Asia

East Asia
Oceania

As the second volume in the series to be published, *Going to School in East Asia* edited by Gerard A. Postiglione and Jason Tan provides an important and timely examination of the educational systems in East Asia, including those in Cambodia, China, Hong Kong, Japan, Laos, Malaysia, Singapore, South and North Korea, Thailand and Vietnam. Through the history of the educational systems in each country and an analysis of contemporary systems, the authors provide a rich description of how schooling is related to national culture, religion, identity, social, political and economic structures, and economic development. Moreover, the book illustrates the importance of historical, philosophical, and sociological perspectives in understanding the similarities and differences among societies and their schools. Finally, the book provides everyday examples of what schools in each country are like and how curriculum and teaching practices reflect the larger cultural, social, religious, and historical patterns of each society.

The authors explore the myths and realities of East Asian academic achievement within a context of globalization. They find that the reasons for high academic achievement are complex and multidimensional and that one must look at national differences as well as continental similarities to get a clearer picture. They argue that universal education has been a difficult challenge, with South Korea and Singapore close to achieving this goal, but others like Thailand and Malaysia much further from it. The chapters also provide an important examination of how differences within and between countries are related to uneven economic development within an international global system.

Going to School in East Asia is emblematic of the series in that it provides students with an understanding that schooling needs to be understood in the context of each local culture, rather than viewed ethnocentrically from a U.S. or Western perspective. We often tend to make broad generalizations about other continents and assume that culture and schooling are uniform across countries. This book demonstrates the importance of examining national systems to uncover differences, as well as similarities.

In *The Japanese Educational Challenge* (1987), Merry White argued that the purpose of studying another country's educational system is not necessarily to copy it, but rather to learn from the lessons of other societies, and where appropriate to use these lessons to improve our own schools, but only in the context of our own culture and schools. *Going to School in East Asia* provides many important lessons, but it also cautions us to understand these in the contexts of national and cultural differences. At a time when policy makers in the United States and elsewhere look to mimic East Asian education in order to improve student achievement and to remain competitive in the global economy, this book reminds us that East Asian achievement must be understood in a historical, sociological and cultural context. Additionally, it reminds us that viewing East Asian education systems as unproblematic successes misses the many challenges they face in the 21st century.

We invite you to continue to explore schooling around the world, this time in East Asia and then the rest of the world, as subsequent volumes are published.

Alan Sadovnik and Susan Semel

REFERENCE

White, M. (1987). *The Japanese Educational Challenge*. New York: The Free Press.

PREFACE: THE EAST ASIAN SCHOOL IN THE 21ST CENTURY

Gerard A. Postiglione

The march of economic globalization is making it increasingly popular within East Asia to view the success of its long-term development strategy as dependent upon its ability to become somewhat like the European Union with a free trade zone, common currency, and convertible educational credentials. It is in this sense that common cultural traditions, historical affinities, and developmental experiences become more valuable. Despite a degree of cultural, especially linguistic and religious, diversity that trumps anything found in Europe, success is viewed by many within East Asia as a function of common themes that emphasize harmony, moral cultivation, social networks, paternal leadership, and political authoritarianism. Despite the strengthening of civil societies, these traditional values resonate to varying degrees across most East Asian belief systems, including Confucianism, Buddhism, Islam, and even Christianity and Communism. East Asia's precolonial era, though certainly not without regional conflicts, is increasingly being viewed as having been a time of free trade amid long periods of harmonious interchange. Colonialism, which carved a deep impression almost everywhere, except perhaps in Thailand and Japan, subsequently affected statehood and forms of governance, as well as having left an indelible cultural marker on language and education. At the same time, colonialism also intensified the salience of cross-national difference; even while education systems laid a foundation for what would later become a relatively convergent form of standardized schooling. The postcolonial era brought with it a surge of Asian values discourse that so dominated the 1980s and 1990s, until it was tempered by the regional economic crisis, which only China seemed to escape. In the Southeast, ASEAN's formation became symbolic of a growing identity and mutual respect. In the Northeast, the powerful economies of Japan, China, and South Korea, though sharing an intimate cultural and educational heritage, found themselves in a complex relationship as they sorted through historical legacies of the 20th century. Yet, these two power centers, north and south, have intensified their educational interchange and cooperation, with China playing no small role. China's massive size, population, and meteoric rise has been accompanied by an astute leadership that emphasizes shared regional prosperity and harmony, alongside an emergent global role, even while the rise of Southeast Asia's other giant neighbor, India, begins to loom larger on the horizon.

Thus, this volume is provided with a key question about how countries use schooling to repackage cultural heritage within shifting sociocultural contexts in order that they may produce a national citizenry and at the same time maintain a common regional affinity necessary to fulfill the penultimate East Asian aspiration—that of being the major sphere of global prosperity in the second half of the 21st century. The East Asian educational model, whether myth or reality, is high on the minds of many international specialists who seek explanations for the declining ability of Western-educated students to compete with the academic high flyers from Hong Kong, Singapore, Japan, China and elsewhere in the region. Among the major drivers in this transformation are global capitalism, neo-liberalism, and corporate investment, which continue to define what constitutes human resource talent.

The rise and transformation of East Asia is unprecedented, but it is an unquestioned assumption that the driving force behind it is a unique brand of East Asian schooling. While there may be some truth in this view, the complete answer is far more complex. While emergent East Asia has a stunning educational tradition that supports much of the hype about its levels of educational achievement, there are complex questions embedded within this success. Contemporary success belongs to those societies that have successfully mounted the manufacturing challenge phase by providing a form of state run schooling anchored in traditional social–cultural values, and emphasizing basic skills and orderly behavior. However, as some countries transfer more of their manufacturing operations to more competitive developing countries with lower wages, the education discourse becomes consumed by the problem of how education must change to suit the needs of the service sector in an expanding knowledge economy. This is a formidable task because it involves major reforms in education that threaten traditional learning patterns—patterns that are viewed as having been the driving forces of success in the earlier phases of development.

There is also another more critical challenge for East Asian schools to overcome. When it comes to ensuring universal education for all, East Asia is less remarkable. For example, while South Korea and Singapore might have achieved this goal, Thailand and Malaysia have not. Indonesia and the Philippines have even further to go. For Cambodia and Laos, the target is barely in sight. Moreover, in countries like China that have nearly reached the goal, their remote regions in places like rural Guizhou and nomadic Tibet would rank near the bottom of the international scale. While many countries have increased their public expenditure on education, some like Thailand have decreased it, especially between 1999 and 2004. Most of East Asia is below the recommended 6 percent expenditure of GDP on education, including China which has hovered near 3 percent. Malaysia, with 8.5 percent of GDP going to education, towers above the rest (UNESCO, 2004).

This book differs from other volumes on East Asian education in its focus on the link between historical sociocultural contexts and contemporary schooling within the midst of economic globalization (Thomas and Postlethwaite, 1983; Tan and Mingat, 1992; Morris and Sweeting, 1995; Cummings and Altbach, 1997; Fung et al., 2000; Mok, 2006). The book combines both an introductory approach to East Asian education systems with selective in-depth analyses and discussions. It is inevitable that several countries will stand out due to their size and regional impact, as well as their level of economic development. However, we have tried to level the countries by providing the same amount of coverage to large and small countries alike. This volume also differs from others in its virtual full coverage of the region. The only country left out is Myanmar where the military regime vets publications for international publication. The tiny 28 square km casino-driven territory of Macao is also missing.

At the very least, this volume reveals the great economic and educational gaps, stunning cultural diversity, and rapidly shifting policies of state schooling across the region. The broad coverage makes clear that East Asia is far from monolithic. Economic globalization and the march of neo-liberal economics has unified educational structures but failed to produce a significant uniformity in educational processes. These remain stubbornly anchored in historical objectivities and experiences strategically resilient to outside influence. We have organized the introduction around shifting clusters of countries to illustrate the major patterns at work and the possibilities for a comparative sociology of education in East Asia that can be connected to other regions of the world through other volumes in the series.

This volume has roots. It grew from a valued collegial relationship with Alan Sadovnik that dates back about 15 years when I wrote about Hong Kong for *The Handbook of International Educational Reform*, edited by Alan and his colleagues (Cookson et al., 1992). This kicked off my link with Greenwood Press that led to publication of *Asian Higher Education* (Postiglione and Mak, 1997). Therefore, I was quick to accept Alan's invitation to edit the East Asian volume for this new series. Having taught sociology of education for a quarter century in East Asia, I felt it an opportune time to pull together cross-regional group of scholars to reflect on the socialcultural dimensions of educational change. Partway into the project I was fortunate to be joined by Jason Tan, professor of comparative education at Singapore's Nanyang Technological University. Together we worked to bring the dual perspectives of East Asia's tiny giants, Hong Kong and Singapore, to bear on the worthwhile task.

Identifying chapter authors was a formidable challenge since, for some countries, there was virtually no academic work available in English about the sociocultural dimension of their education systems. Thanks to Molly Lee of

UNESCO Bangkok, I was put in contact with several highly capable country specialists. I also remain grateful to a number of individuals at Greenwood Press for their assistance, especially Mary Ann Larcada who helped us set sail and Debra Adams who kept us afloat. Finally, Jason and I would like to express our sincere thanks to Mr. Hayes Tang for assisting us with a multitude of communications, checking, and record keeping.

REFERENCES

Cookson, Peter, Sadovnik, Alan and Semel, Susan (eds) (1992). *The International Handbook of Educational Reform*. Westport, CT: Greenwood Press.

Cummings, William K. and Altbach, Philip G. (eds) (1997). *The Challenge of East Asian Education: Implications for America*. Albany, NY: State University of New York.

Fung. Alex C.W., Pefianco, Erlinda C., and Teather, David B. (eds) (2000). "Challenges in the new millenium," *Journal of Southeast Asian Education*, 1(1). Bangkok: SEAMO.

Mok, Ka Ho (2006). *Education Reform and Education Policy in East Asia*. London: Routledge.

Morris, Paul and Sweeting, Anthony (eds) (1995). *Education and Development in East Asia*. New York: Garland Press.

Postiglione, Gerard A. and Mak, Grace C.L. (eds) (1997). *Asian Higher Education*. Westport, CT: Greenwood Press.

Tan, Jee-Peng and Mingat, Alain (1992). *Education in Asia: A Comparative Perspective of Cost and Financing*. World Bank Regional and Sectoral Studies. Washington, DC: The World Bank.

Thomas, R. Murray and Postlethwaite, Neville (eds) (1983). *Schooling in East Asia: Forces of Change*. London: Pergamon.

UNESCO (2004). UNESCO Institute for Statistics. Accessed from http://www.uis.unesco.org/profiles/EN/EDU/countryProfile_en.aspx?code=40313.

Chapter 1

CONTEXTS AND REFORMS IN EAST ASIAN EDUCATION— MAKING THE MOVE FROM PERIPHERY TO CORE

Gerard A. Postiglione and Jason Tan

There may be a good deal of truth to the well-known stereotype about East Asian education (Tu, 1996). School children in Singapore and Hong Kong nearly lead the world in mathematics and science achievement (USDOE, 1999, 2007; OECD, 2000, 2004; Ruzzi, 2005; Thao Lê and Li Shi, 2006). Those in the northeast Asian powerhouse economies of Japan and South Korea are also near the top of the international rankings, and mainland China is rising quickly. Asian students overwhelmingly populate prestigious graduate schools of science and engineering at leading American universities (Johnson, 1993; Nash, 1994; Li, 2006). In short, the school systems of China (including the Mainland, Hong Kong, and Taiwan), Japan, South Korea, and Singapore have already demonstrated the potential to challenge national school systems in other parts of the world. Malaysia and Thailand may not be far behind and fresh attention is being focused on schooling in the vast island nations of Indonesia and Philippines, as well as the transitional economies of Vietnam, Laos, and Cambodia. Though not all countries fit the East Asian stereotype, nonetheless, many are central players in a region that also includes such diverse countries as Brunei, Mongolia, Myanmar, North Korea, and the newest member of the United Nations—Timor Leste. As East Asia continues to consolidate itself within the major regional divisions of the global economy, the education systems of these countries will increase their regional cooperation and interactions (Fung et al., 2000).

Despite the stereotype, education and social development across East Asia has been highly uneven, with each country's sociocultural context contributing differentially to its academic results. Moreover, the massification of schooling has placed added pressure on schools to not only address social development needs but also to promote the capacity for innovative thinking within the volatile global environment of competitive market economies (Suárez-Orozco and

Qin-Hilliard, 2004). While the educational achievements of some nations are highly notable and may be attributed to traditional values, the lack of academic success in other countries has as much to do with the sociocultural context as with traditional values (Cummings, 2003). In each case, it is necessary to consider the way a country weathered colonialism before it strengthened statehood amid new international alliances. Even with the diverse religious and ideological orientations, and rapid sociopolitical transitions, East Asian societies, with few exceptions, are noted for executive-led government, consensus-driven management styles, and gradual but steady struggles to democratize within slowly incubating civil societies (Henders, 2004; Watson, 2004). As the chapters in this volume illustrate, perspectives on cultural values and the historical experiences with colonialism still constitute the context and core of much debate about school reform, especially as countries grapple with overlapping educational philosophies, rapid curriculum change, newly promoted learning methods, bilingual teaching demands, intensified assessment procedures, and school-based management practices (Cookson et al., 1992; Cummings, 2003). Meanwhile, macroscopic themes such as globalization, decentralization, and privatization continue to weave their way into a landscape of discourse on school reform, with results across the region that defy simple generalizations (Mok, 2004; Bjork, 2006).

How East Asian countries reconcile their historical transitions with the contemporary challenges of educational reform within rapidly changing global conditions remains a formidable area for exploration (Thomas and Postlethwaite, 1983; Tan and Mingat, 1992; Morris and Sweeting, 1995; Cummings and Altbach, 1997; Fung et al., 2000; Mok, 2006). Therefore, this volume aims to explore how sociohistorical contexts, including cultural traditions, colonial experiences, and postcolonial transformations, have shaped educational changes. At the very least, the voices in the 17 chapters that follow resist a monolithic viewpoint on education and social change in East Asia. Yet, they confirm that school policies and practices are seldom, if ever, autonomous from their sociocultural contexts. In the case of higher education, the sociocultural context is also driven by a world system in which some Asian nations, with their national flagship universities, aspire to move from periphery to core (Postiglione and Mak, 1997; Postiglione, 2006b).

It is apt to begin this introduction with East Asia's rising giant (Guthrie, 2006). Contemporary China carries the heavy burden of being the oldest continuing civilization on the planet bent on re-attaining the global status it once held (Hayhoe, 1992). As Zhou (Chapter 4) points out, China has the largest school population in the world, with educational practices that are firmly grounded in long held Confucian values. Although China's consciousness of itself as a multiethnic state has become more prominent, its most valued cultural capital is that anchored in the heritage of the majority Han Chinese (Mackerras, 1994, 1995). Its economic rise has meant more funding for education. However, the proportion of GDP for education has remained far below that in other developing countries. Meanwhile, the growing attention that accompanies its economic rise is matched by a growing global interest in its cultural traditions, including the ideal of the Chinese learner (Watkins and Biggs, 1996, 2001). China's educational values and traditional practices span the millennia and have left a deep impression on other regional systems. These not only include the Chinese societies of Hong Kong, Macao, and Taiwan but also Japan, Korea, and Vietnam. The international significance of China's educational values and practices cannot be underestimated, as testified to by the new soft power that has come with the establishment of over 100 Confucian institutes around the world (Yang, 2007).

In a world in which schooling is considered to be an *equalizer*, Chinese cling to the belief that diligent study can overcome social obstacles such as family background, religion, gender, and ethnicity. This idea can be traced back as far as Confucius, who argued that "In education, there should be no distinction of classes" (有教无类) (Legge, 1970). This formed the basis for the imperial examination system with its roots in the Song Dynasty over a thousand years ago. In a study of the Qing Dynasty, the noted historian Chang Cheng-Li (1963) pointed out that: "The examination system did indeed make possible a certain 'equality of opportunity,' but the advantages were heavily in favor of those who had wealth and influence." This view has as much relevance today as it had during the Qing era. Schooling in the socialist market economy of China has become increasingly dependent on household wealth and family income. One of the greatest challenges since the dismantling of the imperial examination system in 1905 has been to establish an education system able to reconcile the essence of Chinese culture with the ways of the outside world. Semi-colonialism left its mark on China and contributed to an ideological battle that lasted beyond the Chinese civil war. Chairman Mao Zedong saw schools as a bulwark against colonialism, capitalism, and dependency, as well as a means to ensure social equality among the masses. Despite the tumultuous years of the Cultural Revolution, China's education system came to be seen by the World Bank as a model for the developing world (Pepper, 1996). The reform and opening of China to the outside world that began in the late 1970s radically changed the direction of schooling (Postiglione and Lee, 1995). Economic reforms that made way for market forces created a larger role for schools in social stratification systems. Fee paying education became the norm and once more, private schools for the middle class families became a reality. Balooning social inequalities place more pressure on schools to provide quality schooling for all, including the children within China's 100 million ethnic minority population (Postiglione, 1999, 2006a). Schools are viewed as playing a key role in restoring China to its historical position as a leading nation, but Chinese have retained the idea that education provides fair and equal opportunity based on merit with diligence and hard work being the key determinants of success.

Small but mighty, Hong Kong has always been a part of China except for 155 years of colonial rule (Postiglione and Tang, 1997). In 1997, it became a Special Administrative Region of China with a great deal of autonomy in most spheres, including education. Hong Kong has not escaped historical traditions superimposed upon a colonial social-cultural landscape. Hong Kong moved from privately resourced schools to a public school system with management by a diverse collection of organizations, especially during the 1970s when nine-year compulsory education was made compulsory (Sweeting, 1990, 2004). Meanwhile, its postsecondary system, including a growing number of universities with high levels of institutional autonomy, correspondingly expanded and diversified. The continuities, as identified by Law (Chapter 5), are "educational developments in response to changing economic and/or sociopolitical needs; a struggle among concerns about access, efficiency, equity, quality, and catering for diverse learning needs; struggles among nongovernment actors in sponsoring and managing public schools; and the controversy of using English or Chinese as the medium of instruction." As an immigrant society under colonial rule, Hong Kong was conservative of many Chinese traditions, but added an overlay of Westernized, largely British school system features (Postiglione, 1991; Zheng et al., 2001). Law remarks on the fragility of mutual trust among education stakeholders in Hong Kong, something that might have roots in the colonial era. While Hong Kong maintains the distinction of being ranked at the top of the world in mathematics achievement, it struggles with how to maintain that status while moving toward promotion of innovative learning styles of the kind it believes can ensure its 21st century survival without natural resources and heavy manufacturing. Its close neighbor Macao, even tinier and wed to a casino-driven tourist economy, has similar baggage from its three hundred-plus-year colonial period under the Portuguese that was severed in 1999. Hong Kong and Macao are the last regions of East Asia in the 20th century to have shed the colonial title. Each was dynastic sovereign territory until foreign settlements became established. In both cases, Chinese schools continued to exist amid colonial governance. Ironically, the retrocession of territorial sovereignty led to a more determined effort to emphasize Western style school reforms, largely due to determined efforts to cultivate problem solvers and innovative thinkers to support a rising economy within the global community. To this day, Hong Kong remains in denial about its educational inequalities, even while its Gini coefficient is one of the highest in the world. Although technically not in Northeast Asia, Hong Kong is included here because it is part of China. Yet, it is a significant integrative economy of Southeast Asia, where it shares a colonial heritage with Singapore and Malaysia, something that has influenced the structure of its school system to this day, including the medium of instruction.

Taiwan continues to be affected by the unsettled cross-straits relationship with the Chinese mainland, but has a common historical tradition influenced by Confucian values. As Chou and Ho (Chapter 15) notes, these include political authoritarianism, the family, examinations, saving habits, local organization, and social networks. Within this configuration of enduring values is the belief that education involves, above all else, hard work and effort. Chinese students were expected to be diligent, persistent, and cultivated. The tumultuous development path taken by Taiwan as it moved from an authoritarian to democratic sociopolitical system of governance did ripple into the arena of school reform and can be seen in debates over many issues ranging from the medium of instruction, the interpretation of Taiwan history and identity, and the degree of managerial autonomy for schools. The policy agenda in more recent times has been deeply affected by the twin ideologies of globalization and localization. Like other East Asian societies with a Confucian heritage, Taiwan has tried to reconcile its traditional stress on examinations with new thinking about what constitutes meaningful learning. Yet, family resources continue to reinforce the school's role as a selection agency with cram school fees becoming a fixed expenditure of Taiwan families. Chou points out that gender equity in access to higher education has steadily increased, but the proportion of indigenous peoples gaining access to higher education is barely half of that within the mainstream population.

Japan continues to be the most successful economy and education system in East Asia. As early as 1905, China used Japan's school system as a model for its early development as a republic. Akira Arimoto reminds us that even before the Meiji restoration, a period associated with the establishment of a modern Japanese education system, the common people of the Tokugawa Era gave education a great deal of attention. Its temples for children's education were effective and literacy rates exceeded those in Western countries. The Meiji restoration's system of compulsory education actually confronted resistance and low enrollment rates in many rural areas. In this sense, Arimoto (Chapter 7) echoes other scholars of Japanese education that "the Tokugawa era became the foundation for modern Japanese education beyond the Meiji Restoration." Eventually, Meiji schooling became viewed as a modern selection system for upward social mobility and tilted Japan's schooling from ascription-based to achievement-based selection. Japan has become, as Arimoto calls it, a degree-o-cratic society with its accompanying educational pathology. Japan is one of the few East Asian countries not colonized, but its education system experienced a major transition from its pre to postwar periods. The postwar educational system was restructured by an education basic law with detailed provisions, for equal opportunity, including for male and female students; compulsory schooling for all; cooperation among school, family, and the community; education for nation-building; religious education; and responsibilities for national and local governments. Japan has demonstrated an uncanny talent for borrowing and adapting knowledge. Centuries of interactions with neighbors, including China and Korea, show a fundamental pattern of placing a high value on mastering and adapting foreign knowledge and techniques. The parts of this process include imitation, examination, criticism, and innovation. The optimism in Japan is wed to the challenges of mastering this process of which education is a part. Looking ahead, there is a renewed emphasis in schools for building patriotism.

Like Japan, Korea has long ago been highly influenced by its neighboring lands (Fairbank et al., 1989). The cultural influence of China's Tang Dynasty remains evident in language and culture. In a different sense, the colonial period of

Japanese occupation is also not easily forgotten or forgiven. Globalization has brought South Korea closer to its traditional neighbors while the North Korean regime remains a question mark, despite some signs of a reform orientation after many years of isolation. After 35 years of Japanese colonial rule, Korea had to dig itself out of the devastation of the Korean War at mid-century that split it in two and resulted in two divergent paths of development that continue to the present. The South Korean peninsula placed its national focus on universal education to overcome mass illiteracy, lasting into the 1970s, after which it moved rapidly into expansion of secondary education to meet the human resource needs of its rapidly developing economy. Amid periodic political turmoil, the public demand for greater education opportunities, including in higher education, led to an expansion that made South Korea virtually the first universal system of higher education in East Asia. Choi (Chapter 14) notes Koreans' positive outlook and unwavering faith in academic credentials. Since the turn of the century, South Korea has been riveted on the educational challenges of the global economy. Korean education is most impressive at the primary and secondary level and least at the tertiary level. South Korea has achieved an extraordinary transformation to become one of the most highly schooled countries in the world. Its elementary and secondary students score high in mathematics and science on international tests and the gender gap has narrowed. Teachers are generally well trained and indicators like dropout rates and school violence are relatively low. University education is subject to extreme competition and low quality. Efforts, including intensive internationalization, are under way in an effort to build world-class universities. An obsession with education created rapid expansion and contributed to both national development and social problems. The linking of educational credentials to the traditional values of Confucian scholars limited the attraction of vocational–technical education. Intense pressure for educational attainment created a competitive entrance examination system. The result was enormous pressure on students and a financial burden on families, as well as a stifled reform effort to promote innovative education. Those unhappy with the system found alternatives in the expanding study-abroad trend. This further intensified social stratification with English-speaking Koreans in an advantaged position.

Meanwhile North Korea continues to inch forward at a snail's pace in educational reform. However, the passion for education in the North is no less intense. With an ideology of self-reliance and self-identity, communism remains a determinate force. Three quarters of the way through the 20th century, the North had achieved universal basic education. Nevertheless, social background played a large part in determining opportunity. Party members and urban residents retain a distinct advantage over others. As Reed and Kim (Chapter 11) makes clear, the striking feature of education in the Democratic People's Republic of Korea (DPRK) is its isolation within a political system virtually bereft of international interface. Most of the economy remains state run, as are schools. However, Reed believes the DPRK is gradually emerging from its isolation with possibly profound implications for education. While globalization is opposed, computer literacy and information technology are heavily promoted, along with foreign language instruction. Without the Soviet Union as the main trusted partner, past practices learned from them are disappearing. Educational differentiation is more apparent. Advanced middle school is a kind of key or magnet school. UNESCO developed a plan with the DPRK ministry that set out goals for all levels of education with a focus on infrastructure and teacher training. As Reed concludes, "Education in North Korea has been remarkably successful in addressing the basic literacy needs of the people. However, the educational system clearly reflects the inflexibility of the political system that it serves."

Mongolia's position in Northeast Asia contrasts sharply with that of North Korea. Though ruled by the communist party for many decades, it is far more reformist than North Korea. The breakup of the Soviet Union affected Mongolia more than North Korea, especially for the school system. Unlike the Koreans who borrowed heavily from China's Tang Dynasty, the Mongols ruled China during the Yuan Dynasty. When Genghis Khan conquered the known world, including Korea, about 800 years ago, he was illiterate. Yet, the record keeping necessitated by his conquests did convince him of the value of education. When Kublai Khan conquered China and established the Yuan Dynasty, he took significant measures to support education, something which also aided Mongol governance of China. Mongol adoption of Tibetan Buddhism lasted through the end of the Yuan dynasty and into its colonization by China's last imperial dynasty. By the start of the 20th century, Mongolia had thousands of monastery schools. When it gained its independence in 1921, virtually all schools were attached to monasteries. As the Soviet influence increased, monasteries eventually became to be viewed as destabilizing and a Soviet-sponsored school system became institutionalized. By the time the Soviet influence waned in 1989, Mongolians were strapped with a Cyrillic alphabet. Efforts to bring back Mongolian script with the help of China which had retained it in Inner Mongolia, were unsuccessful. While the ex-Soviet republics tried various approaches to decentralization of education, Mongolia turned out to be the most successful. Beginning in the 1990s, a series of international development agencies began a series of education projects in Mongolia and donor support remains strong. The focus has turned to sustaining reform and improving school quality and access. As John C. Weidman, Regsuren Bat-Erdene and Erika Bat-Erdene (Chapter 10) note: "The foundation is strong but much remains to be done."

These northeastern members of the East Asia community of school systems have generally been heavily influenced by China at some point in their history. However, the countries of Southeast Asia differ in this respect. With the exception of Vietnam where Confucianism took hold as early as the 10th century, the rest of the region was only close to China through trade. Unparalleled diversity has made it virtually impossible to offer a concise overview of Southeast Asian education. However, economic globalization may be changing that to some degree. Across the region, long entrenched but differing cultural traditions interweave with colonial heritage, multiethnic and religious states, liberal democratic tendencies and socialist regimes in transition (Brown, 1994; SarDesai, 1994;

McCloud, 1995). Nevertheless, there are some pronounced patterns across systems. Beginning with national roots and colonial experiences, the education systems in Singapore and Hong Kong, share an affinity with Chinese intellectual values and, with Malaysia, also share a British colonial heritage. Yet, all have taken on more standardized aspects of global education systems as they aspire to be internationally competitive. While education in Vietnam shares a Chinese heritage with Hong Kong and Singapore, it also has its own indigenous tradition with an overlay of colonial French and Soviet-Russian themes. Indonesia completely shed Dutch colonial influence, where Islam has remained a salient factor in development. Thailand was never colonized, though the debates about future direction wrestle with the issue of globalization and how to emphasize local wisdom in education. The Christian influence on Philippine education remains a salient historical theme as is its American colonial heritage. Meanwhile, Southeast Asian education can hardly escape the increasing effect of its neighboring giants, China and India.

In Vietnam, postcolonial educational expansion has been repeated (Pham, 1988). A state socialist welfare regime developed from the 1940s and 1950s in northern Vietnam, and later on a national basis after the reunification of the entire country in 1975 (Dang, 1997). London (Chapter 18) points out how Vietnam's Communist Party promoted mass education as a basic right of citizenship, and centralized educational governance. Despite these measures, inequalities continued to exist in terms of provision at the regional level, in terms of scope and quality, and access across different population segments. In reality, the provision of social services privileged the political elite and urban-based state-sector workers over all others. While the gradual collapse of the planned economy and the transition to a market economy that began in the 1980s has meant greater investments in mass education and improvements in education access, new inequalities in enrollment and financing have emerged as a result of the unequal distribution of the fruits of economic expansion. Clear differences have emerged between the principles and institutions of the state socialist and Marxist Leninist regimes in terms of education finance. A greater proportion of the burden of education finance has been shifted from the state onto households. This increased household responsibility has in turn fuelled the development and reproduction of inequalities of access to upper secondary education.

The Philippines is atypical of Southeast Asian nations in having a Spanish and American colonial past, in addition to being the only Asian nation with a Roman Catholic majority. Spanish colonization over the course of 333 years left a lasting legacy of religious education and the foundations of higher education. Various religious orders such as the Augustinians, the Franciscans, the Jesuits, and the Dominicans established parish schools to teach Christian doctrine. The Spanish period also saw the establishment of a few colleges such as the Colegio de Santo Tomas, later to become the University of Santo Tomas. The beginnings of a national public school system were inaugurated by the passing of a royal decree in 1863. By the end of the 19th century, the Philippines had a higher literacy level than some European nations. The Americans, who ruled for almost 50 years, further entrenched a national public school system with the passing of the Education Act of 1901. The first quarter of the 20th century completed the template that contemporary Philippine education continues to follow. Another key legacy was the use of the English language as a medium of instruction in a multilingual country that lacked a lingua franca at the time. Despite several attempts over the 1990s to institute reforms such as decentralization of education governance, and improving efficiency and equity of education services, implementation has been patchy. Torralba, Dumol and Manzon (Chapter 12) attribute the patchiness to a lack of political will, political instability, excessive political interference by various parties, and economic constraints.

Singapore presents an interesting case of a city-state with a government that firmly believes in keeping a tight rein on the national education system. The first two postindependence decades were spent centralizing authority over a hitherto disparate set of parallel systems operating in different language media under British colonial rule. Various measures taken included standardizing such aspects as subject curricula, national examinations, teacher qualifications, and eventually making the English language the primary medium of instruction in all schools. The focus began shifting in the mid-1980s toward encouraging more diversity in educational pathways and curricula. These measures included the introduction of independent schools and autonomous schools. Nevertheless, as Tan (Chapter 13) notes, the strong hand of the state remained in order to steer the education system in the direction of supporting national economic development plans and fostering social cohesion (Tan, 2004). From the mid-1990s a series of large-scale educational reforms such as *Thinking Schools, Learning Nation* and *National Education* were launched to meet the perceived needs of the knowledge economy while at the same time fostering social cohesion in a culturally diverse society. There is currently official recognition and support for fundamental changes in teaching and learning. However, the success of undertaking such changes in schools that have been largely driven by traditional notions of examination success remains patchy.

Like Singapore, Malaysia was colonized by Great Britain before gaining political independence. The two countries share a common dilemma of how to integrate an ethnically, linguistically, religiously and culturally diverse populace. Their approaches to this dilemma have diverged considerably over the past four decades. Following ethnic clashes in 1969, the Malaysian government introduced affirmative action policies in employment and education to redress the socioeconomic disparities between the native bumiputera majority and the non-bumiputera ethnic minorities. For instance, bumiputeras received, and continue to receive, preferential treatment in scholarship awards and entry to higher education. In addition, the Malay language was institutionalized as the predominant medium of instruction in national schools. In his chapter, Loo (Chapter 9) points out that although Malaysia has made advances in providing universal access to education, the policy of affirmative action remains highly emotive and controversial. There are allegations that the policy has proved ethnically divisive, and has downplayed individual merit in favor of ethnic affiliation. Furthermore, the national school system has failed as an instrument of national integration. The majority of ethnic Chinese, who constitute about a quarter of the total population, enroll their children in Chinese-medium primary schools, while the vast majority of bumiputera children are enrolled in the national schools. In recent years, the English language has been reinstated as the medium of instruction for mathematics and science in order to boost national economic competitiveness.

Another Southeast Asian country with a British colonial past is Brunei, a tiny oil-rich Malay-Islamic monarchy. Prior to the attainment of full political sovereignty in 1984, there were essentially three parallel education systems: a secular government system, an Islamic system, and a system of Arabic schools. These schools continue to exist currently, in addition to independent schools. Like Singapore, Brunei's government continues to retain British colonial influence in the form of the General Certificate of Education Ordinary and Advanced Level examinations. Tight government control comes in the form of the Melayu Islam Beraja (Malay Islamic Monarchy) national ideology, which is perpetuated through the schools. Upex (Chapter 2) points out several major problems facing Brunei's economy, such as an overdependence on petroleum industry, a bloated public sector, and a mismatch between educational qualifications and labor market needs. The generous welfare system (locally nicknamed Shellfare) is beginning to show cracks due to rapid population increases and internal spending problems. The chapter points out a key dilemma facing Brunei education: reconciling the need to modernize and prepare a skilled knowledge-able workforce with the current emphasis on feudalism and institutionalized religion. Other urgent areas of need include changing the top-down management approach, improving teacher professionalism and morale, and changing the examination-oriented mode of teaching and learning.

Indonesia, like Brunei, has a majority Muslim population. In fact, it has the world's largest Muslim population, even while remaining an officially secular state. Dutch colonialism maintained a centralized and elitist schooling system, with limited opportunities for the poor, rural, or non-European populations. Independence in 1945 brought about a determination to maintain centralized governance in order to hold together a large culturally diverse population spread over 6,000 islands. The government under President Sukarno faced the onerous task of overcoming a massive illiteracy problem while lacking any lingua franca for effective communication. Also lacking were financial resources, physical infrastructure, and trained teachers. Christano and Cummings (Chapter 6) explain that the primary task facing schools was to foster a uniquely Indonesian identity through the use of a common lingua franca, Bahasa Indonesia, and the propagation of the national ideology *Pancasila*. Sukarno's successor, Suharto, continued the policy of having education serve a key nation-building function. The first major step toward loosening tight centralized control of schools nationwide came with the promulgation of regulations in 1994 authorizing local governments to incorporate local content in the official curriculum. The fall of President Suharto in 1998 and his replacement by Habibie initiated one of the most sweeping reforms in Indonesia's history, namely, transforming the country into a decentralized state. This policy thrust was extended to education as well, with the central government's role being restricted to establishing national education policies and defining guidelines for minimum education standards. Individual districts began shifting toward a school-based management system that allowed local schools greater management autonomy.

Timor Leste, the newest nation in Southeast Asia, has had a turbulent political history for the past few decades. This includes 24 years of Indonesian occupation after the withdrawal of the Portuguese colonial government in 1974, and the subsequent violence leading to the eventual withdrawal of Indonesian forces. Under the Portuguese, education provision was conducted in Portuguese mainly in Catholic schools. In addition, the education of women was minimal. Berlie (Chapter 17) asserts that education has been a traditionally neglected sector, and hence the new post-Indonesian government faces an uphill task in reconstructing the schooling system and building teacher capacity. Besides widespread illiteracy, policymakers face the arduous task of choosing a politically acceptable medium of instruction from among Portuguese, English, Bahasa Indonesia, and various indigenous languages. Many Timorese teachers at the primary level have only a senior secondary education, and the situation is worse in rural and remote areas. Despite the best efforts of the government, with the assistance of various international organizations such as the World Bank, UNICEF, and UNESCO, the massive infrastructural and financial issues facing education in Timor Leste persist.

Like Timor Leste, Cambodia shares a recent turbulent political past and is a country engaged in the task of national reconciliation and reconstruction. French colonization began in 1863 and was marked by the introduction of a modern secular education system that served to produce male French-speaking civil servants for the colonial administration. In the 20th century, the colonial government modernized the traditional *wat* schools and expanded educational access outside the urban areas. A Franco-Cambodian education system operated on a 3+3+4 model with French as the medium of instruction. However, no university existed during this period. Furthermore, because monks teaching in traditional *wat* schools were not supposed to have contact with female students, girls' participation in modern education was limited. After the end of French colonialism in 1953, the incoming government began expanding enrollments, but all these gains were almost completely lost after 1970 during the period of the Khmer Republic under Lon Nol, the devastating Khmer Rouge rule from 1975 to 1979, and the Vietnamese occupation in the 1980s. In particular, the Khmer Rouge regarded education of the prewar period as being totally irrelevant to individual or national needs, and viewed educated people such as students, teachers, and professors as dangerous and untrustworthy. Many school buildings were destroyed and many educated Cambodians were killed. Since the 1980s, the task of reconstruction has been proceeding, in large part due to the largesse of development assistance agencies. Educational enrollments have increased at primary, secondary, and higher education levels. In this respect, Sopheak and Clayton (Chapter 3) give particular attention to the education of girls and use this as a prism with which to see the historical transformation of schooling in Cambodia.

Laos shares a French colonial heritage with Cambodia and Vietnam.The French colonial authorities preserved the traditional *wat* schools, which they viewed as a means of preserving traditional religion and culture. Lessons in secular schools were conducted mainly in French. Similar to these two other former French colonies, the various postindependence governments began expanding educational access. The Royal Lao government announced in 1951 that primary education would be compulsory and would be conducted in the Lao language, while secondary education would continue in French. However, secondary enrollments continued to be rather limited. Schooling under the Pathet Lao from the mid-1950s was focused on Marxist-Leninist revolutionary propaganda, and on socializing the non-Lao ethnic minorities into good socialists. The advent of the Lao People's Democratic Republic in 1975 meant that education was to play a major socializing role for national integration and nationalism in a socialist country. Educational access improved tremendously, especially in rural areas. However, educational quality remained rather low, mainly because of a lack of textbooks and skilled teachers. The introduction of the New Economic Mechanism in 1985 meant the reorientation of the education system toward meeting the needs of the free labor market, even while attempting to produce loyal revolutionary socialist citizens. Manynooch Faming (Chapter 8) shows that particular attention was paid to the schooling of non-Lao ethnic minorities in order to integrate and "civilize" them.

Thailand presents an interesting case of a country that has never been formally colonized. In traditional Thai society, centers of learning were houses, temples and the palace rather than schools. Houses prepared children with practical work-oriented skills, temples focused on moral education and ethics, while the palace provided education in governmental ethics. Nevertheless, European ideals of schooling began permeating Thai society in the last quarter of the 19th century, with the formal establishment of the first royal school in 1871 and the first public school in 1884. Over the course of 60 years, schools were established all over the country and a supervisory system put in place to oversee the expansion of schooling. The introduction of democratic institutions in 1932 led to greater attention being paid to equal educational opportunities and expansion of enrollments. Compulsory education was expanded to seven years after World War II, and women's educational opportunities improved. However, as Paitoon Sinlarat (Chapter 16) explains, schooling was largely conducted along the lines of a "one-size-fits-all" model and became increasingly irrelevant to individual and economic needs. The 1999 National Education Act attempted to encourage greater decentralization of management and to promote the idea that learning could take place not only in schools, but also in alternative venues such as homes, community bodies, and other social institutions.

EXPLANATORY FRAMEWORKS AND THE CONTINUED RELEVANCE OF CORE–PERIPHERY

How much is hegemony and how much is self-determination in East Asian education? Is center–periphery still relevant to the analysis of its education systems? (Amos et al., 2002). This is especially apparent in higher education with the quest for world-class universities by China, Korea, and Japan. East Asian higher education systems are closely tied to global markets and follow what sometimes appears to be a dependent pattern of adaptations driven by Western developed economies (Altbach, 1981, 1997, 2004; Altbach and Selvaratnam, 1989; Altbach and Umakoshi, 2004). Yet, there is also a significant amount of resistance. As East Asian countries adapt to ways that help embed economic globalization within their national landscape, the manner in which the adaptation occurs is more selective, open, and democratic than before. Moreover, while global communication with core (center) university systems has been more open and transparent, the system is closed to direct intervention from the outside, making hegemony a less plausible explanation for the manner in which the system is reacting within the new global environment of financial interdependency (Chapman and Austin, 2002).

One does not have to travel far in the region to hear calls to build world-class universities coming from vice-chancellors, ministries of education, and national leaders. Japan, South Korea, and China are particularly prominent in this respect (Min, 2003; Rosen, 2004; Park, 2005). These three countries' national flagship universities are reaching for the gold standard, and the Southeast Asian university systems cannot escape the implications for their own development. As a block, East Asia may be pivotal to the global shift in the center–periphery equation. The region has some of the fastest growing economies in the world with certain linguistic attributes that set it apart.

While the discourse of center and periphery is still relevant to the analysis of university systems, the analytical frameworks from which it has arisen may or may not be. Theories of globalization have done little so far except to provide a thematic framework for the rapid and interdependent changes that increasingly characterize social life. Efforts to analyze the theoretical underpinnings of globalization inevitably return to the well of world-systems theory, neo-Marxism, and institutionalism, where there is also evidence of eclectically combined theoretical elements that derive from one or more of these. Although not theories of globalization, they address transnational structuring. Taken together, world-systems theory and neo-institutionalism help point us in the direction of an answer to the central question about East Asian education: How much is hegemony and how much is self-determination?

With China's rise from the status of a poor developing country to an economy which causes global reverberations, dependency theory seems less relevant than it did in the past. New circumstances and geopolitical realities give the impression that these perspectives are obsolete. While colonialism and dependency have shaped the past, the present appears to be less affected by them, though these ideologies still lurk in the background as shadows of the past and cautions for the future. China, Japan, and South Korea on their own, and the Southeast Asian countries united under the Association of Southeast Asian Nations (ASEAN), have become more emergent in the global knowledge production system and international economic power structure. While the global center has moved toward the United States since the collapse of the bipolar world, a discourse on empire has gained attention, with growing global criticism of foreign interventions and apprehension about what agencies such as the World Bank and International Monetary Fund have done with global inequality.

What kinds of framework can be used to provide explanations of global processes in education, especially higher education, and to make them more congruent with what is actually happening, not only in Northeast Asia but also Southeast Asia, a geographical cluster of countries with smaller populations, diverse cultures, and more island-based and peninsular economies, and which have developed more slowly than their Northeast Asian neighbors? China's own experience in the periphery has made it a flag bearer at times for developing countries, even though its own position in the center–periphery system has clearly changed. Meanwhile, Japan has worked to take on the role of a regional development agency and, by doing so, hopes to distance itself from its widely remembered historical aspirations from the first half of the previous century. South Korea has attained mass higher education faster than any country in the world. With the predominance of center–periphery approaches and their hegemony in discourse and policy, it is imperative to refocus on their explanatory value, especially in light of the changes in global development. Market liberalization has been epitomized in Asia as a contemporary form of civilization that it must catch up with in order to survive. Its switch from opponent to reluctant or willing supporter has had much to do with the end of the Cold War, continued pressure on regimes to deliver on domestic development promises, and the success in the 1980s of the four Asian Tigers (Singapore, Taiwan, Hong Kong, and South Korea). The enforcement of catch-up strategies in higher education enhances our understanding of the new international system, with burgeoning student populations, knowledge-economy discourse, reforms in governance, border-crossing academic programs, overseas study patterns, and new trade in educational services. Proper analysis of the international relations of higher education economies and human capital systems requires grounding in external realities that determine overarching domestic processes of state power and economic reproduction. In general, then, it appears that center–periphery explanations may lose some explanatory value, as part of the process of global transition.

Without a focus on social stratification and educational inequality within East Asian countries, new explanatory frameworks would be severely constrained (Kerchkoff, 2001; Meyer, 2001). New forms of growing inequalities on both domestic and international levels that are being reproduced through compulsory education and the massification of higher education remain the major challenge for any new framework of analysis. However, new economic power in Asia and its deepening global economic integration raise new questions.

There is an increasing need to come to terms with the resilience of poverty and how it finds its way into education in the form of a plurality of reasons for student dropout patterns: economic, informational, social, and cultural handicaps that hamper adjustment to modern learning environments. The major indicator of this phenomenon in East Asia is the new privatization that reaches beyond traditional domestic formats and places profit alongside education. However, the grossly abused privatization discourse does not necessarily entail a move beyond the center–periphery platforms associated with promises of national progress. This is actually part of an international process that pulls East Asian education back into a position that keeps center–periphery platforms relevant. In short, private education has the potential to be part of an exploitative relationship in which core nations are collaborators. Even while the discourse in Asia calls for rejection of selected Western value positions, it has been slower at developing newer analytical categories for schooling-state development experience.

Alternative strategies of development infer rival analytical categories which one can use to frame how the new wealth/elite classes in East Asian capitalist countries maintain state regimes. Thus, any new understanding of relations between states and markets in East Asian education can be realized only through the study of alternative strategies of market capitalist development (ASIHL, 1998, Dumlao-Valisno, 2001; Varghese, 2001). Studies of existing paradigms of dependency, neo-colonialism, and postmodernism are bound to be limiting in certain respects, especially when they focus on the structure of schooling as an incontrovertible and fundamental expression of the essence of national development.

There is a methodological imperative to approach the study of schooling as part of an historical process whose dynamics are internal to it. In the coming decades, East Asia will continue along the path of massification in basic, senior secondary, and tertiary education and its top universities will become more influential both within the national scene and as a symbol of their nations' unique intellectual contribution to the global knowledge economy. In this sense, they are already pushing the limits of the center–periphery equation. But they are not there yet. Much could happen in the coming years to determine whether or not East Asian education will break loose of the limits of core–periphery frameworks.

REFERENCES

Altbach, P.G. (1981). "The university as center and periphery," *Teachers College Record*, 82(4): 601–621.

——(1997). *Comparative Higher Education: Knowledge, the University, and Development.* Boston: Center for International Higher Education.

——(2004). *Asian Universities: Historical Perspectives and Contemporary Challenges.* Baltimore, MD: Johns Hopkins University Press.

Altbach, P.G. and Selvaratnam, V. (1989). *From Dependence to Autonomy: The Development of Asian Universities.* Amsterdam: Kluwer Academic Publishers.

Altbach, P.G. and Umakoshi, Toru (2004). *Asian Universities: Historical perspectives and Contemporary Challenges.* Baltimore, MD: Johns Hopkins University Press.

Amos, K., Keiner, E., Proske, M., and Olaf-Radtke, F. (2002). "Globalisation: Autonomy of education under siege? Shifting boundaries between politics, economy and education," *European Educational Research Journal*, 1(2): 193–213.

ASIHL (Association for Southeast Asian Institutions of Higher Learning) (1998). New Trends in Higher Education: Market Mechanisms in Higher Education Toward the 21st Century. Proceedings, Universitas Indonesia. Jakarta, 22–23, July.

Bjork, Christopher (2006). *Educational Decentralization: Asian Experiences and Conceptual Contributions.* Netherlands: Springer Press.

Brown, David (1994). *The State and Ethnic Politics in Southeast Asia.* London: Routledge and Kegan Paul.

Chang Cheng-Li (1963). "Merit and money," in Johanna M. Menzel (ed.), *The Chinese Civil Service: Careers Open to Talent*, pp. 22–27. Boston, MA: D.C. Heath Co.

Chapman, D. and Austin, A. (eds.) (2002). *Higher Education in the Developing World: Changing Contexts and Institutional Responses.* Westport, CT: Greenwood Press.

Cookson, Peter, Sadovnik, Alan, and Semel, Susan (1992). *The International Handbook of Educational Reform.* Westport, CT: Greenwood Press.

Cummings, William, K. (2003). *The Institutions of Education: A Comparative Study of Education Development in the Six Core Nations.* Oxford: Symposium Books.

Cummings, William, K. and Altbach, Philip, G. (1997). *The Challenge of East Asian Education: Implications for America.* Albany, NY: State University of New York.

Dang, Ba Lam (1997). "Vietnam," in G. Postiglione (ed.), *Asian Higher Education*, pp. 359–372. Westport, CT: Greenwood Press.

Dumlao-Valisno, Mona (2001). "A note on the economic crisis and higher education in the Philippines," in *Impact of the Economic Crisis on Higher Education in East Asia*, pp. 147–155. Paris: UNESCO (IIEP).

Fairbank, John K., Reischauer, Edwin O., and Craig, Albert, M. (1989). *East Asia: Traditions and Transformations.* Boston, MA: Houghton Mifflin.

Fung, Alex, C.W., Pefianco, Erlinda, C., and Teather, David, B. (2000). "Challenges in the New Millenium," *Journal of Southeast Asian Education*, 1(1). Bangkok: SEAMO.

Guthrie, Doug (2006). *China and Globalization: The Social, Economic and Political Transformation of Chinese Society.* New York: Routledge.

Hayhoe, Ruth (1992). *Education and Modernization: The Chinese Experience.* New York: Pergammon Press.

Henders, Susan J. (ed.) (2004). *Democratization and Identity: Regimes and Ethnicity in East and Southeast Asia.* Lanham, MD: Lexington Press.

Johnson, J.M. (1993). *Human Resources for Science and Technology: The Asian Region* (*Surveys of Science Resources Series, Special Report, NSF 93–303*). Washington, DC: National Science Foundation.

Kerckhoff, Alan (2001). "Educational stratification in comparative perspective," *Sociology of Education*, Extra Issue. Sociology at the Dawn of the 21st Century, 3–18.

Komolmas, Prathip, M. (1998). "Thailand: New trends in higher education toward the 21st century," in *New Trends in Higher Education: Market Mechanisms in Higher Education Toward the 21st Century*, pp. 111–125. Jakarta: The Association of Southeast Asian Institutions of Higher Education.

Lê, Thao and Shi, Li (2006). *Chinese-background Students' Learning Approaches*, AARE, Adelaide November, 27. Accessed on April 20, 2007 from http://www.aare.edu.au/06pap/le06370.pdf.

Legge, James (Translated) (1970). *The Four Books; Confucian Analects*, Chapter XXXVIII, p. 357. Taipei: Culture Book Company.

Li, Cheng (ed.) (2005). *Bridging Minds across the Pacific: U.S.–China Educational Exchanges, 1978–2003*. New York: Lexington Books.

Li, Mei (2006) "Beyond push and pull factors: An economic and sociological analysis on mainland Chinese students'outflow to Hong Kong and Macau for higher education." Doctoral dissertation, The University of Hong Kong.

Mackerras, Colin (1994). *China's Minorities: Integration and Modernization in the 20th Century*. Hong Kong: Oxford University Press.

——(1995). *China's Minority Cultures: Identities and Integration Since 1912*. New York: Longman and St. Martin's Press.

McCloud, Donald, G. (1995). *Southeast Asia: Tradition and Modernity in the Contemporary World*. Boulder, CO: Westview.

Meyer, John (2001). "Reflections: The worldwide commitment to educational equality," *Sociology of Education*, Extra Issue. Sociology at the Dawn of the 21st Century, 154–158.

Min, Weifang (2004). "Chinese higher education: The legacy of the past and the context of the future," in Philip G. Altbach (ed.), *Asian Universities: Historical Perspectives and Contemporary Challenges*, pp. 53–83. Baltimore, MD: Johns Hopkins Press.

Mok, Ka Ho (ed.) (2004). *Centralization and Decentralization: Educational Reform and Changing Governance Chinese Societies*. Hong Kong: Comparative Education Research Center and Kluwer Press.

——(2006). *Education Reform and Education Policy in East Asia*. London: Routledge.

Morris, Paul and Sweeting, Anthony (eds.) (1995). *Education and Development in East Asia*. New York: Garland Press.

Nash, M.J. (1994). "Tigers in the lab: Asian-born, U.S.-trained researchers are headed home to challenge the technological supremacy of the West," *Time* (International Edition), November 21, pp. 48–49.

OECD (2000). Knowledge and Skills for Life: First Results from the Organization for Economic Cooperation and Development (OECD), Programme for International Student Assessment (PISA), 2000. OECD Publications, 2, rue Andre-Pascal, 75775 Paris Cedex 16, France. Accessed on January 12, 2007 from http://www.SourceOECD.org.

OECD (2004). Learning for Tomorrow's World—First Results from PISA (Programme for International Student Assessment), 2003, Accessed on January 12, 2007 from http://www.oecd.org/document/55/0,2340,en_32252351_32236173_33917303_1_1_1_1,00.html.

Park, Kyung-Jae (2005). "Policies and strategies to meet the challenges of Internationalization of Higher Education," Paper read at the Third Regional Follow-up Committee for the 1998 World Conference on Higher Education in Asia and the Pacific, Seoul, Korea, July 5, 2005.

Pepper, Suzanne (1996). *Radicalism and Educational Reform in 20th Century China: The Search for an Ideal Development Model.* New York: Cambridge University Press.

Pham, Minh Hac (1988). *Vietnam's Education: The Current Position and Future Prospects.* Hanoi: Gioi Publishers.

Postiglione, Gerard A. (ed.) (1991). *Education and Society in Hong Kong: Toward One Country and Two Systems.* New York: M.E. Sharpe.

——(1999). *China's National Minority Education: Culture, Schooling and Development.* New York: Falmer Press.

——(2005). "Higher education in China: Perils and promises for a new century," in *Harvard China Review*, Spring: 138–143.

——(2006a). *Education and Social Change in China: Inequality in a Market Economy.* New York: M.E. Sharpe.

——(2006b). "Finance and governance in Southeast Asian higher education," in Joaquin Tnes and Francisco Lopez-Segrera (eds), *Higher Education in the World, 2006: The Financing of Universities*, pp. 187–192. New York: Palgrave.

Postiglione, Gerard A. and Lee Wing On (1995). *Social Change and Educational Development: Mainland China, Taiwan and Hong Kong.* Hong Kong: Center of Asian Studies.

Postiglione, Gerard A. and Mak, G.C.L. (1997). *Asian Higher Education.* Westport, CT: Greenwood Press.

Postiglione, Gerard A. and Tang, J.T.H. (eds) (1997). *Hong Kong's Reunion with China: The Global Dimensions.* New York: M.E. Sharpe.

Rosen, Stanley (2004). Beida Reforms, a special issue of the journal *Chinese Education and Society*, 37(6), November–December, New York: M.E. Sharpe.

Ruzzi, Betsy Brown (2005). *International Education Tests: An Overview, New Commission on the Skills for the American Work Force*, National Center on Education and Economy (April). Accessed on January 22, 2007 from http://www.skillscommission.org/pdf/Staff%20Papers/International%20Tests.pdf.

SarDesai, D.R. (1994). *Southeast Asia: Past and Present*, 3rd edn. Boulder, CO: Westview Press.

Sinlarat, P. (2004). "Thai universities: Past, present, and future," in P.G. Altbach (ed.), *Asian Universities: Historical Perspectives and Contemporary Challenges*, pp. 201–220. Baltimore, MD: Johns Hopkins University Press.

Suárez-Orozco, Marcelo, M. and Qin-Hilliard, Desirée Baolian (eds) (2004). *Globalization: Culture and Education in the New Millennium.* Berkeley, CA: University of California Press.

Sweeting, A.E. (1990). *Education in Hong Kong: Pre 1841 to 1941.* Hong Kong: Hong Kong University Press.

——(2004). *Education in Hong Kong: 1941–2001.* Hong Kong: Hong Kong University Press.

Tan, J. (2004). "Singapore: Small nation, big plans," in P.G. Altbach (ed.), *Asian Universities: Historical Perspectives and Contemporary Challenges*, pp. 175–200. Baltimore, MD: Johns Hopkins University Press.

Tan, Jee-Peng and Mingat, Alain (1992). *Education in Asia: A Comparative Study of Cost and Financing*. Washington, DC: The World Bank.

Thomas, R. Murray and Postlethwaite, Neville (eds) (1983). *Schooling in East Asia: Forces of Change*. London: Pergamon.

Tu, Wei-Ming (ed.) (1996). *Confucian Traditions in East Asian Modernity: Moral Education and Economic Culture in Japan and the Four Mini-Dragons*. Cambridge, MA: Harvard University Press.

UNESCO (2004). UNESCO Institute for Statistics. Accessed on January 12, 2007 from http://www.uis.unesco.org/profiles/EN/EDU/countryProfile_en.aspx?code= 40313.

USDOE (1999). "Highlghts from TIMMS, overview and key findings across grade levels," *The Third International Mathematics and Science Study*, National Center for Education Statistics, Office of Educational Research and Improvement, U.S. Department of Education, NCES 1999-081. Accessed on February 4, 2007 from http://nces.ed.gov/pubs99/1999081.pdf.

——(2007). *International Comparisons in Education: Trends in International Mathematics and Science Study*. Washington, DC: National Center for Education Science, National Center for Educational Statistics, U.S. Department of Education.

Varghese, N.V. (2001). *Impact of the Economic Crisis on Higher Education in East Asia*. Paris: UNESCO (IIEP).

Watkins, David A. and Biggs, John B. (eds) (1996). *The Chinese Learner: Cultural, Psychological and Contextual Influences*. Hong Kong: Hong Kong University Press.

——(2001). *Teaching the Chinese Learner: Psychological and Pedagogical Perspectives*. Hong Kong: Hong Kong University Press.

Watson, James (2004). "Globalization in Asia: Anthropological perspectives," in Marcelo Suárez-Orozco and Desirée Baolian Qin-Hilliard, (eds.), *Globalization: Culture and Education in the New Millennium*, pp. 141–172. Berkeley, CA: University of California Press.

Yang, Rui (2007). "China's soft power projection in higher education," *International Higher Education* (46): 24.

Zhang, Victor, Law Kwok-keung and Wong Siu-lun (2001). "The Crisis of Governance in Hong Kong," in S.K. Lau, M.K. Lee, P.S. Wan, and S.L. Wong (eds.), *Indicators of Social Development: Hong Kong 1999*, pp. 1–32. Hong Kong: Institute of Asia-Pacific Studies, Chinese University of Hong Kong Press.

Chapter 2

SCHOOLING IN BRUNEI DARUSSALAM

Stephen G. Upex

Brunei Darussalam is a tiny but affluent Malay-Islamic absolute monarchy on the north coast of Borneo, with a population of *c.* 320,000. Most of the population live on the coastal plain with a few indigenous groups in the interior jungle. The population consists of a variety of Malay groups (67 percent), an entrepreneurial Chinese community who dominate in the commercial life of the country (approx. 15 percent), and a declining number of expatriates consisting of some professionals (mainly Western) in education, health, and aviation and a larger majority of unskilled laborers and servants, mainly from the Philippines, Bangladesh, Indonesia, and Thailand. About 63 percent of the population is of the Islamic faith and the literacy rate defined as for those over 15 who can read and write is 88 percent.

The country is still run under regularly renewed State of Emergency regulations that were introduced in 1962. Parliament was dismissed in December that year and no elections have been held since. Low level censorship is carried out on all media, academic material, and artistic events which might be embarrassing, objectionable, or threatening to the Monarchy or Islam.

The average GNP of just over $20,000 per capita is deceptive, with most wealth in the hands of a small number of families. The great mass of the population are well below the mathematical average but supported through a welfare (locally nicknamed Shellfare) system that is now starting to break down due to rapid population increases and internal spending problems. The economy is supported mainly by petroleum sector revenues (40 percent GDP) which are rather volatile and income from overseas investments which has decreased of late. The government is currently attempting to diversify by developing tourism, agriculture, industry, and establish Brunei as a financial center. The National Development Plan 1996–2000 allocated $7.2 billion to the economic diversification of the economy and gave a major role to education for providing the skilled human resources needed.

Brunei's relationship with the West was very different from that of most of S.E. Asia. It was never colonized but existed as a British Protectorate, with the Sultan receiving "advice" from the British Resident High Commissioner. Since the end of World War II it has been the influence of Islam— not politics— that has shaped the educational system within the country and the rationale behind the present aims of education. Islam permeates and controls all aspects of life in a way parallel to that in the Middle East, rather than that of Malaysia or Indonesia. Also significant is the relatively short period of time in which full time secondary education has been offered and has developed within the country. The first secondary school opened in 1953.

Given the noncolonization of the country and the overriding Islamic controls, the four historical periods which form the themes for the rest of this book do not correlate precisely with the Brunei experience. Educational development within and up to the end of the Protectorate system in 1959 thus forms the first part of this chapter. Then follows an outline of the system of education that developed under the post-Protectorate system and sections on the situation during the Cold War, and more recently with Brunei as a member of ASEAN, focussing on regional issues.

EDUCATIONAL DEVELOPMENT DURING THE BRITISH PROTECTORATE PERIOD (1911–1959)

The Government System

The history of education within the Sultanate is yet to be written in a detailed form. Current research, within the Education Faculty of the University of Brunei, has only just begun to examine the availability of sources and piece together the early years of educational development (Upex, 2000). The very first mention of schools is not made until 1911 when the annual report for that year states that "preparations were made to start a school in the new-year." However the school was not opened until 1914 (Chevallier, 1911; Douglas, 1914). Prior to this period the only education within the country was in the form of some Mosque schools which were run for the sons of the local, wealthier families of the Malay population concentrating almost exclusively on Islamic religious teaching.

The impetus for schooling appears to have been a real shortage of local literate Brunei Malays able to operate the local offices related to the law courts and general government administration that had been set up under the auspices of the British. Such was the need for local, literate administrative staff that an allowance was even made in 1915 for a school for 12 boys to be set up in Muara in someone's house (McArthur, 1987).

The first school in 1914 was located in Brunei Town (later to become Bandar Seri Begawan). By 1918 there were other schools in the Tutong and Belait districts. The shortage of trained teachers was solved by bringing staff in from Malacca (Naim, 1984). By the 1920s–1930s there appeared to be three main factors which influenced the need for the expansion of schools within the country.

First the growing need to provide stable government and administration along a British model was beginning to stretch the imported manpower provision and this, linked with a sense of responsibility to educate the indigenous people and to protect their rights and traditions focused the need on the development of free education (Chong, 1979). The idea of "free education" however had another side, the arrangement was that the British administration would provide only part of the arrangement and the adopted policy is outlined in the 1938 annual report which stipulated that:

the village people themselves...must prove the need and the strength of their desire for a local school by supplying the rough materials...and the labour for the erection of a temporary schoolhouse and teachers quarters. Teacher, equipment, books, etc. are all provided by the government. (H.M.S.O., 1939: 33)

Although this policy may have produced more schools in the growing urban areas, the general trend in the rural areas and up the rivers in the longhouse settlements was to do very little for children who were already working at an early age in various family rural pursuits. By 1930 there were 9 schools in total within the country with a total roll of 688 boys. A temporary girls' school was started in 1930 but it was not until 1932 that the Brunei Town Malay School opened with 13 girls on a more permanent basis (Naim, 1984). Muslim parents were reluctant to send their daughters to school because of the Islamic prohibition of mixing girls and boys and this delayed the development of education of girls (Chong, 1979: 31).

A second major influence in the way that education developed at this period was the growth of the Chinese population. In the 1911 census the Chinese represented 3 percent of the population of the country; by 1931 this figure had risen to 9 percent (*Brunei Statistical Yearbook* 1974/5/6). The ignoring by the local Malays and British of the educational needs of what they saw as an immigrant and perhaps temporary and mobile population, was the catalyst for the Chinese to set up their own schools and by 1921 there was one school in Brunei Town and by 1938 two others in Seria and Kuala Belait. The setting up of these schools through community efforts on the part of the Chinese population brought some conflict with the British administration who would not allow the running of these schools to progress unchecked, so small grants from the administration were made and in return "inspections" were allowed.

The third impetus to the growth of the educational system was the discovery and production of oil in the late 1920s. The development of the oilfields and the expansion of the townships of Seria and Kuala Belait led to the expansion of services for the influx of migrant workers. Amongst such provision was the setting up by Christian missionaries of what become known as the "English schools," simply because the medium of instruction was in English. In 1931 there was one English school but this had been expanded to three by 1938 and all received the support of the British authorities and especially the oil companies who saw the possibility of future recruitment from these schools. The local Muslim population avoided sending their children to these Christian schools on religious grounds. To get around this problem the authorities made a capitation grant to the schools and linked to the grants were conditions which made religious instruction optional for the students. This pleased the Muslim population but restricted the missionary zeal of the schools' governors and ultimately led to the setting up of a totally independent Roman Catholic mission school in Brunei Town in 1933.

Complications were wrought on a basic education system that had barely begun to develop by the wartime influence of the Japanese occupation. The Japanese forced all teachers to learn Japanese, introduced it into the curriculum and then also changed the language of government and administration from English to Malay which allowed local talent to be absorbed into administrative positions more easily.

After the war education was stimulated by the appointment of the first State Education Office in 1949. Then there existed only primary education up to form 4; by 1954 this was expanded to include a secondary provision.

The Islamic System

Islam came to Brunei Darussalam in the 6th century but it was only in 1956 that Islamic religious education for children and adults was established to teach Islamic values. As the state system had developed, the need for a parallel Islamic system became evident. A number of factors prompted this. First, Islamic education was restricted to Mosque schools; these schools were limited in their clientele and religious focus, catering only for the sons of prominent Muslims, and not for ordinary people nor for females.

Second, the religious subjects taught in the vernacular Malay schools run by the then Department of Education were perceived as less thorough and not providing the necessary detail to maintain and enhance a firm Islamic basis to society. This was because the time allocated to Islamic teaching within the school day was quite limited. Moreover, the teachers were reportedly poorly trained and prepared for their duties (Department of Islamic Studies, 1996).

To overcome these shortcomings, and provide a deeper and more meaningful religious education, an Islamic religious education system was developed which involved the building of separate Islamic religious schools. In addition a Ma'had Islam (Islamic college), a religious teachers' college, an Institute of Islamic Studies, and an adult education program to cater for a full range of Islamic education needs was also introduced. Islamic religious teaching was a central feature of all of these institutions and students attended these schools in the afternoon—after they had finished their schooling at the government schools. Thus the school day for students was from 7.30 P.M. until 12.30 P.M. at government schools and then from 2.00 P.M. until 4.30 P.M. at the Islamic religious schools. These schools came under the control of the Ministry of Religious Affairs.

Primary level systematic religious Islamic education for those children whose parents had embraced Islam commenced in 1956, with seven schools being set up. As there were no trained teachers, teachers were seconded from the Malay Peninsula (West Malaysia) and the curriculum, syllabus, and text-books were obtained from Johore. One of the main purposes of the establishment of such schools was to instill in the children Islamic values, and to produce staff who could "Islamise" and uphold Islamic values. A six year religious Primary education was outlined with some schools providing a one year pre-schooling year in addition. In general Islamic primary schools accepted children who attended the primary Level 2 classes in schools run by the Department of Education. The main subjects taught were the Koran, *Jawi* (Arabic script) reading and writing, practical, *Tauhid* (Unity of God), prayers, history, *Adab* (Manners), *Taharah* (Cleanliness/Health Education), *Siam* (Fasting), *Tasauf* (Mysticism), *Tajwid* (Correct Method of Reciting the Koran), *Zakat* (Alms Giving), *Haj*, *Faraid* (Obligations), *Muamalat* (Business Transaction), *Munakahat* (Marriage-related Issues such as contracts), and *Jenayat* (Criminology). Schools had two sessions in the mornings and afternoons with some schools having their own buildings, while others shared buildings with the primary schools run by the Department of Education. Those schools which shared buildings with the Ministry of Education schools had one session.

In 1941 a secondary Arabic school was established in Brunei Town (now Bandar Seri Begawan) although this closed during the wartime occupation. This school was totally separate from the other Islamic and government schools within the country and taught Arabic as a language and other subjects—largely in Arabic. The school, and ones that followed, were set up to produce Arabic scholars within the country and foster the growth of Islam at a higher level. After the war eligible students for Arabic secondary education were sent to Malaya (West Malaysia) and Singapore, and for tertiary education they were sent to the Al-Azhar University in Egypt.

For adult Islamic education after 1956, subjects taught included *Fiqh* (Islamic Jurisprudence), *Tauhid* (Unity of God), *Tafsir* (Exegesis), *Hadis* (Prophetic Tradition), *Tasauf* (Mysticism), Islamic History, Koran and general knowledge. The classes which ran (and still do) for 1–3 years were first held at community halls or private homes although with additional funding the adult classes began to be held in mosques, and *surau*s (small mosques, or prayer rooms).

Thus a range of social and religious factors have been at work within Brunei which influenced the way that ultimately three parallel education systems started and evolved. A government system based on a largely secular curriculum and organized by the Ministry of Education; an Islamic system to foster the understanding and following of Islam organized by the Ministry of Religious Affairs; and Arabic schools, also organized by the Ministry of Religious Affairs, which aimed to produce Islamic clerics and scholars.

EDUCATION IN THE POST-PROTECTORATE
PERIOD (1959–1984)

The setting up of the 1959 Constitution which replaced the British Residential system granted internal self-government to Brunei and mentioned for the first time a "national system of education." This was to include free compulsory education for all ethnic groups using Malay as the medium of instruction and providing equal opportunities within education for the whole population (Aminuddin Baki and Chang, 1959). The government of the day clearly saw that the growing requirement of education was to provide a skilled and educated labor force to implement the country's proposed expansion. Although the aim during the late 1950s was to create a single Malay form of instruction in schools, in practice little appears to have happened after this recommendation and the situation was that both English and Malay were used in State schools, English continued to be used in the Mission Schools, and Chinese in the Chinese schools. After 1978, however, in both government and nongovernment schools there was a common curriculum introduced along with a set of common public examinations, culminating in the adoption of the UK based "O" and "A" level examinations which are still followed.

On March 1, 1966, 46 able students were chosen to attend courses at the *Madrasah* building of the Department of Religious Affairs to start their education in Arabic. The students were chosen from both Islamic and government schools. As the population grew, there was also a need to have bigger schools and two new Arabic secondary schools were opened in 1967. Those students who were housed at the *Madrasah* were moved to these new schools. Subjects are now taught in Arabic, Malay, and English and include Islamic subjects such *Qawaid* (Principles), *Muhadasah* (Discussions), *Mahfuzat* (Memorization), and *Imla'* (Dictation), as well as other subjects such as Science, Mathematics, Geometry, Geography, Malay, and English Language.

In order to cope with the ever-increasing student population, the government felt that it needed to have locally trained teachers. This desire culminated in the establishment of the Seri Begawan Teachers' College in 1972 with an intake of 30 students. Two basic three-year courses were offered depending on qualifications and the courses covered both Islamic and secular subjects as well as education and teaching practice. Running along parallel lines to this government teachers' college was the Institute of Islamic Studies established in 1989 and whose aim was to produce teachers for Islamic Studies. Courses were offered in *Syariah* (Islamic Law), *Usuluddin* (Theology), *Laughah Arabiyyah* (Arabic Language), Koran, and Education.

All this took place against the international background of the Cold War. Not that many Bruneians were aware of it. The only effect of the brief communist uprising in the early 1960s was to entrench the absolute Islamic monarchy into an even stronger position, fortified with internal security regulations that are still in use today to control the country. The Sultan was naturally a staunch ally of the West fearing further communist uprisings. He funded money to President

Reagan's war chest but this appears to have been a personal decision without the knowledge of the Bruneian public to whom he is not accountable. No one would have been aware of this funding but for it being placed in an incorrect bank account. (A similar undisclosed "gift" was provided to a recent short-lived president of Indonesia who was then accused of misappropriation.) Personal bankrolling of what is in the national (read Sultan's) interests is not uncommon. The decision-making processes were and continue to be far removed from the general public and curricula do not reflect or teach material about what has or is being done on their behalf internationally. As the world changed around Brunei, the then Sultan responded by closing down parliament and maintaining an even tighter grip on internal affairs through the feudal system and "rice bowl," rejecting communism absolutely (as do all Islamic states due to the latter's antireligious tenets) and not embracing capitalism apart from the personal investment in oil and other sources of generating personal wealth, out of which the country could also be run as the lower priority. This response to the Cold War was a somewhat unique yet understandable one, maintaining throne and mosque over a deliberately nourished naiveness within the populace.

The only noticeable response within the education system and Islamic society to the Cold War communist threat was to ensure that Islamic religious education was even more firmly entrenched. Thus the culmination of this response to any Cold War influences was the creation of the Islamic religious schools with their commitment to Islamic education and values. The curriculum covered the Koran, Worship, the Unity of God, Manners, and Islamic History, Islamic Jurisprudence, Prophetic Traditions, *Syariah* (Islamic Law), and Theology.

NATIONALISM AND REGIONALISM AFTER INDEPENDENCE (1984–PRESENT)

Brunei resumed full political sovereignty in 1984. National policy continued to be formulated on and by the interests of Islam, the Royal family and a court of senior Bruniean "nobles." Such national, regional, and international changes that independence brought figured little in the school curriculum. Membership of ASEAN and APEC (Asia-Pacific Economic Cooperation) have also had little direct impact on the economy or education since the underlying value system of the present strict Malay Islamic Monarchy philosophy controls all aspects of life, and anything that would conflict with it is unacceptable, disallowed, and expunged.

The Dominant Paradigm: *Melayu Islam Beraja* (MIB) or Malay Islamic Monarchy

Politics, economics, culture, and education now fuse together in a set of Malay-Islamic values that provide a unique philosophy and national ideology, *Melayu Islam Beraja* (MIB) or Malay Islamic Monarchy in which religion and monarchy find mutual support. This ideology, the genesis of which dates back to the 15th century, has been vigorously reasserted since independence to reinforce the presumed legitimacy of the hereditary monarchy and the observance of traditional Muslim values. It ensures absolutism of both religion and sultanate, providing a seamless value system that currently dominates institutional norms and behavior.

The present education system is thoroughly embedded in this MIB value system and is the major vehicle used to uphold and perpetuate it. For example, all students in government schools and university take compulsory MIB courses. Islamic dress codes are prescribed for students at both school and university; all subjects taught at university should have an Islamic input, all children up to third year secondary compulsorily attend classes for religious education each afternoon for several hours after normal classes.

Additionally, overarching the MIB philosophy (and with which there is a comfortable congruence) are those pan-Asian Confucian values of consensus and deference to authority (father figures). Using the concepts developed by management sociologists such as Blunt (1988), Hofstede (1991) and Trompenaars (1993), Brunei Malays can be said to manifest high power distance, strong uncertainty avoidance, and low individualism.

- Power distance—is reflected in Brunei in rigid hierarchy, ascribed status, formal structure of social relations, and social distance between those who wield power and those who are affected by that power. Children are educated to be obedient; teacher-centered education instills order; learning is the transmission of standardized accepted sanitized knowledge. Coercive power is stressed above expert power. Lower level staff avoid decision making, but follow orders and rules rigorously. Long chains of command produce a top-down state organization in all aspects of life.
- Low individualism (or collectivism) stresses "we" as against "I." Western motivation theories emphasizing the satisfaction of individual needs, autonomy, and self actualisation have no place. Efforts focus around consensus, on duties to nation and religion, and on responsibilities within the family and community. Individual rights have low priority.
- Uncertainty avoidance leads to a difficulty in tolerating uncertainty and minimising the possibility by strict laws, a religious/philosophical belief in absolute truth, and an acceptance of divine and political authority. What is different is dangerous; considerable effort is put into "beating the future" and minimizing Western influence (e.g., current banning of concerts).

In all these respects, the Brunei MIB system is little different from general S.E. Asian paternal cronyism, but with strict Islamic overtones. Despite its unique absolute monarchical features, the country shows congruency with the Asian values of authority, deference, and consensus, and reciprocally it is these that permit the survival of the anachronistic feudalism. It is the role of education to maintain this system as is clearly shown by reference to the present aims of education and national education policy.

The Current Aims of Education in Brunei

These aims reflect the location of government education within the MIB context. The focus is on social cohesion and mutually agreed values (such as being a loyal, and responsible citizen, faithful to Islam and the monarchy), and all round skills (physical, mental, and spiritual) rather than those of a specific educational/ intellectual nature. The manpower resource provision is based on national need with the person in the service of the state. In summary these aims are directed,

To inculcate the teaching of Islam.

To cultivate a sense of loyalty to the Monarch.

To cultivate in each individual the values and norms of Bruneian society, centred on the principles of a Malay Islamic Monarchy.

To accelerate the development of manpower resources.

To ensure each individual is fluent in Malay and devoted to the interests of the Malay language as the official language.

To foster the all round development of each individual from the physical, mental, and spiritual point of view . . . to ensure that he or she . . . will uphold the aspirations of the country. (Aims of Education on official government web site, www.moe.gov.bn)

In a similar vein, the National Education Policy seeks to develop the all round potential of the individual in order to bring into being an educated, devout, dynamic, disciplined, and responsible people. Their virtues should be complementary to the needs of the State and be founded on spiritual values which are noble in the sight of Allah. The policy forms a starting point which is oriented toward the specific character of Brunei Darussalam with emphasis on faith and obedience to Allah, priority to the Malay language, and loyalty to Monarch and State (Statement of National Education Policy on official government website, www.moe.gov.bn).

These Malay and Islamic values provide clear requirements for government schools and Islamic religious schools alike, to produce citizens who are faithful and steadfast in their devotion to Islam and to the monarchy. The Sultan in his New Year Royal Address (2000) stated that "we would like to have a country which is excellent in all things by keeping adhered to religious values and noble morals." These underlying ideologies are replete with assumptions about the nature of reality, the purpose of the education and the socioeconomic world.

Academic knowledge and skills are only explicitly stated in the formal curriculum. In certain subjects such as History, Malay, MIB, and Religion, academic material is used to supplement the policies inculcating the required values and attitudes of loyalty, citizenship, and religious obligation. Thus the defining ideology of the Brunei curriculum consists of normative rather than instrumental goals.

The Present Schooling System

Currently there operates a three-fold education system within the country. The government through the Ministry of Education currently operates 29 secondary schools and slightly over 120 primary schools. The Ministry of Religious Affairs runs the 100 or so Islamic religious schools and they also control the six Arabic schools. In addition to these schools there are a number of independent schools run by Western churches, or by local Malays, or which are run as stand alone

International schools. Additionally there are six technical/vocational schools and two tertiary institutions, namely, a university and a technological institute.

The current education system consists of three levels—primary, secondary and tertiary education. At the primary level, children begin at kindergarten and then enter the six-year primary stage. At the end of primary six (grade six), students take a national examination, the *Primary Certificate of Education Examination*, that qualifies them to enter secondary school. Secondary education continues for seven years. At the end of the lower secondary period students sit for the Junior Secondary Assessment which assists in the channeling of students to either vocational schools or to the academic stream. Those in the latter stream follow a two-year program leading directly to GCE "O" level.

Successful students may then follow a two-year course at college for the Brunei-Cambridge A levels, which provide for university entrance. Brunei and Singapore are the only two countries in the world that still stick to "O" levels as even Britain has moved on.

The Vocational schools offer a diverse range of certificate level craft courses leading to National Trade Certificates. The Technical colleges offer technician level courses for the National Diploma to students after the GCE "O" level.

Those who successfully complete "A" level courses may proceed to the Institute of Technology or seek university entrance either in Brunei or study abroad on scholarships (mainly in UK, Australia, and N. America) in subjects not provided at the national university, for example, Law or Veterinary Science. The university which opened in 1987 has a teacher training focus and also provides professional level staff for the public service and petroleum industry. The University also has a Faculty of Islamic Studies and an Academy of Brunei Studies.

All primary and secondary schools follow a common curriculum prescribed by the Ministry of Education (MoE). The emphasis is on book knowledge rather than thinking or skill development, with little room for social, aesthetic, and emotional development. Following independence in 1984, a bilingual education policy (*dwibahasa*) was introduced for students from primary Level 4 to enable all pupils to gain proficiency in both Malay and English. Religious Studies, MIB, and Malay are taught in Malay, whereas subjects such as geography, history, and economics are taught in English. The university provides courses in both media.

To ensure all students in the Tutong District and especially those from the rural districts could obtain Arabic secondary teaching the "Arabic college" or "Ma'had Islam" was built for boys in 1991. The college is at the forefront of Islamic secondary teaching and forms a center of Religious/Arabic secondary education with full board and lodging. Here the classes are divided into prepara- tory, lower secondary, and upper secondary classes and at the end of "O" Level education, eligible students can continue to "A" Level at the Hassanal Bolkiah Arabic Secondary School for boys. Students spend seven years at the college studying Arabic, the Koran, *Tafsir/Hadis* (Exegesis/Prophetic Tradition), Islamic History, and other related areas as well as Malay and English Language, Mathematics, Science, History, Geography, Economics, and Accounts.

The latest development within the education system in the country is the increasing integration of Islamic education with general education. The Institute of Islamic Studies was placed within the Universiti Brunei Darussalam and the Ministry of Education in 1999 and is now known as the Sultan Haji Omar Ali Saifuddien Institute of Islamic Studies and the University is fast becoming an Islamic university. Formerly all Islamic religious schools were controlled by the Ministry of Religious Affairs but in 2001 this control was switched to the Ministry of Education in an effort to reduce the duplication of physical, human, and finance resources and permit closer links and integration between the two elements of education.

At the moment the process of integrating the state and religious systems is taking place but serious questions remain as to how the "new" system will operate and which element—the religious or the secular aspects of education— will dominate. The influence of Islamic teaching and its effect on society grows ever stronger with recent moves to ban singing, concerts, and all aspects of entertainment and at a time that Brunei tries to promote itself as a tourist destination and a player in the global market.

Systematic Problems in the Postindependence Economy

Brunei has been identified as a rentier capitalist state (Gunn, 1993). In such an economy, there is no direct link between production and income distribution as all revenues go to the government which controls and disburses funding, not only for the general running of services but also for subsidised health, housing, cars, and education. Actual personal wages for most are low and supplemented by such subsidies and the benefits of no income tax. It is a welfare state run riot with most things free but dependent on royal generosity and peasant subservience for handouts. The small ennobled group as well as the general public happily maintain the system for their respective benefits.

Moreover, most Bruneians want to work in the public service sector with its entitlements, leaving construction, semiskilled trades and other similar jobs for immigrant workers; this provides no nexus between production, effort, and incentive. The production, import, and consumption of goods and services is not linked to growth in the economy. Most goods are simply imported, while the overloaded public service devours the GNP without contributing much to it. As a result motivation to succeed and competition are both missing in a public service dominated economy; public service jobs in Brunei are a sinecure for life.

The economy is too dependent on the volatility of petroleum prices and diversification is now being sought. Lurking behind both the limited economic base and the education control system is the rapidly increasing population, with a third at school age and below, prognosticating massive future unemployment and social problems.

Already there is a mismatch of school and university graduates to demands of the labor market, with many newly qualified graduates in such subjects as accountancy, tourism, and law, returning from overseas unable to find posts in their specialisms and for lack of anything else and because of government bonding requirements they end up in teaching, whether they like it or not. Unemployment has increased by 6 percent in the last year with 7,500 persons including 100 fresh graduates registered as unemployed with the Labor Department. This problem, coupled with a continuing budget deficit of around 50 percent of GDP and a small, shaky private sector in a government-driven market, provides cause for concern about economic, social, and political stability.

Specific Problems with the Education System

These include

- *Overloaded curriculum and school day.* The school day starts generally at 7.30 A.M. and goes on until 12.30 P.M. In addition all students except those studying for O and A levels must attend afternoon Islamic religious schools. The reported integration (see in the previous section) will alter this in at present unknown ways. Some students are finally subjected at the end of the long day to private tuition to make certain they pass examinations mandatory for advancing to the next year. High rates of repeating have been recorded.
- *Examination focused teacher centered instruction.* Regular assessment occurs but little in the way of diagnostic assessment. Teaching is efficient if it covers the syllabus; the teacher is efficient as judged by the examination results. In such conditions rote learning dominates over understanding, self-direction, and intrinsic satisfaction. It is a verbal reception context offering for most pupils a mainly meaningless diet of information to be rote learned and regurgitated for the examination game in a "banking" concept of knowledge.
- *The lack of professional teachers and professional development.* Many teachers particularly at primary level possess minimal qualifications. The high birth rate has led the government to train more teachers but less qualified ones. Teachers have little autonomy or professional freedom. They cannot with impunity criticise the education system, education policies, or curriculum. The teacher is not a change agent. Within the context of economic efficiency requirements, teachers are technicians and agents of a predetermined curriculum. Yong (1995) found this passivity even in pre-service teachers. The consumer mentality so apparent in the country, exhibits itself in the teacher fraternity (Yong, 1995; Minnis, 1998) with any sense of teacher as reflective practitioner, demonstrating intellectual curiosity, and willingness to try out new ideas being foreign and unwelcome in such a high power distance, uncertainty avoidance, and low individualism context. The professional development depends more on the principal's or Ministry's direction rather than on the teacher's need. The university often finds that many of the teachers sent for upgrading Special Education, Counselling, and M.Ed courses are not keen to do the course but nevertheless attend the classes. Many recent entrants to the teaching profession on interview at the University did not "choose" to enter that profession. They were "chosen" by the government to meet anticipated demand.
- *Language problems.* On school entry, pupils are taught to read in Standard Malay, of which Brunei Malay is a variant. Both of these have Roman scripts which reads from left to right. They are then also required to learn *Jawi*, the Arabic script of the Koran adapted to Malay phonetic symbols, which reads from right to left. Add to this melange English as the medium of instruction for most academic subjects from Year 4 and there is a recipe for disaster.

The existence of this examination-driven system, replete with selection points following a centrally imposed curriculum, teacher centered pedagogy, student language problems, and a highly centralized system of decision making, creates a pursuit of credentialism, a commodity exchange for jobs, and social status, in which the award is more important than the learning. Deep learning, an intrinsic motivation to learn, and individualized development are not sought. Students are rewarded for formal compliance and modest standards and are told what to think and not how to think.

Although much rhetoric is uttered about improving the education system, such as providing computers to every school, and encouraging creativity, the fact is that on many counts little happens to improve the system. It is apparent that, inter alia, school resources are limited, equipment that breaks down is not repaired, the fabric of the school is not maintained, and local teachers have difficulty in teaching in the English medium. The population are given enough basic education to serve the judged needs of the country but there is little indication that an urgency exists to improve the whole sphere of education within the country. However, the systemic shortcomings in the postindependent economy are starting to create problems.

In Brunei a combination of cultural, economic, geographical, and demographic forces are starting to pose challenges. The income from petroleum products and overseas investments has in the past ensured that most Bruneians are provided with jobs, usually in the public service. However, the government now sees the need to reduce the size of this nonproductive area, pull back the hand of government in many services, and offload them onto private ventures, using the public service mainly as a facilitator.

The population pyramid is weighted considerably to the bottom where a high birth rate is locating a disproportionate number of people in the younger age groups. With a third of the population currently below the age of 18, the schooling system is under siege. There will not be enough schools unless more are built quickly. The population is expected to be in the region of 436,000, an increase of 35 percent mainly at the lower age ranges by the end of the next decade. Bruneians tend not to take menial "dirty" jobs which are readily filled by immigrant laborers (45 percent of the workforce in 1999). In this situation, the government has become concerned over the rising unemployment level among young Bruneians who leave school with minimal qualifications. Given the high birth rate, youth unemployment can only get worse at a time when there is an economic fragility in the country with limited alternative economic resources or feasibility for service industry development. The dichotomy between privileged and underprivileged in Brunei could grow even greater as those with money and better education navigate their way through the e-world, leaving the rest as window shoppers.

A Typical Day in the Life of Students in Brunei

It is very difficult to imagine a typical day as Brunei has many diverse social and ethnic groups, including indigenous Malay in urban Brunei Muara, Iban in rural Temburong, Dusun in rural Tutong district and ethnic Chinese in all regions. As an example let us take two secondary school students, Malay children from Brunei Muara. Amir comes from the Kampong Ayer (water village) which is home to some 30,000 people in Brunei's capital, Bandar Seri Begawan, and Rashidah is a land dweller in the same region.

Like nearly all of the population, Amir wakes before dawn as the call to prayer from the local mosque resounds across his village. He may decide to pray but generally his family members are not particularly observant of religion, tending passively to accept but rarely participate in its behavioral and ceremonial demands. He leaves for school at 6.30 A.M. but does not eat before leaving. He walks to school along the maze of interconnecting wooden walkways that rise on stilts above the Brunei river. All the children here walk or travel by boat to school and it is assumed that children will make their own way to and from school. He feels rather tired and hungry but like all the other students here he will probably not eat or drink throughout the school day. The canteen offers one simple meal of rice and chicken but he seldom ever buys any and he cannot afford bottled water.

The children at his school come from one of the poorest and most socially disadvantaged groups in Brunei, although his village is often lauded as an attractive centerpiece to Bandar and the heart of local ethnic culture. His school is very poorly equipped and the stilted buildings are dilapidated and over the weekend some one has stolen all the aluminum frames and the glass from the windows. No one cares much—the building seems cooler without them and as once again the electricity is off, the water supply has failed and the fans are not working, every one is glad of the breeze blowing from the river.

Like his school friends, Amir has a limited and poor diet, and his teachers often complain that their students are mentally and physically lethargic, almost as if they have been "doped," but a combination of inadequate nutrition and lack of sleep—he was up till 1 A.M. watching football on the television—mean he often lacks energy. His family pays little attention to time keeping and punctuality, and regular hours are alien to him.

His school has no proper sanitation and Amir's personal hygiene is very poor and his teeth are bad. Many of his classmates are in a similarly neglected state and as well as being unaware of how to look after themselves they have little concern for their environment either. The school toilets empty straight into the river below the school and Amir and his friends throw their rubbish carelessly into the waters surrounding the school. At low tide the smell and floating rubbish make it an unattractive and unhealthy place to be.

He sits through his lessons, not understanding much, particularly not those lessons that are conducted in English, but he is amiable and obedient though academic aspiration means nothing to him. He likes school as it provides him with social connections and he finds the holidays boring and dull with little for him to do. His day is rather inactive—although the school connects to the land and has a football field there is very rarely any form of physical education in school, so he and his friends pass their days sitting listlessly at their wooden desks. At 12.30 P.M. he walks home—perhaps he will eat some noodles or rice now, and later he may go fishing or sleep for a while.

Rashidah also wakes before dawn and after family prayers and breakfast she does some homework in her room before leaving for school. She and her brothers and sisters are driven to school by their Filipino driver in one of the family's fleet of cars and her driver delivers her right up to the school gates. Like all the children in the city she always travels to school by car and the roads are clogged with traffic as families struggle to deliver several children to various schools around the city before 7.15 A.M. Rashidah attends a girls' high school in the center of town. The buildings are old and rather run down, not many rooms are air-conditioned, and the school has no sports field, but it is a popular school and well thought of for its academic results. She is smartly dressed in her school uniform of long skirt in the school's colors, loose white top and regulation white headscarf—her teachers often find it hard to recognize individual girls in this identity-masking outfit (in classes of 35 to 40 students) and she wonders how many times she will be called by the wrong name today!

Her school is crowded—over 50 years old, it originally housed only a few students, then numbers rose to several hundred and now it has a thousand girls on roll. Buildings have been added piecemeal and rooms divided and the campus is now a hectic and chaotic place but she loves the fun with her friends and the vibrant atmosphere—something is always happening here: competitions, fund raisers, charity events, religious ceremonies. The day starts with prayers and the singing of the national anthem. Rashidah is excited today as her class has been chosen to take part in the annual National Day celebrations and she and her friends will now spend several weeks preparing dance performances with other local schools. She knows this will be a lot of fun and looks forward to appearing on television in her beautiful costume—and to getting out of lessons for a while!

However, generally she values her education and like so many of her friends she hopes to go to university and become a teacher, even to receive a government scholarship and study overseas like her father did. Her parents both speak English to her at home so she does not find the English medium lessons too hard to follow although she is struggling to keep up with the workload. Lessons finish at 12.30 P.M. but today, as so often, she has extra classes in the afternoon. Exam time is approaching and her teachers feel they have not yet covered the syllabus. So, after enjoying lunch in the school canteen where there is a pleasant outdoor seating area, she returns to the classroom for an extra hour of Maths and then of English. It is very hot now and as she sits under the creaking fans she is feeling sleepy and struggling to follow the teacher's instructions but knows she needs to succeed in these exams. It is very worrying for her and she often feels inadequate and lacks confidence. All this work is a chore rather than something she can actively engage in and she shows very little curiosity or interest in class.

She does not mind the afternoon classes though and she is used to it—if she did not have extra classes today she would have gone to the religious school for the afternoon classes. Rashidah's family members are observant Muslims and supportive of the national government and MIB culture which has provided them with free education, free health care, and well-paid work in government offices. Rashidah is not allowed to mix with her friends outside of school so she welcomes extra classes and religious school because they enable her to interact with her peers.

She takes very little, often no, physical exercise. She seldom has PE lessons at school and her schedule allows little time for recreation—no sport, music, drama or creative relaxation. Her life is very sedentary and she is beginning to look rather overweight and unfit.

At 4 P.M. her driver collects her from the school gate and she returns home. The maid has prepared a meal and she eats it while tackling her homework but she is unable to concentrate any longer so soon abandons the Maths and switches on the television. At 7 P.M. her driver takes her to a tuition school where she is attempting to improve her chances in the forthcoming public exams and she works there until 9 P.M. When she returns home the Maths homework is still sitting on the desk accusingly, but she is too tired to face it and guiltily goes to bed, planning to get up very early to finish the homework tomorrow, before leaving for the school.

Education and Social Change in the Future Brunei

Brunei with its small economy and market base has nominally embraced the ASEAN Free Trade Area immediately on gaining independence in 1984, and was a member of both the East Asian Growth Area concept and APEC from their inceptions. But where the doctrines of these bodies conflict with religious or political ends, Brunei ignores them. In terms of education development, ASEAN and other groupings have negligible impact due to the superordinate and controlling role both religion and monarchy play to build, maintain, and increasingly emphasize a traditional Islamic nation. Education is an "in-house" issue. Only at University level where a few overseas ASEAN scholars are present does formal education have much of a link. The other links are in Technical Education where the government of Brunei, well aware of the need for wellfounded development of technical and vocational education, attracted in 1990 the establishment of SEAMEO-VOCTECH in Brunei as the regional center for improving the quality of Vocational and Technical Education through human resource development.

Although neither ASEAN nor APEC per se are having a significant impact on education in Brunei, there are a number of interesting influences permeating the education system in Brunei from within the ASEAN community and more generally from the global arena. For example, Singapore's Smart Schools approach is leading Brunei to consider a similar policy. (Brunei tends to follow Singapore's lead in many things—currencies, defence systems etc.) Brunei plans to develop "Thoughtful Schools" as a collaborative endeavor between the Ministry of Education and the University. The global move to inclusion in schools, has led to a Special Education Unit being established to train teachers in collaboration with the University as Learning Assistance Teachers who have the skills to identify, assess, and develop Individual Education Programmes (IEPs) for learning-disabled pupils currently being integrated into normal classes. The University has developed an in-service counselling course to provide trained personal and career counsellors for schools. The RELA language program has been instituted in all primary schools to develop English language and reading skills as English skills are seen as essential in a global and computerized world. This is supported by direct recruitment of around 240 expatriate teachers of English as a Foreign Language through a private company, CfBT. Computer courses for teachers at secondary level and the training of specialist computer teachers is now ongoing. A start has been made to provide some general portable skills by including in Technical and Vocational Education programs a Common Skills element, which aims to teach learners to be self-motivated, be adaptable, and assume responsibility for their own learning and career development. The University in 2000 instituted an Entrepreneurial Development Unit to develop and strengthen the private business sector through training and strategy development as future job creation is seen to lie almost totally within a currently small, and in a business sense, naïve private sector. Lifelong education, a new and vital element in most nations' educational planning is making a cautious start at the University with a limited introduction of extra mural courses in 2002.

But many of these regional and global influences and directions are scrupulously mediated and diverted toward Brunei's MIB policy. There is a world of difference between the Singapore concept of "Thinking" schools in which creativity and questioning are encouraged and the subtle variation to "Thoughtful" schools, whose underlying aim is not opening minds but encouraging Islamic thought and reflection onto whatever is being taught. Even academics at the university are expected where possible to incorporate Islamic input in the content of what they teach, which counters attempts by the University of Brunei to update its teacher education program in 1999, placing more emphasis on teaching praxis and greater integration between theory and practice to better the teaching–learning context. Direct recruitment of expatriate teachers other than those with ESL skills has ceased as the focus moves to localization to produce a mainly Islamic profession to influence young minds. The new University counselling course is deeply imbued with Islamic input in which religious underpinnings to personal renewal are as much emphasized in removing unacceptable behaviors or thoughts as Skinnerian behavior modification, while Rogerian self actualization and personal choice are viewed with some trepidation in the context of a deterministic religious philosophy. Career education tends to focus on techno-rational and behaviorist skill formation and human resource development in line with presumed manpower requirements to turn out persons with required skills for collective goals and state policy agendas rather than enable individual choice and personal vocational satisfaction.

Many other developments in the country reflect the delicate base of the economy rather than ASEAN and APEC imperatives. The recent establishment of the Brunei Economic Council mandated to steer the country toward economic recovery, and an educational think tank, the Negara Brunei Darussalam National Council for Education (September 1999) may provide the opportunity for changes to the education system that will enable Brunei to cope with its changing economic base and remove the excessive import of foreign labor. The Economic Council is also promoting development through the provision of government funded projects, especially in light industry, agriculture, tourism and the privatization of government services. This impetus associated with a parallel drive toward localization in jobs is leading to the decline in the dominance of the state sector, with its guaranteed jobs for most Bruneians, and an opening up of jobs at all levels across the economy which were formerly the repose of expatriates. Efforts are now directed to the technical–vocational education sector to achieve closer correspondence between the workplace and the education and training system (Government of Brunei, 1996). This will assist in developing an economy that must build closer ties with education and training. While most of these changes and developments are somewhat cosmetic, the national education system is seen as the engine for supplying that change with human capital. But there are considerable doubts whether any of this is possible given the underlying values that determine the education system (Williams, 1999).

Females are not discriminated against in education or the economy and many hold senior jobs not only in the education service but throughout the public service. Nearly two-thirds of university entrants are female. This may be a response to utilize the skills and abilities of all members of what is a small population rather than any considered acceptance of equity issues, given the strength of Islamic values in Brunei. Brunei strongly promoted one of the main thrusts of the APEC Heads of Government meeting held in Brunei November 2000—that of facilitating the role of women in entrepreneurial SMEs.

The Brunei Dilemma—Reconciling Tradition with the Future

Thus a small start has been made to change the face of Brunei education and enable it to go further along the road to developing a skilled, knowledgeable workforce that is computer literate, well grounded in English, as well as possessing enhanced numeracy and scientific and literacy skills. However, currently missing are the personal skills needed to cope with rapid change or as Toffler (1980) so aptly put it, "future shock," changes to the top-down management approach, eradication of the bureaucratic "by the book culture" that stifles small businesses and initiative, attempts to increase teacher professionalism and morale, and a lessening in emphasis on the rote learning examination-oriented approach. The current and future problem facing the Brunei government is to balance traditional and conservative approaches to education with the need to maintain and enhance Brunei's place in the global economy and regional alliances such as ASEAN and APEC, and be regarded as a realistic player on the world stage. The current emphasis on feudalism and institutionalized religion will impede Brunei's adaptation to current and future developmental needs.

There is a social cost to be met whichever way Brunei proceeds. Maintenance of orthodoxy will damage its ability to deal with the future, while adaptation will undermine the traditional way of life. This is exemplified in the realization that tourism could benefit the economy. However, the obverse is that many Bruneians view with trepidation incursions of tourists with alien values and the need to provide "leisure" services and activities that are "harmful" (*haram*) to the culture. Brunei cannot avoid increasing exposure to "foreign" values, ideas, role models, and behaviors which challenge and confront the "local" ones. Internet and satellite TV are ever present. But liberalization that has already occurred has produced a resulting counter reaction by traditionalists and clerics who are gradually imposing more restrictions to protect a stricter Islamic lifestyle with increasing social conditioning on local radio and television, the issuing of required Islamic dress standards for university students when on campus, banning "decadent" concerts, and increasing vigilance over issues of non-halal foods. TV footage of ASEAN and APEC meetings usually focus on the importance of the Sultan, providing the local populace with "evidence" of the importance of their monarch and country. The main agendas of the conferences are relatively ignored.

Students practicing for national day celebrations. Courtesy of Sylvica Upex.

The major challenge for Brunei is finding a balance between the traditional and the developing needs of the country to meet global escalating change. The overarching values have served the narrow interests of Bruneian national cohesion well, but given rigorous implementation they are counterproductive to addressing new economic realities and needs, and simply fossilize the country in a time warp of religious, social, and political practices that belong more to the 15th century than the present one.

REFERENCES

Baki, Aminuddin and Chang, P. (1959). *Report of the Education Commission Brunei.* Brunei Darussalam: Brunei Government Press.

Blunt, P. (1988). "Cultural consequences for organisation change in a Southeast Asian state: Brunei," *Academy of Management Executive,* 1: 235–240.

Brunei Statistical Yearbook 1974/5/6. Brunei Darussalam: Economic Planning Unit.

Chevallier, H. (1911). *Annual Report on the State of Brunei for the year 1911.* Singapore: Government Printing Office.

Chong, N.C. (1979). "An examination of dysfunctional roles and problems of education in national unity and development with special reference to Brunei Darussal." Unpublished M.Ed. thesis, University of Hull.

Department of Islamic Education (1996). *Pendidikan Ugama Di Negara Brunei Darussalam* (Islamic Religious Education in Brunei Darussalam). Brunei Darussalam: Government Printing Department.

———(1998). *Laporan 10 Tahun 1986 Hingga 1995 Jabatan Pengajaian Islam* (The 10 Year Report: 1986 to 1955 Department of Islamic Education). Brunei Darussalam: Government Printing Department.

———(2000). *Kegiatan Tambahan Jabatan Pengajaian Islam—Taklimat Jabatan Pengajaian Islam Kepada Pelawat-Pelawat Dari Kmenterian Hal Ehwal Ugama Johor Malaysia* (Extra Activities of the Department of Islamic Education—Briefing to Visitors from the Ministry of Religious Affairs Johore Malaysia). Brunei Darussalam: Government Printing Department.

Department of Islamic Studies (1996). *Sejarah Persekolahan Ugama Bersistem Di Brunei* (The History of Systematic Religious Education in Brunei). Brunei Darussalam: Ministry of Religious Affairs.

Douglas, F.W. (1914). *Annual Report on the State of Brunei for the year 1914.* Singapore: Government Printing Office.

Government of Brunei (1996). *7th National Development Plan 1996–2000.* Brunei Darussalam: Government Printing Department. The Government of Brunei Official Government Website, www.moe.gov.bn.

Gunn, G. (1993). "Rentier capitalism in Negara Brunei Darussalam," in K. Hewison, R. Robison, and G. Rodan (eds), *S.E. Asia in the 1990's: Authoritarianism, Democracy and Capitalism,* pp. 95–132. London: Allen and Unwin.

HMSO (His Majesty's Stationery Office) (1939). *Brunei Education System.* London: HMSO.

Hofstede, G. (1991). *Culture and Organisations.* London: McGraw Hill.

McArthur, M.S.H. (1987). *Report on Brunei in 1904.* Ohio University Monograph in International Studies. S.E. Asian series No. 74, Athens, OH: Ohio University.

Minnis, J. (1998). "Brunei's 7th National Development Plan 1996–2000: Implications for policy and practice," *Asia Pacific Journal of Education,* 18: 25–37.

Naim bin Haji Tuan (1984). "The development of education in Brunei." Unpublished Teachers Certificate Dissertation. Gadong: Sultan Hassanal Bolkiah Teachers College.

Office of the Permanent Secretary (1992). *Education in Brunei Darussalam.* Brunei Darussalam: Ministry of Education.

Toffler, A. (1980). *The Third Wave.* London: Collins Naisbett.

Trompenaars, F. (1993). *Riding the Waves of Culture.* London: Blackwell.

Upex, S.G. (2000). "An outline of some of the sources for research into the development of education within Brunei Darussalam," in M. Clements, H. Tairab and K. Wong (eds), *Science, Mathematics and Technical Education in the 20th and 21st Centuries,* pp. 356–364. Gadong: Universiti Brunei Darussalam.

Williams, R. (1999). "Planning for economic diversification in Brunei: Can schools help?" *Studies in Education,* 4: 39–51.

Yong, B. (1995). "Teacher trainees' motives for entering into a teaching career in Brunei Darussalam," *Teaching and Teacher Education,* 11: 275–280.

Chapter 3

SCHOOLING IN CAMBODIA

Keng Chan Sopheak and Thomas Clayton

Located in Southeast Asia and sharing borders with Vietnam, Laos, and Thailand, Cambodia is a country of about 13 million people with a land area of 181,035 square kilometers. The Cambodian population is predominantly Khmer and Buddhist. With a per capita gross domestic product (GDP) of US$315 and a human development index of 0.571, Cambodia ranked 130th among 177 countries in the 2005 United Nations Development Programme's *Human Development Report* (United Nations Development Programme, 2005). Cambodia shares many cultural similarities with other Southeast Asian nations, among them the relatively high status of women in society (Chandler, 1992; Ledgerwood, 1996). Women keep household resources, manage household finance, and do most of the trading and small business in the market (Ledgerwood, 1996). Despite having important roles both at home and in the economy, however, Cambodian girls and women have not enjoyed equal opportunity in education. Cambodia's history of social unrest, wars, and tragedy has further inhibited the educational advancement of girls and women.

Unlike the other chapters of this volume, this one chooses to take a special focus on the the history of education for girls and women in Cambodia since the modern education system was introduced during French colonization.[1] More specifically, after a brief discussion of traditional education in Cambodia, this chapter discusses educational development across six periods: French colonization (1863–1953), postcolonial Cambodia (1954–1969), the Khmer Republic (1970–1975), the Khmer Rouge regime (1975–1979), post–Khmer Rouge Cambodia (1979–1990), and the contemporary era.

The French introduced modern education to Cambodia, but provided no significant opportunities for girls. Almost a century after the introduction of modern education, girls and women were still effectively excluded from it. Only during the period of educational expansion following the departure of the French did girls begin to catch up. After 1970, wars, destruction, and isolation stalled girls' progress in education. It was only toward the end of the 1990s and the turn of the new millennium that attention began to be paid to girls' schooling. Despite notable recent progress in representation of girls in the education system, much remains to be accomplished relative to gender inequity in Cambodian education today.

TRADITIONAL EDUCATION IN PREMODERN CAMBODIA

What we know today as Cambodia began as the Kingdom of Funan in the 1st century A.D. Funan was subsumed in the 6th century by the Chenla Empire, whose border spread to what is now China. Split by internal conflict, Chenla fell to the Indonesian-Malayan Srivijayan Empire in the 8th century. Cambodia regained independence during the Angkor period (802–1431), when successive kings built many splendid temples. The Angkor Empire ended with the Thai invasion in 1431, after which Cambodia entered a period of decline. From the end of the Angkor period to the arrival of French in 1863, Cambodia was sporadically invaded and controlled by neighboring Thailand and Vietnam (Chandler, 1992).

Prior to the introduction of modern education in the 19th century, Cambodian boys attended schools in Buddhist monasteries, or *wats*. When boys reached a certain age, they were sent by their parents to their local *wat* for a period of education. They entered as monk novices, and they lived with monks for periods of time ranging from a few months to a few years; the duration of a boy's novitiate depended on how long his family could afford the loss of his labor. Every morning, a group of boys would traverse the village with a monk or a group of monks to accept offerings from local villagers according to the traditional practice of Cambodian Buddhism. In the afternoon, boys learned to read the *Sastra* (the Buddhist sacred text) and to observe and be guided by Buddhist principles, rules of propriety, and moral and traditional values; in addition, boys gained manual skills by working as apprentices with monks on projects such as crafts, construction, and carpentry (Bilodeau, 1955; Kalab, 1976; Gyallay-Pap, 1989; Sorn, 1995; Tully, 1996; Ayres, 2000).

Some commentators describe *wat* schools as deficient due to their absence of defined curriculum and lack of systematic organization and supervision (Bilodeau, 1955). They also totally excluded girls, who according to Cambodian customs were not allowed to have the close contact with monks that characterized *wat* education. Because of this prohibition, most girls were illiterate when the French arrived in the region (Tully, 1996).

FRENCH COLONIZATION AND MODERN EDUCATION

France established a protectorate over Cambodia in 1863. Driven by the sense of civilizing mission, the *mission civilisatrice*, the French engineered many changes in Cambodia during their 90-year colonial presence. Of particular importance to the current discussion, France introduced a modern secular education system in the country. In principle, French education allowed for the participation of girls, but in fact it largely neglected them. During the 19th century, France used education to produce male civil servants for the colonial administration. In the 20th century, the French modernized the *wat* schools and in the process expanded educational offerings outside the country's urban centers, though few village girls were able to enroll in these schools.

France introduced modern education to Cambodia with the establishment of a French-language primary school in 1873 under the supervision of Ferry Rolles, a French military officer (Morizon, 1931). The French opened a few more schools over the next several decades, and by 1902 there were four French-language schools in the country; the College of the Protectorate in Phnom Penh enrolled 430 pupils, while approximately 60 students studied in each of three other schools in three provincial capitals (Tully, 1996). In the 19th century, French schools sought to produce young men capable of speaking French and "assist[ing] the French authorities [in] their work of colonization" (Bilodeau, 1955: 16). During this early period of very limited educational development, schools catered to male children of the European, Vietnamese, and Chinese communities; only a few Cambodian elite families sent students to French schools. Early educational statistics testify to the ethnic imbalance that existed in French schools in the 19th century: In the late 1880s, only eight Cambodians could be found among the 100-plus pupils attending the College of the Protectorate, then known as the School of the Protectorate (Forest, 1980; Tully, 1996).

Modern education began to expand at the turn of the 20th century with the establishment of the Franco-Cambodian education system. Franco-Cambodian schools operated on a "3 + 3 + 4" model. Elementary schools (the *écoles élémentaires*) provided the first three years of primary education; complementary schools (the *écoles complémentaires*) included both the elementary cycle and the three-year complementary cycle of primary education. By 1939, 107 elementary schools and 18 complementary schools were providing education in Cambodia (Bilodeau, 1955). Graduating from primary education, students could enter the four-year advanced primary education (*enseignement primaire supérieur*) cycle. In 1933, the Collège Sisowath (formerly the College of the Protectorate) became the Lycée Sisowath; this school introduced a full secondary curriculum in 1935 (Népote, 1979). Following this innovation, graduates of advanced primary education could proceed to three years of secondary education, which "terminat[ed] with an examination equivalent to the French *baccalauréate*" (Tully, 1996: 245). French served as the language of instruction in Franco-Cambodian schools. Although there were a number of skills-training centers, no universities provided education in Cambodia until after the country gained independence from France in 1953.

The Franco-Cambodian school system remained very small during the early decades of the 20th century, and girls benefited little from it. According to John Tully (1996), for example, girls composed only around 6 percent of the 3,700

Cambodians studying in Franco-Cambodian schools in 1922. In the decades that followed, girls continued to be underrepresented in Franco-Cambodian schools, despite some sluggish growth. In 1931, 982 girls attended Franco-Cambodian schools, most at the 13 girls' schools established in Phnom Penh and provincial capitals (Morizon, 1931). In this year, girls made up 11 percent of primary school students; the proportion of girls rose to 17 percent in 1941 and to 21 percent in 1951 (Steinberg et al., 1957).

Thomas Clayton (1995) argues that low enrollments in French schools represented resistance on the part of Cambodians to modern education, rather than a purposeful restriction of education by the colonial administration. In an effort to draw more Cambodians into modern education, particularly in areas outside urban centers, in the early 20th century the French "modernized" the *wat* schools. Despite some difficulties at the beginning, this reform spread rapidly around the country after 1924. By 1931 and 1939, respectively, 101 and 908 modernized *wat* schools were providing education to Cambodian children in cities, towns, villages, and rural areas throughout Cambodia (Bilodeau, 1955). In modernized *wat* schools, pupils received instruction equivalent to the three-year elementary cycle in Franco-Cambodian primary schools. Children attended schools from 2:00 P.M. to 5:30 P.M. to avoid conflict with the morning religious rituals of monks (Sorn, 1995). Khmer served as the medium of instruction in modernized *wat* schools (Bilodeau, 1955). The curriculum in *wat* schools mainly concentrated on reading and spelling in Khmer language; only one hour per week was devoted to reading and writing French (Tully, 1996).

In principle, modernized *wat* schools served as a bridge to the Franco-Cambodian education system. In reality, however, very few students from modernized *wat* schools crossed this bridge. In order to be admitted to Franco-Cambodian schools for further study, *wat* students had to pass the examination for the *Certificat d'Etudes Elémentaires Indigenes* (CEEI) and then attend a preparatory course to learn French. School statistics show that a relatively small proportion of modernized *wat* school students graduated with the CEEI. In 1933, for example, out of 4,764 enrolled students in Kampot province, only 585 registered for the examination, and only 240 passed it; in that year, only 33 percent of all students in the country who took the exam received a passing grade. Reasons for low success rates for modernized *wat* pupils included high absenteeism and dropout rates, the distance from villages to provincial town centers where examinations took place, and the low quality of instruction in topics including mathematics (Sorn, 1995).

Modernized *wat* schools relied heavily on monks to provide education. Because it was considered inappropriate for monks to have contact with girls, this segment of the Cambodian school-aged population was effectively barred from obtaining education in modernized *wat* schools (Tully, 1996). Thus, even when the French attempted to expand opportunities for modern education beyond the Franco-Cambodian school system and urban centers, girls' participation was inhibited. For Tully (1996: 243), the *de facto* prohibition against girls in modernized *wat* schools combines with disproportionate representation of girls in Franco-Cambodian schools to form a significant theme during the colonial period:

The neglect of girls' education is one of the greatest blots on the French record in Cambodia. Even if we acknowledge the indifference and hostility of the Cambodians themselves to girls' education, and even if we recognize that feminist consciousness was at a low level in European society at that time, this is still an abysmal record.

GIRLS AND EDUCATION AFTER INDEPENDENCE: MASS EXPANSION

The French colonial period officially ended in Cambodia in 1953. As in many newly independent states, the leaders of the Kingdom of Cambodia perceived education to be integral to achieving their goals of modernization and nation building. Consequently, they engineered a great expansion of the education system in the postcolonial period. This rapid expansion brought a surge of girls into the formal education system, mostly at the primary level.

The postcolonial government of Cambodia, led by Prince Norodom Sihanouk, worked relentlessly to improve the small formal education system left by the French administration. Expenditures for education, for instance, rose to more than 20 percent of the national budget in the years 1956–1959 (Fergusson and Masson, 1997). As one important consequence, the number of secular public schools (both former Franco-Cambodian schools and converted modernized *wat* schools) increased dramatically, as did the number of children attending them. The tally of primary schools rose from 787 in 1952, to 2,001 in 1960, and to 5,275 in 1969. Meanwhile, primary enrollments jumped from around 200,000 in 1952, to nearly one million by the end of the 1960s. Whereas five secondary schools had been established by 1952, this number had expanded to 35 and 146 by 1960 and 1969, respectively. From approximately 1,000 students at the end of the 1940s, secondary enrollment rose to 13,000 by 1957 and to 150,000 by the end of the 1960s (Bilodeau, 1955; Duvieusart and Ughetto, 1973; Whitaker et al., 1973; Népote, 1979; Gyallay-Pap, 1989). By the end of the 1960s, nine universities had opened in Cambodia, six in Phnom Penh and three in provincial capitals, and they enrolled 5,753 students (Fergusson and Masson, 1997).

The growth of secular public schools brought many girls into formal education, particularly into primary schools. For example, the proportion of female students among total primary school enrollees steadily accelerated from a mere 21 percent in 1951 to more than 40 percent in 1968 (Steinberg et al., 1957; Watts et al., 1989). While this progression toward parity clearly illustrates a positive trend, hurdles to education remained for girls, notably for advancement beyond the first few years of primary school. Even as the number of secondary schools increased in Cambodia, for example, the proportion of girls attending decreased; girls accounted for only 15 percent of secondary enrollments in the early 1960s (Eilenberg, 1961). This trend accelerated in higher education. According to data collected by the United Nations Educational, Scientific, and Cultural Organization (UNESCO), for instance, women accounted for only 11 percent of students attending university in Cambodia between 1952 and 1963 (cited in Fergusson and Masson, 1997).

It is notable that in the postcolonial era, the representation of Cambodian women dropped rather than increased at each successive level up the educational ladder. There may be many reasons for this trend, including the lack of attention given to gender issues by policy makers distracted by other educational projects, notably the language policy reform that began to replace French with Khmer as the instructional medium. Cultural attitudes relative to girls' expectations in life may also have contributed. Michael Vickery (1984: 176), for instance, examines this period and explains that the

place of women was definitely considered to be in the home and, for peasant women, in the fields; and formal schooling for them had not traditionally been seen as necessary. At most, basic literacy was seen as desirable; and as late as 1960s few girls outside of Phnom Penh persisted beyond the six years of primary school. In fact many got married soon after that, and . . . at that time . . . male students and teachers frequently remarked that too much schooling tended to turn girls into whores.

Whether it can be explained by the inattention of educational policy makers, cultural attitudes, or other reasons, the decreasing rate of participation in successive higher levels of schooling tempered the significant educational progress achieved by and for girls and women in the period of postcolonial educational expansion.

EN ROUTE TO DESTRUCTION: EDUCATION IN THE KHMER REPUBLIC

The year 1970 marked a turning point in Cambodian history. Resentment over Prince Sihanouk's corrupt government, economic mismanagement, left-leaning political agenda, and inability to prevent Cambodia from becoming embroiled in the conflict in neighboring Vietnam led to his overthrow by General Lon Nol. Cambodia's new government, the Khmer Republic, sided with the United States in the escalating war in Southeast Asia (Chandler, 1992; Corfield, 1994). However, Cambodia deteriorated significantly during the five years following 1970. The period saw "substantial human devastation and material destruction, with Cambodian Republicans, Cambodian Communists, Vietnamese Communists, their South Vietnamese enemies, and the United States all inflicting extensive damage on the rural Cambodian countryside" (Ayres, 2000: 69). Though an ally, the United States bombed Cambodia heavily in the late 1960s in an attempt to disrupt the movement of Vietnamese troops and supplies along the Ho Chi Minh Trail in the eastern part of the country (Etcheson, 1984). The economy also declined as a result of heavy deficit spending and hyperinflation that dropped the value of Cambodia's currency by 462 percent by 1974 (Duggan, 1996).

Educational progress came to a halt, and in most cases it was actually reversed. The Khmer Republic era saw many school buildings and educational materials destroyed or damaged by heavy U.S. bombing; other schools closed either because the government had lost territory to the rebels or because heavy fighting in the region made it too risky for pupils to attend class. According to Whitaker et al. (1973), by 1971 approximately 80 percent of the country's 5,275 primary schools had closed, as had half of the nation's 146 secondary schools. Of the country's nine universities, only Phnom Penh University remained open. The war also slowed or stopped the educational reforms of the postcolonial period. The significant progress made during 1970 and 1971 to institute Khmer as the language of instruction in secondary schools halted, for example; primary schools had completed the shift to Khmer by the end of the 1960s. Similarly, many committees that had been formed within school districts to translate educational materials into Khmer ceased functioning as their members fled dangerous areas (Ayres, 2000).

It is difficult to assess the impact of the war on girls' education during the Khmer Republic, given that so few records survive. Considering the vulnerability of girls to social insecurity and their fragile status in education at the beginning of the period, it is likely that many withdrew from education. At least some advancement in girls' educational participation in the postcolonial years, then, may have been reversed by the calamities of the early 1970s.

The Khmer Rouge and Education

The Khmer Republic collapsed in April 1975, when the Khmer Rouge led by Pol Pot took over the country by force. Until the end of 1978, Cambodia was ruled by the government of Democratic Kampuchea, and the regime was infamously known for its brutality, massive killings, and abrupt social changes. The Khmer Rouge sought to transform Cambodian society by eliminating the international influence, social injustice, inequality, and exploitation they believed to have prevailed in the earlier periods (Chandler, 1992). Many institutions and structures associated with previous regimes were abolished, among them markets, currency, and religion, and many people who sympathized with previous ways of life were killed (Mysliwiec, 1988). Many others died after having been relocated from urban to rural areas, where they were subjected to hard labor under the merciless supervision of Khmer Rouge cadres.

The modern education system introduced by the French and advanced by Sihanouk in the postcolonial period ceased to function in Democratic Kampuchea. The Khmer Rouge regarded education of the prewar period as useless and unrelated to individual or national needs, and they viewed educated people such as students, teachers, and professors as dangerous, untrustworthy, and unreliable (Vickery, 1984; Chandler, 1992; Ayres, 2000). As a result, the new government destroyed many school buildings after 1975, while leaving others to deteriorate or converting them into prisons or warehouses. At the same time, the Khmer Rouge purposefully killed many Cambodians suspected of having been educated. Though likely inflated, official records of the government that succeeded Democratic Kampuchea report that the Khmer Rouge destroyed 90 percent of existing school buildings and killed 75 percent of the teaching force, 96 percent of tertiary students, and 67 percent of primary and secondary students (Clayton, 2000). Given the immense destruction in the education sector, many commentators conclude that education was nonexistent during the Democratic Kampuchea period.

Other scholars and historians, however, have found evidence of some formal education during the period. Indeed, the Khmer Rouge declared their dedication to providing primary education for young children, and a limited number of primary schools did operate in some parts of the country between 1975 and 1979, though no consistency existed across regions (Vickery, 1984; Clayton, 1998; Ayres, 2000). Where it could be found, schooling took place in rice barns, in buffalo stables, and in the open air. Teachers earned positions on the basis of their "revolutionary attitude," as opposed to experience or university credentials (Vickery, 1984: 171). Children spent more time singing revolutionary songs than learning the Khmer alphabet, and as a result most were reported to have been illiterate at the end of the decade (Clayton, 1998; Ayres, 2000). Beyond the limited primary schooling for young children, the Khmer Rouge provided political education for the general population, training for Khmer Rouge cadres, and reeducation for the middle classes of the previous regime (Clayton, 1998).

It is difficult to draw conclusions about the education of girls in Democratic Kampuchea. However, given the fact that the Khmer Rouge treated men and women equally, it would be reasonable to expect that girls and boys would have received similar educational treatment. Unfortunately, since children learned almost nothing even if they lived in areas where Khmer Rouge schools operated, girls and boys would have emerged from school equally illiterate. Thus, the devastating Khmer Rouge years exacerbated the educational decline begun during the Khmer Republic, and the advances made by and for girls in postcolonial Cambodia weakened further.

FROM VACUITY TO ISOLATION: EDUCATION IN POST-KHMER ROUGE CAMBODIA

Democratic Kampuchea came to an end on January 7, 1979, when a group of former Khmer Rouge cadres, who had earlier defected and fled to Vietnam, toppled the regime with military support from the Vietnamese army (Chandler, 1992). Vietnam quickly installed a new government, the People's Republic of Kampuchea; like its Vietnamese patron, the People's Republic of Kampuchea adopted socialism as Cambodia's official state ideology. From camps on the Thai border, the regrouped Khmer Rouge and several other armed factions—including one led by Prince Sihanouk—launched a military campaign against the

Vietnamese occupation. Cambodia suffered from this draining civil war throughout the 1980s.

The destruction of social structures and institutions from 1975 onward left the People's Republic of Kampuchea little to start with in 1979. "There were no institutions of any kind—no bureaucracy, no army or police, no schools or hospitals, no state or private commercial networks, no religious hierarchies, no legal system," one commentator wrote of the period (Gottesman, 2003: x). As if this were not enough, Western nations, the People's Republic of China, and the member states of the Association of Southeast Asian Nations condemned the continuing Vietnamese military presence in Cambodia and, as a consequence, refused to provide development assistance to the country, despite the devastation the people had endured in the 1970s (Chandler, 1992). One Western aid worker described the results of this international pressure well in the title of her study of life in the early 1980s: *Punishing the Poor: The International Isolation of Kampuchea* (Mysliwiec, 1988). Eastern-bloc nations, on the other hand, provided considerable development assistance to Cambodia in the 1980s.

In spite of the difficult situation it inherited, the government of the People's Republic of Kampuchea demonstrated a strong commitment to education, beginning with the restoration and expansion of the formal education system. In the fall of 1979, the Ministry of Education opened a "4 + 3 + 3" education system, with four years of primary schooling being followed by three years each of lower and upper secondary education; the primary cycle expanded to five years in 1987 (United Nations Children's Fund, 1990). At the completion of each cycle, students sat for a national examination; successful candidates obtained diplomas and could advance to the next school level (Galasso, 1990). With support from Communist-bloc nations, notably Vietnam and the Soviet Union, the Ministry of Education gradually reopened the country's universities, beginning with the Faculty of Medicine and Pharmacy in 1979 and the Teachers' Training College in 1980. While Khmer served as the medium of instruction in primary and secondary schools, some universities, those where Vietnamese and Soviet professors had replaced those killed by the Khmer Rouge, provided instruction in Vietnamese and Russian.

With the goal of universalizing primary education by 1991, primary enrollments expanded rapidly during the 1980s; by the end of the decade, 1.3 million Cambodian children were attending primary schools (Watts et al., 1989). Secondary education also expanded dramatically as the Cambodian Ministry of Education worked to make the first eight years of education compulsory. By 1989, more than 330,000 Cambodians were studying in secondary schools (289,000 and 35,000 at the lower and upper secondary levels, respectively; Watts et al., 1989). As universities opened throughout the 1980s, the number of tertiary students increased, ultimately reaching 5,479 by the end of the decade (Ministry of Education, 1990). The People's Republic of Kampuchea also worked to provide education to adults, particularly to those who had been denied formal schooling during the Khmer Rouge regime. As of 1991, nearly

70,000 adults were participating in complementary equivalency education, which included material equivalent to that learned in formal primary and secondary schools; adults studied either full time during the day or part time at night on the premises of formal schools (Galasso, 1990; United Nations Children's Fund, 1990; Yos, 1991).

The expansion of education posed significant difficulties for the Cambodian Ministry of Education. To begin, the ministry faced a severe shortage of school facilities. In populated areas, surviving schools operated double or triple shifts, or organized multigrade classrooms, in an attempt to accommodate exploding student demand (Galasso, 1990). In other areas, children studied in ruined buildings or under trees; in 1980, for example, one commentator observed a "grade one class tak[ing] place under a tree but need[ing] to be closed as soon as the rainy season starts" (Reiff, 1980, annex IV: 2). Many schools operated without tables, chairs, or teaching and learning materials such as teachers' guides, students' textbooks, pencils, or notebooks (Galasso, 1990; United Nations Children's Fund, 1990). From this difficult beginning, thousands of schools arose throughout the country, often built by members of the community served by the facility. By the end of the decade, 4,773 primary, 394 lower secondary, and 61 upper secondary schools had been repaired or constructed (Ministère de l'Education, 1990). By 1989, seven institutions were providing university education in Cambodia.

Additionally, many teachers had little formal training. During the emergency period of the early 1980s, teachers were recruited without regard to educational background according to the motto: "Those who know a lot teach those who know little [and] those who know little teach those who know nothing" (Gottesman, 2003: 72–73). One Cambodian who had worked with the Ministry of Education in the early 1980s explained:

In order to open the school year 1979, we called all survivors, even if they had a very low academic background, even if they only had a primary education. We had to call these people to be volunteer teachers. We gave them one or two or three weeks of training. We gave them some ideas about pedagogy and classroom management. With these volunteers, we reorganized the system of education. (cited in Clayton, 2000: 114)

As the ministry succeeded in reopening the country's system of teacher training colleges with Vietnamese assistance, however, trained teachers began to enter Cambodia's schools. By the end of the 1980s, several tens of thousands of Cambodians had graduated from these pedagogical institutions and had joined others trained more perfunctorily in the early 1980s in a 50,000-strong teaching corps (United Nations Educational, Scientific, and Cultural Organization, 1991).

Infrastructural and pedagogical problems in Cambodian education in the 1980s perhaps explain the high rate of attrition in Cambodia's schools: For every 100 students who enrolled in Grade 1 in 1981, only 14 reached Grade 5 in 1985 (Watts et al., 1989). The pressing demands for new school buildings and teacher training programs may also have distracted the Ministry of Education from addressing gender equity issues directly, for issues of girls' and women's education do not feature prominently in educational policy documents from the 1980s. Nevertheless, some progress appears to have been made in this arena compared with the postcolonial period. In the 1980s, girls accounted for 45 percent of the primary enrollment; this figure exceeded the 40 percent proportion of primary school girls in the 1960s (Watts et al., 1989). Girls made up 31 percent of the student body in secondary schools in 1989, dramatically higher than the 15 percent they composed in the 1960s (respectively, Ministère de l'Education, 1990; Eilenberg, 1961). The trend continued in higher education. In 1989, 16 percent of entering university students were women; in the 1950s, women had accounted for only 11 percent of the university population (respectively, Ministry of Education, Youth, and Sport, 1993; Fergusson and Masson, 1997).

One could argue that the 1980s constituted Cambodia's second great period of educational expansion, after the first in the 1950s and 1960s. In each era, the number and proportion of girls and women in schools and universities increased overall, while at the same time decreasing in successive levels of education; girls' and women's educational opportunities appear to have been somewhat higher at all levels in the 1980s than in the earlier era. Immediately prior to the Education for All initiative, then, Cambodia appears to have reestablished the positive trajectory toward gender equity in education begun in the postcolonial period.

ENTERING THE GLOBALIZATION AGE: GIRLS' EDUCATION SINCE THE EARLY 1990s

The waning of the Cold War in the late 1980s and early 1990s brought many changes to Cambodia. These changes included the substantial reduction of financial and technical support from the Eastern bloc, the withdrawal of the Vietnamese army, the abandonment of central economic planning in favor of the free market, and the influx of development assistance agencies from Western countries. Negotiations between the People's Republic of Kampuchea and the other factions in Cambodia's civil war led to the Paris Peace Accords, signed in 1991. Though the Khmer Rouge ultimately withdrew from the peace agreement and continued fighting, Cambodia held its first democratic election in 1993 under international supervision; other general elections followed on the five-year schedule mandated by the 1993 constitution, in 1998 and 2003.

Change also occurred for girls in Cambodia's education system. Since the early 1990s, considerable attention has been given to gender inequity in education and, more specifically, to the participation of girls in basic education. The government's overt concern for girls' education manifests itself in agreements to and adoptions of various frameworks for which educational gender equality is central. For example, the Royal Government of Cambodia officially endorsed the goals of Education for All adopted at the World Conference on Education for All in Thailand in 1990 and the World Forum on Education for All in Senegal in 2000. Both world forums highlight the importance of girls' education and gender equity in schooling (Inter-Agency Commission, 1990; United Nations

Educational, Scientific, and Cultural Organization, 2000). In 2000, Cambodia also became a signatory to the United Nations' Millennium Development Goals; Goal Two emphasizes universal completion of primary education, and Goal Three proposes gender equality in all spheres by 2015 (United Nations Department of Public Information, 2005).

Guided by these global initiatives, Cambodian leaders have articulated local goals for girls' educational participation in broad development plans such as the First Five-Year Socio-Economic Development Plan 1996–2000 (Royal Government of Cambodia, 1997), the Second Five-Year Socio-Economic Development Plan 2001–2005 (Royal Government of Cambodia, 2002b), and the National Poverty Reduction Strategy 2003–2005 (Royal Government of Cambodia, 2002a); all have advocated gender equity in education. Equal access to education for all groups, including girls, also emerges as a primary objective in plans specific to the education sector, such as the Basic Education Investment Plan 1995–2000 (Royal Government of Cambodia, 1994), the Education Strategic Plan 2001–2005 (Ministry of Education, Youth, and Sport, 2001b) and its supporting Education Sector Support Program 2001–2005 and 2002–2006 (Ministry of Education, Youth, and Sport, 2001a, 2002a), and the Education for All National Plan 2003–2015 (Royal Government of Cambodia, 2003).

Despite the articulation of gender equity in education as a goal in Cambodia's development plans, however, few dedicated programs to accomplishing it were unveiled until very late. In the 1990s, the Ministry of Education, Youth, and Sport appears to have assumed that girls' participation would automatically improve with the development of the education system as a whole. For example, in the major education plan of the 1990s, the Basic Education Investment Plan 1995–2000, the ministry listed investments in school infrastructure, teacher training, curriculum development, and textbook distribution among interventions intended to achieve equitable access to basic education (Royal Government of Cambodia, 1994). A similar lack of preferential treatment for girls can be observed in the recent Education Strategic Plan 2001–2005, in which specific measures to increase girls' participation in education are few. For instance, among 12 Priority Action Programs laid out in the Education Sector Support Program 2002–2006, only the final addresses gender equity, through its focus on providing scholarships to secondary school girls in danger of dropping out of school (Ministry of Education, Youth, and Sport, 2002a).

Only at the beginning of the 21st century did the Ministry of Education, Youth, and Sport establish the Gender Working Group to address gender equity issues in education. The secretariat of the group, consisting mainly of ministry officials, produced the Five-Year Gender Mainstreaming Strategy 2002–2006 (Ministry of Education, Youth, and Sport, 2002b). The strategy comprises three main goals: (1) achieving gender equity in access to education; (2) achieving gender equity in educational management and service delivery; and (3) strengthening gender technical capacity in educational programming and policy making. Activities initiated by the Gender Working Group include reviewing all departmental plans within the ministry for the integration of gender related issues, gender awareness raising, and the promotion of measures to increase the representation of women in educational management positions (Ministry of Education, Youth, and Sport, 2002b). In addition to the ministry's actions supportive of educational equality, many donor agencies have also implemented projects and programs to enhance the education of girls in recent years (for a review of these projects, see Bredenberg et al., 2003).

The commitment to providing education to all children, coupled with recent concrete activities dedicated to girls' educational participation, have resulted in increases in the number of girls enrolled in schools and in the proportion of girls in education. As illustrated in Table 3.1, the number of primary school girls has steadily increased since the beginning of the 1990s; by 2004–2005, more than twice as many girls were attending primary schools as in the early 1990s. The 45.08 percent share of girls in primary education in 1991–1992 represented a similar proportion to that in the late 1980s (see previous section); girls' participation in primary education rose to 45.81 percent at the end of the 1990s and then to 47.22 percent in 2004–2005 (Ministry of Education, Youth, and Sport, 1995/1996–2004/2005). Although the percentage of female students in secondary schools in the early 1990s decreased from the late 1980s (see previous section) and then stagnated during the later half of the 1990s, it has since improved dramatically. By 2004–2005, girls represented nearly 42 percent of the secondary population; this proportion is 51 percent higher than in 1991–1992, when girls represented only slightly more than one-quarter of the secondary population. In absolute terms, the number of girls enrolled in secondary schools has more than quadrupled since 1991–1992.

Table 3.1
Girls' Share in Total Enrollment in Primary and Secondary Education

Year	Primary Level				Secondary Level			
	Total	Boys	Girls	Girls %	Total	Boys	Girls	Girls %
1991–1992	1,371,694	753,357	618,337	45.08	236,882	171,040	65,842	27.80
1992–1993	1,468,958	809,217	659,741	44.91	239,363	160,240	79,123	33.06
1993–1994	1,621,685	894,625	727,060	44.83	285,779	208,402	77,377	27.08
1994–1995	1,703,316	947,181	756,135	44.39	297,555	185,757	111,798	37.57
1995–1996	1,805,631	1,002,273	803,358	44.49	288,075	174,512	113,563	39.42
1996–1997	1,918,985	1,058,285	860,700	44.85	327,566	207,484	120,082	36.66
1997–1998	2,011,772	1,104,945	906,827	45.08	302,951	197,511	105,440	34.80
1998–1999	2,094,000	1,137,916	956,084	45.66	308,167	202,999	105,168	34.13
1999–2000	2,211,738	1,198,604	1,013,134	45.81	341,491	222,559	118,932	34.83
2000–2001	2,408,109	1,294,738	1,113,371	46.23	388,664	250,383	138,281	35.58
2001–2002	2,705,453	1,447,764	1,257,689	46.49	465,039	292,691	172,348	37.06
2002–2003	2,747,411	1,463,551	1,283,860	46.73	543,885	334,520	209,365	38.49
2003–2004	2,747,080	1,455,827	1,291,253	47.00	613,744	366,006	247,738	40.37
2004–2005	2,682,129	1,415,709	1,266,420	47.22	706,069	409,697	296,372	41.97

Source: Ministry of Education, Youth, and Sport, 1995/1996–2004/2005.

Advancement can also be observed in higher education, particularly after 1999 when the government began to allow private universities to operate (United Nations Development Fund for Women, World Bank, Asian Development Bank, United Nations Development Programme, and Department for International Development/United Kingdom, 2004). The proliferation of universities, especially in provinces outside Phnom Penh, has made it possible for some young women who were earlier constrained by the cost of traveling and other distance-related concerns, to pursue higher education. The share of female students in higher education increased from 16.7 percent in 1996–1997, a figure compatible with that of the late 1980s (see previous section), to 22.9 percent in 2001–2002 (Bredenberg et al., 2003).

Thanks to the greater attention given to girls' education and efforts made by the Cambodian government and other institutions and organizations, girls and women have made remarkable gains in educational participation in the current era. That girls continue to lag behind boys, however, suggests that more work needs to be done. Several studies describe the complex web of factors that impede contemporary girls' participation and progress in education. These factors include parental preference for boys' education, higher perceived opportunity cost of girls' education, the lack of latrine facilities for girls at schools, and the absence of positive female role models (Fiske, 1995; CARE and Ministry of Education, Youth, and Sport, 1998; Velasco, 2001, 2004). Further, Esther Velasco (2001) illustrates how the expectation for girls to become homemakers prevails among parents, teachers, and even girls themselves. The dynamic combination of gendered attitudes, economic necessity, and school factors appears to be contributing to lower participation by girls than boys in education in Cambodia.

Given the many obstacles that girls face, progressing through schooling to a level above primary education remains a difficult journey. The description that follows illustrates how one Cambodian girl struggles against these obstacles on a daily basis to get education.

A DAY IN THE LIFE OF A RURAL GIRL IN CAMBODIA TODAY[2]

Davy (a pseudonym) is a Grade 9 student currently enrolled in Kondeang lower secondary school in Kondeang district, in Cambodia's Pursat province. She lives about eight kilometers from her school. Because Kondeang district is located in the plains surrounding Tonle Sap lake, people in Kondeang, including Davy's family, make their living from both farming and fishing. Davy is the eldest of four siblings. Born to a relatively poor family, Davy has to help her parents earn cash to cover various expenses, including those related to her and her brothers' education. Early in the morning every other day, Davy sells vegetables in a small market a few hundred meters from her school before school starts. She grows the vegetables for sale in her own garden, or buys or forages them from around her neighborhood.

Today is a market day, so Davy gets up at 4:30 A.M. It takes her 20 minutes to wash, tie up her hair, put on her uniform, and eat some rice for breakfast. The journey from home to the market takes her about 20 minutes by bicycle. Because the day starts early in Cambodia, many housewives and farmers are already in the market to shop for vegetables and meat at 5:30 A.M. Davy sets up her baskets and sells most of her vegetables by 6:45 A.M. She then quickly sells off the few items remaining in her basket and hurries to school by 6:50 A.M. She does not have time to notice that her uniform has gotten dirty in the muddy market place. Davy would have wrapped up her sale 15 minutes sooner if it had been Monday, when all students arrive early in the school yard to honor the national flag and sing the national anthem, or if it was her turn to sweep the classroom. At school, Davy leaves her basket with the lady who runs a food stall in the school canteen and with whom Davy has become acquainted through her frequent lunches at the lady's shop.

School starts at 7:00 A.M. Classes normally last from 7:00 A.M. to 11:00 A.M. in the morning and from 2:00 P.M. to 5:00 P.M. in the afternoon. Officially, students eat lunch from 11:00 A.M. to 2:00 P.M. Not many of Davy's classmates take the three-hour lunch break, however. Most opt to spend only 30 minutes for lunch either at home, for those who live nearby, or at the school canteen, for others. Then, they return to their classrooms for private supplementary tutorial classes for Chemistry, from 11:30 A.M. to 12:30 P.M., and for Mathematics, from 12:30 P.M. to 2:00 P.M. Today, Davy eats her lunch at the canteen and then attends both Chemistry and Mathematics supplementary classes, which are offered by her classroom teachers. She then sits in classes for another three official hours before returning home at 5:00 P.M.

Davy finally arrives home at 5:30 P.M. Though tired, she does not indulge herself with a rest, but instead helps her mother cook dinner. Davy's family eats dinner at 6:00 P.M. After doing the dishes and some other housework, Davy again sets off to a teacher's house in the neighborhood for her private English lesson, from 7:00 to 8:00 P.M. Davy, like many other students, does not take private English lessons for the sole purpose of getting high scores in her secondary school leaving examination, but rather for its own importance. She believes that if she could speak English, she could find a job in the city. Davy not only takes private English lessons on weekdays, but also spends four hours each weekend in English classes offered free by a local nongovernmental organization. Davy returns home at 8:00 P.M., does some homework, and goes to bed around 10:00 P.M. On days before market days, Davy must pick, buy, or forage vegetables for sale between the time she returns from school and the time she leaves for her English lesson.

Going to school and at the same time earning some money to supplement her family's income is a daily challenge for Davy. Davy aspires to finish high school and go to the teacher's training college in nearby Battambang province. Given both the direct cost of college education, and the indirect cost to her family from the loss of her income, Davy realizes that achieving her dream will not be easy.

AN UNFINISHED HISTORY

This chapter has examined girls' and women's education in Cambodia across several historical periods. As we have seen, Cambodian girls and women have made great progress in education over the course of the last several centuries, though complete equity in educational participation has not yet been achieved.

In premodern Cambodia, boys studied with monks in Buddhist monasteries or *wats*, while girls were prohibited from interaction with monks and, hence, from education. The French introduced a small system of modern education in Cambodia in the 1870s, though throughout the 19th century few Cambodians, and fewer Cambodian girls, enrolled in it. The French expanded modern education beyond the urban centers in the early 20th century by modernizing the *wat* schools. While this reform brought many Cambodians from rural areas into the modern education system, cultural prohibitions against girls' participation remained, and as a result relatively few girls received education. Indeed, after nearly a century of French colonial control, in the early 1950s, only about one-fifth of Cambodian girls were attending school. It seems an understatement to conclude that boys benefited disproportionately from education during the French colonial period, while girls lagged far behind.

In the immediate postcolonial period, Cambodia undertook a massive expansion of the formal education system. For many girls, the expanding secular educational infrastructure provided the first opportunity to attend school, and both the numbers and proportion of girls in education increased dramatically. Despite the fact that the Ministry of Education did not discuss gender equity in educational policy documents, and despite the lack of specific interventions designed to increase girls' and women's educational participation, by the end of the 1960s girls approached par with boys in Cambodia's primary schools; fewer girls than boys continued to higher levels of education, however, as the educational statistics from secondary schools and universities indicate. Unfortunately, the progress achieved by girls in the postcolonial period faltered after 1970, as the war escalated and the Khmer Rouge came to power. In these years, schools were destroyed or left to decay, and the modern education system ceased to function. Girls and boys appear to have been treated equally in such schools as did exist in Democratic Kampuchea, though the focus of education was such that both groups remained illiterate.

Cambodia entered a second period of educational expansion in the post–Khmer Rouge period, during which the government of the People's Republic of Kampuchea and its Eastern-bloc patrons, Vietnam and the Soviet Union, directed considerable resources and effort into the restoration of the education system. As schools were opened and teachers trained to replace those destroyed and killed by the Khmer Rouge, the education system expanded with the goal of universal primary schooling. In the process of expansion, significantly larger numbers of girls enrolled in education than ever before. By the end of the 1980s, the proportion of girls nearly equaled that of boys at the primary level, while girls' share in secondary and tertiary education surpassed that of the immediate postcolonial period. Perhaps because educational policy in the 1980s did not specifically address gender equity in education, enrollment rates for girls and women nevertheless lagged those of boys and men, particularly after primary school.

Cambodia experienced significant change relative to economics, politics, and development assistance in the late 1980s and early 1990s. Change also occurred in education, as the Royal Government of Cambodia became a signatory to

Santhormok high school during lunch break. Courtesy of Keng Chan Sopheak. This picture is dedicated to all Cambodian students who have coped with all obstacles in the pursuit for more education.

international goals such as Education for All. As a direct result, girls' education began to receive dedicated attention for the first time in history. Though the government and development assistance agencies have begun to translate the goal of educational equality into concrete programs designed to achieve equity only relatively recently, results can already be observed. Indeed, both the number and proportion of girls in all levels of education has increased remarkably since the early 1990s. As a result of gendered attitudes, economic imperatives, and school facilities, however, girls' and women's educational participation still lags behind that of boys and men, particularly in secondary and tertiary education. It will only be through continued programming by the government and development assistance agencies that equity will be achieved for girls and young women in education in Cambodia.

NOTES

1. Original research for this chapter was conducted by the first author in March and April 2005, based on data collected from school observations and interviews with local education officials, teachers, and students.

2. In March 2005, the first author asked several secondary students to write a one-week diary of their daily lives both in and outside schools. This student diary was selected on the basis of its comprehensiveness and its accurate depiction of Cambodian rural life.

REFERENCES

Ayres, David (2000). *Anatomy of a Crisis: Education, Development, and the State in Cambodia, 1953–1998*. Honolulu, HI: University of Hawai'i Press.

Bilodeau, Charles (1955). "Compulsory education in Cambodia," in Charles Bilodeau, Somlith Pathammavong, and Lê Quang Hông (eds), *Compulsory Education in Cambodia, Laos and Viet-Nam*, pp. 9–67. Paris: United Nations Educational, Scientific, and Cultural Organization (UNESCO).

Bredenberg, Kurt, Somanee, Lon and Sopheap, Ma (2003). *Gender and Education in Cambodia: Historical Trends and the Way Forward*. Phnom Penh: Oxfam.

CARE and Ministry of Education, Youth, and Sport (1998). *Survey on Girls' Education in Cambodia*. Phnom Penh: CARE and Australian Agency for International Development.

Chandler, David (1992). *A History of Cambodia*, 2nd edn. Boulder, CO: Westview Press.

Clayton, Thomas (1995). "Restriction or resistance? French colonial educational development in Cambodia," *Education Policy Analysis Archives I*, 3(19). Accessed on June 23, 2004 from http://epaa.asu.edu/epaa/v3n19.html.

——(1998). "Building the new Cambodia: Educational destruction and construction under the Khmer Rouge, 1975–1979," *History of Education Quarterly*, 38: 1–16.

——(2000). *Education and the Politics of Language: Hegemony and Pragmatism in Cambodia, 1979–1989*. Hong Kong: Comparative Education Research Center, University of Hong Kong.

Corfield, Justin (1994). *Khmers Stand Up! A History of the Cambodian Government 1970–1975*. Clayton, Australia: Monash University Centre of Southeast Asian Studies.

Duggan, Stephen (1996). "Education, teacher training and prospects for economic recovery in Cambodia," *Comparative Education*, 32: 361–375.

Duvieusart, Baudouin, and Ughetto, R. (1973). *République Khmère: Projet de Restructuration du Système d'Education*. Paris: United Nations Educational, Scientific, and Cultural Organization (UNESCO).

Eilenberg, Jeanette (1961). "New directions in Cambodian education," *Comparative Education Review*, 4: 188–192.

Etcheson, Craig (1984). *The Rise and Demise of Democratic Kampuchea*. Boulder, CO: Westview Press.

Fergusson, Lee, and Le Masson, Gildas (1997). "A Culture under siege: Post-colonial higher education and teacher education in Cambodia from 1953 to 1979," *History of Education*, 26: 91–112.

Fiske, Edward (1995). *Using Both Hands: Women and Education in Cambodia*. Manila: Asian Development Bank.

Forest, Alain (1980). *Le Cambodge et la Colonisation Française: Histoire d'une Colonisation sans Heurts (1897–1920)*. Paris: Editions L'Harmattan.

Galasso, Elisabetta (1990). *Education in Cambodia: Notes and Suggestions*. Phnom Penh: Redd Barna.

Gottesman, Evan (2003). *Cambodia after the Khmer Rouge: Inside the Politics of Nation Building*. New Haven, CT: Yale University Press.

Gyallay-Pap, Peter (1989). "Reclaiming a shattered past: Education for the displaced Khmer in Thailand," *Journal of Refugee Studies*, 2: 257–275.

Inter-Agency Commission (1990). *World Declaration on Education for All and Framework for Action to Meet Basic Learning Needs*. New York: Inter-Agency Commission.

Kalab, Milada (1976). "Monastic education, social mobility, and village structure in Cambodia," in Craig Calhoun and Francis Ianni (eds), *The Anthropological Study of Education*, pp. 61–74. The Hague: Mouton Publishers.

Ledgerwood, Judy (1996). *Women in Development: Cambodia.* Manila: Asian Development Bank.

Ministère de l'Education (1990). *Bulletin de Statistiques de l'Education de l'Etat du Cambodge.* Phnom Penh: Ministère de l'Education.

Ministry of Education (1990). *Education: State of Cambodia.* Phnom Penh: Ministry of Education.

Ministry of Education, Youth, and Sport (1993). *Education: Statistics and Training.* Phnom Penh: Ministry of Education, Youth, and Sport.

——(1995/1996–2004/2005). *Education Statistics and Indicators* (annual volumes). Phnom Penh: Education Management Information System.

——(2001a). *Education Sector Support Program 2001–2005.* Phnom Penh: Ministry of Education, Youth, and Sport.

——(2001b). *Education Strategic Plan 2001–2005.* Phnom Penh: Ministry of Education, Youth, and Sport.

——(2002a). *Education Sector Support Program 2002–2006.* Phnom Penh: Ministry of Education, Youth, and Sport.

——(2002b). *The Five-Year Gender Mainstreaming Strategy 2002–2006: From Commitment to Action.* Phnom Penh: Ministry of Education, Youth, and Sport.

Morizon, René (1931). *Monographie du Cambodge.* Hanoi: Imprimerie d'Extrême-Orient.

Mysliwiec, Eva (1988). *Punishing the Poor: The International Isolation of Kampuchea.* Oxford: Oxfam.

Népote, Jacques (1979). "Education et Développement dans le Cambodge Moderne," *Mondes en Développement*, 28: 767–792.

Reiff, Hans (1980). *Educational Emergency Assistance and Rehabilitation in Kampuchea.* Bangkok: United Nations Educational, Scientific, and Cultural Organization (UNESCO).

Royal Government of Cambodia (1994). *Basic Education Investment Plan 1995–2000.* Phnom Penh: Royal Government of Cambodia.

——(1997). *First Five-Year Socio-Economic Development Plan 1996–2000.* Phnom Penh: Royal Government of Cambodia.

——(2002a). *National Poverty Reduction Strategy 2003–2005.* Phnom Penh: Council for Social Development.

——(2002b). *Second Five-Year Socio-Economic Development Plan 2001–2005.* Phnom Penh: Royal Government of Cambodia.

——(2003). *Education for All National Plan 2003–2015.* Phnom Penh: Royal Government of Cambodia.

Sorn, Samnang (1995). *L'Evolution de la Société Cambodgienne entre les Deux Guerres Mondiales (1919–1939).* Unpublished Ph.D. Dissertation, University of Paris.

Steinberg, David, Bain, Chester, Burlingham, Lloyd, Duff, Russell, Fall, Bernard, Greenhouse, Ralph, Kramer, Lucy, and McLellan, Robert (1957). *Cambodia: Its People, Its Society, Its Culture.* New Haven, CT: Human Relations Area Files.

Tully, John (1996). *Cambodia under the Tricolour: King Sisowath and the "Mission Civilisatrice" 1904–1927.* Clayton, Australia: Monash Asia Institute.

United Nations Children's Fund (UNICEF) (1990). *Cambodia: The Situation of Women and Children.* Phnom Penh: UNICEF.

United Nations Department of Public Information (2005). *UN Development Millennium Goals*. Accessed on July 15, 2005 from http://www.un.org/millenniumgoals/index.html.

United Nations Development Fund for Women, World Bank, Asian Development Bank, United Nations Development Programme, and Department for International Development/United Kingdom (2004). *A Fair Share for Women: Cambodia Gender Assessment*. Phnom Penh: United Nations Development Fund for Women, World Bank, Asian Development Bank, United Nations Development Programme, and Department for International Development/United Kingdom.

United Nations Development Programme (2005). *Human Development Report 2005*. New York: UNDP.

United Nations Educational, Scientific, and Cultural Organization (UNESCO) (1991). *Inter-Sectoral Basic Needs Assessment Mission to Cambodia*. Bangkok: UNESCO.

——(2000). *The Dakar Framework for Action: Education for All: Meeting Our Collective Commitments*. Paris: UNESCO.

Velasco, Esther (2001). *Why Are Girls Not in School? Perception, Realities and Contradictions in Changing Cambodia*. Phnom Penh: United Nations Children's Fund (UNICEF) and Swedish International Development Cooperation Agency.

——(2004). "Ensuring gender equity in education for all: Is Cambodia on track?" *Prospects*, 34: 37–51.

Vickery, Michael (1984). *Cambodia 1975–1982*. Boston, MA: South End Press.

Watts, Kenneth, Draper, Charles, Elder, David, Harrison, John, Higaki, Yoichi and Salle, Jean-Claude (1989). *Report of the Kampuchea Needs Assessment Study*. New York: United Nations Development Programme.

Whitaker, Donald, Heimann, Judith, MacDonald, John, Martindale, Kenneth, Shinn, Rinn-Sup, and Townsend, Charles (1973). *Area Handbook for the Khmer Republic (Cambodia)*. Washington, DC: U.S. Government Printing Office.

Yos Son (1991). *Report on the Situation of Basic Education in Cambodia*. Opening speech at the National Conference on Education for All, September, Phnom Penh.

Chapter 4

SCHOOLING IN CHINA

Zhenzhou Zhao

INTRODUCTION

It is impossible to underestimate the importance of education's role in cultural transmission for China—the longest continuous civilization in the world. In the canonical *Daxue* (the Great Learning), one of the most prominent pieces of classical literature in ancient China, education is described as a mechanism for "cultivating oneself, regulating the family, as well as administering state affairs and ensuring national security (*xiushen qijia zhiguo pingtianxia*)" (see Liu, 1998: 121).

As Reed (1988: 3) states, "Respect for education was reputedly the hallmark of traditional China." Throughout Chinese history, education has also played a prominent role in upward social mobility. In the modern society, educational reform was closely bound with political change (Pepper, 1996).

Learning the Confucian orthodoxy and receiving a post in officialdom through civil service examination, known as the *keju*, began in ancient China around 1,300 years ago (Borthwick, 1983). Since the mid-19th century, continuous defeats in the wars with Western nations and Japan made the Qing court realize the deficiencies of the traditional Chinese education system in science and technology and the imperative need for learning from the West (Pepper, 1990, 1996).

Accordingly, a modern school system was established and students were sent abroad for Western training (Ding, 2001). In 1905, the *Keju* was abolished. In modern China, education is regarded as a driving force for social transition from an "agrarian, family-based society to a modern, industrialized nation" (Borthwick, 1983: xvi). The notion of "saving the country through education" (*jiaoyu jiuguo*) predominated throughout the past century (Peterson et al., 2001). Indeed, during the early 20th century, education had been an arena where the most innovative social transformations (i.e., new ideas and social structure rose) (Peterson et al., 2001).

After the foundation of the People's Republic of China (PRC), the government put emphasis upon the development of scientific and technological talents for building a strong, modern and prosperous China, while education was utilized as a tool of political struggle in the era of Mao Zedong (Gu, 2001). In 1983, Chinese leader Deng Xiaoping put forward a new vision, "education should face modernization, the world, and the future" (Ding, 2001: 174). During the past two decades, China witnessed tremendous economic, political, and educational reforms (Kewin and Xu, 1989).

From the 1990s, the central government considered science and education, knowledge economics, and human resources as an impetus for the rejuvenation of China (Gu, 2001). Yet, in contemporary Chinese society, schooling faces many challenges in an age of accelerated globalization: vitality of traditional Chinese culture and a promotion of Western modernization, the cultivation of talented people who are politically loyal to the government but have innovative capacity, the pursuit of equal education, and so on (see Gu, 2001; Peterson et al., 2001; Postiglione, 2006; Yang, 2006).

This chapter will present a chronological overview of schooling in China, and discuss how societal and cultural momentum influenced the development of education over time. Attention will be given to formal and informal education and the issues of class, gender, and ethnicity. Levels of schooling covered will be pre-school through higher education. The chapter ends by concluding that education is employed for "personal advancement and national self-strengthening effort" (Reed, 1988: 4).

HISTORICAL ROOTS

We will review the historical roots of China's education. Four periods are included: Ancient times (the Pre-Qin Period); the classical times, covering from the Han dynasty to the late the Qing, namely Confucian China; the modern times (1849–1949); and the contemporary society (1949–present).

The Ancient Times

It is argued that the earliest schools in China may be traced back to the Shang dynasty (*c.* 1766–1122 B.C.) when the symbols recorded on oracle bone indicated that school existed (Lee, 1985). The official in charge of education was called *situ* (Huang, 2005). In the Western Zhou dynasty (*c.* 1066–771 B.C.), schools were of two types: the state schools (*guoxue*) for noble slave owners; and community schools (*xiangxue*) for common slave owners (Wang et al., 1985). Yet, educational opportunities were only limited to the governors (*xuezai guanfu*) (Lee, 1985; Wang et al., 1985).

Owing to wars between princes, the public schools declined in the Spring and Autumn Period/Warring States Period (770–221 B.C.). The books and records kept in the state were disseminated in the civil society, and some intellectuals became private teachers (Wang et al., 1985). This allowed a niche for the boom of private schools by philosophers and scholars. The most famous ones followed the ideas of one or more of the influential Chinese philosophers, especially Confucius, Mengzi, Mozi, and Xunzi. They argued about the nature of human beings, the philosophy of education, and how to govern society (see Lee, 1985). "It was a time of free thinking and free expression, of invention and discover" (Chuang, 1922: 5). Confucius, the most influential of all, advocated that "the government should educate everyone without class or racial distinction; all men are born with equal potential for goodness" (*you jiao wulei*) rather than only the ruling class (Lee, 1985: 6). His disciples recorded the sayings and actions of Confucius in the "Analects" (*lunyu*), which is one of the "Four Books" (Chuang, 1922). During the Qin dynasty (221–206 B.C.) which made the first attempt to conquer foreign regions and unite China, ancient books, including the classics of Confucius were burned and scholars were persecuted by a cruel and tyrannical emperor, Qin Shihuang (Chuang, 1922). However, during the following Han and subsequent dynasties, Confucianism has become the primary source of ethical teaching and social philosophies in China (Lee, 1985). China had entered the Confucian age, where it would remain for most of its history.

The Classic Time: The Feudal Society

In Confucius' view, education should be based on ethical rectitude. Thus, morally superior people are eligible to govern the state and become the ruling class of a hierarchic society (Lee, 1985). In this sense, education is regarded as an approach for upward social mobility. From the standpoint of the state, functions of education are twofold: "the transformation of the masses (*jiaohua*) and the cultivation of the talent for office (*yucai*)" (Borthwick, 1983: 4). The former was accomplished through schooling, the latter was through the civil service examination (*kejue*).

Historically, schooling in ancient China involved two parts: institutions of higher learning (involving different levels of state schools according to the civil service examination and some private institutions) and basic education (mainly private schools) (Lu, 1983; Wang et al., 1985). The earliest complete schooling system took shape in the end of the Period of Disunion (A.D. 220–589) (Lee, 1985).

The first central organized institution was established in 124 B.C. in the Han dynasty, called the *Taixue* (the Imperial University). Its graduates would be appointed to a position in the officialdom (Lee, 1985; Wang et al., 1985). The following dynasties followed and further developed the system (Lee, 1985). In the Sui dynasty (A.D. 516–618), the Central University (*guojijian*) was established (Gao, 1999; Zhong and Hayhoe, 2001). It functioned as "the highest level of academic institution and the highest administrative organ for education" (Zhong and Hayhoe, 2001: 268). In addition, another form of institution of higher learning was the academy (*Shuyuan*). The earliest academy appeared as the central library in the Tang dynasty (A.D. 618–907) (Wang et al., 1985). From the Song (A.D. 960–1279), it became an independent institute for teaching and research (Wang et al., 1985; Zhong and Hayhoe, 2001). The succeeding dynasties witnessed the boom of academies around the country. Yet, the government had attempted to place academies under government control (Borthwick, 1983). The Ming court tried to abolish academies four times (Wang et al., 1985). Most academies were located in isolated mountain areas, far from cities and townships (Lee, 1985; Zhong and Hayhoe, 2001). Some were funded by the government, yet they were largely private institutions (Zhong and Hayhoe, 2001).

By the Song dynasty, apart from the central state institutes, the government established two levels of local schools (numbering 588 in total), prefectural and subprefectural (county) (Lee, 1985). Schools for basic learning have several forms, such as community schools (*shexue*), charity schools (*yixue*), and private elementary schools (*sishu*) (Borthwick, 1983). The school curriculum involved the Hundred Surnames (*bai jia xing*), the Thousand Character Classic *(qianzi wen)*, the Four Books (*sishu*), the Five Classics (*wu jing*), and so on. The main teaching method was rote memorization of these classics, primary history, ethics, general knowledge, all of which appeared remote from most students' experiences (Chuang, 1922; Borthwick, 1983). Moreover, students learned to behave like an "educated man" (Borthwick, 1983: 33; see also Schneewind, 2006). In general, the majority of the population was still illiterate or semiliterate (Pepper, 1996).

The civil service examination system started in the late 6th century during the Sui dynasty (A.D. 581–618). Before that, the selection was based on recommendations from aristocrats and officials. In general, the candidates were mainly composed of the children of the elite. As Chang Chung-Li (1963: 22) pointed out:

> The examination system did indeed make possible a certain "equality of opportunity," but the advantages were heavily in favor of those who had wealth and influence.

Confucian orthodoxy was the foundation of the national civil service examination system (Chuang, 1922). It aimed to examine whether candidates (only male adults) had mastered the classics. As a result, students had to memorize a great number of materials, that is, orthodox commentaries (Reed, 1988). In the Ming (A.D. 1368–1644) and Qing (A.D. 1644–1912) dynasties, the examination prescribed writing the essay in accordance with strict rules, called the "eight-legged essay," since it was made up of eight parts (Chuang, 1922). Indeed, rather a limited number of students could pass the examination, which was determined by national and provincial quotas (Reed, 1988). The successful candidates at different levels of examinations achieved certain titles, *shengyuan, xiucai, juren,* and *jinshi* (Borthwick, 1983; Lee, 1985; Zhong and Hayhoe, 2001). A small fraction of *jinshi*, less than a third, became members in the Hanlin Academy, the body of highest government officials (Borthwick, 1983). As Chuang (1922: 5) notes, "education became a supplementary part of the examination, and the content of education became narrowly confined to the Confucian classics." It seems that the examination provided equal opportunities for every candidate to ascend officialdom, yet the commoners were still disadvantaged compared with members of elite families (Lee, 1985).

Modern China (1840–1949)

This section will review educational transition in the last Qing dynasty and school system in the Republican era prior to focusing on education for ethnic minorities and women before the establishment of the PRC.

Transition from Traditional to Modern Education (1840–1912)

The defeat of China in the Opium War in 1840 urged the Qing court to initiate educational reforms. Later, several schools to train interpreters and mechanical, medical, telegraph, and military talents were built around the country (Edmunds, 1919; Chuang, 1922). In 1898, Kang Youwei, Liang Qichao, and other reform-minded leaders launched a political reform, known as the *Wuxu Reform* or the Hundred Days' Reform (see Zheng, 2001). It had a significant impact on the establishment of a modern education system in China. At the end of the 19th century, modern subjects, such as mathematics and science were introduced into schools and the state examinations ran parallel with the classical learning (Chuang, 1922). In 1905, the traditional civil service examination, which was used for 1,300 years in ancient China, was abolished. Meanwhile, the Qing government established a Ministry of Education imitating that of Japan. Originally, education was included in the Board of Rites, and this was the first time that the government set up an independent education department (Lu, 1983). The Imperial Regulations of 1902, also modeled on those in Japan, made an attempt to build a modern education system that included primary school (lower and higher), middle school (including lower normal school), and higher education (university, research school, higher vocational school, school of language, and higher normal school) (Bailey, 1990). Moreover, according to the 1904 regulations, primary and normal schools run by the government were free (Borthwick, 1983). The new schools adopted the organization of modern school education, for example, having at least two teachers (rather than one in the old *sishu*), a division of class, as well as the Western calendar (Borthwick, 1983). Yet, classics and literary subjects still played a large role in the curriculum (Chuang, 1922). At the end of the Qing dynasty, the number of schools reached 50,000, at all levels and types; and students enrollment reached 1,500,000 (Chuang, 1922).

Missionaries played a pioneering role in establishing modern schools and colleges (Edmunds, 1919). W.A. Martin (Ding Weiliang), an American missionary, became the first president of the Imperial Capital University (the predecessor of Peking University) in 1869, and took this position in decades that followed. In particular, missionaries made a great contribution to female education, which will be detailed later. From 1876 to 1920, the number of students in missionary schools rose from 4,909 to 245,049 (Tian, 2004).

Another indication of the emerging modern education system in China was the growing number of students studying overseas (Chuang, 1922). From the 1860s to 1890s, the Qing court sent about 200 students to America and Europe (Tian, 2004). The Tsing Hua College was established in 1911 as a preparatory school for Chinese students to study in America with "indemnity scholarships" (Edmunds, 1919). After Japan defeated China in the Sino-Japan War (1905), a large number of students went to Japan (Edmunds, 1919).

Education in the Republican Era (1912–1949)

In the Revolution of 1911, the Qing dynasty collapsed and the Republic of China was established by Sun Zhongshan (Sun Yat-sen) in Nanjing. There were two influential measures implemented by the new Ministry of Education: permitting coeducation in lower primary school and removing the classical learning from the curriculum of primary school (Edmunds, 1919; Chuang, 1922). Moreover, the new government promulgated that lower primary education was compulsory in the 1912 school system (Bailey, 1990). According to Chuang (1922), new teaching methods (i.e., self-study, problem work) were increasingly used in schools, a correlation between different subjects was established, and new textbooks with teachers' manuals were published. In the New Culture Movement of 1919, the classical written language was replaced by Beijing-based vernacular, originally called Mandarin and renamed as the "national language" (*guoyu*); thus, spoken and written languages were consistent (Zheng, 2001). Soon, the old textbooks at all educational levels were rewritten in the vernacular (Zheng, 2001). In 1919, John Dewey visited China, and some contend that his educational ideas had a strong influence upon the establishment of a new system of education in 1922 (Ding, 2001). The 1922 school system imitated the American 6–3–3 pattern (Ding, 2001; Zhong and Hayhoe, 2001). The formation of this system "marked the maturation of China's modern school system" (Zheng, 2001: 209). In the same year, the Curriculum Standard of the New School System was implemented (Huang, 2005). After the Nationalist Party took power in 1927, the central government shaped uniform regulations for primary, secondary schools, and even universities and colleges (Zheng, 2001). During the Nationalist period, higher education boomed. By 1947 there were 20,133 faculty members and 20,133 students in 207 higher education institutions (61.4 percent public and 38.6 percent private) (Zhong and Hayhoe, 2001).

After presenting education in ancient times and Republican era, we will focus on education for ethnic minorities and women before the foundation of the PRC.

Minority Education before the PRC

The concept of China, *Zhongguo*, means the middle kingdom in the Chinese language. As Postiglione (2005) notes, "the Chinese state originated with the Qin Dynasty (221–207 B.C.), which both unified the Han Chinese states and absorbed non-Han Chinese states." In general, Central China was controlled by the imperial dynasties of Han, except of course, the Yuan (established by Mongols, 1280–1368) and the Qing Dynasty (by Manchu, 1644–1911). However, these two groups adopted many Han governing norms and became culturally assimilated (Postiglione, in press).

Historically, the Han held a contemptuous attitude toward non-Han groups and labeled them as barbarians (see Postiglione, 1995; Jenner, 2001). Confucianism, advocated by the ruling class since the Han dynasty, emphasized "non-violent assimilation" of the groups through learning the Confucian classics rather than by their extermination (Postiglione, in press). The main education programs were absorbing a small quantity of non-Han group members to study in the central area. As early as in Eastern Han (25 A.D.–220 A.D.), Xiong Nu sent their students to study in the Imperial University (Wang et al., 1985). This means few special and large-scale education programs were offered to ethnic minorities by the central government in ancient society. This situation continued until the end of the last Qing imperial dynasty in Chinese history (Mackerras, 1998, 2003). In the Republic of China, the modern state education by the central government emphasized Han domination ideology, the Han Chinese, and even subjects in accordance with schools in Han areas (Mackerras, 1998). Apart from state education implemented by the Han, many ethnic groups had their own educational approaches (e.g., church school) (Mackerras, 1998).

Education for Women before the PRC

In the ancient feudal society of China, women's role was to raise children, serve their husbands and other family members, and they were deprived of access to school (Jin, 2000). Girls were primarily educated by the mother and nurse within the family. However, girls from aristocratic and rich families received the instruction of private tutors together with their brothers at home before the age of puberty (Borthwick, 1983). In fact, there are some famous intellectual women whose works were highly respected in China's history (Li and Wang, 2000). The entrance of women into the school system owed much to missionary schools (Jin, 2000). The first missionary school for girls was opened by M.A. Aldersay, a British missionary, in Ningbo in 1844 (Tian, 2004). Until half a century later, the first modern school for girls under Chinese auspices (*jingzheng nuxiao*) appeared in Shanghai, 1898 (Edmunds, 1919). Yet, schooling for girls was not provided for in the 1904 new school system by the Qing court (McElroy, 2001). In 1907 the Qing dynasty began to build schools for girls, involving primary and normal schools that trained teachers (Zheng, 2001). Moreover, women were granted some scholarships for study in Japan, Europe and America (Edmunds, 1919; Tian, 2004). The numbers of girls and women in school greatly increased from 1,307 in 1876, to 9,929 in 1907, to 57,256 in 1917 (Edmunds, 1919). During the late Qing dynasty and early Republican period, schooling for women emphasized the differences between women and men (McElroy, 2001). Household management (*jiazheng*) played a large role in the curriculum of normal schools for girls (McElroy, 2001). The school texts contained both the traditional and modern images of women, yet women's role as citizens was increasingly emphasized (McElroy, 2001).

The Contemporary Society: Under the PRC (1949–Present)

The People's Republic of China was founded in 1949 after the Chinese Communist Party took power. This section will review educational development in three periods, reorganization, reform, and expansion (1949–1966), the Cultural Revolution (1966–1976), and Post-Mao Period (1977–).

Reorganization, Reform, and Expansion (1949–1966)

After the founding of the PRC, the central government reorganized the past school system and built a new one heavily influenced by the Soviet Union (Reed, 1988). At the end of 1952, private schools and universities, including those run by the religious bodies, were taken over and reorganized into a new school system (Price, 1979; Lofstedt, 1980).

The new school system included primary schools, middle schools (junior and senior), and higher education institutions (universities and specialist institutes) (Cleverley, 1991). Similar to the Soviet Union, independent research institutes were established under the Academy of Sciences (Reed, 1988). In 1954, the Constitution guaranteed that citizens had the right to education (Price, 1979: 28). In the Great Leap Forward (1958–1959), education experienced a rapid expansion (Lofstedt, 1980). In 1958, 40,000 more students were enrolled in universities and colleges than in 1957 (Lofstedt, 1980). Numerous schools and classes were opened by communes, but were of very low quality (Cleverley, 1991). Political activities and labor production played a large role in ordinary teaching (Cleverley, 1991). The transformations in educational areas followed Chairman's Mao's dictum: "Education must serve proletariat politics and be integrated with productive labor" (Gu, 2001: 93; see also Gu and Liang, 2000).

The Cultural Revolution (1966–1976)

In the mid-1960s, Mao launched the Cultural Revolution (Great Proletarian Cultural Revolution), for the purpose of transforming education and the cultural field (Cleverley, 1991). This movement lasted for 10 years until Mao died in 1976. During this period, education was employed as a tool of class struggle (Gu, 2001). The old school system was severely criticized (Lofstedt, 1980). Political activities (i.e., studying the thought of Mao Zedong), physical labor in factories and on farms, and military-inspired projects by the People's Liberation Army played a crucial role in schooling (Cleverley, 1991). During reeducation, intellectuals, teachers, and cadres were sent to the countryside to practice productive methods with peasants (Cleverley, 1991). Recruitments to university and colleges were based on peer recommendation; in this context, a huge number of worker-peasant-soldier college students were enrolled (Lofstedt, 1980). During the 10 years, a total of 160 million young people did not receive a high-quality education, and were barely literate (Reed, 1988).

The Post-Mao Period (1977–)

After the aftermath of the Cultural Revolution, the educational system was restored in accordance with that in the mid-1960s (Pepper, 1996). Under the leadership of China's new leader, Deng Xiaoping, major reforms were launched that came to transform Chinese society and the education system. In 1977, the university entrance examinations were reinstated. Deng stated that "science and technology are the key to modernization, and education is the means to developing science and technology" (Gu, 2001: 112). After that, teachers gained equal status as workers and intellectuals (Cleverley, 1991). In 1985, the first major set of reforms of the education system were undertaken including nine-year compulsory education, decentralization of educational finance, expansion of senior secondary level vocational–technical schools, and increased autonomy for colleges and universities. "The Law of Compulsory Education" was promulgated in 1986. In 1993, the central government declared that education should be given even greater priority (Hao, 1998). At the end of 1990s, the government advocated science and education to revitalize the nation in the 21st century (Gu and Liang, 2000; Peterson et al., 2001).

LEVELS OF EDUCATION

China's formal education system involves four levels, preschool, primary, secondary, and tertiary education. As of 2004, there were approximately 21 million children in kindergarten, 112 million primary students, 101 million secondary students, and 20 million tertiary students (Yang, 2006). The types of institutions and student populations are shown in Figure 4.1. Kindergartens normally cater

Figure 4.1
Numbers of Students Enrolled at Different Educational Levels

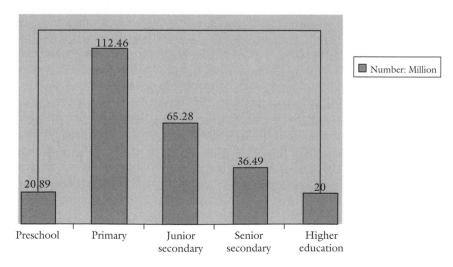

for kids aged 3 to 7 years; primary schools admit students at the age of 6 or 7, and last for 5 or 6 years; secondary education covers junior (3–4 years) and senior middle schools (2–4 years) (Teng, 1994; Hu, 2005). In 1986, the National People's Congress stipulated that primary and lower-secondary education are compulsory (Teng, 1994; Ding, 2001). By 2005, nine-year compulsory education had covered over 95 percent of the relevant age group in China (Ministry of Education, 2006). Graduates of senior middle schools sit the National College Entrance Examination for enrollment in higher education. The length of tertiary programs ranges from 2 years to 5 years. The candidates attend national examinations for master and doctoral programs, which usually last for 2–3 years and 3 years respectively.

Junior secondary education is provided in general (having a predominant proportion, over 98 percent) and vocational schools (Hu, 2005). At the senior secondary level, general school students account for 60.8 percent of the total and the rest are in vocational education (Yang, 2006). By 2005, the admission rate to higher education had reached 19 percent (Yang, 2006).

Basic Education (*Jichu jiaoyu*)

The basic education program (*Jichu jiaoyu*) involves preschool, nine-year compulsory education (primary and junior secondary), and senior secondary education. Vocational education at junior and senior secondary levels will be detailed in the following section.

Preschool

Preschool education normally caters for the age range 3 to 6 (Pang and Richey, 2007). The central government is committed to achieving universal three-year (ages 3 to 6) preschool education throughout the country (Levine, 2005). Preschools have diverse forms, including kindergartens (mainly in the urban areas), nursery classes (mainly in the rural areas), seasonal kindergarten children activity centers, game groups, and mobile aid centers (Cai, 2006; Pang and Richey, 2007). The past decade witnessed a sharp increase of private preschools, despite an overall decrease in the number of preschools (Levine, 2005; Cai, 2006). In 2004, the number of private preschools reached 62,000, which was 4,000 more than the number of public preschools (Cai, 2006).

As of 2004, there were around 759,600 preschool teachers, and an increasing number of them have obtained a postsecondary degree (Cai, 2006). However, more and more qualified teachers tend to leave pubic preschools owning to low salaries (National Education Inspection Group, 2005). Moreover, there are less qualified teaching staff in rural than in the urban areas (ibid.). The curriculum of preschool education has changed from the subject-centered approach in the 1950–1970s to an integrated approach in favor of play-based learning in the late 1980s (Li and Rao, 2005). According to the Guidance for Kindergarten Education issued by the Ministry of Education in 2001, the content of preschool education entails "five domains of development (health, language, society, science, and art)" (Li and Rao, 2005: 237). Specific requirements and suggestions were detailed in the *Guidance* (ibid.). Until now, diverse curriculum approaches, for example, the project approach, have been used in China (Tang, 2006). The programs primarily consist of "games, sports, classroom activities, observation, physical work projects, and daily activities" (Teng, 1994: 751).

In the past, instructions directly from the teacher for the entire group were emphasized in preschool classrooms (Vaughan, 1993). As a result, little attention was given to develop students' emotion, creativity, independence, critical thinking, as well as individualism (Vaughan, 1993; Pang and Richey, 2007). Since the late 1990s, more Western teaching methodology is increasingly employed in preschool education (Pang and Richey, 2007). Teachers play a collaborative and supportive role, and are more sensitive to children's interests and needs (Pang and Richey, 2007; Tang, 2006). Students are free to "choose materials, ways to play and opportunities to interact with peers and teachers" (Pang and Richey, 2007: 5) It should be noted that the new teaching methods tend to be used more in the urban areas (Pang and Richey, 2007).

General Primary and Secondary Schools

From the founding of the PRC to the mid-1980s, China's curriculum followed the model of the Soviet Union. Schools nationwide used one set of textbooks published by the People's Education Press in Beijing (Bray, 2003). Under centralized management, the instructional plan and guidelines were uniform (Liu and Maxey, 2005). The old curriculum was subject oriented and put an emphasis on basic knowledge and skills, bearing little relevance to students' real lives; the classroom was teacher-centered; student interaction and hands-on activities were very few (Liu and Maxey, 2005). Furthermore, a teacher's priority was to prepare students for examinations (Liu and Qi, 2005). As a result, the curriculum and teaching methods were geared toward examination success.

The latest curriculum reform covers primary, junior, and senior secondary education. The reform for primary and junior secondary education (Grades 1–9) was initiated in 2001 with the *Outline of Reform on Curriculum in Basic Education* by the Ministry of Education. The new curriculum was piloted in 38 experimental areas and then gradually implemented nationwide (Liu and Qi, 2005). Compared with the past curriculum, the new one aims to cultivate well-rounded students, and highlight students' understanding and application of knowledge and integration of the subjects which were separate in the past (Liu and Qi, 2005). Two new comprehensive subjects were created: integrated liberal arts, involving history and society (history and geography) and arts (music and fine arts), and integrated science (physics, chemistry, and biology) (Liu and Qi, 2005). Moreover, besides the state-selected courses, the new approach would assign 16–20 percent of the total class hours to local and school-selected courses. More specifically, in the lower primary school, the courses consist of moral education and life, Chinese language, mathematics, physical education, arts (music and fine arts), and so on. In the upper primary schools, integrated science, foreign language (mainly English, Russian, Japanese, etc.), and comprehensive practical activities and research are included in the courses. The courses in general junior secondary schools are composed of moral education, Chinese language, mathematics, foreign language (mainly English, Russian, Japanese, etc.), integrated science (physics, chemistry, and biology), history and society (history and geography), physical education and health, arts (music and fine arts), and comprehensive practical activities and research. The new curriculum for senior secondary education was piloted in Shandong, Ningxia, Guangdong and Hainan in 2004. Up to now, 10 provinces have been involved. The subjects entail Chinese language, mathematics, foreign language (mainly English, Russian, Japanese, etc.), physical education and health, arts (music and fine arts), physics, chemistry, biology, history, geography, computer education, comprehensive practical activities, research-oriented study, and technology. Besides, optional subjects are offered.

The new curriculum requires a change in the authoritarian role of teachers in the classroom. As Liu and Maxey (2005: 169–170) note, "teachers will change from knowledge brokers to helpers, from administrators to guides, from a commanding position to a position equal with their students." Moreover, diverse teaching methods, in particular with the aids of information technology, need to be employed. Instead of rote learning, independence, individualism, participation, and cooperation are emphasized (Liu and Qi, 2005).

The new curriculum diversifies assessment methods, and new evaluation approaches are employed, for example, portfolio (Liu and Qi, 2005). Primary students do not need to sit for examination for admission to the junior secondary school and attend the nearest junior secondary school. Graduates of the junior secondary education need to pass an entrance examination to the senior secondary school administered by provinces and autonomous regions.

The national university entrance examination has gone through tremendous changes since its restoration in 1978. Originally, the examinations were divided into two types, one for candidates of liberal arts and the other for natural sciences. The former involves six subjects: politics, Chinese, mathematics, history, geography, and foreign language. The latter involves seven subjects: politics, Chinese, mathematics, physics, chemistry, biology, and foreign language (Reed, 1988). Reforms in higher education entrance examinations were initiated in Guangdong province in 1999, reducing the subject tests from 6–7 tests to "3+X." The new model meant that the examinees would have to take three required subjects (Chinese, English, and mathematics), plus one optional subject based on their interest and university major requirements. In that year, another four provinces joined the pilot under another model. The new pilot model was in the "X" subject, requiring that an "integrated humanity" and an "integrated science" was necessary for selection by candidates (Zhu, 2000). Subsequently, a new form of examination was adopted nationwide in the following year. This new measure intended to eliminate examination orientation in schools, and thereby increase equality in selection.

In terms of teaching forces, *The Teacher Law* promulgates that primary school teachers should obtain a degree of a secondary normal school and acquire a national teacher certificate; the secondary school teachers should have a college degree and teacher certificate as well. As of 2004, there were 6 million primary school teachers, 3.5 million junior secondary school teachers, and 1.2 million teachers in regular senior secondary schools. At the elementary level, the average student/teacher ratio was 19.98:1; the secondary level student/teacher ratio was 18.65:1 (Ministry of Education, 2006).

Higher Education

China has the largest higher education system in the world (Liu and Liu, 2005). As mentioned in the previous section, the enrollment in higher education institutions numbered over 20 million by 2004. Under Soviet influence, China's higher education system was composed of comprehensive and specialized institutions of higher learning (Hayhoe, 1996). Recent decades have witnessed tremendous changes in higher education, through restructuring and merging (Mok, 2005). The universities and colleges are run and administered by the Ministry of Education, by different departments of the central government, and by provincial and other local authorities (Mok, 2005).

Since the mid-1980s, China's higher education has experienced fundamental changes. Regarding the elitism mode and the examination orientation in higher education, the central government embarked on a series of reforms to improve educational efficiency and equality since the 1990s. *The Outline of the Reform and Development of China's Education* issued in 1993 by the central government offered higher education institutions considerable autonomy (Ding, 2001). Universities and colleges were urged to "establish mechanisms of self-regulation and responsibility" (Zhong and Hayhoe, 2001: 276). As a result, universities and colleges enjoy autonomy in organizing teaching activities, student admissions, issuing diplomas and certificates, allocating funds, hiring personnel, and so on (ibid.). Moreover, the government increased the proportion of the relevant age groups in higher education from 9.8 percent to 15 percent from 1998 to 2004, and planned to reach 21 percent by 2006. The expansion of higher education involves increasing students' enrollment in regular higher education institutions and adult higher education, upgrading secondary schools into higher specialized colleges, approving private higher education colleges, and so on. The ratio of students to teachers is 16.22:1 at the tertiary level (Ministry of Education, 2006).

A small number of institutions of higher education started to charge tuition since the mid-1980s. At that time, university students fell into three categorizes: state assignment, students financed by the unit where they have to serve after graduation, and the self-supported (Reed, 1988: 64). Since 1995–1996, students are charged tuition fees nationwide, except for several teacher and military universities. Recently, students are being required to pay 25 percent of the total expense of higher education (Williams et al., 1997). In the meantime, students are granted a right to seek jobs in the labor market, rather than being assigned a position by the state (ibid.). Additionally, the university students can get monthly subsidies from the government, which cover part of the expenses for their living and books (ibid.). The students who have excellent academic performance are offered scholarships, and the ones with financial difficulties can apply for grants-in-aid and loans from the state (ibid.). After that, more and more universities have begun to charge tuition fees to students, which became a stable income for higher education institutions (Chen, 1999).

Additionally, internationalization of higher education is emerging in China. The central government administered "Project 211" in 1995, selecting and developing 100 institutions of higher education for world-class universities in the early 21st century (Mok, 1999). In 1998, the Ministry of Education advanced a plan, named "Project 985," an "Action Plan for Education Development of 21st Century," in which certain universities would be supported to become world-class universities (Yang, 2003). At present, 34 universities have been involved in this project (ibid.). Moreover, internationalization manifests itself in the fact that Chinese universities increasingly adopt international subject content, foreign university textbooks, and teaching in English (Huang, 2006).

With regard to curriculum and research, similar to basic education, the syllabus and curriculum for university teaching was unified in China until the mid-1980s. Yet, higher education institutions have gained more autonomy since 1993, as mentioned earlier. According to the *Law of Higher Education* issued in 1998, the academic committee of the university determines the formation of disciplines, majors, curriculum and syllabuses, research plan, and so on, based on social needs and particular conditions. Compulsory and elective courses are offered in higher education institutions. There are two groups of compulsory courses for university students (Marxist theory and, morality and ideology), called "Two Lessons" (*liangke*). Despite the prevalence of political and ideological indoctrination, general education is receiving growing attention from various universities which offer courses, hold seminars, and organize activities (Zhou and Chen, 2003).

Vocational Education and Adult Education

After suspension in the Cultural Revolution (1966–1976), vocational education as "an effective pillar of support for socioeconomic development," has been greatly improved (Ding, 2001: 176). Despite the fact that the Chinese school system is liberal-arts-dominated, the development of vocational education has been highly supported by the Chinese government for meeting the needs of the labor force in the Socialist market economy (Lin, 1993: 61).

The vocational education system covers junior secondary, senior secondary (specialized secondary, vocational senior secondary schools, skilled-workers training schools), and tertiary levels. Junior vocational schools, primarily located in rural areas, occupy less than 2 percent at junior secondary level. At the senior secondary level, the students in vocational secondary schools account for 14.09 million, occupying nearly 40 percent of the total enrollment in 2004 (Yang, 2006). At the higher education level, there were 1,047 tertiary vocational institutes with an intake of around six million students by 2004. The proportion of students in tertiary vocational education reached 46.82 percent of the student population of higher education. Similar to preschool education, private schools are playing an increasingly important role in vocational education (He and Geng, 2006). As of 2004, private secondary vocational schools number 1,633, and their enrollment covers 7.9 percent of the secondary vocational education (He and Geng, 2006).

Adult education covers secondary and higher learning levels. Adult higher education comprises radio and TV universities, advanced staff development colleges, farmer's colleges, and the higher education self-study examination systems (Teng, 1994). At secondary education level, adult education mainly refers to adult senior secondary schools. By 2004, there were 505 adult higher learning institutions and 955 adult senior secondary schools. The central government has been committed to achieving universal nine-year compulsory education for school-aged children and eliminating illiteracy of youths and adults, famously known as "Two Basics" (*liangji*). By 2004, 93.6 percent of the Chinese population has reached this goal.

After discussing the education system, this chapter will offer a brief introduction of education of minorities and women in the next two sections.

Education of Ethnic Minorities

The PRC has 56 designated ethnic groups, in which the majority are the Han and the remainder are referred to as ethnic minorities. These minorities accounted for over 100 million people in total, but form less than 10 percent of the national population. Since the foundation of the PRC in 1949, the central government has implemented a variety of educational measures specifically for ethnic minorities, including making laws and regulations to guard the implementation of ethnic education (e.g., "Ethnic Regions Autonomy Law" in 1984); setting up various types of schools to meet the needs in different areas, including ethnic primary and middle schools, universities or colleges for nationalities, and so on; implementing bilingual education and preferential policies for ethnic minority students' enrollment and work assignments, and so on (Sautman, 1999; Postiglione, in press; etc.).

As a result, education of the ethnic minorities developed competently during the past 50 years in China. At different levels of schooling, the students belonging to the ethnic minorities increased significantly. Ethnic minority students numbered 10.97 million in primary school, 6.76 million in general secondary school, and 0.8 million in institutions of higher education; the proportions reach 9.76 percent, 7.78 percent, and 5.70 percent respectively (Ministry of Education, 2006). However, literacy rates of almost all ethnic groups are below that of the Han majority owing to poverty and remoteness (Postiglione, 2000, 2005). At the tertiary sector, minority students are still quantitatively underrepresented, especially in terms of top universities (Postiglione, in press). Moreover, the textbooks in the minorities' own languages, seldom offer ethnic minority groups' history or literature (see Upton, 1999; Mackerras, 2003; Postiglione, in press).

Education for Girls and Women

The Chinese Communist Party (CCP) promotes a policy of gender equality. Mao Zedong, put forward a famous statement, "Women can hold up half the sky" (Liu and Carpenter, 2005: 277). Most schools in China are coeducational. China's Program for the Development of Chinese Women (1995–2000) and its Goals 2000 give special importance to female education (Ross, 2001). The female illiteracy rate dropped from more than 90 percent in 1949 to 14.9 percent (15 years of age and above) in 2004 (Gu, 2005). Up to 2004, 98.93 percent of girls attended primary schools and junior schools, roughly equaling boys' attendance rate of 98.97 percent. At the tertiary level, the enrollment of women also experienced an unprecedented growth, rising from 17.8 percent in 1947 to 45.65 percent in 2004 (Gu, 2005).

Nevertheless, educational opportunities for poor and rural girls are limited, owing to traditional cultural and social gender biases (Rao et al., 2003). Gender inequality in education is closely related to poverty and disparities between urban and rural areas in China. Lavely et al. (1990: 61) argue that, during the past five decades, the increase in educational attainment of women "occurred first in cities, then in towns, then in the better-endowed rural areas and, finally, in poorer peripheral areas." In addition, despite the government embracing gender equality, gender stereotypes prevail in teaching materials and classrooms (see Shi, 2004; Liu and Carpenter, 2005). In higher education, female students tend to study in the disciplines of social sciences, humanities, medicine, and teacher education; rather than natural sciences and engineering (Gu, 2005).

A STORY OF GUOGUO[1]

Guoguo is a senior secondary student in Chongqing city. She is in Grade 3. This story, which takes place on November 2, gives her daily routine.

At 6:50 A.M., the alarm clock goes off. Guoguo is still asleep when her mother gets up. At 7:07, she reluctantly gets up after continuous calls from her mother. At 7:20, Guoguo leaves for her school and buys a piece of bread as breakfast on the way.

Upon arrival at school, the first thing she does is to submit the assignment. Today's self-study class in the morning is for the Chinese language. Students recite an ancient masterpiece, *Chushibiao*, but Guoguo is unable to focus. She keeps thinking of the breakfast in her bag. Finally, after the morning class is dismissed, Guoguo eats the bread during the break.

The first class, English, starts at 8:30. The teaching content is vocabulary and grammar. Guoguo loves English, so she is very attentive. The teacher gives a vocabulary and spelling test before the class is over. The second class is for

Chemistry. Guoguo had not prepared well, so she seems lost in the class. She takes notes on the book and plans to ask the teacher to clear her doubts, but is unable to do so as unfortunately, many of the students are waiting there. After two classes, it is time for students to take a gym break on the ground. Guoguo prefers to use this period to ask questions or do the assignment. The third class is usually the most difficult time for Guoguo, since she always feels sleepy at this time. Today it seems worse because the class is for physics. The final class, Chinese, is to review *Chushibiao*. The teacher finds some tests for students from extracurricular readings, since the teaching materials do not contain any exercise for this text.

Before students leave for home at noon, the English teachers ask students to correct the errors in the morning test. Guoguo finishes it very soon. Just before she leaves the classroom, Guoguo suddenly remembers a mistake in the Mathematics assignment. She corrects it and goes home contentedly. Fortunately, the teachers do not give assignments this morning. Guoguo prays, "I hope there was no assignment in the afternoon, and I can go to sleep early today."

At 12:30 P.M., Guoguo gets home. She takes a nap after having lunch. This was the happiest time of the day for her.

Guoguo goes back to school at 1:40 P.M. to perpare for a test. The first afternoon class is for history. The second class is for information. However, the classes of information and physical education are usually replaced by the major subjects (i.e., Chinese, English and Mathematics). Today's class is changed to English. The final class is for mathematics on the topic "parabola." The exercises in the textbook are very easy and Guoguo finishes quickly. However, when the teacher presents more questions, Guoguo gets confused. At the end of the class, the teachers give the assignments. It seems that Guoguo's hope is being snatched away.

It is time for cleaning. The classroom is dusty, but Guoguo prefers to complete the assignment indoors rather than going out for a break. At 4:40 P.M., the first evening self-study class starts. Students finish a test. The teacher gives an assignment. Guoguo thinks that she will probably finish her homework by 12 midnight.

During the break, her father sends Guoguo dinner. It is fish and bean curd, Guoguo's favorite. Yet, she finishes dinner in 15 minutes and begins to do her assignments.

The second evening self-study class, physics, lasts from 6:30 to 8:30 P.M. Guoguo does not enjoy this subject, and had failed in several past examinations. She worries about it very much and pushes herself to concentrate. The physics teacher also assigns homework.

Guoguo begins to do the assignments as soon as she gets home: one hour for English, one hour for mathematics, and two hours for physics. It is 1 o'clock when Guoguo completes all homework. The monthly examination is approaching. Guoguo has to spend another hour preparing for it. When she finishes all the work and goes to sleep, it is 2 o'clock nearing dawn.

A middle school classroom.

MAJOR EDUCATIONAL REFORMS

China launched economic reforms in 1978. Market economic mechanisms were introduced to replace the original planned economy (Mok, 1997, 1999). In the education sector, the CCP adopted a policy of decentralization (Mok, 1999). Accordingly, China's education is more involved in a process of privatization and marketization (Mok, 1997). This chapter will present three major educational reforms, decentralization, marketization and pursuit of educational equality.

Decentralization

In order to enhance modernization and lessen regional disparities, the central government proposed reforms to the education system, namely "diversification of educational provision and decentralization of educational administration" (Hu, 2005). Since then, a decentralized school system took shape (Teng, 1994). After the reforms, enterprises and social communities have greatly expanded and improved the provision of education (Teng, 1994). By 2004, there appeared around 78,500 private schools and institutions at various levels nationwide, enrolling 17.69 million students (Yang, 2006). More specifically, at the tertiary level, private regular higher learning institutions and adult colleges constitute 0.47 percent; at the secondary level, private schools reached 8.21 percent (Yang, 2006). In addition, as mentioned earlier, primary and secondary textbooks have been decentralized. Provinces and municipalities are permitted to produce their own textbooks based on a national syllabus (Hu, 2005).

In the decentralized system of educational administration, local authorities are responsible for managing and financing basic education while the Ministry of

Education determines the policy and regulation at the macro level (Teng, 1994). Higher education institutions enjoy considerable autonomy (Ding, 2001; Zhong and Hayhoe, 2001). Furthermore, school leadership has changed (Lin, 1993). In the past, the party secretary and the committee of the CCP were responsible for school administration; in order words, the party secretary was considered to be the principal (Lin, 1993). The reform implemented the Principal Responsibility System, in which the party secretary's power is limited only in guiding political activities (Lin, 1993).

Marketization

In 1978 the Third Plenum of the Eleventh Central Committee of the CCP decided that the tenet of education policy in the Post-Mao era is "a crucial basis for a drive toward economic and technological modernization" (Yin and White, 2002: 410). As a result of the market economy prevailing in the larger society, in 1985, the "Decision on the Reform of the Educational System" relaxed control in educational provision and administration (Bray, 2003). As mentioned earlier, private schools have proliferated during the past two decades and occupy a considerable proportion at various levels. According to Kwong (1997), an essential reason accounting for emerging market forces within the education sector is that the government failed to cater to the demand for education of the populace.

The marketization plays an increasingly prominent role at the tertiary level, since institutions of higher education have to adjust to market needs and graduates' demands for employment (Mok, 1999). Meanwhile, the funds of universities become diversified, rather than just government budgetary allocations (Mok, 2005); tuition fees and other fees collected from students, donations from social forces, and budgetary allocation of the government at all levels (Mok, 1999). Moreover, the institutions of higher education are encouraged to open business firms to increase their funds (ibid.). Higher education, therefore, has become an important venue to practice marketization of education (Yin and White, 2002). This manifests itself in four areas, "the emergence of fee-paying students, partnership with industry, pressures for the curriculum to become more practical, and the diversification of management system" (ibid.: 217).

Toward Educational Equality

Since the mid-1980s, educational decentralization and rising market forces exacerbate the regional disparity in public educational investment (Xue and Shi, 2001; Hannum, 2003). The central government is devoted to universalizing nine-year compulsory education, yet the major challenge is the huge gap between urban and rural areas in basic education (Hawkins and Su, 2003). Between 2002 and 2003, the public educational expenditure in urban areas was nearly twofold higher than that in rural areas (Zhou, 2006). According to a national survey by Peking University in 2005, children's school spending accounted for 12 percent of family expenditure at primary level and 18 percent at junior secondary level; half of the household budget was devoted to expenditures on college students in township; the educational expenditures were far beyond the household income in the rural areas *(Liaowang*, 2005). Students were exempt from tuition fees in Chinese higher education before China's economic reform in 1978. Yet, tuition fees have increased over 25 times during the next two decades.

There is an imperative for the Chinese government to redress education inequality. The measures for enhancing the universalization and quality of compulsory education in poor rural areas include initiating governmental projects for poverty reduction (i.e., funding allocation for poor areas and transferring resource between provinces and cities and townships and counties), mobilizing community resources, and involving international aid (Zhang and Zhao, 2006). In September 2003, the State Council implemented the Policy of "Two Exemptions and One Subsidy" (exemption of miscellaneous fee and textbook fee; subsidy for boarding) for impoverished children. Since then, provinces have adopted various strategies to move toward free compulsory education in poor rural areas (see Zhou and Shen, 2006). Moreover, the "One Fee for All," aiming to strictly regulate collection of fees by primary and secondary schools and relieve the economic burden of parents has taken effect since 2004 throughout the country. In the tertiary sector, the government provides tuition fee loan schemes, scholarships, and subsidies for university students from poor families.

CONCLUSION

In ancient China, education functioned as a mechanism for individuals to achieve higher social status, and for the government to regulate the people and maintain social hierarchy. Confucian learning, imperial power, and bureaucratic authority were closely interlinked and formulated a well-developed education system (Pepper, 1996). During the first half of the last century, in the last days of the Qing dynasty, the Republican government made significant effort to build a modern school system (Zheng, 2001). With the foundation of the PRC, the Chinese government enhanced and expanded opportunity for the populace, especially for women and ethnic minorities. With China's economic reforms, private schools and institutions of higher learning are booming in contrast to their abolition in the 1950s. On one side, the central government is dedicated to improving quality education and cultivating innovative talents (e.g., through the new curriculum reform); on the other side, it struggles to alleviate increasing educational inequality resulting from decentralization and marketization. From the Self-Strengthening Movement at the end of the imperial government, to the New Culture Movement of 1919, the contemporary Chinese government's advocating science and education to revitalize the nation in the 21st century, the education system has been geared to cater for China's industrialization and modernization (Pepper, 1990).

NOTE

1. This story was retrieved from the People's Daily (*Renmin ribao*) by Muyi, November 24, 2005, and also presented in Yang (2006: 459–460).

REFERENCES

Bailey, P.J. (1990). *Reform the People: Changing Attitudes towards Popular Education in Early Twentieth-century China*. Edinburgh: Edinburgh University Press.

Borthwick, S. (1983). *Education and Social Change in China: The Beginnings of the Modern Era*. Stanford, CA: Hoover Institution Press.

Bray, M. (2003). "Control of education: Issues and tensions in centralization and decentralization," in Robert F. Arnove and Carlos Alberto Torres (eds), *Comparative Education: The Dialectic of the Global and the Local*, 2nd ed., pp. 204–228. Lanham, MD: Rowman & Littlefield.

Cai, Y.Q. (2006). "Zhongguo you'er jiaoyu fazhan zhuangkuang (The situation of China's preschool education)," in Yang Dongbing (ed.), *Jiaoyu lanpishu: 2005 nian zhongguo jiaoyu fazhan baoguo* (Blue Book of Education: The Development of Report of China's Education, 2005), pp. 94–108. Beijing: Shehui kexue wenxian chu ban she.

Chang, Chung-Li. (1963). "Mcrit and Money," in Menzel, Johanna Margarete (ed.), *The Chinese Civil Service: career open to talent?*, pp. 22–27. Boston: Health.

Chen, Y.K. (1999). "Shi lun gaodeng jiaoyu de gongping yu xiaolu wenti (The issue of equality and efficiency in higher education)," in Chen Xuefei (ed.), *Zhongguo gaodeng jiaoyu yanjiu 50 nian* (Higher Education Research in China for 50 Years), pp. 788–790. Beijing: Jiaoyu kexue chu ban she.

Chuang, T.H. (1922). *Tendencies toward a Democratic System of Education in China*, 2nd edn. Shanghai: Commercial Press.

Cleverley, J.F. (1991). *The Schooling of China: Tradition and Modernity in Chinese Education*, 2nd edn. Sydney: Allen & Unwin.

Ding, G. (2001). "Nationalization and internationalization: two turning points in China's education in the twentieth century," in Glen Peterson, Ruth Hayhoe, and Yongling Lu (eds.), *Education, Culture, and Identity in Twentieth-century China*, pp. 161–186. Hong Kong: Hong Kong University Press.

Edmunds, C.K. (1919). *Modern Education in China*. Washington, DC: Government Printing Office, 1919. Taipei: Ch'eng Wen, 1973.

Gao, S.M. (1999). *Zhongguo jiaoyu zhidu shilun* (History of China's Educational System). Taiwan: Lianjing chuban shiye gongsi.

Gu, M.Y. (2001). *Education in China and Abroad: Perspectives from a Lifetime in Comparative Education*. Hong Kong: Comparative Education Research Centre, University of Hong Kong.

Gu, M.Y. and Liang, Z.Y. (2000). *Shijie jiaoyu daxi zhongguo jiaoyu* (Education in the World: China's Education). Jilin jiaoyu chubanshe.

Gu, N. (2005). "Jianguo yilai nuxing jiaoyu de chengguo, wenti ji duice (Achievement, problems and suggested measures of female education after the foundation of PRC)," *Dangdai zhongguo shi yanjiu* (Contemporary China History Studies), 1(6): 56–64.

Hannum, E. (2003). "Poverty and basic education in rural China: Villages, households, and girls' and boys' enrollment," *Comparative Education Review*, 47(2): 141–159.

Hao, K.M. (1998). *Zhongguo jiao yu ti zhi gai ge 20 nian* (Reforms of China's educational system during the past 20 years). Zhengzhou: Zhongzhou gu ji chu ban she.

Hawkins, J.N. and Su, Z.X. (2003). "Asian education," in Robert F. Arnove and Carlos Alberto Torres (eds), *Comparative Education: The Dialectic of the Global and the Local*, 2nd ed., pp. 338–356. Lanham, MD: Rowman & Littlefield.

Hayhoe, R. (1996). *China's Universities, 1895–1995: A Century of Cultural Conflict*. Hong Kong: The Comparative Education Research Center, University of Hong Kong.

He, Z. and Geng, J. (2006). "The opportunities and challenges of vocational education," in Yang Dongbing (ed.), *Jiaoyu lanpishu: 2005 nian zhongguo jiaoyu fazhan baogao* (Blue Book of Education: The Development Report on China's Education, 2005), pp. 109–122. Beijing: Shehui kexue wenxian chubanshe.

Hu, G.W. (2005). "Reforms of basic English-language education in China: An overview," *International Journal of Educational Reform*, 14(2): 140–165.

Huang, F. (2006). "Internationalization of curricula in higher education institutions in comparative perspectives: Case studies of China, Japan and the Netherlands," *Higher Education*, 51(4): 521–539.

Huang, J. (2005). *Zhong wai jiao yu shi* (History of Education). Gaoxiong Shi: Gaoxiong fu wen tu shu chu ban she.

Jenner, W.J.F. (2001). "Race and history in China," *New Left Review*, 11: 55–77.

Jin, Y.L. (2000). *Jin dai Zhongguo da xue yan jiu: 1895–1949* (Study on University in Modern China: 1895–1949). Beijing: Zhong yang wen xian chu ban she.

Kewin, K. and Xu, H. (1989). "Rethinking revolution: Reflections on China's 1985 Educational Reforms," *Comparative Education*, 25(1): 7–17.

Kwong, J.L. (1997). "The reemergence of private schools in socialist China," *Comparative Education Review*, 41(3): 244–259.

Lavely, W., Xiao, Z.Y., Li, B.H., and Freedman, R. (1990). "The rise of female education in China: National and regional patterns," *The China Quarterly*, 121 (March): 61–93.

Lee, T.H.C (1985). *Government Education and the Examinations in Sung China*. Hong Kong: Chinese University Press.

Levine, M.H. (2005). "Take a giant step: Investing in preschool education in emerging nations," *Phi Delta Kappan* (November): 196–220.

Li, G.J. and Wang, B.Z. (2000). *Zhongguo jiao yu zhi du tong shi* (General History of China's Educational System). Jinan Shi: Shandong jiao yu chu ban she.

Li, H. and Rao, N. (2005). "Curricular and instructional influences on early literacy attainment: Evidence from Beijing, Hong Kong and Singapore," *International Journal of Early Years Education*, 13(3): 235–253.

Liaowang (2005). "Jiaoyu chengben: jiating ying chengdan duoshao (Education cost: how much the family should afford?)," *Liaowang Xinwen zhoukan* (*Weekly Journal of Outlook*) (48), p. 29.

Lin, J. (1993). *Education in Post-Mao China*. Westport, CT: Praeger.

Liu, J. and Carpenter, M. (2005). "Trends and issues of women's education in China," *The Clearing House*, 78(6): 277–281.

Liu, N.C. and Liu, L. (2005). "University rankings in China," *Higher Education in Europe*, 30(2): 217–226.

Liu, P. and Qi, C.X. (2005). "Reform in the curriculum of basic education in the People's Republic of China: Pedagogy, application, and learners," *International Journal of Educational Reform*, 14(1): 35–44.

Liu, S.J. and Maxey, S. (2005). "Are Dewey's educational ideas involved in China's education once again?" *International Journal of Educational Reform*, 14(2): 162–177.

Liu, Y.K. (1998). "Educational utilitarianism: Where goes higher education?" in Michael Agelasto and Bob Adamson (ed.), *Higher Education in Post-Mao China*, pp. 121–140. Hong Kong: Hong Kong University Press.

Lofstedt, J.I. (1980). *Chinese Educational Policy: Changes and Contradictions, 1949–79.* Stockholm: Almqvist & Wiksell.

Lu, H.J. (1983). *Zhongguo jin shi de jiao yu fa zhan, 1800–1949* (Educational Development in Modern China: 1800–1949). Hong Kong: Hua feng shu ju.

Mackerras, C. (1998). "The minorities: Achievements and problems in the economy, national integration and foreign relations," in J.Y.S. Cheng (ed.), *China Review 1998*, pp. 281–311. Hong Kong: The Chinese University Press.

———(2003). *China's Ethnic Minorities and Globalisation.* London: RoutledgeCurzon.

McElroy, S.C. (2001). "Forging a new role for women: Zhili first women's normal school and the growth of women's education in China, 1901–21," in Glen Peterson, Ruth Hayhoe, and Yongling Lu (eds), *Education, Culture, and Identity in Twentieth-century China*, pp. 348–374. Hong Kong: Hong Kong University Press.

Ministry of Education (2006). "Educational statistics issued by the ministry in 2004," in Yang Dongbing (ed.), *Jiaoyu lanpishu: 2005 nian zhongguo jiaoyu fazhan baogao* (Blue Book of Education: The Development Report on China's Education, 2005), pp. 264–272. Beijing: Shehui kexue wenxian chu ban she.

Mok, K.H. (1997). "Marketization or quasi-marketization: Educational development in post-Mao China," *International Review of Education*, 43(5–6): 1–21.

———(1999). "Education and the market place in Hong Kong and Mainland China," *Higher Education*, 37(2): 133–158.

———(2005). "Globalization and educational restructuring: University merging and changing governance in China," *Higher Education*, 50(1): 57–88.

National Education Inspection Group (Guojia jiaoyu dudaotuan) (2005). "You'er jiaoyu dudao jiancha gongbao (The report of inspection on childhood education)," in Yang Dongbing (ed.), *Jiaoyu lanpishu: 2005 nian zhongguo jiaoyu fazhan baogao* (Blue Book of Education: The Development Report on China's Education, 2005), pp. 291–294. Beijing: Shehui kexue wenxian chu ban she.

Pang, Y.H. and Richey, D. (2007). "Preschool education in China and the United States: A personal perspective," *Early Child Development and Care*, 177(1), 1–13.

Pepper, S. (1990). *China's Education Reform in the 1980s: Policies, Issues and Historical Perspective.* Berkeley, CA: Institute of East Asian Studies, University of California.

———(1996). *Radicalism and Education Reform in 20th-century China: The Search for an Ideal Development Model.* New York: Cambridge University Press.

Peterson, G., Hayhoe, R., and Lu, Y.L. (eds) (2001). *Education, Culture, and Identity in Twentieth-century China.* Hong Kong: Hong Kong University Press.

Postiglione, G.A. (1995). "National minorities and nationalities policy in China," in B. Berberoglu (ed.), *The National Question*, pp. 259–279. Philadelphia, PA: Temple University Press.

———(2000). "National minority regions: Studying school discontinuation," in Judith Liu, H.A. Ross, and D.P. Kelly (eds), *The Ethnographic Eye: Interpretive Studies of Education In China*, pp. 51–72. New York: Falmer Press.

Postiglione, G.A. (ed.) (2006). *Education and Social Change in China: Inequality in a Market Economy*. Armonk, NY: M.E. Sharpe.

———(in press). "Ethnicity and the role of education as a mechanism for national unity in China," in Santosh Saha (ed.), *Ethnicity and Socio-political Change in the Contemporary World: Politics of Identity*. New York: Macmillan/Palgrave.

Price, R.F. (1979). *Education in Modern China*, 2nd edn. London: Routledge and Kegan Paul.

Rao, N., Cheng, K.M., and Narain, K. (2003). "Primary schooling in China and India: Understanding how sociocontextual factors moderate the role of the state," in Mark Bray (ed.), *Comparative Education: Continuing Traditions, New Challenges, and New paradigms*, pp. 153–176. Dordrecht: Kluwer Academic Publishers.

Reed, L.A. (1988). *Education in the People's Republic of China and U.S.–China Educational Exchanges*. Washington, DC: NAFSA.

Ross, H. (2001). "Historical memory, community service, hope: Reclaiming the social purposes of education for the Shanghai McTyeire School for girls," in Glen Peterson, Ruth Hayhoe, and Yongling Lu (eds), *Education, Culture, and Identity in Twentieth-century China*, pp. 375–402. Hong Kong: Hong Kong University Press.

Sautman, B. (1999). "Expanding access to higher education for China's national minorities: Policies of preferential admissions," in Gerard A. Postiglione (ed.), *China's National Minority Education: Culture, Schooling, and Development*, pp. 173–210. New York; London: Falmer Press.

Schneewind, S. (2006). *Community Schools and the State in Ming China*. Stanford, CA: Stanford University Press.

Shi, J.H. (ed.) (2004). *Zoujin jiaocai yu jiaoxue de xingbie shijie* (Gender Analysis of Teaching Materials and Classroom). Beijng: Jiaoyu kexue chubanshe.

Tang, Feng, L. (2006). "The child as an active learner: Views, practices, and barriers in Chinese early childhood education," *Childhood Education*, 82(6): 342–346.

Teng, T. (1994). "China, People's Republic of: System of education," in Torsten Husen and T. Neville Postlethwaite (eds), *The International Encyclopedia of Education*, 2nd edn, pp. 750–755. Oxford: Pergamon.

Tian, Z.P. (2004). *Zhong wai jiao yu jiao liu shi* (Sino-foreign Educational Exchange History). Guangzhou Shi: Guangdong jiao yu chu ban she.

Upton, J.L. (1999). "Development of modern Tibetan language education in the PRC," in Gerard A. Postiglione (eds), *China's National Minority Education: Culture, Schooling, and Development*, pp. 281–340. New York: Falmer Press.

Vaughan, J. (1993). "Early childhood education in China," *Childhood Education*, 69 (4): 196–200.

Wang, B.Z., Guo, Q.J., Liu, D.H., He, X.X., and Gao, Q. (1985). *Jian ming Zhongguo jiao yu shi* (A Brief History of Education in China). Beijing: Beijing shi fan da xue chu ban she.

Williams, G., Liu, S.S., and Shi, Q. (1997). "Marketization of higher education in the People's Republic of China," *Higher Education Policy*, 10(2): 151–157.

Xue, L.R. and Shi, T.J. (2001). "Inequality in Chinese education," *Journal of Contemporary China*, 10(26): 107–124.

Yang, D.P. (ed.) (2006). *Jiaoyu lanpishu: 2005 nian zhongguo jiaoyu fazhan baogao* (Blue Book of Education: The Development Report on China's Education, 2005). Beijing: Shehui kexue wenxian chubanshe.

Yang, J.Y. (2003). *Zhongguo dalu gaodeng jiaoyu zhi yanjiu* (The Study of China Higher Education). Taibei Shi: Gao deng jiao yu wen hua shi ye you xian gong si.

Yin, Q. and White, G. (2002). "The 'Marketisation' of Chinese higher education: A Critical Assessment," in F.N. Pieke (ed.), *People's Republic of China*, Vol. I, pp. 409–429. Aldershot, England/Burlington, VT: Ashgate.

Zhang, T.D. and Zhao, M.X. (2006). "Universalizing nine-year compulsory education for poverty reduction in rural China," *Review of Education*, 52: 261–286.

Zheng, Y. (2001). "The status of Confucianism in modern Chinese education, 1901–49: A curricular study," in Glen Peterson, Ruth Hayhoe, and Yongling Lu (eds), *Education, Culture, and Identity in Twentieth-century China*, pp. 193–216. Hong Kong: Hong Kong University Press.

Zhong, N.S. and Hayhoe, R. (2001). "University autonomy in twentieth-century China," in Glen Peterson, Ruth Hayhoe, and Yongling Lu (eds), *Education, Culture, and Identity in Twentieth-century China*, pp. 265–296. Hong Kong: Hong Kong University Press.

Zhou, H.Y. and Chen, Q.B. (2003). "Zhongguo dalu yu Taiwan daxue gongshi jiaoyu kecheng de bijiao (A comparison of general education in universities between Mainland China and Taiwan)," in Koo Ding Yee, Ramsey, Wu Siu Wai, Li Siu Pang, and Titus (eds), *Jiao yu fa zhan yu ke cheng ge xin* (Education Development and Curriculum Innovations), pp. 46–58. Xianggang: Gang Ao er tong jiao yu guo ji xie hui.

Zhou, H.Y. and Shen, G.C. (2006). "Nongcun mianfei yiwu jiaoyu de tuijin (The promotion of free compulsory education in rural areas)," in Yang Dongbing (ed.), *Jiaoyu lanpishu: 2005 nian zhongguo jiaoyu fazhan baogao* (Blue Book of Education: The Development Report on China's Education, 2005), pp. 48–57. Beijing: Shehui kexue wenxian chu ban she.

Zhou, J.Y. (2006). "Zouxiang junheng fazhan de yiwu jiaoyu (Strive to balanced development of compulsory education)," in Yang Dongbing (ed.), *Jiaoyu lanpishu: 2005 nian zhongguo jiaoyu fazhan baogao* (Blue Book of Education: The Development Report on China's Education, 2005), pp. 58–71. Beijing: Shehui kexue wenxian chu ban she.

Zhu, Wenqin (2000). "'3+x'shenhua gaokao gaige de fang'an (The reform plan of '3+x' for higher education)," *Guangming Daily*, March 22, 2000.

Chapter 5

SCHOOLING IN HONG KONG

Wing-Wah Law

INTRODUCTION

Education shapes and is shaped by social change, and social change is reflected in and refracted into education. The case of Hong Kong is no exception. This chapter focuses on how education in Hong Kong was shaped by its economic and sociopolitical contexts before and after World War II. During these periods, Hong Kong made significant shifts: It moved from relying completely on private sources for funding education to developing a public educational system; it developed diverse sources of school sponsorship; it promoted universal education at the primary and junior-secondary levels; and it universalized and diversified postcompulsory education. Parallel to these changes were important continuities that constituted the basic features and issues of a dynamic Hong Kong educational system. These continuities included educational developments in response to changing economic and/or sociopolitical needs; a struggle among concerns about access, efficiency, equity, quality, and catering for diverse learning needs; struggles among nongovernment actors in sponsoring and managing public schools; and the controversy of using English or Chinese as the medium of instruction.

This chapter comprises three major parts. The first part presents the emergence of Hong Kong's educational system and colonial education policy before World War II. In particular, it focuses on some features that continue to affect Hong Kong education today, such as the complicated relationship between government and nongovernment actors in sponsoring education, the tension between diversification of school sponsorship and the government's control over school education, and the competition for status between English and Chinese language education. The second part examines the expansion of education in response to changing economic needs and sociopolitical conditions in Hong Kong since

World War II. In particular, it discusses the Hong Kong government's strategies and rationales for providing nine years of universal, compulsory basic education in the 1970s, and expanding and diversifying postcompulsory education since the 1980s. The third part discusses five major, recent education initiatives in Hong Kong: the cultivation of new local and national identities through citizenship education, curricular reform for economic globalization, the launch of the Direct Subsidy Scheme to enhance parental choice, the introduction of an unprecedented policy of medium of instruction in secondary schools, and the pursuit of quality and accountability in public school education.

THE FORMATION OF COLONIAL EDUCATION IN HONG KONG BEFORE WORLD WAR II

Before ceding from China's Qing Dynasty to Britain in 1842, Hong Kong had no public education, but some small, traditional, private Chinese schools (*si shu*) offered elementary education to foster moral character formation, equip children with basic skills such as reading and writing, and provide basic knowledge of Chinese classical texts in preparation for China's longstanding civil service examination (which was abolished in 1905). Between 1842 and World War II, Hong Kong, under British colonial rule, began to develop a semblance of an educational system, which became a foundation for contemporary education in Hong Kong. The foundation included diversified school-sponsoring bodies (including local social organizations and Western religious bodies) that would provide education; the beginning of a three-tiered academic structure; and the emergence of a tripartite school system by funding mode (comprising government, aided, and private schools). During this period, the Hong Kong government gained more control over school education and reinforced the importance of English, leading to struggles with school-sponsoring bodies.

The Birth of Public Education and Diversified School Sponsorship

At the beginning of its colonial rule, particularly between 1841 and 1860, the government adopted a minimalist approach to education. This approach enabled the government to exert a modicum of control over schools in exchange for their providing nominal resources, leaving nongovernmental sponsoring bodies to run their schools. Initially, the government wholly relied on foreign religious bodies and local charity organizations to provide mainly free primary education. The government allowed Western religious bodies to move their schools (e.g., Morrison Memorial School from Macau in 1842 and the Anglo-Chinese Ying Wa College from Malacca in 1843) to Hong Kong and also permitted them to establish private missionary schools (such as St. Paul's College in 1851). These schools were unique in admitting girls. While these schools might have allowed women to provide male graduates with educated wives who would have Christian families, Ting (1993) argued that the schools helped improve women's social status and fought against a traditional cultural value against female education epitomized in the phrase: "It is a virtue that women have no talent" (*nu zi wu cai bian shi de*).

Many local Chinese people did not want to send their children to these missionary schools because they perceived the British administration as a foreign power and these schools as a means to consolidate colonial leadership and spread Christianity. To meet the Chinese community's needs, the colonial government allowed local charity organizations to run private Chinese primary schools, which offered mostly free education and emphasized the study of classical texts, such as the Trimetrical Classic and the Thousand Words Classic. The demand for these Chinese private schools intensified because of a large influx of Chinese refugees who had escaped the uprisings in the southern part of Mainland China and chose to live in Hong Kong in the early 1850s. This created a demand for Chinese teachers which was met by refugee teachers who accompanied the influx to Hong Kong.

In the second half of the 19th century, Hong Kong gradually began to further develop public education, comprising subsidized private schools and government schools. After recognizing the unpopularity of missionary schools, in 1847 the government began subsidizing three private Chinese vernacular schools with minimal grants (e.g., HK$10 per month each) by supporting teachers' salaries and providing classrooms and facilities (Cao, 1997). In return, the schools were subject to the Education Committee's supervision. Moreover, because of the large influx of Chinese immigrants and increasing concern about the poor quality of private schools, in the mid-1850s the government began developing the government school sector by first converting some aided primary schools into government schools and putting them under its direct management, and later establishing its own government schools. As a result, the number of government schools increased from 10, with a student enrollment of 400 in 1855, to 19, with a total of over 900 students, at an annual cost of £1,200 in 1859 (Wong, 1993; Yau et al., 1993). These schools offered lessons in elementary Chinese, Chinese classics, geography, and the English language. Students paid only a small tuition fee. Later, government schools were reorganized. Some schools were merged to form the Central School in 1862 (which was renamed as Queen's College in 1889) and then incorporated into the civil service sector so that they were directly managed by the government; their staff enjoyed better benefits, similar to those of civil servants.

From the last quarter of the 19th century, the colonial government began to extend its scale and scope of subsidies to private schools. In 1873, the government introduced the Grant-in-Aid Scheme to provide eligible missionary schools with land and financial subsidies. As explained later, the response of missionary schools was cool at first, but quite positive later. The number of grant schools increased from six in 1873 to 100 in 1898, with a total of nearly 6,000 students (Wong, 1993). The share of public expenditure on education increased from 0.3 percent in 1853 to 4 percent in 1893 (Cao, 1997). In the 1920s, the government began to give monthly subsidies to Chinese private schools in accordance with the inspector's report, and this marked the beginning of the aided school sector, which remains the largest of the school sectors.

During the first half of the 20th century, the government found subsidizing educational institutions to be a useful strategy for providing education. The government thought that establishing more government schools would be redundant. Consequently, the number of government schools was kept low. Of the 649 schools for 118,000 students in 1941, only nine were government schools; 91 were grant schools, 20 were aided schools, and 529 were private schools (Wong, 1993). To complete the academic structure, the government also allocated land and earmarked HK$ one million for establishing in 1911 the University of Hong Kong, which comprised faculties of medicine, engineering, and the arts. Its establishment not only constituted a full academic structure, but it also sped up the expansion of senior-secondary education in Hong Kong. All of these developments marked the beginning of public education with a three-tiered academic structure and the tripartite school system by mode of funding (government, grant/aided, and private schools).

The Emergence of the Government's Colonial Educational Policy

In Hong Kong, the diversification of school sponsorship did not mean a reduction in or the retreat of government control over education. On the contrary, the government gradually formulated its colonial education policy and increased its administrative control over education. This in turn created tensions between the government and school-sponsoring bodies, and between Chinese education and English education. Both domestic and external factors contributed to the emergence of Hong Kong's colonial educational policy before World War II. Domestically, the Hong Kong government lacked mechanisms for monitoring and controlling education, and thus different religious bodies and local organizations mostly took charge of the schools. Many schools, particularly those in remote areas, were criticized for their poor facilities and low teaching standards. However, the government had only minimal, if any, control over their curricula and management, and could not force, for example, missionary schools to open up their curricula by offering to the masses secular education instead of Christian education.

Moreover, the Hong Kong government was confronted with strong, anti-British sentiments. The initial confrontation was reflected in the local people's objection to the legalized exploitation of Chinese workers by exporting them to other countries in 1857, and the people's 1899 resistance in the New Territories (located in the northern part of Hong Kong and leased to Britain for 99 years in 1898) to occupation by the British army, which later was used to suppress Hong Kong residents, some of whom were killed. In 1925, the Chinese people's dissatisfaction with colonial rule was intensified by the "May 30th Tragedy," in which the British army shot Chinese students who took to the streets to protest the killing of workers. The students' deaths triggered a territorywide boycott in nearly all sectors for over a year.

In addition to domestic challenges, the Hong Kong government faced external challenges to its leadership from Mainland China in the first half of the 20th century. Hong Kong had been known as a base in the 1911 revolution that led to the Kuomintang's (KMT) overthrow of the imperial Qing Dynasty and the founding of the Republic of China, under the leadership of Sun Yat Sen, who was one of the Hong Kong Central School's "old boys" and a graduate of the College of Medicine for the Chinese (which was founded in 1887 and later merged into the newly established University of Hong Kong in 1912).

In the years around 1911, the KMT organized many activities in Hong Kong society, particularly in local Chinese schools. Between the 1920s and 1940s, the KMT and the Communist Party of China (CPC) (which was established in China in 1921) competed for political support, especially in Hong Kong's educational sector. Moreover, many Chinese private schools adopted the Mainland's 6–3–3 academic structure (i.e., 6 years of primary education, 3 years of junior-secondary education and 3 years of senior-secondary education). They used the curricular standards issued by China's Ministry of Education, although they also followed the local colonial curricula, including the teaching of English, Chinese, mathematics, and other practical subjects, such as bookkeeping. Most subjects were taught in Mandarin, supplemented with Cantonese. Some of these private schools were registered with both the Hong Kong government and the Chinese government. Such double registration enabled them to obtain financial help and expertise from the Chinese government, and their graduates' qualifications could be recognized for further studies in Mainland universities. However, this inevitably strengthened Chinese influences on Hong Kong education.

The Hong Kong government saw both domestic and external challenges as serious threats to its colonial rule. The government used four major measures to consolidate its leadership and gain control over education. First, in the second half of the 19th century, the government began to establish mechanisms of administrative control over schools. For example, it established the Education Committee to monitor subsidized, local, private schools (1847); then it restructured the Education Committee into the Education Department to oversee education (1860). It also established a textbook committee to review and approve schools' textbooks and teaching materials (1873), and formed a school inspection team.

Second, the government used laws to regulate education and particularly to reduce the KMT government's influence in Hong Kong education. In 1913, the government enacted the unprecedented Education Ordinance, requiring compulsory registration of all public and private schools with the Department of Education and putting them under its supervision. More importantly, this ordinance gave it the power to close schools that the Director of Education deemed unacceptable. This drastically extended the Department's territory from 60 to over 1,200 schools. In 1932, the government promulgated 25 Education Regulations to regulate maximum class size, safety facilities, allocation of curriculum time, and punishment of students. Despite many amendments over time, the Ordinance and Regulations remain as the major legal bases for governing Hong Kong's schools.

Third, the government used economic means to gain control over private schools and to provide more school locations. The first target group was missionary schools. The original intent of the Grant-in-Aid Scheme was to require participating missionary schools to become public primary schools that would offer four hours of daily secular, rather than religious, education in exchange for government grants (Yau et al., 1993). Only a few Christian schools joined the scheme, and no Catholic school took part. To ease the tension with missionary schools, the government revised the scheme in 1879 so that schools would provide secular education, but also were allowed to teach Biblical knowledge. The revision encouraged more missionary schools to join the scheme, and religious bodies established more grant schools. Most of them offered Chinese vernacular education and not English. Since then, the control over missionary schools has been transferred from the church to the government, and their curricula have focused more on secular education than Christian education.

Fourth, the government introduced a policy of emphasizing English education and downplaying Chinese education. Because more English-speaking firms were moving from Mainland China to Hong Kong, the demand for interpreters and clerks who could communicate in English had increased substantially. The government initially lengthened the lesson time for English from four to five hours and shortened that for Chinese from four to two hours in Queen's College (a prestigious secondary school); later, it made English compulsory and Chinese an elective, with English becoming the medium of instruction (EMI) under a revised grant code in 1890 that denied grants to schools that did not use EMI (Yau et al., 1993). At the same time, the government closed 40 percent of the 28 Chinese vernacular schools in 1892 and abolished Chinese vernacular lessons in government schools between the mid-1890s and 1902. Private Chinese schools continued Chinese education. However, this was only because they were not subsidized by the government, but rather supported by local charitable organizations and the Chinese community.

In the early 20th century, the importance of English education in the school sector was further intensified by the support of prominent Chinese people, who asked the government to establish a Chinese secondary school that would offer English education for Chinese children of well-off families. They also asked for the establishment of the only university, the University of Hong Kong, that was an EMI institution. As a result, most missionary schools came to adopt EMI. The scope of EMI was extended to include other academic subjects in many schools. Despite this, Chinese schools managed to grow because in the early 1910s, many Chinese scholars went to Hong Kong to seek refuge and establish study clubs and classes for Chinese classics.

Then in the 1920s, the government began to adopt a softer approach to colonization by promoting Chinese vernacular education with a view to easing anti-British sentiments in the Chinese community and addressing the local demand for improving Chinese students' proficiency in Chinese. First, the government gave monthly subsidies to Chinese schools. Second, the government reinstated Chinese vernacular education by establishing the first Chinese government school (the Government Vernacular Middle School established in 1926 and renamed Clementi Secondary School in 1951). Third, the government supported the establishment of the Department of Chinese at the University of Hong Kong in 1927 for graduates from Chinese schools. Fourth, famous Chinese schools were allowed to move from Mainland China to Hong Kong because of the Sino-Japanese wars in the 1930s; for example, the Pui Ching Middle School moved from Guangdong to Hong Kong in 1933.

British colonial education in Hong Kong ended temporarily when it was occupied by Japan during World War II. The number of schools decreased from about 650 to 30, and Hong Kong's student population dropped significantly from 110,000 in 1941 to 3,000 in 1945 (Zhang and Kong, 2005). Despite this, the Japanese occupation administration "Japanized" Hong Kong education. For example, it used Japanese as the medium of instruction, forcing students to learn Japanese four hours a day, teaching students Japanese cultures and rituals, and using Japanese textbooks. The "Japanization" of Hong Kong education ended with Japan's surrender in September 1945.

EDUCATIONAL DEVELOPMENTS IN HONG KONG AFTER WORLD WAR II

After resuming leadership in 1945, the British colonial administration in Hong Kong began to rebuild the city's infrastructure and institutions and improve people's living conditions. Demographically, the population of Hong Kong rose from less than 6,000 in 1841 to seven million in mid-2005. Those of Chinese descent are the majority (95 percent), most of whom, or whose ancestors, migrated from the Mainland, some before, but most after the PRC's founding in 1949. The rest are of other nationalities, the largest groups being Southeast Asians (Filipinos, Indonesians, Thais, Indians, and Nepalese) and Westerners (including from the United States—Americans, Canadians, Australians, and British). In 1974, Chinese was made an official language alongside English, the previous sole official language of Hong Kong.

In education, the Hong Kong government developed a systematic academic structure by adopting both the British comprehensive school system and British university structure.

The academic structure is 6 + (3 +2) + 2 + 3: six years of primary education (P1–P6 for 6–12 age cohort), three years of junior-secondary education (S1–S3, 12–15 age cohort), two years of senior-secondary education (S4–S5, 15–17 age cohort), two years of matriculation in preparation for university education (S6–S7, 17–19 age cohort), and three years of university education (cohort aged 19–22) (see Figure 5.1). The first two tiers constitute nine years of free and compulsory basic education. Early education for children aged 3–6 is offered in

Figure 5.1
The Academic Structure of Hong Kong

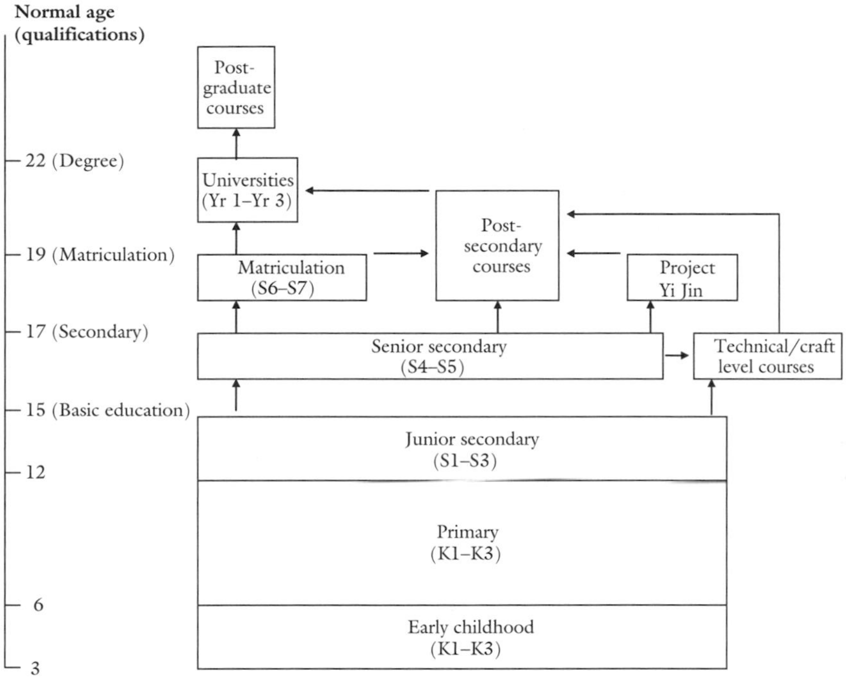

Source: Redrawn from Education Commission (2004).

kindergartens. This academic structure is a result of the gradual expansion of education by levels in different development stages, as will be discussed later.

By the beginning of the 21st century, the school system still consisted of both local and nonlocal sectors. The local school sector, comprised over 1,200 schools, offers to most students (900,000 in 2004) a curriculum focused on local public examinations. The other sector offers nonlocal curricula, in a number of international schools (American, British, Canadian, German-Swiss, Japanese, Singaporean, Jewish, and Korean), and prepares students for overseas study. In 2004, there were about 60 subsidized British Schools, with about 33,000 students. Many parents see nonlocal schools as a better alternative to local mainstream schools and offer an escape from competitive local examinations. The higher-education sector has 12 degree-awarding institutes; of them, seven universities and one teacher training institute are funded by the government through the University Grants Committee (UGC), one academy of performance arts is publicly funded, one open university is self-financed, and two other colleges are totally private. The UGC-funded higher-education institutes offer a total of 14,500 first-year-first-degree places, accommodating about 18 percent of the 17–20 age cohort.

EDUCATION FOR ALL IN HONG KONG: ACCESS, EFFICIENCY, AND EQUITY

In Hong Kong, a basic education of nine years has been provided for all children since the late 1970s. Basic education is often taken as a synonym for the level of schooling that is stipulated by law as free and compulsory (Grover, 2004). Since World War II and particularly since the 1990 Jomtien Declaration (UNESCO, 1990), the provision of basic education has been a long-standing aspiration across the globe and is seen as a useful strategy enhancing the basic quality of human capital and human life, particularly under the movement of Education for All (UNESCO, 2000a). While the United Nations is striving hard to promote these concepts and urging for the provision of universal primary education for all children across the globe by 2015 (UN Millennium Project, 2005), Hong Kong, under the British colonial administration, already had achieved universal, nine-year, compulsory education by the 1970s. As argued in this section, the framework for providing education for all in Hong Kong has been mainly driven by economic and sociopolitical needs, and various strategies have been used to deal with the problems of access, efficiency, and equity.

Economic and Sociopolitical Considerations of Education for All

In Hong Kong, the present framework for universal, compulsory basic education is very similar to UNESCO's framework of Education For All. In the Education for All movement, UNESCO spelled out a powerful triumvirate of arguments for universal basic education: rights, freedoms, and development benefits (UNESCO, 2002). Education is a human right and a means of securing good health, liberty, security, economic well-being, and social and political participation. Similar to Amartya Sen's (1999) concepts of human capabilities and development, UNESCO (2002) sees education as a means to help people gain freedom by equipping them with basic skills that are conditions and outcomes of development, reducing child labor, and empowering the disadvantaged. As a productive investment, education can lead to an increase in self-employment in both urban and rural areas and enhance the quality of human life through lower fertility rates and healthier diets. In Hong Kong, the Board of Education (1997) referenced the 1990 Jomtien Conference on Education for All, and spelled out the need for compulsory education in Hong Kong as a human right for all people and as a means to protect this human right; a means to protect children by helping them develop the ability to make informed, rational, and reasoned decisions; and an important factor contributing to the community's economic development by enhancing the quality of human resources and enhancing an individual's employment opportunities.

Despite the present framework, the provision of nine-year, compulsory basic education in the 1970s was more a response to a concern about economic development than one about people's rights and freedoms. After World War II, Hong Kong had a very strong need for local social and economic redevelopment.

This was complicated by the large influx of immigrants from Mainland China due to its political instability and/or economic difficulties during three major climaxes of immigration: around the CPC's assumption of power and the founding of the People's Republic of China in 1949, economic difficulties after the Great Leap Forward Movement in the late 1950s, and after the disastrous Cultural Revolution (1966–1976). It was estimated that the first two climaxes brought in over one million people from Mainland China. As a result, the Hong Kong population increased from about 1.5 million in 1946 to five million in 1979 (Hong Kong Government, 1980).

These sudden population increases supplied capital and cheap manpower to help develop the labor-intensive economy. They also brought forth "immense" demands on the social, economic, and financial resources (Hong Kong Government, 1974). In particular, most of these immigrants had low educational levels and poor vocational skills. According to the 1961 census, the illiteracy rate of people over age 10 was 25 percent (Census and Statistics Department, 1962). Many children did not have education and child labor was common. In 1961, the primary and secondary enrollment rates of the cohorts aged 6–11 (54 percent and 16 percent, respectively) and 12–18 (53 percent and 23 percent, respectively) were low (Census and Statistics Department, 1972). If these immigrants and their children lacked education and training, the new population could become a liability, rather than an asset, to economic and social development. To prevent this and provide semiskilled labor for the postwar economy, Hong Kong increased its school enrollment from 50,000 in 1945 at an annual rate at the peak of about 45,000 primary places in the 1950s and 1960s (Hong Kong Government Secretariat, 1981). In 1964, nearly all children of primary-school age were given places in government-aided or private schools. However, only 18 percent of primary graduates could receive subsidized places in government or aided schools, and about half were enrolled in private schools without government subsidies (Hong Kong Government, 1964).

Unlike UNESCO's framework for education for all, the need for sociopolitical stability in the colony has been an important consideration for providing free and compulsory basic education, particularly in the late 1960s. Schooling has been a device for promoting social order (Ross, 1900) and a political tool for encouraging conformity to social, cultural, and moral norms (Peden, 1977; Rickenbacker, 1999). Schools can be used as a means of indirect social control for regulating individual or group behavior by passing on to students such values as discipline and obedience, and preparing them to be law-abiding citizens and productive, disciplined workers (Ballantine, 2001).

In Hong Kong during 1966 and 1967, many young people participated in social unrest and riots that challenged social stability and the colonial administration's legitimacy and authority (Law, 2004). As a result, the Hong Kong government adopted a two-pronged approach. First, the government intensified its management of and control over society by, for example, enacting the Public Security Ordinance in 1967, which required people to apply to the police in advance of any public gatherings or else face imprisonment (Legislative Council, 2000). In schools, any flag, songs, symbols, uniforms, dances, symbols, or activities of a political nature were forbidden (Hong Kong Government, 1971).

Second, the government wanted to ease social dissatisfaction and contradictions by improving social welfare; this included a 10-year plan for public housing and more educational opportunities. In particular, the government's youth policy was intended to improve social structure, increase recreational facilities, enhance youth's social participation, strengthen moral education, and create emotional outlets for children and teens (Hong Kong Government, 1967). The government's intention to instill among students the concept of being a responsible citizen for an orderly society was reflected in the Education Department's (1981) guidelines on promoting moral education in primary and secondary schools, which aimed to help students "acquire desirable habits, attitudes and values which will enable them to become responsible members of society" and cope with youths' problems, including juvenile delinquency.

Strategies for Providing Education for All

In Hong Kong, the quest for education for all was complicated by interrelated concerns about access, equity, efficiency, and quality. How to strike a balance among these concerns is a hot topic of the Education for All movement (UNESCO, 2002, 2003, 2005). Equal opportunity for all requires a sufficient provision of school places. Such provision must be financially affordable to both education providers (particularly the government) and consumers (including students and parents), and requires the efficient deployment and use of available, but limited resources. The provision also needs to address the issue of educational quality because it "determines how much and how well students learn, and the extent to which their education achieves a range of personal, social and development goals" (UNESCO, 2005). In Hong Kong, six major strategies have been used to address the issues of access, efficiency, and equity in universal basic education.

First, after World War II, the Hong Kong government began providing access to primary education to as many students as possible by optimizing its very limited resources. In the early 1950s, the Hong Kong government began running both morning and afternoon sections for two different groups of primary students with two separate teaching staff teams. It also allowed social organizations (such as churches) to establish and run primary schools on the rooftops of public resettlement estates until the 1970s (Chung and Ngan, 2002; Chu, 2003) and charged students tuition fees to share the cost of education.

Second, the government gradually shifted its reliance on nongovernment sources from private to aided schools. Before the late 1970s, the government continued the prewar policy of relying heavily on private schools for providing education. However, the quality of private schools varied greatly and many of them were profit making. Their tuition fees were higher than those of government or subsidized schools, and the number of public-school openings was very limited, particularly in junior-secondary education, which prevented many children of poor families from attending. To tackle the shortage of public-school places and improve the quality of private schools, in the mid-1960s, the government began to modify its funding policy by buying places from private secondary schools, about 1,500–2,000 per year, as estimated in the late 1960s (Hong Kong Government, 1965). As a result, the number of private, government-bought places increased from 46.4 percent of total student enrollment in 1979 to 51.2 percent in 1980 (Hong Kong Government Secretariat, 1981). This helped increase the opportunity of children from poor families to access junior-secondary education.

Moreover, the government decided to make aided schools the major constituent of the public-school sector. The government considered that public education was "provided more economically in aided than in government schools" and decided that government schools would be established only "where an aided school cannot be provided" (Hong Kong Government, 1965). As a result, in the mid-1970s and 1980s, the government established many aided schools. Most of these schools were sponsored by the Catholic Church and the Protestant Church, which had gained the favor of the government and more educated people to take up the duty of school management; whereas a minority was taken up by organizations associated with other religions (such as Buddhism and Taoism) and local social organizations that did not share the Christian Churches' favorable conditions (Luk, 2004). The government also invited non-profit-making private secondary schools with satisfactory operating standards to be converted into aided schools. In 1982, about 60 such private schools were converted into aided secondary schools. As a result, the number of aided schools (including grant schools) grew from 340 in 1954 to 756 in 1977, 849 in 1992, and 1,040 in 2001. The expansion of aided schools and the introduction of free, compulsory, nine-year schooling diminished the role of private schools and ended their historical mission in paving the way for education for all in Hong Kong. Most private schools were closed, and only a minority managed to survive. The percentage of private schools dropped from about 70 percent of all schools in the early 1970s to about 50 percent in the late 1970s, and then to 8.2 percent (103 schools) in 2001. In a similar manner, the number of government schools first increased from 40 in 1954 to 112 in 1978, but dropped to 88 in 1992 and 78 in 2001. Despite the provision of education for all in the public sector, a small proportion of students (e.g., less than 10 percent in 2000) opt for private schooling (Hong Kong Government, 2001).

Third, as the economy grew, the government increased its financial responsibility for education. It increased the percentage of public expenditure on education from 8.5 percent in 1951 to 19 percent in 1971, and the percentage was kept at an average of 17.5 percent between 1974 and 1979 (Hong Kong Government Secretariat, 1981; Wong and Ho, 1996). The percentage of the GDP of the government expenditure on education rose from 0.7 percent in 1951 to 2.1 percent in 1971 and 2.67 percent in 1978. The gradual increase in educational financing enabled the government to raise the target percentage of primary-six leavers to receive subsidized junior-secondary education from 15–20 percent of the cohort in 1965 to 50 percent in 1970, and 100 percent in 1978 (Hong Kong Government, 1974). It also reduced the financial burden on poor families by abolishing tuition fees in public, junior-secondary forms in 1978 and then subscription and other charges in junior-secondary classes in 1979.

Fourth, the government used legal means to ensure access to and equity in education, and this has had binding effects on both the government and parents. By law, all children between the ages of 6 and 15 are obliged by law to receive free, but compulsory, nine-year education (or to complete F.3, whichever is earlier) (Hong Kong Government, 1980). The access to such education in the public sector is made available to "all children of the right age, irrespective of sex, ethnic origin, religion or ethical belief, family status and physical or mental ability" (Board of Education, 1997). Moreover, since the introduction of free compulsory education in 1978, the Education Ordinance has given the government (specifically the former Director of Education and now the Permanent Secretary for Education and Manpower) legal power to enforce the school attendance of children of the right age (Hong Kong Government, 2006). Moreover, in the 1970s, the government issued separate codes of aid, both stipulating its financial commitment to four types of aided/grant schools (primary schools and secondary schools in the mainstream and special education sectors) and prescribing the rules and conditions governing financial grants to such schools (Hong Kong Government Secretariat, 1981). These codes helped reduce the disparity among government and aided/grant schools in educational expenditures, facilities, and teachers' qualifications and therefore provided students with learning opportunities in environments with similar standards.

Fifth, the provision of a common core curriculum for general education and written assessment is used to ensure further equity in students' promotion from primary to junior-secondary education. Primary–secondary students mainly follow a common general education curriculum, with an emphasis on three core subjects (Chinese language, English language, and mathematics). In junior-secondary education, students are required to study academic and practical subjects in both grammar-secondary schools (which is the majority, 440 in 2000) and secondary-technical schools (19 in 2000) (which also offer a senior-secondary curriculum). The two types differ in the percentage of practical subjects: about 10–20 percent in grammar-secondary schools and about 25–30 percent in technical schools (which have provided technical education since the 1930s) (Education Department, 1997b) (see Table 5.1). Because both grammar and technical-secondary schools provide a 5-year curriculum leading to the Hong Kong Certificate of Education Examination, many technical schools dropped the word "technical" from their school names. Moreover, two of the practical subjects, home economics and design and technology, which were offered separately to female and male students, were criticized for sexual

Table 5.1
The Percentages of Practical and Technical Subjects in Different Types of
Junior-Secondary Education

Type of School	Form 1–Form 3	Form 4–Form 5
Grammar schools	10–20	Not fixed
Technical schools	25–30	Not fixed
Pre-vocational schools	40–50	30 in information technology
Practical schools	45	—
Skills opportunity schools	40	—

Sources: Board of Education (1997); Education Department (1997b).

discrimination in the late 1990s. As a result, most secondary schools, which are coeducational, now offer both subjects to both genders.

Sixth, in the mid-1960s, the government began to take a two-pronged approach to meeting the needs of students with different disabilities and learning abilities, which is concomitant to the concern with equal opportunity in education for all. In the mid-1960s, the government adopted a segregation approach for students with severe mental and physical disabilities, placing them in special schools separated from mainstream schools. Churches had offered special education; for example, missionaries established the first special school (for the deaf) in 1935. Then in the 1970s, the government began using a traditional, integration approach to help students with mild disabilities and diversified learning abilities participate in the general education curriculum in mainstream schools. The government gave additional resources (such as resource teachers) to ordinary schools for providing special classes for children with less-severe handicaps (such as those partially sighted) and resource classes for ordinary children of slow learning; in 1977, these two class types had 4,095 and 3,840 places, respectively (Hong Kong Government, 1977). To address individual differences in the mainstream-school sector's common-core curriculum, an activity approach has been encouraged in primary schools, along with remedial teaching, and additional teachers have been introduced in both primary and secondary schools to assist students with weak academic performance.

THE EXPANSION AND DIVERSIFICATION OF POST-COMPULSORY SCHOOLING SINCE THE 1980s

Unlike basic education, access to senior-secondary education and tertiary education in Hong Kong has been a choice rather than a right or an obligation. Despite this, Hong Kong gradually expanded these two tiers of education in the 1980s and 1990s, respectively. Similar to the provision of basic education in the 1970s, the expansion of postcompulsory education has been geared toward changing economic needs and sociopolitical considerations. The Hong Kong government adopted similar strategies to strike a balance among access, efficiency, equity, and catering to diverse learning needs.

The Provision of Virtually Universal Senior-Secondary Education from the 1980s

Before the enactment and attainment of nine-year compulsory education in 1978, the Hong Kong government (1974) foresaw the community's strong need for expanding senior-secondary education, and noted the financial constraints that might inhibit such an expansion. The government expected to increase the percentage of the 16–17 age cohort from 40 percent in 1974 to over 70 percent in 1986 (Hong Kong Government Secretariat, 1981). Later, the Hong Kong government (1978) made four important policy decisions that have affected the development of senior-secondary education since the 1980s.

First, the government decided that postcompulsory education should be available to people on a voluntary basis, but that consumers of such education (namely students and their parents) should bear a reasonable share of the costs. Since that time, those pupils who wish to continue secondary education beyond secondary-three must pay fees. To ensure that no student is prevented from continuing education in the public-school sector because of inability to pay fees, the government has a fee remission scheme that subsidizes eligible students' school fees and books.

Second, the government diversified the senior-secondary curriculum to include both grammar and vocational tracks. The former prepared students for the examination for admission to universities or other tertiary institutes, while the latter was for preparing a limited number of junior-secondary leavers who were capable of becoming technicians for direct entry into the labor market after taking craft-level courses at technical institutes (now amalgamated into the Institute of Vocational Education). Most secondary-three leavers would receive two more years of subsidized, senior-secondary education (secondary four and five), and a minority would receive basic craft courses of vocational education at technical institutes. Under the pressure of discrimination against vocational education, the proportion of students in subsidized grammar and vocational tracks changed respectively from 85.4 percent of 80,628 leavers and 5 percent in 1997 to 92.1 percent of 73,640 leavers and 3.2 percent in 2001–2002 (Hong Kong Government, 1998, 2002).

Third, because of the expansion, the government decided to adopt the Junior Secondary Education Assessment (JSEA) System to allocate subsidized secondary-four places based on parental choice and students' performance in school internal assessments during the last year of the junior-secondary curriculum. Most eligible students are allocated whenever possible to their original secondary schools (if, as most do, it has senior-secondary education), but a minority of them who cannot get a place in their original schools must take part in the central allocation for subsidized places in other secondary schools that have spare places or craft courses in technical institutes. However, under normal circumstances, secondary-three leavers are not allowed to take part in the JSEA exercise more than once.

Fourth, the government set a limit on the quota of subsidized places in the two-year, secondary-six curriculum leading to the Hong Kong Advanced Level

Examination, which has been used as a major mechanism for selecting students in degree and subdegree programs. Subsidized secondary-six places are made available for up to one-third of students entering subsidized secondary-four places two years previously. In other words, the promotion rate is limited to 33 percent. In 2001–2002, there were slightly over 24,000 subsidized secondary-six places (Hong Kong Government, 2002). This policy has made secondary-six education a bottleneck in the academic structure because the competition for a secondary-six place is keener than that for a university place, particularly after the expansion of higher education in the 1990s.

In the 2000s, subsidized senior-secondary education was further expanded. As part of education reform, any secondary-three leavers from publicly funded schools who have the ability and want to pursue further studies are given an opportunity to receive subsidized senior-secondary education of secondary five and six or vocational education. Secondary-five leavers may enroll in the self-financing Project Yi Jin program as an alternative route to increase their continuing education opportunities (Hong Kong Government, 2005a). Graduates of this program are awarded a qualification equivalent to five subject passes in the Hong Kong Certificate of Education Examination (including Chinese and English) for the purposes of employment and further study (such as associate degree courses). Moreover, universal senior-secondary education is expected to be achieved when the new academic structure of senior-secondary education and higher education is implemented in 2009; the former will become three years and the latter four years (Education and Manpower Bureau, 2005c). By that time, the bottleneck at the secondary level will disappear, and anyone who wishes to and has ability will be provided a subsidized place in the new three-year senior-secondary curriculum. Senior-secondary students also will be given the opportunity to choose their own combinations of academic and vocational components (namely, Career-Oriented Studies), according to their needs and the availability of the latter in their schools (Education and Manpower Bureau, 2006a).

The Gradual Shift from Elitist to Universal Higher Education Since the 1990s

After expanding senior-secondary education, Hong Kong began to increase its higher educational opportunities in the 1990s. Formerly, access to higher education in Hong Kong was very restricted and limited to a very small percentage of high achievers in public examinations. For example, the two universities (the University of Hong Kong and the Chinese University of Hong Kong) offered "first-year, first-degree" (FYFD) places to only slightly over 2 percent of the 17–20 age group between 1975 and 1981 (Llewellyn, 1982).

Sociopolitical and economic considerations were major causes of higher education's expansion. In the late 1980s and 1990s, Hong Kong's economy faced two major problems: a brain drain and a need for economic restructuring. After the signing of the 1984 Sino-British Joint Declaration that returned

Hong Kong from the United Kingdom to China in 1997, many Hong Kong people worried about the political future and began to emigrate to other countries to seek political safety. This reached a head in 1989 as many talented Hong Kong residents emigrated after the military suppression following the Tiananmen Square incident in Beijing. As a result, the average number of emigrants per year drastically increased from 20,000 in the early 1980s to 60,000 in the early 1990s. Many of these emigrants were highly trained personnel. For example, of the 43,100 emigrants in 1995, nearly 40 percent (15,700) were managers, administrators, professionals, and associated professionals. The exodus abated near the handover in 1997; thus the number of emigrants decreased from 40,300 in 1996 to 19,300 in 1998. Many Hong Kong emigrants repatriated to Hong Kong after they had obtained the right of abode in other countries. It was estimated that at least 12 percent of people who had emigrated before 1994 returned to Hong Kong (Hong Kong Government, 1997).

Moreover, by the early 1990s, Hong Kong had been transformed from a labor-intensive economy into a capital- and technology-intensive and service economy. The total manpower requirement was estimated to increase by about 434,000 jobs, about half of which would come from various business services, import/export trade, and off-site construction. The information and communication-technology sector was seen as an emerging and urgent area that needed a large quantity of trained personnel. The economic transformation, in turn, created a mismatch between job requirements and workers' qualifications. It is estimated that by 2007, the manpower supply at the upper-secondary level and below will be at a surplus of 231,500, but at shortage at the "post-secondary level" and "first-degree and above" by about 65,200 and 36,500, respectively (Hong Kong Government, 2003).

To compensate for the brain drain and sustain the transforming economy in the early 1990s, the Hong Kong government expanded tertiary education to train more high-level professionals, using two strategies (Cheng, 1996). The first strategy was to massively expand subsidized higher education. In 1989, the government decided to raise the number of FYFD places from 1994–1995 to no less than 18 percent of the 17–20 age cohort or about 15,000 places, which was later reduced to 14,500, according to the 1991 population census (University Grants Committee, 1996b). As a result, FYFD places were drastically increased from less than 4,000 (less than 4 percent of the age cohort) in 1985–1986 to 14,253 (17.4 percent) in 1994–1995; since then, the figures have been maintained roughly at this new level (e.g., 14,719 places in 2004–2005) (University Grants Committee, 1996a, 2005). In the meantime, the government expanded programs leading to diplomas that were granted mainly by the two polytechnic institutes (which were upgraded to universities in the mid-1990s) and technical institutes. In both degree and subdegree programs, priority was given to social work, information technology and computer engineering, business administration and management, and hospitality management (University Grants Committee, 1996b).

Another strategy was to extend subdegree programs to include associate degree (AD) programs in the early 2000s. Between 1991 and 2001, the expansion of higher education increased the proportions of the population aged 15–24 and 25–34 enrolled in higher education from 13.7 percent to 19.3 percent and from 15.5 percent to 29.5 percent, respectively (Census and Statistics Department, 2001). However, the figures were still far below those of developed economies, such as the United States and Britain. To catch up with them, in 2000, the Chief Executive created a policy to provide postsecondary education for 60 percent of the 17–20 age group, for about 55,000 places per year from 2010 (Hong Kong Government, 2000). This meant that additional postsecondary places would increase from 6,500 in 2001 to about 28,000 in 2010. Instead of expanding undergraduate education, the government strongly promoted self-financing AD programs while expanding other subdegree courses. To attract providers to offer self-financing AD education, between 2001 and 2005, the government lent over HK$ four billion to existing public tertiary institutes, and allocated five pieces of land to build community college campuses. As a result, nearly all universities made use of this loan to establish their community colleges. The expansion of AD education also boosted the overall postsecondary participation rate for the 17–20 age group from about 30 percent in 2000–2001 to 53 percent in 2004 and 66 percent in 2005–2006, five years earlier than the target date (2010) (Hong Kong Government, 2005b). However, such drastic expansion led to questions about, for example, quality control over AD programs and the legitimacy of AD diplomas in the labor market (Fung, 2005; Lam, 2005; Lee, 2005).

OTHER MAJOR EDUCATIONAL REFORM INITIATIVES AND RELATED ISSUES

Changes in the domestic and international economic, social, and political contexts of Hong Kong have redefined its needs and requirements for its labor force, thus leading to educational reforms. They include the promotion of new local and national identities through education; curricular reform to prepare students for the challenges of economic globalization; the introduction of a medium of instruction policy; the increase in parental choice and strengthening of private education; and the democratization of school governance.

Decolonization and the Cultivation of New National and Local Identities

In the late 1980s, the Hong Kong government began to redefine the school curriculum's sociopolitical component by equipping students with a new political identity. This can be seen as part of its strategy to ease anti-British sentiments and match the gradual institutionalization of representative government (as discussed earlier); it also was a response to the sociopolitical change from being a British colony to becoming a special administrative region (SAR) of the People's Republic of China in 1997. The colonial government deregulated political control over schools. Formerly, the government had suppressed political activities in schools, as mentioned earlier (Hong Kong Government, 1971). In the 1990s, the Education Regulations were revised to allow schools to organize activities that do not have adverse effects on students' welfare and education and to disseminate "unbiased" political information and opinions (Hong Kong Government, 1991).

The colonial government also changed its curriculum policy from delocalization to localization (Law, 2004). Formerly, students were not allowed to learn about their local history and how they had been colonized and governed. Instead, they were taught about the political systems and cultural traditions of other countries, which were mainly British allies. In the 1980s, the government introduced such subjects as Social Studies and Economics and Public Affairs, with a view to enhancing students' understanding of the government's structure, policymaking processes, political elections, and local affairs. In the late 1990s, the history curriculum incorporated an independent topic, Hong Kong history, which covers different phases of development, ranging from the rural life centuries ago to 20th-century economy and society.

Moreover, in the mid-1980s, the colonial government promoted citizenship education to prepare students for their dual citizenship, both local and national. Formerly, the school curriculum had distanced Hong Kong students from the Chinese mainland by describing it as a northern neighbor and not incorporating its contemporary developments. In 1985 (one year after the signing of the Sino-British Joint Declaration in 1984 that sealed Hong Kong's return to China), the colonial government issued unprecedented school guidelines on civic education (Education Department Curriculum Development Committee, 1985). Under the increasing pressure of sovereignty transfer, the guidelines were revised in 1996 (Curriculum Development Council, 1996). The 1996 revised guidelines differed from the original ones by providing an explicit conceptual framework of citizenship education and civic learners and officially recognizing the importance of nationalism and patriotism to fostering a national identity, a sense of belonging, and national cohesion (Lee, 2004).

Despite these differences, the two sets of guidelines had two major similarities. First, they shared a common vision about promoting civic awareness, skills, and attitudes amongst students, and both encouraged students to develop critical thinking skills and schools to adopt a values clarification approach (rather than an indoctrination approach) to citizenship education. Second, they both promoted a tripartite framework for citizenship education with a view to equipping Hong Kong students with triple citizenship in the Hong Kong SAR, China, and the world. The local dimension included developing a sense of belonging to Hong Kong, an appreciation of the local cultural heritage, and respect for law and order, which are important foundations of Hong Kong's success, as well as articulating Hong Kong citizens' basic rights, freedoms, duties, and responsibilities.

On the national level, in 1985, the colonial administration first referred to China as the "nation." Students were encouraged to foster a sense of national identity and belonging, love for the nation, and pride in being Chinese. The global dimension covered such themes as appreciation of world civilizations, respect for different peoples and cultures, the importance of cooperation, the interdependence and interconnectivity of peoples in the world, and concerns about world issues and problems. However, the promotion of citizenship education was not as successful as the authorities expected for various reasons, including teachers' fear about the political sensitivity of citizenship education, the marginalization of citizenship education in an examination-oriented culture, the cross-curricular approach, which emphasized everyone's responsibility for citizenship education, but later became no man's land, and the lack of teacher training (see also Leung, 1995). To improve citizenship education, in 1998 schools were allowed to introduce civic education as an independent, time-tabled subject in the junior-secondary school curriculum on a voluntary basis.

Despite the tripartite framework for citizenship education, the SAR government emphasizes the national components more than the local and global ones, and political identity more than cultural identity (Law, 2004). Since the handover in 1997, the SAR government has intensified its efforts on shifting curriculum policy from deaffiliation to reaffiliation with the Chinese Mainland. First, the government issued guidelines and encouraged schools to enact national rituals, which included displaying the national flag on important days, such as National Day (October 1) and Handover Day (July 1), and playing the national anthem on important school occasions, such as graduation day. Second, in extracurricular activities, elements of Chinese culture, such as Chinese music and martial arts, were introduced. Third, students were sponsored to attend activities in the Chinese mainland, such as national education programs in Beijing, visits to sites that were designated for patriotic education, and other activities that helped them learn more about China's recent developments and achievements. Fourth, in history textbooks, the triangular relationship among Hong Kong, China, and Taiwan was redefined. China is no longer described as the northern neighbor, but as a sovereign power over Hong Kong, and Taiwan is no longer presented as a separate entity called the Republic of China, but as an integral part of China. Textbooks also record the intent of China's authorities to unite Taiwan under the principle of one China. Fifth, in the curricular reform of the early 2000s (see more later), moral education and civics were designated as key curricular topics and national identity was identified as a priority value to be fostered among students. Sixth, in mid-2004, the Working Group on National Education was established to help promote national education outside schools. As a result of its efforts, China's national anthem, "Our Home Our Country," has been played on Chinese-language television channels before the broadcast of the evening news.

Curricular Reform in a Global Age: A Challenge to Equal Educational Participation

Besides equipping students with new local and national identities, in the early 2000s Hong Kong's school curricula, as in many other societies (such as China,

Taiwan, the United Kingdom, and the United States), were reformed so as to prepare students to face the challenges of the 21st century, especially those associated with the dawning of a global era during which capital, people, goods, and services flow easily across borders. Another major challenge is Hong Kong's competition with cities from the Chinese mainland, which has joined the World Trade Organization. The increasing opening up of Chinese cities, such as Shanghai, has reduced Hong Kong's role as a bridge between China and the rest of the world.

The Hong Kong government (2000) recognized these challenges and reformed the curricula to help deal with them. At the levels of primary and secondary education, the curricular reform proposal shares many themes and emphases that are similar to the global imperatives for education advocated in many other countries, particularly UNESCO's (1996; 2000b) four pillars of learning: learning to know, learning to do, learning to live together, and learning to be. In the new curricula for primary and junior-secondary education (Curriculum Development Council, 2001), learning to learn is the overarching theme of curricular reform. An important curricular task is to help students develop a culture of self-learning and master nine generic skills (collaboration, communication, creativity, critical thinking, information technology, numeracy, problem solving, self-management, and study skills). Another important task is to equip all students with a broad knowledge base and essential lifelong learning experiences. To rectify Hong Kong's examination-oriented culture and give students more space for all-round development, the government attempted to shift the relation between assessment and learning. In this regard, the government introduced a territory-wide system assessment to evaluate students' basic competence in Chinese, English, and mathematics at primary-three, primary-six, and junior-secondary-three levels in 2004, 2005, and 2006, respectively.

Although the territorywide assessment was intended to help schools improve the quality of educational provision by knowing the performance of their students, it has unfortunately reignited examination pressure. Many schools reintroduced drilling exercises to prepare their students for the assessment because they were afraid that the overall school performance might affect the quality of their student intake and even the school's survival particularly under the pressure of school closure, which has begun due to a significant, anticipated drop in the primary school-age population (aged 6–11) by 82,600 (17 percent) between 2001 and 2010 (Education and Manpower Bureau, 2003).

Moreover, the new basic education curricular reform challenges the principle of equal educational participation and puts students from low-socioeconomic-status families at a disadvantage. The use of information technology for interactive learning and the promotion of reading have been set as two (of the four) key curricular tasks (Curriculum Development Council, 2001). Schools are also encouraged to provide students with more school-based, off-campus, and after-school, life-wide learning activities (such as learning musical instruments, visiting museums, and going to concerts). However, all these require more financial resources and therefore increase the financial burden on low-income families.

The Policy of Medium of Instruction: The Institutionalization of Linguistic Stratification

With the return of sovereignty from the United Kingdom to China in 1997, the debate on the use of the CMI and EMI in secondary schools has intensified and become more complex. Unlike its predecessor, which attempted to interfere with schools' medium of instruction (MoI) policies by using grants to force them to use EMI in the late-19th century, the 20th century colonial government adopted a laissez-faire language policy in secondary education until the mid-1990s. Although the Hong Kong government (1974) recognized the dilemma between the importance of using Chinese in junior-secondary forms on educational grounds and the need to maintain the English standard for economic reasons and to meet many parents' expectations, it allowed individual school authorities to "decide whether the medium of instruction should be English or Chinese for any particular subject in junior secondary forms." Because of parents' strong preference for English over Chinese, many originally CMI schools switched to EMI, and this led to the expansion of the EMI-school sector and the contraction of the CMI-school sector. Despite this, the Hong Kong government had been urged to promote CMI, particularly in junior-secondary forms by the international panel led by Llewellyn (1982) and the Education Commission (1984; 1986; 1990).

However, in the mid-1990s, the Hong Kong government, under the British administration, slowly began to change its MoI policy for secondary education from nonintervention to intervention. Major reasons for this change included complaints about the decline of students' English standards and widespread, mixed-code instruction (switching between and mixing English and Cantonese) in EMI schools (Johnson, 1998; Evans, 2000). Immediately after the transfer of sovereignty in 1997, the new Hong Kong government introduced a general language policy of biliteracy and trilingualism (i.e., to be literate in both Chinese and English, and proficient in English, Cantonese, and Putonghua [the national oral language]).

Moreover, in 1997, the new Hong Kong government enforced the unprecedented MoI policy to institutionalize the streaming of secondary schools into either CMI or EMI. Three major criteria were used for granting EMI status to a secondary school (Education Department, 1997a). First, at least 85 percent of students in the secondary-one intake were capable of learning through both English and Chinese. Second, teachers were capable of teaching in English. Third, the school had sufficient support to promote learning in English. As a result of these new criteria, 114 secondary schools (which were already competitive schools) were allowed to continue to be EMI and about 300 secondary schools were forced to change their medium of instruction to CMI (i.e., Chinese textbooks and examinations, and Cantonese in oral communication).

After a series of public consultations between 2003 and 2005, the government accepted the Education Commission's (2005) recommendations for continuing the bifurcated streaming policy, and agreed to implement a series of revised MoI arrangements to be put into effect beginning September 2010. Regarding students' ability, in an ordinary EMI school at least 85 percent of its secondary-one intake must be EMI-capable (i.e., they must be among the top 40 percent of secondary-one students). A "through-train" secondary school can have two thresholds of EMI-capable students: 75 percent for entrants from the linked primary school, but 85 percent for those from nonlinked primary schools. Regarding teachers' capability, EMI-capable teachers of any subject must have minimum qualifications in English proficiency equivalent to a grade of C in English language (syllabus B) on the Hong Kong Certificate of Education Examination (HKCEE) or a D in the Use of English on the Hong Kong Advanced Level Examination (HKALE). They are also required to attend a minimum of 15 hours of EMI-related professional-development activities every three years. EMI schools are required to incorporate support measures in their school development plans and annual reports (which are basic documents made accessible to the public and used in school reviews by the Education and Manpower Bureau or an external agency under the quality-assurance mechanism). In general, secondary schools can opt to change their MoI in 2010 based on their results on the HKATs of 2008 and 2009. Schools can opt for a change every six years. Those CMI schools that meet the revised criteria can apply for a switch to EMI, and those EMI schools that fail to meet the criteria are required to change to CMI.

Based on the Education Commission's recommendations, the government agreed to introduce a policy of positive discrimination for schools that continue to use CMI or opt for CMI. First, provided that other, nonlanguage subjects in CMI and the normal progress of teaching and learning are not undermined, CMI schools are allowed to raise gradually the proportion of teaching time for English from 15 percent in secondary one to 20 percent in secondary two and 25 percent in secondary three, so as to enhance students' exposure to English (Education and Manpower Bureau, 2005d). Second, funding is tilted toward CMI schools to help them improve their English learning environment. However, successful CMI schools are required to sign a "performance contract" that includes the targets of improvement over six years with interim milestones of achievement, for example, by raising the overall percentage of their students that pass (or credit and above) in English language on the HKCEE by 10 percent three years after the receipt of funding. If they fail to achieve this target, funding can be withheld. The positive discrimination for CMI led to public criticism by the Association for the English Medium Secondary Schools (Lour, 2006).

As compared with English, the promotion of Putonghua is less vigorous. For most Hong Kong people, Putonghua is a new (oral) language. After the return of Hong Kong to China, Putonghua quickly was introduced as a timetabled subject into primary and secondary schools across the territory. However, only a minority of primary and secondary schools use Putonghua as the MoI, in only Chinese language or in all non-English subjects. As shown in a survey, the reasons for the low use of Putonghua as an MoI in schools include an insufficiency of Putonghua proficiency in both teachers and students, a shortage of appropriate teaching materials, and a lack of the necessary language environment (Education and Manpower Bureau, 2005a). Although the government has put effort and resources into promoting Putonghua, the scale and amount are relatively low as compared with those for English.

The Direct Subsidy Scheme: A Challenge of Equity versus Choice and Diversity

Since nine-year compulsory schooling began in the 1970s, the quality of public school education in Hong Kong has been questioned. To address this, in the 1990s the government began to use two strategies: to strengthen the private education sector and increase parental choice, and reform school management in public schools. In the 1970s and 1980s, the policy of reliance on aided schools in the provision of education not only promoted equal access to education, but also helped equalize the allocation of resources among schools (Luk, 2004). However, the aided-school policy increased the government's financial burden and weakened private education's role as a good alternative to public schools. The egalitarian approach to financing the public school sector reduced the motivation of many public schools to strive for school improvement. As a result, parents had limited choices when seeking quality schools for their children. To rectify this, in 1991 the government strengthened private education with the provision of the Direct Subsidy Scheme (DSS) for private schools and aided schools to provide greater parental choice and more diverse schools (Director of Education, 2001). There are three types of DSS schools: those converted from private school status, those converted from aided school status, and those that started as brand-new DSS schools. The DSS initiative is expected to encourage the privatization of education (Tse, 2005).

However, the DSS is not a genuine case of privatization; rather, it subsidizes private education. Ex-private DSS schools that were formerly excluded from the government's subsidies can receive financial help from the government based on the number of eligible students and the average unit cost of an aided school place in the respective grade levels. The DSS initiative also can be seen as a movement toward the partial deregulation of aided schools. While receiving government subsidies, ex-aided DSS schools, unlike government or aided schools, can make autonomous decisions regarding their curriculum, fee standards, admission requirements, medium of instruction, and salary and personnel matters. DSS schools are not totally free from the government's control, however. They must sign a service contract with the government, which later serves as the basis for an evaluation on school performance to determine whether the contract will be renewed with or without modifications to the agreement terms (Director of Education, 2001).

Despite its advantages, the DSS did not receive good responses from schools in the 1990s. It managed to attract mainly eligible private schools that faced increasing financing difficulties because of the phasing out of the bought-place scheme (through which the government bought secondary one to three private schools to provide free universal basic education) by the end of the 1990s. Aided schools did not support the scheme because of strong pressure and objections from teachers, principals, and even school-sponsoring bodies. They feared that the conversion might bring many problems, including the instability of school income, which mainly comes from student fees; lower quality of student intake, stronger competition among schools for students, teachers' unstable income and lower job security, complexity in the arrangement of the teachers' provident fund, and increasing demands on school management committees (whose members are volunteers) to manage and run the schools.

However, in the early 2000s, the DSS suddenly received a warm welcome, particularly from aided secondary schools. The number of DSS schools offering local curricula increased from 18 in 1999–2000 to 59 (including 45 secondary, 11 primary, and 3 secondary-cum-primary) in 2005–2006. There are three major reasons for the sudden rise. First, the government modified the DSS by giving new DSS schools government-built premises (rather than asking them to purchase or lease buildings) and granting them land at a nominal charge. Second, the government gave priority to brand-new DSS schools rather than existing aided schools in the allocation of new school sites. Third, the educational reform of the late 1990s and early 2000s was another driving force of the DSS because it enabled some famous aided secondary schools whose school places were highly competitive to escape the adverse impact of educational reform. In particular, some feared that the new allocation system would greatly reduce the schools' control over the admission of primary one students and therefore the quality of student intake of their affiliated primary schools. Conversion to the DSS, which allows schools to have their own entrance requirements and Hong Kong-wide student recruitment, was seen by these famous aided secondary schools as a preventative measure to guard against the potential lowering of the quality of their student intake. Some of their affiliated aided primary schools also made this conversion to DSS status.

The increase in the number of DSS schools has broadened the diversity of the school sector and given parents more choices. The scheme also allows schools to obtain additional financial resources (namely government subsidies for ex-private DSS schools and student fees for ex-aided DSS schools) to improve their facilities, students' learning environments, and teachers' working conditions, for example, by reducing class size.

However, it is too early to determine whether the DSS has improved the quality of education in Hong Kong because most DSS schools are still very new. Furthermore, the conversion of famous aided schools to DSS schools reveals a puzzle that deserves further reflection: whether they will make their students successful or their students will make them successful. Though it may be a "chicken-and-egg" problem, DSS schools undeniably need good students to maintain good reputations.

Moreover, the DSS has been severely criticized for challenging the principles of equal opportunity for educational access and the equalization of educational resources. Yuen (2004), who was a representative of a major school-sponsoring body, criticized the government's policy for allowing those who can afford DSS (and private education) to enjoy the diversity of education, but denying those who cannot afford it. This criticism seems to be valid when it is applied to the nine-year compulsory schooling, which is totally free. In 2005–2006, the annual school fee of DSS schools ranged from HK$8,000 to HK$48,000 in the primary school sector, from free to HK$48,000 in the junior secondary school sector, and from about HK$5,000 to HK$98,000 in the senior secondary sector (Education and Manpower Bureau, 2006b). Tuition fees can be a barrier for students from poor families. Five DSS schools do not charge junior secondary students a school fee, but whether parents and students are willing to choose these schools is another issue. Besides, the likelihood that students will gain access to their preferred schools outside of their geographic areas is increased because DSS schools can recruit students from across Hong Kong.

However, this criticism should not be overexaggerated. When it is applied to the senior, postcompulsory, secondary level, only a very small minority of DSS schools charges high tuition fees (e.g., over HK$20,000 a year) (see Table 5.2). They dare to do so because they are famous ex-aided schools and can still attract parents and students. There is no point for them to lower the entrance requirements in exchange for more income; otherwise, they would not have needed to be converted into DSS schools. Most DSS schools do not charge tuition fees that are much higher than aided schools whose fee standards were, for example, HK$5,320 and HK$9,100 for senior secondary four and five students and secondary six and seven students, respectively, in 2005–2006 (Education and

Table 5.2
Number of DSS Schools by Education Level and Range of Annual School Fee, 2005–2006

Annual School Fee (HK$)	Primary One to Six	Junior Secondary One to Three	Senior Secondary Four to Five	Senior Secondary Six to Seven
Below 10,000	2 (14.3%)	26 (59.1%)	26 (68.4%)	13 (39.4%)
10,000–19,999	6 (42.9%)	9 (20.5%)	8 (21.1%)	16 (48.5%)
20,000–29,999	2 (14.3%)	5 (11.4%)	1 (2.6%)	2 (6.1%)
30,000 or above	4 (28.6%)	4 (9.1%)	3 (7.9%)	2 (6.1%)
Number of DSS schools*	14 (100%)	44 (100%)	38 (100%)	33 (100%)

Note: * By 2005–2006, many DSS schools had not offered a full program yet because they were new or in the process of conversion.

Source: Calculated from Education and Manpower Bureau (2006b).

Manpower Bureau, 2006c). Unlike famous DSS schools, many "ordinary" DSS schools do not have strong selling points to attract students, and some even have difficulty competing with aided schools for students.

Public Schools' Struggle to Balance Quality, Accountability, and Autonomy

The concern about the quality of public schools became more acute when the government gradually institutionalized economic rationalism—market concepts, mechanisms, practices, and values—in public administration, including educational administration and the management of publicly funded schools. Since then, schools' internal management and the processes of ensuring the quality of teaching and learning have been under attack by the government and the public. To address this problem, the government has introduced a series of "managerialist strategies and quasi-market mechanisms" to reform public education (Tse, 2005). In particular, the education authority has attempted to change its role in educational administration from detailed control to supervision. It also has begun to devolve some powers to schools, empower parents and teachers in school governance, and use external school review to force schools to improve their quality of management, teaching, and learning. As a result, schools are caught in a tension among quality, accountability, and autonomy.

In the early 1990s, poor school management was regarded as a major reason for the poor quality of education in Hong Kong. In the School Management Initiative (SMI), the Hong Kong government admitted that the school system was not cost-effective and that there were ineffective and under-performing schools (Education and Manpower Branch and Education Department, 1991). Major causes included inadequate management structures and processes; poorly defined roles and responsibilities of the education authority, sponsoring bodies, supervisors, and principals; a lack of clear frameworks for responsibilities and accountability; and the inadequacy of schools' performance measures.

Since 1991, the government has gradually initiated a series of measures to reform school management in the public-school sector. First, the government imposed on public schools a broad framework for school development and accountability with a view to reengineer school management to improve teaching and learning outcomes (Quality Assurance Division, 2005). Second, the internal mechanisms of management and accountability in public schools were revamped or created so as to increase the transparency and accountability of schools to education stakeholders. Schools are required to have explicit statements of their visions and missions, establish mechanisms to report school development in annual school plans and achievements in annual school profiles and reports, and develop performance assessments and staff-appraisal systems. Third, the government attempts to enhance the participation and power of key stakeholders, such as parents and teachers, on school affairs in aided schools by incorporating them into school management committees. This proposal received cool responses and even resistance from schools in the 1990s (Wong, 1995). By 2003, only 16 percent of schools had both parent and teacher representatives on school management committees (Li, 2004). In 2004, the government managed to enact the Education (Amendment) Bill 2004, which came into effect on January 1, 2005 (Legislative Council, 2004). Existing aided schools are given a grace period of five years, and by July 2009 they must establish an incorporated management committee (IMC) that includes school-sponsoring body managers (up to 60 percent of membership), the principal as an *ex-officio* member, at least one teacher-manager, at least one parent-manager, at least one alumni-manager, and at least one independent manager. Teacher-managers and parent-managers must be elected through a fair and transparent election process. The amended ordinance gives the Permanent Secretary the power to nominate a public officer to attend and offer advice in the school's management meetings if this is conducive to the school's operation and performance.

There has been a spectrum of views on the mandatory establishment of IMCs. The government and its supporters (including many parents) see the amendment as a step toward democratizing school management. This new framework is expected to help schools increase their management's transparency and accountability and ensure that the public annual subsidies of HK$22 million to each primary school and HK$38 million to each secondary school are put to the best use (Education and Manpower Bureau, 2004). However, the enactment has encountered much public opposition from major sponsoring bodies, including the Catholic Church (which had over 320 schools in 2004), the Hong Kong Sheng Kung Hui (the Anglican Church) (about 90 schools), and the Methodist Church of Hong Kong (18 schools). These churches object to requiring all schools to have the same composition and management committee structure. They also object to the devolution of power from school-sponsoring bodies to the individual schools' IMCs, as well the centralization that could result from making the IMCs directly answerable to the government. These schools doubt whether their visions and missions (such as providing religious education) can be maintained and realized if each school's constitution must be approved by the government; and they worry about possible negative effects on school administrations by involving parents at the highest decision-making level, as well as the conflict of interests of teachers, who play a dual role as employees and members of the IMC, which has personnel power to determine the employment, promotion, and dismissal of staff.

Unlike their objections to the Education (Amendment) Ordinance, the oppositional, school-sponsoring bodies have not shown any strong resistance to the government's introduction of top-down, external, quality-monitoring mechanisms because the pressure is more on school principals and teachers than on school management committees. In 1997, the government began to conduct quality assurance inspections (QAI) in schools across the territory. The distribution of the assessment was: school's self-assessment (20 percent) and on-site full inspection (including all subjects) by an external team for about one week (80 percent). As a result of the labor-intensive nature of QAI, between 1997 and 2002, only 294 (about 25 percent) primary schools and secondary schools were assessed (calculated from Quality Assurance Division, 2004; Quality Assurance Inspection Section, 1998, 1999, 2000, 2002). To speed up the process, in 2003, the QAI was simplified into an external school review (ESR) by shortening the on-site activities to four days and reducing the number of reviewers from about 10 to 5, asking schools to contribute more in their self-assessment (80 percent), and redefining the nature of the external review from a full inspection to a validation of the school's self assessment (20 percent).

In both QAI and ESR, the basis for assessment is a prescriptive set of 29 performance indicators in four major domains (management and organization, learning and teaching, student support and school ethos, and student performance) (Quality Assurance Division, 2002). Each domain is subdivided into areas, and every performance indicator has one or more components; this adds up to 14 areas and 82 subperformance indicators (which are further subdivided). These indicators can be grouped into process indicators and outcome indicators; and the former are expected to reveal "the school's capacity in providing a desirable learning environment conductive to the development of quality education," whereas the latter is intended to reflect the effectiveness of education provided by the school. The scale of assessment includes four levels of performance: excellent, acceptable, unacceptable, and unsatisfactory. At the end of the review, a full, written report is given to the school, and the summary report is made available to the public on the government's website. The result of the assessment is expected to help the reviewed school reflect on its strengths and weaknesses, shape its development plan, and plan staff development to serve the school's needs (Education and Manpower Bureau, 2005b). This kind of review is seen to have positive impacts on schools, such as an increased sense of competition and motivation to improve (Clarke et al., 2005). However, QAI and ESR also have been criticized for being top-down and prescriptive, distracting teachers from teaching, and overloading schools with documentation and numerous internal meetings in preparation for the review exercise. Despite these criticisms, most schools take this external review seriously because their summary reports will be available online to the public and the full reports to parents and related education stakeholders on campus, and this in turn may affect their future student intake and school survival.

CONCLUSIONS

This chapter has presented developments in Hong Kong's education and identified some major changes and continuities since the 1840s. The educational developments, such as educational expansion by stages, were responses to changing economic and sociopolitical contexts and were achieved through various strategies. In particular, frameworks for education for all and postcompulsory education took sociopolitical considerations into account. The Hong Kong government has regarded education as helpful to promoting economic development and sociopolitical stability, which have been equally important to consolidating its rule.

In the Hong Kong case, access, efficiency, and equity have been interrelated, and the issue of quality arose mainly after basic concerns about quantitative provision had been addressed. The larger the government's financial commitment to subsidizing education, the higher is the children's equal opportunity to have access. However, the government alone might not be able to provide education for all levels and thus may require the concerted effort of local organizations and private entities, particularly at the initial stages of the provision. With the government's increasing financial commitment to education for all, laws in Hong Kong can play an important role in ensuring access and equal opportunity by legally binding all stakeholders to protect the rights and properly administer its duties, particularly for universal, compulsory education.

Hong Kong education also has been confronted by longstanding, deep-seated issues that are related to its historical and sociocultural contexts. Despite the emphasis on the fostering of China's national identity in education and society, the return of Hong Kong from the United Kingdom to China did not demote, but consolidated the status of English as an MoI. The MoI policy in Hong Kong reinforces the function of education as a vehicle of cultural reproduction. The choice of MoI, as argued by Tsui (2004), is central to language policy decisions because it determines who will participate in the competition for wealth and power. In addition to their communication function, languages can carry different social and cultural values and have different socioeconomic and cultural statuses in various societies. Proficiency in a preferred language is a cultural asset for accessing higher educational qualifications and attaining better employment opportunities in the labor market. In Hong Kong, the compulsory streaming of secondary schools by MoI and the measures of positive discrimination for CMI schools are *de facto* modes of institutionalizing educational stratification and consolidating the status of English as important socioeconomic and cultural capital. Moreover, the MoI policy is a *de facto* policy for streaming students by ability into both CMI and EMI schools. Most students who attend the latter are considered by the government to be not only EMI-capable, but also high achievers with the motivation to learn (Education and Manpower Bureau, 2005d). In contrast, most students in CMI schools are average or low achievers, and are put in a disadvantaged position for acquiring higher-value cultural capital and attaining upward social mobility (Cheng, 2005). These are more likely to reinforce, rather than minimize, the labeling effects on secondary schools and their students, as well as teachers, and make education an instrument to maintain inequalities in a capitalist economy.

Hong Kong consistently has upheld the policy of aided schools since the 1920s, and therefore it has developed a significant aided-school model to enhance cooperation between government and nongovernment actors in sponsoring and managing publicly funded schools. The school-sponsoring bodies of aided schools act as "brokers" of the government in the provision of public education. However, longstanding cooperation between the government and school-sponsoring bodies does not necessarily exclude their competition and conflict for control over school management and the quality of education. When the sponsoring cannot guarantee the effective use of public money, the government can make use of other means such as the DSS, the school management initiative, and high-stakes performance measures to monitor and ensure the quality of aided schools (as well as government schools). Moreover, the recent debate on the reform of school management committees in aided schools reveals that the government, school-sponsoring bodies, teachers, and parents lack mutual trust. Major school-sponsoring bodies fear parents (more than alumni and independent managers) becoming involved at the decision-making level. They do not trust the government despite its promises and fear that losing direct power over schools may prevent them from realizing their vision and mission. This leads to two important questions that deserve further exploration: Why is the mutual trust among education stakeholders so fragile? And can the new political ecology in educational administration and school management enhance the mutual trust among different education stakeholders? It is unfair to attribute the causes of these problems to any single party (such as the government, school-sponsoring bodies, school leadership, teachers, parents, or the community). To ease or solve these issues, each party must reflect on what needs to be done, and all must work together to enhance the quality of educational services for students.

Four aided schools and two DSS schools in a small community in Hong Kong. Courtesy of Wing-Wah Law.

REFERENCES

Ballantine, Jeanne, H. (2001). *The Sociology of Education: A Systematic Analysis*, 5th edn. Upper Saddle River, NJ: Prentice-Hall.

Board of Education (1997). *Report on Review of 9-year Compulsory Education*, revised version. Hong Kong: Government Printer.

Cao, Tai Sheng (1997). "Xianggang Jiaoyu Zhidushi Yanjiu, 1840–1997 (The history of Hong Kong education system, 1840–1997)," *Huadong Shifan Daxue Xuebao Jiaoyu Kexueban (East China Normal University Journal, Educational Sciences)*, 2: 1–15.

Census and Statistics Department (1962). *Hong Kong Population Census, 1961: Main Report*. Hong Kong: Government Printer.

———(1972). *Hong Kong Population Census, 1971: Main Report*. Hong Kong: Government Printer.

———(2001). *Briefing on the Summary Results of the 2001 Population Census Relating to Education Matters*. Hong Kong: Legislative Council.

Cheng, Kai Ming (1996). "Efficiency, equity and quality in higher education in a time of expansion," in M.K. Nyaw and S.M. Li (eds) *The Other Hong Kong Report 1996*, pp. 409–418. Hong Kong: Chinese University Press.

Cheng, Yin Cheong (2005). "Jiaoxue Yuyan De Wenhua Ziben Yu Jieji Liudong (Medium of instruction, cultural capital and social mobility)," *Ming Pao*, February 24, p. A19.

Chu, Sau Lin (2003). "Tiantai Xuexiao Yu Jiaohui (Rooftop schools and church)," *Xuan Xun (Christian and Missionary Alliance Church of Hong Kong Monthly Magazine)*, 42: 1.

Chung, Chak, and Ngan, Ming Yan (2002). "From 'Rooftop' to 'Millennium': The development of primary schools in Hong Kong since 1945," *New Horizons in Education*, 46: 24–32.

Clarke, Paul, West, Mel, and Ainscow, Mel (2005). *Using an Established School Improvement Programme to Build Capacity at School and System Level: The Hong Kong IQEA Programme*. Accessed on February 2, 2006 from http://www.aare.edu.au/05pap/cla05195.pdf.

Curriculum Development Council (1996). *Guidelines on Civic Education in Schools*. Hong Kong: Government Printer.

———(2001). *Learning to Learn: The Way Forward in Curriculum Development*. Hong Kong: Printing Department.

Director of Education (2001). *Direct Subsidy Scheme, A Circular to Supervisors / Heads of all Secondary Schools and Primary Schools (excluding ESF Schools and International Schools)*. Hong Kong: Education Department.

Education and Manpower Branch, and Education Department (1991). *The School Management Initiative: Setting the Framework for Quality in Hong Kong Schools*. Hong Kong: Government Printer.

Education and Manpower Bureau (2003). *Consolidation of High Cost and Under-utilized Primary Schools* (LC Paper No. CB(2)1826/02–03(01)). Hong Kong: Legislative Council.

——— (2004). *Leaflet on School-based Management: "Committed Parents, Quality School."* Hong Kong: Printing Department.

———(2005a). *Injection into the Language Fund*. Hong Kong: Legislative Council.

———(2005b). *Inspection Handbook for Schools*. Hong Kong: Government Logistics Department.

Education and Manpower Bureau (2005c). *The New Academic Structure for Senior Secondary Education and Higher Education: Action Plan for Investing in the Future of Hong Kong.* Hong Kong: Printing Department.

———(2005d). *Review of Medium of Instruction for Secondary Schools and Secondary School Places Allocation.* Hong Kong: Legislative Council.

———(2006a). *Action for the Future: Further Consultation on Career-Oriented Studies and the New Senior Secondary Academic Structure for Special Schools.* Hong Kong: Government Logistics Department.

———(2006b). *List of Direct Subsidy Scheme Schools 2005/06.* Hong Kong: Education and Manpower Bureau.

———(2006c). *Revision of Senior Secondary School Fees.* Hong Kong: Education and Manpower Bureau.

Education Commission (1984). *Education Commission Report No. 1.* Hong Kong: Government Printer.

———(1986). *Education Commission Report No. 2.* Hong Kong: Government Printer.

———(1990). *Education Commission Report No. 4: The Curriculum and Behavioural Problems in Schools.* Hong Kong: Government Printer.

———(2004). *Education Statistics 2004.* Hong Kong: Printing Department.

———(2005). *Review of Medium of Instruction for Secondary Schools and Secondary School Places Allocation.* Hong Kong: Government Logistics Department.

Education Department (1981). *General Guidelines on Moral Education in Schools.* Hong Kong: Government Printer.

———(1997a). *Medium of Instruction: Guidance for Secondary Schools.* Hong Kong: Education Department.

———(1997b). *Review of Prevocational and Secondary Technical Education.* Hong Kong: Education Department.

Education Department Curriculum Development Committee (1985). *Guidelines on Civic Education in Schools.* Hong Kong: Government Printer.

Evans, Stephen (2000). "Hong Kong's new English language policy in education." *World Englishes* 19(2): 185–204.

Fung, Wai Wah (2005). "Fuxueshi Paomo Baopo (The bursting of the bubble of associate degrees programs?)," *Ming Pao*, September 14, p. A21.

Grover, Sonja (2004). "Secondary education as a universal human right," *Education and the Law,* 16(1): 21–31.

Hong Kong Government (1964). *Education Policy.* Hong Kong: Government Printer.

———(1965). *Education Policy.* Hong Kong: Government Printer.

———(1967). *Yijiu Liuliu Nian Jiulong Saodong Baogaoshu* (Report on the Riots in Kowloon in 1966). Hong Kong: Government Printer.

———(1971). *Education Regulations: Subsidiary Legislation, Chapter 279.* Hong Kong: Government Printer.

———(1974). *Secondary Education in Hong Kong over the Next Decade.* Hong Kong: Government Printer.

———(1977). *Integrating the Disabled into the Community.* Hong Kong: Government Printer.

———(1978). *The Development of Senior Secondary and Tertiary Education.* Hong Kong: Government Printer.

———(1980). *Hong Kong 1980.* Hong Kong: Government Printer.

———(1991). *Education Regulations: Subsidiary Legislation, Chapter 279.* Hong Kong: Government Printer.

———(1997). *Hong Kong 1997*. Hong Kong: Printing Department.

———(1998). *Hong Kong—A New Era: A Review of 1997*. Hong Kong: Printing Department.

———(2000). *The 2000 Policy Address: Serving the Community Sharing Common Goals*. Hong Kong: Printing Department.

———(2001). *Hong Kong 2000*. Hong Kong: Printing Department.

———(2002). *Hong Kong 2001*. Hong Kong: Printing Department.

———(2003). *Manpower Projection to 2007*. Hong Kong: Printing Department.

———(2005a). *Hong Kong 2004*. Hong Kong: Printing Department.

———(2005b). *The 2005 Policy Address: Working Together for Economic Development and Social Harmony*. Hong Kong: Printing Department.

———(2006). *Education Ordinance: Chapter 279*. Accessed on March 1, 2006 from http://www.justice.gov.hk/blis_ind.nsf/CurAllEngDoc?OpenView&Start= 27&Count=30&Collapse=279.1#279.1.

Hong Kong Government Secretariat (1981). *The Hong Kong Education System*. Hong Kong: Government Printer.

Johnson, Robert Keith (1998). "Language and education in Hong Kong," in M.C. Pennington (ed.), *Language in Hong Kong at Century's End*, pp. 265–281. Hong Kong: Hong Kong University Press.

Lam, Pun Lee (2005). "Fuxueshi Dayuejin Zhizao Duanzhuang Xuesheng (The crisis of the Great Leap Forward movement of associate degrees education)," *Ming Pao*, September 28, p. A20.

Law, Wing Wah (2004). "Globalization and citizenship education in Hong Kong and Taiwan," *Comparative Education Review*, 48(3): 253–273.

Lee, Siu Fu (2005). "Suan Yi Suan Fuxueshi De Hutu Zhang (Editorial: Reviewing the messy associate degrees education)," *Pinggu Ribao (Apple Daily)*, December 28.

Lee, Wing On (2004). "Citizenship education in Hong Kong: Development and challenges," in W.O. Lee, D.L. Grossman, K.J. Kennedy, and G.P. Fairbrother (eds), *Citizenship Education in Asia and the Pacific: Concepts and Issues*, pp. 59–80. Hong Kong: Comparative Education Research Centre, University of Hong Kong.

Legislative Council (2000). *Official Record of Proceedings of Council Meeting on 21 December 21*. Hong Kong: Legislative Council.

———(2004). *Education (Amendment) Ordinance 2004*. Hong Kong: Legislative Council.

Leung, Sai Wing (1995). "Depoliticization and trivialization of civic education in secondary schools: Institutional constraints on promoting civic education in transitional Hong Kong," in P.K. Siu and T.K. Tam (eds), *Quality in Education: Insights from Different Perspectives*, pp. 283–312. Hong Kong: Educational Research Association.

Li, Arthur, K.C. (2005). *Jiaoyu Tongchouju Juzhang Yu Lifahui HuiyiShang Jiu 2002 Nian Jiaoyu Xiuding Tiaoli Caoan Huifu Erdu De Zhici Quanwen (Speech by Secretary for Education and Manpower in LegCo on Education (Amendment) Bill 2002*, July 8, 2004. Accessed on January 11, 2005 from http://www.info.gov.hk/gia/ general/200407/08/0708258.htm.

Llewellyn, John (1982). *A Perspective on Education in Hong Kong*. Hong Kong: Government Printer.

Lour, Tsang Tsay Lawrence (2006). "On question of language the real message is in the medium," *South China Morning Post*, February 11, p. 13.

Luk, Bernard, H.K. (2004). "Xianggang Banxue Zhidu Huigu (Review on the school sponsorship system in Hong Kong)," *Si (Reflection)* No. 92, pp. 5–10.

Peden, Joseph, R. (1977). *Education and the Political Community*. Menlo Park, CA: Institute for Humane Studies, Center for Independent Education.

Quality Assurance Division (2002). *Performance Indicators for Hong Kong Schools*. Hong Kong: Government Logistics Department.

———(2004). *Inspection Annual Reports, 2002–03*. Hong Kong: Government Logistics Department.

———(2005). *School Development and Accountability*, December 13, 2005. Accessed on December 18, 2005 from http://www.emb.gov.hk/index.aspx?langno=1&nodeID=174.

Quality Assurance Inspection Section (1998). *Quality Assurance Inspection Annual Report 1997–98*. Accessed on October 5, 2001 from http://www.ed.gov.hk/qai/eqai_sum9798/qai_rpt.htm.

———(1999). *Quality Assurance Inspection Annual Report 1998–99*. Accessed on October 5, 2001 from http://www.ed.gov.hk/qai/eqai_sum98–99/qai_sum.htm.

———(2000). *Quality Assurance Inspection Annual Report 1999–2000*. Accessed on October 5, 2001 from http://www.ed.gov.hk/qai/eqai_sum9900/qai_sum.htm.

———(2002). *Quality Assurance Inspection Annual Report 2001–02*. Hong Kong: Printing Department.

Rickenbacker, William, F. (ed.) 1999. *The Twelve-Year Sentence: Radical Views on Compulsory Education*. San Francisco, CA: Fox & Wilkes.

Ross, E.A. (1900). "Social control. XIV. Education," *American Journal of Sociology*, 5(4): 475–487.

Sen, Amartya (1999). *Development as Freedom*. New York: Knopf.

Ting, Joseph, S.P. (1993). "Preface," in S.K. Yau, K.L. Leung and S.L. Chow (eds), *Xianggan Jiaoyu Fazhan: Bainian Shuren (Education in Hong Kong: Past and Present)*, pp. 8–11. Hong Kong: Urban Council.

Tse, Kwan Choi (2005). "Quality education in Hong Kong: The anomalies of managerialism and marketization," in L.S. Ho, P. Morris and Y.P. Chung (eds), *Education Reform and the Quest for Excellence: The Hong Kong Story*, pp. 99–123. Hong Kong: Hong Kong University Press.

Tsui, Amy, B.M. (2004). "Medium of instruction in Hong Kong: One country, two systems, whose language?" in J.W. Tollefson and A.B.M. Tsui (eds), *Medium of Instruction Policies: Which Agenda? Whose Agenda*, pp. 97–116. Mahwah, N.J.: L. Erlbaum Publishers.

UNESCO (1990). *World Declaration on Education for All: Meeting Basic Learning Needs*. Paris: UNESCO.

———(1996). *Learning: The Treasure Within*. Paris: UNESCO.

———(2000a). "The Dakar framework for action, education for all: Meeting our collective commitments," paper read at World Education Forum, April 26–28, at Dakar, Senegal.

———(2000b). *Globalization and Living Together: The Challenges for Educational Content in Asia*. Paris: UNESCO.

———(2002). *Education for All: Is the World on Track?* Paris: UNESCO.

———(2003). *Education for All Global Monitoring Report 2003/4: Gender and Education for All—The Leap to Equality*. Paris: UNESCO.

——(2005). *Education for All Global Monitoring Report 2005: The Quality Imperative.* Paris: UNESCO.

University Grants Committee (1996a). *Facts and Figures 1995.* Hong Kong: University Grants Committee.

——(1996b). *UGC Quadrennial Report 1991–95.* Hong Kong: Government Printer.

——(2005). *Facts and Figures 2004.* Hong Kong: University Grants Committee.

UN Millennium Project (2005). *Toward Universal Primary Education: Investments, Incentives, and Institutions.* London: Earthscan.

Wong, Ho Wing (ed.) (1993). *Xianggang Jiaoyu Shouce (Hong Kong Education Handbook)*, revised edn. Hong Kong: Commercial Press.

Wong, Ho Wing and King On Ho (1996). *Jinri Xianggang Jiaoyu (Education Hong Kong Today).* Guangzhou: Guangdong Education Press.

Wong, Kam Cheung (1995). "School management initiative in Hong Kong— The Devolution of Power to Schools, Real or Rhetoric?" in K.C. Wong and K.M. Cheng (eds), *Educational Leadership and Change: An International Perspective*, pp. 141–154. Hong Kong: Hong Kong University Press.

Yau, Siu Kam, Leung, Kit Ling, and Chow, Siu Lun (1993). *Xianggan Jiaoyu Fazhan: Bainian Shuren (Education in Hong Kong: Past and Present).* Hong Kong: Urban Council.

Yuen, Tin Yau (2004). "Xiaoben Guanli Tiaoli Zhihou: Jiaohui Banxue De Fansi (Reflection on the church's policy of school sponsorship after the introduction of school-based management bill)," *Si (Reflection)*, No. 92, pp. 23–27.

Zhang, Hui Zhen, and Qiang, Sheng Kong (2005). *Cong Shiyiwan Dao Sanqian: Lunxian Shiqi Xianggang Jiaoyu Koushu Lishi (From 110000 to 3000: Oral History on Hong Kong's Education under the Japanese Occupation).* Hong Kong: Oxford University Press.

Chapter 6

SCHOOLING IN INDONESIA

Rita Oswald Christano and William K. Cummings

INTRODUCTION

Indonesia is a country of great diversity. Located along the equator, it is the world's largest archipelago spanning 5,000 kilometers and comprising more than 17,000 islands, 6,000 of which are inhabited. The population of Indonesia ranks fourth in the world, 60 percent of whom live on the island of Java. While the country boasts the world's largest Muslim population, it remains a secular state. More than 250 languages are spoken by more than 300 different ethnic groups, the largest of which is the Javanese. The variety of human experiences within the country is also quite extensive, ranging from youth in big cities using cell phones, sending emails, and playing computer games at internet cafes to families in more remote areas living traditional lifestyles. Indonesia's diversity poses considerable challenges for educational policy and implementation. Since independence, the initial planning relied on a centralized approach, while in recent years there has been a greater reliance on regional leadership and local participation.

HISTORICAL CONTEXT

In order to understand the contemporary schooling structure better, it is helpful to examine how the educational system has been transformed over time. Each of the six periods noted in the following sections was instrumental in the development of Indonesia's national education system.

Precolonial Era

Commerce with traders from India and China brought new cultural and religious traditions to the archipelago. In fact, as early as the first few centuries A.D.,

Buddhist and Hindu influences were present throughout the region. The area was dominated by a number of Hindu-Javanese kingdoms, the last and most powerful of which was Majapahit, until around 1300 when trade between the Islamic world and the Majapahit Hindus of Java began increasing. As the Majapahit kingdom eventually weakened and collapsed due to internal conflicts, various kingdoms, many of them Muslim (i.e., the Islamic Kingdom of Demak), were established in its place. Nine key Islamic saints, the *Wali Sanga*, are credited with the spread of Islam to various parts of the region.

Because of the importance placed on education in the Islamic tradition, this period of Islamic expansion saw a proliferation of religious education centers, with the establishment of the first known *pesantren* or Islamic boarding schools (Lukens-Bull, 1997; Buresh, 2002). These *pesantren* provided a nonformal, religious education for the indigenous population, particularly in rural Java (the location of most *pesantren*), at a time when virtually no other educational opportunities were available. The purpose of these original *pesantren* was to train scholars in Islamic religious teachings so that they could then spread Islam to other kingdoms. These institutions taught mainly Islamic religious teachings and the Arabic language in order to read holy texts like the Qur'an.

The campus of the *pesantren* centered around the mosque, which at times served as the classroom, sleeping quarters, or as a place of study (Dhofier, 1999). *Santri* (students of *pesantren*) were taught by a *kyai*, the leader and founder of their *pesantren*, who maintained close contact with his *santri* in order to monitor and better guide their religious and social development. Because most *kyai* specialized in a particular branch of Islamic study, *santri* would travel from one *pesantren* to another in order to gain a broader knowledge base, resulting in a rather extensive and tightly knit religious community (Rachman, 1997; Dhofier, 1999). For this reason, most *santri* came from wealthier families in rural areas because of the heavy costs associated with supporting a traveling student. In addition, a wandering scholar was unable to provide additional income for his family, so few families could afford to spare a child for educational or religious objectives.

Dutch Colonial Era (Early 1600s–1942)

The next major period in Indonesian educational history occurred from the early 1600s to 1942 with the arrival of and colonization by the Dutch. During this period, the Dutch gradually increased their presence and control in the region, despite their very small numbers of about 70,000 compared with an indigenous population in Java of about 20 million (Cote, 2001). The creation of a restrictive social hierarchy segregated individuals based on ethnicity, starting at the top with Europeans, followed by the native aristocracy and Eurasians, individuals of Chinese descent, and finally the indigenous population. Thus, class divisions typically corresponded with ethnic differences. Disparities developed not only between the Dutch and other groups, but also across the indigenous peoples (Sirozi, 2004). Schooling throughout the region also reflected this system of social stratification instigated by the Dutch colonial power.

These divisions affected education under Dutch control in many significant ways. The Dutch provided schooling predominantly for children of Dutch families in addition to a limited number of Javanese aristocrats whom they trained for positions within the colonial administration. A quality education was generally only available to Europeans, while schooling for the native population was generally either separate and unequal, or entirely nonexistent.

Throughout the era, the Dutch maintained a centralized educational system. As a result, the development of the educational process was not collaborative; Indonesians had little or no voice in how to participate in the system. Instead, educational opportunities were designed by and for Dutch interests. For example, most schools in the region were virtually carbon copies of those belonging to the educational system in the Netherlands, providing instruction through Dutch language and employing pedagogical methods typical in European counterparts.

The educational structure supported and promoted a number of Dutch colonial interests. First, it provided opportunities for the Dutch population to receive a quality education and severely limited the options of the native population. This ensured Dutch status, power, and security in Indonesia (Cote, 2001). The educational system was exclusive and elitist, allowing only a select few from the native population to participate. In this way, the Dutch could easily maintain social order, since it was felt that education would only inspire independence movements among indigenous groups and instigate tension. This could lead further to the native population eventually competing for jobs in fields not previously accessible to them (Sirozi, 2004). It was important for the Dutch to preserve their domination over the Javanese elites who served them, and one way to accomplish this objective was by severely limiting education.

In addition, schools were a mechanism for the Dutch to spread their Christian faith. For example, the Dutch, intending to convert the local population to Protestantism, opened a school located in the Moluccas Islands in 1607 (Purwadi and Muljoatmodjo, 2000). Replacing the predominant religions of the region (Hinduism, Buddhism, and Islam) with Christianity was another important function of the Dutch colonial education system (Rahman, 1997).

Those who were poor, lived in rural areas, or were non-European had few educational opportunities. In fact, during the colonial era, a *pesantren* education provided one of the few educational options for indigenous males. Even then, though, the Dutch interfered. As the colonial rulers increased their control and governance over the kingdoms of Java, they gradually removed the *kyai* and other indigenous authorities from participation in local government affairs and instead forced the *pesantren* to relocate to the rural areas of Java (Buresh, 2002). Despite these barriers, the *pesantren* maintained a strong presence and continued as one of the few educational options for the native population.

Japanese Occupation (1942–1945)

In 1942, the Netherlands, occupied by Nazi Germany and greatly weakened militarily, surrendered power of the archipelago to the Japanese without a physical struggle. As the region's new ruling power, Japan defended its military occupation by self-designating its role in the world as "the leader of Asia, the protector of Asia, the light of Asia," a popular slogan of the Japanese government at the time. Japanese propaganda frequently espoused working together with the native population of the archipelago to create a better, stronger Asia, when actually the regime's motives were much more economic in nature. Like the Dutch before them, they too wanted access to oil and other natural resources in order to support their war effort.

In their short three-year reign, the Japanese commenced the transformation of the Dutch colonial education system toward a national system of education. First, the Japanese endeavored to refashion the educational system into a less socially stratified and more equal system. In addition, they began the transition from instruction that was typically provided in Dutch toward a classroom that used Indonesian or Malay. In fact, the Japanese even prohibited the use of Dutch books (Buchori and Malik, 2004). Finally, they introduced a new component to the traditional curriculum: military training. While their presence on the islands was brief, their policy of permitting Indonesians to arm themselves facilitated the indigenous population's preparation for an independence movement. The purposes of education under the Japanese were mainly to promote nationalistic interests (Rahman, 1997) and "to facilitate the formation of an economic region led by Japan" (Purwadi and Muljoatmodjo, 2000: 81).

Independence and Reconstruction (1945–1966)

Indonesian nationalists declared their independence on August 17, 1945 following the Japanese surrender. Sukarno became the first president of the newly autonomous country and Mohammad Hatta his vice-president. The Dutch, however, vigorously fought to regain possession of their former colony. Following four years of fighting, the Dutch finally acknowledged Indonesia's sovereignty in 1949. The period was marked by a continued spirit of nationalism; the prospects of independence were exhilarating, and there existed a strong sense of enthusiasm to make Indonesia great. The principal challenge at independence was national unity, specifically how to develop a sense of nationhood amongst such diversity. Sukarno favored a national structure in which the central administration governed the various provinces. The country's motto "unity in diversity," has represented the dual goals of the government to recognize the country's varied citizenry while maintaining a unified national perspective (Turner and Podger, 2003). The country's new leaders recognized the prominent role that education would need to play in the development of Indonesia.

The tasks facing the new government were overwhelming. An unfortunate legacy of the Dutch colonial era was the enormous illiteracy problem, as the

Dutch administration had invested almost none of its prosperity on educating the indigenous population. The implications of this colonial policy were far reaching; how does a country begin to govern itself when virtually no one has an education? With a soaring illiteracy rate at independence and only a handful of individuals trained for leadership positions within a government setting, the circumstances were daunting (Eels, 1952). In observing the desperate circumstances besieging the country Van Der Kroef noted, "Indonesia has a desperate need of high-school and college graduates, and the job of creating them in sufficient numbers goes far beyond the government's resources" (1955: 372). Indonesia had to assume the task of educating an entire population, both children *and* adults, who were scattered over a large, diverse land. Most of its citizens at the time spoke only their regional language; the idea of a single language of instruction was still new, and there were few, if any, books written in Indonesian. It should also be noted that at the time, this fledgling country lacked financial resources, sufficient physical facilities for schooling, and trained teachers, further adding to the difficult nature of the task.

Education at this time mainly served nationalistic purposes; it was a mechanism for nation-building and functioned to unify and integrate societal differences of race, ethnicity, and class (Sirozi, 2004). Its major role was to fashion a uniquely Indonesian identity from the range of diversity spanning the archipelago. In addition, the founders also constructed the system in such a way as to develop moral, responsible citizens that supported and observed the country's founding principles of the *Pancasila* (Buchori and Malik, 2004). Defined as Indonesia's national ideology, the *Pancasila* consists of the following values: (1) monotheism; (2) humanism; (3) nationalism represented by the unity of Indonesia; (4) representative government; and (5) social justice. Teaching *Pancasila* moral values to all Indonesian children was a way to conduct nation-building activities via the education system, socializing its citizens to subscribe to the same set of beliefs. The development of a national education system facilitated the transition from loyalty toward one's ethnic group, religious affiliation, or class toward the nation state.

Yet another delicate educational issue at the time was mediating the secular–religious conflicts that were brewing, and that were jeopardizing the formation of a unified national system of education (Sirozi, 2004). Secular nationalist groups and Islamic religious leaders each advocated for what they believed should be the core features of the system. In response, the government developed an educational system which addressed the concerns of individuals from both persuasions.

New Order Era (1966–1998)

The New Order era represented the period from 1966–1998 during the dictatorship of Suharto. Under his regime, Suharto extended Sukarno's vision of nation-building, and the interventionist strong central state gave him complete authority over all levels of government, as well as increased power and proximity to resources. Suharto's heavy hand was matched by an equally powerful military as well as an almost nonexistent civil society, such that the development of individual capacity to take part in democratic practices eluded most (Emmerson, 1999). Corruption pervaded the administration, and practices of nepotism meant that the best deals and business transactions went to a favored few, further filling the pockets of the Suharto family (Frost, 2002).

In spite of Suharto's repressive reign, improvements in the country's development did occur. In fact, as a result of the revenues received from the oil boom of the 1970s, the central government allocated a portion of its profits toward education, namely SD-INPRES (Presidential Instruction for Primary Schools). It designed one of the largest and most rapid primary school construction programs, building more than 61,000 new schools within a six-year period and increasing educational accessibility and attainment as a result (Duflo, 2001). In the 1980s and much of the 1990s, Indonesia benefited from high rates of economic growth, a reduction in poverty, and improvements in the health and education of the population (World Bank, 1998).

The purpose of education throughout the New Order era continued to be one of nation-building, and preserving the unity, cohesion, and social stability of the country (Nielson, 2003). Bjork describes Indonesian educational institutions as the "socialisers of patriotic citizens" (2004: 256). Such a highly centralized system often tended to produce educational approaches of the "one size fits all" type (Nielson, 2003). Very little variation could be found amongst schools throughout the country.

Present Day (1998–Present)

Many anticipated Indonesia's relative economic prosperity of the 1990s to continue. Then, in late 1997, the country was unexpectedly hit with a falling *rupiah*, an incredibly elevated inflation rate, and a drastically weakened economy. In addition, Suharto's corrupt practices and his use of unsecured loans from State banks to finance his various enterprises caught up with him, bringing serious repercussions upon the country's economic sector. Together, these circumstances came to be known throughout Indonesia as *Krismon* (*krisis moneter*, or monetary crisis). While much of Asia felt the effects of the financial crisis, Indonesia was one of the hardest hit countries, with a drastically depreciated *rupiah* in just a matter of months (Pritchett et al., 2002). The social effects of *Krismon* were immediate.

In early 1998, as food and oil prices continued to rise, inflation soared and civil unrest began increasing. In an effort to mitigate these disastrous circumstances, the International Monetary Fund (IMF) presented the government of Indonesia with a loan package, intended to aid the country in resuscitating its economy. Indonesia accepted the offer. However, attached to this loan scheme were stipulations, including a rapid reform of Indonesia's financial sector, which ultimately triggered the closing of numerous failing banks. This action actually turned out to have disastrous effects on the Indonesian economy, creating massive debt, and increasing the political chaos (Emmerson, 1999).

Suharto managed to remain in power; however, an especially intense month of student demonstrations and mass riots finally brought about his resignation. On May 21, Suharto transferred authority to his vice-president, B.J. Habibie, a fellow New Order crony. Since then the country has experienced various political transitions and short-lived presidencies. It comes as no surprise, then, that the present day educational system could be characterized as one in transition. It underwent a far-reaching decentralization reform that on paper appeared to generate significant changes (see section entitled *Major Education Reforms*). However, much is unknown at this point regarding the degree to which the system will make tangible, substantial changes rather than remaining a highly centralized, bureaucratic system.

In spite of the country's recent political and economic turmoil, a major focus of the national education system continues to be the development of human resources as well as the transmission of cultural and national values expressed in the *Pancasila*. The government maintains its emphasis on the importance of producing Indonesian-speaking citizens who are devoted to the policies and goals of the state (Nilan, 2003).

SECTORS AND LEVELS OF EDUCATION

Two Parallel "Public" Systems

The colonial period fostered two distinctive educational traditions: the colonial institutions focusing on European-oriented content and located primarily in Java on the one hand and on the other hand the Islamic institutions focusing on Islamic content and located throughout Indonesia with perhaps the most prominent schools in Sumatra. Following independence, one possibility was to merge these two traditions, but the differences seemed too great. So a compromise evolved of allowing two separate systems to operate in parallel.

Both essentially employed a 6–3–3–4 structure consisting of primary, junior secondary, senior secondary, and postsecondary. The Islamic schools were made responsible to the central Ministry of Religious Affairs whereas the European-oriented schools became the responsibility of the Ministry of Education; additionally, most private schools are regulated by the Ministry of Education. This distinction has essentially continued down to the present. The central government has tended to provide much more generous support to the Ministry of Education, and hence the schools under its sponsorship have expanded more rapidly and enjoyed greater resources. However, over time there has been increasing collaboration between the two systems in terms of curricular expectations (religion is taught in the MOE schools and an increasing proportion of the Islamic curriculum is devoted to secular subjects such as science and mathematics) and the sharing of scarce resources, most notably teaching personnel.

Public/Private Education

Within each of the four levels of schooling (primary, junior secondary, senior secondary, and postsecondary levels) in Indonesia, both private and public options are available. Particularly, at the primary and junior secondary level, the great majority of places are provided by public schools; however, at the upper secondary level, about half the places are provided by private schools and at the tertiary level at least two of every three places are in the private sector. However, the distinctions between private and public institutions are quite blurry (Duncan, 2000). In fact, both sectors share many similarities, largely due to centralized requirements, such as the national curriculum, the national examinations, and some overlap of public and private funding; most public schools charge fees (including contributions to parent teacher associations) and many private schools accept public subsidies.

There exist two types of private education: private secular and private religious institutions, such as the *Muhammadiyah, pesantren,* or Christian schools, among others. Private schools in Indonesia have provided educational alternatives for the poor and those living in more remote areas, and are sometimes the only options for these students. Of course, the stereotypical exclusive private school does exist in Indonesia, but the overwhelming majority of private institutions provide educational services for those who would otherwise be denied access (Jones and Hagul, 2001). However, Duncan acknowledges that the quality of private schools has been an issue, and laments that "while the private sector in one sense has performed a most valued service to the rural and urban poor over the years by providing educational services to which they might otherwise have had no access, in another sense it perpetuates a type of system level discrimination that is quite inequitable" (2000: 155). In other words, because the poor have very few educational options at the secondary level and those that are available are of very poor quality, a rather segregated system has resulted.

Nonformal Education

In addition to the choices of private and public education, formal and nonformal programs are available for students at each level as well. In the context of Indonesia, nonformal education refers to out-of-school programs designed to eradicate illiteracy, to provide equivalency certificates, or to provide continuing education beyond basic education. Some of the goals of nonformal education include providing students with basic literacy skills to advance their income or employment level, supporting the community in ways which are not currently being addressed by the local school system, and preparing learners to be able to continue their education at the next level. Participants in nonformal education programs are often located in rural areas where access to a nearby school is lacking or financial constraints exist and the family cannot afford a formal education. Indonesia's parallel nonformal system provides equivalency while allowing students to transfer back into the formal system if they choose to do so.

Programs for adult illiteracy eradication enroll over one million people per year in Indonesia, 60 percent of whom are women (World Bank, 1998). Women are particularly attracted to these programs due to their flexible schedules, incorporation of income-generating activities, and their consideration of local community issues. Nonformal education in Indonesia usually takes the forms of either distance education using radios or television, or a direct method using learning groups or small classes. Indonesia has a variety of distance education programs available including *SLTP Terbuka* (junior secondary level) and *Universitas Terbuka* (postsecondary level).

Programs with more direct methods include the literacy curriculum of *Kejar Paket A* (and now *Pakets B*, and *C* as well), originally designed as a literacy program for those who have never completed primary school. Using learning groups as its primary method of instruction, it also integrates an income generation component into the program. Indonesia's Ministry of Education and Culture first implemented the program in 1977 whose goals included the acquisition of literacy skills, continued learning, and the application of newly learned skills to the workplace. Completion of *Kejar Paket A* is the equivalent to a primary school (6th grade) education. A variety of next steps are available for the learner, including advancement to *Kejar Paket B* (the lower secondary equivalency) or enrolling in a junior secondary school. A third equivalency package, *Kejar Paket C*, is also now available for students.

Teacher Education and Pedagogy

For most of Indonesian educational history, teachers have been employees of the state. As civil service employees, a central aspect of their position as teachers has been to promote and display loyalty to the state ideology. Their classrooms have typically reflected New Order principles of respect and reverence for those in authority, such as teachers. Classroom instruction has traditionally concentrated on the development of students' cognitive skills, and employed pedagogical methods of rote learning that stressed memorization and repetition.

Requirements for teacher certification have gradually been upgraded. In the 1950s teacher certificates were conferred to individuals who participated in a teacher training program at the junior secondary school level. A number of Institutes of Teacher Training and Education (*Institut Kegurauan dan Ilmu Pendidikan*/IKIP) now provide preparation and in-service training for teachers, with programs ranging from two to four years depending on the level of certification awarded. While teacher qualifications have risen, educators continue to be inadequately trained both in the subject matter they teach and in recent pedagogical methods.

Curriculum and National Examinations

A nationally mandated curriculum at all levels has been employed in order to promote consistency and stability. In addition to typical subjects of mathematics, physical and social sciences, and Indonesian, both secular and religious schools include a religious component in the curriculum at all levels. During their religious education class, students are typically separated according to religious affiliation and provided separate instruction related to their respective religions.

The educational system is highly regulated and includes a national school leaving exam, *Evaluasi Belajar Tingkat Akhir Nasional* or EBTANAS, which is a standardized test given to all students in both public and private schools at the end of a school cycle (i.e., the sixth year of primary school, the third year of junior secondary, and the third year of senior secondary school). The exam assesses students' competencies relative to the nationally mandated curriculum. EBTANAS scores are then used to determine students' continuation to the next educational level, entrance to another school, and graduation and the receipt of a diploma from one's current educational level. EBTANAS scores are also used to categorize and rank schools (both public and private) as well as individual students according to their grade level, school, and geographical region. The exams have been advocated by the government as legitimate measures of educational quality as well as a tool to ensure that students are ready and able for the next instructional level; however, the integrity and validity of these exams is questionable (Oey-Gardiner, 2000).

Preschool

While preschool education is not included in the national commitment to universal education, most young people in urban areas attend some form of preschool education, especially those living in urban areas. Preschools vary widely in their curriculum with some being academically intensive while most place more stress on social and psychomotor skills. Many of the preschools are organized by religious groups, and provide an introductory exposure to the religious principles of their founders.

Primary

Educational access has rapidly and significantly expanded at the primary level, partly due to the school construction programs implemented by former President Suharto. As a result, universal primary education (grades 1–6) was achieved in the mid-1980s. Impressive progress was made in providing access, enrolling students, and narrowing educational attainment gaps between girls and boys. The rural/urban and rich/poor disparities that currently exist are relatively minimal at the primary level but are greatly amplified as students progress through the system to secondary levels (Oey-Gardiner, 2000).

While primary level educational access has drastically improved, persistence in the system has not. According to Jones and Hagul, "even now only about 70 percent of pupils entering primary school actually graduate from grade 6. Primary education is universal only in the sense that almost all children spend some time in primary school" (2001: 207). Additionally, enormous disparities exist between provinces in completion rates for primary school.

Junior and Senior Secondary

In recent years, more children have participated in educational programs at the junior secondary, and to some extent senior secondary level. Unfortunately the numbers are still low. In addition, the relationship that exists between students' socioeconomic background and their likelihood to enroll in school intensifies as students progress to the secondary level (Jones and Hagul, 2001). Private schools, such as the *madrasah* and *pesantren*, play an especially important role at the secondary level by providing additional slots not available through the public system. Additionally, many parents feel more comfortable allowing their daughters to attend these types of religious schools possibly "because more conservative Muslim families consider the religious orientation of the curriculum, as well as the school's social environment, to be more appropriate for girls" (Duncan, 2000: 146).

As previously noted, the curriculum is quite centralized; moral and civics education is taught at the secondary levels as well, in addition to the ideals of the *Pancasila*. However, this nationalistic orientation and emphasis on producing respectable citizens does not sufficiently respond to the needs of the country. Nilan asserts that the existing curriculum is "oriented toward producing clerks and civil servants" and feels that enormous disparities exist between the type of education students receive and the necessary skills students must possess for the workforce (2003: 566).

At the senior secondary level two tracks or streams of education are made available: general and technical/vocational. The general stream prepares students for more academically oriented programs at subsequent levels. Also a three-year program, the technical track enrolls more than 39 percent of all senior secondary students, some examples of which include cooking, agriculture, graphics, business, music, and so on (Purwadi and Muljoatmodjo, 2000).

Postsecondary

When Indonesia realized its independence, higher education was almost exclusively for Dutch nationals and classes were conducted in Dutch. Perhaps less than 1,000 Indonesians had completed a first degree. But those privileged to receive higher education and gain a university teaching post were committed to building a meaningful higher educational tradition. In the years following independence, many university professors and their students played a prominent role in the revolutionary struggle to send the Dutch occupiers home. At the same time, they laid plans for a new university system that would foster Indonesian national development.

The new system that evolved came to have two strands, a main strand under the Ministry of Education and a parallel strand under the Ministry of Religious Affairs. The main strand included several national institutions that had been founded in the colonial period (the University of Indonesia in Jakarta, the University of Airlanga in Surabaya, the Bogor Institute of Agriculture, and the

Bandung Institute of Technology) as well as Gadja Mada University of Yogyakarta that was established by the revolutionaries. Within a short time, several religious groups also established universities that observed the regulations of the Ministry of Education; these set the precedent for private secular legal bodies to establish higher educational institutions, a practice that became very common from the 1980s. Alongside the universities, a variety of specialized institutions also were founded to train engineers, teachers, health personnel, and other professionals. The second strand of religious-oriented institutions, primarily Islamic, were initially only allowed to form specialized higher educational institutions in the field of teacher training.

Over time the system has rapidly expanded and some of the distinctions that once were maintained between different institutions have become somewhat blurred. An important element in the expansion has been the central government's determination to have a public university in every province, no matter how large or small the province's population. Many of these new universities involved the merger of several specialized institutions; by the late 1970s this vision of a university in every province was realized. Building on these local national universities, higher educational institutions have been established throughout Indonesia. Currently Indonesia has nearly 1,000 institutions of higher education and upwards of 10 percent of the 18–22 aged cohort attend these institutions; over two-thirds of the places are in the private sector.

A CHRONOLOGY OF THE DAILY LIFE OF A STUDENT

It is the mid-1980s, and Santoso is a nine-year-old boy in the third grade living in Central Java. Every morning Santoso rises to the sound of the call to prayer resounding from the nearby mosques adjacent to his home. Before heading off to school, he eats a quick breakfast of *nasi goreng*, a typical Indonesian dish of fried rice often accompanied by a fried egg. Selecting his clothes for the day is an easy task because he is required to wear a uniform, which his mother purchased at the start of the school year in July. All passersby will know he attends elementary school because students at each grade level wear a distinct uniform. Primary level students like Santoso are required to wear red shorts (red skirts for girls) and a white shirt with black shoes. On the side of his right sleeve is sewn a patch with the name of his school and its address.

Santoso attends SD Negeri I, one of the local public elementary schools in his small town. He usually walks to school; however, this morning Santoso is behind schedule, so he will hire one of the pettycabs passing by his street to take him to school. Classes start promptly at 7 A.M., and he doesn't want to be late!

Today is Monday, an important day of the week for the school system. When Santoso arrives at school he starts his day with a special flag ceremony, just like every other child attending school on Monday morning in Indonesia. The ceremony is marked by formality, militarism, and nationalism. It is well-choreographed and meticulously prepared. Students march from their classrooms to the area where the flag pole is located. As the designated student leader for the day, Santoso must position his classmates on the field in straight rows and columns. After the students from all the classrooms have been appropriately positioned, the raising of the flag begins with the unfurling of the flag. As the flag is hoisted up the flagpole, the national anthem is sung by a student choir and concludes just as the flag reaches the top of the pole. The ceremony also includes a time of remembrance, a recitation of the *Pancasila* and the preamble, as well as speeches and announcements by the principal. As the ceremony draws to a close, the head student leader dismisses the children for return back to their classrooms.

Inside his classroom are hung separate pictures of the president and vice-president, with the national emblem (the *garuda* bird) centered between them. There is also a map of Indonesia and portraits of national heroes, such as Sukarno, Hatta, and Kartini, and a poster containing the five principles of the *Pancasila*. There are a few windows, none of which have screens, but they occasionally allow a gentle breeze to enter the classroom and provide some relief from the sweltering heat.

While Santoso typically speaks Javanese at home and with his friends, both his teachers and textbooks provide instruction in Indonesian. The textbooks issued to Santoso at the beginning of the school year were designed by the government and were distributed to all third grade students in the country. The mandated curriculum is quite dense, and includes the study of civics, *Pancasila* moral education, as well as religion. In fact, although Santoso attends a public elementary school, he is required to participate in some form of religious instruction catered to his particular religious affiliation. So, while Santoso attends a class on Islam his fellow classmates receive lessons in their respective religions.

The classroom environment is characterized by strictness and formality. Santoso's teachers firmly discipline those who misbehave and maintain their authoritarian position at all times. Santoso is taught to memorize facts using routine and repetition; there is very little space to debate or discuss the "whys" of the lecture. Instead, Santoso is instructed to listen, comply, and repeat what he is taught. Santoso's teachers only have a year or two of postsecondary education, and some have no university training at all. Because they barely earn enough to provide for their families, most of his teachers are forced to find other ways to supplement their meager incomes. For example, one of his teachers sells *satay* on the street in the evenings and another provides after-school tutoring for struggling students.

Santoso's school day ends at one o'clock in the afternoon. He walks home and as he enters his home he smells the aroma of the fried fish and rice which his mother prepared for his lunch. After finishing his homework, Santoso will have the afternoon free to ride his bike or go to the neighborhood soccer field to fly home-made kites with his friends. His school day may appear short, but don't forget that Santoso attends school Monday through Saturday—six days a week!

MAJOR EDUCATION REFORMS

Universal Nine-Year Basic Education (1994)

The government's emphasis has shifted from a focus on primary education toward the secondary levels of instruction. Because universal primary education was generally considered to have been achieved, the government set a new educational goal in 1994 that would extend access to all children for nine years of basic education. While enrollments at the junior secondary schools have increased, this new goal has yet to be realized for a variety of reasons. First, there is still a limited availability of student places and physical facilities at the junior secondary level. Private schools have mitigated this challenge to some extent by providing additional spaces for students. Second, while most students spend some time in primary school, completion rates continue to be low (Duncan, 2000). The issue of retention prevents access to secondary levels of education, as entrance to junior secondary school requires a passing EBTANAS score from primary school. Third, financial barriers continue to be problematic as the costs of tuition, school fees, uniforms, and so on can be a burden for families, particularly those who need the additional income their children might supply. Finally, in order for the government's goal of universal nine-year basic education to be realized, parents and students must perceive education at the secondary level to be necessary and beneficial (Jones and Hagul, 2001).

Local Content Curriculum (1994)

Even prior to the recent decentralizing reforms, the central government began to recognize the merits of curricular content that was responsive to local culture and needs. In that spirit, regulations were introduced in 1994 that authorized regional governments to localize their curricula entitled "Local Content Curriculum." This strategy was to be achieved by inserting local content (history, literature, stories, examples, place names, and so on) at appropriate points in the curriculum, and by either replacing or adding to the content developed by national curriculum experts. Local content was to become 20 percent of the overall curriculum. Many local governments took modest steps to localize their curricula and instructional materials, but progress was hampered by the lack of assistance and training from the central government, teachers' deep-rooted perceptions of their functions and responsibilities as civil servants, and then by the political turmoil associated with the demise of the New Order government (Bjork, 2004). It is expected that greater progress will be made in the future to enhance local content as political and economic conditions become more stable and more favorable to local initiatives.

Decentralization

The range of cultures, languages, and ethnicities found throughout Indonesia is immense. Such a diverse environment would seem to require the formation of a decentralized nation state for reasons of efficiency and effectiveness (Turner and Podger, 2003). Instead, over the past 50 years the country has developed into one of the most centralized nations in the world (World Bank, 2000). However, by the turn of the century, Indonesia made the decision to rapidly decentralize its political and economic authority in a "big bang" manner.

While there have been a few meager attempts to introduce a decentralized governmental structure in the past, none have actually been implemented. Consequently, since its independence from the Dutch in 1945, Indonesia remained a central state. Suharto's autocratic practices prompted individuals to push for reforms, like decentralization. Under Suharto, the locus of power rested in Jakarta, reflecting Javanese priorities, goals, and customs and ignoring the significant regional diversity of the country. Jakarta also received most of the income generated from resource-rich provinces like Papua and Aceh before it was then disbursed according to the priorities of Jakarta's elite. Furthermore, the money that did return to the local community was often misappropriated or squandered by local village officials appointed by the New Order. Because local communities in these provinces felt powerless to respond to such practices, hostility and bitterness toward the center intensified.

Suharto eventually stepped down and transferred his power to B.J. Habibie, who was regarded as incapable and unwilling to generate authentic reform. Instead, Habbie oversaw the creation of one of the most sweeping policy reforms in the country's history: that of transforming Indonesia from a central-ized to a decentralized state, despite the fact that his term lasted only 17 months. Habibie's desire to decentralize the government during a time of political crisis at first appears counterintuitive. Why would Habibie choose to promote legislation that would seem to lessen his power and control under these circumstances? Amidst this economic and political chaos, Habibie needed to actively demonstrate that he had severed ties with Suharto and to provide assurance that his administration would be radically different from the previous one (Ferrazzi, 2000). Numerous provinces expressed tremendous dissatisfaction with what they perceived as Jakarta's pilfering of their financial and natural resources without an equal return on their "contribution." The strengthening of various independence movements in these provinces began to threaten the unity of Indonesia to the point that their calls for sovereignty could no longer be ignored. Organized movements in Aceh and Papua, suppressed under Suharto, now had the opportunity to more vocally proclaim their desire for sovereignty. The Indonesian populace was vigorously calling for true democratic governance.

Habibie was thus in the difficult position of needing to extinguish regional resistance and secessionist movements, but also wanting to appear democratic as the elections loomed in the near future. In an effort to appease these regions and to give legitimacy to his precarious new role as interim president, Habibie approved two pieces of decentralization legislation that called for a transfer in the responsibility and accountability for public service delivery to local governments.

This act helped to disassociate him with the New Order and signified his commitment to reform.

Indonesia's decentralization reform measure was presented to the legislative body (DPR) in April 1999 and ratified the next month. Habibie's strategy was to decentralize swiftly and radically in a "big bang" style so as to ensure implementation before any subsequent administrations could quash their efforts (Hull, 1999). The crafting of the policy, however, took place in a style typical of the New Order government; discussions took place internally, with little or no input from the regions (Ferrazzi, 2000). In fact, Suharyo termed the policy formation process as an "in-house exercise" (2000: 15). He also found that the few ways in which the central government did involve local communities were mainly to disseminate information under the guise of discussion, but that typically almost no authentic dialogue occurred. The end result of this undisclosed process was the creation of two major laws: Law 22 on Local Autonomy and Law 25 on Fiscal Relations between Central and Local Governments.

Law 22 of 1999 devolved a number of political powers to local governments. According to this decree, two major governing structures exist: the central government of the President and his or her Cabinet, as well as the sovereign local government of *Kabupaten* (Districts) and *Kotamadya* (Cities). The provinces also became autonomous; however, their main purpose was to serve as coordinators between the central and local governments. This shift toward the district level as the main unit of government power has given local government a wide range of functions.

Law 25 of 1999 concerns the financial aspects of decentralization and recognizes that local governments require resources in order to adequately perform their new duties. This law allows local governments to tax and creates a structure whereby the central government transfers portions of its tax revenue back to localities. The old system was characterized as one that dictated every expenditure via earmarked grants to local governments. While the general system of transfers from the central to the local government remains, the central government no longer has the authority to determine how and when districts spend their funds.

The decentralization policy briefly outlined earlier has major ramifications for Indonesia's education system because it altered the roles and responsibilities of all stakeholders involved. Under the new provisions, the role of the central government has been restricted to establishing national educational policies that define minimum guidelines for educational standards. Districts, rather than the central government, are now assigned the responsibility to provide and manage educational services. Many schools are in the process of transitioning toward a School-Based Management system (SBM) which coincides with the devolution of responsibilities already taking place throughout the system. SBM involves shifting authority from the central government to local schools to determine matters such as class size, schedules, curriculum content, textbook selection, and school maintenance (Usman, 2001).

In addition, the Ministry of National Education manages the largest number of civil servants (teachers), previously funded by the central government. Usman states that "one outcome of the decentralization process is a massive excess of around 2.1 million central government employees who are being transferred to regional levels of government" and approximately half of them are teachers (2001: 12). Most education personnel were already situated in local districts rather than Jakarta prior to decentralization, and will thus not need to be relocated. However, what has changed is that they are now employed by local educational systems, a rather significant difference.

Under these new decentralization guidelines, fiscal responsibility for education resides with local governments. The manner in which funds are allocated to different sectors, such as education, is now dependent upon district leaders. This refers not only to the exact sum allotted for education, but also to the ways in which that amount is prioritized within the education budget (Yonezawa and Muta, 2001).

Essentially the decentralization policy has transformed the roles of those involved with the education system. As the Ministry's role has diminished in terms of its breadth, the local government and education administrators have acquired new responsibilities, such as educational finance and spending, teacher recruitment, and the provision of educational services.

The decentralization process in Indonesia has been met with a variety of challenges which have seriously impacted its education sector. First, capacity at the local level to assume responsibilities from the central government is lacking. The decentralized system in Indonesia has devolved numerous new responsibilities to districts; as autonomous regions they no longer have the type of support and assistance as in the past, requiring a new level of ability at the district level. Unfortunately, more than 30 years of Suharto's repressive regime virtually killed all attempts at civil society development. The structure of the centralized system conditioned individuals to follow orders from the top, implementing, rather than initiating or designing policy. Due to the newly changed structure, the administrative functions of district officials, principals, and teachers require a level of vision, initiative, and ingenuity not previously demanded of them. In addition, in undertaking their new role as financial managers, administrators must possess the skills to stretch their modest funds to accommodate their educational needs.

The reform delegated new responsibilities to local leaders, many of whom were, understandably, unprepared for the task. Few of the local districts (*kabupaten*), many of which are small, rural locales, have sufficient experience in self-governance. In order to perform their new duties, such as curriculum selection, teacher recruitment, facility management, and budget creation, local leaders need to acquire skills in policy planning and design, service delivery, and fiscal management. The combined lack of local expertise and experience, as well as weak and disorganized community groups and political parties, and virtually no central government efforts to develop capacity at the district level have resulted in a disastrous combination. These conditions have created an environment ideal for corruption, potentially disrupting the delivery of essential services like education (Suharyo, 2000). This structure, if not amended, has the potential to merely mimic Suharto's corrupt, central government on a miniature scale in districts throughout the country.

A lack of capacity and weak accountability structures will greatly reduce the efficiency and effectiveness with which the education system can operate. A smoothly operational education system is unlikely if principals and other local educators lack experience in planning, inventing, and evaluating. These essential skills are necessary for their new decision-making responsibilities regarding the curriculum, evaluation methods, staff, and professional development needs. They will also need skills in the development and administration of financial budgets as they collaborate with local officials on these issues.

Capacity and accountability also affect how much and in what ways local districts allocate their financial resources and invest in various enterprises. As a result of the decentralization policy, local leaders almost exclusively manage the distribution of funds with few accountability mechanisms; consequently, there exists great potential for unprincipled and unscrupulous behavior. District leaders may disregard certain community priorities such as education or even make decisions based on bribes or other corrupt practices which are unlikely to be mitigated by civil society. Thus, the specific amount designated for the education budget and the level of education which is prioritized, such as primary, secondary, tertiary, or nonformal education, will vary from district to district; the central government's role as an equalizer between regions no longer exists.

If decentralization in Indonesia is to be a successful endeavor, efforts must be taken to develop civil society and build capacity not only for the current administration, but also for its future leaders. The education system will perform a key role in developing students' skills, such as critical thinking and leadership, which are essential for effective leaders. In addition, community, political, and religious organizations must be strengthened in order to ensure a strong, functioning, autonomous local government because such groups play an important role in demanding accountability and voicing the local community's aspirations and needs. The development of civil society through education is possible if the system models democratic practices through its management and approach.

CONCLUSION

Perhaps no other country encompasses the range of geographic, ethnic, and cultural–religious diversity as Indonesia. A largely illiterate nation on the eve of its declared independence in 1945, great strides have been taken over the past several decades to expand basic education so as to achieve near universal coverage. The variegated education system includes secular and religious streams as well as public and private provision. Over the past decade, Indonesia has experienced an important transition from the authoritarian New Order government toward a more democratic political system that is promoting greater decentralization of social services. In this new environment, administrative reforms are encouraging greater public participation in the shaping of educational policy. Perhaps the greatest challenges in the years ahead will be to improve the quality of education and increase its relevance while preserving Indonesia's impressive record in providing universal access to basic education.

REFERENCES

Bjork, C. (2004). "Decentralisation in education, institutional culture and teacher autonomy in Indonesia," *International Review of Education*, 50(3): 245–263.

Buchori, M. and Malik, A. (2004). "The evolution of higher education in Indonesia," in P. Altbach and T. Umakoshi (eds), *Asian Universities: Historical Perspectives and Contemporary Challenges*, pp. 249–277. Baltimore, MD: Johns Hopkins University Press.

Buresh, S.A. (2002). *Pesantren-based Development: Islam, Education, and Economic Development in Indonesia*. Ph.D. dissertation, University of Virginia.

Coté, J. (2001). " 'Administering the medicine': Progressive education, colonialism and the state," *History of Education*, 30(5): 489–511.

Dhofier, Z. (1999). *The Pesantren Tradition: The Role of the Kyai in the Maintenance of Traditional Islam in Java*. Tempe, AZ: Arizona State University, Program for Southeast Asian Studies.

Duflo, E. (2001). "Schooling and labour market consequences of school construction in Indonesia: Evidence from an unusual policy experiment," *The American Economic Review*, 91(4): 795–813.

Duncan, W. (2000). "Basic education in Indonesia: A partnership in crisis," in Y. Wang (ed.), *Partnerships in the Social Sector: Issues and Country Experiences in Asia and the South Pacific*, pp. 144–167. Tokyo: Asian Development Bank.

Eels, W.C. (1952). "Educational progress in Indonesia," *School and Society*, 75(1951): 297–299.

Emmerson, D.K. (ed.) (1999). *Indonesia beyond Suharto: Polity, Economy, Society, and Transition*. London: M.E. Sharpe.

Ferrazzi, G. (2000). "Using the 'F' word: Federalism in Indonesia's decentralization discourse," *Publius*, 30(2): 63–85.

Frost, N. (2002). *Indonesia: An Oxfam Country Profile*. Dorset, UK: Oxfam.

Hull, T.H. (1999). "Striking a most delicate balance: The implications of Otonomi Daerah for the planning and implementation of development cooperation projects." Indonesia–Australia Population-Related Research for Development Planning and Development Assistance Project. Accessed on July 10, 2005 from http://wbln 0018.worldbank.org/eap/eap.nsf/Attachments/hullreport/$File/hullreport.pdf.

Jones, G. and P. Hagul (2001). "Schooling in Indonesia: Crisis-related and longer-term issues," *Bulletin of Indonesian Economic Studies*, 37(2): 207–231.

Lukens-Bull, R.A. (1997). *A Peaceful Jihad: Javanese Islamic Education and Religious Identity Construction*. Ph.D. dissertation, Arizona State University.

Nielson, H.D. (2003). "Reforms to teacher education in Indonesia: Does more mean better?" in E.R. Beauchamp (ed.), *Comparative Education Reader*, pp. 391–410. New York: Routledge Falmer.

Nilan, P. (2003). "Teachers' work and schooling in Bali," *International Review of Education*, 49(6): 563–584.

Oey-Gardiner, M. (2000). "Schooling in a decentralized Indonesia: New approaches to access and decision making," *Bulletin of Indonesian Economic Studies*, 36(3): 127–134.

Pritchett, L., Sumarto, S., and Suryahadi, A. (2002). *Targeted Programs in an Economic Crisis: Empirical Findings from Indonesia's Experience*. Jakarta: The SMERU Research Institute.

Purwadi, A. and Muljoatmodjo, S. (2000). "Education in Indonesia: Coping with challenges in the third millennium," *Journal of Southeast Asian Education*, 1(1): 79–102.

Rachman, H.A. (1997). *The Pesantren Architects and their Socio-religious Teachings*. Ph.D. dissertation, University of California, Los Angeles.

Rahman, A. (1997). *Social Class, School Structure, and Schooling Outcomes in Indonesia*. Ph.D. dissertation, Florida State University.

Sirozi, M. (2004). "Secular–religious debates on the Indonesian National Education System: Colonial legacy and a search for national identity in education," *Intercultural Education*, 15(2): 123–137.

Suharyo, W. (2000). *Voices from the Regions: A Participatory Assessment of the New Decentralization Laws in Indonesia*. New York: United Nations Support Facility for Indonesian Recovery.

Turner, M.M. and Podger, O. (2003). *Decentralization in Indonesia: Redesigning the State*. Canberra, Australia: Asia Pacific Press.

Usman, S. (2001). *Indonesia's Decentralization Policy: Initial Experiences and Emerging Problems*. London: The SMERU Research Institute.

Van Der Kroef, J.M. (1955). "Higher education in Indonesia," *The Journal of Higher Education*, 26(7): 366–377.

World Bank (1998). *Education in Indonesia: From crisis to recovery* (Report No. 18651-IND). Washington, DC: World Bank.

———(2000). *Indonesia's Decentralization after Crisis* (PremNotes Number 43). Washington, DC: World Bank.

Yonezawa, A. and Muta, H. (2001). "Financing junior secondary education in decentralized administrative structures: The Indonesian example," *Journal of International Cooperation in Education*, 4(2): 109–124.

Chapter 7

SCHOOLING IN JAPAN

Akira Arimoto

VIEWPOINTS ON THE JAPANESE EDUCATION SYSTEM

Historical Viewpoint

Modern Japanese schools were created with the introduction of a new school system during the Meiji Restoration in 1872 (Meiji 5), in which compulsory education required all six-year old children to attend elementary schools. In fact, initially enrollment was low in many places because people objected to sending their children to these schools. Opposition, especially in rural agricultural areas, even led to the destruction of schools. This contrasts with an earlier period at the time of the feudal Tokugawa *Bakufu* (Tokugawa government), when the common people gave education much attention when it was mainly conducted in *terakoya* (temples for children's education). The literacy ratio at that time reportedly reached a higher level than those found in Western countries (Dore, 1970). Reflecting this traditional respect for education, the enrollment rate soon improved in the new schools despite the initial objections. Among the Western scholars who studied Japanese education, H. Passin and R.P. Dore note that the Tokugawa era became the foundation for modern Japanese education beyond the Meiji Restoration (Passin, 1969; Dore, 1970, 1978).

One reason people may have been persuaded to accept the schools was their perceived value as a modern selection system, one that could guarantee the opportunity of upward social mobility. This new school system moved Japan beyond the feudal social system in which "ascription" rather than "achievement" had defined social mobility.

Social and Cultural Viewpoints

In the Edo age before Japan became a modern nation and the Tokugawa *Bakufu* government ruled the country, there were no modern universities comparable to those in the West. Some schools such as Hanko and a part of Gogaku provided a higher education for people in the elite classes, shogun and daimyo. These schools were solely for the children of the ruling "sword" class within the basic four social categories of feudal society—sword, farmer, craft, and merchant. However, the common people did have access to elementary education, which was fairly popular in the rural agricultural areas. It was customary to have a *terakoya*[1] in which a teacher taught the 3Rs: reading, writing, and arithmetic, to several children. Accordingly, the literacy rate among common people was fairly high even in feudal society and it is reasonable to assume that the existing culture provided a climate that encouraged education.

It is certainly true that the culture as well as a climate suitable for development of education and acceptance of modern schooling was already established at the time of the early Meiji era when the wave of modernization rushed into Japan from the West. We can identify this as one of the important reasons why high enrollment was achieved in such schools so rapidly in an Asian developing country. A further reason can be seen to lie in the fact that it was urgent for Japan to import the advanced models of schools and education from the Western civilized countries: several attempts actually took place in order to realize this goal. From observing China's colonization under the foreign countries, it was seen as a crucial problem for the Japanese government to construct a nation strong enough to be able to stand among these advanced Western nations.

Some key leaders understood the logic that in order to build a strong nation and economy, it would be necessary to make an intensive investment in human resources. This is reflected in a slogan of the early Meiji era: "fukoku kyohei," or "a rich nation with strong military forces." Under these circumstances, the climate for modernization and speculation about the future through importing the advanced Western models in the form of schools and education was in accord with Japan's national originality and identity. As a consequence, however, as Donald Dore points out, it brought about "late development effects, a disease of this new civilization. In short, it led to a degree-o-cratic society with its accompanying educational pathology" (Dore, 1978). From a later viewpoint, many effects, both positive and negative can be seen to have resulted. In terms of the concepts identified by Robert Merton, they include both manifest and latent functions and dysfunctions (Merton, 1968).

HISTORICAL CONTEXT

Ancient and Classical Ages

In ancient times, when the cultural priority was to serve the gods, political and military affairs were thought to be of great importance. This ideological structure was unconsciously conveyed from one generation to another. At the time, there was no formal or systematic education. The first useful writing and cultures were imported to Japan from countries such as Shiragi and Kudara on the Korean peninsula.

By the middle of the 7th century, Buddhism had reached Japan from China by way of the Korean peninsula, and became a factor in the ruling society and government. Famous monks such as Ganjin, facilitated the import of Chinese culture. Immigrants from China and the Korean peninsula, "kikajin," introduced cultures related to Buddhism and Confucianism, together with aspects of their civilization, as well as their construction technology.

Buddhism came earlier to the society of the common people (Takahashi, 1978: 55). At a time when Shotokutaishi, who was the most famous leader in the ancient era, compiled the 17 chapters of the first constitution in 604, many students, such as Onono Imoko, Takamukono Kuromaro, and Minamibuchi Shoan were sent to the Sui dynasty in China. In the ruling class, a considerable degree of intensive training and education oriented to Buddhism were conducted. After the Reformation of Taika in 645, the first school, in Otsukyo near Kyoto, attached to the government was established in approximately 667 introducing education oriented to Confucianism (Takahashi, 1978: 65). Following establishment of this school, a series of the first universities were founded in the capital and other local areas on the basis of a "school order" set in the law of Taiho (Taihoritsuryou) in 701. These universities were quite different from modern universities. An ancient university, called a Daigakuryo, was a bureaucratic place in Shikibu-sho (Ministry of Shikibu), consisting of clerks, called *kami, suke, ju, zoku,* and academic staff, called *meikyo, On, Sho, San,* or also known as *hakase* (doctor), being equivalent in status to a modern professor, and, at a lower level of academic staff, a post of *jokyo* (Takahashi, 1978: 68–69). [The name of *jokyo* was reintroduced as the title of one grade in the new organization of university academic staff—consisting of *kyoju* (professor), *jun kyoju* (associate professor), *jokyo* (assistant professor), *koshi* (lecturer), and *joshu* (assistant)—by the CEC (Central Education Council) in 2005.] These positions were located in the upper social class and students were restricted to descendants of the classes higher than fifth class and the descendants of *kikajin*.

This meant that the power of the *kikajin* was still strong. After the start of the Heian era in 794, dependency on *kikajin* was no longer necessary, as symbolized in 894 by abolition of *kentoshi*, (acknowledgment by a Japanese envoy of the status of the Chinese emperor) to the Tang dynasty. It is clear that enrollment of students from classes other than the aristocracy was difficult. However, in 1177 *daigakuryo* were abolished. A number of reasons contributed: children of the aristocracy had little inclination for learning; they objected to the strict entrance examination; and it had become possible for them to be promoted easily to higher positions on the basis of ascription without any hard study (ibid.: 107).

Japan also imported written languages from abroad. *Kanji*, the Chinese characters, were gradually imported from the time of the Nara era[2] and then institutionalized to the extent that it has become the core of the written Japanese language. All the other syllabaries including *katakana*, and *romania* other than *hirakana*, which was originally invented in Japan, were either imported from abroad or modified from an imported script. Cultural education was restricted to men (ibid.: 120) so women did not learn *kanji*. Women, though, did learn three subjects including music, Japanese sonnet, and calligraphy. Even so it is clear that in the Heian era women's culture was fairly high in some areas related to aristocratic palace culture. For example, women such as Murasaki Shikibu and Seishonagon contributed to a world class literature. As a result, from an early historical stage, Japanese culture and education were to a large extent formed by the strong influence of foreign cultures, even though the effects were evident only in some limited areas.

Taking a historical and retrospective overview of education, we can recognize that a kind of conscious education was apparently undertaken in the cases of *daigakuryo* and *kokugaku* by a process similar to that of many other countries where it was started by a king's family and relatives, aristocratic people, scholars, politicians, and monks. Equally, the common people did not receive any systematic education. But even so, in the Nara and Heian eras, the people in the higher classes enjoyed limited access to education in the private tutorial-type schools such as *shijuku* and *kajuku* where family members or invited teachers took part in teaching. But more widely the development of *Kana* including *katakana* and *hirakana*, a Japanese system of syllabic writing, enabled a much wider spectrum of the common people to be somewhat involved in education in the Heian era.

Given the cultural pattern of the ancient and feudal eras, cathedral schools of the Western type and universities like Bologna, Paris, Oxford, Cambridge, were never established in Japan (cf. Rashdall, 1936 [1970]). *Daigakuryo* belonged to one part of the bureaucratic structure, but even though it called itself a "university" by restricting its teaching to politics and morals, its scope was narrow compared with that of Western universities. *Shugeishuchiin*, which Kukai or Kobodaishi (774–835)—a famous monk—built in Kyoto in 828, was not comparable to the European Middle Age universities, though it was a product of the Middle Age in Japan.

Tokugawa *Bakufu* Era

After the early modern age, including the Nara, Heian, Kamakura, Muromachi, and Civil War eras the Tokugawa *Bakufu*, or Edo era (1603–1867), emerged in the 17th century and lasted approximately 260 years. The Tokugawa *Bakufu* encouraged Confucianism as an ideology sustaining the political regime of feudalism. Some members of the Hayashi family became teachers and bureaucrats of Confucianism in the *Bakufu* successively after Razan Hayashi, an initiator of the *shushigaku* faction and its position in *Bakufu*. Criticism of the *shushigaku* brought about proclamation of other factions, such as *yomeigaku*, *kogaku*, and *kokugaku*.

The former adopted the role of sustaining feudal society; *yomeigaku* proclaimed the equality of human beings; *kogaku* reconsidered the importance of classics and made much of knowledge based on experience; *kokugaku*, also emphasized the study of ancient Japanese thought and culture. Norinaga

Motoori completed this school of study. On the other hand, from the middle of Edo era, study of *yogaku* (Western learning) became active. Originally started by study of Danish medicine, its field broadened to English, French, German learning, proclaiming rational and positive ideas that prepared the way for study of the sciences in the Meiji era (Inoue, 1977: 86–87).

Meanwhile, various kinds of schools were established responding to the development of learning. Considering higher education, at the time of Tsunayoshi, the fifth Shogun, *shoheigaku* was founded. This was developed as an educational organization into *Shoheizaka Gakumonsho*, a school at Shoheizaka, which was directly controlled by the *Bakufu*. First, *Shushigaku* was taught by the Hayashi family as described earlier, and then a series of practical education organizations were founded: *Kaiseisho* for comprehensive education, *rikugunsho* for military education, *kaigunsho* for navy education, *igakusho* for medical education. Eventually it developed and led to the establishment of Tokyo University in 1877.

Hanko, or clan schools (for clans such as Meirinkan, Nisshinkan, Koudoukan, Meidoukan, Koujokan, Zosikan), were established for the education of *hanshi*, clan warriors, which provided education in *jugaku*, or learning for Confucianism, and *bugei*, or Art for warriors, as the central subjects. In response to the rising need for education, some famous scholars founded *juku* (private schools). As in the case of *kangakujujku* (schools for the study of Chinese learning), there were some schools such as Tanso Hirose's Kangien, Shoin Yoshida's Shokasonjuku; for *kokugakujuku* (schools for the study of ancient Japanese thought and culture), there was Norinaga Motoori's Suzunoya; for the study of Dutch learning (*rangakujuku*) there was Koan Ogata's Tekijuku. At the end of the Edo era, Yukichi Fukuzawa founded Keiogijuku from which Keio University, one of the leading universities in Japan, was developed.

In contrast, institutions at the level of elementary and secondary education were established only after transplantation of Western concepts and modes following the Meiji Restoration. Previously, *terakoya*, which were the educational institutions for common people described earlier, equivalent to elementary education, had developed from around the Kyoho era. The main subjects were the 3Rs (consisting of reading, writing and arithmetic). These were private schools, but *Gogaku*, which were close to public elementary schools and were managed by the local community, also existed. Their curriculum was almost similar to that in the *terakoya*. From a historical perspective there were few secondary schools, although the old type of lower secondary school and high school were developed at an intermediate level between elementary school and upper secondary school.

From the 17th century to the 19th century in the Edo era, *terakoya* and *gogaku* developed at the level of the common people, while *Shoheizaka Gakumonsho* and *Hanko* developed for the elite class or warrior level. At that time, educational contents differed to a great degree according to the students' class and position in the social stratification. It was said that the type of education was determined according to a person's position and gender. Later, after Meiji Restoration, realization of integration of people in the framework of the modern educational system by providing all people with similar curricula and educational institutions became a focal problem.

Meiji Era and Modernization

In the Meiji era (1868–1912), by the Imperial University Law of 1887 and, in the Taisho era (1912–1926), by the University Ordinance of 1917, modern higher education was systematically started and developed. Some institutions such as Keio, Waseda, Doshisha, and Ritsumeikan Universities, which were not authorized at all by the government until the latter Ordinance, were promoted to the status of university as private universities. On the basis of this historical development, a two dimensional structure of double statuses, consisting of the national and private sectors, and the university and professional schools, was intentionally formed and lasted until the end of World War II in 1945 (Amano, 1986). In this context, a hierarchy in the form of an academic pyramid with Tokyo University and Kyoto University at its pinnacle was built politically and sponsored by the government (Clark, 1983). This structure has persisted until today regardless of the restructuring due to the postwar academic reforms.

Establishment of primary and secondary education systems was undertaken after the decision to introduce a new educational system in 1872. The school system was promoted around 1886 when the school law provided for a period of four-years of compulsory education. Primary school became compulsory education and gradually developed in accordance with a structure of *jinjo-shogakko* and *koto-shogakko*. "After just a quarter of a century, compulsory education was virtually as advanced as in any Western country. In no other non-Western nation did such rapid change occur"(Rohlen, 1998: 11). By 1900, the school system had established the following sequence: *yochien* (3–5 year-old), *jinjo-shogakko* (6–9 year-olds), *koutou-shogakko* (10–11 year-olds), *chugakko*, or lower secondary school (12–16 year-olds), *koutou-gakko*, or senior higher school (17–20 year-olds), *Teikoku Daigaku*, or Imperial University (20–23 year-olds), *daigakuin*, or graduate school (24+ year-olds).

Historically, the primary school was an institution opened to provide educational opportunity to the masses, while the university was for the elite. From a perspective of integration of educational institutions, which were separated into elite and mass provisions until the Edo era, it is evident that the prewar system still retained the same closed and segmented characteristics.

There developed a structure in which selection of elite class students was made at the lower secondary schools and later they went from the senior higher schools to the universities. In addition to a vertical differentiation in the whole educational system, there was a horizontal differentiation, between public and private institutions at the higher education level.

Postwar Era and Education Reforms

The prewar educational system was dramatically restructured by the introduction of the postwar educational system. This was essentially defined by the education basic law, in which there were many elements ranging from the basic ideal of education to detailed provisions for implementation. Its prescriptions include: equal opportunity for education; compulsory education; equal education for male and female students; school/teachers; family education; social education; linkage and cooperation of school, family, and the community; education to support society and nation-building; religious education; responsibilities of national and local government (MEXT, 2004).

From these basic aims, schools and education have developed to overall modernization at all levels of primary, secondary, and higher education. An emphasis on modernization has been particularly evident in the postwar period, though changes in the prewar period had already achieved much with introduction of basic principles of the equality of educational opportunity, coeducation, and nine-year compulsory education. Reform of the school system in 1945 broke the old dual school system, introducing a single, compulsory 6–3 school system, which has a basic school system consisting of the six-year primary education and the three-year lower secondary school, followed by provision of a three-year upper secondary school, and a four-year university. In addition, the basic school system included nursery schools at the preschool level, two-year junior colleges and the graduate schools at the higher education level. Figure 7.1 outlines the organization of the school system in Japan in 2005.

Figure 7.1
Organization of the School System in Japan

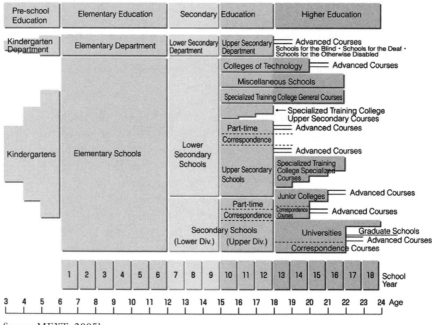

Source: MEXT, 2005b.

As of 2004, the number of institutions is 14,061 at kindergartens, 23,423 at the elementary schools, 11,102 at lower secondary schools, 5,429 at upper secondary schools, 508 at junior colleges, 709 at universities. The number of primary schools and secondary schools is on the decline as schools merge or close due to the low childbirth rate. However, the number of universities has increased consistently. Figure 7.2 shows the trends in the number of institutions.

The new school system of 1947, transformed the old universities, which were modeled on the German university, to new universities based on the American university model. The new universities were called "daigaku" (university) and were created by gathering and amalgamating institutions from a variety of the old categories, such as senior schools, professional schools, normal schools, and universities. As the numbers attending the universities increased, they grew beyond the threshold of 15 percent of the 18-year-old cohort, identified by Martin Trow as marking a transition from elite to massified higher education (Trow, 1974).

Figure 7.2
Trends in Number of Institutions

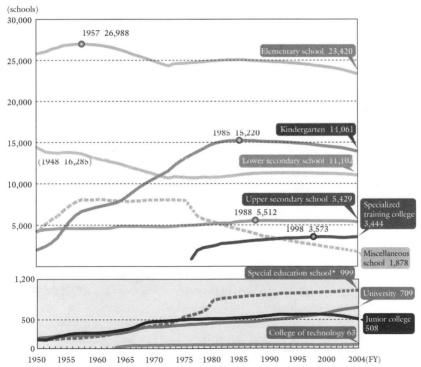

Note: * Schools for the blind, for the deaf and other disabled.
Source: MEXT, 2005b.

In 2004, there are 2,809 thousands students at universities and 234 thousands students at junior colleges as shown in Figure 7.3 detailing the trends in number of students. By 1967, universities, including junior colleges, numbered as many as 821 and enrolled more than 1 million students, equivalent to 20 percent of the age cohort. The rate of growth was impressive: the 48 prewar universities enrolled only 100 thousand students. About this time also turmoil in the universities was widespread, often occurring through conflicts due to discrepancies between orientation of elite and mass higher education.

The private university sector largely sustained the shift to massification by the gradual increase of enrollments in private universities to 73.4 percent and junior colleges 91.7 percent of the total in 2004, as shown in Figure 7.4 detailing the percentage distribution of students enrollments: national, public, private (2004), when the participation ratio in universities and colleges in Japan reached 51 percent.

Reform of university education became one of the notable problems from the late 1960s when massification became a dominant phenomenon but no adequate reforms were undertaken. Today, after 40 years, when the system has reached a stage of universal access, academic and educational reform, has become an even more crucial problem requiring resolution as soon as possible.

Figure 7.3
Trends in Number of Students

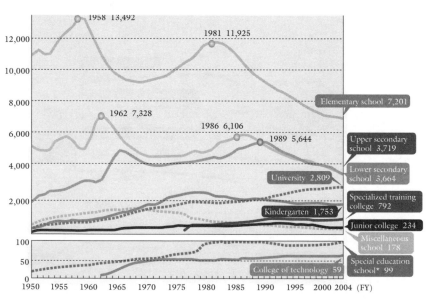

Note: * Schools for the blind, for the deaf and for the other disabled.
Source: MEXT, 2005b.

Figure 7.4
Percentage Distribution of Student Enrollments: National, Public, Private (2004)

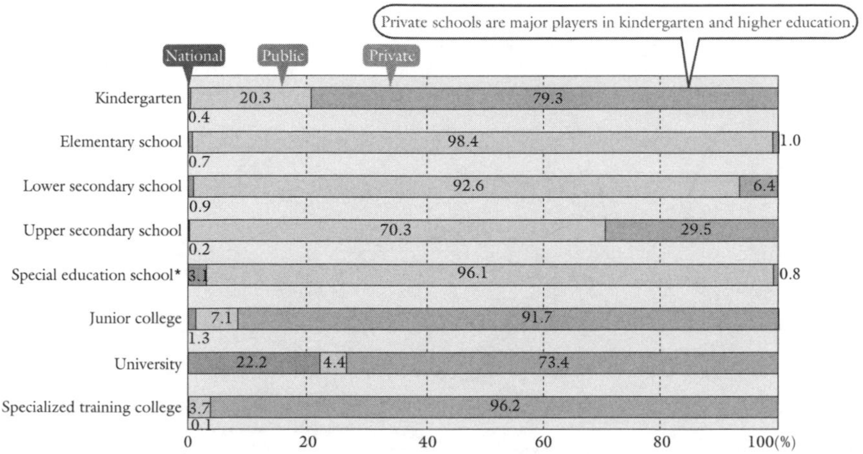

Private schools are major players in kindergarten and higher education.

	National	Public	Private
Kindergarten	0.4	20.3	79.3
Elementary school	0.7	98.4	1.0
Lower secondary school	0.9	92.6	6.4
Upper secondary school	0.2	70.3	29.5
Special education school*	3.1	96.1	0.8
Junior college	1.3	7.1	91.7
University	22.2	4.4	73.4
Specialized training college	0.1	3.7	96.2

Note: * Schools for the blind, for the deaf and for the other disabled.
Source: MEXT, 2005b.

The number of full time teachers is at the massification stage at all levels as you see in Figure 7.5 showing the number of full-time teachers. In 2004, 415 thousands at elementary schools, 256 thousands at upper secondary schools, 250 thousands at lower secondary schools, 159 thousands at universities, 13 thousands at junior colleges, and so on. As far as higher education is concerned, it is true to say that enhancement of quality is necessary not only in students but also teachers in universities and colleges.

LEVELS OF EDUCATION

Preschool

Students

The preschool system comprises a dual structure of nursery schools (*Hoikuen*), controlled by the Health and Labor Ministry, and kindergartens (*Yôchien*) controlled by the MEXT (Ministry of Education, Culture, Sports and Technology). This dual system has lasted for a long time and integration of the two systems into one system under the MEXT is now under consideration. Children of various ages, from less than 1 year-old to 5 years-old (i.e., up to the age of attendance at elementary school), go to the nursery schools. Kindergartens aim at helping preschool children develop their mind and body by providing a sound educative environment for them. Kindergartens cater for children aged 3, 4, and 5, and provide them with one- to three-year courses.

Figure 7.5
Trends in Number of Full-Time Teachers

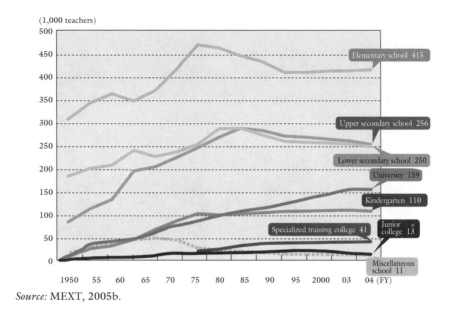

(1,000 teachers)

Source: MEXT, 2005b.

As of 2004, there were 14,061 kindergartens including 49 national, 5,649 private establishments, with approximately 1.8 million children and approximately 110 thousand teachers (MEXT, 2004: 169).

Teachers

In the nursery school, *hoikushi*, or nursery teachers, who have been awarded certificates or passed examinations at the nursery schools, conduct teaching. In the kindergarten, too, teachers who have received similar certificates from courses at universities and colleges and passed examinations usually conduct teaching.

Curriculum

The government controls curricula at nursery school as well as kindergarten. In the case of kindergarten, there is a guideline as follows: "(1) Communicating with teachers and friends, and acting with a sense of stability; (2) Moving the body fully through engaging in various kinds of play; (3) Playing outdoors willingly; (4) Becoming familiar with various activities and engaging with joy; (5) Acquiring a healthy pattern of life; (6) Maintaining cleanliness and becoming self-efficient in activities essential to life, such as changing clothes, eating, and using the bathroom; (7) Understanding the ways of life in the kindergarten, and organizing the life space of kindergarten without adult assistance; (8) Acquiring curiosity in one's health and carrying out activities willingly necessary for preventing illness; (9) Understanding where danger is, what dangerous play is, and how to act in case of catastrophe, and to take actions with regard to safety."

Teaching Method

Adequate methods of teaching deemed appropriate to meet development of infants are used.

Elementary Schools

Students

Elementary schools (*Shôgakkô*) aim at giving children between the ages of 6 and 12 primary general education suited to the stage of their mental and physical development. In Japan, all schools, universities, and colleges start the academic year in April when the cherry blossom is in full bloom and end it at the end of March. This custom differs from that in other northern hemisphere countries where the year usually starts in September and ends in June. Consideration of altering the dates occurs often but to no effect, largely because the tradition has been well and truly institutionalized deeply in the system for many years.

Elementary school has six grades, from the first to sixth. Again differing from other countries, there are in principle no dropouts and it is usual for students to graduate at the sixth grade after having progressed through the grades step by step every year.

In general, quality assurance of elementary education has been thought to be excellent in an international context as on average students graduate with high achievement scores. However, decline of achievement among pupils has become one of the issues recently identified as "7–5–3 education": that is, the proportion of students in elementary school who understand the curriculum is 70 percent, in lower secondary school it is 50 percent and in upper secondary schools 30 percent. Accordingly it may now be that as many as 30 percent of pupils in the elementary schools are inclined to become dropouts as underachievers.

Teachers

Recruitment of teachers is made from those who have been awarded licenses to teach in elementary school after completing courses at teacher training colleges and after having passed the recruitment examination conducted by the education committee of each prefecture. Today, recruitment of teachers has fallen due to a decrease in the number of children. Accordingly, many students who graduated from the teacher training colleges and possess teaching certificates too are unemployed, or "paper teachers," with few chances of recruitment. Recruitment of graduates from some teacher training colleges has declined to as little as 30 percent; and the category of part time teachers, waiting for permanent employment, is increasing. However, recently, a new surge is gradually increasing recruitment, from requirements for more teachers in the large cities such as Tokyo, Osaka, and Nagoya, where many teachers of the "dankai no sedai," or baby boom generation, are coming to the retirement age.

Trends in average age of full time teachers are now increasing with over 40 in all schools other than kindergartens. "The oldest average age of teachers is at Upper Secondary Schools at 43.8 years. At the higher education level, the average age of teachers has risen in recent years in all but the graduate schools, with the average age of junior college teaching staff now over 50 at 51.0" (MEXT, 2005b: 25).

The ratio of male to female teachers is usually in the range 4/6, or 3/7. In the large cities, the numbers of female teachers and also female school principals are gradually increasing. Elementary and secondary school teachers are considered to belong to the middle class, or the lower middle class. Female teachers especially are apt to come from the middle class, because regional middle class families want their daughters to attend teacher training colleges in their region and to become teachers in the same region rather than move to the large cities.

Curriculum

According to a learning guideline reformed in 1998, the aggregate standard time of the teaching classes through six years of elementary school was 4,025 hours. After reform, in 1999, the equivalent guideline for three years in lower secondary school was 2,450 hours (ibid.: 16). As these numbers indicate, teaching class hours in elementary and lower secondary schools are determined by the government and implemented on the basis of such decisions. This is also true for teaching contents. In elementary schools, teaching comprises Japanese, social studies, mathematics, science studies, life, comprehensive learning, and others. In lower secondary schools, it includes Japanese, social studies, mathematics, science studies, foreign language, elective subjects, and comprehensive learning (ibid.: 16). Accordingly, teaching contents are almost the same in both public and private schools throughout the country. However, recently it has become possible to recognize some new trends. The government is introducing "special education districts" which are expected to practice new curricula: for example, in one typical case, teaching of English language is being introduced from the first grade in elementary school. Indeed, even in the regular public elementary schools, introduction of English into fifth and sixth grade is under consideration. In general, it is true to say that deregulation of curriculum is now prevailing owing to the effects of the market in the field of education as well as its effects on policy, the economy, and culture which date from around the 1990s.

Educational Method

Elementary school teachers are recruited after having passed prefectural examinations and completed their systematic training for four years in teacher training colleges and universities for the degree necessary to enter the teaching profession. In their courses, it is necessary for students to take a series of credits specified for the teaching profession in addition to the necessary classes: these include a five-week basic practice teaching, a two-week subject practice teaching, and writing a dissertation for graduation. Accordingly, the educational methods to be used by teachers who have met these requirements are considered to satisfy the expected standard.

Educational Pathology

However, it is becoming clear that there are also symptoms of educational pathology. These can be categorized under two headings: educational pathology and pathological education. Under educational pathology, there are educational failures, including school dropouts; school phobia; bullying; truancy (students who refuse to attend schools); school violence; property damage; class interruption; neurosis; and suicide. For example, "violent incident occurrence in junior high school is the highest or 24,000 in 2003. The total number of such incidents across elementary to upper secondary schools rose to 31,000 in 2003, for the first time in three years." In recent years, truancy has been decreasing: in 2003, the total amounted to 126,000 cases including 24,000 cases in the elementary school and 102,000 in the lower secondary school, that is, one in every 280 pupils in elementary school and one in every 37 students in lower secondary school. Reports of bullying have decreased over the recent 10 years, but there are still approximately 23,000 cases, including 6,000 cases in elementary schools, 15,000 cases in lower secondary schools and 2,000 cases in upper secondary schools (MEXT, 2004: 146).

The heading, pathological education, covers failings derived from education itself. These include: excessive competition in entrance examinations, emphasis on intellectual education, *hensachi* education or education that places too much dependence on examination results. This has created a need for counseling, guidance, supplementary lessons, remedial education, and/or precautionary specialist remedy. The number of schools with school counselors has increased rapidly every year over the past eight years from 154 in 1995 to 6,941 in 2003 (MEXT, 2005b: 19).

There is also a collapse of class and school discipline in elementary and lower secondary schools where even experienced teachers are barely able to control classes adequately.

Around 1990, Yasumasa Tomoda pointed out the following facts. "One teacher is appointed to each of the classes, and this teacher is in charge of the class members. S/he teaches almost all the subjects including music and physical education in primary schools. For this reason, not only the relationship between teacher and students, but also that between students tends to become very familiar. Soon, a teacher become quite familiar with the characteristics of the students in her/his class" (Tomoda, 1988: 87–88). How to explain the current phenomena of collapse, though this observation is likely to be basically adaptable to the classes in primary schools?

To some extent this can be attributed to the dramatic changes in children's worlds due to factors ranging from rapid social changes, an acceleration of children's unbalanced physical and mental development, and insufficient discipline and training in family and regional community.

Anxiety symptoms are also recognizable in the decline of children's physical strength. Over the past quarter century, the average height of eleven-year old boys has increased from 142.3 cm to 145.1 cm, and that of girls from 144.4 cm to 147.0 cm. Yet the time they take to run 50 m has increased from 8.80 to 8.91 seconds for boys and from 9.10 to 9.25 seconds for girls; and the distance they can throw a softball has diminished from 34.0 m to 30.42 m for boys and from 19.60 m to 17.19 m for girls. The decline of their physical strength in spite of an increase in their stature is notable (MEXT, 2005b: 6).

School collapse seems to be caused by factors related to both children and teachers. It is evident that an individual variation in abilities is found among teachers. Testimony to this is provided by the approximately 200 teachers who are judged by the government to be inadequate teachers each year. Rethinking of introducing a new teacher training system in universities and colleges is increasingly seen to be one of the problems in urgent need of solution.

How does this relate to the trends in average class size? Classes in both elementary and lower secondary school types had an average size of 45 students in 1950. That ratio was down to 26.3 students per class in elementary schools and 31.0 students per class in lower secondary schools by 2004. If we make an international comparison, it is still high. "Japan had 28.8 students per class in primary education and 34.3 per class in Lower Secondary School in 2001, both in excess of the OECD country mean and one of the highest levels for any OECD country" (MEXT, 2005b: 23).

Secondary School

Students

All the children who have completed elementary school are required to study in lower secondary school (*Chûgakkô*) for three years until the end of the school year in which they reach the age of 15. Lower secondary schools give children between the ages of 12 and 15 a general secondary education suited to the stage of their mental and physical development, on the basis of the education given in elementary school. There are three grades in lower secondary school, the first to the third. As at elementary school, attendance is compulsory.

Those who have completed nine-year compulsory education in elementary and lower secondary school may go on to upper secondary school (Kôtô-gakkô). Students must normally take entrance examinations to enter upper secondary school. In addition to full-day courses, there are also part-time and correspondence courses. Full-day courses last three years, while both part-time and correspondence courses last three years or more. The last two courses are mainly intended for young workers who wish to pursue their upper secondary studies in a flexible manner in accordance with their own needs. All these courses lead to a certificate of the upper secondary education. In terms of the content of teaching provided, the Upper Secondary School courses may also be classified into three categories: general, specialized and integrated courses. (MEXT, 2005b)

Traditionally, most students work very seriously so as to get either a good job placement or to go to the upper secondary schools and also to universities and colleges. However, we can observe recently not only functional but also dysfunctional phenomena. For example, truancy is still not small in number, though it is decreasing in the lower secondary schools as in the elementary schools. In 2003, approximately 102,000 cases of lower secondary school truancy were reported. In the upper secondary schools drop outs have been declining for the last few years but numbered approximately 82,000, or 2.2 percent of all students (MEXT, 2004: 147). There is increasing recognition of educational pathological anomie evident in bullying, motorcycle gangs, blackmail, delinquency, runaway boys and girls, suicides, and at the extreme, homicides.

Teachers

Those who pass the examinations for teacher recruitment as well as graduating with the necessary credits from teacher training course in universities and colleges are recruited as the lower secondary school teachers. An elementary school teacher is usually required to teach all subjects, but a lower secondary school teacher is appointed to teach a designated subject, such as Japanese, mathematics, sciences, Japanese history, world history, or music.

Just as in the elementary schools, examples of educational pathology are increasingly observable in the lower secondary schools. Truancy, school collapses, and various kinds of pathologies are also increasing.

Problems with teachers who have difficulty in teaching and controlling class-rooms increase: in 2003, 481 cases were recorded throughout the country (ibid.: 153). Some of these teachers have succumbed to a "burnout syndrome" but others are clearly inadequate teachers. These problems attract much attention across society to the extent that the government has started to introduce various measures including improving teacher training, strengthening provision for teaching practice, and establishing professional schools of education.

This trend may suggest changing environment of teachers as well as Japanese traditional society, if we compare the environment which was described by Merry White some two decades ago as follows:

One might set the view of a teacher's life in Japan against the view of the lives of old people. For both, tradition emphasizes respect, reverence, and support from both family and community. Recently, however, the lives of the aged (especially those who cannot live within extended families) have been shown to be less than "golden," just as teachers have been regarded as being under siege. Both have suffered, it seems, from the erosion of traditional values. However, the aged who have fallen through the cracks in Western societies might still envy the old people of Japan, who have only in statistically rare cased been abandoned. Similarly, most Western teachers would probably prefer the generally well socialized Japanese child and the predicable, rewarding career of the Japanese teacher over what they now have. (White, 1987: 91)

Curriculum

As in the elementary schools, curriculum in the lower secondary schools is controlled by the government. It follows that the curriculum content to be taught shows much similarity across schools throughout the country. Overall the curriculum is less unified than in each class in elementary schools, as the designated subjects are taught by individual teachers according to their specialization in Japanese, mathematics, science, and so on. The possibility of limited student achievement in the schools if the quality and ability of teachers in their subject areas is insufficient is seen as a growing concern. Accordingly, how to attract excellent teachers is becoming an important problem in all schools as well to their Parent Teacher Associations (PTA). In some school districts in Tokyo, for example, schools are advertising in open competition for recruitment of teachers and head hunting and scouting for good ones.

Educational Method

Uniformity of the practices and methodology of qualified teachers in lower secondary school is accepted throughout the country. But innovation in teaching methodology can rapidly achieve prominence. In this sense, the GP (good practice) program, which government introduced in 2003 to universities and colleges to promote improved teaching in higher education, may also be useful as a means of improving the training of upper as well as lower secondary school teachers, where, as students, they have been taught in the innovative GP programs in a university or college.

At the level of upper secondary school, a new development has been "sogo gakka," or a comprehensive department. This was introduced in 1996 to cater for the needs of schools with diversified students. It offers an innovative curriculum based on acceptance of student diversity in terms of, typically, their ability, aptitude, interest, concern, career. By 2004, approximately 100,000 students were following the new curriculum in 248 schools nationwide (MEXT, 2004: 161–162). Each comprehensive department in 2003, for example, distributed its time, 72.8 percent on the general course, 24.0 percent on a specified course, and 3.2 percent on the comprehensive course (MEXT, 2005a: 5).

In addition to the above categories, secondary schools (*Chûtô-kyôiku-gakkô*) was introduced in April 1999 as a new type of six-year secondary education school system. Secondary schools combine lower and upper secondary school education in order to provide lower secondary education and upper secondary general and specialized education through six years. The lower division in the first three years provides lower secondary school education and the upper division in the latter three years gives upper secondary school education.

Other than these school systems, special education schools (*Tokushu-kyôiku-gakkô*) aim at giving children with disabilities, education suited to their individual needs. There are schools for the blind, deaf, and other disabled. Schools for the other disabled may be further classified into three types: those for the mentally retarded, those for the physically disabled, and those for the health impaired. Special education schools comprise four levels of departments, namely, kindergarten, elementary, lower secondary, and upper secondary. Special classes in ordinary elementary, lower, and upper secondary schools cater to disabled children whose disabilities are not so serious (MEXT, 2005b).

Generally speaking, some innovations are observable in high school educational system as described earlier. However, some important questions such as how to build ability related to creativity, expressive and critical thinking, and problem resolution, for example, remain to be solved in Japanese education in the stage of high school as well as the other stages. With respect to this problem, Thomas Rohlen even made a comparative study of teaching between high schools in Japan and the United States, and critically discussed the instructions almost entirely made by lecture.

American teaching should not be idealized, but crucial differences remain between Japan and the United States. The American ideal for high school instruction is that it should stimulate the students' interest and cause them to think, to question, and to want to learn more. Class discussions are an important part of our strategy to attain these goals....Our goal is the stimulated student (attentive, intelligent, and expressive) who is developing critical judgement (a mark of independence)....In the Japanese view, expressive and critical skills generally emerge later and progress gradually throughout adulthood. In sum, the lecture format in Japanese high schools teaches patient listening. (Rohlen, 1983: 245)

Basic categories of human development are not necessarily sorted out the same way in every society. A case in point is what Japanese call "spritiual training" (*seishin kyoiku*), a range of experience based on forms of instruction that entail a mixture of physical ordeals, lessons in social morality, and character building. (Rohlen, 1995: 51)

Postsecondary Education, Higher Education

Students

Those who graduate from the upper secondary schools, or pass a certification examination are eligible to apply to enter universities and colleges (*daiken*). Students are able to enroll by passing entrance examinations consisting of a preliminary unified entrance examination held by the university entrance examination center and a secondary entrance examination held by individual universities and colleges, although some institutions conduct only the latter examination. There are four-year universities and colleges and two-year junior colleges: students graduate from the former with the degree of either B.A. or B.Sc., or from the latter with an Associate degree.

As of 2004, 49.9 percent of the 1,410,000 students in the18-year old cohort get enrolled in universities and colleges and as a result it is said that Japanese higher education is coming to a universal stage of higher education development. As of 2005, the share of enrollment in all postsecondary education is already 74.5 percent, though that is still 51 percent in universities and colleges as previously described, and it is clear that, beyond the massification stage, the universal stage has already been fully realized.

A large majority, as many as 545 institutions, or about 80 percent, of the 709 universities and colleges in 2004 had established graduate schools. Graduate student numbers are approximately distributed as 160,000 in masters' courses, 70,000 in doctoral courses, and 8,000 in professional degree courses (MEXT, 2004: 195). The proportion of graduate students to undergraduate students is approximately 10 percent, which is low in comparison to the figure of about 20 percent in the United States, the United Kingdom, and France (ibid.: 196).

Teachers

Most university teachers are recruited by an examination conducted by every institution after students have graduated from masters' or doctoral courses; for appointment, though, it is not essential to possess such certification. CEC (Central Education Council) recently proposed to change the title of academic staff from *joshu* (assistant), *koshi* (lecturer), *jokyoju* (assistant professor), *kyoju* (professor) to *joshu*, *koshi*, *jokyo* (assistant professor), *junkyoju* (associate professor), *kyoju* (full professor). The major change is that *jokyo* is now thought to be a career path for promotion to *junkyoju* which is an independent position comparable to *kyoju*, though formerly *jokyoju* was thought to be assistant to *kyoju* (CEC, 2005).

The academic marketplace has had a closed structure peculiar to Japan with academic nepotism and inbreeding for about one century, because a pinnacle of university pyramid hired their own graduates into faculty members with high inbreeding ratio of more than 90 percent as seen in Tokyo University and Kyoto University. However, this trend is gradually improving owing to an international pressure for institutional competitiveness (Arimoto, 2005a).

We should pay attention to the persistently small share of female teachers. Trends in percentage of females among full time teachers have been improving slightly but not sufficiently for many years. In 2004, of all school types, the one with the most female teachers is kindergarten, 93.9 percent, followed by elementary school, 62.7 percent, specialized training college, 51.2 percent, junior college, 46.3 percent, lower secondary school, 41.0 percent, miscellaneous school, 37.9 percent, upper secondary school, 27.5 percent, university, 16.0 percent (MEXT, 2005b: 21).

Curriculum

At undergraduate level, students are required to obtain 124 credits for graduation. Following introduction of a deregulation policy in 1991, all institutions were responsible to integrate the curriculum for general education and professional education in the undergraduate course. Many institutions set a level of 40–50 credits in general education in all curricula totaling 124 credits in all undergraduate education; recently, though, the weighting assigned to general education has been declining in many institutions. CEC discussed in 2002 this situation from a perspective of the need to strengthen general education in the undergraduate curriculum (CEC, 2002).

Educational Methodology

Teaching takes place with the usual conventional methods, such as lectures, seminars, laboratory experiments, field studies, and preparation of dissertations. Lectures are the most traditional method by which a professor can teach more or less than 50 students in class rooms of average size, and occasionally more than 100 students in lecture theatres. Recently, there has been a tendency to introduce small class teaching for groups of less than 20 students in order to enhance the morale and achievement of individual students.

Remedial or developmental education, as well as faculty development (FD) is needed to respond to these diversified students who are now increasingly coming to universities and colleges in the massification stage of higher education. The number of institutions introducing FD is gradually increasing every year, having risen now from 183 (national sector 47, public 1, private 135) in 1996 to 458 (96, 41, 321) in 2002 (MEXT, 2005b: 213).

The share of student placement in employment recovered to 92.8 percent in 2004, although it had dropped to 90.5 percent in 2000 (ibid.: 218).

PUBLIC EXPENDITURE ON HIGHER EDUCATION

Finally, it is true to say that government financing to higher education is desired to be improved to a considerable degree in an international comparison, although Japan is now slightly recovering from a long economic recession. Even the MEXT says in its recent white paper as follows:

Public expenditure on school education is 3.5 percent of GDP in Japan, which is in the lower group among OECD countries. Public expenditure on higher education is particularly low and at 0.5 percent, in the lower end among OECD countries. One reason is that public expenditure accounts for a low proportion of GDP in Japan overall, and another is that it is likely that the majority of higher education is privately-run. (ibid.: 57)

It is an important problem for Japan how to raise the share of governmental financing to higher education from 0.5 percent of GDP to more than 1.0 percent equivalent to the United States, Canada, Australia, and European countries, though private financing is already more than 1.0 percent, a high share comparable to the United Sates, for example (Arimoto, 2005b: 176–187).

A CHRONOLOGY OF THE DAILY LIFE OF A STUDENT

School

In general, elementary school pupils walk to school in groups, which parents usually take turns to guide. Supervision of this traditional custom has recently been reinforced as a response to the death of some elementary pupils during their journeys to and from schools. Around 8:30 A.M., teaching starts in class rooms throughout the country. School lunch is provided at lunch time, around 12 o'clock. Around 3 P.M., school is over and club activity starts. Pupils also return home in groups. Many pupils go to cram schools and coaching classes, while some of them go to the supplementary private schools for lessons and exercises in piano, violin, *koto*, abacus, tea ceremony, and flower arrangement.

Home tutors (katei Kyoshi) are also employed if a child is having trouble in a subject. In addition, there are two basic types of extra schooling (juku): private remedial classes (gakuashu juku), for those who have fallen behind, and the better-known examination cram classes (shingaku juku), for those who can work at or ahead of the classroom pace and who want to get into a good university. In the latter, the child learns more advanced material to gain an exam advantage over children who study only the regular curriculum. (White, 1987: 145)

Elementary school pupils as well as junior and senior high school students have busy days because of such activities.

All pupils used to wear uniforms, for a variety of reasons—economy, control, unification, and so on. Students in junior and senior schools also used to wear uniforms. Merry White described the school regulations related to the case of the junior high schools.

School uniform skirts should be centimeters above the ground, no more and no less. (This differs by school and region.) / Wear your school badge at all time. It should be positioned exactly./ Going to school in the morning, wear your book bag strap on the right shoulder; in the afternoon on the way home, wear it on the left shoulder. Your book case thickness, filled and unfilled, is also prescribed. (White, 1993: 223–225)

But, today commonly they wear casual dress instead of uniforms in many more places nationwide, especially in the elementary schools. (University students wore uniforms until the 1960s; during the campus turmoil around the late 1960s and 1970s they gradually changed to the current casual style.)

Lower secondary school pupils usually go to school individually, not in groups. They enjoy club activity after the end of classes longer than the elementary school pupils. They also go to the cram schools longer and it is not unusual for them to be at such schools until around 10 P.M.

Involvement in club activity is higher for high school students, as also is the time spent at cram schools by senior students. The description *jukenjigoku*, or "the hell and war of the entrance examination," has been notorious for many years from around the 1960s in the Japanese degree-o-cratic society. Some 20 to 30 years ago, this was quantified as "shito goraku," or "four hours pass and five hours fail," in the sense that those who sleep four hours in the night can pass the entrance examination but those who sleep five hours will fail. William Cummings even discussed the quality of adolescent life related to the examination system.

The growing public concern with the examination system is based on the fear that involvement and competition it generates have caused a decline in the quality of adolescent life. Various sources report the ill effects of the examination system. Young children report being lonely after school because most of their playmates attend a juku. Parents report that their children have become so accustomed to organized activities, whether at the the juku or at school, they forget how to play by themselves. Almost 40 percent of all sixth graders now wear glasses, over double the proportion in the late 1950s. (Cummings, 1979: 90)

The situation is now changing because of open door enrollment started since 2007 when applicants to less competitive institutions are likely to be more relaxed in preparation.

Universities and Colleges

The less prestigious universities are becoming less competitive in the hierarchical pyramid of higher education institutions. Since 2007, entrance to university has, in effect, been through an "open door": the number of school-leavers seeking enrollment in universities and colleges is expected to be approximately 650 thousand, and equal to the number of places available. As a result the university entrance examination is necessarily serving different roles determined by the polarization of the social and academic differentiation among universities and colleges.

Students in the universities and colleges usually enjoy more freedom than those in the elementary and secondary schools, a natural consequence of their greater maturity. Recently, the number of adult students has been increasing, a novel situation in Japan, in accord with an increasing orientation toward lifelong learning. The majority of students in the fields of humanities and social sciences are women, and in the field of the sciences men; relatively few women enroll in engineering.

The social class of students is higher in the group of the universities and colleges enrolling the most able students (students achieving high "hensachi"[3]). A sort of "kakusa-shakai" (differentiated society), or society with a gap between rich and poor, is becoming evident in the stratification of higher education reflecting the growing gap in social stratification. In addition, among the low *hensachi* group, proportionately fewer enrollments occur due to an apparent decline of students' learning abilities and achievements. In 2006, almost 40 percent of all private universities and colleges experienced well below full enrollment, and some face the likelihood of being closed. As pointed out by P. Bourdieu, "a cultural reproduction" is occurring in the pyramidal system of higher education institutions as well as in society in total (Bourdieu, 1991).

What is occurring in the campus life of students experiencing such social changes inside and outside academic institutions? In general, classes start at 9:00 A.M. Serious students attend class punctually, while dull students attend less promptly and less frequently. According to a recent national survey, students became more serious in their attitudes following the collapse of the bubble economy in the 1990s (Takeuchi, 2003: 119–138). They perceive a need to obtain good grades in order to improve their employment prospects during a period of economic recession.

While some students live in dormitories, the majority commute: in comparison with students in China, where most live on campus, in Japan commuting can take a long time. Students are inclined to eat "brunch" rather than breakfast. Club activity is fairly popular but political activity has declined after its peak in the 1960s.

In accordance with the diversification of students accompanying massification, the learning ability and achievement of most students, is said to have leveled down though perhaps about 20 percent of students still demonstrate high ability, achievement, and dedication. Teaching reforms, especially institutionalization of FD has to a large extent become inevitable in order to permit students' ability and achievement to attain the levels of the teaching goal to which each institution aspires (Arimoto, 2005).

MAJOR EDUCATIONAL REFORMS: ANALYSIS AND CONCLUDING REMARKS

It is appropriate to locate discussion and analysis of the key educational reforms within their social and cultural context. The main educational reforms can be categorized this way: the Meiji restoration, in which modern education was institutionalized; the period after World War II, when the postwar reforms were taking place; and the contemporary educational reforms seeking a 21st century vision. The contemporary issues of rapid change include (1) knowledge based society, (2) globalization, (3) marketization, (4) population decline, (5) lifelong learning. Structural education reforms are necessary to cope with these great social changes.

Knowledge-based Society

It is self-evident that rapid access to more information has led to a significant increase in knowledge in society. Accordingly, it is necessary to reform the curriculum and use of educational technology through the reconstruction of knowledge in schools and universities. For universities, this has meant a focus on developing Centers of Excellence (COE) in individual institutions as well as across the national system.

Globalization

Attainment of global educational standardization has become important in the process of globalization. In the context of the worldwide educational competition, Japanese school education has revealed symptoms of decline against two criteria: first, OECD's student achievement survey, PISA 2003, which covered approximately 4,700 upper secondary school students; and second, an international survey of the trend in mathematics and sciences called, TIMSS 2003, which covered approximately 4,500 elementary pupils and approximately 4,900 lower secondary school students (MEXT, 2004: 133). PISA 2003 revealed that "Japan's 15-year olds (first year upper secondary school students) were in the top class internationally. The reading literacy of the Japanese students, however, is dropping in rank and is not considered the world's top class." The MEXT has identified a need to develop educational content, teaching methods, and teachers' quality in order to enhance student's achievement. It plans to introduce an achievement test that will be administered nationally.

As for the creation of knowledge, the research productivity of Japanese scientists is increasing to a considerable degree as shown by indicators such as the science citation index (SCI), and the number of published papers. For example, SCI of Japanese scientists in the worldwide indicators increased from 6.3 percent to 8.4 percent, with higher speed compared to that in the United Kingdom, Germany, and France, and in 1993 was second only in the world after the United States (MEXT, 1997: 150). However, much greater improvement in attainment of educational ability to an international level is desired as educational productivity has not been similarly high thus far.

Marketization

The policy of deregulation in education has led to a trend that emphasizes coordination between demand and supply as part of the process of marketization. The key concepts are gradually shifting from the categories of nation, government, control, preevaluation to those of region, institution, freedom, and postevaluation. In other words, it is changing from nationalization to decentralization. All institutions and individuals are required to realize their own uniqueness and identity. In the case of higher education, for example, the national government controlled the system of higher education by way of introducing the preevaluation to institutions and also the advanced model in the modernization process for about 130 years. It tried to control quality of the system so as to meet with the advanced model. On the other hand, marketization was introduced to the system through 1990s deregulation process to the extent that tendencies of initiative, autonomy, freedom, and identity were encouraged in accordance with introducing postevaluation. In this process, national university (*kokuritsu daigaku*) was transformed to national university corporation (*kokuritsu daigaku hojin*) in 2004 as an intermediate position between national and private sectors, in which quality assurance of institutions is to be conducted on the basis of their involvement in tendencies such as initiative, autonomy, freedom, and identity. Postevaluation was introduced to all institutions by the newly established accreditation system in 2004. As observed internationally, market mechanism is apparently working in this process, possessing invisible hand with efficiency (cf. Teiseira et al. (eds.), 2004: 2–3). It is not clear whether the transformation of traditional higher education policy from stressing the preevaluation to one stressing the postevaluation was successful or not.

Population Decline

As a series of simulations predicts a population decline from 130 millions today to 80 millions by the mid-21st century, the development of human resources becomes an educational issue of the highest priority. The planning of what is appropriate for total society in terms of the development of human resources will need to become coordinated at the levels of elementary, secondary, higher, and lifelong education.

Lifelong Learning

A commitment to lifelong education demands the constant, systematic, and sustainable provision of the opportunity of education and learning to the full range of communities and societies beyond individual schools. In Japan where the participation rate in higher education now surpasses 50 percent, this places an age of universal access to higher education within reach so that all people should be able to enjoy lifelong learning through schools, universities and colleges, communities, and societies.

Structural Reforms

Based on these five points, the realization of educational reforms has become an essential challenge if educational visions corresponding to the demands and forces of the middle and long term time span are to be met. The national constitution and the basic education law define the current education structure. In its central provisions, the basic educational law has operated for 60 years from its introduction of the postwar educational reforms until the present day. One of the pressing issues to be faced today is the reform of the law. According to a white paper released by the MEXT, the framework of educational reform is as follows:

1. establishment of reliable school education;
2. promotion of academic reforms appropriate to the needs of the 21st century as a century of knowledge;
3. the regeneration of educational ability at family level and promotion of cooperation between school, family, and community to generate a nexus;
4. encouragement of peoples' consciousness and attitudes toward substantial participation in public affairs;

5. respect for Japanese tradition and culture, and the encouragement of an attitude of a caring community and nation, and the encouragement of an awareness of membership of international society;
6. realization of a society committed to lifelong education;
7. policy making of the education promotion basic plan. (MEXT, 2004: 100)

At present these plans have not gained unequivocal support among the Japanese people: the components 3, 4, and 5 are viewed as controversial. The trend of argument that has led to rethinking of the law is that in the process of Americanization, a commitment to Japanese traditional culture has been ignored so that there has been a tendency for decrease in: participation in public affairs, respect for traditional culture, and a caring community and nation.

It is not an oversimplification to suggest that in the 21st century it is an important matter for Japanese people to establish their own national identity and at the same time to realize educational reforms to train and educate human resources able to accept responsibility for a harmonious development of social and individual demands.

Finally, Thomas Rohlen's observation of Japan in the historical perspective is likely to be valuable if we think about Japan's identity for the future in the 21st century.

The Japanese had long demonstrated a talent for borrowing knowledge. Centuries of periodic apprenticeshisp to China and Korea established fundamental patterns that placed a high value on the capacity to master foreign knowledge and techniques. Painstaking imitation, followed by careful examination and criticism, leading increasingly to greater independent innovation describes the typical process, whether we consider the seventh and eighth centuries or the nineteenth and twentieth. (Rohlen, 1995: 5)

A highly educated population and a work force engaged in continuous learning make for impressive and regular gains in productivity. Such a population constitutes a strong platform for continued adaptive change. This capacity for learning is still today a major cause for optimism regarding the country's likelihood of successfully meeting the extraordinary challenges of the future. It is sobering to recall, however, that Japan has never before in history succeeded in being an international leader in cultural, scientific, or political terms. The challenges and contradictions ahead truly momentous and should not be underestimated. (ibid.: 41)

NOTES

1. Itinerally, *terakoya* originally started from the later Muromachi era in early 16th century when monks taught students, or *terako*, in *tera* (temple) and so it meant *terakoya*, or houses of teaching for *terako*, which became substantially educational organizations of ordinary people in the Edo era and especially at the later Edo era it dramatically increased not only in large cities but in local areas throughout the country. The number of it was roughly estimated as many as 30 to 40 thousands, while the counterpart of elementary schools today is approximately 25 thousands. Owners of *terakoya* which were usually ordinary people such as *chonin* (town people) and *nomin* (farmers) hired teachers who were called as *shisho*.

2. Nara era (710–794) indicates 84 years from 710 (Wado 3) when Emperor Genmyo set up city in Heijokyo (Nara) to 794 (Enreki 13) when Emperor Kanmu set up city in

Heiankyo (Kyoto) starting the Heian era (794–1185). The name of Nara era derived from Heijokyo Nara. In this era, Taihorituryo (the Law of Teiho) was modified to cope with the national situations in an attempt to construct a centralized nation, while Tenpyobunka (Nara culture) flourished.

3. *Hensachi* (standard score) is a figure which shows certain position in denominator. It expresses that mean score is 50 and standard deviation is 10. If we say simply *hensachi*, it usually means *gakuryoku hensachi* (achievement standard score) which reveals results of the tests of achievement and is broadly used to indicate the possibility of passing entrance examinations.

REFERENCES

Amano, I. (1986). *Koto Kyoiku no Nipponteki Kozo* (Japanese Structure of Higher Education). Tokyo: Tamagawa University Press.

Arimoto, A. (1984). "Gendai Shakaito Kyoiku Byori (Modern society and educational pathology)," in M. Shinbori and S. Tuganezawa (eds), *Environment of Education and Pathology*, pp. 35–67. Tokyo: Daiichi Houki Publishing Co.

———(ed.) (2003). *Daigaku no Curriculum Kaikaku* (Academic Curriculum Reforms). Tokyo: Tamagawa University Press.

———(2005a). *Daigaku Kyojushoku to FD: America to Nippon* (Academic Profession and FD: USA and Japan). Tokyo: Toshindo Publishing Co.

———(2005b). "Structure and functions of financing higher education in Asia," *Higher Education in the World 2006: The Financing of Universities* (GUNI Series on the Social Commitment of Universities), pp. 176–187. Houndmill, Basingstoke, Hampshire, and New York: Palgrave Macmillan.

Bourdieu, P. (Translated by T. Miyajima) (1991). *Saiseisan: Kyoiku, Shakai, Bunka* (Reproduction: Education, Society, and Culture). Tokyo: Fujiwara Shoten Co.

CEC (Central Educational Council) (2002). *Kyoyou Kyoiku no Kaizen* (Improvement of General Education). Tokyo: Central Education Council.

———(2005). *University Teachers Organization*. Tokyo: Central Education Council.

Clark, B.R. (1983). *The Higher Education System: Academic Organization in Cross-national Perspective*. Berkeley and Los Angeles, CA: University of California Press.

Cummings, W.K. (1979). "Expansion, examination fever, and equality," in W.K. Cummings, K. Kitamura, and M. Nagai (eds), *Changes in the Japanese University: A Comparative Perspective*, pp. 83–106. New York: Praeger Publishers.

Dore, D. (Translated by H. Matsui) (1970). *Edojidai no Kyoiku* (Education in Edo Era). Tokyo: Iwanami Publishing Co.

———(1978). *Gakureki Shakai—Atarashii Bunmeibyou* (Degree-o-cratic Society: Diploma Disease). Tokyo: Asahi Shinbunsha.

Inoue, H. (1977). *Nippon no Kyoiku Shiso* (Educational Ideology of Japan). Tokyo: Fukumura Publishing Co.

Merton, R.K. (1968). *Theory and Social Structure*. New York: The Free Press.

MEXT (1999). *Kyoiku Hakusho* (White Paper). Tokyo: MEXT.

———(2001). *National Curriculum Standards for Kindergartens*. Tokyo: MEXT.

———(2004). *Kyoiku Hakusho* (White Paper). Tokyo: MEXT.

———(2005a). *Kyoiku Hakusho* (White Paper). Tokyo: MEXT.

———(2005b). *Japan's Education at a Glance 2005*. Tokyo: MEXT.

Passin, H. (Translated by M. Kunihiro) (1969). *Nippon no Kindaika to Kyoiku* (Modernization of Japan and Education). Tokyo: Saimaru Publishing Co.

Rashdall, H. (Translated by T. Yokoo) (1936 [1970]). *Daigaku no Kigen* (The Universities of Europe in the Middle Ages). Tokyo: Toyokan Publishing Co.

Rohlen, T.P. (1983). *Japan's High Schools.* Berkeley and Los Angels, CA: University of California Press.

———(1995). "Building character," in T.P. Rohlen and G.K. LeTendre (eds), *Teaching and Learning in Japan,* pp. 50–74. Cambridge: Cambridge University Press.

———(1998). "Introduction," in T. Rohlen and C. Bjork (eds), *Education and Training in Japan,* Volume 1, pp. 1–45. London and New York: Routledge.

Shinbori, M. (ed.) (1981). *Nippon no Kyoiku* (Education of Japan). Tokyo: Yushindo Publishing Co.

Takahashi, S. (1978). *Nippon Kyoiku Bunkashi* (Japanese Cultural History). Tokyo: Kodansha Publishing Co.

Takeuchi, K. (2003). "Gakusei to Daigaku Kaikaku (Student and university reform)," in A. Arimoto and S. Yamamoto (eds), *Daigaku Kaikaku no Genzai* (University Reform Today), pp. 119–138. Tokyo: Toshindo Publishing Co.

Teiseira, P., Jongbloed, B., Dill, V., and Amaral, A. (eds) (2004). *Markets in Higher Education: Rhetoric or Reality?* Dordrecht: Kluwer Academic Publishers.

Tomoda, Y. (1988). "Politics and moral education in Japan," in W.K. Cummings, S. Gopinathan, and Y. Tomoda (eds), *The Revival of Values Education in Asia and the West,* pp. 75–91. New York: Pergamon Press.

Trow, M. (1973). "Problems in the transition from elite to mass higher education," *Conference on Future Structures of Post-Secondary Education, General Report, Policies for Higher Education,* Paris, June 26–29, 1973, pp. 51–101.

White, M. (1987). *The Japanese Educational Change: A Commitment to Children.* New York: Free Press.

———(1993). *The Material Child: Coming of Age in Japan and America.* New York: Free Press.

Chapter 8

SCHOOLING IN THE LAO PEOPLE'S DEMOCRATIC REPUBLIC

Manynooch Faming

Education is certainly a key tool for national development, including economic, political, and sociocultural improvement, particularly in new nation states. Gellner provides a notion of nationalism that relates to education, namely, that it is "a political principal, which maintains that similarity of culture is the basic social bond ... [to maintain and] legitimize the similarity of culture ... " (1997: 3). This certainly requires legitimate people (i.e., citizenship) of the society to be educated with the shared values of patriotism and culture. Education is also the very tool to precondition social participation and acceptability appearing in textbooks at all extents, from hidden to manifest presentation of the texts and contents at various levels, depending on the individual government's political ideology and situations in order to integrate larger diverse groups of population (Bocock, 1986). This is also true in the case of the Lao People's Democratic Republic (or Laos). National education is believed to produce skilled members of the labor force and modern citizens, who ideally feel no ethnic biases, are no longer saddled with backward religious beliefs, and are willing to play a part in national patriotism. The country can improve its economy and thus bring about modernity. After the formal independence proclamation of the Lao People's Democratic Republic (1975), the Lao government has paid close attention to restructuring the country's educational system as a way to "civilization or to reach 'socialism' as the ultimate goal."[1] This is a civilizing mission that has become a national focus to expand the national education system throughout the country as part of national economic development. This is aimed not only at the peasant majority ethnic *Lao Loum* but also at ethnic minorities living in border regions.

The purpose of this chapter is to explore the educational system of Laos, particularly the contemporary system of nationalism through "Laoization," focusing more specifically on ethnic minorities who comprise more than 50 percent of the total population. Ethnic groups in Laos are also commonly referred to as *Lao Loum* (Lowlander), *Lao Theung* (Upperlander) and *Lao Soung* (Highlander) to refer to nonethnic Lao (the dominant). I argue that education in the Lao PDR is another civilization mission that aims at "Laoization." This mission has been politically successful but less so with regard to social and cultural aspects. The national education system carries not only the messages of nationalism and being "educated persons" but also "cultural production" (Levinson and Holland, 1996) or "Laoization" as representing modernity. However, many ethnic minority students as the subjects to be civilized by this modern education view Lao society and culture as less modern. This is because the education system has offered students certain freedoms and opportunities to access various forms of modernity within and outside Laos. In addition, the formal and modern education teaches students to be "Lao" rather than citizens of the Lao PDR, unlike the education during the French period that taught students to be part of colonial Indochina, not to be "French."

"Laoization" is a process of adopting major *cultural symbols* of what is called "Lao culture," including conversion to Buddhism, wearing traditional ethnic Lao dress (particularly the *Sinh* or Lao skirt), living in an off-ground house, eating sticky rice, playing and singing Lao songs and instruments, and speaking Lao language. For example, some ethnic minorities who fail to speak Lao language are regarded as "uneducated," and thus "backward." On the contrary, many ethnic minorities are educated. For instance, many *Hmong* can read and write in their own language. However, when they lack knowledge of Lao language, they are officially regarded as being uneducated. Finally, this chapter provides an account of a day at school of an ethnic *Mouteun* male student.

THE COUNTRY AND ETHNIC MINORITIES

The LPDR is a landlocked country surrounded by Burma, China, Vietnam, Cambodia, and Thailand, with a population of about 5.8 million, and an area of 236,800 square kilometres. The country is divided into 18 administrative provinces. Due to the country's rugged mountainous geography, only 3.3 percent of land area is arable, and the majority of the people are scattered, particularly in the hilly and mountainous areas.[2]

Laos is still regarded as one of the "least developed countries" in the world. Its estimated per capita income was US$390 in 2004.[3] The country's economy is highly dependent on agriculture and natural resources and foreign aid. Eighty five percent of the population are subsistence farmers (mainly rice growers), and social and educational progress is still low. The human development indicators published by UNDP show that the population has high mortality and fertility rates, with an average life span of 51 years and the average number of lifetime births by women of child-bearing age being 6.5. In terms of formal education, the census also shows that 23 percent of ethnic Lao have never attended school. The figure is much higher for minority groups, for example, for *Phutai* 34 percent, *Khmu* 56 percent, and *Hmong* 67 percent, while it is 94 percent for *Koh* and 96 percent for *Museu*.

According to the 1995 census the LPDR has 47 different ethnic groups or "Son Phao" in Lao. They are also linguistically diverse. After 1975, the terms *Lao Loum* (lowland Lao), *Lao Theung* (midland Lao), and *Lao Soung* (highland Lao) were used officially and originally derived from the French colonial categorization. Ethnolinguistically, the *Lao Loum* covers the *Tai* groups, *Lao Theung* covers *Mon-Khmer* and Austronesian groups, and Tibeto-Burman and *Hmong-Yao* groups are under *Lao Soung*. The three terms are misleading because some ethnic groups under the same category live in more or less different geographical areas and share few linguistic or cultural similarities (Chamberlain, 1995). The Lao government maintained these official ethnic identifications until the early 1990s.

HISTORICAL BACKGROUND OF SCHOOLING AND EDUCATION IN LAOS

Modern education is a relatively new social phenomenon in Laos. It was first introduced during the French colonial period in the early 1900s but secular primary education was made compulsory only in 1951 (LeBar, 1967). Prior to French colonization (which began during the 1800s), there were traditional temple (*Wat*) schools available for Buddhist Lao men, but not for non-Buddhist ethnic minorities. Among the latter, traditional education was transmitted from mothers to daughters and from fathers to sons, until modern government schools entered the villages. The advent of government school also came to affect the Lao traditional temple school system.

Traditional Buddhist *Wat* Schooling

There were three forms of Buddhist temple education. The first form was more informal (commonly seen in the past but rare nowadays). A boy or a man lived in a *Wat* and took part in events at the *Wat*, such as in ceremonies, caring for the temple yard and buildings, and so on. He would learn how to read and write Lao language along with monks and novices in informal classes taught by more senior monks or "Khru," roughly equivalent to a Guru. The second form was "Sangha School." This form of schooling had a national curriculum and consisted of formal classes taught by monk teachers, under the supervision of the Ministry of Education. The third form was only teaching Pali language. The purpose of this form of education was to produce competent monks, knowledgeable about the Buddhist teachings (Wilder, 1972: 60–61). Only Lao men and boys who became monks and novices could attend this form of schooling. Most of them were also students of "Sangha School." The temples provided sufficient knowledge to be heads of families, jacks-of-all-trades, farmers, and to be Lao language teachers. However, it was not enough for the administrative jobs during the colonial period. This caused a decrease in numbers of students in traditional temple-based schools. According to Wilder (1972: 61), a survey done during 1960s showed that 43 percent of the 34 year-old male population had spent some time in a Buddhist temple, with 80 percent of this group having spent more than six months in a *Wat*. In 1961–1962, there were 252 *Wat* schools accounting for about 22 percent of all elementary schools in Laos. In 1966–1967, there were 241 (about 4 percent) *Wat* schools. This indicated that government secular schools were increasing rapidly, causing *Wat* schooling to lose its attractiveness to Lao men. Although, in 1935, the *Wat* schools modernized their curriculum to try to compete with the French elementary schools, the move did not change the trend of losing their students to the French schools. This was because of the demand for positions within the government, which required skills in reading, writing, and speaking French that a *Wat* school could not offer (ibid.: 62).

Traditional education was also unavailable for girls and women. However, they could be accepted into a Buddhist temple as nuns. As the mainstream Lao culture relied on religious doctrines, Lao women were raised to be wives and mothers. Somlith Pathammavong wrote in a UNESCO report in 1955 that "girls were brought up simply to be good housewives" (Pathammavong, 1955: 82). The male children of the housewives studied in the *Wat* schools. It was also a traditional Buddhist belief that the supportive mothers and wives received merits through their sons and husbands' monkhood. This is because passing through monkhood also meant moving from being a normal man to becoming a respectable "maha" with knowledge of dharma and skills of reading and writing Lao language (LeBar, 1967: 79). Therefore many Lao women were less eager about going to school, as they relied on their men for their livelihood.

Schooling under the French

Prior to World War II, the importance of the secular schools in villages was limited. After World War II, government secular schools were introduced to the villages in increasing numbers. When the French first came in during the 1890s, *Wat* schooling system was widespread. The French had no intention to intervene as they relied on it for a continuation of "moral" education and a tool to preserve traditional religion and culture. Lockhart (2001) writes:

The fundamental objective was to utilize the traditional educational function of Lao monks to impart a more updated curriculum, including doses of Western science and math along with the moral values and religious teachings with constituted the core of temple-based schooling. This approach allowed the French to integrate a bit of their "mission civilisatrice" with the preservation of traditional culture, yet it also reflected the reality that the colonial regime simply did not require a large number of Lao subjects with a Western-style education.

The secular schooling system grew slowly as the needs of the French civil service were relatively small, there being a group of more educated Vietnamese working in the Lao government. In 1915, there were only 10 elementary schools with a total enrollment of 260 students (see Table 8.1).

Table 8.1
Number of Primary Schools and School
Enrollments in Laos, 1915–1944

Year	Enrollments	Schools
1915	260	10
1920	931	28
1925	1,585	39
1930	3,223	n/a
1932	7,035	70
1933	7,066	91
1934	6,667	87
1935	6,537	84
1936	6,210	85
1937	6,320	84
1938	6,765	85
1939	7,026	92
1941	n/a	94
1942	7,901	121
1943	9,508	138
1944	11,401	163

Source: Reproduced based on phammavong's UNESCO
report in 1955.

A French decree in 1917 made the schools in Laos part of a common Indochina education system, in which each commune had one official primary school. There were five courses offered in this primary cycle, which was divided into two levels: grades 1–3 and 4–6 (LeBar, 1967: 80). The first level or cycle was also called the "preparatory and elementary courses," which provided graduates with a primary Indo-Chinese school certificate. The second cycle was the complementary primary cycle, including second grade intermediate courses and senior courses. This led students to receive a "certificate of complementary primary Indo-Chinese studies." Teachers were former Buddhist monks or graduates from *Wat* or "sangha schools." In 1932, there were 70 schools with 7,035 students including 976 girls. This figure included some ethnic minority students of whom 110 were *Thai Neua*, 65 were *Kha*, 43 were *Meo*, 35 *Phu Noy*, 33 *Phu Thai*, and 7 *Red Thai* (Evans, 2002: 49). The sizable number of ethnic minority students implies that the French regarded Laos as part of a wider Indochina colony, not as a nation state; thus the ethnic Lao were treated equally along with other ethnic minorities in terms of education opportunity. The available data showed that by 1944, there were 163 primary schools with 11,401 students (Pathammavong, 1955: 90). Table 8.1 shows the enrollments and numbers of primary schools since 1915 to 1944.

There was a period of decreasing enrollment during 1934–1938, from 7,066 in 1933 to 6,210 in 1936, for example. According to Pathammavong (1952: 89) this was because it was difficult to pass the three-year elementary cycle. Although during this period French studies were not made compulsory, many students graduated at the age of 15. Many dropped out before being granted the certificate for economic reasons.

By 1946 there were 24,057 students in 509 schools, including three new secondary schools. They were established in Pakse (1945), Luang Prabang (1946), and Savannakhet (1947), in addition to the Pavie Collége at Vientiane (1925). In 1944, the "tribal schools" were founded for ethnic minority peoples. There were six schools with an enrollment of 250 and 600 at the "mobile schools." This form of schooling served seminomadic ethnic groups. The *Meo* population and students living near Xiengkhouang Province were encouraged to enroll in the main town schools. There were also a few "Laotheung boarding schools" with 215 students. Some schools for ethnic minorities were established in a form of half hospital and half school as a teacher training center and medical school (Pathammavong, 1955: 92 and LeBar, 1967: 81). Before the Royal Lao Government (RLG) time, the secondary schooling was developed into two stages: grades 7–10 as the first cycle and grades 11–13 (see Figure 8.1). There were few reports on secondary schools in Laos during the French colonial period. During the entire decade of the 1930s, there were 148 graduates, of whom 96 were Vietnamese and 52 were Lao (Wilder, 1972: 65). Some sources reported that a reason for the small number of secondary Lao graduates was because many of them were former students of traditional *Wat* schools, which did not conduct lessons in French, the language of government. Nonetheless, a few select students from this modern secondary education cycle were sent to Hanoi, Saigon, or Phnom Phenh for their secondary education.

Lessons for both elementary and secondary education were conducted mainly in French. Apart from mathematics and natural sciences, history and geography carried contents about Laos as part of the French Indochina protectorate.[4] Teachers of all government schools at that time were mostly native French speakers and some were graduates of the French schooling system, particularly in Vietnam.

Schooling under the RLG[5]

The period between 1946 and the 1960s, witnessed relatively rapid growth in the modern secular education system while the traditional *Wat* school modernized its curriculum to include mathematics, sciences, and French. The two forms of schooling were under the Ministry of Education but were administered by two different offices.

On the one hand, the experience gained from the French, the building of schools and the extension of large parts of formal education provided the RLG the basis to greater education development. Primary education remained the same as during the French period but the government announced in 1951 that primary education would be compulsory and be conducted in the Lao language; while French would be retained for secondary education. Similar to the data presented in Table 8.1, Table 8.2 demonstrates two decreases in enrollment, one in 1953, about 8 percent lower than the previous year, and another in 1961, nearly 10 percent lower than in 1960. This was because of the decreasing aid

Figure 8.1
Education System Organization Chart under the RLG

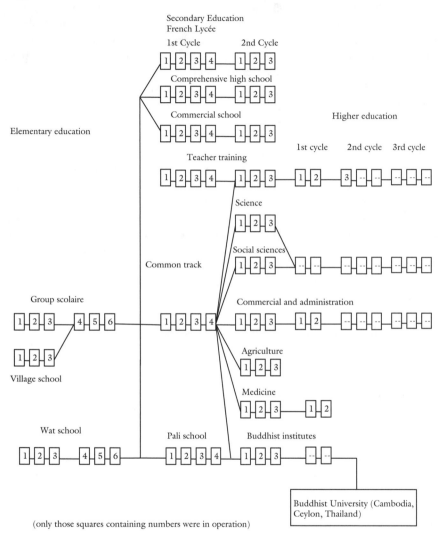

(only those squares containing numbers were in operation)

money from international donors and French subsidies.[6] Many students dropped out as their parents could not afford it during a period of high unemployment. The French experience was also a good basis for a clearer establishment of a formal education system, including primary, secondary, higher education, and sport and youth. Vocational education was placed provisionally under the Ministry of Public Works. Primary education was a six-year cycle (grades 1–6), secondary education was a seven-year cycle (grades 7–13), and higher education

Table 8.2
Number of Primary (Grades 1–6) Schools and
Enrollment from 1946 to 1969

Year	Enrollment	Number of Public Elementary Schools
1946–1947	24,057	509
1947–1948	31,414	507
1948–1949	36,517	604
1949–1950	38,331	641
1950–1951	34,087	662
1951–1952	36,902	741
1952–1953	41,412	866
1953–1954	33,357	852
1954–1955	43,274	923
1955–1956	63,950	1,021
1956–1957	75,167	1,235
1957–1958	77,204	1,269
1958–1959	95,957	1,464
1959–1960	99,302	1,567
1960–1961	91,313	1,573
1961–1962	88,312	1,646
1962–1963	108,603	2,172
1963–1964	117,111	2,410
1964–1965	128,040	2,498
1965–1966	142,269	2,636
1966–1967	156,481	2,742
1967–1968	166,159	2,863
1968–1969	185,724	n/a

Source: Wilder, 1972: 67.

took another three years. Higher education included teacher's training and technical training education (see also Figure 8.1).

On the other hand, during the first decade of this period, the RLG encountered teacher shortages because many Vietnamese, who were working in the government or as teachers, were asked to leave. Lao staff in government service occupied minor positions, and had been denied access to teaching jobs. There was no solution to the teacher shortage problem except to accept people who had only meager qualifications. Thus, education of this period, similar to the present, was highly criticized by many outsider educators for its poor quality, besides the standard of teachers, school buildings, and teaching–learning materials. Nonetheless, the system managed to produce literacy rates of 41 percent for men and 13 percent for women in the urban areas, and about 37 percent for rural men and 10 percent for rural women by 1968 (Whitaker, 1972: 78).[7]

Secondary education was rather limited, with only a small number of primary graduates continuing to this level of education. There were two cycles: grades 7–9 (3 years) and grades 10–13 (4 years). In 1955, a total of 652 students enrolled in secondary schools. By 1968, there were 9,699 enrollments with 185 in their four final years of the second cycle. This is because there were only five schools providing a three-year lower secondary education. They were in Luang Prabang, Thakek, Savannakhet, Xieng Khouang, and Pakse. These secondary schools were also called *collèges* after the French. There was only one at Vientiane, *Lycée Pavie*, that provided the final four years of secondary education. The curriculum of *collèges* included ethics and civics; French, Lao, and English; history and geography; mathematics; physical culture; drawing; music; and handicraft. All lessons, except Lao language, were conducted in French. *Lycée Pavie* carried a curriculum similar to those offered in a French modern and classical *lycée* at that time (ibid.: 84). Before 1952, final written examinations took place in Vientiane while oral examinations were held in Hanoi. Then, both examinations were parts of the *Baccalauréat* in Vientiane (Mauger, 1959: 446).

Students who had finished the first cycle could continue in either *Lycée Pavie* or enroll in teacher training education or the National Military School for Officers in Laos; or Medical Officer's School, the Public Works, or Agriculture and Forestry in Cambodia; or go to France to complete their secondary education. Graduates of *Lycée Pavie* in Vientiane could proceed directly to higher studies in Vietnam or other foreign countries. Between 1955 and 1959, 171 students were sent to France under French scholarships while the RLG sent another 104 students to various countries. By 1967, there were about 400 Lao students studying outside the country.

Vocational and Teacher Training

Vocational education had already existed during the French colonial period. The buildings, facilities and curriculum remained unchanged after independence. For example, *École Atelier* was to train carpenters, masons, auto mechanics, and metal workers. In 1955, an *École Artisanant* was founded in Savannakhet. These two schools, which were equivalent to *Lycée Techniques*, operated with rather low enrollments, 300 in a span of 10 years. In the mid-1960s, Germany sponsored more modern and practical training courses. Thus, vocational education during the RLG grew slowly due to low enrollment and inadequate relevant employment opportunities.

After the autonomous government asked the Vietnamese workers to leave the country, RLG education encountered teacher shortages. The RLG then tried hard to train graduates from the *Wat* schools to be teachers based on facilities left after the French time. This also included, similar to vocational education, the half-hospital half-teacher training schools, a common form of education in Xieng Khouang among the *Méo*. The RLG established also more lower secondary schools which were also teacher training colleges with increasing enrollments. However, there was low motivation amongst those students to become teachers due to the low social prestige and relatively poor hopes of career advancement that the job offered.

Curriculum revisions were made, for example, to the content in history and geography subjects to include greater coverage about Laos as a "sovereign country" with its own "legendary" history[8] and land (Pathammavong, 1955: 97). The RLG government also printed textbooks in Lao language, but encountered problems of standardization, particularly with regard to the spelling system. There was no solution to this but to print Lao textbooks with the spelling by custom or according to individual preference. What is interesting is that ethnic minority children had to learn about ethnic Lao history in Lao language in the same way that the Lao students had had to learn in French language during the colonial period. Pathammavong writes:

The pre-eminence of Laotian as the national language has never been questioned, although in Laos there were several branches of the same "thai" race. Nowhere, over the whole area of Lao territory has any national, to whatever ethnic group he may belong, ever thought of raising the question of using another language. [The] language of primary education is thus Laotian, and any attempt to replace it by another language would be calculated to prejudice Lao national unity ... [In] the matter of spelling, however, discussion about the various systems proposed tends to go on interminably; but it will come to an end once the means of printing have been developed. (1955: 104–105)

The message, comparatively, made French colonial education sound more accommodating toward ethnic minorities. That is, they were placed on an equal footing with the ethnic Lao because they all have to learn through nonmother tongue education. Education for ethnic minorities during the RLG period was rather "negligible, although, for example, the Khmu who lived close to urban centers were aware of the value of education and in a few cases requested the services of a Lao teacher" (LeBar, 1967: 83). In addition, Lockhart (2001: 11–14) noted that the RLG's textbook and education reforms of 1962 were of no use to ethnic minorities living at the margin. For example, nationalism and "Laoization" content in Lao textbooks sent mixed signals to all students, including nonethnic Lao, about their glorious Lao heritage, symbolized by the royal elephant flag and their shared Buddhist faith.

Schooling under the Pathet Lao (Mid-1950s–1960s)[9]

Schooling under the Pathet Lao could be considered generally as "education"[10] or "literacy program" rather than as schooling, in the case of the nonethnic Lao. Although there is little work available about education in this area, Lockhart (2001) mentions that schooling was organized in the Pathet Lao liberated zone through the support of the Vietnamese and almost every country in the socialist bloc. What happened was "children and adults went to Vietnam for schooling and/or training and many Vietnamese cadres came to advise and to teach in the revolutionary educational camp in Sam Nua" (ibid.). On the other hand, most education was conducted informally at local community centers, army camps, or bunkers, particularly in operation caves (Chagnon and Rumpf, 1982). Chagnon and Rumpf (1982: 167) quote the experience of a "cave school teacher" as "it was a hard life. The caves were always dark, damp and cold. Often we didn't have enough paper or chalk, so students had to memorize a lot." On the other, the aim was to teach basic communication skills in Lao language for ethnic minorities who joined the communist movement of the Pathet Lao. Bouasy, a former *Makong* ethnic graduate from Sam Nua education camp told me during an interview on April 25, 2001:

I was in Sam Neau for two years and there was an order to move the school down to Xieng Khuang. We all had to walk for 7 days. I graduated from there. Sometimes in the mid 1960s, I could not remember exactly which year but I did remember that there was aerial bombardment. The Pathet Lao had not yet taken over the government and the soldiers were still working along the borderline. I taught for one year. The classes were set up within a cave. The curriculum used to be divided into different subjects but then it was cramped into one big unit without specialization in any subjects. The teacher's training institute belonged to the regional central administration but then the military took over the management. There were two educational institutions that the military looked after: the teacher's training and nursing and medical school. I was asked to teach both Composition and Lao Literature and it turned out that I was to all intents and purposes the expert for the two subjects. Actually, Ban Na Lao Kham [Khammouan Province] was my ethnic group village. I was sent back to teach at a Lao Theung village, my home, Makong (his voice went soft and low). Most of them are Makong and some were ethnic Lao. I normally use Lao language to teach them. The purpose was to get to learn how to read and write Lao language and some basic mathematics. All of this could be equivalent to grade three. Many were sent off to Vietnam to complete their primary education and came back to be teachers like me.

Therefore, education under the Pathet Lao was more focused on "literacy programs" involving Lao literacy. And, the target groups were various ethnic minority populations with an emphasis on ethnic solidarity as a way to conquer the battle field.

The education under the Pathet Lao also focused on the Marxism-Leninism revolutionary propaganda or "revolutionary culture." Their students learned from watching documentary films about revolution in eastern bloc countries and Vietnam, and about fighting for "working class." The textbooks carried content that contrasted with that used in RLG schools. For example, as Lockhart (2001) writes, "[terms] such as 'patriotism' and 'helping the nation' constitute an alternative and competitive national discourse, buttressed by derogatory references to the 'masters and lords' who have traditionally taken the people's land and to the American 'bandits' who have brought war to the country." Many textbooks, however, made no mention of Buddhism but talked about the solidarity among various ethnic minorities and carried pictures of a Pathet Lao soldier treating a sick *Hmong* child. This type of message was reproduced in many textbooks of primary schools after 1975.

Schooling under the Lao People's Democratic Republic (LPDR) (1975–1985)

After December 2, 1975, the National Assembly proclaimed the LPDR with a new flag, anthem, and Lao as the national language. The Lao People's Revolutionary Party (LPRP) and the government unanimously felt that to develop Laos into a socialist country, education had to be the most important task. In addition, the LPRP and the government announced their educational policy

1. Take education one step as the key to widen the door to the rapid and successful renovation and building up socialism;
2. Identify the fundamental concepts on education of the LPRP:
   a. Schools are the tool of the dictatorship of the proletariat
   b. Education must serve the revolutionary tasks and directions of the LPRP
   c. Education must serve productivities (both social and agricultural or even industrial)
   d. Education is the obligation of working class people
   e. Teachers are personnel of the Party.[11]

As a result, this message formed the central purpose of education during this period. Students were, then, trained to exhibit revolutionary characteristics.

The reach of the education system expanded rapidly in this period, especially to the rural areas. Similar to the Pathet Lao, education in this period was focusing on what is now called "informal education and literacy eradication." The new Lao government spent their efforts to make education of all forms available as well as making it compulsory and free for all. Yet, quality and quantity were growing in two opposite directions (Chagnon and Rumpf, 1982).[12] As cited in Chagnon and Rumpf (1982: 168), the World Bank reported in 1979 that within 5 years after 1975: "The literacy rate among adults aged 15 to 40 has doubled from 40 percent to 80 percent. 75 percent of 5 to 11 years old population currently attend primary school as opposed to less than 50 percent in 1974. The number of schools and teachers has increased 182 percent and 427 percent respectively. The number of teacher-trainees has risen by 125 percent." This impressive educational improvement was highlighted along with the fact that the quality had not improved. The main reasons for this poor quality were that many qualified personnel, including teachers, had fled Laos, textbooks were insufficient, and teaching-learning materials were inadequate (ibid.).

The LPRP held strongly to their political agenda of promoting national integrity. A nonformal education scheme was heavily targeted at ethnic minorities and those who marry early, to teach them how to read and write Lao. Once again, many ethnic villagers felt that it was less relevant to their agrarian lifestyle. All families with children of eight years old and above had to send them to school, which they regarded as taking their family workforce away from home. For example, in Thakek, there were times when some soldiers came to villages and checked every house to see if there were any children staying at home. Those soldiers would tell the parents to send all their children to the school. Many parents were willing to do so because the government promised that it was free of charge, and that the children were better off serving in the military as a way to express patriotism.

The New Economic Mechanism (NEM) and the New Phase of Laos's Educational Development (1985–1990)

The collapse of the former Soviet Union was the starting point for the Lao PDR to launch the so-called all round reform, the NEM introduced by Kaysone Phomvihane in mid-1980s.[13] The introduction of this NEM was to get the moribund Lao economy off the ground and to find more national income channels under state-enterprise mechanisms so as to maintain the socialist political will and ideology of equality and working class society.

At this time, education was to be open to the idea of *free labor market*,[14] which had never previously been a feature of education in Laos. The gradual economic policy and practice changes pushed the Ministry of Education (MOE) to make changes. Unlike the previous 10 years, Laos's educational development became more organized so as to handle pressures from the outside world, as well as local demands. The development of education at this time expanded around secondary and vocational training education as to produce a pool of workforce for the free labor market. Yet, what students learned from the content of education remained more nationalistic and catered less toward the practical needs of the market. For instance, students in upper secondary school or higher education learned through taking notes as teachers read aloud from textbooks. Some contents of many social subjects carried the praise of national heroes and how the revolution had caused them to have free access to education. Every month, teachers and students had a meeting to learn about "socialism" directions and propaganda from the LPRP. During the first month of each new semester, upper secondary students were all put through a one-day military skill training course as part of training for national security. At the same time, many investors from other countries requiring well-trained employees found Lao "educated" labor disappointing. Ironically in the Fourth National Congress and Politbureau Meeting of June 1987, the LPRP stated that: "from now on, we shall still operate our education task as the core to cultural and moral revolution as to produce new socialist people." Kaysone also expressed his concerns as directions for Laos's education as in the education policy under NEM:

1. Education plays an important role in the country's revolutionary affairs
2. [we should] Design education based on varieties and characteristics of economy and society of each working unit and of each locality
3. People must receive basic education at the primary level (compulsory education)
4. Raise the quality and effectiveness of education
5. Raise the importance and status of teachers among local community
6. Urge the community to participate in the implement in accordance to the strategic educational goals, particularly in building new young men and women to be new socialist people

7. Increase the leadership of the party and the government toward educational affairs, as they are the leaders with good attentions and visions.[15]

That is, all students, including ethnic minorities were to learn "how to be a new revolutionary citizen of the Lao PDR." Women and ethnic minority groups received relatively open opportunities and access to education. In a 1990 Ministry of Education report, by 1988 there were 571,630 primary students, of whom 254,042 were girls. 15.65 percent or 89,434 (with 35,739 girls) were "Lao Thueng" (*Mon-Khmer* linguistic groups) while nearly 4 percent or 22,185 (with 5,743 girls) were "Lao Soung" (*Hmong-Yao* linguistic groups). Lao education of this period was hoping to produce an educated and skilled workforce in line with the capitalist labor market even as the government maintained the need for "nationalism-socialism" that manifested nearly every textbook and that students had to learn by rote and apply in their social life at school.

CONTEMPORARY EDUCATION

In the 1990s with the entry of a wide range of foreign aid donors, the government's vision of Human Resource Development (HRD)[16] was further developed (MOE, 1998b). For instance, the whole educational system was more established and better structured as a result of the "Education For All" (EFA) project. However, the core idea of "educating youths of Laos" for national integration and nationalism remained strong.

In 1990, MOE representatives attended the UNESCO World Conference on Education For All for the first time. That meeting resulted in a few key proclamations. For instance, *Article 1: Meeting Basic Learning Needs* mentions that everyone, young as well as adults, benefits from education. The same article also defines the scope of "education" to include knowledge and skills for survival, developing professional capacities, living and working in dignity, access to the basic right of self decision making, and "to participate fully in development." Second, it must empower individuals' decision making (in socioeconomic matters and politics) through "*their collective, linguistic and spiritual heritage*... and to work for international peace and solidarity in an independent world." Third, "education development is the transmission and enrichment of *common cultural and moral values.*"[17] The two highlighted points interestingly and clearly fit well within the Lao nationalistic education policies of the two prior periods, particularly the term collective, linguistic, and spiritual heritage, since ethnic Lao culture and Buddhism that have already been defined as the national character and identity are specifically mentioned in Section IX of the 1991 Constitution of the Lao PDR. Thus, the EFA brought few changes to the Laos' educational policy except to modernize the nationalism concept, which was used to integrate ethnic minority populations.

Another example of how the EFA modernized the Lao nationalism concept in education is clearly shown in the Lao Education Laws issued in 2000. Article 1 of EFA carries the key words related to the concept of basic learning (including knowledge, skills, values, and attitudes) for survival as well as participation in development, which is determined by the individual countries. Articles 1 and 2 of the Education Laws of the Lao PDR read as follows:

Article 1: Role of Education Law
The role of Education Law is to define the principles, regulations, and various measures related educational activities so as to develop people to be good citizens who are equipped with a correct understanding about the Party's direction, the state's laws, social morality, patriotism, democracy, solidarity amongst ethnic groups [who] love and care for the beautiful and unique cultures and traditions which are the heritage of the country . . . [T]his is to equip people to participate in the [security] protection and development of the country as so to gradually base national progress on the concept of national education, science, progress, and modernity.

Article 2: Concept of Education
Education is the learning process with the purposes of educating people about national policies, perceptions, morality, wisdom, arts, physical education, and other activities. The main task of education is to continuously provide general and all round knowledge to Lao people of all ethnic groups. This is to develop the conditions for all Lao citizens to be able to develop themselves within the society effectively according to one's rights and obligations.[18]

Although the Education For All scheme probably encouraged the adoption of the Law, the passage's emphasis remains on nationalism. Similar to the directions for education pronounced by Kaysone Phomvihane in 1979, the emphasis remains on "education" as an apparatus to produce "socialism" people for the government and the Party. The concept of "socialism" is also expanded into the modern knowledge of sciences, technology, politics, economics, society, and culture that one is supposed to have as stated in Article 2. *Modern* knowledge, as defined by both the Lao government and International organizations, is based on "Western" economic development concepts. That is: people are poor because they do not have "education." In other words, people are "*backward*," and lack "*knowledge*" that can be used to survive in their daily life as well as to "participate in the country's development" (Article 1 of EFA). Thus, both the EFA and the Lao Education Law are developed based on a shared "discourse of education" as a solution to all social problems. This discourse permeates all levels of formal education in Laos.

The education discourse is being modernized every time Laos encounters foreign education consultants who contribute their knowledge, particularly their worldview on *poverty*. Ethnic minorities are immediately considered as being "poor" although sometimes the "majority" is "poorer" than some "ethnic minorities." Yet, what marks them as "ethnic," "minority," or "poverty" has origins in French colonialism (Anderson, 1987: 1). The concept of "poverty reduction" has spread throughout Laos in the past five years. This concept is intensely discussed in Vientiane before being translated into detailed plans for implementations of all provinces. Most people in Laos focus on poverty reduction among ethnic minorities. For instance, according to an MOE report on *National Education for All* (2004: 28), "72 out of 142 districts have been identified as poor. Most of these districts are located in mountainous areas (habitats of ethnic population)."

Preschool Education

Preschool education is believed to be a solution to the chronically low quality of education in Laos. According to the MOE, children will perform better in primary schooling if they have been to kindergarten schooling for at least a year or two (MOE, 2000). From 1975 to mid-1985, the purpose of preschooling was to share childcare between parents and government. Preschooling was also designed and set up as to share the childcare burden from parents, particularly mothers, so they could participate more in the revolutionary tasks in schools, factories, cooperatives, and hospitals (ADB, 1992: 10; Dolittle, 1998: 28). This is in contrast to the MOE report, where the concept of preschooling was part of a general discourse of education as a solution to all social problems. That is, when a child is better and more prepared in his/her early years, s/he performs qualitatively in the next level of education; thus, growing up as a quality person within the society.

Preschool education is set up for a target group of children between two–six years old, with a maximum nurturing time of three years (see Figure 8.2). Most preschools are also located near large construction projects, agricultural and forestry projects, and farms. In 1989, there were 188 daycare centers and 638 kindergartens throughout the country, all of which were government-run. From 1991 onward, the MOE allowed the private sector to provide preschooling.

Figure 8.2
Structure of the Education System of the Lao PDR

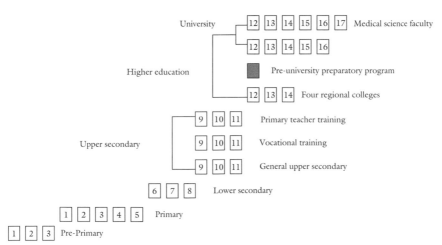

In 1997–1998, preschools increased 11.8 percent with the total number of 39,187 students as reported by the MOE. However, this figure was collected from kindergartens, which are mostly located in urban or more populated areas, such as the main town of each province, where there are more nuclear families and more parents can afford preschool education. In the rural areas parents are mostly nonethnic Lao and have different concepts of their young children's formal education due to their cultural traditions (i.e., a "baby" may be between 2–4 years of age in a *Mouteun* village).

Primary Education

Primary education is a five-year cycle in urban areas and a three-year cycle (incomplete primary education) commonly exists in remote areas. The age of students of this level of education are from 6–15, depending on the location of the schools. In urban areas, their ages are 6 years old in grade 1 and 10–11 by the time they finish grade 5. In rural areas, children start to enroll in grade 1 when they are about 7–8 years old and by the time they finish grade 5, some would be 12–15 years old. This is due to the high dropout and grade retention rates. According to the data from MOE, there were 317,126 primary level students in 1975, 463,098 in 1980, and 561,806 students in 1985.[19] In 1990–1991, there were 590,801 students and 762,539 students in 1995. In 2000–2001, there were 829,887 students attending 8,192 primary schools throughout the country. In other words, the number of students increased from 1990 to 1995 by 3.44 percent, and 11.32 percent from 1995 to 2000. These statistics are less impressive when compared with the population growth rate of 70 percent. This is because the majority of the population are still living in rural areas. These groups of people normally have more children than those living in the urban areas of Laos.

The primary education curriculum is strongly focusing on Lao language, mathematics, and "the world around us." Lao language takes up 45 percent of the total instructional hours while mathematics takes 23 percent and "the world around us" and other supplementary subjects, such as handicrafts, physical, and performing arts, take the rest out of 726 hours of grades 1–2 and out of 759 hours of grades 3–5. This seems less problematic for ethnic Lao students who live in the urban areas but the most difficult thing to implement for teachers and students in the rural areas and ethnic minority students who are non-Lao speakers. For example, a teacher from a Phonesoung boarding school for ethnic minorities complained that ethnic students (mostly *Xo* and *Slang* under the *Mon-Khmer* linguistic group) could not understand Lao language lessons and had to be retained in the same grades for at least one more year.

The primary education curriculum is designed within the Lao national context (i.e., ethnic Lao culture and Buddhism), which is less relevant to the life of ethnic minority children. For example, many lessons in the Lao language textbook of grade 2 are illustrated with pictures of "good children/students of their parents/teachers" wearing Lao skirts with their palms together showing respect to their parents after arriving home (lesson 18: 47). The homes and houses illustrated are typical Lao style houses (lesson 20: 52). They also learn that Vientiane is the capital, where the *civilization* exists. This message is transmitted through the topic "visiting my uncle in Vientiane." This topic takes three lessons illustrated with pictures of a playground with rides and a merry-go-round at That Luang (a Buddhist stupa that is now the national symbol), and a picture of a *road with traffic lights* near That Luang square (lessons 30–32: 80–87). The texts of the three lessons introduce students to vocabulary related to national symbols, such as the Jade Buddha statue, which is now located in Bangkok. In the same lesson, the term "vatthanatham" or "culture" is translated as "modernity" (p. 88). Primary students of all ethnicities within the Lao PDR start to learn how to be Lao at a very early stage of their formal education. These lessons, in addition, are delivered by ethnic Lao teachers.

The next issue for primary education is the quality of teachers. Most trained teachers graduate from primary education before continuing in teacher training for 4 years under a 5 + 4 system. The latter teachers graduated from lower secondary schooling before taking teaching courses for 4 years (i.e., 8 + 4). Some teachers in rural schools, particularly the incomplete primary schools,[20] have finished only grade 3 or 5. They have never undergone teacher training but are assigned to teach because they are the only locals who know how to read and write and who have migrated elsewhere. These teachers are mostly ethnic minorities themselves and are considered "unqualified" or "untrained" teachers. This problem still exists as the MOE does not have many choices because the teacher training graduates do not want to teach in rural schools. Thus, primary education in the last decades has faced a lack of teachers that was a big problem during the RLG period.

Secondary Education

Before 1995, secondary education was divided into two levels, three years of lower and another three years at the upper secondary education. Nowadays, the two levels have been combined within a six-year cycle. However, similar to primary schooling, there are three types of secondary schooling: schools that provide years 1–3, schools that provide years 4–6, and another where students undergo all 6 years within the same school compound. This change, however, remains the same as lower and upper secondary schooling, except the last type. Secondary education grew rapidly after 1978, from 11 schools with 2,517 students in 1975 to 107 schools with 38, 794 students in 1978. During the first eight years under the new government, lower secondary student enrollment increased 27.07 percent per year, from 38,794 students to 69,226 students in 1985. Upper secondary education was the least developed of all formal education areas during that time. However, comparatively the increasing data of students of this level was the most impressive. From 2,517 students in 1975 to 20,093 in 1985, the enrollment growth rate was 97.53 percent per year. In 1990, there were 122,718 students and 156,704 students in 1995.

The curriculum at this level of education has changed very little. In 1990, the MOE introduced a new secondary curriculum that "political studies" was replaced with "population studies." Other subjects, including mathematics, chemistry, biology, history, Lao language and literature, and geography remain unchanged in terms of instructional hours and the importance of the subjects. Some content has been edited in Lao language and literature. History and geography carry the same texts used after 1975. These two subjects are now combined under a new term, "Social Sciences." This subject is for secondary 1–3, while "Population Studies" starts to be introduced to students of secondary 4–6.

The content of "Social Sciences" subjects are designed to provide students at the ages of 12–20 with a more solid knowledge of "commonness" through many lessons comparing various peoples of Laos, and also Laos with the outside world. For example, a text on population in secondary year 1, provides a definition of "Sat" (nation or country) as "a country and people who hold citizenship of residing country; a group of people are biologically related, sharing same race, religion, language, history, culture, and live under the same government" (p. 157). The teacher later elaborates that it is the Lao nation and Lao peoples of various races, sharing the first king myth and legend of *Fa Ngum* and that it is a *Buddhist* country as stated in the Constitution.[21] Interestingly, Fa Ngum, who was the first king of Lane Xang Kingdom is considered the king of the entire Lao PDR, even though it was the French who consolidated political control over the entire country. Thus, all students regardless of their ethnic background learn that this is their shared history although many of them are non-Buddhists. The teachers are graduates of a three-year teacher training course or 11 + 3 system (i.e., 11 years of regular schooling plus 3 years of teacher training).

By 2000, there were 283,713 students with 44,604 lower secondary graduates, and 20,452 upper secondary graduates in 2001. Many of these students continue with higher education in private or public schools. In fact, many ethnic minority students, particularly girls drop out before reaching secondary year three or six. This is because of the irrelevance of the national curriculum. In addition, ethnic minority parents hold different cultural views on their daughters' formal education and future life. At the same time, many ethnic Lao teachers as well as revolutionary educators believe that ethnic students deserve only primary education because, according to a teacher at Phonesoung primary school, "they will not need it while in the field. Knowing how to speak and count in Lao should be sufficient unless they want to join the national military."[22] However, this does not mean there is no effort to promote higher levels of education for ethnic minorities. The MOE as well as the LPRP have established three ethnic minority secondary boarding schools throughout the country.

Boarding Schooling for Ethnic Minorities (1998–Present)

Boarding schools for ethnic minorities are established in two separate levels, a primary level belonging to the Provincial Education Office (PEO), and a secondary level managed by the MOE. There are three regional ethnic minority boarding schools in Oudomxay, Savannakhet, and Saravan. They offer a complete six-year secondary education. There are 14 primary level schools that are under Provincial Education Offices in the remaining 14 provinces. The curriculum at both levels is the same as the national curriculum used throughout the country. The instructional language is Lao. There is no bilingual option. Teachers are usually native Lao speakers, mostly from the central regions. However, many teachers are ethnic minorities themselves but they feel shy to speak their native languages to their students. Partially, this is because of a discourse that considers ethnic minorities poor and backward. Thus, a teaching position requires an "educated person" who should speak more Lao language and lead his or her life under the scientific guidance of the LPRP.[23] After students finish their formal education in the boarding schools, they are expected to return to their home villages.

In neighboring China and Vietnam boarding schools have become a crucial part of the government's strategy for minority education. Anthropologist Mette Halskov Hansen, in her excellent study of minority education in southwestern China, says these schools are regarded positively by the local government and educators because:

The boarding school has more control over students, who cannot easily leave; students spend more time studying because they live at school; their parents have no influence on what they do in their spare time; they cannot participate in time-consuming religious activities; and they use the Chinese language more than they would at home. All minority secondary boarding schools are situated in country or prefectural capitals, where students from various minority ethnic groups and villages are gathered and subjected to a standardized education.[24]

Hansen is neither in favor of nor against the boarding schooling in south China but feels that the structure of boarding schooling facilitates the transmission of certain values and social practices to students who live far away from home for years. Teachers as well as students soon create a sense of commonality and shared experience among students from various ethnic backgrounds (Hansen, 1999: 22). This is, to all intents and purposes, national integration.

In the Laotian case, Mr. Vongphachan Vilayhom, the Head, Ethnic Education Division, explains the role of boarding schools in this way:

The establishment of Ethnic Minority Boarding Schools is based on socio-economic development demands in remote areas. This [form of schooling] develops ethnic personnel for the government, ethnic technicians for society as well as to develop solidarity, equality, and the ongoing drive to provide school access for ethnic minorities. It is an institution for teaching basic knowledge and skills, for growing morality and sensitivity towards the changing and sciences or the world, for training patience, and for preparing them to whole heartedly participate in local development, and to be a source of knowledge about the state, heritage of the country, basic rights and obligations as Lao citizens, independence, and the *civilized* lifestyle.[25]

Vongphachan is also a former Ph.D. graduate from Vietnam. He views that education for ethnic minorities in Laos can be accomplished through this boarding schooling. When asked why there is only this specific boarding schooling program available for ethnic students, he told me that it was the government policy as so to provide them "scientific knowledge," particularly the knowledge that would help them to increase their agricultural productivities. He continued "a number of ethnic minorities are still living off the land and are ignorant. We need to bring them *civilization*." When I asked for clarification of the term, he simply told me "civilization is buildings, cars, roads, electricity, clean Water supply, technology, and information, particularly, from international broadcasting channels." Thus, the Laotian education for ethnic minorities through boarding schooling seems to be education of the backward.

Vongphachan as well as other graduates from Vietnam view theVietnamese government as having been successful with its boarding schooling for ethnic minorities. He also complained that Laos does not invest enough in making this boarding schooling work well like in Vietnam. I then asked whether or not ethnic students should attend normal schooling as part of the EFA scheme launched by the MOE with funding from external sources. I also asked this question to Mr. Ly Tu, and Mr. Khamhoung, the Director of the General Education Department in the MOE. Both Khamhoung, and Ly Tu replied, as Vongphachan had, that "ethnic minorities need *special treatments* because they are 'poor' and live in inaccesible areas. Only the government and LPRP personnel devote their energy and sincerity to bring education to those ethnic children as well as adults. It is also the responsibility of the LPRP and the government. This is because they are descendants of *Lao peoples of all ethnic groups*."[26] It is, therefore, evident that the boarding schooling concept is not only for schooling for the backward but also to facilitate national integration as well as political control of minorities in Laos.

Teacher Training, Vocational and Higher Education

Teacher Training

The LPRP and the government recognize the shortage of teachers as posing a big problem for Laos. From the late 1970s to early 1980s, many primary graduates and most secondary graduates were sent to nearby teachers' colleges. There were a great number of teacher graduates at that time. As a requirement and obligation, they had to teach for some years under the allocation of the government. Some of them were allocated back to their hometown; while some were sent to remote areas with a small compensation and incentive package. The quality of their training was poor and patriotism oriented. After the introduction of NEM and the WB, IMF, ADB prescription of restructuring the government administration, there was a huge lay off of government employees, including teachers. Teachers in remote areas now enjoy more flexible job choices that offer more income than teaching. As a result, the government continues to lose both qualified and nonqualified teachers.

In 1989, there were 59 teachers' colleges, including 41 for preschool and primary teachers (5 + 1, 5 + 2, 5 + 3, 8 + 1, 8 + 2, 8 + 3), 17 for lower secondary (5 + 3, 8 + 1, 8 + 3) and one for upper secondary, which is at Dong Dok (11 + 4). The enrollments at that time were high. Over 4,000 students were in primary teacher training, 3,000 in lower secondary, and nearly 3,000 in Dong Dok These new graduates were more than adequate to fill vacancies in school at all levels. The one major challenge was how to retain them within the profession. Many teacher trainees decided to drop out for economic and family reasons. The completion rate was, however, still high at 72 percent in 1990 (ADB, 1992: 20). Currently, the MOE is redesigning the teacher training curriculum and reducing the number of training institutions. There are now 13 teacher training colleges remaining throughout the country. According to the government, this is to reduce expenses and to focus on the quality of students. A practical problem that remains is that new graduates are not given teacher guidebooks to help them teach the new curriculum.

The curriculum of teacher training education is designed by the National Research Institute for Sciences and Education (NRIES). The NRIES is the only central office in charge of curriculum at all formal education levels in Laos. At this level of education, the curriculum aims to provide teaching pedagogical methods to students. It provides little upgrading of students' content of knowledge in the subject areas they will teach. This is because students are assumed to have learned the necessary content during their own secondary education. Many students lack confidence to teach because they feel unsure of the content.

Teachers in these colleges are former graduates of Dong Dok teacher training college and some are former graduates from the former Eastern bloc and Vietnam. However the traditionally low prestige of teachers results in many of them leaving after returning from short or long term training abroad. Many who decide to stay are posted to administrative positions.

Vocational–Technical Education

The new Lao definition and policy on vocational and technical schooling is to provide skills and to prepare youths for the labor market. This is based on the national development plan that aims to eradicate poverty from the country by the year 2020 (MOE, 2004). Students graduating from grade 5 and grade 8 (lower secondary year 3) can continue with this education, in addition to upper secondary and/or university education. Vocational and technical education of the Lao PDR during 1975–1995 provided training that was sufficient enough for civil service work. Graduates of this period received certificates equivalent to the upper secondary education level. The training was only available in forestry (Nabong Forestry School), accounting (Dong Kham Xang School), and a two-year polytechnic school. There was also one private accounting school (Pakpasak School) in Vientiane. Higher education equivalent to university was unavailable. There was only the Medical University of Vientiane offering a seven-year course. Dong Dok Teacher Training University was not a full university but a teacher training college offering a 4–5 year course. Graduates of this institution became teachers in upper secondary schools. There were Polytechnic and Architecture colleges providing 4–5 year courses. After the establishment of the National University of Laos (NUOL) in 1995, the structures of these schools were also changed. Dong Dok became the main campus for the NUOL while the medical university, polytechnic, architecture, and forestry colleges became faculties within it.

At present, there are two separate systems of vocational training: private and state-funded schools. Private schools are to prepare students to work for the private sector while the state ones are to prepare students to work as government employees. Sometimes, state vocational schools are located within various ministries, such as Agriculture, Public Health, Construction and Post, Culture and Information, and Finance. In fact, most of the time, these departments have their own vocational–technical school, but under the support and management of the MOE. Recently, the private sector has been permitted to take part in this field. There are more English language and accounting training centers open today.

There are 6,630 new graduates from lower and upper secondary education enrolled in the existing vocational schools. The most popular area of training is Communication-Construction and Post with 3,672 students in 2000. The training under this provides skills needed by electricians, mechanics, secretaries, and typists. Over 2,300 are enrolled at Dong Kham Xang Accounting School. This school trains students in basic accounting used in the Customs Office, Ministry of Finance. About 1,566 students are enrolled in Agriculture and Forestry, while 580 students are enrolled in Arts and Music.

Teachers in these vocational and technical schools are former graduates from the Eastern bloc. This is sometimes an issue for the quality of graduates. That is, many private companies and the government require market-oriented knowledge, once regarded as the negative side of the capitalist world by many former socialist countries. However, they are now being updated with new technology and information from Thailand (with which Laos shares linguistic and cultural similarities).

In regard to ethnic minority students, the boarding school principals, whom I interviewed, as well as Mr. Vongphachan, share a common discourse about ethnic minorities as uncivilized people, and that "vocational training would show them more modern and civilized methods of agriculture" (June 5, 2003). They believe that graduates of the boarding schools are better suited to vocational and technical training rather than a higher level of education. However, many ethnic students at the Oudomxay Boarding School have dreams of continuing at the NUOL or even abroad. One *Khmu* student told me that he wanted to study Law and French after his graduation.

The National University Of Laos (NUOL)

The NUOL was established in 1995 with nine faculties. It has set up a curriculum with the national economic development goal of producing qualified lecturers and researchers. A bachelor's degree may be obtained within four years of study. Sometimes, this process takes longer depending on the areas and subjects of studies, for instance, five years for architectural school and seven years for medical school. During the first few years of its operations, NUOL admitted students through the "quota system"[27] and open entrance examination. In 1997, there were 4,305 students enrolled in the bachelor's degree program.[28] There are also students enrolled with *certificate* and *special section*, which made the total number of students 8,053.[29] However in recent years, the number of students has been increasing steadily. According to the NUOL's newly created website, the statistics show that the total number of students was 22,624 in year 2004–2005, and 26,673 in year 2005–2006. These figures indicate that 50 percent of all admissions are through the "quota system." Fifteen percent of all quota students are successful students with outstanding performances during their secondary school leaving examination. Twenty percent are students who are government civil servants. Ten percent are top students from the provinces while 5 percent is reserved for ethnic minorities from the three secondary boarding schools. Nonquota admissions are for students who have successfully taken the entrance examination, which is open to every student. For example, there were 11,879 students in year 2004–2005 or a little over 50 percent of the total number of students, while in year 2005–2006 a little more than 40 percent or 14,141 of the total students were under nonquota admissions. The top 5 percent of entrance examinees receive tuition fee waiver awards till their graduation. The rest are obliged to pay 50–80 percent more than the regular fees set by the university.

One related concern provided by the University Dean is the distribution of students in different faculties. The most popular faculties among students are medical sciences, economics and management, engineering and architecture, law, and foreign languages, especially English and French. The least popular faculty for students is education because of the low esteem for teaching. However, the number demonstrated in Table 8.3 shows a higher number of students. This is because of the NUOL's new policy on issuing scholarships to all students who enroll in this Faculty. The number has been increased from a little over

Table 8.3
Faculties within the National University of Laos and Students by Faculties in the Years 2005–2006

1	School of Foundation Studies	2,766
2	Faculty of Sciences	889
3	Faculty of Engineering	4,984
4	Faculty of Agriculture	960
5	Faculty of Medical Sciences	1,321
6	Faculty of Letters	3,326
7	Faculty of Education	3,636
8	Faculty of Economics and Business Administration	3,295
9	Faculty of Architecture	792
10	Faculty of Laws and Political Sciences	2,273
11	Faculty of Forestry	1,381
12	Faculty of Social Sciences	773
13	Environment Development Center	277
	Total	26,673

Note: See www.nuol.edu.la.

300 students in year 1998–1999 to 3,326 students in 2005–2006. However, over 70 percent or 2,703 students belonging to the "special section" are also eligible for the scholarship. Thus, the Faculty of Education will remain unattractive but for the provision of scholarships to a large number of students.

David Chapman (2002) states that the establishment of a national university is to fulfill three national development agendas: (1) as a symbol of national identity and international prestige, (2) to gain funding, and (3) to strengthen the quality and relevance of the education provided at the university. He argues that in the case of Laos the NUOL has been less than successful in the last agenda because of lacking "re-examination of the relationships of the university to the national government and of university employees to their institution" (Chapman, 2002: 93). However, this chapter is concerned with nationalism of Laos within the context of education, which is the first agenda. This is because, with regard to the second agenda, it is obvious that Laos is a "third world" country, lacking its own funding and relying heavily on international funding (Evans, 1998, 1999b, 2000, and 2002). The first agenda for the NUOL has been more successfully attained. Many international consultants visiting Laos as part of international funding projects had suggested that Laos should have its own higher education institution to train Lao citizens. The establishment of NUOL, thus, has assisted Laos in developing and strengthening the social-economic and cultural symbols of national identity. For example, Chapman (2002) provides that this agenda is implemented through the use of Lao language as the only instructional language at the NUOL although the language has not been standardized.[30] Certainly this pride is in contrast with the French colonial period, when higher education was conducted only in French and was unavailable inside Laos.

Another issue facing the NUOL is the level of academic knowledge of teachers and lecturers. According to an MOE report (MOE, 1999), there are 1,043 teachers. 102 teachers have vocational certificates, 7 have technical diplomas, 6 have higher technical diplomas, 665 have bachelors' degrees, 2 are postgraduates, 180 have masters, and 81 have doctoral degrees. These people are trained in various former Eastern bloc countries as well as Vietnam and China. Upon their return to Laos, they have brought along diverse knowledge, teaching styles, and cultures. As a result, curriculum has been based on individuals' personal academic experiences, which have not been organized systematically and conceptually; thus, diluting the knowledge delivered to students. The NUOL still faces the problem of insufficient capacity to train researchers and lecturers as well as their students while achieving the task of strengthening the national identity.

A DAY AT SCHOOL IN A SECONDARY BOARDING SCHOOL FOR ETHNIC MINORITIES (OUDOMXAY PROVINCE)

A Day at School: Bocher, a *Mouteun* Student

Bocher first experienced formal education when he was 12 in 1992. He was the only one from his village to attend school. Bocher has a special talent in learning how to speak many different languages in a short time. His father was the head of the village at that time. His father was officially obliged to send him, to a primary school in a *Lue* village, about four km away from his village. He completed third grade or the final year of the Lue incomplete primary school. He was sent to a complete primary boarding school for ethnic minorities in Na Mor district of Oudomxay province. Bocher was there only for one year before being sent to a newly opened boarding school for ethnic minorities in the main town of Oudomxay. Since 1997, he has been a student at the Oudomxay boarding school. Bocher graduated last year. Now, he is in a preparatory year at the NUOL.

A day at the Oudomxay boarding school for ethnic minorities of Bocher begins at 5:30 A.M. The weather is rather dark and gloomy as it is a typical winter day with fog and mist floating down the hills of a northern province of Laos. Bocher and other students look cold and sleepy. They walk slowly to the playground for the morning physical exercises, which many students are not keen on in such weather regardless of how healthy it is for them and what they have learned from their basic natural sciences class. They feel sleepy while trying to raise their arms and then reach their feet. They finish their morning exercises within five minutes. Bocher is more awake than other students because it is his turn to lead other students for the daily playground cleaning. Students do it quickly and finish by 6:00 A.M. By this time, they are all awake although many of them return to their beds. Bocher as well as many other students get themselves ready for classes. The school has stopped providing breakfast for the last two years. They get their breakfast from the neighbors who happen to be their teachers and who own either cooked food or snack stands in front of their houses. Their salary (between US$30 to 50 per month) is available to them once in three months and that lasts only one month. They have economic reasons to make extra money from their students as they realize well that many parents of their ethnic minority students earn more than many teachers do. Bocher also has a monthly allowance from the school (around US$9 per month) besides the money sent by his parents. In the morning, Bocher always has a bowl of instant noodle soup, costing him around 1,000 kip (about 10 cent of a US dollar), which he can easily afford, since his father is relatively rich. Other students do odd jobs for their teachers in exchange for food security. Breakfast for these students consists of steamed sticky rice and some chilly paste, just enough to start off the day.

Students are in a hurry today because it is Monday morning, when the whole school gathers for the weekly meeting and to salute the national flag. Today is also ethnic dress day. All students are supposed to wear their traditional dress. Yet, there are times when students do not have any idea how distinctive their "ethnic tradition" dresses are, particularly the *Lue*, *Thai Dam*, *Thai Khao*, ethnic Lao from *Khmu*. They have to wear something to show that they are "ethnic minorities." Their solution is to borrow a blouse or dress from *Khmu* or *Hmong* friends, who have distinctive and colorful dresses. On other days students have to wear their uniform of white shirt and black or dark blue long pants for boys or Lao skirts for girls. Teachers, too, wear their uniform (grey-brownish safari suits) only on Mondays. Today, Bocher borrows a dress from his *Hmong* class-mate as it is his turn to report in front of all students and teachers about who breaks the school regulations. Before his report begins, all students have to sing the national anthem and to wait for all teachers to arrive at the podium. After all teachers are seated around 8:05 A.M., Bocher reads his report. The report is a template of which students have been good or bad. Bad students are those who have missed their morning exercises or classes or evening school activities, or have cooked food by themselves, or have had inappropriate relationships with their schoolmates or teachers. Then, the principal comes up to present the weekly plan and deliver propaganda education, particularly the importance of the boarding school for ethnic minorities. What he emphasizes most is the meaning of being ethnic minority students or special students. They are special because they are "ethnic minorities" who are poor and they need this education for a better life to break away from the "superstitious beliefs," and unscientific and backward lives of their parents. They are special and need this education so they will gain "scientific" knowledge to improve the "quality of life" for their home villages and their parents.

The meeting continues till 9:00 A.M. Students are allowed to go to their class-rooms according to the daily schedule. This morning Bocher has a "population study" class. The teacher comes to the class a little later than normal. He makes an excuse that he was busy taking care of his new baby and that he has just returned from foraging for food in the forest. He starts the lesson by asking students where he left off the last time before continuing to read the text from the textbooks. Today's lesson is about the structure of the National Parliament of Laos and Legislation, which he appears to find confusing as he was trained as a Chemistry teacher in Vietnam. This is not surprising. Oudomxay town has a population of only 30,000 people, who are mostly nonethnic Lao. Ethnic Lao are a minority there. A large number of "Lao Loum" or the mainstream group do not know much about the government because they are living in the areas where official central power has less control over their life.[31] On the other hand, the local government appears to remain equally irrelevant to local ethnic minority people. Of course, the government is aware of this. Thus, the boarding school has been set up to train ethnic minority youths to help maintain the central government's power. However, boarding school students have also observed the irrelevance of government to the people. Thus, they pay less attention to what the teachers say and memorize this lesson in order to pass the final examination rather than seeing it as useful knowledge. And, this is the routine of teaching and learning that happens at this school as well as in many others in Laos.

The morning classes break for lunch around 12:00 P.M., but teachers tend to end the classes earlier as they have to prepare for their own lunch at home. The school prepares lunches and dinners for students at the canteen, where all students stand while eating. I asked the teacher in charge why there were no chairs. He replied, "there are enough chairs for all students but they do not know 'table manners.' These students are special because some of them have parents while some do not have. They are all from rural areas where sitting on a chair and eat[ing] meals on the table is not part of their 'cultures.' So, to treat all of the[m] equally, we let them stand and later they will be taught 'table manners.' This process takes time." I asked him to clarify. He says "education and to civilize them." However, students do not view it as a way to civilization but rather as oppression. Bocher's eating culture is to sit on a long knee-high bench with food on a table. He eats rice (not sticky rice) in a small bowl with chopsticks (similarly to the Chinese style). Yet, he learns what is civilization through the culture of eating by having meals with his Lao teachers. They show him the "Lao" way of eating. That is, sitting on the floor next to a rattan round shaped tray, about 12 inches off the floor. Bocher learns to use his hands to hold sticky rice in one of his palm and how to dip the rice in various dishes on the tray. He enjoys the food and the eating style while his teachers tell him that it is the "educated and civilized" way of eating, not the standing style nor the rice bowl and chopsticks.

Two nonethnic Lao students are steaming sticky rice, the national staple food symbol, at the school backyard and behind a teacher's residence. This photo is showing a labor exchange for food between students and their teachers. Courtesy of Manynooch Faming.

Afternoon classes start at 2:00 P.M. and last till 4:00 P.M. This afternoon, Bocher learns about the national history of Laos. The teacher is a *Hmong* who graduated from the History Department of the NUOL in 2004. Initially, he was hoping to work for the Lao National Front for Construction (LNFC)[32] at its Oudomxay office. He tells me, "I hoped to apply my historical knowledge of the Hmong to help the LNFC develop policies for the Hmong. But, LNFC thinks that I am better off teaching at this boarding school because of my degree in history. The policies at present are good the way they are. So, they sent my c.v. to the boarding school." I ask what he finds in the history textbook, meaning the content. He says that it is just the same as what he learned at the NUOL. That is, the history started with Fa Ngum in the 13th century, then the French came and finally the American neo-colonialism. He told me that he did not like the French period because it separated "Lao people" into three different groups: "Lao Loum," "Lao Theung," and "Lao Soung." He claimed that this categorization came attached with socioeconomic status, for example, the *Hmong* were to be growing opium for the French. I asked if he included this in his teaching. He said yes. Thus, Bocher learns a national history that does not include his ethnic group while expressing sympathy for the French oppression of the *Hmong*.

The only *Hmong* teacher is teaching his "ethnic minority" students about the national history of Laos. This hour he is teaching about the invasion of the French, how the *Hmong* and other ethnic groups joined the revolution and how they helped to conquer the French. Courtesy of Manynooch Faming.

Soon after 4:00 P.M., all students are dismissed. Some go back to their dorm rooms while some go to the football field, and many go into the wood to find bamboo shoots for their dinner. Dinner prepared by the school is never enough nor good. Cooking in or outside the canteen is illegal but there is no punishment. This is because the teachers themselves realize well how bad the school cook is. They do not mind hosting students at their houses for dinner some time or letting them cook for themselves occasionally. Thus, Bocher is learning not only in the classroom but also sharing his life outside school with the *Lao Loum* teachers. The latter play a major role in "Laoizing" Bocher and other nonethnic Lao or *Lao Loum* students. This is also a hidden agenda of the boarding school for ethnic minorities.

Bocher has to return for the evening tutoring classes (with no teachers unless students pay extra money to the teachers) till 8:00 P.M. These evening classes are nothing but another social gathering for them. He has to go to bed at 9:00 P.M. His roommates and other students must be silent around 9:30 P.M., when a teacher in charge checks each room. Before Bocher falls asleep, he and his roommates share details of their personal lives, such as families and future dreams after graduating from this boarding school. The most popular stories shared amongst them relate to their future. For Bocher, he wants to work for a governmental office and marry a Lao wife, settle down and have a house in the main town of Oudomxay or in a bigger town rather than going back to his village. He views it as "backward" and "uncivilized" although it is only 4 km from the Chinese border, where there are more "modern" products available. As a result of living near the Chinese border, Bocher is exposed to a different "modernity." Every time he comes back from his home visit, Bocher has a new hair cut that looks closer to a Chinese pop singer on a poster. He wears a pair of jeans and a jacket made in China during the weekend. He views the school uniforms and the way the teachers dress as being "out of date." Thus, Bocher is not only experiencing modernity defined within the boarding school and the main town of Oudomxay, but also the one in Thailand (through watching Thai television programs) and China, which is modernizing quickly and certainly faster than Laos.

CONCLUSION: THE LONG ROAD TO LAOIZATION

Formal education in Laos has, since its first introduction there, carried a nationalist purpose. During the French period, modern education was "mission civilasatrice." French formal education, in other words, was to produce local staff for administration work while developing a sense of "greater Indochina." The instructional language was French while classes were available initially only from grades 1–3 and later included the lower secondary education level (lycée). The common sense of Indochina and language of instruction, on the contrary, provided opportunities for ethnic minorities to be on a par with the dominant ethnic Lao in terms of formal education, unlike the traditional Buddhist temple-based schooling which was unavailable for non-Buddhist ethnic minorities and women. Although the education provided by the French was criticized by the subsequent Royal Lao Government for the French nationalism–colonialism content of education, the French had successfully set up basic modern educational facilities for both regimes.

The RLG benefited from this. This resulted in the rapid expansion of primary formal education during late 1950s to early 1960s. The number of primary students increased remarkably. The RLG announced some education reforms, particularly ones in reaction to the French system. These included sending the Vietnamese teachers back to Vietnam, causing the RLG to lose a large number of qualified teachers. This problem has persisted to the present. Another reform was the adoption of the Lao language as the national language and the language of instruction. This was in contrast to its lack of use in instruction during the French colonial period. However, the Lao language was used at the primary education level while secondary and higher education remained in French. The content of history was redesigned by including the myth of first Lao King, Fa Ngum. These attempts at "Laoization" disadvantaged nonethnic Lao students as they lacked "socio-cultural capital" compared to the ethnic Lao students. Formal education in general was well developed up to higher education level but very little was provided for ethnic minorities.

During the late 1960s, the Pathet Lao provided ethnic minorities within their liberated zone a nonformal and informal education focusing on education for literacy rather than formal schooling. The content of the textbooks was geared toward Leninism-Marxism doctrines while the instructional language was still Lao. However, unlike the RLG, the Pathet Lao could recruit more ethnic teachers to teach their own people, a more effective way to deliver the revolutionary propaganda. After their cave education, students of Pathet Lao also had an opportunity to study abroad, particularly in countries in the former Eastern bloc, China, and Vietnam.

After 1975 when the country officially became the Lao PDR, education was once again the object of reform, and was subject to both internal and external influences. There were attempts to imbibe revolutionary inspiration to attain socialism. Efforts were made to improve equity of participation among women and ethnic minorities. The number of students increased sharply during the first 10 years of LPDR while the quality of education remained weak due to the lack of teaching materials and qualified teachers, who had mostly fled the country after the new regime took over. After the introduction of the NEM during the mid-1980s, the LPDR government revised the concept of "human resources development," aiming to produce workforce for the "labor market." This proved superficial as the curriculum and content of textbooks remained unchanged. The contents manifested the messages of patriotism and revolutionary zeal rather than exposing students to labor market oriented education.

The external influences came from various directions, particularly from international donor-funded development projects. These projects brought international consultants into the country. These consultants were mostly experts in education who hoped to make a change while in practice they both consciously and unconsciously helped the LPDR achieve its national agenda of "Laoization" through all forms of education. For example, the Education For All (EFA) Conference of 1990 forced the LPDR to issue the first Education Laws in 2000 based on a shared discourse that education is the solution to all social problems. That is, people are poor because they lack (modern) knowledge that can be used to survive in their daily lives (Article 1 of EFA). In addition, the concept of "poor" was targeted at ethnic minorities. Education was to provide them with modern knowledge under the guidance of the government.

This resulted in the establishment of boarding schooling for ethnic minorities. Students in these schools used textbooks designed by the central government or the NRIES. The content of textbooks changed very little, except for the covers and more pictures illustrating the national characters, such as *That Luang*, contrasting pictures of urban and rural areas, Lao style houses in comparison to "Lao Theung" and "Lao Soung." Like many other nonboarding school students, Bocher is an example of a boarding school student who has been learning from this type of textbook for 11 years. His case is more intense than students of regular schooling because he has been sharing his social life with students and teachers who are not from the same ethnic group. His school mates and he learn to adopt "Lao Buddhist culture," saluting the flag and the symbolic national characters through textbooks while in practice he learns more through sharing his life with his "Lao Loum" teachers. On the other hand, the teachers view their ethnic minority students as poor and backward, and needing to be civilized. However, these teachers fail to realize what civilization or modernity their students have also been exposed to outside of school.

Education in the LPDR in the last decade has been focusing on "poverty" and less on meeting the needs of the "labor market." Although there has not been an announcement of educational reform, the education system in the LPDR has been changing dramatically, particularly under the influence of the capitalist world. There has been greater private sector investment in all levels of formal education while the MOE takes care of the NUOL and boarding schooling for ethnic minorities. At the same time, this education provides students an opportunity to be "educated persons" within Lao society. However, there are times students go beyond the bounds of the government education agenda, in terms of modernity that they have been exposed to via mass media and crossing the border to neighboring countries. Therefore, in sum, regardless of how education under the LPDR has been re-conceptualized toward international modernity, the core purpose remains unchanged, that is, the mission of civilizing ethnic minorities. Education is not only a tool to provide modern knowledge that is supposed to be a solution to their poverty but also a tool for national integration among ethnic minorities and to have control over them through the hidden agendas of Lao social class, castes, and gender restrictions.

NOTES

1. One can find similar messages on the front pages of local newspapers, particularly where there are speeches made by the government leaders on special occasions such as the National Day of Laos in December of every year. This particular message is excerpted from

the speech of the Deputy Prime Minister of Laos made during the National Educational Meeting in August 2004.

2. Asian Development Bank, 2005, accessed on August 26, 2006 from www.adb.org/Documents/Books/Key_Indicators/2005.

3. Ibid.

4. See *Education in Laos in Historical Perspective* by Bruce M. Lockhart (2001). In this chapter he provides some discussions on the content of History that explains the context of "Lane Xang lost its civilization" and the French rebuilding the Laos state.

5. The transition to the Royal Lao Government regime took place after independence from the French in 1946 but for the first few years the regime remained unchanged. However, Lockhart (2001) claims that during the first 18 months of the 1945–1946 period, Laos had four regimes: "the French (with Japanese presence), the Japanese (after overthrowing the colonial government), the anti-French Lao Issara, and the French once more (with the Lao monarchy)." Full independence came in 1954, at the same time as the territorial expansion of the Lao revolutionaries (or Pathet Lao) led by the Vietnamese communist front in the northern provinces of Laos (Evans, 2002: 92).

6. For an example of the dependency of the RLG on aid money for national development provided by America during the 1950s, see Evans, 2002: 98–105.

7. However, it should be noted that the majority of people in Laos were peasants living in the rural and remote areas. Thus, actual numbers of literate women in rural areas may have been greater than the corresponding numbers among urban women. And, of course, these rural literate women were mostly ethnic Lao.

8. The Lane Xang Kingdoms were unified and founded by King Fa Ngum during the 13th century. For more details and discussion, see Evans, 2002.

9. Pathet Lao originated from the Indochinese Communist Party founded during the late 1940s. The Pathet Lao controlled two northern provinces, Huaphan and Phongsaly of Laos; thus, it had its own agenda for education in that region, which influenced the education reform of the present government, particularly during 1975 and onward.

10. Levinson and Holland (1996: 2) distinguishes education from schooling as two forms of knowledge. He defines "schooling as a state-organized or regulated institution of intentional instruction." This includes both formal and nonformal education for the young and adults. The Pathet Lao was not considered as a government in charge of the whole country of Laos at that time, but rather of two northern provinces. In addition, much of the literature on Laos state that formal schooling under the Pathet Lao was mostly occurring in Vietnam (Langer, 1971, Evans, 1998, 1999a, Goscha, 2000, and Lockhart, 2001).

11. See LPRP, 1979: 6–8.

12. See Chagnon and Rumpf, 1982: 163–180.

13. See Grant Evans (1991: 84–130), for the discussion on the origins of this adopting concept from the former USSR, and how it is applied and operated in the Lao economy.

14. This concept is referred in Lao language as "market." This is because of some political sensitivity that the local government felt not ready to lose political control. After 1975, all businesses were taken over by the government so as to ensure that no corruption and unfair trading (the negative sides of capitalism) existed in the Lao socialist regime. Thus, the term "free labor market" was changed to "market." Yet, the contradiction was that during this period there were not enough foreign investors to provide employment to Lao graduates of all levels. Their only choice was to work in the civil service, which posed

financial problems for the government (Public Administration Reform Project, UNDP: Vientiane, 1995).

15. MOE, 1998a.

16. Human Resources Development or *Karn Patthana Supphanyakorn Manut* was first introduced in 1996 and adopted as the Eighth Priority for the national development in the Sixth Party Congress (March 17–20, 1996), and by the National Assembly in its subsequent sessions. In August 1996, a National Review Conference on Human Resource Development (HRD) identified the most urgent related areas: (1) value formation and training civil servants, (2) quality of education, (3) building the labor force, (4) culture and information, (5) health, and (6) mass organizations such as the Youth Organization, the Lao Women's Union, and the Trade Unions.

17. Extract from "World Declaration on Education For All" in *World Conference on Education For All Report*. See UNESCO (Thailand) (1990).

18. See Lao National Assembly, 2000. The English text is my translation.

19. ADB, 1993.

20. Incomplete primary schools provide education to students of grades 1 to 3 of primary schooling. Some of these schools conduct multigrade courses. That is, a teacher teaches different subjects concurrently to students of grades 1, 2, and 3 in one classroom. This form of schooling is highly recommended by international aid organizations.

21. An observation made at Oudomxay boarding school during February 2004.

22. June 28, 2001.

23. An observation and personal conversation with teachers from Oudomxay and Phonesoung boarding schools during February and May 2005.

24. See Hansen, 1999: 21–22.

25. This quote is excerpted from an article written by Mr. Vongphachan, with his permission. See Vongphachan, 2003: 2.

26. The interviews of Khamhoung, Vongphachan, and Ly Tu were conducted separately—Khamhoung in April 2000, Vongphachan in July 2002 and March 2003, and Ly Tu in April 2003. This quote is a transcription from an interview with Vongphachan in March 2003.

27. Students under the "quota system" receive the government scholarships which they have to pay back by working for the government or in the public sector after their graduation. Forty five percent of these scholarships are given to top students from schools of secondary education in the capital Vientiane, 25 percent to ethnic minorities from boarding schools, and 35 percent is for the top five students from each secondary school from other provinces throughout Laos.

28. This number is excerpted from Chapman, 2002: 93–106.

29. "Certification" courses offer students with a three to four year period of study, available only in three Faculties: Engineering, Agriculture, and Forestry. On the other hand, the "special section" takes a similar idea to private evening colleges in Laos, particularly in the capital of Vientiane, where students are required to pay 50–80 percent extra over and above the normal NUOL tuition fees, but they are not required to attend the courses from School of Foundation Studies. Thus, students of this section graduate one to two years faster than normal NUOL students. The "special section" courses, depending on the individual departments' curriculum, start from early afternoon and go on till late evening. Students who graduate from this section obtain degrees equivalent to the ones offered by NUOL.

30. For a discussion on the standardization of Lao language, see Enfield, 2000: 258–290.

31. The traditional power or Mandala administrative system of Laos still exists alongside socialism. For a discussion, see Evans (2002) or Stuart-Fox (1998).

32. LNFC is the only governmental organization that works on issues relating to ethnic minorities, such as relocation, education, and pension policies. Recently, the LNFC issued a publication on the official category of ethnic minorities of the Lao PDR.

REFERENCES

Anderson, Benedict (1991). *Imagined Community: Reflections on the Origin and Spread of Nationalism*. London: Verso.

Asian Development Bank (ADB) (1992). *Education Development in Asia and the Pacific Series*, Vol. 1: Lao People's Democratic Republic. Manila: Asian Development Bank.

——(1993). *Education Development in Asia and the Pacific Series, Vol. 1: Lao People's Democratic Republic*. Manila: Asian Development Bank.

——(2000). *A Country Report: Lao PDR*. Manila: ADB.

Berman, E.H. (1992). "Donor agencies and the Third World educational development: 1945–1985," in R.F. Arnove, P.G. Albach, and Gail Kelly (eds), *Emergent Issues in Education: Comparative Perspectives*, pp. 57–74. New York: SUNY Press.

Bocock, Robert (1986). *Hegemony*. Chichester: Horwood.

Chagnon and Rumpf (1982). "Education: The prerequisite to change in Laos," in Martin Stuart-Fox (ed.), *Comtemporary Laos*, pp. 163–180. Queensland: University of Queensland Press.

Chamberlain, James, R. (1995). *Indigenous People Profile: Lao People's Democratic Republic*, CARE International, Vientiane, Prepared for the World Bank, December 1995.

——(2002). *Participatory Poverty Reduction Report*. Manila: Asian Development Bank.

Chapman, David (2002). "When goals collide: Higher education in Laos," in D.W. Chapman and A.E. Austin (eds), *Higher Education in the Developing world: Changing Contexts and Institutional Responses*, pp. 93–106. Westport, CT: Greenwood Press.

Chapman, D.W. and Austin, A.E. (eds) (2002). *Higher Education in the Developing World*, April. Westport, CT: Greenwood Press.

Enfield, Nick (2000). "Lao as national language," in Grant Evans (ed.), *Laos: Culture and Society*, pp. 258–290. Singapore: ISEAS.

Evans, Grant (1991). "Planning problems in peripheral socialism: The case of Laos," in Zasloff and Unger (eds), *Laos: Beyond the Revolution*, pp. 84–130. London: MacMillan.

——(1998). *The Politics of Ritual and Remembrance: Laos since 1975*. Honolulu, HI: University of Hawaii Press.

——(1999a). "Apprentice ethnographers: Vietnam and the study of Lao minorities," in G. Evans (ed.), *Laos: Culture and Society*, pp. 161–190. Chiang Mai: Silkworm Books.

——(1999b). "Ethnic change in the Northern Highlands of Laos," in G. Evans (ed.), *Laos: Culture and Society*, pp. 125–147. Chiang Mai: Silkworm Books.

——(2002). *A Short History of Laos: The Land In Between*, pp. 98–105. Chiang Mai: Silkworm.

Gellner, Earnest (1997). *Nationalism*. London: Weidenfeld.

Goscha, Christopher E. (2004). "Vietnam and the world outside: The case of Vietnamese communist advisors in Laos (1948–62)," *South East Asia Research*, 2(12), 141–185.

Government of Laos (1997). Government Report: Sixth Round Table Meeting (signed by Bounyang Vorachit, Deputy Prime Minister, June 7, 1997).

Hansen, Mette Halskov (1999). *Lessons in Being Chinese: Minority and Ethnic Identity in Southwest China*. Hong Kong: Hong Kong University Press.

International Labor Organization (2000). *Lao PDR: Policies on Indigenous Peoples of Laos*. Geneva: ILO.

Ireson-Doolittle, C.J. (1996). *Field, Forest, and Family: Women's Work and Power in Rural Laos*. Boulder, CO: Westview Press.

Langer, P. (1971). *Education in the Communist Zone of Laos*. Santa Monica, CA: Rand Corporation.

Lao National Assembly (2000). *Education Laws* (Vientiane, April 8, 2000. Ref: 03/LNA).

LeBar, F.M. (1967). "Education System," in LeBar and Suddard (eds), *Laos: Its People, Its Society, Its Culture*, pp. 79–90. New Haven, CT: HRAF Press.

Levinson and Holland (1996). "The cultural production of the educated person: An introduction," in Levinson, Foley, Holland (eds), *The Cultural Production of the Educated: Critical Ethnographies of Schooling and Local Practices*, pp. 1–56. New York: State University of New York Press.

Lockhart, Bruce (2001). "Education in Laos in historical perspective." Unpublished Paper, National University of Singapore.

LPRP (1979). *Politbureau's Resolutions Regarding Education Tasks of the New Revolutionary Era*. Vientiane: Ministry of Education, Sports and Culture.

Mauger, M. (1956). L'Enseignement secondaire. In *Présence du royaume lao*, R. de Berval (ed.) (pp. 1112–1113). Saigon: special issue of *France-Asie* (no. 118–120).

MOE (1998a). "An evaluation of educational planning and implementation from Year 1991–1997." Draft. Vietntiane: MOE.

——(1998b). *Capacity Building for Public Management and Community Development*. Vientiane, Laos: MOE.

——(1999). *Education Sector Development Plan: 2000–2005, and 2001–2020*. Vientiane, Laos: MOE.

——(2000). "The Education Strategic Vision: A Draft Discussion Paper." Prepared for the Education Donors' Meeting. Vientiane, Laos: MOE.

——(2004). *National Education For All*. Vientiane, Laos: MOE.

NUOL (2006). *Enrolment Data by ethnic group and major of year 2004–2005*. Accessed on August 25, 2006 from http://www.nuol.edu.la/temp5.jsp?id=6&lc=en.

——(2006). *Total student numbers of year 2000–2005*. Accessed on August 25, 2006 from http://www.nuol.edu.la/temp5.jsp?id=6&lc=en.

Ogbu, J. (1978). *Minority Education and Caste*. New York: Academic Press.

Pasaxon Newspaper (2002). "Banyakaad, or National Assembly member election atmosphere," February 28, p. 3. Vientiane: Laos.

——(2003). International cooperation: The educational cooperation between Laos and Vietnam year 2003, May 28, p. 3. Vientiane: Laos.

Pathammavong, S. (1955). "Compulsory education in Laos," in C. Bilodeau, S. Pathammavong, and Lê Quang Hông (eds), *Compulsory Education in Cambodia, Laos and Vietnam*, pp. 71–111. Paris: UNESCO.

Postiglione, G. (2000). "Introduction: State schooling and ethnicity in China," in G. Postiglione (ed.), *China's National Minority Education: Culture, Schooling and Development*, pp. 3–20. New York: Falmer Press.

Stenhouse, L. (1981). *An Introduction to Curriculum Research and Development*. Bungay, Suffolk, Great Britain: Richard Clay Ltd, p. 5.

Stuart-Fox, Martin (1998). *The Lao Kingdom of Lan Xang: Rise and decline*. Bangkok: White Lotus Press.

UNDP (1995). A Report: Public Administration Reform Project. Vientiane: UNDP.

UNESCO (Thailand) (1990). "World declaration on education for all," in *World Conference on Education For All Report*. Bangkok: UNESCO.

Vongphachan, Vilayhom (2003). "Some thoughts for ethnic minority education development." Unpublished Document, Vientiane.

Whitaker, Donald, P. (1972). *Area Handbook for Laos*. Washington: U.S. Government Printing Office.

Wilder, Bernard, D. (1972). "An Examination of the Phenomenon of the Literacy Skills of Unschooled Males in Laos." Ph.D. Thesis, Michigan State University, College of Education, Ann Arbor, Michigan.

World Bank (1996). Preparation of an Implementation Plan for Human Resources Training and Capacity Building: Lao People's Democratic Republic, April. Vientiane: World Bank.

WEBSITES

http://www.adb.org/Documents/Books/ADO/2006/documents/lao.pdf (accessed on October 9, 2006).

http://www.adb.org/Documents/Books/Key_Indicators/2005/pdf/LAO.pdf (accessed on August 25, 2006).

http://www.adb.org/LaoPDR/default.asp (accessed on July 20, 2005).

http://www.ecotourismlaos.com/maps_khammouane.htm (accessed on August 25, 2006).

http://www.ecotourismlaos.com/maps_oudomxay.htm (accessed on August 25, 2006).

http://www.nuol.edu.la (accessed on August 25, 2006).

http://www.nuol.edu.la/temp1.jsp?id=145&lc=en (accessed on August 25, 2006).

http://www.nuol.edu.la/temp5.jsp?id=6&lc=en (accessed on August 25, 2006).

Chapter 9

SCHOOLING IN MALAYSIA

Seng Piew Loo

INTRODUCTION

Malaysia occupies the southernmost peninsula of Southeast Asia and the
northern one-third of Borneo. It became a nation on September 16, 1963
when Singapore, Sabah and Sarawak joined Malaya which had earlier gained
Merdeka or independence from the British on August 31, 1957 to form a single
Federation (Singapore left the Federation in 1965). Malaysia has a democratically
elected government with a constitutional monarch.

Malaysia has a multiethnic population consisting of native (bumiputera)
and "immigrant" (non-bumiputera) ethnic groups. The Malays are the main
indigenous ethnic group. The main "immigrant" groups in Malaysia are the
descendents of Chinese and Indians[1] who settled in Malaysia during colonial rule
when the British encouraged large scale immigration of workers from China and
the Indian subcontinent to provide labor for the mining and plantation sectors
of the economy respectively. Consequently, at the time of independence in 1957,
Malays were reduced to a bare majority (55 percent). Of the non-bumiputeras,
the Chinese originally made up 34 percent of the population, Indians accounted
for another 10 percent while the remainder consists of other groups.

Over the past five decades, the population growth rate of Malays and other
bumiputeras outpaced that of non-bumiputeras due to differential rates of
fertility. Consequently, the proportion of bumiputeras in the population rose to
60.6 percent in 1991 and 65.1 percent in 2000. Correspondingly, the proportion
of Chinese in the population fell to 28.1 percent in 1991, and 26.0 percent in
2000 (Department of Statistics 1995, 2001). Similarly, the proportion of Indians
fell to 7.9 percent in 1991 and 7.7 percent in 2000.

After ethnicity, the next most important demographic parameter in Malaysia's
population structure is domiciliary location according to urban and rural
settlement. Rapid economic development over the past four decades has led to

increasing urbanization of the population. The urban population increased by an average of 4.4 percent per annum from 9.5 million (50.7 percent) in 1991 to 13.6 million (62.0 percent) in 2000. The proportion of rural dwellers dropped from 49.3 percent in 1991 to 38.0 percent in 2000.

HISTORICAL CONTEXT OF EDUCATION IN MALAYSIA

The history of Malaysia is summarized in the chronological chart as given in Figure 9.1.

Primitive and Feudal Period (35,000 B.C.–1786)

Malaysia's early history is shrouded in mystery because of the dearth of archeological evidence or historical records. The little available archeological evidence reveals that the first human beings arrived in East Malaysia around 35,000 B.C. and in West Malaysia around 25,000 B.C. On the peninsula, the aboriginal people are collectively known as the *Orang Asli*. The *Orang Asli* are not a homogenous group. For example, the *Negrito* people who are related to Australian aborigines settled in Peninsular Malaysia around 25,000 B.C. while the *Senoi* who arrived between 3,000 and 2,000 B.C., are of Mongoloid origin.

A more technologically advanced group migrated to the peninsula from a region now called *Yunnan* in China *c*. 2,500 B.C. Called the Proto-Malays, they were seafarers and farmers, and their advances forced the *Negritos* away from the coastal area into the interior. The modern Malays are the descendents of the Deutero-Malays—an amalgam of many early ethnic groups including Indians, Chinese, Siamese, Arabs, and Proto-Malays. The Deutero-Malays heralded the arrival of the Iron Age in Malaysia.

The earliest Indian record of civilization in Malaysia mentions a place called *Savarnadvipa*—the Land of Gold. Lured by the search for gold, early Indians established a Hindu kingdom in what is now known as the state of Kedah *c*. 100 B.C. A succession of Indo-Malay and Malay kingdoms followed.

Figure 9.1
Chronological Chart of the History of Educational Development in Malaysia

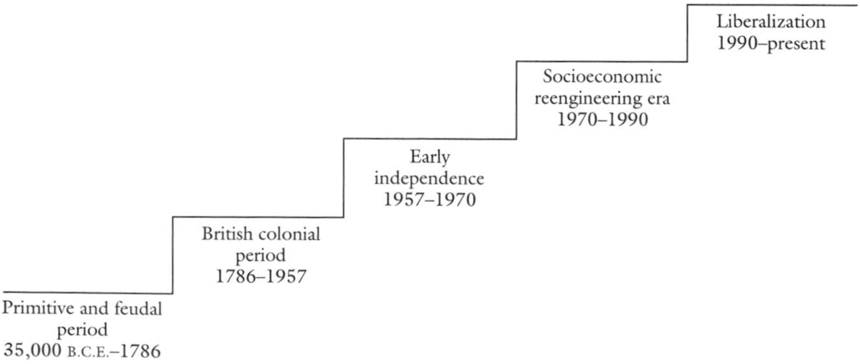

During the 13th century, a great maritime kingdom called Srivijaya emerged in the Malay Archipelago. However, as other ports emerged toward the end of the 13th century, Srivijaya's influence declined and paved the way for the Malays to emerge as the dominant power in the Malay Archipelago.

According to the Malay Annals, Malacca was founded in 1400 by Parameswara, a prince from Sumatra who was fleeing from the wrath of his king. The strategic location of the port of Malacca at the narrowest part of the Straits of Malacca allowed it to control the lucrative spice trade. Revenue from port taxes and services greatly enriched Malacca. With the success it enjoyed, Malacca built a large army and navy and eventually controlled large parts of the Malay Peninsula and Sumatra. Muslim traders from Arabia and India brought Islam to Malacca. Soon after establishing his kingdom, Parameswara converted from Hinduism to Islam.

Ironically, at the height of its power, Malacca fell to the Portuguese in 1511. The Portuguese were content to control no more than the city and port of Malacca and did not venture to try to conquer the rest of the kingdom. Thus, whilst the Portuguese were the first European power to establish a colony in Southeast Asia, the Portuguese era did not mark the true beginning of the colonial era in Malaysia. Nor were the Dutch who defeated the Portuguese and conquered Malacca in 1641 the first colonial overlord of Malaysia. It was in fact the British who colonized all of Malaysia. The Portuguese built a formidable fort to defend Malacca. Despite repeated attempts by the deposed sultan and his descendants to retake the city, the Portuguese and later on the Dutch prevailed because of their superior military technology. Eventually, the sultanate of Malacca broke up into a number of Malay kingdoms.

Education during this period was typical of feudal societies. Only members of the royalty and nobility had the benefit of formal education that prepared them for ruling the masses. Education for the rest of society was largely of an informal nature involving the passing down of traditional life skills from generation to generation. However, the Islamic clergy established a small number of Qur'anic schools or *pondok* for the purpose of religious education.

The British Colonial Period (1786–1957)

The British colonial period began when Captain Francis Light of the British East India Company convinced the Sultan of Kedah to allow them to build a fort in Penang, an island off the northwestern coast of the Malay Peninsula in 1786. When France captured the Netherlands in 1795, the British took over Malacca because, rather than handing Malacca over to the French, the Dutch government-in-exile agreed to let England temporarily oversee the port. The British handed back Malacca to the Dutch in 1808, but it was soon ceded to the British in a trade for Bencoolen in Sumatra. Another colony was established in Singapore by Sir Stamford Raffles. Penang, Malacca, and Singapore collectively came to be known as the Straits Settlements.

The British colonial period in the Malay Peninsula started as a commercial venture but soon became a Crown matter. Civil war in the West Malaysian state of

Perak during the 1860s gave the excuse for the British government to intervene and force the Malay rulers to sign a peace treaty known as the Pangkor Agreement in 1874. The treaty paved the way for the British to colonize the rest of the Malay Peninsula or what was then called Malaya. British rule in Malaya was abruptly interrupted by the Japanese occupation from 1941 to 1945.

Like on the peninsula, East Malaysia did not begin as Crown protectorates. In 1877 the Sultan of Brunei and the Sultan of Sulu ceded large tracts of territory in North Borneo to Baron von Overbeck and Alfred Dunt. Overbeck and Dunt later formed the British North Borneo Company in 1881 to administer what is now known as the state of Sabah until 1941, when the Japanese invaded and took control. After World War II, the British returned and turned Sabah into a Crown colony. Sarawak, on the other hand, has a very unique colonization history. In 1842, the Regent of Brunei ceded a large part of Sarawak to James Brooke and gave him the title of "Rajah" for helping suppress a rebellion against the sultanate. Over the next 104 years, the Brookes consolidated their power and extended their control over the rest of Sarawak. The rule of the "White Rajahs" was interrupted by the Japanese occupation from 1941 to 1945. In 1946, Charles Vyner Brooke ceded Sarawak to the British Crown.

During the colonial period, the main concern of the British was to maintain peace and order to facilitate the exploitation of the economic resources of Malaysia, especially tin and rubber. As mentioned earlier, the demographic structure of Malaysia changed drastically during the colonial period because with their typical tendency to racial stereotyping, the colonialists regarded the Malays as amiable but rather lazy (Alatas, 1977). Consequently the British encouraged mass immigration of workers from China and India to work in the tin mines and rubber plantations respectively. Rapid urban development took place during the booming colonial economy. For the most part, the Malays remained in rural areas whilst the towns were dominated by the Chinese and a minority of Indians who eventually controlled commerce and industry.

Educational development during the colonial period can be divided into three phases: 1786–1941, 1941–1945, and 1945–1957.

1786–1941

The British adopted an educational policy that is, at best described as *laissez faire*, or at worst, divide-and-rule. During the colonial period, four types of schools existed—English schools where English was used as the medium of instruction and three types of vernacular schools, namely, Malay, Chinese and Indian.

On the whole, the colonial government did not see the need to set up good schools for their colonial subjects but established a few English schools to condition Malay royalty and nobility for limited leadership roles under British rule as well as to recruit and supply personnel for the colonial civil service. Besides the government, Christian missionary groups also established English schools in the major towns. Of the four types of schooling, English education was the best as it consisted of both primary and secondary levels and students could potentially further their education until university level in England or at the Raffles College, which was established in the 1930s in Singapore. As all missionary schools were established in urban areas, school enrollment was dominated by the Chinese and the Indians.

Although the colonial government did not feel the need to build schools for the masses, for the Malays at least, the British felt some form of patronizing and paternalistic obligation to provide a basic form of education designed to teach them to be better able to carry on in subsistence farming and fishery as well as to develop habits of punctuality and good behavior in order that they not disturb the peace. Evidence of this is provided by James Birch, the British administrator of the state of Selangor in his Annual Report (Malaya, 1893: 46):

Vernacular education is in my opinion useful in so far as it makes the Malay regular and cleanly in his habits, but where it exalts boys, as it often does, above the calling of their fathers, who for the most part will remain small agriculturists or fishermen, it does more harm than good.

Loh (1969: 162) reports that 189 Malay vernacular schools with a total enrollment of 7,218 pupils had been set up by 1892.

In the case of the Chinese and Indians who were considered as transient subjects, the British largely left them to their own devices to establish their own vernacular schools. The Chinese community actively established their own schools and imported curricula, teachers and textbooks from China. The Indians, on the other hand, were left at the mercy of the rubber plantation owners. Plantation owners who built schools for the children of their workers only saw it fit to provide a rudimentary form of terminal primary education in dilapidated buildings.

To summarize, four separate education systems existed in colonial Malaysia. The best education was available in English schools. More nonnatives were able to benefit from English schools than natives. The quality of Malay, Chinese, and Indian vernacular schools was generally poor and the curricula focused on their respective motherlands. Thus, the population became divided, and remained so for more than 150 years.

1941–1945

Japanese occupation of Malaysia during World War II was too brief to have had much impact on education in Malaysia. Nevertheless, the defeat of the British at the hands of Asians shattered the myth of white superiority and led to a surge of nationalism in colonial Malaysia.

1946–1957

After the Japanese Occupation, the British initially tried to cling on to power by persuading the Malay sultans to surrender what little was left of their sovereignty and uniting the British-protected Malay states with the Straits Settlements into a single British colony called the Malayan Union. The first attempt to reform the education system was made through the Cheeseman Plan, which advocated primary and secondary education in the four existing languages—English, Malay, Chinese, and Tamil. Chinese and Tamil language teaching were to be made available in the English schools, and at the same time the teaching of English was to be made compulsory in all vernacular schools.

Malay nationalists organized mass protests against the Malayan Union and demanded independence. The British realized that they would have to accede to the demands for independence. Before independence could be granted, it was necessary to undo the divisive legacy of colonial education and forge a sense of shared national identity amongst Malaysia's multiethnic population through education. The Cheeseman proposal was abandoned in 1949 with the demise of the Malayan Union. The search for a blueprint for national integration began in earnest.

The Barnes Committee was set up in 1950 to look into reforming and integrating the educational system. The Barnes Report (Malaya, 1951a) recommended that all existing schools should be transformed into National schools in which children of the various ethnic groups would be taught through the medium of Malay and English. Not surprisingly, the Chinese saw the Barnes Committee proposal as an attempt to eliminate their languages and cultural identities and protested vehemently against it. To appease the Chinese, another committee called the Fenn-Wu Committee was formed in 1951 to look into their needs. The Fenn-Wu Committee was sympathetic toward Chinese vernacular education and recommended a bilingual policy where Malay and English would be used as media of instruction, but at the same time provisions would be made for the learning of Chinese and Tamil in schools.

The Report of the Central Advisory Committee (Malaya, 1951b) took into consideration the collective wisdom of the Barnes and Fenn-Wu committees. Its recommendations formed the basis for the Education Ordinance of 1952 in which a bilingual national system of education with a common curriculum was established based on only one type of school—the National School. Malay and English were placed on an equal footing as media of instruction in the national school but Tamil and Chinese were taught as third languages. Chinese and Tamil vernacular schools were not accepted as part of the national system.

Early Independence (1957–1970)

Immediately after the first national elections in 1955, the government-elect immediately started work on drafting the constitution of the Federation of Malaya. The constitution, the product of political accommodation between the natives and nonnatives, divided Malaysians into two classes of citizens—natives and nonnatives.

In exchange for accepting the "special rights" of the Malays spelt out in Article 8(1) of the Federal Constitution, Chinese and Indians were granted citizenship. The "special rights" of the Malays in principle and practice refer to their inalienable right to benefit from preferential economic and educational policies. Such is the importance attached to the "special rights" of the Malays that the term "Malay" is a clearly defined constitutional term. According to Article 160(2) of the Federal constitution, a Malay

means a person who professes the religion of Islam, habitually speaks the Malay language, conforms to Malay custom and—
(a) was before Merdeka born in the Federation or in Singapore or born of parents one of whom was born in the Federation or in Singapore, or is on that day domiciled in the Federation or in Singapore, or
(b) is the issue of such a person.

When Sabah and Sarawak joined Malaya to form the expanded Federation of Malaysia in 1963, the term *bumiputera* was created as a more inclusive term for all native Malaysians. Both *Orang Asli* and East Malaysian natives were accorded "special rights" alongside the Malays. The "special status" accorded to aboriginal natives, however, does not give them legal rights over ancestral land. Under the Aboriginal Peoples Act (APA) of 1974, the aboriginal people of Malaysia who have resided on the land of their ancestors for thousands of years are no more than "tenants at will" (Jumper, 1999; Nicholas, 2000) who may be evicted at any time at the discretion of the state, the unconditional landlord. In all fairness, the position of the Malaysian government with respect to the status of native ancestral land rights is consistent with international land litigation practice, which whilst adhering to the rule of law is not necessarily just, for example the *Terra Nullius* Principle applied by the government of Australia.[2]

The most important educational documents that have had the most impact in shaping educational policy in Malaysia are contained in a number of Cabinet educational reports and educational legislation.

The Razak Report and the Education Ordinance of 1957. The government-elect moved swiftly to draft Malaysia's first educational policy just before independence was granted in 1957. The Report of the Education Committee, 1956 (Malaya, 1956), popularly known as the Razak Report was the government's educational blueprint for postindependence Malaysia to create a national education system aimed at fostering national integration. The Razak Report resulted in Malaysia's first legislation on education as an independent nation—the Education Ordinance of 1957.

There are two major differences between the education ordinances of 1952 and 1957. Under the former, Chinese and Tamil vernacular primary schools existed outside the national education system but under the latter, such schools were integrated within the national education system as national type primary schools. Thus, the 1957 Ordinance favored the interests of the non-bumiputeras more than the 1952 Ordinance.

The conciliatory tone of the Razak Report that acceded to the wishes of the nonnatives, however, came at a price—the acceptance of the Malay language as the sole national language and dominant medium of instruction. Whilst mother-tongue instruction was allowed to continue in primary schools, it was implicit in the report that vernacular secondary education would eventually be phased out.

More importantly, Malay nationalists who had long regarded English-medium schools as the symbol of colonial oppression that paved the way for nonnatives to dominate education and the economy moved immediately to phase out English-medium schools from the education system. The status of English, which was equal to that of the Malay language under the Education Ordinance of 1952, was diminished to that of a second language taught as a school subject under the Education Ordinance of 1957.

The Rahman Talib Report and the Education Act of 1961. Four years after the Razak Committee completed its report, an Education Review Committee headed by Rahman Talib was charged with the task of reviewing the progress of the implementation of the Razak Report. The Committee found that there was little progress in implementing the use of the Malay language as the main medium of instruction in Malaysian schools and phasing out English-medium schools. There were still four media of instruction—Bahasa Melayu, English, Chinese, and Tamil. The Report of the Education Review Committee, 1960 (Malaya, 1960) resulted in the Education Act of 1961.

The most significant outcome of the Education Act of 1961 was that a definite timetable was set to phase out English-medium schools and convert government-aided Chinese-medium secondary schools into Bahasa Melayu-medium secondary schools. It is important to note that the Rahman Talib Report forcefully implemented the government's Bahasa Melayu policy without violating the inalienable right of non-bumiputeras to mother tongue instruction under Article 152(1b) of the constitution. Although all government-aided Chinese-medium secondary schools were also converted to Bahasa Melayu-medium national secondary schools, the use of Chinese and Tamil as media of instruction was maintained in the respective national type primary schools.

Socioeconomic Reengineering Era (1970–1990)

Non-bumiputera domination of the economy accelerated after independence resulting in increasing interethnic tensions which culminated in the violent interracial riots of May 13, 1969. A national emergency was declared to restore public order. After public order was restored, a stunned nation was left to contemplate the solution to the root cause of the bloody conflict—dissatisfaction of the Malays over economic disparities. The government launched a 20-year plan in 1970 called the New Economic Policy (NEP) to regulate and restructure the economy. In particular, ownership of equity capital of bumiputeras, non-bumiputeras, and foreigners would conform to a ratio of 30:40:30. In essence, economic redistribution was to be achieved as the economic cake expanded rather than through forced appropriation. The government has achieved considerable success in increasing the numbers of bumiputeras in professional and managerial occupations and raising the average income level of bumiputeras.

The ratio of mean income for bumiputeras vis-à-vis the Chinese improved from 56.7 percent in 1985 to 58.8 percent in 1990. In the restructuring of the corporate sector, the share capital of bumiputeras increased from 3 percent in 1970 to 18.5 percent in 1985 and 20.3 percent in 1990.

Socioeconomic reengineering also impacted on education in the form of educational policies that discriminated in favor of the bumiputeras. A racial quota system was set up in which entry requirements in institutions of higher learning were lowered for bumiputeras in order to forcibly increase the number of bumiputeras in tertiary education. Other preferential practices were the construction of elite fully residential schools reserved for bumiputeras and the near total bumiputera monopoly of government scholarships.

It was also during this period that the national language policy laid down by the Rahman Talib Report was implemented without any further delay; nor was it resisted by the non-bumiputeras. Table 9.1 summarizes the government's schedule to implement the Bahasa Melayu (which was renamed Bahasa Malaysia) policy during this period.

Another important educational development that took place during this period was massive reform in the primary and secondary school curricula. School curriculum reform was prompted by the Report of the Cabinet Committee to Review Educational Policy (1979), popularly known as the Mahathir Report.

The Report of the Cabinet Committee to Review Educational Policy (1979). The Committee took almost five years to publish its recommendations. The terms of reference of the Committee were to recommend steps to improve the implementation of the Education Act of 1961. In particular, the Committee was charged with reviewing the existing primary and secondary school curricula.

Table 9.1
Key Milestones in the Implementation of the Bahasa Malaysia Policy

Year	Event
1970	The phased conversion of English-medium national type primary schools to Bahasa Malaysia-medium national type primary schools was started in the first year of primary school.
1975	The conversion of English-medium national type primary schools to Bahasa Malaysia-medium national type primary schools was completed.
1976	The phased conversion of vernacular and English national type secondary schools to Bahasa Malaysia-medium national type secondary schools was started in the first year of secondary school.
1981	The conversion of vernacular and English national type secondary schools to Bahasa Malaysia-medium national type secondary schools was completed. The use of Bahasa Malaysia as the medium of instruction in the first year of all university degree programs was started.
1983	The use of Bahasa Malaysia as the medium of instruction in Form 6 was completed.
1985	The use of Bahasa Malaysia as the medium of instruction in Malaysian universities was completed.

The Mahathir Report concluded that the existing primary school curriculum was too content-heavy and did not give enough attention to the balanced development of the individual child. It recommended that more attention should be given to the development of basic literacy and competency skills as well as the inculcation of moral and spiritual values.

In response to the Mahathir report, the Curriculum Development Centre had to work at a feverish pace to design and implement a new primary school curriculum. The New Primary School Curriculum, now called the Integrated Primary School Curriculum (KBSR),[3] was introduced in 1982 as a pilot project in 302 schools. In the following year, KBSR was implemented nationwide. To maintain curriculum continuity between the KBSR and the secondary school curriculum, the Integrated Secondary School Curriculum (KBSM)[4] was pilot tested in 1988 and implemented nationwide in 1989. Like KBSR, KBSM was guided by liberal arts ideals.

Liberalization and Globalization Era (1990–Present)

Although the aim of carving out a 30 percent share of the economy for the bumiputeras by 1990 was far from being achieved, the government decided that enough momentum had been built up to justify the easing of government regulation of the economy. In 1991, the National Development Policy (NDP) was launched which allowed for a limited liberalization of the economy. The rationale for not extending the NEP was that foreign investment during the 20-year period was not as high as had been hoped for. The reason is that under the NEP, foreign investors were required eventually to reduce their share capital to 30 percent. In other words, foreigners had to surrender control of companies to Malaysians. New rules now allow foreigners to maintain 100 percent control.

The limited liberalization of the economy attracted a big inflow of foreign investment. Before the East Asian economic crisis of 1997–1998 struck, economic growth during the first seven years of the NDP averaged 8.2 percent per annum. Foreign corporate equity ownership increased substantially from 25.1 percent in 1990 to 31.8 percent in 1998. Foreign equity ownership surged from RM (Malaysian ringgit) 27.6 billion in 1990 to RM93.6 billion in 1998.

Although the government's effort to liberalize the economy is commendable and consistent with the current climate of free trade in an open and highly competitive global economy, a considerable amount of government regulation of the economy remains. Preferential economic and educational policies that favor the bumiputeras are still enforced. For example, the government awards the overwhelming majority of contracts for public works to bumiputera companies and the education system remains highly ascriptive rather than meritocratic. The implication is that the increase of bumiputeras in professional and managerial occupations has been largely accomplished through lower university entrance requirements than ability *per se*.

Two major pieces of educational legislation were passed in 1996. The most important impact of the Education Act of 1996 was to incorporate preschool education within the national education system. The Private Higher Educational

Institution (PHEI) Act which was also passed in 1996 aimed to increase private sector participation in tertiary education. The PHEI Act allows the private sector to establish degree awarding institutions. It also allows foreign universities to set up branch campuses in Malaysia.

LEVELS OF EDUCATION

Malaysia has a centralized system of education. Until recently, overall control of the entire education system was in the hands of the Education Minister who is ultimately answerable to the Prime Minister. Since March 27, 2004, however, the Education Ministry has been split into two—the revamped Ministry of Education which encompasses most of the original divisions and departments, and the Ministry of Higher Education. The Ministry of Higher Education oversees the Institutes of Higher Education Management Division, the Polytechnics and Community Colleges Management Division, the National Accreditation Board, the Tunku Abdul Rahman Foundation as well as 17 universities and university colleges.

Structure and Curriculum

Malaysia's current system of education can be described as a P–13 system, that is, 13 points or year levels of education preceding university education. The P–13 system is subdivided into 6–3–2–2 levels consisting of 6 years of primary schooling, 3 years of lower secondary education, 2 years of upper secondary education and 2 years of preuniversity education. Under the Education Act of 1996, preschool education of children of age 5+has been incorporated within the national system of education.

Students in government-aided schools follow a common national curriculum taught in Bahasa Malaysia from the secondary level onwards. National examinations are conducted at the sixth year of primary schooling (Primary School Assessment Test or *Ujian Penilaian Sekolah Rendah*—UPSR), the third year of secondary schooling (Lower Secondary Assessment or *Penilaian Menengah Rendah*—PMR), the fifth year of secondary schooling (Malaysian Certificate of Education or *Sijil Pelajaran Malaysia*—SPM) and the second year of postsecondary schooling (Malaysian Higher School Certificate or *Sijil Tinggi Persekolahan Malaysia*—STPM). However, students who enter colleges or polytechnics do not sit for the STPM. Also, there is a highly selective intake of students for the matriculation program who circumvent the same examination. The matriculation program is designed specially for bumiputeras for entry into first degree science, technology, and accountancy programs. University education for most programs lasts between three and four years. The levels of education in Malaysia are summarized in Figure 9.2.

The Ministry of Education released plans to transform Malaysia's education system into a P–12 system where lower secondary education will be reduced from three years to two years (Ministry of Education, 2001) but until now no date has

Figure 9.2
Structure of the Educational System of Malaysia

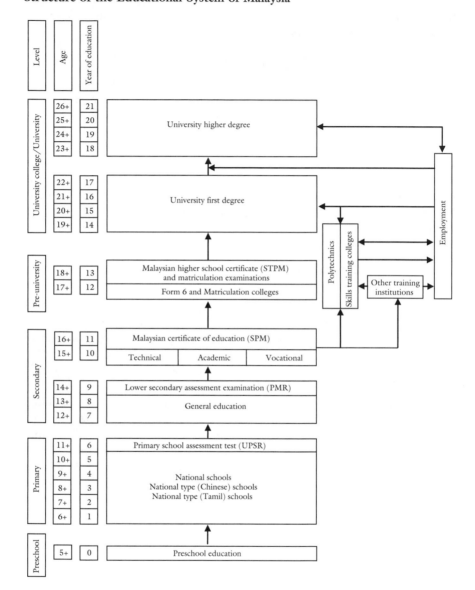

been set for implementation. It would appear that the plan for the P–12 system has been deferred indefinitely and replaced by a new five year educational blueprint (Ministry of Education, 2006) jointly launched on January 16, 2007 by the Prime Minister and Minister of Education. Perhaps the most important of the six thrust areas in the new educational blueprint is the intention to create "cluster schools." "Cluster schools" are somewhat vaguely defined as "niche areas" schools that can mean anything from existing niche area schools identified according to medium of instruction, special education needs, school type (elite selective residential schools, elite selective nonresidential schools, and nonelite, nonresidential schools), and so on, to new "clusters of excellence" schools. Most significantly, the new niche area schools will be given autonomy in terms of selecting up to 10 percent of their student enrollment in accordance with the specific fields or niche areas the schools would like to develop, which was previously denied under the centralized school curriculum. Such schools will also be allowed to offer subjects *out of* the national school curriculum and teaching/learning methods suited for the needs of the targeted niche areas. Also, cluster schools will be allowed to implement teaching and learning times which are more flexible.

Preschool Education

Preschool education is offered both by government agencies and the private sector. The overall aim of preschool education is to provide a firm foundation for primary school education. Specifically, the preschool curriculum promotes the holistic intellectual, social, psychomotor, and spiritual development of the child. All preschool centers have to abide by the curriculum guidelines set by the Ministry of Education under the Education Act of 1996.

Although Malaysia has achieved near universal primary education (exceeding 96 percent), the preschool enrollment rate at 64.0 percent is much lower (Ministry of Education, 2001). However, it is envisaged that this will increase to 95 percent by the year 2010. As might be expected, the participation rate in rural areas is lower than that in urban areas.

Primary School Education

It was only in 2003 that Malaysia implemented a policy of compulsory primary education. Nevertheless, since independence the government has affirmatively and relentlessly pursued a policy of universal primary education. The enrollment rate for primary education increased steadily from 93 percent in 1991, 94 percent in 1992, 95 percent in 1994, and 96 percent in 1995 (Sahara, 2000) and is expected to reach 99 percent by 2010 (Ministry of Education, 2001). As with preschool education, both government and private interest groups are involved in the provision of primary education.

The primary education system is divided into the national schools (*Sekolah Kebangsaan* or SK) and vernacular or national type schools (*Sekolah Jenis Kebangsaan* or SJK). The medium of instruction in the SKs is Malay. Chinese vernacular schools or SJKC conduct classes in Mandarin and Indian vernacular schools or SJKT use Tamil.

Recently, attempts have been made to establish vision schools (*Sekolah Wawasan*). Vision schools share facilities among two or more national and national type schools, ostensibly to encourage closer interethnic interaction. One possible reason for the creation of vision schools is the failure of the national school as a catalyst for national integration. In 2004, the prime minister said "the national school, the main catalyst for the integration process in the young generation, has begun to lose its popularity as a school of choice, particularly among Chinese students." He went on to say that only about 2 percent of Chinese students attended SKs (Wiki, 2005). Nevertheless, the prime minister had an apparent change of heart concerning the Vision School because he recently reaffirmed that the SK is Malaysia's "school of choice" (Ministry of Education, 2006).

The financing of public primary schools is somewhat complicated. Schools where the land on which the school buildings are located belongs to the government are given full federal aid—both grant-in-aid and capital grant. Many former Christian missionary schools, SJKCs, and SJKTs where the land has not been alienated to the government are only given partial aid in the form of grant-in-aid. The large numbers of partially aided vernacular schools is borne out by the imbalance in development funds for government-aided primary schools. Between 1996 and 2000, the Seventh Malaysia Plan allocation for primary education development allocated 96.5 percent to SKs which had 75 percent of total enrollment. SJKCs (21 percent enrollment) received 2.4 percent of the allocation while SJKTs (3.6 percent enrollment) received 1 percent of the allocation.

Independent schools are schools that do not receive any federal aid. Independent Chinese primary schools are one example of such schools. Another example is the Community Religious School or *Sekolah Agama Rakyat* (SAR) operated by Islamic Religious Councils under the jurisdiction of the state governments or private Islamic religious bodies. SAR schools attract the patronage of Muslim parents who are keen on maintaining a more rigorous form of Islamic religious education for their children.

The curriculum of all primary schools within the national education system is KBSR. It appears to have been hastily planned and implemented. A number of sharp departures from the old curriculum were made but were reversed after some time. One of the most astonishing decisions made by the Ministry of Education was the banning of the use of textbooks and workbooks by teachers. Cummings (1986) attributed this to the differences in philosophical bases of KBSR and the old curriculum, the former anchored in humanistic psychology and the latter in behaviorist psychology. For some reason the Ministry naively believed that teachers could change their mindsets overnight and use their creativity to design customized curriculum materials to suit the individual differences of children. This was a disastrous move as teachers were highly dependent on prepared curriculum materials and were not adequately trained to design their own instructional materials. Also the average class had about 40 children and it was unrealistic to expect teachers to prepare customized instructional materials for so many children. In the end, public agitation over the lack of instructional materials forced the Ministry to approve the use of textbooks and supplementary workbooks mass-produced by commercial firms.

Another major departure from the old curriculum was the removal of science from the primary school curriculum. The curriculum developers overzealously integrated curriculum content to the extent that science and humanities subjects were integrated into a single subject called Humanity and the Environment taught in Year 4. Pressure soon mounted on the Ministry of Education to review the subject because the teachers who taught the subject were either specialists in science or humanities, but not both. As such, many of them were at a loss on how to teach the subject. In 1994, a decision was made to split Humanity and the Environment into two separate subjects—Science and a humanities subject called Local Studies—thus restoring the traditional divide between science and the humanities. The swing back to science in the primary curriculum was completed in 2003, when it was reintroduced in Year 1.

Secondary School Education

Apart from severely mentally and physically disadvantaged students, learners are streamed into three types of lower secondary schools, regular day schools, fully residential schools, and MARA[5] Junior Science Colleges. Fully residential schools and MARA Junior Science Colleges are elite schools reserved largely for bumiputera students. Competition for places in such schools amongst bumiputeras is very intense and UPSR results are used as the main criterion for selection. Rural bumiputeras are given preference over their urban counterparts although some studies seem to indicate otherwise (e.g., Siti Zahara, 1975; Mustapa, 1989). All other students are channeled into regular nonresidential schools.

Lower secondary education for most students lasts three years. However, all students from the SJKC and SJKT, apart from those who achieve excellent results in Bahasa Malaysia in the UPSR, are retained in "Remove" classes for a year before commencing secondary schooling. The purpose of the "Remove Year" is to enhance the Bahasa Malaysia foundation of Chinese and Tamil learners to prepare them for secondary education that is delivered in Bahasa Malaysia.

Entry into upper secondary education depends on the learners' performance in the PMR. Upper secondary education is divided into three streams—the academic, technical, and vocational streams. There are four kinds of upper secondary schools in the academic stream—regular day schools, fully residential schools, Science Secondary Schools, and MARA Junior Science Colleges. Again, as in lower secondary schools, the last three are elite schools largely reserved for bumiputeras.

The vocational stream offers practical training in trade skills for less academically inclined learners. The technical stream, on the other hand, provides training in highly specialised technical skills. Until 1996, vocational schools existed separately from technical schools. Vocational schools, however, have proven highly unpopular because of the stigma of being associated with low-wage, blue-collar careers and not being tailored closely to the specific, changing, and complex needs of the trades industry. Many students prefer to drop out of such schools and immediately take up on-the-job vocational training as apprentices in workshops and small industries. To overcome this problem, the government started phasing out vocational schools and absorbing the vocational stream within technical schools in 1996.

At the end of the two years of upper secondary education, students sit for the SPM, a national examination equivalent to the British General Certificate of Secondary Education.

In Malaysia's centralized educational system, all secondary school students follow the KBSM curriculum. Under the previous secondary school curriculum, pupils were streamed into science and arts streams, whereby they had to select more or less preset science or arts subject packages. For example, under the old curriculum, science students were usually required to take a "hard" science subject combination of Biology, Physics, Chemistry, and Additional Mathematics (besides Modern Mathematics which was compulsory) and allowed to pick only one nonscience elective subject (e.g., Geography). Under KBSM, pupils are allowed to select between two and four elective subjects from a minimum of two elective packages: Humanities, Vocational and Technological, Science, and Islamic Studies.

Liberalization of subject choice under the elective system has had a deleterious effect on Malaysia's Vision 2020—the goal of Malaysia to achieve the status of a fully developed nation by the year 2020. The ratio of students enrolled in science versus nonscience electives in KBSM dropped alarmingly from 31:69 in 1986 to 20:80 in 1993 (Lee et al., 1996). The drift away from science also impacted badly on the demand for secondary school science graduate teachers. For example, the School of Educational Studies in Universiti Sains Malaysia had to scrap its Bachelor of Science with Education program and introduce a rather awkward program called Program B between 1990 and 1995—a Bachelor of Arts with Education program where teacher trainees majored in one humanities subject and one science subject.[6] In response, the Ministry of Education has set a target of reversing the trend of falling enrollment in science by setting a target of achieving a science: arts ratio of 60:40. Consequently, enrollment in science is picking up again and science teacher education has been revived.

Another curriculum pendulum swing that has recently occurred is the shift in the language policy. As pointed out earlier, the status of the English language which was paramount in colonial Malaysia has been much diminished after independence. In 2002, the outgoing premier, Mahathir Mohamed, proposed bringing back English for the teaching of science and mathematics in school beginning with the first years of primary school, secondary school, and Form 6. The proposal was put into action in less than a year in time for the start of the new school year in 2003. The move was founded on the conviction that Malaysia's competitiveness in the global economy depends on the level of scientific and technological knowledge of its citizens and to achieve that it is necessary for the two subjects to be taught in English, the dominant language of science in the world.

Postsecondary/Tertiary Education

Postsecondary education is divided into college, polytechnic, and preuniversity education. Students who only wish to pursue their studies up to the certificate and diploma levels enter Teacher Education Colleges, Polytechnics, and the Tunku Abdul Rahman College where professional courses are offered. Preuniversity postsecondary education again highlights the dichotomy of educational opportunities between privileged bumiputera students and not-so-privileged non-bumiputera students. Government matriculation colleges offer more-or-less guaranteed entry for bumiputera students into choice science, technology, and accountancy programs in Malaysian public universities. Non-bumiputera students, on the other hand, enter Form 6 where entry is dependent on performance in the STPM. The STPM and matriculation serve as two parallel filters for university entrance. The two systems of examinations are not equivalent as the matriculation program is internally examined by the individual matriculation colleges while the STPM is examined according to a central standardized system. The dual meritocratic carriageway of two separate examination systems opens university entrance to potential distortion.[7] It has been commonly argued that the Form 6 preuniversity program is more rigorous in academic content than the matriculation program and the STPM is more difficult than the matriculation examinations. Nevertheless, a perfect CGPA score of 4.00 in the STPM is apparently not as good as a similar score in matriculation. For example in 2004, 128 students who obtained the perfect score in the STPM were denied their first choice of course—medicine. In contrast, judging from the absence of any complaints by aggrieved matriculation students, it may be assumed that every matriculation student with the perfect CGPA who applied for medicine was successful. The only common denominator in the group of unsuccessful 128 STPM students was that they were all non-bumiputeras. It was only after a huge public outcry that the Minister of Higher Education was forced to personally intervene to get a number of them accepted for medical studies in public higher education institutes (HEIs). The rest secured offers from private medical colleges but many were forced to give up their ambition for a medical career because of the high fees charged by private HEIs.

In a move to slowly reintroduce meritocracy in preuniversity education, the government has opened up a token 10 percent of the intake in government matriculation colleges to non-bumiputeras since 2002. Nonetheless, the system of higher education remains largely geared toward the sponsored mobility of bumiputeras. This has forced many non-bumiputera students to further their education in high-fee private HEIs that offer twinning and credit transfer programs leading to degree courses in foreign universities on a 2+1 basis (2 years in a local host institution and 1 year in the parent foreign university overseas). Recently many colleges have started to offer preuniversity courses leading to 3+0 programs which allow the entire degree program to be conducted in a local host institution. With the passing of the PHEI Act of 1996, foreign universities are now allowed to set up branch campuses in Malaysia. Currently, five foreign university branch campuses have been established in Malaysia. For the period 1998–2002, the student enrollments in private HEIs have increased by a hefty 75 percent while the increase in public HEIs has been only 35 percent. The total enrollment in private HEIs now stands at 294,600 while public enrollment stands at 325,000 students.[8] As at December 1999 the proportion of bumiputera students enrolled in degree and diploma level courses in private HEIs constituted only 36.1 percent of the total enrollment (Malaysia, 2001: 198). This is almost a mirror reverse image of the enrollment by ethnicity in public HEIs because according to a report by *Bernama*, the official national news agency on June 24, 2005, the Higher Education Department director Dr Hassan Said announced that, in total, 24,837 bumiputeras were offered places in public universities, representing 63.8 percent of the total number of seats available for 2005.

Teacher Education

Preservice teacher education in Malaysia is divided into graduate and nongraduate teacher training. Virtually all secondary school teachers are university graduates but most primary school teachers are trained in teacher training colleges under the jurisdiction of the Teacher Education Division (TED) of the Ministry of Education.

Currently the TED controls four preservice teacher education programs conducted in teacher training colleges (TTC) under its jurisdiction—the Malaysian Teaching Diploma Course (KDPM), the Post-Degree Teacher Training Course (KPLI), the Special Program for Nongraduate Teachers (PKPG) and the Bachelor of Education (PISMP). KDPM was introduced by the Ministry of Education in 1996 to replace the Basic Teachers Certificate Course (KPA) for preservice primary school teacher education. KPDM is a preservice program targeted at secondary school leavers and lasts three years. KPLI, on the other hand, is a preservice diploma program targeted at university graduates who wish to pursue a career in teaching. The duration of KPLI is one year. PKPG is a special in-service three year program offering degrees to nongraduate teachers and other education officers in the Ministry of Education or other agencies. The first year is spent at a teacher training college, while the second and third years are spent at a public HEI. In mid-2004, the TED implemented a five-year post-SPM B.Ed. twinning program entirely conducted by the TTCs in partnership with a public or private HEI. PISMP is divided into a 1½ year diploma component and a 3½ year degree component. At the time of writing, details of the "mother university" for the degree component of the PISMP had not emerged.

The long-term plan of the Ministry of Education is to achieve a staffing target of 50 percent of graduate teachers in primary schools by 2010 (Ministry of Education, 2001). This entails a daunting figure of 100,000 graduate primary school teachers to be trained in a period of 10 years. Although the TED is involved to a limited extent in graduate teacher training, it is in fact the public HEIs that are primarily responsible for graduate preservice and in-service teacher education as only universities and university colleges are empowered to award degrees under Malaysia's Universities and University Colleges Act (UUCA) of 1971. The creation of the Ministry of Higher Education in March 2004 has hampered the long-term plan of the TED announced by the Minister of Education (as reported in *The Star* of February 22, 2004), to convert teacher training colleges into degree awarding institutions as control of such institutions would have to be surrendered to the new ministry. In such an event, the very existence of the TED within the Ministry of Education would be untenable. It is expected that the TTCs will eventually be converted into degree-awarding institutes of teacher education (IPG) through an amendment of the UUCA by an Act of Parliament. The first concrete step toward making IPGs a reality was taken when the Prime Minister announced the allocation of funds to set up the IPGs in Budget 2006. Nevertheless, whether IPGs will emerge as degree-awarding institutions not affiliated to universities remains to be seen.

A DAY IN THE SCHOOL LIFE OF NUR ATHIRAH ROS AZMI

My name is Nur Athirah Ros Azmi. Both my parents are school teachers. I am 11 years old and the eldest of three children. I live in an apartment at Section 18, Shah Alam, the capital of the state of Selangor. I go to school at Sekolah Kebangsaan, Section 19, Shah Alam. I am now in Standard 5 Juara. My school is a mixed gender school. Most of the students here are Malays. Indians make up around 10 percent of the enrollment but there are very few Chinese as most Chinese parents prefer to send their children to Chinese primary schools.

Every morning, after breakfast, mum drops me at school. School starts at 7:30 A.M. sharp. All students must wear school uniforms. Boys have to wear white shirts and dark blue trousers. The uniform that most Muslim girls wear consists of a white *baju kurung*[9] and *tudung*[10] while the uniform for non-Muslim girls is a sky blue pinafore and a white blouse. As I am a school prefect, I have a special school uniform consisting of a light purple blouse, *tudung*, dark brown vest, long skirt, and matching tie.

On Mondays, we have school assembly before the commencement of classes, where we sing our national anthem, *Negaraku*. After assembly, we proceed to our classrooms in an orderly manner. When the teacher enters the class, the monitor will ask all the students to stand up and greet the teacher. Only then do the lessons start. Each lesson is approximately 40 minutes long.

The school day continues with different subjects and different teachers until eventually recess arrives and that is break time for the students and teachers after a hard morning. Before I eat, I say a quick prayer thanking Allah for all that He has given me. After recess, we go back to class and the lessons will continue until the end of the day.

I love school because the teachers here make learning fun with lots of hands-on activity, inquiry learning, and project work.

School ends at 1.10 P.M. but sometimes I have to stay back to attend cocurricular activities such as sports, club, and society meetings and so on. I attend

Islamic religious classes five times a week in the nearby SAR in the afternoon because mum says what I learn in school is not enough.

ANALYSIS AND CONCLUSION

National Integration and Equity Issues

Malaysia has made tremendous strides in terms of creating an integrated national system of education from the chaotic legacy of the British colonial administration. At the same time, Malaysia's record in providing universal access to education regardless of social and cultural background is good.

Out of necessity, the government was forced to suspend meritocracy in 1970 and implement a preferential education selection policy in favor of Malays and other bumiputeras to enable the bumiputeras to catch up economically with the non-bumiputeras. The Malays have made tremendous strides in education and a vibrant professional, managerial, and entrepreneurial bumiputera class has emerged. Nevertheless, the progress made in education amongst the bumiputeras has been uneven. The drop-out rate from primary schools for the *Orang Asli* and minority *bumiputera* communities in Sabah and Sarawak stands at a staggering 62.0 percent against the national average of 3.1 percent in 1995 (Ministry of Education, 2001).

On the larger question of national integration between natives and nonnatives, the national school has clearly failed in its role as the catalyst for national integration as it is only attended by 2 percent of the Chinese school-going population. Worse still, the preferential educational policy has created a dual meritocratic carriageway where entrance into choice university programs is apparently made easier for bumiputeras through the matriculation track while non-bumiputeras have to take the more challenging route. The dual meritocratic system is also evident in the sharp dichotomy that exists in enrollment in public and private HEIs where the former is attended mainly by bumiputeras and the latter by non-bumiputeras. By whatever measure, it is difficult to dismiss the argument that the educational system of Malaysia is, to a certain extent, a form of state-sponsored separatism, which bears some semblance to the much condemned divisive educational system of the colonial era.

Article 8(1) of the Federal Constitution decrees that all Malaysians "are equal before the law and entitled to the equal protection of the law." However, unequivocal equality of Malaysians under the constitution is negated by Article 153(1) which grants special rights to bumiputeras and Article 153(8A) which accords preferential university and college entrance privileges to bumiputeras. In a speech at the UMNO[11] General Assembly of 1992, Dr. Mahathir Mohamed, the former prime minister, articulated his vision of the "New Malay," a new breed of Malays who are "capable of meeting all challenges, able to compete without assistance ... [and] through their own efforts and skills ... will achieve progress." Similarly, during the tabling of the Second Outline Perspective Plan in Parliament on June 17, 1991 Dr. Mahathir lamented the dependency syndrome that has

Table 9.2

Enrollment in Government and Government-Assisted Educational Institutions by Grade and Level of Education as of June 30, 2004

Level of Education	Male	Female
Primary	1,603,500	1,517,386
	(51.38 %)	(48.62 %)
Lower secondary	666,743	626,234
	(50.81 %)	(49.19 %)
Upper secondary	363,443	387,468
	(48.40 %)	(51.50 %)
Postsecondary (Form 6 and Matriculation)	52,781	104,492
	(33.56 %)	(66.44 %)
College and Polytechnic	61,944	59,914
	(50.83 %)	(49.17 %)
University/University College	116,799	179,412
	(39.43 %)	(60.57 %)

Source: Ministry of Education, 2004.

taken hold amongst bumiputeras and warned bumiputeras that they "cannot expect economic policies to always favor them" and that "they must learn to face competition [in business]."

Any form of state-sponsored protection, be it fuel subsidies or in this case discriminatory educational policies, is ultimately unsustainable in the global economy as it is costly to maintain and decreases efficiency; it is also against the global civil society principle of equitable access in education. It is not suggested that the safety net, so to speak, that protects the natives should be removed straight away. As soon as the gap between the natives and nonnatives has sufficiently narrowed, the dual meritocratic track based on the dual citizenship class system should be dismantled in order to realize true national integration.

Where educational access by gender is concerned, Malaysia has more than achieved gender parity in educational access. In fact, as can be seen in Table 9.2, the participation of males decreases as they move up the educational ladder until females account for more than 60 percent of the enrollment in public universities.

Nevertheless women's domination of Malaysia's universities does not correspond with occupational success. Nik Kamariah and Filzah (2004) pointed out that only about 5 percent of women are working in managerial and professional positions in Malaysia.

Language Issues

Language has always been an emotional issue in Malaysia because of the cultural attachments amongst Malaysia's ethnic communities toward their respective mother tongues. The right of nonnatives to mother tongue instruction is nonnegotiable as it is enshrined in the federal constitution. While vernacular secondary schools have ceased to exist within Malaysia's public education system, nevertheless the SJKC and SJKT continue to flourish and independent Chinese secondary schools continue to thrive outside the national education system with the support of the Chinese community.

The Malays, on the other hand, are divided into the hardcore nationalists and the progressive modernists. The former have fought successfully for the Malay language to be maintained as the sole national language and medium of instruction in public educational institutions. The latter, whilst remaining true Malays at heart, have nevertheless opined that the English language which was sidelined since independence has to be brought back to a limited extent as a medium of instruction as it is the dominant language of global commerce as well as science and technology. Surprisingly, the architect of the small swing back to English was Mahathir Mohamed who accomplished the mission shortly before he retired as prime minister. This is surprising because Mahathir's inspirational influence through the publication of *The Malay Dilemma* (Mahathir, 1970) was instrumental in launching Malaysia into the socioeconomic reengineering era of the New Economic Policy from 1970 to 1990. To reconcile the two contrasting images of Mahathir, perhaps he can be described as a visionary pragmatist. When he stepped into office as prime minister in 1981, the winds of globalization and liberalization had just begun to sweep around the world. In the end, he remained true to his heart in transforming the mindset of the Malays in order to stand tall on the global stage even if it meant that they would have to relax their emotional attachment to their language.

A backlash from the ultranationalists was sounded when the Second Malay Education Congress organized by the Malay Education and Development Organization on March 26–27, 2005 in Kuala Lumpur adopted a unanimous resolution urging the government to halt the implementation of the policy of teaching science and mathematics in English, and reinstate the Malay language as the medium of instruction for all subjects. The call was based on the alarmist and unsubstantiated revelation that half a million Malay students might drop out of science and technology programs if the policy of teaching science and mathematics in English were to continue. In a knee jerk reaction, Prime Minister Abdullah Ahmad Badawi promised to review the policy. In response, Mahathir, his political mentor and former premier, stoutly defended the dilution of the language policy which he had proposed three years earlier (Rencana, *Utusan Malaysia*, March 29, 2005). Following that, Education Minister Hishammuddin Hussein, in deference to the long shadow cast by Mahathir on the Malaysian political arena, hastily declared that the language policy would continue until the end of 2007 without any review whatsoever.

The ad hoc announcements and retractions of the government as it reacted to the waxing and waning of the political winds surrounding the language issue do not bode well for the long-term well-being of the school curriculum. More needs to be done to reduce language–culture sensitivities in education. The example of Northern Ireland shows that homogeneity of language does not guarantee harmony in society. In contrast, a country like Switzerland where three languages share equal status as national languages serves as a model for multicultural harmony.

Curriculum Upheaval

The centralized educational system of Malaysia has one thing in common with giants of folklore—it creates massive upheavals on the landscape whenever it stirs. Major curriculum reforms are often hastily planned and implemented, resulting in damaging repercussions which have had to be reversed at high cost back to status quo, for example, the pendulum swing away from science and back again. School textbooks and science were abruptly taken out of primary schools and then reintroduced. The swing back to science toward a science:humanities enrollment ratio of 60:40 may have been overcompensatory because according to an IIEP study, the economic benefits of an upper secondary science enrollment exceeding 50 percent is not justified by the associated high cost of science education (Caillods et al., 1996). Another hastily enacted curriculum turnaround, the reintroduction of English as the medium of instruction for science and mathematics in 2003, is also in danger of being reversed once again. One observation that is often raised in informal conversation amongst Malaysians is that every Malaysian premier apart from the first had at one time occupied the education ministry but the reverse is not necessarily true. Given the importance placed on education with respect to national integration, the education portfolio is a testing ground for potential prime ministers. There is no evidence to suggest that an aspiring premier or even an outgoing one feels pressured to leave behind a huge personal legacy in education. However, if that is true perhaps little can be done to avoid cataclysmic changes in Malaysian education.

Unanticipated Consequences of Past Policies and Possible Unintended Consequences in Future

The greatest challenge faced by the leaders of newly independent Malaysia in 1957 was to forge a sense of national identity amongst the nation's multiethnic communities. Education was seen as the silver bullet, so to speak, to achieve the said purpose. It was the intention of the nation's founders to create a national system of education and a common school curriculum in order that Malaysian children from all cultural communities could interact freely and ultimately develop a sense of national belonging and destiny. The SK was originally singled out as the sole vehicle of national integration. Alas, the Durkheimian functionalist scenario of organic solidarity in Malaysia could not be realized because of the delicately balanced politics of the country. The nonnative Chinese and Indian communities which formed sizeable minorities fought hard for the maintenance of vernacular schools as the said schools were seen as fundamental toward the survival of the respective cultures. In the end, a political compromise was achieved. In exchange for recognizing the special rights of the natives, the SJKC and SJKT were integrated as national type schools within the national school system. At the same time, English-medium schools were eliminated from the national school system and the English language was relegated to the status of a second language taught as a school subject. The outcome was unsatisfactory to both bumiputeras and non-bumiputeras but, by and large, with the exception of the violent interethnic riots of May 13, 1969, the process of political accommodation that had existed since independence continues to thrive. Far from moving toward a national destiny, Malaysia continues to dominated by divergent communitarian agendas. Nevertheless, as the political power of the nonnatives is eroded by the continual decline in the proportion of the nonnatives in the population, it appears inevitable that the national type schools will eventually be eliminated from the national school system. On the other hand, the role of the English language appears to be on the upswing in the prevailing atmosphere of nationalism amid globalization.

NOTES

1. Indians refer to immigrants from the Indian subcontinent, including Pakistan, Bangladesh, and Sri Lanka.

2. *Terra Nullius* literally means, "This land belongs (or originally belonged) to no one." The principle was used to legally nullify aboriginal ancestral land claims in Australia.

3. KBSR is the Bahasa Malaysia abbreviation for *Kurikulum Bersepadu Sekolah Rendah.*

4. KBSM is the Bahasa Malaysia abbreviation for *Kurikulum Bersepadu Sekolah Menengah.*

5. MARA schools fall under the jurisdiction of the Ministry of Entrepreneur Development, not the Ministry of Education. MARA (*Majlis Amanah Rakyat*) is a statutory government agency charged with developing entrepreneurship amongst bumiputeras, especially those in rural areas.

6. Program A was the "normal" Bachelor of Arts with Education program where students double-majored in the humanities.

7. On May 28, 2004, an opposition party leader called upon the government to scrap the dual preuniversity examination system and establish a common examination for university entrance. He pointed out that 1,774 students obtained the maximum Cumulative Grade Point Average (CGPA) of 4.0. Among the STPM students, 527 obtained the maximum CGPA—Chinese (503), Indians (23), and Bumiputera (1). For matriculation, there were 1,247 students with the maximum CGPA—Bumiputera (789), Chinese (419), and Indians (39). In all, 70 percent of top scorers were bumiputera matriculation students, which seems to cast some serious doubts on whether the two examinations are equivalent.

8. Keynote Address: *International Education: The Effects of Globalisation—Needs, Challenges & Strategies* by Dato' Mustapa Mohamed, Executive Director, National Economic Action Council (NEAC) at the International Conference on Globalization: Effects of Globalization, Sunway Lagoon Resort, Petaling Jaya, October 9, 2003.

9. A loose-fitting full-length female Malay dress consistent with the requirements of modesty in Islam.

10. A head scarf for Muslims.

11. UMNO—the United Malays National Organization is the dominant political party in the ruling coalition.

REFERENCES

Alatas, Syed Hussein (1977). *The Myth of the Lazy Native*. London: Frank Cass.

Caillods, François, Göttelmann-Duret, Gabrielle, and Lewin, Keith (1996). *Science Education and Development: Planning and Policy Issues at Secondary Level*. Paris: International Institute for Education Planning.

Cummings, William K. (1986). *Low-cost Primary Education: Implementing an Innovation in Six Nations*. Canada: International Development Research Centre.

Department of Statistics, Malaysia (1995). *Population and Housing Census of Malaysia 1991: General Report of the Housing Census*. Malaysia: Government Press.

——(2001). *Population and Housing Census of Malaysia 2000: Population Distribution and Basic Demographic Characteristics*. Malaysia: Government Press.

Jumper, Roy Davis Linville (1999). *Orang Asli now: The Orang Asli in the Malaysian Political World*. Lanham, MD: University Press of America.

Lee, Molly Nyet Ngo, Yoong, Suan, Loo, Seng Piew, Zon, Khadijah, Ghazali, Munirah, and Lim, Chap Sam (1996). *Students' Orientations towards Science and Mathematics: Why are Enrolments Falling?* Penang, Malaysia: Universiti Sains Malaysia.

Loh, Fook Seng (1969). *The Malay States 1877–1895: Political Change and Social Policy*. London: Oxford University Press.

Mahathir, Mohamed (1970). *The Malay Dilemma*. Kuala Lumpur: Times Books International.

Malaya (1893). *Report of the Protected Malay States, January, 1893, Cd.6568*. London: HMSO.

——(1951a). *Report of the Committee on Malay Education*. Kuala Lumpur: Government Press.

——(1951b). *Report on the Barnes Report on Malay Education and the Fenn-Wu Report on Chinese Education*. Kuala Lumpur: Government Press.

——(1956). *Report of the Education Committee, 1956*. Kuala Lumpur: Government Press.

——(1960). *Report of the Education Review Committee, 1960*. Kuala Lumpur: Government Press.

Malaysia (2001). *Third Outline Perspective Plan, 2001–2010*. Kuala Lumpur: Government Press.

Ministry of Education, Malaysia (2001). *Pembangunan pendidikan 2001–2010: Perancangan bersepadu penjana kecemerlangan pendidikan* (Education Development Plan 2001–2010: Generating Educational Excellence through Collaborative Planning). Malaysia: Ministry of Education.

——(2004). *Educational Statistics of Malaysia, 2004*. Malaysia: Ministry of Education.

——(2006). *Pelan Induk Pembangunan Pendidikan 2006–1010* (Educational Development Blueprint 2006–2010). Malaysia: Ministry of Education.

Mustapa, Kassim (1989). "Preferential policy in higher education in Malaysia: A case study of Malay graduates at the University of Science, Malaysia." Ph.D. dissertation, University of Wisconsin.

Nicholas, Colin (2000). *The Orang Asli and the Contest for Resources: Indigenous Politics, Development and Identity in Peninsular Malaysia*. Denmark: International Work Group for Indigenous Affairs.

Nik Kamariah, Nik Mat, and Filzah Md Isa (2004). "Phantom women graduates: Where are they?" Paper presented at the international conference on management education, June 28–29, 2004 in The Legend Hotel, Kuala Lumpur.

Sahara, Ahmad (2000). *Education for all (Malaysian country report)*. United Nations: UNESCO.

Siti Zahara, Sulaiman (1975). "MARA Junior Science College: Students selection and its implication for educational development in Malaya." Ph.D. dissertation, University of Cornell.

Wikipedia (2005). *Education in Malaysia*. Accessed on August 15, 2005 from http://en.wikipedia.org/wiki/Education_in_Malaysia.

Chapter 10

SCHOOLING IN MONGOLIA

John C. Weidman, Regsuren Bat-Erdene, and Erika Bat-Erdene

The contemporary Republic of Mongolia is the world's largest landlocked country. It has an area of 1.5 million square km consisting mainly of high plateaus across the western, northern, and eastern regions, and the Gobi desert in the southeast. Mongolia has bitterly cold winters tempered by moderate summers. With a total population of just over 2.5 million, it is the world's least densely populated country. Among the population, 41 percent of people live in rural areas. Urban drift over the past decade has resulted in 37 percent of the population residing in the capital city of Ulaanbaatar, while another 22 percent live in urban areas including the cities of Darkhan and Erdenet (*Mongolian Statistical Yearbook*, 2004, Table 3.1). Almost three times more people of Mongolian descent live within the borders of China (primarily in "Inner Mongolia") than in the Republic of Mongolia.

Extreme weather conditions and accompanying population movements are major factors that make it very difficult to provide adequate resources for education. The World Bank classifies Mongolia as a lower middle-income developing country but this general classification disguises a highly diverse socioeconomic environment ranging from very poor populations in peri-urban and isolated rural settings to high income enclaves in prosperous neighborhoods of Ulaanbaatar.

From 1911 until 1990, Mongolia, though independent from 1921 and never a constituent republic of the U.S.S.R., was closely aligned with the Soviet Union from whom it received significant economic aid, including support for education. Russian language was a required subject and Mongolian textbooks were printed in Cyrillic script. After the U.S.S.R. collapsed, Mongolia embarked on a path to reform in all spheres of political, economic, and social life, including the education sector.

This chapter takes as its historical starting point the year 1206 when Genghis Khan unified the Mongolian tribes and embarked on a series of conquests continued by his descendents that significantly altered the geopolitical situation of the globe. It illustrates the respect for learning held by Mongolians that persisted over the ensuing centuries and mentions some of the ways in which ideas and approaches from other countries were incorporated into their education.

The main focus of the chapter is the evolution of Mongolian schooling since 1990 as the legal and policy frameworks to build the current educational system were developed, establishing the structures and mechanisms for schooling that would support the transition from a command to a market economy. The reflections of a Mongolian college student provide insights into the daily life of school children in the 1990s. The chapter concludes with a discussion of the directions in Mongolian education is moving and the prospects for sustaining reform initiatives.

THE IMPERIAL PERIOD—13TH AND 14TH CENTURIES

The year 2006 marked the 800th anniversary of the unification of the Mongol tribes by Genghis Khan and the onset of the largest conquest of the globe ever experienced. Genghis, the first of the "Great Khans," and his descendents built an empire that, according to historian David Morgan, can be described as follows:

The Mongol Empire of the thirteenth and fourteenth centuries was the largest continuous land empire that has so far existed. At its greatest extent it stretched from Korea to Hungary, including, except for India and the south-east of the continent, most of Asia, as well as a good deal of eastern Europe. As a whole it lasted for well over a century, and parts of it survived for very much longer. It was merely one, albeit by the far the most extensive, of a series of great steppe empires; and it should be seen in the context provided by its predecessors. The major difference between the Mongols and previous conquerors is that no other nomad empire had succeeded in holding both the Inner Asian steppe and the neighboring sedentary lands simultaneously. (1986: 5)

Genghis Khan was illiterate, but he recognized the importance for managing his conquests of being able to write down directives and regulations. While there is some question about whether or not his decrees actually constituted a legal code (Morgan, 1986: 96–99), he did arrange to write down decrees so that they could easily be communicated to rulers at the far reaches of the empire. Genghis Khan brought a Uighur scholar to his court for the explicit purpose of writing down decrees and ordinances for the management of the empire. Hence, Uighur script was used for writing the Mongolian language and Mongol children and governing officials were required to learn it (Juvaini, 1260: 25). The appropriation of the Uighur script is an early illustration of an openness to and propensity toward drawing from others certain cultural and educational practices that served useful purposes within the Mongolian context, what has been called more recently "educational import" (Steiner-Khamsi and Stolpe, 2006).

Recognizing the necessity for an effective system of communication over the vast expanse of the empire, the precursor to the modern postal system was established by Genghis Khan and refined by his son and successor, Ogedei. Messages were carried by riders on sturdy steppe horses via post stations located at stages equivalent to a day's journey (40–50 km, more in desolate areas) where fresh horses were kept. Urgent messages could go as far as 200–300 miles per day (Morgan, 1986: 103–107), depending on the terrain.

In 1260, the grandson of Genghis Khan, Kublai, was named the "Great Khan." By this time Kublai had already begun his conquest of China, having established the place where modern Beijing sits as his capital. In 1272, Kublai Khan established the Yuan Dynasty which ruled until 1368 (Morgan, 1986: 135). It might be said that Kublai Khan set the progress of education in China back when he did away with the Chinese civil service examination system in 1260 (Morgan, 1986: 111). There was, however, a very pragmatic reason for this: Kublai Khan needed to have Mongols administering the dynasty, but they were vastly outnumbered by the Chinese (according to Rossabi, 1988: 71–72, by as many as 200 to 1). He could not risk having to appoint civil servants on the basis of tests that would favor the Chinese majority. However, while Kublai Khan did not appoint Chinese to the highest administrative offices, he recognized that "lower-ranking civil servants had to be allowed to continue with their job if government was to function at all" (Morgan, 1986: 110).

There is also evidence that Kublai Khan was a strong supporter of education. As early as 1269, he founded a special office to print books. In 1286, he offered land grants to academies to support the printing of books (Rossabi, 1988: 163). He supported craftsmen, as well, and during his reign the blue and white porcelains often associated with the Ming Dynasty actually originated (Rossabi, 1988: 170). Even though Kublai Khan favored Tibetan Buddhism, like most Mongol rulers he tolerated religious diversity (Morgan, 1986: 124–125; Badamsambuu, 2006, chapter 3). Kublai Khan also made certain that the history of the Mongol conquests was recorded so that it could be passed on to future generations, bringing the Persian historian Juvaini (1260) to his court and even giving him administrative responsibilities in the Yuan Dynasty.

He was open to receiving foreign visitors, the most famous of whom was Marco Polo. It is quite likely that Marco Polo brought both printing and porcelains to Europe from the court of Kublai Khan in Beijing. According to Morgan (1986: 111):

The Mongols, then, would adopt any institution and employ any potential servant that seemed likely to facilitate effective government; the effectiveness would be measured chiefly by the revenue receipts. There is little that can be regarded as identifiably "Mongol" in the governmental institutions of the Mongols' empire, except for the way in which they put it all together and made such an extraordinarily disparate assemblage actually work. The principal constraint on this free and easy approach was the consideration that nothing should be allowed to endanger Mongol military supremacy.

When the Chinese overthrew the last Mongol ruler of the Yuan Dynasty in 1368 and established the Ming Dynasty, the descendents of the Mongolian Khans returned to their homelands in the north and the nomadic way of life punctuated by a series of tribal skirmishes, but never again ascendancy to a unified force.

THE MANCHU COLONIZATION (17TH–19TH CENTURIES)

By the middle of the 16th century, conversion of the various Mongol tribes to Buddhism was proceeding rapidly, with the first "Dalai Lama" being named in 1578. The form of Buddhism adopted "was the Tibetan denomination of the Yellow Hat, better known as Lamaism... It was famous for its extreme monasticism, theocracy eventually symbolized by the person of the Dalai Lama reigning from Lhasa, and a complex system of reincarnation" (Soucek, 2000: 168).

By the end of the 17th century, the eastern Mongol tribes were under the control of the Manchu Dynasty. Continued incursion by the Manchus colonized the western tribes as well.

The tribes living in what would evolve in Inner Mongolia had been annexed since the rise of the Manchus as early as 1644. For Inner Mongolia, incorporation in the Chinese empire proved a permanent arrangement, on both the political and demographic levels: politically, it outlasted the Manchu Dynasty beyond its demise in 1911 and exists today as the Inner Mongolian Autonomous Region of the People's Republic of China; demographically, the Mongol population has been swamped by Chinese settlers. In Outer Mongolia, Chinese suzerainty lasted until the twentieth century—until 1911 or later dates depending on interpretation, the latest *terminus* being 1945—but without the demographic transformation that befell Inner Mongolia. (Soucek, 2000: 171)

The Manchu set up just enough schools to train a small number of clerks for routine management tasks in the Mongol provinces. However, religious education became increasingly popular among Mongolians during the Manchu period. By the beginning of the 20th century, 25–30 percent (18,000 to 20,000 total) of school-aged boys studied in 700 big and 1,000 small monastery schools (Badamsambuu, 2006, chapter 3). In addition, families continued a longstanding tradition of conducting schooling for their children at home (Badamsambuu, 2006, chapter 3).

The sons of the well-to-do studied either in the family or under a tutor. It was a good idea for a tutor to take on, now and then, a clever boy from a very poor family. Then he would be able to do a good turn for a well-off family, if it had a son summoned for service, by providing an acceptable substitute. (Lattimore, 1962: 83)

This situation continued more or less uninterruptedly through 1911 when the Manchu Dynasty collapsed as well as through the following decade of a religious government established in what was to become modern Ulaanbaatar. At independence in 1921, Mongolia had only one elementary school not attached to a monastery (Lattimore, 1962: 169).

In an effort to solidify independence from the Chinese, the Mongolian religious leader sought closer ties with its neighbor to the north, Russia. By 1915, a Russian owned printing house was publishing books and the first Mongolian newspaper in the capital city.

RUSSIAN INFLUENCE, 1921–1989

The People's Revolution in 1921 freed Mongolia from external occupation by the Chinese military force that invaded in 1920. The "white" Russians supporting the 1921 revolution seemed at the time to be liberators from Chinese dominance. However, the "red" Russians defeated them. Consequently, the now commonly accepted interpretation is that the "white" Russians were occupants, as well. Following the 1921 revolution, a theocratic state with a religious leader as the head of the state was established (Baabar, 1999). Even after the theocratic government was deposed with the establishment of the Mongolian Peoples' Republic in 1924, Tibetan Buddhism was firmly entrenched and the feudal system of monasteries and their lamas that had evolved over the centuries continued to flourish. In the mid-1920s, literacy in the Mongolian language was estimated at just 1 percent of the population. Another 9 percent were literate in languages like Tibetan and Chinese (Lattimore, 1962: 110–111). The fledgling communist government began establishing public schools in order to establish its own preeminence over religious education which was perceived to be antirevolutionary. In 1924, the first two "secondary specialized schools" were established and by 1930, there were 122 state-funded elementary schools (Lattimore, 1962: 169). The government opened the first professional school to train teachers in the mid-1920s.

However, the Tibetan Buddhist monastery structure was entrenched and continued to exert strong religious and economic influence into the 1930s. The monastic schools had a tradition of being open to all males and were well-integrated into the pastoral society, providing room and board in or near the monasteries for children from nomadic families (Steiner-Khamsi and Stolpe, 2006: 29). In 1936, 11 percent of the total population was lamas, including 40 percent of the adult males of the country. To the detriment of Mongolian children, the church was committed to the prestige of religious books written in Tibetan and "obstinately opposed to the teaching of the Mongol written language, and to all modern education" (Lattimore, 1962: 137).

Persisting economic influence was reflected by the income of the church and individual lamas in 1935–1936, that "was equivalent in amount, when compared to the annual national budgets of 1932–1936, to percentages ranging from 68 per cent to 93 per cent of the national income" (Lattimore, 1962: 138). The government, strongly influenced by Soviet Communists, increasingly viewed the monasteries as undermining Marxist principles. Consequently, in 1938 and 1939, monasteries were suppressed, systematically destroyed, and monastic schools were forced to close.

State-funded schools were expanded considerably in this period. By 1940, there were 331 government elementary schools (Lattimore, 1962: 169). In 1941, the traditional Mongolian script that had evolved from the Uighur script introduced by Genghis Khan, was replaced by Cyrillic. In 1942, the Mongolian State University was established in Ulaanbaatar (Government of Mongolia, 1993). By the end of World War II and the successful reassertion of Mongolian independence from China with the help of Russia, the transition to a Soviet-style education system was fully underway.

Table 10.1 shows the enrollment growth in the Mongolian educational system beginning in 1940. Compulsory education consisted of four years of primary education followed by a secondary (middle school) education that lasted for three years (four years duration between 1974 and 2005) . After completing compulsory education, graduates had to be promoted to the next level or allowed to leave to get employed, or enter professional schools for such careers as teacher, nurse, accountant, and so on. An additional three years (two years since 1974) were required to complete secondary education, with the option of going on to an advanced professional or higher education program after completing the full secondary cycle. By 1989, almost 447,000 Mongolian children were enrolled in general secondary education (grades 1–10). Another 55,000 were enrolled in one of three types of vocational schools:

those providing two years of training for eighth grade graduates of general education schools, those offering one year of training for tenth grade completers of secondary schools, and those (called "specialized secondary schools" which offer an equivalent to associate degree programs designed to train mid-level professional and technical person-nel) at the secondary level providing two to three years of training depending on enrollees prior school completion (either 8 or 10 years). This system worked reasonably well until 1990 when Mongolia embarked on a program of transition to a market economy. Because the system was designed to meet the exigencies of a planned economy it encountered difficulties meeting the training and retraining needs of the transitional economy. (Government of Mongolia, 1993, chapter 6: 3)

By the mid-1980s, Mongolia began feeling the effects of a declining socialist economy and collapsing of the totalitarian regime as well as increased pressure for social and political reform:

In 1986, Mongolia became one of the first socialist countries to launch a program of political openness and restructuring. This program had five goals: a) acceleration of development; b) application of science and technology to production; c) reform of management and planning; d) greater independence of enterprises; and e) balance of individual, collective and societal interests. (Government of Mongolia, 1993, chapter 4: 2)

Anticipating the coming transition, the 5th Congress of Mongolian Teachers, held in June 1989, proposed administrative decentralization of education, increas-ing involvement of stakeholders in school management, and creating a favorable environment to support independent learning by students. For more details about

Table 10.1
Enrollment in Mongolia by Level of Education, 1940–1999

Year	Kindergarten	General–Secondary (Grades 1–10)	Vocational Education and Training (VET)	Specialized Vocational Education	Diploma Programs	Higher Education on Bachelors Programs	Postgraduate Degree Programs
1940	146	24,311		1,332		197	
1945	576	34,543		1,744		309	
1950	1,800	68,614		3,186		1,476	
1955	3,878	83,334		4,493		3,039	
1960	9,738	107,204		8,811		6,909	
1965	24,450	155,780	4,761	9,231		10,677	
1970	29,613	230,406	10,628	11,121		8,427	
1975	36,974	301,936	13,483	13,465		13,643	
1980	49,807	372,112	22,109	18,734		23,214	
1985	62,470	415,168	27,718	22,978		24,549	
1986	69,746	423,545	29,276	23,212		23,516	
1987	70,594	430,540	32,053	23,992		22,647	
1988	81,029	438,152	33,797	22,556		20,723	
1989	88,274	446,665	34,137	20,534		19,504	
1990	97,212	440,986	29,067	18,478		17,338	
1991	95,715	411,696	19,252	15,779		16,801	
1992	85,700	384,069	11,685	8,703		19,827	192
1993	59,909	370,302	8,317	5,799		24,247	383
1994	60,959	381,204	7,555	5,943		27,870	435
1995	64,086	403,847	7,987	5,584		31,973	804
1996	67,972	418,293	11,308		3,730	39,157	1,201
1997	70,035	435,061	12,320		4,426	44,864	1,671
1998	74,299	447,121	11,650		4,094	59,444	1,734
1999	78,630	470,038	11,245		4,371	67,554	2,100

Source: MECS, 2001.

Mongolian education in the 1921–1989 period, interested readers are referred to the excellent historical accounts of primary and secondary education by Khamsi-Steiner and Stolpe (2006) and of higher education by Badamsambuu (2006).

EDUCATION UNDER THE MONGOLIAN REPUBLIC (1990–THE PRESENT)

Mongolia's first multiparty elections were held in 1990 and a new constitution approved in 1992 that incorporated the principles of a democratic society based on a market economy and the guarantee of fundamental human rights, including the right to education. The constitution has been the basis for political and legal development in Mongolia, including the education sector. The government has granted the education sector a premium role, both in the Soviet era and since, because Mongolians have traditionally regarded education as an important asset. The rapid social and economic changes from 1990 included legal and policy reforms necessary for moving the education system away from one that was suited to a centrally planned society. This required fundamental reorientation of the education sector (Yoder and Weidman, 2003).

Legal and Policy Frameworks

Similar to other countries in Central Asia that had been former Soviet republics, Mongolia had to develop the legal and policy frameworks necessary for reforming and regulating its educational system (Asian Development Bank, 2004). The *Mongolian Government Education Policy* (Government of Mongolia, 1995a) lays out the basic principles for education reform, stating: "the Mongolian government recognizes that the source for Mongolia's future progress is the continually developing, creative citizen with high levels of education as well as intellectual abilities and skills, so it considers education as a priority sector of society." This document also indicates that "education is the source for sustainable and accelerated economic and social growth, science and technology progress, intellectual and social welfare, national sovereignty and security." Accordingly, education reform is established as a political priority in the national development agenda of Mongolia in order to respond to new demands for providing students with the knowledge and skills necessary for the emerging market economy.

The Mongolian government wanted to deal with the possibility of vast income differences among citizens that could accompany economic transition and privatization of government enterprises. Education was considered to be a key instrument for fighting poverty, improving living standards, and enhancing economic capacity. The *Education Policy* and *Education Law* (Government of Mongolia, 1995a,b) identify the following principles governing the rights of people to education as well as government responsibility for its provision:

- education is to be developed as a priority sector; the government will continually support and nourish it while monitoring and coordinating its activities;
- the government will provide free basic education for all;

- citizens will be provided with an equal opportunity to learn in their own mother tongue by not discriminating on account of social origin, status, race, color, age, sex, wealth, job, position, or religious belief;
- any educational or training activities contradictory to the interests, health, and security of individuals and of society or contradictory to democratic beliefs are prohibited;
- the government will support education institutions without discriminating on the basis of ownership; and
- to guarantee sustainability, 20 percent of government revenues are to be allocated to the education sector.

The Parliament of Mongolia (Great Khural) has amended the comprehensive set of laws governing the education sector periodically since 1995 as new contingencies arise. Despite the problems of coping with an economic transition from a command to a market economy, Mongolia has maintained an educational system which reaches a widely dispersed population and boasts of one of the highest literacy rates in the world (more than 90 percent).

Mongolia Education and Human Resource Master Plan (1993–1994)

In 1993, the Asian Development Bank (ADB) provided a grant to fund a comprehensive Sector Review and Master Plan process designed to serve as the foundation for supporting assistance to the education and human resource sector in Mongolia as it moved through the difficult transition from a command to a market economy. The documents resulting from this activity, the *Mongolia Education and Human Resource Sector Review* (Government of Mongolia, 1993) and the *Mongolia Education and Human Resource Master Plan* (Government of Mongolia, 1994), described all sectors of the educational system in place at that time and established strategies for its development through 1999. The 1994 *Master Plan* (Government of Mongolia, 1994) identified six areas of specific concern:

- enhance basic and general education
- reform higher education for national development purposes
- rationalize systems for vocational training
- provide learning opportunities of out-of-school children and youth
- improve educational management
- increase the efficiency of the Ministry of Science and Education structure and operations.

Education Sector Development Strategy (1999)

In 1999, the ADB supported development of the *Education Sector Development Strategy, 2000–2005* (MECS, Government of Mongolia, 1999). This document extended the 1994 *Master Plan* and contained the basic direction for the education sector in the new millennium, identifying four areas of greatest strategic priority:

- alleviating deficiencies with buildings and facilities
- providing teacher training and re-training

- developing curriculum and providing textbooks and other educational materials
- increasing student participation in education.

An underlying goal of the government in this process has been to reduce poverty by increasing access to education in areas with the lowest enrollment rates as well as reducing income and poverty deprivation by improving access to quality preschool and basic education (Grades 1–8) in poorer rural and urban areas.

While the 1994 *Master Plan* emphasized investment in human resource development across the entire education system, the 2000–2005 *Sector Strategy* concentrated on primary and secondary education, adding an emphasis on investments in school buildings and material resources along with continuing capacity building among teachers. The Mongolian tradition of welcoming visitors, its strategic location, its democratic government, its relatively successful transition to a market economy, and its historical ties to both Europe and Asia have made this small country very attractive to donors from around the world.

In addition to the ADB investments, there have been a variety of projects funded by grants from donors including DANIDA, UNESCO, UNICEF, the Mongolian Foundation for Open Society (MFOS-Soros Foundation and its successors, the Mongolian Education Alliance-MEA and the Open Society Forum), the Australian Agency for International Development (AusAID), the European Union, the Korean International Cooperation Agency; the World Bank; World Vision; and the Save the Children Foundation (UK). There are agreements with the Government of Germany in the area of technical and vocational education, and with the Japanese International Cooperation Agency (JICA) for renovation of school buildings. Of the total investment in the education sector over the four-year period between 2000 and 2003, 54 percent came from donor grants, 10 percent from soft donor loans, and 36 percent from national and local government.

Mongolia has also benefited from long- and short-term training of educators and educational officials. Before the transition, many Mongolians studied in the former Soviet Union. Since 1993, other agencies have included the German Academic Exchange Service (DAAD), American programs such as Fulbright, Humphrey, and IREX; the Australian Government, the Japanese Government, and the Soros Foundation.

Structure of the Mongolian Education System

Figure 10.1 shows the structure of the Mongolian education system prior to 2004 when a complete cycle was 10 years. An 11th year of the complete general secondary education cycle was added in 2004 by optional enrollment of 7-year-olds into the first year of school. Full implementation began in September of 2005 with an expectation of moving to a 12-year system (6 years primary, 3 years lower secondary, and 3 years upper secondary) in 2008 by enrolling 6-year-olds in Grade 1. The number of years of compulsory education will also be changed from eight to nine years. The number of years for postsecondary degrees will not

Figure 10.1
The Educational System of Mongolia (10-Year General Secondary)*

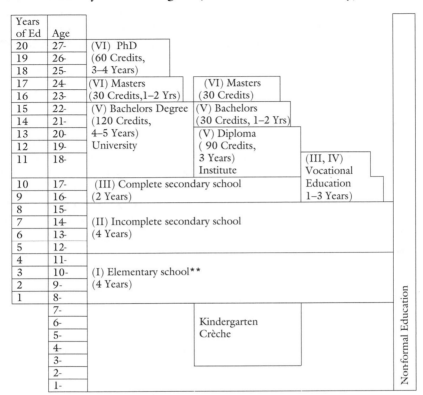

Notes: * Beginning in September of 2005, the formal transition to a 12-year general secondary education system was phased in with the enrollment of 7 year-olds in the first year of an 11-year system, followed in 2007 by enrollment of 6 year-olds into the first year of a 12-year system.
** The Roman numerals in parentheses represent UNESCO ISCE categories designating the level of education represented.

Source: Erdenechimeg, et al., 2005.

change but, because of the introduction of a 12-year preparatory cycle, the content and rigor of degrees will be strengthened. Technical and vocational education is offered in both vocational schools and postsecondary diploma programs housed in higher education institutions. Nonformal and distance education programs span the entire educational system.

Enrollment Patterns

The enrollment patterns shown in Table 10.1 reflect the effects of the social and economic transition of the late 1980s and early 1990s. Kindergarten enrollments grew until 1990 (97,212), followed by a small drop in 1991 and then a large drop in 1993. This was due largely to elimination of government subsidies to families for enrolling their children in kindergartens and accommodating them in boarding facilities in rural areas. Enrollment in general secondary education (Grades 1–10) reached 446,665 in 1989 and then dropped to 370,302 in 1993. The cumulative school dropout rate of children aged 8–15 (average expected age range for the eight years of compulsory education at that time) was estimated to be just 4 percent in the 1988–1989 school year, but by 1992–1993 the cumulative dropout rate had increased to 18.6 percent (Government of Mongolia, 1993, chapter 4: 4–14). By 2004, enrollment had climbed to 557,346 students.

Vocational education and training (VET) was introduced in vocational–technical schools in 1965 and enrollment grew until 1989 (34,137), dropping to a low of 7,555 in 1994 as the job placement structure that had existed within the command economy collapsed and vocational education struggled to provide students with skills required for employment in a market economy. In an effort to keep up VET enrollments, vocational–technical schools were restructured as vocational training and production centers with the aim to increase their capability to generate additional income producing, marketable goods. This also allowed them to respecialize and open new programs, including postsecondary diploma programs. In some places this types of institutions merged with other institutions. Some former specialized secondary schools were restructured to operate as two- to four-year colleges, thereby increasingly delivering more marketable undergraduate programs.

Table 10.2 provides a summary of several basic indicators of the education sector in Mongolia from 2000 through 2004. Higher education has experienced the most rapid enrollment expansion of any level of education in Mongolia over the past four years. While enrollment in private higher education institutions has more than doubled over the past four years, there have also been large enrollment increases in public sector institutions. In 1994, the Mongolian government required public higher education institutions to charge tuition at levels sufficient to cover the cost of academic staff salaries. This resulted in a large reduction in the government budget for higher education. Presently, the only support provided by the government to higher education is through the State Training Fund which grants loans and scholarships to students enrolled in accredited institutions of higher education, both public and private.

Enrollments at all other levels of Mongolian education have also been increasing, but at much slower rates. Only kindergarten and secondary vocational education enrollments in 2004 were lower than they had been prior to 1990. Limited government funding for preschool and kindergartens seems to be the major reason for the continuing lag in enrollments at that level. The vocational education sector is still struggling with implementing reforms appropriate for meeting the needs of the emerging market economy.

It is anticipated that the government mandate to change the general secondary education cycle from 10 to 12 years by 2008 will also increase enrollments over

Table 10.2
Students and Teachers in Mongolian Education, 2000–2004

	2000	2001	2002	2003	2004
Kindergartens	653	665	655	687	696
Pupils	79,294	83,578	87,711	90,215	82,674
Annual rate of change (%)	0.8	5.4	4.9	2.9	−8.4
Teachers	3,056	3,177	3,257	3,267	3,424
Pupil/teacher ratio	26	26	27	28	24
Secondary schools, of which	683	700	688	686	710
Primary schools (standalone)	113	106	95	72	75
Secondary schools (grades 1–10)	570	594	593	614	635
Pupils	494,544	510,291	527,931	537,398	557,346
Annual rate of change (%)	5.2	3.2	3.5	1.8	3.7
Percentage of dropouts (%)	2.8	2.8	2.4	2.5	2.3
Teachers	19,223	20,076	20,752	20,792	21,458
Pupil/teacher ratio	26	25	25	26	26
Vocational and technical education schools (VTPC/VETC/Branch schools)	36	32	31	32	35
Students	12,177	15,051	19,493	21,574	21,911
Annual rate of change (%)	8.3	23.6	29.5	10.7	1.6
Teachers	865	843	955	1,098	1,160
Student/teacher ratio	14	18	20	20	19
Higher education institutions (universities, institutes, colleges)	172	171	178	176	178

Table 10.2 (Continued)

	2000	2001	2002	2003	2004
Students	84,970	90,246	98,031	108,268	123,824
Teachers	4,910	5,251	5,650	5,962	6,309
Public higher education institutions	38	41	42	47	43
Public higher education institutions' share (%)	22.1	24.0	23.6	26.7	27.5
Public higher education students	56,906	60,382	66,834	74,134	84,041
Public higher education students' share (%)	67.0	66.9	68.2	68.5	67.9
Annual rate of change (%)	11.5	6.1	10.7	10.9	13.4
Public higher education teachers	3,455	3,655	3,882	3,999	4,187
Public higher education student/teacher ratio	16	17	17	19	20
Private higher education institutions	134	130	136	129	135
Private higher education institutions share (%)	77.9	76.0	76.4	73.3	72.5
Private higher education students	28,064	29,864	31,197	34,134	39,783
Private higher education students' share (%)	33.0	33.1	31.8	31.5	32.1
Annual rate of change (%)	22.2	6.4	4.5	9.4	16.5
Private higher education teachers	1,455	1,596	1,768	1,963	2,122
Private higher education student/teacher ratio	19	19	18	17	19

Sources: 1. NSO, 2004, 2005, 2. MECS, 2004, 3. MECS, 2000 and 2003.

the short term. Previous enrollment increases have been accommodated through restructuring, renovation, and more efficient use of schools without adding new buildings. However, the capacity of buildings is a concern to MECS as they provide only 62.6 percent of the required places. Consequently, in Ulaanbaatar and 18 other *aimags* there are general secondary schools which operate on three shifts per day.

Mongolia is different from most other Asian countries with respect to the gender balance of enrollments. While equal numbers of boys and girls start school, by the end of secondary school girls outnumber boys in both general secondary and vocational schools. In higher education, 62 percent of the students in public institutions and 66 percent of the students in private institutions are female. With respect to the gender distribution of teachers, 96 percent of kindergarten and crèche teachers, 80 percent of primary and secondary teachers combined, 63 percent of secondary vocational teachers, 53 percent of public university teachers, and 58 percent of private higher education institution teachers are female.

Current Economic Conditions Affecting Education in Mongolia

Since the 1990 collapse of the Soviet Union, Mongolia has become increasingly open politically and economically. In the early 1990s, the Mongolian economy experienced severe shocks when the government initiated a transition from the former command or centralist controlled to a market economy, initially experiencing hyperinflation and devaluation of the local currency. With substantial international donor support, Mongolia was able to weather the transition and achieved the unique status of enjoying strong relationships with the major neighboring economies of Russia and PR China as well as other Asian, European, and North American countries.

While the legal foundation for and the transition to a market economy has generally been successful (ADB, 2004), a major concern continues to be the relatively high incidence of poverty in both urban (30 percent) and rural (43 percent) areas. Poverty is lowest (around 27 percent) in Ulaanbaatar and the larger cities, where half of the population resides, and highest (51 percent) in the western region (World Bank, 2005).

According to the 2003 Government of Mongolia *Economic Growth Support and Poverty Reduction Strategy* (EGSPRS), key priorities are improvement of the quality of and access to basic education and health services, thereby supporting employment and income-generating activities as well as strengthening social safety net coverage. The country continues to experience significant demographic changes, accelerated rural migration to urban areas (Batbaatar et al., 2005) and structural changes in the labor market, including: (i) increased demand for workers trained to work with new technology replacing outdated equipment from the Soviet era; (ii) smaller numbers of herders involved with livestock and farming; (iii) need for improved public and private sector managers;

and (iv) a rapidly expanding mining and extraction industry environment which relies on labor and skills from other countries. In implementing social sector activities, the government has tried to ensure that poor and vulnerable groups have access to basic social services that also support opportunities for employment.

A World Bank (2005) analysis of data from the 1998 (NSO and UNDP, 1999) and 2002 (NSO, 2004) Living Standards Measurement Surveys (LSMS) found that the negative impact of poverty on dropout rates from school is significant at every level of schooling, even at the primary level where completion rates are near universal, with the largest effect on upper secondary school dropout. Despite Government figures suggesting overall dropout rates under 2.5 percent, research suggests that the problem is much more extensive (del Rosaria, 2005).

Improvements in school attendance were also evident, however, during this period: among rural children of primary school age (8–12) in the poorest two quintiles, the enrollment rate increased from 84 percent in 1998 to 91 percent in 2002; among all rural primary school children, the corresponding rates were 82 percent and 91 percent. For secondary school-age (13–17) children in the poorest two quintiles, enrollment rates also increased, but from 61 percent to 66 percent; among all rural children enrollment rates were 65 percent in 1998 and 74 percent in 2002. Between 1998 and 2002, the proportions of out-of-school children fell from 11.7 percent to 5.7 percent among primary school children and from 24.2 percent to 14.5 percent among secondary school children. An interesting feature of education in Mongolia is that the quality of teaching influences parental decisions whether to keep their children in school or not and teacher *attitude* is increasingly recognized as a major influence on school dropout patterns (World Bank, 2005).

Unfortunately, progress in enrollment has been offset by other factors. Migration from rural areas to peri-urban areas has escalated. Rural families in search of enhanced opportunities including better education, health and other services, and income earning opportunities have drifted to the larger towns (Batbaatar et al., 2005). Now, 7 percent of children in the 8–15 age cohort are out-of-school. Nearly 11 percent of eight-year-olds do not attend school and urban schools are characterized by overcrowding and high absenteeism. High migration rates are also associated with poor student performance in schools. Further, educational quality as measured by examination results is significantly lower in rural areas, with children from poorer *soums* performing worse than those from richer *soums* (World Bank, 2005).

Fees for preschools and boarding facilities are proving to be prohibitive for *aimag* (provincial) and *soum* (district) households. Because the cost of schooling increases significantly for grades 9 and 10, it is not surprising that poorer families are underrepresented in upper secondary education in both rural and urban areas. In effect, poverty is the single most important factor in determining whether a child is enrolled in school or not. Without unhampered access to quality education, opportunities for earning a reasonable income and rising above the poverty line are restricted. To be sure, those with at least completed secondary education in Mongolia are significantly less likely to be poor (World Bank, 2005).

Education Planning Frameworks since 2000

Economic Growth Support and Poverty Reduction Strategy (2003)

The following policy objectives are recommended to develop the educational sector in the *Education Growth Support and Poverty Reduction Strategy* (EGSPRS) report (Government of Mongolia, 2003: 131):

- Upgrade the education quality of all stages of schools and to educate a citizen capable of living in the society with a market economy ... It is appropriate to start these actions from conducting diagnosis through monitoring, analyzing, and evaluating the performances of students and activities of schools and teachers, and through assessing the conditions and the environment which influence educational quality.
- Set up a system where educational services are accessible in all areas, particularly in rural areas, and support the needs of low income groups to obtain education and the possibility to provide them with education services.
- Improve the management capacity of central and local educational institutions of all levels.

In order to implement the policy objectives, the following strategies are recommended for consideration (Government of Mongolia, 2003: 131–132):

- Strengthen management capacity of the state central administrative organization in charge of educational issues and of educational institutions in *aimag* and local areas.
- Reduce dropouts and increase the coverage of basic education up to 90.5 percent by 2006. Gender disparities in secondary and higher education should be addressed by increasing the enrollment rates of both sexes. In this regard, education facilities, teachers and other personnel need to be motivated and trained more effectively and actions should be taken to improve access and quality of services. It is necessary to aggregate efforts of government, public organizations, community institutions, business entities, citizens, parents, teachers, and schools in this work.
- Improve the teacher training system, fully provide rural schools and kindergartens with teachers, and rationalize the actions to improve and upgrade teachers' professional and methodological skills.
- Improve the education content of schools at all levels and kindergartens so they can provide job orientation and life skills to the students, and transfer to an 11-grade system starting in 2005.
- Expand the coverage of preschool education by achieving 62.0 percent by 2006, improve the training environment of rural kindergartens, and describe rational methods and forms of preparing children of herder families for school.
- Expand conditions and possibilities to fully cover the children from herder and poor families, and the children with development difficulties (such as deaf, blind, disabled, etc.) in the schools, improve dormitory supply and provision, and upgrade service quality.
- Provide literacy education for children, youth, and citizens who have dropped out from school, and encourage and expand all methods and forms of obtaining professions.
- Expand the scope of training professional workers who can meet market demands through improving education content and the material environment of VTCs (Vocational Training Centers) and involve unemployed young people in vocational training.

- Improve the quality of the accreditation process for higher education institutions and upgrade the level of higher education to international standards.
- Continue the renewal of general secondary school textbooks and fully supply students with handbooks and textbooks.
- Improve the training environment by maintaining, expanding and building new schools, kindergartens and dormitories, strengthen the training material base, and computerize and connect the schools to the internet.
- Monitor and evaluate the performance of students in general secondary schools, study the basic factors affecting their performance, and improve the quality of basic education.

Millennium Development Goals (2004)

The strategies for improving education put forth in the EGSPRS are reinforced by the international Millennium Development Goals (MDG) effort supported by the United Nations Development Program. MDG 2 is "Achieve universal primary education." Target 4, "Provide primary education to all girls and boys by 2015," for which attaining this goal is discussed in the *National Report* (Government of Mongolia and UNDP, 2004: 20–23). Several priorities that address this target are mentioned, including improving: access by reducing direct and opportunity costs of schooling borne by families, teacher training, curriculum and student assessment, physical plant and resources of schools, availability of extracurricular activities, community involvement in schools, inclusion of disabled and special needs children, and opportunities for dropouts of all ages to reenter schools or nonformal educational activities.

MDG 3, "Promote gender equality and empower women," includes Target 5, "Eliminate gender disparity in primary and secondary education by 2005 and in all levels of education no later than 2015." Because Mongolian females already exceed males in school completion at all levels, the strategy for doing this is to continue improving the secondary school completion rate of males and increasing their enrollment in higher education.

Government of Mongolia Action Plan (2004)

The *Government of Mongolia Action Plan, 2004–2008* (Government of Mongolia, 2004) lays out an ambitious agenda for improving education in Mongolia that parallels what appears in the EGSPRS and MDG reports. Three major objectives are specified in this document: (1) improve quality and competitiveness; (2) establish closer linkages between training, research and industry; and (3) create wider opportunities for citizens to get education and training. Under these three objectives, a long list of activities to be undertaken is presented:

- Further deepen legal reforms in the education, science and technology sectors;
- Develop a new Education Master Plan of Mongolia;
- Rationalize structure and location of general secondary schools and dormitories, including supply of dormitories;
- Improve professional capacity and status of teachers, focus education sector budget expenditures more on teachers and decrease management costs;

- Implement new standards of general secondary education and ensure preparation for transfer to 12 year schooling system;
- Encourage rights of parents and teachers to choose from alternative textbooks that meet standards;
- Implement new standards for preschool, primary and secondary schools, reform the primary and secondary school system, and increase enrollments in the preschool and basic education subsectors;
- Make appropriate changes in the curriculum, invest in teacher training and increase number of volunteer teachers in connection with the preparation to make English an official language;
- Expand coverage and improve quality of basic and complete secondary education;
- Support educational programs in the areas of English language, natural science, engineering, and information technology;
- Expand vocational, part-time, and distance training;
- Support civil society initiatives to provide reeducation services for out-of-school children and adults who were unable to attend schools;
- Continue the provision of free-of-charge school stationery for one child of vulnerable, low income families and households with three or more children studying in school at same time;
- Provide special state support to engineering and technology education, including incentives for private sector investments in such education;
- Strive to align program accreditation with international standards;
- Continue management privatization in the education sector;
- Support internationally accepted ethical norms in academic and research activities at the higher education level, and improve quality and effectiveness of academic training and research;
- Introduce ITC in higher and middle levels of education;
- Improve competitiveness and status of Mongolian higher education;
- Pilot and introduce a confidentiality system for students' grades;
- Support forms of an "Open University" designed for people to be trained while working;
- Develop vocational education and improve its quality through renewal of vocational education curriculum and standards, improvement of teaching and learning environments, and activate social partnerships;
- Use proximity of schools to students as a criterion for urban development in order to have normal class size;
- Provide computers to general secondary and vocational schools and gradually connect to a network according to approved standards;
- Undertake construction, expansion, and rehabilitation of school and dormitory buildings;
- Provide access to education for disabled children and youth, increasing capacity of schools and providing classes with appropriate equipment;
- Reform of tuition loan and grant system administered by State Training Fund;
- Support campus-based (towns including student dormitories) universities and Vocational Training and Production Centers (VTPC);
- While training researchers and young scholars in developed countries, also support initiatives to establish branches of high ranking foreign universities and colleges, to provide and export quality education services; and
- Promote initiatives to establish "Learning Palaces" that provide comprehensive education services in cities and rural areas, and create efficient legal and financing systems.

Many of these activities are well underway, but there are insufficient government funds to support all of them at a high level. A major problem with the development of such lists is the Mongolian Government has been reluctant to establish priorities among the items. Since so much is perceived to be needed to bring the Mongolian educational system to the desired level of quality and international competitiveness, the Government is reluctant to restrict its approaches to donors in any way.

Mongolia EFA (UNESCO) Assessment (2005)

Another influential driver of educational policy in Mongolia is the Education for All (EFA) program, an initiative of UNESCO. A team from MECS is charged with conducting an assessment and developing strategies for attaining EFA goals (MECS, 2005). The basic framework being used for the EFA assessment was developed during the World Education Forum held in Dakar, Senegal, in April 2000 and applies to the period from 2000 to 2015. During a forum held in Ulaanbaatar in November 2005, an initial assessment was presented on the status of Mongolia with respect to each of the six EFA goals (MECS, 2005).

1. Expanding and improving comprehensive early childhood care and education, especially for the most vulnerable and disadvantaged children. In Mongolia, the net enrollment ratio for early childhood education is 34.1 percent. The only schools serving children with disabilities and special needs are in Ulaanbaatar.
2. Ensuring that by 2015 all children, particularly girls, children in difficult circumstances and those belonging to ethnic minorities, have access to and complete, free and compulsory primary education of good quality. The net enrollment ratios for Mongolian primary (grades 1–4) and complete basic education cycle (grades 1–10) are 90.2 percent and 91.4 percent, respectively. Among the out-of-school children, 61 percent are boys.
3. Ensuring that the learning needs of all young people and adults are met through equitable access to appropriate learning and life-skills programs. A National Curriculum of Equivalency Education in accordance with national standards has been adopted for Mongolia. Nonformal and distance learning opportunities are proved at local centers. Vocational Training and Production Centers (VTPCs) provide occupational training and linkages with employers. Opportunities for both nonformal and vocational education are significantly better in urban than rural areas.
4. Achieving a 50 percent improvement in levels of adult literacy by 2015, especially for women, and equitable access to basic and continuing education for all adults. According to the 2000 Census, 98 percent of Mongolian adults were literate.
5. Eliminating gender disparities in primary and secondary education by 2005, and achieving gender equality in education by 2015, with a focus on ensuring girls' full and equal access to and achievement in basic education of good quality. In Mongolia, girls have higher participation in education at all levels than boys, a problem that is especially acute in rural areas.
6. Improving all aspects of the quality of education and ensuring excellence of all so that recognized and measurable learning outcomes are achieved by all, especially in literacy, numeracy and essential life skills. In 2005, competency-based education standards and an accompanying national curriculum (content frameworks, teaching plans, textbooks, methods of evaluating student achievement, etc.) were implemented.

Like its Central Asian neighbors that were former Soviet republics, Mongolia has had to reform its educational system in accordance with changing social, economic, and political conditions (ADB, 2004). These countries had to approve new constitutions as well as develop new laws and policies related to education as they transitioned from government-driven command economies to private sector driven-market economies. New standards and curricula had to be developed along with reforms of both preservice and in-service education to prepare teachers to deliver the curricula. Vocational education had to be restructured to fit more closely to labor market demand rather than government mandate. Those countries that had primary and secondary school systems of less than 12 years increased the length of schooling. Most of the countries tried various approaches to decentralization of education (Yoder and Weidman, 2003). In all of these things, Mongolia has been among the most successful among the former Soviet republics of Central Asia (ADB, 2004; Weidman et al., 2004).

While financial restraints on the education system remain substantial, donor support has continued to be strong. In the future, however, sustaining reform and improving quality of and access to education will require much better coordination of efforts across Government agencies and among donors, a so-called sector wide approach. Some efforts along these lines to date have been very promising (Weidman, 2001). Priorities will have to be agreed upon and educational investments driven by them. The foundation is strong but much remains to be done.

SCHOOL DAYS OF A MONGOLIAN GIRL IN ULAANBAATAR (ERIKA BAT-ERDENE)

To provide a sense of schooling in the Mongolian capital of Ulaanbaatar as experienced by a student, we conclude this chapter with a reflection written by Erika Bat-Erdene.

September 1, 1993, was the day on which I set out on the long and winding road of my life as a student. I was seven years old then but I remember that day as clearly as if it were yesterday. At that time, it seemed as if I'd waited for the moment forever. Finally, when that day came I was extremely happy but a bit nervous at the same time. In Mongolia, September 1, no matter which day of the week, is always the first day of school for all students of all ages. The day becomes a day for the celebration of students and scholars. Thus, I felt very grown up and proud of myself to be taking a part in such a big, important, and exciting event.

I wore my school uniform, a requirement for all students during that time. For girls, the uniform consisted of a brown dress with a black apron in the front. On holidays, such as the first day of school, the black apron was replaced by a white apron. At the top of the dress we wore a white lace collar that was removable and could be washed separately, because the collar was always supposed to be clean. The boys wore navy blue pants and jackets.

So, around 8:00 A.M. in the morning, holding fresh flowers in my hands for my homeroom teacher, carrying a book bag, and accompanied by my family,

I approached my school, the 10-year Special Public School of Foreign Languages Number 23 in Ulaanbaatar, or simply known as School Number 23. This school is special in the sense that it provides extended foreign language classes from the early grades as compared to other typical primary and secondary schools. The rest of the classes are the same as in public schools. It was a huge white building with four floors and already many people were gathered there. All the teachers dressed in formal wear with handfuls of flowers were outside, too, heading their class queue of students. The school principal addressed the crowd with a welcoming speech for the students about the new school year. The school doors opened to the students when two of the youngest and oldest representatives of the student body walked in front of the school doors ringing a bell. Everything seemed to be going very fast for me, but as soon as I followed my class queue and entered through the glass doors of my school, I looked at the morning sun, it was very bright and beautiful, and then somehow I realized from that moment on I was taking on a big responsibility of my life.

From then on, every day was pretty normal with various classes and examinations. Within the 10-year school system there were three levels: grades 1–4 were elementary school, grades 5–8 were middle school, and grades 9–10 were high school. Middle and high school level classes were scheduled in the morning from 8:00 A.M. to 1:00 P.M. The elementary level classes were in the afternoon from 1:00 P.M. to 5:00 P.M. Each grade had 4–6 groups (cohorts), depending on the number of students in each grade level. Every group at the elementary level had about 40 students. Each group had a label, for instance, group "1.a" would mean group "a" of the first grade level, and grade "1.b" would mean group "b" of the first grade level, and so on. School #23 was an urban school so the labels extended as "a, b, ve, ge" (in the order of the Russian Cyrillic alphabet). This form of dividing the student body into different groups carries on throughout the 10 years of secondary school. In other words, those who stand in the same queue on the first day of school and sit in the same classroom with you will be, after 10 years, the same folks you'll be with on the day of your graduation as you get in line to receive your diploma. Pretty neat, don't you think? Regarding gender diversity within classrooms, there was always the tendency for the girls to outnumber the boys. The other three groups of my grade level (called "parallel groups") all had a 3:1 ratio of females to males. In the case of my group I was very lucky because it had exactly 20 girls and 20 boys.

My school days were always very interesting. During my elementary school years, I would wake up around 9 in the morning. Then I would make sure I'd done all of my homework. I had five classes a day, each about 45 minutes long. Recess was about 10 minutes long. We did not have free lunch or any lunch break. We either bought some snack or simple food from the school cafe or brought something to eat from home. I think I had about 11 or 12 subjects, most of them taught by my homeroom teacher. Only subjects such as physical education, music, and art were taught by a different teacher. Every day we had some variation in our schedules, but the primary classes such as maths, language arts, and English were scheduled for every school day. Our three parallel groups had Korean, Japanese, and Russian as their special foreign language. Each of the groups started to learn its particular foreign language in the second grade. Our first English teacher was a man from the Philippines. I remember everyone being very excited to have a foreign teacher. During that time, school days included Saturdays.

Once we advanced to fifth grade, our homeroom teacher changed and all classes were taught by different teachers. At that time we were taking as many as 18 different subjects in one term, all of which were regarded as providing basic knowledge for an educated individual, so all of the subjects were taken seriously. During my school years, many changes were happening in the education system. The old grading system consisted of numbers, with "two" being the lowest and "five" being the highest. The new system consisted of percentages and English letters "A, B, C, D, and F." It was not very difficult to adapt and students were able to look into their evaluations more clearly. One other change was in the use of the old Mongolian script. Starting in middle level classes, Cyrillic script was used in all textbooks for all subjects but we still had to study the old Mongolian script through to graduation. It was very confusing and we often questioned why we should keep on learning it. However, now I think about it and I understand that it was a big part of our culture and our identity as Mongolian people.

As the grades advance, the subjects and examination become more and more difficult. Final examinations took place at the end of May. The greatest importance was placed upon mathematics and Mongolian language arts subjects. In my school, foreign languages were taken very seriously as well. Final examinations were very difficult, because students had little knowledge of what to expect. Students had to prepare particularly well for the nationwide exams required for advancing to the next level of schooling (i.e., 4th to 5th grade, 8th to 9th grade, and at the end of 10th grade). They were particularly important, because if one could not pass the exams, it might not be possible to advance to upper levels and continue an education. This kind of testing got a little bit easier to prepare for when I was in my 6th and 7th grades, because many books and magazines were published to help students prepare for those tests. Those books served the same purpose as the SAT Prep books in the United States.

As the days passed and I moved into the high school level, I realized I was changing and growing up, too. Class days began in the morning and finished in the afternoon (by that time school days were from Monday to Friday). The winter was the hardest time with mornings in Ulaanbaatar very cold (-25 to -30 degrees Celsius) and dark. We usually took a public bus to school. As the years went by my classmates become closer friends. We often went to picnics in the countryside and celebrated holidays such as the New Year together. I remember becoming an "upper classman" and taking the responsibilities to keep control in school in various ways, such as being the doorkeeper. It was a very responsible job, and I felt very grown up doing it. Eventually, the school that looked that so huge and wide on my first day of school looked small and simple.

REFERENCES

Asian Development Bank (ADB) (2004). *Education Reforms in Countries in Transition: Policies and Processes*. Six Country Case Studies Commissioned by the Asian Development Bank in Azerbaijan, Kazakhstan, Kyrgyz Republic, Mongolia, Tajikistan, and Uzbekistan. Manila, Philippines. Accessed on July 27, 2006 from http://www.adb.org/Education/educ-reforms-countries.pdf.

Baabar, B.B. (Translated by D. Sukhjargalmaa et al., edited by C. Kaplonski) (1999). *Twentieth Century Mongolia*. Knapwell, UK: White Horse Press.

Badamsambuu, Khishigbayar (2006). "The external influences on the development of Mongolian higher education system." Unpublished Ph.D. Dissertation, Graduate School for International Development and Cooperation, Hiroshima University, Japan (March).

Batbaatar, M., Bold, Ts., Marshall, J., Oyuntsetseg, D., Tamir, Ch., and Tumenast, G. (2005). *Children on the Move: Rural–Urban Migration and Access to Education in Mongolia*. CHIP Report No. 17. London: Childhood Poverty Research and Policy Centre (CHIP), Save the Children (U.K.).

del Rosario, Mercedes, Donrov, B., Bayarsaihan, B., Tsetsegee, B., Batmonkh, D., Sengedorj, T., Tseveen, Ts., and Delger, E. (2005). *The Mongolian Drop Out Study*. Ulaanbaatar: Mongolian Education Alliance.

Erdenechimeg, D., Baljinnyam, R., Batchuluun, Ye., Dorknamjin, B., and Nyamdavaa, Yo. (2005). *Nonformal and Adult Education Study Team Report*. Prepared to support the 2005 Education Sector Review and 2006–2015 Master Plan. Ulaanbaatar, Mongolia: Asian Development Bank and Ministry of Education, Culture and Science of Mongolia.

Government of Mongolia (1993). *Mongolia Human Resource Development and Education Reform Project: Sector Review*. Prepared for the Government of Mongolia by the Ministry of Science and Education; the Academy for Educational Development; the School of Education, University of Pittsburgh; and DanEduc Consulting (contributing author). This activity was funded by the Asian Development Bank with financial support from the Japan Special Fund. December 21.

———(1994). *Mongolia Education and Human Resource Master Plan*. Prepared for the Government of Mongolia by the Ministry of Science and Education and the Academy for Educational Development. This activity was funded by the Asian Development Bank with financial support from the Japan Special Fund. February 24.

———(1995a). *The Mongolian Education Law*, 1995, amended 1998. Ulaanbaatar.

———(1995b). *The Mongolian Government Education Policy*, Parliament Resolution No.36 of 1995.

———(2003). *Economic Growth Support and Poverty Reduction Strategy*. Ulaanbaatar (July).

———(2004). *Action Plan of Mongolian Government, 2004–2008*. Appendix to Parliament Decree No. 24, 5 (November).

Government of Mongolia and UNDP (2004). *Millennium Development Goals: National Report on Status of Implementation in Mongolia*. Ulaanbaatar.

Juvaini, Ata-Malik (1260). *Genghis Khan: The History of the World Conqueror*. Translated from the text of Mizra Muhammad Qazvini by J.A. Boyle. Seattle: University of Washington Press (1977, original translation published by UNESCO in 1958).

Lattimore, Owen (1962). *Nomads and Commissars: Mongolia Revisited*. New York: Oxford University Press.

MECS (Ministry of Education, Culture and Science) (2000 and 2003). *Statistical Bulletin for the Education, Culture, Science, and Technology Sector.* Ulaanbaatar, Mongolia: MECS.

———(2001). *Foundation of the Education Sector in Mongolia and its Development in 80 Years.* Ulaanbaatar, Mongolia: MECS.

———(2004). *Information Reference for the Education, Culture and Science Sector, 2000–2004.* Ulaanbaatar, Mongolia: MECS.

———(2005). *EFA Assessment of Mongolia* (November). Ulaanbaatar, Mongolia: MECS.

Morgan, David (1986). *The Mongols.* Oxford: Basil Blackwell.

MOSTEC (Ministry of Science, Technology, Education and Culture), Government of Mongolia (1999). *Mongolia Education Sector Strategy 2000–2005.* Ulaanbaatar, Mongolia: MOSTEC.

NSO (National Statistical Office) (2004). *Mongolian Statistical Yearbook 2003.* Ulaanbaatar: NSO.

———(2005). *Mongolian Statistical Yearbook 2004.* Ulaanbaatar: NSO.

NSO and Asian Development Bank (2004). *Main Report of Labour Force Survey 2002–2003.* Ulaanbaatar: NSO and ADB.

NSO and ILO (International Labour Organisation) (2004). *Report of National Child Labour Survey 2002–2003.* Ulaanbaatar: NSO and ILO.

NSO and UNDP (1999). *Living Standards Measurement, 1998.* Ulaanbaatar: NSO and UNDP.

NSO, World Bank, and UNDP (United Nations Development Programme) (2004). *Main Report of "Household Income and Expenditure Survey/Living Standards Measurement Survey, 2002–2003."* Ulaanbaatar, Mongolia: National Statistical Office (NSO) of Mongolia.

Soucek, Svat (2000). *A History of Inner Asia.* West Nyack, NY: Cambridge University Press.

Steiner-Khamsi, Gita and Stolpe, Ines (2006). *Educational Import: Local Encounters with Global Forces in Mongolia.* New York: Palgrave Macmillan.

Weidman, John C. (2001). "Developing the Mongolia education sector strategy 2000–2005: Reflections of a consultant for the Asian Development Bank," *Current Issues in Comparative Education* ([Online], 3(2), May 1). Accessed on May 29, 2007 from http://www.tc.columbia.edu/cice/Archives/3.2/32weidman.pdf.

Weidman, John C. and Bat-Erdene, Regsurengiin (2002). "Higher education and the state in Mongolia: Dilemmas of democratic transition," in David W. Chapman and Ann E. Austin (eds), *Higher Education in the Developing World: Changing Contexts and Institutional Responses*, pp. 129–148. Westport, CT: Greenwood Press.

Weidman, John C., Chapman, David W., Cohen, Marc, and Lelei, Macrina C. (2004). "Access to education in five newly independent states of Central Asia and Mongolia: A regional agenda," in Stephen P. Heyneman and Alan J. DeYoung (eds), *Challenges for Education in Central Asia*, pp. 181–197. Greenwich, CT: Information Age Publishing.

World Bank (2005). "Being left out of upper secondary schooling: Mongolia's rural poor." Draft for discussion with the Government of Mongolia. East Asia and Pacific Region. Washington, DC. (June 22).

Yoder, Brian L. and Weidman, John C. (2003). "Neo-Liberalism as an analytical framework to examine the educational policies of two countries in transition: Mongolia and Uzbekistan." Paper presented at the Annual Conference of the Comparative and International Education Society (CIES), New Orleans, LA.

Chapter 11

SCHOOLING IN NORTH KOREA

Gay Garland Reed and Yoon-Young Kim

JUCHE STYLE EDUCATION FEVER IN NORTH KOREA

Education fever is the term that is commonly used among South Koreans to describe their passion for education ignited by the perception that education is the avenue to social advancement (Seth, 2002). Despite a radically different educational climate and political system, the passion for education in the North is equally fierce. A Democratic People's Republic of Korea (DPRK) Ministry of Education document describes the fever this way, "In the DPRK there is no one who has not received education or gives up study. All people without exception study the whole of their life" (2004: 19). The document notes that "all people, whether they work in factories, enterprises, scientific, cultural or educational establishments, study for two hours after their day's work" and Saturday is also set aside as study day (Ministry, 2000: 18). Among the world's communist states, the North Korean Workers' Party's emblem is unique in that it shows not only the mandatory hammer and sickle but also a calligraphy brush, signifying the value of knowledge (Cohen, 2001). This lifelong education fever North Korean style encompasses formal, nonformal and informal approaches.

The term *Juche* in the heading of this section refers to the unique political ideology formulated by former leader, Kim Il Sung and later articulated by his heir, Kim Jong Il. *Juche* is nominally defined as "self-sufficiency" but the term has been elaborated and expounded upon in volumes of work by the great leader Kim Il Sung and his son, Kim Jong Il. Since the objective of North Korean education is the creation of "Juche type revolutionaries," and *Juche* is the principle which undergirds the political and economic systems, it is useful to understand what this term means and to discuss its implications for the education system.

Juche is most often translated as "self-reliance" or "self-identity" but the meaning is imprecise and it can also refer to national pride, national assertiveness, or national identity, depending on the context (Bunge, 1981: 76). Kim Il Sung was clear that *Juche* represented the independent stance of rejecting dependence on others and fostered the belief in one's own strength.

The principle is further illuminated in Kim Il Sung's *Theses on Socialist Education* which was released at the 14th Plenary Meeting of the Fifth Central Committee of the Worker's Party of Korea on September 5, 1977. This document is perhaps the most quoted of all education documents in North Korean writings dealing with the educational system. In the theses, Kim Il Sung reiterates themes which are discussed in his collected works and encapsulates his views on the principles, pedagogy, content, and policies of North Korean socialist education. The document also stresses that the *Juche* principle is a "scientific and revolutionary world outlook indispensable for men of a communist type" (Kim Il Sung, 1977: 7). In the *Theses on Socialist Education, Juche* appears to be synonymous with communism although at a later time he suggests that it actually supersedes communism.

The guiding idea of our socialist education is communism, the *Juche* idea. Communism, the Juche idea, is the ideological, theoretical and methodological basis of socialist education. Communism, the Juche idea, gives correct answers to all theoretical and practical problems arising in educational work and shows the direction in which socialist education should develop.

Later in the same document, Kim Il Sung explains that the unique environmental, social, and cultural characteristics of a nation demand that it train its people to conform to that reality and thus, education must focus on the history, culture, nature, and geography of one's own country. Even subjects like science and technology which are imported from other countries should be studied from the standpoint of the Korean situation. "The purpose of learning and introducing foreign things should always be to get better acquainted with our own things and to carry out our revolution and construction more efficiently" (Kim Il Sung, 1977: 12).

In August of 2005, the *Minju Chosen (People's Korea)* published a piece that reveals the continuing role of education, both formal and informal, in furthering *juche* ideology which is currently equated with socialism instead of communism. In this iteration, "what counts most . . . is to dye the whole society one color by arming all members of society with the socialist ideology" (Ch'oe, 2005: 1).

The work defines imbuing the whole society with the socialist ideology as the primary duty of the ideological work and assumes the indoctrination in the *chuch'e (juche)* idea, including education in collectivism, education in the spirit of loyalty to the party, education in party policy, education in revolutionary traditions, and education in socialist patriotism as its content.

This coincides nicely with the Democratic People's Republic of Korea's Socialist Constitution which was initially adopted in 1948 (revised in 1972, 1992, and 1998) that states: "The State shall put the principles of socialist education into practice and raise the new generation to be steadfast revolutionaries who will fight for society and the people, to be people of a new communist type who are knowledgeable, morally sound and physically healthy" (Chapter III, Article 43).

The genesis of the *Juche* principle and its unique cultural features are an expression of Korea's historical experience.

HISTORICAL CONTEXT

Education in the DPRK shares its historical roots with South Korea. For the purpose of this study the history of North Korean education is divided into five periods which are labeled as: Confucian period, Japanese period, Pre-Korean War period, Destruction and Massive Expansion period (Kim, Dong-Kyu, 1990: 103) and *Juche* period. The periods are presented in a linear fashion as if the influences begin and end abruptly when in fact, to varying degrees, the influences continue into the present even if they have been officially repudiated. Historical legacies and continuing influences are acknowledged throughout this section on the historical context.

Confucian Period (Ancient Korea to 1910)

Like other countries in Northeast Asia, Korea has Confucian roots. Chinese thought and culture had an enormous impact on Korea, especially among the *yangban* (aristocratic) class. Although the Korean alphabet (*hangul*) was developed by a group of scholars during the reign of King Sejong in 1446, Chinese characters were imported into the Korean written language and used in official documents, scholarly texts and poetry. To be educated was to know the Chinese classics. *Sodang* (village schools) were common throughout the Korean peninsula and families who could afford it, sent their male children to these schools for training in the classics and Chinese calligraphy to prepare them to take the civil service examinations. The pedagogy was teacher-centric with students memorizing and reciting the Confucian classics. Calligraphy was learned by mastering each stroke and copying the work of famous calligraphers of the past. Educated people were held in high esteem in traditional Korea and teachers were respected.

In the waning years of Confucian dominance, Western missionaries made their mark in Korea by establishing a number of schools throughout the peninsula. The missionary influence permeates education in South Korea but never returned to the DPRK after the Japanese occupation and subsequent division of Korea. Although the missionary influence lost its hold in the North, the educational legacies of Confucianism can be traced to the present. We might say that they are part of the imbedded social grammar that informs interaction and thought. Paternalism, authoritarianism, and respect for learning are aspects of Confucianism that continue to influence educational thought and pedagogy in North Korea. Chinese characters are one aspect of traditional Confucian education that disappeared when the DPRK instituted the exclusive use of *hangul* immediately following the Japanese occupation as a means of ridding the country of the legacies of past feudalism.[1] However, elements of conservative state Confucianism are still apparent despite the communist repudiation of Confucianism as a feudalistic belief system which denigrates manual labor and maintains class stratification. Korea maintained a system of very sophisticated Confucian schools for many centuries until the Japanese occupation which began in 1910.

Japanese Occupation (1910–1945)

Always vulnerable to the influence of China and Japan, Korea maintained her political and cultural sovereignty until 1910 when she was annexed by Japan. The period from 1910 until 1945 was a period of systematic deculturalization. Korean children were forbidden from speaking Korean at school and educational opportunities for Koreans were limited. There was strong resistance to colonization both at home and abroad where Korean churches became the sites of political resistance and language and cultural traditions were kept alive (Reed and Choi, 2001: 175–190). Segregated elementary and secondary public schools existed until April 1938 when the new policy of "One Nation, One School" was instituted (Mansourov, 2001: 50).

Higher education in the modern sense did not exist until the establishment in 1925 of Kyoungsung Imperial University, the predecessor of Seoul National University. Although this institution for higher learning was built on Korean soil, the majority of the students who attended were Japanese. Access to tertiary education for Koreans was limited to those rare few who were willing to become loyal servants of the Japanese. Since most higher order jobs were taken by Japanese, there was little need to provide the local Koreans with tertiary education. Nevertheless, a few Koreans went to Japan for study.

The annexation left deep psychological scars and this experience was relived for decades in the speeches of Kim Il Sung contributing to the formation of the *Juche* principle which became the central feature of Korean communism.

Brief Expansion Period (1945–1950)

Although brief, the period after Liberation from the Japanese and before the Korean War (known as the "Fatherland Liberation War" in North Korea) was marked by enormous advancements in the DPRK in eradicating illiteracy.[2] Adult schools, evening schools, workshop schools, and Korean alphabet schools were set up all over the country for this purpose.[3] North Koreans designate this period as the "peaceful building up period and democratization of schools and education."

While schools in the South were pressured to adopt an American model of education, in the North the Soviet influence began to be felt in schools. Pictures of Russian heroes appeared in Korean schools and students were exhorted to "learn from the Soviet Union" (Yang and Chee, 1963: 126). Famous Soviet pedagogues such as Krupskaya, who was the wife of Lenin, and Makarenko were stressed in North Korean educational materials used in teachers' colleges. The combination of theory and practice and collectivism in education, which are major themes in North Korean education, originate from these sources (Kim H.C., 1990: 102; Kim D.K., 1990: 76–77).

All schools, including those that had been used by the Japanese living in Korea, those which had religious affiliations, and those which were privately owned were consolidated into a single government controlled system. Educational advisors, some of whom were Soviet-Koreans, went to North Korea to revolutionize the system (Scalapino and Lee, 1972: 900) These Soviet educational advisors trained teaching cadres in teachers' colleges. At the same time, college students from DPRK went to the Soviet Union for higher education (Yang and Chee, 1963: 127).

Period of Destruction and Massive Expansion (1950–1975)

Over the next 25 years Korea was plunged into the destruction and confusion of war, then rebuilt and expanded its education system as a completely divided country. This period from the beginning of the Korean War in 1950 to 1975 when the 11 year compulsory education policy was fully implemented in North Korea, solidified the differences between the communist North and the capitalist South.

The Korean peninsula was devastated by the war which lasted from 1950 to 1953. Cultural and educational facilities were nearly all destroyed and 850,000 students from the north, about half the total number, were mobilized for the war effort (Yang and Chee, 1963: 127).

The period following the Korean War was marked by successive reforms in the field of education. Universal primary education was established in 1956 (Scalapino and Lee, 1972: 1105). The formal commitment to education was gradually increased over the next two decades until 1972 when the 11 year system was introduced. The period between 1972 and 1975 was marked by massive expansion in the educational sector. State investment increased 1.7 times, 60,000 teachers were trained, and 30,000 more classrooms were built. By 1975 there were 60,000 kindergartens and nurseries, 4,700 primary and 4,100 senior middle schools in the DPRK (*Indo-Korean Friendship*, 1981: 12).[4] By 1975, the period of massive educational expansion in North Korea was slowing and the country realized the full implementation of the 11-year compulsory educational system.

Juche Education (1975–Present)

The year 1975 is designated here as the beginning of the *Juche* period even though the seeds were sown much earlier. North Korea traces the origin of *Juche* to the Manchu armed resistance period and, as indicated earlier, the desire for self-determination was a natural response to Japanese colonialism. Kim Il Sung who was established as North Korean Premier and Chairman of the Korean

Workers' Party (KWP) in 1948 and ruled until his death in 1994 made national dignity and identity objectives of his political movement very early on (Yang and Chee, 1963: 127). The official adoption of *Juche* as a statement of principle was made in 1970 in a Korean Worker's Party resolution and again in 1972 in the North Korean constitution (Hwang et al., 1990: 129). On the occasion of the First Youth Day on August 26, 1991, Kim Jong Il, son of Kim Il Sung, made the statement: "The *Juche* idea is the sole guiding ideology of our revolution and the lifeblood of our nation. All the revolutionary struggle of our party and our people is to implement the *Juche* idea," in a "Letter to Young People and Workers of the League of Socialist Working Youth" (*North Korean Quarterly*, 1991: 257). This narrow focus on self-interest and self-study was remarkably successful in sustaining the personality cults of Kim Il Sung and Kim Jong Il and the themes are reiterated to the present.

According to Oh and Hassing, access to schooling in the 1980s depended to a large degree on class standing. Those who belonged to the hostile class which in 1984 constituted 20–25 percent of the population had very limited opportunities to attend good schools. The greatest educational opportunities were reserved for KWP members and those who belonged to the core class, the top loyalty group (2000: 133).

LEVELS OF EDUCATION

As Table 11.1 indicates there are four main levels of schooling in the DPRK: kindergarten, primary, secondary, and tertiary. Universal compulsory 11-year education encompasses the first three categories, but it would be appropriate to note that nonformal ideological and work-study education beyond these levels is also mandatory for every individual. The distinctions between compulsory and mandatory are thin.

During the first four years of primary school students study about the childhood exploits of Kim Il Sung and Kim Jong Il. They also learn communist morality, Korean language, mathematics, history, science, physical training, music, drawing, and basic engineering. At the secondary level the ideological curriculum focuses on the revolutionary activities of Kim Il Sung and Kim Jong Il, communist party policies, communist morality, Korean language, mathematics,

Table 11.1
Levels of Education

Grade Level	Years	Age(s)	System
Kindergarten (Pre-school)	1–2 years	4–5 years	Formal/one year compulsory
Primary school	4 years	6–10 years	Formal/compulsory
Secondary school	6 years	11–16	Formal/compulsory
College and University	2–12 years	Adult	Formal/informal

Source: Adapted from Ministry of Education Document, 2004.

history, geography, physics, chemistry, biology, physical training, music, drawing, electrical technology, and engineering. There are special activities for girls and increasingly, students are learning English and Chinese at the direction of the present leader "Dear Leader" Kim Jong Il. His rationale is that North Korean people have to learn English for earning foreign currency from international trade and that people need to know Chinese characters in order to read South Korea's policy for reunification.

School enrollment in the late 1990s declined precipitously due to food shortages, natural disasters and economic difficulties (see Figure 11.1).

Mansurov reports that the population growth rates in the DPRK slowed to less than 1 percent in the 1990s reaching approximately 22.622 million in 1994, then moving into a decline as of 1995 (Mansurov, 2001: 56). He attributes these declines to falling birth rates, increased infant mortality and generally increasing death rates due to the profound economic depression that began in 1990. This population decline was brought on partially by a series of natural disasters like the floods in 1995 and 1996 followed by drought in 1997. These disasters and the malnutrition that resulted, left the general population reduced by about 2 million and a consequent decline in the number of students attending school (from 4.9 million in 1991 to about 4 million in 1997). The decline in population was accompanied by a corresponding decline in the number of educational facilities from 10,769 in the beginning of the 1990s to about 8,400 in 1997 (Mansurov, 2001: 57). Seven years later in 2004 the DPRK Ministry of Education indicated a total number of students in elementary and secondary schools at 3.9 million (1.65 million in 4,948 primary schools and 2.25 million in 4,825 secondary) all at state expense (Ministry of Education, 2004: 8). At the same time the Ministry indicates that more than 1,523,000 children are brought up at over 28,000 nurseries and about 757,000 children attend 14,312 kindergartens (ibid.: 7).

Figure 11.1
Enrollment in North Korea (1965–1998): Elementary School, Middle School, University

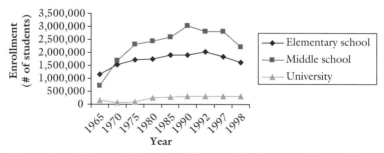

Source: Adapted from Ministry of Education, Ministry of Unification in Cho and Zang, 2002: 73–111. Figure designed by Jane Pak, 2004.

Educational access is not even throughout the DPRK. Children in remote provinces are less likely to receive the same educational opportunities as their urban counterparts. The DPRK Ministry of Education is working with UNICEF on educational projects to support the development of an educational management information system that will be used as a primary tool to plan educational services for children. They also aim to ensure that children receive essential information and learning on child rights and prevention of HIV/AIDS. During the 2004–2006 period, they planned that all boys and girls in the three most vulnerable provinces and in kindergartens nationwide will receive textbooks and basic school supplies (UNICEF DPRK, 2005). UNICEF and the DPRK Ministry of Education have also identified 10 focus counties/districts where they will implement school physical and quality improvement plans, to bring them up to national scale.

Table 11.2 indicates the multiple models of tertiary education in the DPRK.[5] Some courses of study are completed in as little as two years and others might take as long as 12 years if the student moves through all of the levels to take the terminal doctoral degree.

As the chart in Table 11.2 indicates there are a variety of options for tertiary education. Political elites of the KWP are trained at special schools which include the Socialist Working Youth University, the Politics University of the North Korean CIA and the Kim Il Sung High Level Elite School (Sun Ho Kim, 1990: 292).

Table 11.2
Tertiary Education Formal and Informal

Formal Higher Education	*Years*
Specialized schools	2–3 years
Universities and colleges	4–6 years
Informal higher education	*(Study while working)*
Factory colleges	4 years
Farm colleges	4 years
Fishermen's college	4 years
Evening courses at regular universities	5 years
Correspondence at regular universities	5 years
Licensing at specialized schools	3–4 years
Licensing at teacher training colleges	3–4 years
Licensing at universities of education	4–6 years
Postgraduate courses	
Masters Course* (full time/correspondence)	3–4 years
Doctorate* (full time/correspondence)	2–3 years

Note: The DPRK uses the term "informal." The term "nonformal" is more commonly used to describe this form of organized education outside the formal system.

* Special Masters and Doctoral post-graduate courses of one year also exist.

Source: Adapted from DPRK Ministry of Education and DPRK National Commission for UNESCO Document, 2003.

Most colleges and universities have daytime, evening, and correspondence classes. Higher education expanded significantly in the 1980s. The number of colleges and universities including teachers' colleges and factory colleges was 170 in 1980, but in 1989 the number reached 270. Two and three year junior colleges increased from 516 to over 600 during the same period (Sun Ho Kim, 1990: 279–296; Chung Gak Lee, 1990: 292–294).[6]

Expansion of the tertiary education system continued into the 1990s when a combination of failed economic planning and natural disasters slowed all growth in the DPRK. In April 1994, the Minister of Finance of the DPRK, Yun Ki-chong, delivered a report on the 1993 budget in which he indicated that more than 20 universities and colleges made their appearance in 1993 including universities of technology, agriculture, and physical education (SWB, 1994). The Ministry of Education reports that the total number of universities had increased to over 300 in 2003 (DPRK MOE and National Commission for UNESCO, 2003: 4).

Without doubt, North Korea's most prestigious institution of higher learning is Kim Il Sung University (KISU) which was founded in 1946, two years before the official establishment of the North Korean government. As of 1980, KISU had 50 departments in 13 schools and 10 research institutes with 1,200 faculty members. The 13 schools are: History, Philosophy, Politics and Economy, Law, Foreign Languages and Literature, Korean Language and Literature, Mathematics, Energy and Dynamics, Physics, Chemistry, Biology, Geography and Geology, and Automation Science (Kim and Ahn, 1993: 33).

The UNESCO statistical yearbook of 1992 indicates that in 1987 there were 390,000 students enrolled in higher education institutions. UNESCO also notes that 2,468,000 students were enrolled in secondary education in the same year. Given the large number of institutions of higher education, including factory colleges, and the national emphasis on tertiary education for all, the enrollment in secondary schools is surprisingly low. An important point to note is that 70 percent (Dong-Kyu Kim, 1990) of the freshman class is comprised of those who have been recently discharged from compulsory military service which ranges from three to ten years.

Teacher Training Colleges offer licensure for kindergarten and primary school teachers. Each region or city has its own teachers' college and there are a total of 13 throughout the country. Students preparing to teach at the secondary level take a four-year course of study at Education Universities. There are 19 of these institutions offering four-year courses throughout the DPRK (Han Man-Gil et al., 2001). Table 11.3 gives details of the number of teachers including percentage of female teachers.

According to the Ministry of Education the student–teacher ratio in 2003 was 1:21 in general education and female teachers made up 57 percent of the total teaching force.

In order to improve teacher quality, all teachers receive retraining in the "reed-ucation institute." There are retraining periods of one, three, and six months. In addition, every summer or winter vacation, all teachers are tested to evaluate their

Table 11.3
Number of Teachers and Percentage of Female Teachers

Teacher Level	Number of Teachers	Percentage of Females
Kindergarten	37,000	100
Primary	69,000	86
Secondary	112,000	58
Colleges	Not available	23
Universities	Not available	19

Source: Adapted from the DPRK Ministry of Education and DPRK National Commission for UNESCO Document, 2003.

ideological correctness. Oh and Hassing refer to this as the DPRK's own version of "high stakes testing" (2000: 142). They comment that:

The North Korean people are constantly tested in their beliefs. To determine if information has been memorized and understood, people are quizzed in political study sessions; those who fail to demonstrate understanding and commitment receive black marks on their political record. To translate learning into commitment and action, people undergo criticisms and self-criticisms.

Such displays of commitment are part of everyday life in the DPRK. Admittance to institutions of higher education is based on political considerations and scholastic achievement, in that order (Kwon, 1993). In the past the applicants to college sent their documents, including a list of five preferred colleges or schools, to the education department of the local administrative committee in the city or county of their residence. The applications included recommendations by an employer or school, performance record, an evaluation of political attitude written by the chairman of the local youth league, a statement of social origin (peasant, worker, or intellectual), family situation, "trend of thought," and general caliber. Screening of the applications was done by a selection committee composed of Party cadres and staff members of the administrative, social and educational organizations of that district. This committee then assigned the applicants to colleges based on the quota set by the provincial organizations. Once assigned to a college, the student took the entrance examination. The results of this examination, along with the student's social status and political activities determine whether or not s/he would be accepted (Vreeland, 1976: 118).

Far less prestigious than Kim Il Sung University or any of the other established provincial universities and colleges throughout the country, are the study-while-working colleges whose numbers have grown exponentially over the last several decades. Theoretically, 100 percent of factory workers attend school part time while they are working (Scalapino and Lee, 1972: 1289). The study-while-working model is attributed to an on-the-spot inspection by Kim Il Sung at Kim Chaek Engineering College in 1960. At the time he noted that study was detached from practical production and proposed the union of education and productive work with an emphasis on technical training.[7] Besides promoting technical expertise, these schools also served the ideological purpose of "critiquing exploitive capitalism" where workers are deprived of educational opportunity.

In 1977 in the *Theses on Socialist Education*, Kim Il Sung suggested that tertiary institutions which promote the "ideological, technical and cultural revolutions" should be distributed in rural as well as urban areas and in industrial and agricultural zones so as to maintain a developmental balance throughout the country and address unique regional characteristics (1977: 45). He was clear that the intellectualization of the society would only be complete when higher education became compulsory. In 1992 the process of "assimilating the whole society to intelligentsia" was reiterated at the sixth congress of the KWP. At that time it was noted that within the last decade alone, over 100 higher education institutions had been expanded or set up in cities, industrial zones, rural areas, and fishing villages (FBIS, 1992: 22). Most of these institutions were factory- or farm-attached colleges.

The curriculum of factory colleges is divided into two broad categories: theoretical training which includes political training and technical training. In the past, political training consisted of five hours a week studying Kim Il Sung's *History of Struggle* and the history of the KWP; four hours a week for foundations of Marxism-Leninism and five hours a week of Russian Language training. This accounted for 60 percent of the time. The rest of the time was spent in specialized technical training.

A CHRONOLOGY OF THE DAILY LIFE OF A STUDENT

Kim In-shik is a third year senior middle school student who lives in Wonsan, a city of 274,000, located on the east coast of the DPRK on the East Sea. He was born in 1990. When he was one-year old his grandmother died from hepatitis and his parents, who both work full time, placed him in a *t'agaso* (nursery) until he was old enough to attend Kindergarten. The *t'agaso* is indispensable for some families like his where there are no grandparents to take care of the children. It was in the *t'agaso* that In-shik was first introduced to "Father Kim Il Sung" whose portrait greeted him every morning.[8] This was the beginning of his ideological education and it has helped him in his later schooling. Kim In-Shik comes from a good family, nevertheless they have faced difficult times. They survived the famine years of 1995–1999 by eating two meals a day of *juk* (a watery rice porridge made of roots) and whatever his mother could find. He is small for his age as are most children in North Korea. In this respect he is like a lot of his classmates.

Like his classmates he wears a uniform to school as he has done for all his school career. When he completes his senior middle school, he will fulfill his military service obligation which can last from 3–10 years depending on the service that he is assigned. In-Shik is a diligent student but struggles with the work because of his health. The only tests that In-Shik has ever taken are essay tests because there are no multiple choice tests in schools in the DPRK.

Although he would like to go on to college some day to study computer science he suspects that his test scores will not be high enough right now and he will have to wait until he returns from military service.

The following chronology is a day in the life of Kim In-Shik.

Kim In-Shik's Day

6:00–6:45 A.M.	Gets up/helps his mother with some chores/eats
6:45– 7:15	Walks to school
7:30–8:00	Group exercises to patriotic songs/salute to Kim Jong Il
8:00–12:00	Five 45-minute classes: history, communist morality, biology, maths, and chemistry
12:00–1:30 P.M.	Goes home for lunch (no lunch facilities at school)
2:00–5:00	One afternoon class: English or Chinese/sports activities
5:00–6:00	Children's place for computer study one day a week
6:00–7:00	Returns home/eats a light dinner
7:00–9:00+	Studies for classes
10:00	Lights out (electricity must be conserved)

In the secondary school, all classes start at 8:00 A.M. as in primary school. Classes at the Middle school level last for 45 minutes and there are six classes a day, five in the morning and one after they return to school in the afternoon after lunch break. All classes and school activities are over at 5:00 P.M.

When Kim In-Shik was in primary school during the late 1990s sometimes he went to school in the morning and found that his teacher was not there. He knew that she wanted to teach the students but her family needed her to find food. She said she was sick but he heard that she went to the fields to work to make extra money for her family. Some people said it was a kind of "school collapse" because so many teachers and students were absent. In-Shik thinks that things are getting much better than they were before and he looks forward to serving the Fatherland and the Dear Leader General Kim Jong Il.

In-Shik knows that he is lucky to be living in the fatherland "under the loving care of the fatherly leader" who cares deeply for him and his family (Martin, 2004). Although he knows that countries like South Korea and China are richer than the Fatherland, he has learned that their governments do not care about the people and some groups are discriminated against. Every year in school he has learned about the selfishness and decadence of the West, particularly the U.S., and he feels fortunate to live in the DPRK.

MAJOR EDUCATION REFORMS

The following Table 11.4, drawn from multiple sources, highlights the major educational milestones in the DPRK. The table integrates major historical events with educational reforms and policy initiatives and shows how educational progress was punctuated by setbacks due to war, national disasters, and public policy failures.

Table 11.4
Major Educational Policy Reforms and Setbacks in North Korea (1945–2000)

Year	Educational Policy Reforms and Setbacks
1945–1950	Locally built elementary schools resulting in growth of 300 percent
1950–1953	Korean War—Loss of 72 percent of schools during the war
1956	4 years of compulsory primary education introduced
1958	3 years of compulsory middle school introduced, totaling 7 years of compulsory schooling (this included the building of more secondary schools)
1959	Tuition fees abolished; free education implemented (in 1959, this affected 8.5 million school children and students)
Late 1950s	Transition from general high schools to 2 years of technical and 2 years of technical high school, based on government's greater emphasis on technical education
1966/1967	Compulsory, free 9-year education introduced (secondary school (of 3 years) and technical school (of 2 years) merged, resulting in 5 years of postelementary schooling)
1972	11 years of compulsory education implemented; school entry age moves from 7 to 6 years old; addition of 1 year to the 5-year postelementary schooling
1977	*Theses on Socialist Education* (codification of existing policy)
1990s	School population significantly reduced by famine
2001	National Campaign for Information Technology
2003	National Plan of Action on Education for All with UNESCO

Sources: Chang, 1995; Lankov, 2000; H. Lee, 2001; UNICEF, 2003; Pak, 2004. Materials related to family life were drawn from a variety of sources including the Library of Congress country study. Much of the material for this section is inspired by the work of Chung, 2003: 191–211.

One of the striking features of education in the DPRK is its isolation from the global community. In reviewing the changes in North Korean higher education which have taken place over the last five decades it is useful to keep in mind that the political structure of the DPRK has functioned almost without interfacing with the international community. While much of the world considers the benefits and liabilities of living in a time of globalization, North Korea has, until recently, held a very negative view of the process (Reed, 1997: 167). For the most part, North Korea has maintained its own internal path of change and development.

Ninety percent of the DPRK economy remains under state control (Far East and Australia, 2005: 506). Nevertheless the country seems to be inching toward greater openness. With the market economy pressing from all directions, the DPRK is gradually emerging from its isolation and the implications for education are staggering. The economic picture influences the educational picture in terms of curriculum content, the structure of the system, allocations for infrastructure improvement, and attitudes toward the outside world.

Since 1999 the government has begun to stress the importance of computer literacy. Information Technology is mentioned numerous times in a Ministry of

Education document from 2004. Increased foreign language instruction is another indication of the growing awareness of the need to develop international connections. The collapse of the Soviet Union, the DPRK's closest international partner, has brought about a different international focus and a realization that past practices are no longer viable or desirable.

One example of this is a new focus on educational differentiation. In the service of egalitarianism, there were no special classes or schools for children with special intellectual gifts in the past. As of 1999 special schools for gifted students have begun to appear. These schools are supposed to be better equipped and class sizes are smaller than regular schools (25/class as opposed to 40/class).[9] They are known as advanced middle schools and would be somewhat equivalent to key schools in China or magnet schools in the United States. Children's places, like the famous Mangyondae, Pyongyang, and Kumsong First and Second Junior High Schools are sites for advanced educational opportunities for gifted children. This is no longer restricted to music, sports, and art but also includes computer technology. A 2001 report indicates that 600 children were selected from all parts of the country to receive training in computer technology at the Kumsong First Junior High School. The interest in Information Technology is supported by the newly formed Ministry of Electronic Industry (1999) (*Strategic*, 2001).

There have been other changes in education in the 21st century. The DPRK National Commission for UNESCO and the Ministry of Education developed a National Plan of Action on Education for All in 2003 that clearly addresses a host of educational issues. This document includes a medium Educational Development plan for the 2004–2008 period and a long-term plan that extends to 2015. The 62-page document sets goals for all levels of education from nurseries and preschool through university including infrastructure development and a focus on teacher training and in-service refresher courses. The document includes provisions for monitoring and evaluating the ongoing changes. The most striking aspects of this document are the strong emphasis on science education and information technology. As daunting and difficult as they have been in the past, perhaps the greatest educational challenge that North Korea faces is the prospect of reunification. Although mutual accommodation will be inevitable, the DPRK will carry the greater educational burden because it will not only be accommodating to South Korea but to the global community as well. Education in North Korea has been remarkably successful in addressing the basic literacy needs of the people. However, the educational system clearly reflects the inflexibility of the political system that it serves. Literacy is only part of the task of creating an educated populace. As awareness of the world grows, the political task of indoctrination will likewise increase.

NOTES

1. The choice to give up Chinese characters was part of the emphasis on independence from outside influences that characterizes *Juche* ideology. Unfortunately it also creates difficulty for scholars and students seeking to read old texts. Furthermore, it could become

a formidable educational challenge as the two Koreas work toward unification, since educated South Koreans read between 1,500 and 2,000 characters.

2. Some estimates place the literacy rate of North Korea at 99 percent making it among the highest in the world.

3. At the end of World War II, Korea, which was regarded as a Japanese territory, was divided into two military occupation zones. The Soviet Union controlled the North and the United States controlled the South. Military governments were temporarily set up on either side of the 38th parallel and this division of Korea was the foundation of two politically, economically, and educationally estranged societies.

4. Thirty years later the numbers for primary and middle schools are remarkably similar raising questions about whether the 1975 numbers were a bit inflated.

5. Some of the material from this section was published in an earlier paper on higher education in North Korea. See Reed and Chung, 1997.

6. These numbers are consistent with statistics found in Kim, Ransoo, and Yong Sop Ahn (1993).

7. Note that a similar model was introduced by Russian advisors and that Chinese educators also placed a strong emphasis on melding the theoretical and the practical.

8. According to French (2005) only about 14–16% of students go directly to college after graduation.

9. Note that this number is different from the DPRK MOE document that listed the teacher student ratio as 1:21.

REFERENCES

Bunge, Frederica M. (1981). *North Korea: A Country Study*. U.S. Secretary of the Army.

Cho, M.C. and Zang, H. (2002). "North Korea's education policy and system, and external cooperation with international organizations," *Journal of Asia-Pacific Affairs*, 3(2): 73–111.

Chung, Byung-Ho (2003). "Living dangerously in two worlds: The risks and tactics of North Korea refugee children in China," *Korea Journal*, 43(3): 191–211. Korean National Commission for UNESCO.

Cohen, David (2001). "Academics in South Korea ponder a future tied closely to the North," *The Chronicle of Higher Education*. Reprinted and available online; accessed on August 21, 2002 from http://www.educationusa.or.kr/english/news/chronicle-north-korea-ed.html.

DPRK Ministry of Education and DPRK National Commission for UNESCO (2003). *Democratic People's Republic of Korea National Plan of Action on Education for All*. Accessed on February 22, 2004 from http://portal.unesco.org/education/en/ev.php-URL_ID=30256&URL_DO=DO_TOPIC&URL_SECTION=201.html.

Far East and Australia (2005). 36th edn. London: Europa Publication.

Federal Broadcast Information Service (FBIS) EAS (1992). October 19, p. 22.

Federal Broadcast Information Service (FBIS) EAS (1993). February 16, p. 19.

French, Paul (2005). *North Korea: The Paranoid Peninsula—A Modern History*. London: Zed Books.

Han, Man-Gil, Yun, Jong-Hyeok, and Lee, Jeoung-Kyu (2001). "Analysis of the Realities and Changes of North Korean Education." Monograph, Korean Educational Development Institute (KEDI), Seoul, Korea, pp. 57–89.

Im, Eric Iksoon and Mansourov, Alexandre Y. (2001). "Contemporary general and vocational education in the Democratic People's Republic of Korea," in Lee-Jay Cho and Eric Iksoon Im (eds), *North Korean Labor and Its Prospects*. Northeast Asia Economic Forum, pp. 81–112. Honolulu, Hawaii: East-West Center.

Indo-Korean Friendship (1981). "Universal eleven-year compulsory education," 12(8–9), August–September. New Delhi: Om Prakos Mantri.

Kim, Il Sung (1977). *Theses on Socialist Education*. Pyongyang, Korea: Foreign Languages Press.

Kim, Ransoo and Yong Sop Ahn (1993). "Higher education in South and North Korea," *Higher Education Policy*, 6(2): 29–36.

Mansourov, Alexandre Y. (2001). "Evolution of education and continuing training in the DPRK since the 1950s," in Lee-Jay Cho and Eric Iksoon Im (eds), *North Korean Labor and Its Prospects*. Northeast Asia Economic Forum, pp. 47–79. Honolulu, Hawaii: East-West Center.

Martin, Bradley K. (2004). *Under the Loving Care of the Fatherly Leader: North Korea and the Kim Dynasty*. New York: Thomas Dunne Books.

North Korea Quarterly (1991). Nos. 61 and 62, Summer/Fall. Hamburg, Germany: Institute for Asian Affairs.

Oh, Kongdan and Hassing, Ralph C. (2000). *North Korea Through the Looking Glass*. Washington, DC: Brookings Institution Press.

Pak, Jane (2004). "Socio-political influences on educational goals in North Korea: An analysis of Kim Il Sung and Kim Jong Il's works on education (1946–1986)." Unpublished Monograph, International Educational Administration and Policy Analysis, School of Education, Stanford University.

People's Korea (2001). "Strategic plan for IT Revolution in the DPRK," August 25. Accessed on July 27, 2005 from http://www.hartford-hwp.com/archives/55a/177.html.

President Kim Il Sung and Development of Education in Korea (1992). Pyongyang: Kyowon Sinmun.

Reed, Gay Garland (1997). "Globalisation and education: The case of North Korea," *Compare*, 27(2): 167–178.

Reed, Gay Garland and Choi, Sheena (2001). "Confucian legacy, global future: Values education policy in South Korea," in William Cummings, Maria Teresa Tatto and John Hawkins (eds), *Values Education for Dynamic Societies: Individualism or Collectivism*, pp. 175–190. Hong Kong: University of Hong Kong Press.

Reed, Gay Garland and Chung, Bong Gun (1997). "North Korea," in Gerard Postiglione and Grace Mak (eds), *Asian Higher Education: An International Handbook and Reference Guide*, pp. 231–244. Westport, CT: Greenwood Press.

Scalapino, Robert and Lee, Chong-sik (1972). *Communism in Korea: Part II The Society*. Berkeley, CA: University of California Press.

Seth, Michael J. (2002). *Education Fever: Society, Politics and the Pursuit of Schooling*. Honolulu, HI: University of Hawaii Press and Center for Korean Studies, University of Hawaii.

Summary of World Broadcasts (SWB) (1994). BBC, April 9, D/5.

U.S. Library of Congress (2003). *North Korea*. Accessed on July 22, 2004 from http://countrystudies.us./northkorea/42.htm.

Vreeland, Nena (1976). *Area Handbook for North Korea*. Washington: U.S. Department of the Defense, Department of the Army.

Yang, Key P. and Chee, Chang-boh (1963). "The North Korean educational system: 1945 to the present," in Robert Scalapino (ed.), *North Korea Today*, pp. 125–140. New York: Praeger.

Korean Language References

Han, Man-Gil, Yun, Jong-Hyeok, Lee, Jeoung-Kyu (2001). "*Pukhan Kyoyuk ŭi Hyeonsilgwa Byeonhwa* [Analysis of the Realities and Changes of North Korean Education]." Korean Educational Development Institute (KEDI). pp 57–89.

Hwang, Chung-kyu (1990). *Pukhan kyoyuk ŭi Jomyeong* [*Spotlight on North Korean Education*]. Seoul: Bobmunsa.

Kim, Chang-ho (1990). *Chosŏn kyoyuksa* [*History of North Korean Education*]. Pyongyang: Social Science Publishing.

Kim, Dong-kyu (1990). *Pukhan ŭi kyoyukhak* [*Pedagogy of North Korea*]. Seoul: Mun Maek Sa.

Kim, Hyong-chan (1990). *Pukhan ŭi kyoyuk* [*North Korean Education*]. Seoul: Ulyoumunhwasa.

Rhee, Dong-gun and Choi, Su-il (1979). [*Juche Ideology in the Ideological amd Methodological Foundation of Socialist Education*]. Pyongyang: Science Encyclopedia Publishing.

Chapter 12

SCHOOLING IN THE PHILIPPINES

Antonio Torralba, Paul Dumol, and Maria Manzon

INTRODUCTION

The Philippines is an archipelago of 7,107 islands stretching from the south of China to the north of Borneo. Its strategic location has made it not only as a bridge between East and Southeast Asia, but also between Europe and America as its colonial history reveals. Hunt (1993: 68) described it as "a cultural crossroads, a place where Malays, Chinese, Spanish, Americans and others have interacted to forge that unique cultural and racial blend known to the world as Filipino." A home to over a hundred linguistic, cultural, and racial groups, the Philippines is, however, a relatively homogeneous society. In a country of over 83 million people, comprised mainly of Christian Malays, 85 percent of the population is Roman Catholic, a feature that distinguishes it from its Asian neighbors.

Geographic size and uneven demographic and economic features across the archipelago as well as disruptive discontinuities in the country's political and economic governance have posed major challenges to national development. Amidst these discontinuities has been the challenge of equity in educational access and outcome.

This chapter commences with a discussion of the major historical periods which have shaped contemporary policy and practice in Philippine education. The chapter then provides a macroscopic description of the current structure of schooling in the country and complements this with a vivid example of a typical day in the life of a Filipino student. The penultimate section analyzes educational reforms since the 1990s.

HISTORY OF PHILIPPINE EDUCATION

The history of education in the Philippines can be divided into three major periods: the colonial era under Hapsburg Spain (1565–1700), the colonial period under post-Hapsburg Spain (1700–1898), and the transition to the 20th century starting with American colonial rule (1898–1946) leading to the establishment of the Philippine Republic (1946–present). While education during these periods exhibited marked shifts, features of the past are recognizable in the contemporary system and help understand its genealogy. A summary of major historical events in Philippine education is given in Table 12.1.

Philippine Education under Hapsburg Spain (1565–1700)

The history of schooling in the Philippines begins with the parish schools founded by missionaries. The first to arrive were Augustinian friars who came in 1565, followed 12 years later by the Franciscans, and subsequently by the Jesuits (1581), Dominicans (1587), and the Augustinian Recollects (1601). The parish schools were intended to teach Christian doctrine. If they also taught reading and writing, it was because these skills were considered necessary for studying the faith. These schools were primary schools, attended by boys and girls in separate groups. There were no other sorts of schools (secondary or tertiary) to be found in native communities until the second half of the 19th century.

Spain has been sometimes criticized for neglecting the education of native Filipinos, but that is to misunderstand the nature of Spanish presence in the Philippines, at least under Hapsburg Spain (and Hapsburg policies persisted into the 19th century). The only justification for Spanish presence in the Philippine Islands under the Hapsburgs was to support the missionaries in their evangelization of the native peoples. Some 20 years after the official establishment of a Spanish colony in Manila in 1571 and partly in reaction to the abuses committed by Spanish soldiers to whom natives and territory were entrusted, the policy was adopted of keeping Spanish contact with the native peoples to the minimum—daily contact with the missionary and annual contact with the *alcalde mayor* who collected tribute on behalf of the King of Spain. Spaniards resided in Manila and in a few garrison towns. Spain exercised direct rule only over the communities of Spaniards. The Philippines for most of Spain's history in the islands was a colony of two societies—native and Spanish.

The native towns were autonomous communities, linked to Spain by pacts. They were ruled by natives and continued to follow customs and traditions that were not considered incompatible with the Christian faith. The towns were founded by the missionaries: prior to their coming, Filipinos lived only in villages. Where the missionaries founded towns they opened schools, and because they fanned out through the archipelago, parish schools were to be found from north to south, east to west. It is estimated that a thousand such schools were established (Bazaco, 1953). To them must be credited at least in part the formation of the Filipino Christian culture that characterizes most of the peoples of the Philippine islands to this day. Instruction was carried out in the vernacular of the region. This contributed to the preservation and development of native languages and all that this implies with respect to the native mind: the so-called Hispanization of indigenous Philippine culture was not the result of the

Table 12.1
Major Historical Events in Philippine Education (1565–Present): A Detailed and Useful Chronology

The Philippines under Hapsburg Spain (1565–1700)	The Philippines under Post-Hapsburg Spain (1700–1898)	The Philippines under the United States of America (1899–1946)	The Philippines under Japan (1941–1945)
1565: Parish schools (PS) in Filipino towns	1820: Escuela de Náutica (VS); Escuela de Dibujo y Pintura (VS)	1901: Establishment of a public school system with free primary instruction (Grade 1 to 7); English as MoI	1941–45: Elementary school curricula radically changed to include Japanese militaristic and racist dogmas; Nippongo replaced English; textbooks censored
1587: Colegio del Parian (SS) for boys of Chinese and Filipino parents	1859: Jesuits take over the Ateneo Municipal de Manila (later Ateneo de Manila) (SS for boys)	1901–1926: Establishment of higher education institutes. 1901: Philippine Normal University, Silliman University, and San Beda College; 1906: St. Scholastica's College; 1908: University of the Philippines; 1910: Centro Escolar University; 1911: De La Salle University; 1912: St. Paul's College; 1913: College of the Holy Spirit; 1919: Philippine Women's College and Jose Rizal College; 1925: Mapua Institute of Technology; 1926: Maryknoll College 1926: Establishment of the Bureau of Private Schools	1945: Pilipino is a required subject in elementary and secondary education
1594: Colegio de Santa Potenciana (SS) for Spanish girls; 1601: Colegio y Seminario de San Jose (SS) for Spanish boys	1863: Royal Decree establishing a public primary school system (obligatory from ages 6 to 12)		The Philippine Republic (1946 to present)
1611: Colegio de Nuestra Señora del Santo Rosario (Colegio de Santo Tomás from 1617 onwards) (SS) for Spanish boys; 1619: Papal privilege for Santo Tomás to confer degrees	1864: Escuela Municipal for girls (SS)		1974: Filipino to be used as MoI for Social Studies in basic education
1620: Colegio de San Juan de Letran (SS) for boys of Spanish parents or Spanish *and Filipino* parents	1865: Normal School for male teachers opens under the Jesuits		1978: Licensure exams for elementary and secondary school teachers required
	1870: Moret decree secularizing the University of Santo Tomás (UST)		1988: Mandated free public secondary education
	1875: Colegio Normal de Nueva Cáceres (NS for female elementary teachers); programs		

Table 12.1 (Continued)

The Philippines under Hapsburg Spain (1565–1700)	The Philippines under Post-Hapsburg Spain (1700–1898)	The Philippines under the United States of America (1899–1946)	The Philippine Commonwealth (1935–1946)	The Philippines under Japan (1941–1945)
1623: Colegio de Santa Isabel (SS) for Spanish girls.	in Medicine and Pharmacy opened in UST; UST is charged with overseeing secondary education for boys		1935: Constitutional provision for free public primary instruction and for the development of a Philippine national language	
	1650s: *Filipino boys* admitted to secondary schools		1937: Tagalog chosen as base for the national language (later called Filipino). 1939: Use of vernacular as an auxiliary MoI in the primary grades	
	1877: Moret decree retrieved			
1696: Beaterio Colegio de Santa Catalina (SS) for *Filipino girls*	1892: La Asuncion: first higher normal school for women		1940: Double-shift schooling and abolition of Grade 7	

Notes: Legend: PS—primary school; SS—secondary school; VS—Vocational school; NS—Normal School for teachers; MoI—medium of instruction.
Sources: Bazaco (1953); Isidro and Ramos (1973).

imposition of a foreign culture, but rather of one people's willing assimilation of another's culture through the sieve of the people's native language.

In the Spanish city of Manila, on the other hand, Spaniards transplanted their educational tradition for the benefit of their own community. Manila, for a city of its size, had an abundance of schools. Aside from primary schools, there were secondary schools for boys and girls, though the two sexes never mixed, as was the custom then. Of these, three schools established in the 17th century deserve mention since they continue to exist today: the Colegio de Santo Tomás founded in 1611 and authorized to grant university degrees in 1619; the Colegio de San Juan de Letran founded in 1620; and the Colegio de Santa Isabel founded in 1632. The first two were schools for boys; the third, for girls. The schools were for Spaniards, but Letran admitted the children of Spanish soldiers by native women. Eventually, by the middle of the 17th century, the children of the native aristocracy coming from the ethnic groups that lived around Manila— the Pampangos and Tagalogs—were also admitted into the secondary schools. The number of native students, however, was small. A few studied for the priesthood; in the 18th century, some took up law.

Philippine Education under post-Hapsburg Spain (1700–1898)

The worlds of Spanish Filipinos and native Filipinos remained separate until the 19th century. Close to the middle of the 19th century, native Filipinos other than Pampangos and Tagalogs sought admission to the Spanish secondary schools and the University of Santo Tomás in ever-increasing numbers. These were the children of natives who had grown wealthy by trade with the British and Americans. This interest in secondary and university education was the sign of a new tendency among natives—to enter the world of Western Europe and America, and it coincided with a change in Spanish colonial policy: Philippine towns were no longer considered autonomous communities, but communities directly under Spanish rule. The new colonial policy was implemented gradually, gaining momentum in the 1860s. Aware of the demand for education, school-masters opened schools in the towns, providing an alternative to the parish schools and the schools in Manila. The desire for education beyond primary school filtered down from the upper classes to the lower. It is to this period in Philippine history that we should trace the perception among the lower classes, still extant in the Philippines, of education as a way out of poverty and a way to acquire social dignity. This perception involved above all university education.

The graduates of the lone university in Spanish Philippines in the second half of the 19th century, the University of Santo Tomás, would shape modern Philippines at the turn of the century (Schumacher, 1991). From the university graduates, few though they were, would come the great movement for change that would shake the Philippine colony in the late-19th century. They would lead a press campaign for political reforms in Europe that would eventually meta-morphose into the Revolution of 1896. Many of them would join the resumption of the Revolution in 1898. Jose Rizal, the foremost Philippine national hero, noted in his death cell that he owed his patriotism to his education in the Ateneo de Manila, then a secondary school, and the university, and yet the education he received was the same liberal education Spanish Filipinos received. This liberal education, imparted to native Filipinos in the Spanish language, produced a sophisticated version of Filipino culture that may aptly be called "Europeanized" and which survived roughly to the middle of the 20th century, coexisting with the "Americanized" Filipino culture that would be the fruit of the school system set up by the Americans.

Secondary education and university education were well beyond the means of most Filipinos, but Filipinos from the lower class would sacrifice to send their children at least to secondary school. Andres Bonifacio, the founder of the secret society that would launch the Revolution of 1896, finished a couple of years of secondary school; Emilio Jacinto, his subaltern, was a student in Letran when the Revolution broke out: both were from the lower middle or lower class. Apolinario Mabini, the foremost thinker of the Revolution of 1898, was likewise from the lower class and finished law while on financial assistance from the Dominicans.

In 1863 a royal decree was passed in Spain, establishing a public school system in the Philippines. A normal school for male teachers was opened in 1865 under the direction of the Jesuits, while secondary schools for girls were authorized to give a two-year course that would prepare female teachers. In 1875 the Colegio Normal de Nueva Cáceres was opened, a normal school for female elementary teachers, followed 17 years later by a higher normal school for female teachers, La Asunción. In 1897, a year before Spanish rule ended in the Philippines, there were 2,153 primary schools in the Philippines. The literacy level in the Philippines by the end of the 19th century was higher than in some European nations. In his history of education in the Philippines under the Spaniards, Evergisto Bazaco (1953) lists 193 secondary schools by the end of Spanish rule distributed throughout the archipelago, all of them private, but subject to inspection by the government.

Philippine Education in the 20th Century

The American occupation of the Philippines, which began in 1899, would change the situation of education radically. America opened public schools as early as 1900 with soldiers as the first teachers. A year later 600 American teachers, who came to be known as the Thomasites after the ship they rode in, took over. The Education Act of 1901 established a public school system and a normal school which exists to this day—the Philippine Normal University.

The American passion for education may be traced to their justification of their acquisition of the Philippines: they were, they claimed, bringing civilization to the less civilized. (The small group of university-educated Filipinos smarted under that.) As well, having noticed the feudal structure of native Philippine society (a few rich and very many poor), the Americans thought to bring about its dismantlement by providing education to as many as possible. In line with their protestation that they were in the Philippines only while Filipinos were not ready to rule themselves, Americans made Filipino preparation for self-government an avowed goal of public education (May, 1984). Public schools were established in all towns, with the curriculum following American practice; secondary schools were established in select towns; and in 1908 the University of the Philippines opened its doors.

The first 25 years of the 20th century saw the template completed that Philippine education has followed ever since. Changes in the template have been few and slow, despite the defects noted in it as early as 1925. The major defect was the gap between official intentions and available resources, particularly qualified teachers (BES, 1925). This was not helped by the inclusion in the Philippine Constitution of 1935 of free elementary education. In 1940, two shifts were instituted in the use of classrooms with a lessening of time spent in school; Grade Seven was abolished and has never been restored. The gap noted in 1925 persists to the present day.

The Americans made a decision whose impact Filipinos still feel today: the use of English as the medium of instruction. The wisdom of the decision has been challenged ever since (see BES, 1925; JCCE, 1951; and PCSPE, 1970). It was not as absurd as it might sound, however: at the beginning of the 20th century, there was no lingua franca in the Philippines (Spanish was spoken by only a small fraction of the population, precisely by those who had gone to secondary school and the university), and the suggestion that one Philippine language be chosen over all others as the lone medium of instruction of all public schools elicited vigorous protests. On the other hand, the use of the local language as the medium of instruction would have meant substantial expense in the production of teaching materials. (The Philippines has some 80 languages and more than 120 dialects.) The decision meant, however, having to instruct many Filipino teachers in a foreign language as quickly as possible to be able to supply the numbers needed by schools: this was not easy and continues to be difficult. The level of spoken and written English among the population at large has deteriorated steadily since the departure of American teachers more than 70 years ago. In 1937, Tagalog was chosen as the basis of a national language which was to be developed and was to include words from other Philippine languages. In 1940, Tagalog became part of the basic education curriculum. Over the years, the use in the mass media of the national language (called "Pilipino" since 1959) and the vernacular in non-Tagalog-speaking regions grew, making it more difficult for children to pick up English from the environment. In 1974, it became obligatory to teach Social Studies, Work Education, and Physical Education in Pilipino. Unfortunately, the result is often only a superficial knowledge of both English and Pilipino, now called "Filipino" ever since the letter F was admitted into the alphabet of the national language in 1987.

The use of English opened the world of the Filipino to America. As early as the 1930s Filipinos schooled under the Spaniards rued the rise of an Americanized Filipino culture and the consequent alienation of Filipinos from their neighbors.

This was blamed as well on the elementary school curriculum which was lifted from American schools; textbooks were superficial adaptations of American originals. Today, however, with the increasing influence of America in East Asia and Southeast Asia, it is clear that the Americanized Philippine culture of the 1930s was simply an early sign of what is today called "globalization."

The public school system spread out over many islands necessitated a highly centralized administration that in turn relied on the uniform implementation of lesson plans. This was lamented by a team of American experts that surveyed Philippine education in 1925, noting how this led to an education that was not much in touch with local realities and which stifled creativity in the teacher (BES, 1925). This aspect of Philippine education has been extremely slow to change, but the pressures to change have not gone away.

All the aforesaid observations applied particularly to elementary education throughout the 20th century, in which the majority of students were enrolled. Unfortunately, most would stop schooling at Grade Four. The result has been much wastage of resources, as the Department of Education itself has observed that at least six years of schooling is needed for functional literacy.

Though small in comparison to the student population in elementary schools, enrollment in secondary schools and colleges grew apace in the 20th century, far beyond the capacity of the public school system to satisfy. Roman Catholic religious orders, Protestant missions, and private citizens—some motivated by love of country, others by profit—moved to fill the gap and opened secondary schools, colleges, and universities. In 1926, the Bureau of Private Schools was established. It closed down 23 percent of private schools for falling below minimum standards; the next year it closed down 15 percent more (JCCE, 1951). This did not lessen the establishment of new private schools, many more of which were opened after World War II, but the government office to regulate them was there and it would move from time to time to close down the worst.

Professional education has been provided by private education in many fields unavailable (at least initially) in state universities. Private schools had the clear advantage over public schools because of their relatively greater freedom in curricular offerings. The higher salaries they paid teachers meant as well that they attracted more talented and qualified teachers. Experimentation in pedagogical technique was also easier in private schools. By 1970 half of the high school students in the country were being educated in private schools, and nine out of ten college students, in private institutions (Isidro and Ramos, 1973). Private education, however, especially in the better schools, was and is expensive, so much so that in 1970 good education in the Philippines at the tertiary level was available only to the top 2.6 percent of Philippine society (PCSPE, 1970). It is the products of this education as well who speak English with fluency. It has been claimed that the greatest divide in Philippine society is between those who speak English fluently and those who cannot. Many more job opportunities are available to the former. As well, there are noticeable cultural differences between the two groups.

As early as 1925, however, the mismatch between secondary and tertiary education on the one hand and the economic needs of the nation on the other was already clear. This mismatch was rooted in the economic aspirations of the people (PCSPE, 1970). There had always been vocational schools—schools offering education in agriculture and industry, but enrollment in these schools remained low, and their graduates would invariably go to college. The steady increase of enrollment in secondary and tertiary schools reflected the persistence of the perception that secondary and tertiary education would rescue families from poverty or (at least) keep them in the middle class. Graduates preferred to move away from farms and rural areas: the monstrous growth of what is now called Metro Manila is graphic proof of this. With globalization, however, the mismatch has taken on a new look: the previously unemployed graduates of high schools and colleges now work overseas with English as their passport. Unfortunately, among the Filipinos working overseas are teachers and even principals, exacerbating the already bad situation of Philippine education.

This section has discussed five centuries of the history of schooling in the Philippines. The Spanish colonizers have left a lasting legacy of religious education and one of the oldest European style universities in Asia. The Americans established a public school system and teaching in English. By the end of its 40-year governance of the Philippines, the basic structure of formal education was complete, from primary to tertiary education. Postwar independence government was to retain that structure, making only minor modifications, as discussed in the next section.

To conclude this section on the historical context of Philippine education, the evolution of the language policy in the Philippines is taken as a case in point to illustrate the interaction between colonial history and ethnic diversity, a pattern echoed in other postcolonial societies. The introduction of Tagalog into the grade school and high school curriculum and its subsequent use as medium of instruction in some subjects have been mentioned. In 1939, the vernacular was allowed as an auxiliary medium of instruction in the first two grades; in 1955, it was allowed as the medium of instruction in those same grades. Schooling today in the Philippines continues to be bilingual in Tagalog areas and tri-lingual in non-Tagalog areas where English, Filipino and the local non-Tagalog language are used. The fortunes of Spanish in the Philippine university curriculum likewise make for an interesting tale. Under Spanish colonial rule, the vernacular was used in parish schools whereas Spanish was reserved for the few local elite who were able to study in Spanish secondary schools and universities. This elite, typified by Manuel Quezon, the first nationally elected President of the Philippines, ruled Philippine society under the Americans. In 1952, the study of Spanish was made obligatory in colleges and universities by Philippine law. The new Philippine Constitution of 1987 rescinded this law. What had happened in between? The 1952 law was the work of a generation alarmed by the death of a strain of Philippine culture: the Hispanic culture that reached its apogee precisely during the American era, the culture of the parents of the lawmakers. The 1987 constitution was the work of the children of these same lawmakers, raised in the postcolonial nationalism of the 1960s and 1970s with no particular love for their grandparents' Spanish heritage.

THE PHILIPPINE EDUCATION SYSTEM

The educational system of the Philippines may be divided into the formal and nonformal education, both of which have their public and private sectors. Formal education follows a 6–4–4 structure built on the three levels of education: elementary, high school, and higher education or technical–vocational education (see Figure 12.1).

Basic education consists of six years of compulsory elementary education (referred to as Grade One to Six) and four years of secondary education (referred to as first to fourth year high school). After high school, a student may proceed to higher education (from four to ten years) or take a postsecondary technical–vocational course. This latter alternative was intended for those who could not afford to go to college for reasons either of financial limitations or lack of appropriate academic competence.

Figure 12.1
Philippines: Structure of the Formal Education System

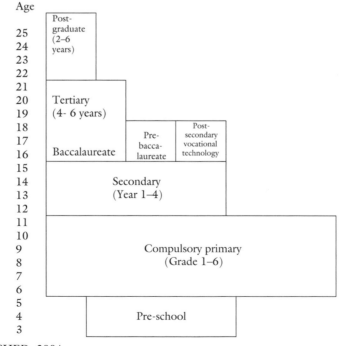

Source: CHED, 2004.

During the American occupation, education consisted of seven years of elementary schooling; this was reduced to six in 1940 in the public school system. Private schools followed suit, and presently, Grade Seven is limited to a handful of private high schools.

There have been attempts since the 1970s to add a school year either to the elementary or the secondary level in public schools, but the cost burden to the government as well as to the parents who would have to postpone their children's productive employment failed to bring about positive results.

Public and Private Schooling

Philippine schools are either *public*, that is, put up and directly supervised by government and funded by public funds; or *private*, that is, established and funded by private entities. Public schools are of five types: elementary, secondary, integrated elementary–secondary, technical–vocational, and state colleges and universities (SCUs). Private schools and universities are either sectarian (that is, denominational or church schools run by religious orders and congregations, dioceses, or parishes), nonsectarian (that is, nonconfessional schools owned and run by families, corporations, or foundations), or lay (that is, schools that teach the doctrine of a particular faith without falling under the jurisdiction of any church or religious entities). Among the private schools are the *madrasah* for the Muslim youth and the schools for indigenous peoples. There are also schools catering to the Chinese community from Taiwan and southern China which offer the basic education curriculum side-by-side with classes taught by Chinese teachers in Chinese language and literature. Management of these schools is mostly in the hands of denominational groups or families.

Education Governance

The Philippines, for political administration as well as education governance, has been divided into 17 political regions. Direct supervision of *public basic education* and the minimum quality monitoring of *private basic education* fall under the Department of Education (DepEd). The DepEd governs basic education through the Bureau of Elementary Education (BEE) and the Bureau of Secondary Education (BSE), and nonformal education through the Bureau of Non-Formal Education (BNFE). BSE also supervises all schools offering vocational secondary curriculums, whether agriculture, fisheries, or trade.

Postsecondary education is governed by two educational bodies. Technical–vocational schools offering postsecondary courses fall under the Technical Education and Skills Development Authority (TESDA), while higher education is covered by the Commission on Higher Education (CHED). State colleges and universities have their own charters, with CHED commissioners simply chairing or forming part of the respective boards of directors.

Basic education, deemed a constitutional right of every Filipino child, is a huge government responsibility that is given its corresponding (but never enough) budget allocation. Looking at the magnitude of basic education alone, the single biggest Philippine bureaucracy includes close to 50,000 schools; beyond 19 million students; and close to 550,000 teachers (DepEd, 2006).

Public education, whose teacher and other personnel salaries are still funded from the national budget or the General Appropriations Act has been significantly decentralized in other expense items, sourced out from funds from local tax collections. For instance, 1 percent of the real estate tax collection is allotted to the operations of a local school board in cities and towns and in the maintenance and operating expenses of the schools, with amounts depending on enrollment. Several local governments add to the support of the schools in their constituencies either through infrastructures or salaries. Schools are allowed to supplement their budget requirements through canteen and other similar operations. Collecting from students and parents, however, is frowned upon by government.

LEVELS OF EDUCATION

Formal education, specifically a college diploma, is top priority among Filipino families, yielding carefully laid out plans to ensure the schooling of *all* siblings even if this means postponing the weddings of older ones, alternating the schooling of the siblings over the years, or selling farm animals and real property. The responsibility of the eldest, whether male or female, to put the younger ones to school, is a grave obligation. No wonder, some three decades ago, the Philippines was second only to the United States in the ratio of college to total population.

A typical Filipino child goes through 10 years of basic education, one of the shortest in Asia, and, depending on the course one is taking, four (for most) to ten years (for medicine) of higher education.

Preschool Education

Private schools have the students go through two to four years of preschool education, invariably called nursery, kindergarten and prep, with "junior" and "senior" attached to either nursery or kindergarten.

Increased attention to the importance of early childhood education in the public school system was catalyzed by various studies undertaken by the then Department of Education, Culture and Sports (DECS) in collaboration with UNICEF (in 1991) and the World Bank (in 1995). These studies demonstrated lower dropout rates in basic education among students with preschool education (Hernandez, 2006). Thus in early 2000, the DepEd introduced a one year Kindergarten level in the public schools. Under the scheme, pupils enter preschool for one year at age five in the hope of equipping them with the necessary skills for the big school. These public preschools adopt a uniform curriculum: the Preschool Integrated Core Curriculum (ICC), which was pilot-tested in 2003 in Metro Manila schools.

In 2002–2003, around 77 percent of a total of 2.2 million five-year old children were served by formal preschools and day care centers. Private preschools enrolled one out of five students in the age cohort served (NEDA, 2004).

Basic Education

Elementary education is free and compulsory. Children aged 6 to 11 go through six years of grade school. In 2004–2005, there were more than 41,650 elementary schools, with a student enrollment of 13 million (93 percent in public schools and 7 percent in private schools).

The Philippines is on track in its Millennium Development Goal of achieving universal primary education by 2015. In 2002–2003, the Philippines reported a net participation rate in the elementary level (both public and private) of 90.05 percent for boys and girls (NEDA, 2004). Nevertheless, survival and completion rates stood at about only 70 percent, with girls doing slightly better than boys in both categories. However, large disparities exist across geographic areas in the country.

Secondary education is free but not compulsory. Children at the age of 12 go through four years of high school. In 2004–2005, a total of 8,100 secondary schools enrolled 6.3 million students (80 percent in public schools and 20 percent in private schools). In 2002–2003, the net participation rate in secondary education was 58 percent and completion and cohort survival rates were 60 to 65 percent, respectively (NEDA, 2004). In both categories, girls scored higher than boys (e.g., 67 percent completion by girls as compared to 52 percent completion by boys).

The world's biggest high school, with a population of more than 22,000 students, arranges its classes according to intellectual achievement, giving the school in each year level a highly advanced and brilliant Section One and a so-so diploma-bound Section 75. The public science schools, and even the science sections of regular schools, perform creditably well in national and even international competitions, but the students from this type of environment hardly comprise 5 percent of the total student population.

Postsecondary Education

After high school, a student has three options (aside from idling, which is not really an acceptable option): (a) to take a postsecondary technical–vocational course, (b) to take higher education, or (c) not to proceed with schooling and be gainfully employed. Except for self-employment or entrepreneurship which requires substantial investments, the prospects for the third alternative are not as strong as they were in the 1950s and 1960s.

Technical–vocational schooling is taken either in private or public schools and lasts anywhere from one year (short courses lasting for one or a few months do not fall under this category) to three years. Certificates or diplomas are awarded at the end of these nondegree courses. Depending on the course of studies approved by TESDA, the curriculum invariably has its general education component (e.g., English, Civics, and Values Education) and the related skills courses. Entry into technical–vocational programs has hardly required passing any national or school-based tests.

The competency levels observed by the world of technical–vocational education have been three traditionally, with a fourth one a more recent introduction, still not a degree course:

1st Level Courses (one year)—Operator
2nd Level Courses (two years)—Craftsman
3rd Level Courses (three years)—Technician
4th Level Courses (four years)—Licensed or Master Technician

There has been a traditional societal bias against technical–vocational education in the Philippines where families, whether rich or poor, aspire for their children to have a college degree. The lack of equivalency between technical–vocational education and training (TVET) and higher education also added to the negative perception attached to TVET (Johanson, 1999). Ladderized interface between TVET courses and college degrees has been made possible by a presidential executive order in 2004 mandating TESDA and CHED to develop and implement a unified national qualifications framework, enabling technical–vocational graduates to proceed to related degree courses.

One example of a technical–vocational curriculum is the dual-training program of a food and beverage course for the hotel and restaurant industry. Lasting for 24 months, the first six months are spent in school for what is deemed an optimum combination of general education and specialization courses. In the next months the students alternate between school and on-the-job training in partner hotels and restaurants in periods of three months. In the end, the graduate is expected to be capable of carrying out any or all five skilled jobs: waiting at tables, bussing, pantry, bartending, and basic accounting. Some colleges and universities allow graduates of this school to proceed to Hotel and Restaurant Management courses.

In 2003, TESDA reported a total of 3,397 TVET providers, 60 percent of which were private institutions. Of a total enrollment of 1.3 million students, 37 percent (492,000 students) were in school-based TVET programs and 43 percent (568,000) were in community-based training programs; male and female students were almost equal in proportion.

Degree programs in colleges and universities comprise higher education, which can last from four to ten years. Most Bachelor of Arts or Bachelor of Science courses last for four years; engineering lasts for five years; prelaw and law together lasts eight years excluding the bar review and examination; medicine lasts anywhere from six years (a shortened course called Intarmed offered at the premier state university) to ten years. A course that was developed in 1995 offers three years of liberal education[1] and two years of specialization, a total of five years, leading immediately to a Masters degree. Masters degrees ordinarily last two years for full time students with a little occupational work load, although there are Masters programs that last for two summers and two semesters (14 months) if the students go full time with their studies. Finally, doctoral students as full time or almost full time students stay anywhere from two to six years in the university, including dissertation.

Higher education is largely delivered by the private sector. In 2005–2006, the total number of higher education institutions (HEIs) stood at 1,647 (excluding 271 satellite campuses of state universities and colleges); 89 percent were private (CHED, 2006). Private institutions enrolled two-thirds of the 2.4 million higher education students in 2003–2004. Of these 2.4 million students, 10 percent were in prebaccalaureate, 86 percent in baccalaureate, 4.2 percent in master's and doctoral programs, and 0.09 percent in other postbaccalaureate programs (CHED, 2004). Although the Philippines reports high gross enrollment rates in tertiary-level education, along with Asian neighbors (Singapore, Hong Kong, Taiwan, and Thailand), it has been characterized as a system where quantity is higher than quality (Gonzalez, 1997).

State colleges and universities, which are created and funded by Congress from the General Appropriations Act, have their own respective charters and enjoy a great deal of autonomy in their policy and operations. The chairman or other commissioners of the Commission of Higher Education either chair the school boards or sit in them.

While the number of private higher education institutions has the upper hand over their public counterparts, financial strains in recent times make a good number of students opt to go to state colleges and universities.

The Education of the "Magister"

More and more preschoolers, especially in private schools, are taught by graduates of child education courses. Grade school pupils are handled by teachers who have graduated from their four-year Bachelor of Elementary Education (B.E.Ed.), which hardly has any specialization. High school students, on the other hand, are handled by those who have completed their Bachelor of Secondary Education (B.S.Ed.) cum major, for example, English, Chemistry, Social Studies or Mathematics. College graduates who wish to teach in grade school and high school but did not take up B.E.Ed. or B.S.Ed. can still teach provided they complete 18 units of undergraduate education: Foundations of Education, Curriculum Development, Teaching Strategies, Research and Evaluation, Theories of Learning, and where still necessary, for those with no teaching experience, Practicum.

Education courses, which can include specializations in elementary education, secondary education, library sciences, tourism (in some universities), or child education, has core subjects, professional subjects, and major subjects, not to mention general education subjects. Core subjects refer to the most basic education subjects such as Foundations of Education, Research Methods, and Statistics. Professional subjects are those directly related to teaching, such as Testing and Measurement, Curriculum and Development, and Methods of Teaching. And major subjects are those that pertain to one's field of specialization.

Apart from the college degree, teachers are required either before employment or in time to pass the Licensure Examination for Teachers (LET) under the supervision of the Teacher Education Board of the Professional Regulation Commission (PRC).[2]

At the postsecondary education level, technical–vocational students are taught either by graduates of Bachelor of Science in Industrial Education (B.S.I.E.), or by craftsmen or technical–vocational masters. University students are taught by professionals, practitioners, or subject specialists who in all probability never took up pedagogy or education formally, much less possess postgraduate academic qualifications. Gonzalez (1997) noted that graduate programs and research are underdeveloped in the Philippines. In 2003–2004, only 9 percent of university teaching staff held a doctorate and 30 percent a Masters degree.

Curriculum of Basic Education

Curriculums in Philippine schools have lasted more or less 10 years or more over the past four decades. Until 2004 the elementary school and high school curriculums were crafted almost independently of (rather than simultaneously with) each other. For secondary education, for example, the Revised Secondary Education Program (RSEP) of 1972 was changed to the New Secondary Education Curriculum (NSEC) in 1984. Both were written separately from their elementary education counterparts, with the general impression among some educators of the Minimum Learning Competencies (the term used for grade school) not bridging the Desired Learning Competencies (the term used for high school).

The latest curriculum in use is the Basic Education Curriculum of 2004 (BEC, 2004). Under the previous curriculum, there were eight subject areas that came in varied names depending on whether they refer to the elementary or secondary curriculum: English, Mathematics, Filipino, Science, Social Studies, Values Education, Work Technology and Home Economics, and Physical Education-Health-Music.

BEC 2004, prompted by the relatively poor Philippine performance in English, Mathematics, and Science in the international arena, reduced the eight subjects to five learning areas from Grade One to Fourth Year high school. The five areas are as follows:[3]

English
Mathematics
Science
Filipino
Makabayan

The fifth learning area "Makabayan" (translated as Citizenship Education) was an attempt to put together four (or five) subjects of secondary importance to English, Mathematics, Science, and Filipino.[4] These subjects include (a) Social

Studies, (b) Values Education, (c) Work Education, (d) Physical Education and Health, and (e) Music and Arts.[5] There has been some attempt to actually integrate the five fields into one, but to date the four or five subjects remain to be taught as four or five distinct subjects by maybe four different teachers who hardly meet to plan and implement integrative work.

It is observed that school instruction in many if not a big majority of Philippine schools develops more the students' retention skills than imagination and much less critical thinking. The crème-de-la-crème in public (and even private) schools do enjoy tremendous opportunities to hone their comprehension and expression skills and to expose themselves to analytical knowledge, but the much bigger "bottom" suffer misery in comparison.

The Philippines boasts of high literacy rates (over 90 percent basic literacy, and over 80 percent functional literacy), and ranks among the highest in Southeast Asia. Yet, despite innovative programs and improved budgets, achievement in 2004–2005 in Grade Six in the learning areas ranged from a high national average of 62 percent in Filipino (the study of the national language) to a low of 54 percent in Science for an aggregate achievement rate of 59 percent. On the other hand, achievement in Fourth Year is from a low of 39 percent in Science to a high of 51 percent in English. These low achievement scores had and continue to have a telling effect on Philippine performance against other countries.

Consider the above data from another perspective by noting the numbers in different levels of mastery groups in English and Maths in the National Achievement Test of 2005, respectively, for grade school and high school graduates (Table 12.2). We then notice the steep increase in the *no mastery group* size from Grade Six to Fourth Year in both English and Math. High school continues to be the missing link. And high school is the end of formal basic education, for a few with eyes toward higher education and for the great majority with eyes toward the world of work.

A great variety of human and material environments confronts Filipino students, many of whom are able to meet natural and man-made challenges with

Table 12.2
Levels of Mastery, National Achievement Test 2005

	Grade Six (%)	Fourth Year (%)
English		
Mastery Group	26	7
Near Mastery	43	49
No Mastery	31	44
Mathematics		
Mastery Group	31	16
Near Mastery	36	31
No Mastery	34	53

Source: Abad (2005).

fortitude, singular pursuit of goals, cheerfulness, and resilience. One such example, perhaps not one of outstanding heroic proportions (yet), is Charise.

CASE STUDY: A DAY IN THE LIFE OF CHARISE

A typical day in the life of a Filipino student is not easy to come by or describe because the "typical" day is as varied as the "typical" Filipino student.

Who then are the "typical" Filipino students?

The upper class young man and young woman in college;

The middle class young man and young woman in college;

The lower class young man and young woman in college;

The lower class young man and young woman who cannot afford to go to college and who instead (or deliberately for a very few) take technical–vocational education;

Multiply the four "typical" groups above by five for "typical" days in (a) highly urbanized metropolis, (b) urbanized cities, (c) semi-urbanized cities, (d) small commercial towns, and (e) farming-fishing towns, and we find 20 "typical" days;

Multiply the 20 "typical" groups above further by four for typical days of a male or female in (a) a college or university, (b) technical–vocational education, (c) high school, and (d) grade school, and we increase the number of "typical" days to 80.

Finally, multiply the 80 "typical" groups by an indeterminate number of temperament and personality types, and we have an indeterminate number of "typical" days in the life of Filipino students.

But behind the great variety of types is one composite of a Filipino student: hardworking, diligent in studies, fun-loving. Such is Charise, a student in a recently established public high school located some 20-minute ride from her residence in one of the major cities of Metropolitan Manila. Vying for graduation honors, she is in Fourth Year high school and belongs to the top section of her year level.

Charise's typical class day schedule starts as early as 6:30 A.M. Hence, she has to wake up at 4:00 A.M. to fix the bed, cook for herself and her siblings, eat, wash dishes, and dress up for school, and be able to leave the house between 5:30 and 5:45 A.M. for the 6:15 flag raising ceremony and short remarks, reminders and announcements from the school principal.

At 6:30 Charise and the rest of her 46 classmates[6] brace for Physics, then English, then Math, at one hour periods each, and a 20-minute recess that starts at 9:30 A.M.

By 9:50 A.M. Charise and classmates go back to class for the tandem of Social Studies (Monday to Thursday) and Values Education (Friday), then Filipino, then the compendium of Music (Monday)—Physical Education (Tuesday)—Health (Wednesday)—Arts (Thursday)—Community Advanced Training (Friday),[7] then Technology and Livelihood Education.[8] Classes are over by 1:50 P.M., but not the day.

From 2:00 to 4:00 or 5:00 P.M. is frequently given to library work, cocurricular activities, and going home time to arrive between 5:00 and 6:00 P.M., depending on the requirements of the parents on any given day. Home at 5:00

could mean a one hour rest and sleep, followed by cooking and eating dinner. Beyond the household chores are doing of assignment and recreation, which can include television watching, free "unlimited" mobile calls courtesy of a service provider, guitar strumming, all depending on the interest at the moment. Friday nights of course means longer rest and recreation period: volleyball, visiting houses of classmates, in effect "unwinding."

Sleeping time can be anywhere between 10:00 P.M. and midnight.

Charise's typical weekday schedule differs somewhat from that of some male classmates, or some of those who are well-off to get the services of stay-in helpers, or those who are less endowed than her family is, or some of those who belong to the lower section. It is commonly observed and theorized with facetiousness that the poorer one is, the lower one's class section is, and the more prone one becomes to idling around with the peer group, referred to in the native language as *lakwatsa*, defined by Charise as "doing things that are either unnecessary or contribute nothing significant to one's personal and social development." This theory, of course, still demands further scrutiny and validation.

From a bright young girl's perspective, activities with friends, even if these be in malls, parks, or other places of interest, are matters of culture and social development . . . they are, therefore, not *lakwatsa*. Saturdays, apart from being given to cleaning the house, laundry work, consequently include "malling" (an anglicized Filipino term for the act of going to malls), computer games in shops, "gimmicks" or carrying on girl-talk with friends. Finally, Sunday means church, home-stay, completion of school assignments, and sleep for more energy accumulation.

That's Charise, different from many and yet as typical as the same many. Like parents of most teenagers her age, her own parents repeatedly admonish her: "Don't come home late! Focus on studies! Make sure your friends inspire rather than distract you! Not too much *lakwatsa*! Clean the house!"

And, as a result, her wish list for her parents: Wish they could be more patient! Wish they would not be too strict! Wish they'd increase my daily allowance! Wish they'd realize how tiring school can be and how much rest I need!

The little joys of childhood . . . the little joys of schooling . . . the little joys of being Filipino.

EFFORTS AT REFORMS

The Philippines has been actively launching education development thrusts and reforms. These include the decentralization of education governance as well as the moves to improve the efficiency and equity in education services. In the decade of the 1990s alone, five study teams had been commissioned to undertake a comprehensive review of the education sector.[9] Yet, political consensus on the reforms and their actual implementation has been slow in coming. The reasons for this phenomenon will be examined later. Meanwhile, some of the attempts at reform will be discussed, highlighting both government-initiated reforms as well as private sector initiatives in education.

Decentralization of Education Governance

Governance of Philippine education has undergone major and minor modifications since the 1980s, all in an effort to manage more efficiently the giant bureaucracy that education is. Until 1994–1995, the then Department of Education, Culture and Sports (DECS) was exercising governance responsibilities over basic, higher, technical–vocational, and nonformal education, as well as culture and sports. In 1994, tri-focalization reforms care of an Education Commission created for comprehensive education reforms, distributed the functions of the DECS to three bodies: DepEd for basic education, TESDA for post-secondary technical–vocational courses, and CHED for higher education. Since 2001, with the education governance act, sports and culture affairs have been under separate units in the executive department, respectively, the Philippine Sports Commission (PSC) and the National Commission for Culture and the Arts (NCCA).

Indeed, recent Philippine education history has been characterized by changes and intended reforms in management and governance, most particularly, decentralization. With these arises the wish that policy and thrusts be more stable than the leadership of such key institutions as DepEd, TESDA, and CHED, that comes and goes with less-than-comfortable frequency.

Improving the Quality of Basic Education

Among the many reforms introduced by the DepEd in the public school system, one that has been given much attention was the addition of one preschool curricular level, Kindergarten. As discussed earlier, the DepEd hopes that by enhancing early childhood care education, strong foundations for basic education could be laid and educational outcomes at the later levels could be improved.

Other major reforms involved the curricular reform of basic education, with a stronger emphasis given to English, Mathematics, and Science at the elementary and high school levels. As discussed earlier, this involved the revision and implementation of the Basic Education Curriculum of 2004. An earlier initiative was the *Bridge Program*, initiated in 2003, which intended to put some 50 percent of post elementary school pupils in a one-year pre-high school where focus would be in English, Science, and Mathematics. In effect, the students taking the Bridge Program would take five years of high school, inclusive of one pre-high school preparatory year.

Expected to go through the Bridge were those who fail to get 75 percent or higher in a pre-high school enrollment test crafted for the purpose. The results, however, were such that to ensure a distribution of 50–50 between the Bridge and the regular First Year, the cut-off score had had to be reduced to 30 percent. The former cut-off of 75 percent would have relegated more than 90 percent of the high school entrants to the Bridge. In the end, the abysmal results of the tests, as well as the then forthcoming 2004 national elections, weakened political will, and the Bridge Program was made voluntary on the part of the parents. Three years down the roll-out of the Bridge, only a handful few are still offering the program for the sake of the handful of parents who wish the best for their children.

The DepEd leadership, prior to the vacancy created by the politically related resignation of the previous secretary, cited the three R's of back-to-the-basics thrust of the department: (a) Reduce Resource Gaps, (b) Reengineer Systems and Structures, and (c) Raise Learning Outcomes, each of which is characterized by well-laid-down strategies (Luz, 2005). These targets and recommendations are well and good, but political will is deemed an absolute necessity to ensure their attainability. The general public still has to hear sustained efforts and initial results from these thrusts, directions, and recommendations. The parents' association in a public school observed that, for a change, it would perhaps be pleasant to hear, "And now the implementation plans and their deadlines . . . " and soon after, "And now some positive results . . . "

The light at the end of the tunnel is premised not only on the leadership of young local government executives who are now taking a more and more active role in ensuring education within their constituencies, but on private business and the rest of the private sector contributing directly to ensuring education reforms. One of several cases in point is *Synergeia* Foundation, Inc., which initially served in 1999 as a learning circle for Ford Foundation grantees.[10] After seven years and with more than a hundred key leaders from education, government, and private sectors, it has been a catalyst for reforms that establish quality basic education as a universal right and as a foundation for economic development and poverty alleviation. Its mission is to ensure the effectiveness and sustainability of reform programs in basic education and to disseminate reform processes and results coherently and collectively. Add to *Synergeia* several business corporations and social enterprises that work directly on either adopting schools or supporting human development efforts in the public school system, and there is a sound moral basis for hoping that the Philippine education system will eventually overcome obstacles to effective education.

Individual schools or school systems have come up with innovative thrusts addressing specific challenges posed by limited, sometimes extremely limited, resources. Among many, four of these can be cited.

Home-School Collaboration. A deliberate, well-laid out effort to involve parents in their primary responsibility of educating their own children and of working hand-in-hand with the school in realizing the multi-stakeholder nature of child education. In the private sector, a spearhead of this effort is the schools under the Parents for Education Foundation, Inc. (PAREF) and a parents' initiative called, Education for the Upbringing of Children (EDUCHILD).

Dual Training. A system of technical–vocational training where the students alternate between the school and on-the-job training for the duration of their schooling. Training thus is closely coordinated between the school and the business firm.

Youth Summer Institutes and Congresses. A national association of secondary school administrators, in collaboration with the Bureau of Secondary Education, holds annual congresses involving student campus and academic leaders. Campus leaders are formed in the spirit of effective service, while academic leaders are prepared to help foster and mount intellectual life in the campus through a buddy system.

National Culture of Excellence. A nationwide effort to establish a system of building excellence in the school campus and in education offices through champions ensuring sound criteria for personal integrity, family solidarity, civic responsibility, and universal charity.

Improving Equity in Basic Education and Beyond

Despite improvements in enrollment rates, the Philippines reported 11.6 million people in the age cohort of 6 to 24 who are not attending school (NSO, 2003). The top three reasons for being out-of-school were: looking for employment, lack of interest, and high cost of education. Disaggregated ratios by region reveal that a lack of interest in schooling is salient among surveyed populations in East Visayas and Muslim Mindanao, the two regions with the highest rural population in the country. These are also conflict-affected areas which make continuity and quality in education delivery difficult.

Among the targets of the government is to close the classroom gap in the public school system by building more classrooms and expanding its educational subcontracting program and financial assistance for high school students to study in private schools. One such scheme is the Government Assistance to Students and Teachers in Private Education (GASTPE). As for students in underserved, high-risk and disadvantaged areas, the DepEd aims to expand its existing distance learning program. It also aims to formulate and implement a standard curriculum to improve the quality of *madrasah* education for the Muslim population in the Philippines (mainly based in Mindanao) and to strengthen indigenous peoples' education (NEDA, 2004).

Improving Efficiency and Equity of Higher Education

Orbeta (2003) reviewed the higher education reform proposals from 1990 to 2000 and noted that they converged on two themes: efficiency and equity. In the domain of improving internal efficiency, the reports called for the rationalization of public investments in higher education by reaffirming the role of the private sector and concentrating public funds on a few priority study/research areas. Some steps had been taken to implement these. A moratorium was called on the creation and conversion of provincial secondary institutions to state universities and colleges, which during the Aquino administration was observed, but was reversed with the adoption of a laissez-faire approach under the Ramos administration (Gonzalez, 1997). As for providing financial incentives to priority fields of study, schemes such as the GASTPE for higher education students studying these priority courses helped, but on a small scale (Maglen and Manasan, 1999).

In terms of external efficiency, reform proposals urged better manpower planning to address the mismatch between the country's needs and the supply and quality of graduates. It also encouraged strengthening linkages between academe and industry. Dealing with the underemployed college graduates has been and is a problem in the country. In 2006, the underemployment rate stood at 21.3 percent while the unemployment rate was 8 percent (NSO, 2006). The problem, however, goes beyond the confines of the education system and needs to be addressed by systemic changes in the country's economic planning.

With respect to improving equity, instead of direct provision of public higher education to give access to the poor, expanded scholarships to low-income students was suggested as a better way to improve equitable access to higher education.

This section has shown that the Philippines is not lacking in attempts to reform its education system. Study after study has been undertaken, but a lack of political will (or, conversely, excessive political interference by "interested" parties) has deterred the implementation of reforms, if not their sustainability. Economic constraints also had their share in posing limits to reforms. One big challenge is the changes in policy and major programs accompany changes in the leadership of educational bureaucracies, which are in tandem with changes in the country's political leaders and their political platforms. Policies and thrusts thus come and go with changes in the post of Secretary of Education, and the movements have been rather frequent in the past 20 years under the post-Marcos era. A further hurdle is posed by the need to receive legislative support in order to actualize reform proposals. The quite highly politicized nature of the legislative system in the Philippines, coupled with political and economic instability (and consequent limited budget for education), and the occurrence of sporadic natural calamities, have impeded the realization of education reforms. A stronger political will on the one hand, and lesser political interference (for private interests) in education on the other, are desirable for the sustainability of education reforms. The question then arises: "Why is there a lack of political will?" The issue is a complex one and would need a deeper examination not only of the political and sociological structure of education reforms (e.g., Tan, 2001), but also of the transformative role of education in nation-building. What is the role of Philippine education in the formation of its indigenous political elite? Could the relative neglect of the civil service, of the teaching profession, of quality higher education be the reasons halting the country's definitive take-off? How can a "virtuous cycle" be initiated and sustained in the Philippine education system?

CONCLUSION

The Philippines has gone quite a long way since the beginnings of formal schooling in the archipelago in the 16th century. From a Spanish colonial legacy that focused on universal religious education for the entire Filipino populace, but which limited access to secondary and higher education in what would be the oldest Spanish university in Asia, the Philippines entered an era of mass basic

Classmates of Charise in the senior year, San Joaquin–Kalawaan National High School, Pasig City, Phillippines after a Friday co-curricular activity. Courtesy of Michelle de la Cruz of University of Asia and the Pacific.

education introduced by its American colonizers. The local elite that inaugurated the Philippine Republic in 1946 inherited a national education system that was virtually complete in its structure from basic education to higher education, partly modeled after the American template. Public investment in basic education has led to high literacy rates among Filipinos as compared to their Asian counterparts.

However, limited economic resources and a weak political will (where political intervention is required) have left serious imbalances which continually strain the system. There were mismatches between "popular expectations and educational standards; facilities and enrollment; the supply of graduates and demand for specific manpower skills; location of educational facilities and actual regional development needs; and national investments in economic enterprises." Such was the scenario in 1970 described by the Presidential Commission to Survey Philippine Education. These observations, despite positive developments across time, generally remain valid after almost four decades.

The Philippine education system is a microcosm which reflects the tensions taking place at the wider national system. The wide gap between rich and poor, between the powerful and the powerless are of great concern. While in times past, elitism was externally introduced into the educational system, elitism is now an internal feature of the local society. A continuing challenge for the country's educational planners is the achievement of equity in access and in outcomes. Stronger political governance in collaboration with private sector initiative could provide a ray of hope to the younger generation of Charise.

NOTES

1. "Liberal education" is distinguished from "general education" by the integrative approach ensured in teaching the nevertheless distinct disciplines of the former.

2. This is a government body in charge of ensuring sustained quality in 43 professions, including teaching, through tests and continuing professional education endeavors.

3. The curriculum of vocational high schools is differentiated by an addition of two or three subjects in agriculture, fisheries, or trade depending on the "specialization" of the respective students.

4. Filipino, as a subject, takes up the grammar, syntax, usage, and diction of the national language called Filipino. The use of Tagalog-based Filipino has put the nationalists in contrapuntal with those who see English as the Philippine advantage in the world labor and employment market.

5. Since 1984–1985, Physical Education (PE), Health, Music and Arts have been rolled into one, with the teachers oftentimes PE majors but with less-than-fair level of music education, or music majors with hardly any training in physical education.

6. Class size ordinarily is 50, can reach 60 to 70, and in a multi-grade setting even 100. Classrooms in public schools are made for 40. Teacher–student ratio is 1:36 in elementary school and 1:41 in high school. This seemingly good news becomes a dampener if we consider that these ratios would mean that there is only one teacher for 36 pupils or 41 students throughout the school day. The more expensive private schools would have teacher–student ratio of as low as 1:12 or even 1:8.

7. Previously Philippine Military Training or Citizen Military Training, this once-a-week subject has been transformed to community service.

8. Except for Filipino the postrecess subjects comprise the learning area called *Makabayan*.

9. Orbeta (2003: 1) cited these studies: (1) the Congressional Commission on Education (EDCOM), 1990–1992; (2) the Congressional Oversight Committee on Education (COCED), 1995; (3) the Task Force on Higher Education of the Commission on Higher Education (TF-CHED), 1995; (4) the ADB-World Bank (ADB-WB), 1998–1999; and (5) the Presidential Commission on Education Reforms (PCER), 2000.

10. A significant part of Synergeia seed funding initially came from the Ford Foundation when the latter left the Philippines in 2003. Synergeia remains strong, with several education reform projects carried out in consonance with international foundations, local governments, and private business.

REFERENCES

Abad, F. (2005). Presentation by the Education Secretary, Iloilo City, Philippines, June 2.

Asian Development Bank and World Bank (1999). *Philippine Education for the 21st Century: The 1998 Philippine Education Sector Study.* Manila: Asian Development Bank.

Bazaco, E. (1953). *History of Education in the Philippines,* 2nd rev. edn. Manila: University of Santo Tomas Press.

Board of Educational Survey Created under Acts 3162 and 3196 of the Philippine Legislature (BES) (1925). *A Survey of the Educational System of the Philippine Islands.* Manila: Bureau of Printing.

Commission on Higher Education (CHED) (2004). *Higher Education Statistical Bulletin. Academic Year 2003–2004.* 5th Revision as of September 30, 2005.

——(2006). *Overview of the Higher Education System.* Accessed on June 28, 2006 from www.ched.gov.ph/hes/.

De Dios, E. (ed.) (1995). *If We're So Smart, Why Aren't We Rich? Essays on Education and Economic Success.* Manila & Quezon City: Congressional Oversight Committee on Education (COCED), Congress of the Republic of the Philippines.

Department of Education (DepEd) (2006). *Basic Education Statistics. Fact Sheet 2006.* Updated March 28.

Gonzalez, A. (1997). "Philippines," in Gerard A. Postiglione and Grace C.L. Mak (eds), *Asian Higher Education: An International Handbook and Reference Guide.* Westport, CT: Greenwood Press, pp. 265–284.

Hernandez, I.C. (2006). "An evaluation of the integrated core curriculum and its implementation in selected schools of San Juan, Metro Manila." Unpublished Manuscript. Manila: University of Asia and the Pacific.

Hunt, C. (1993). "The society and its environment," in Ronald Dolan (ed.), *Philippines: A Country Study.* Washington, DC: Federal Research Division, Library of Congress, pp. 65–116.

Isidro, A. and Ramos, M. (1973). *Private Colleges and Universities in the Philippines.* Quezon City: Alemar-Phoenix Publishing House, Inc.

Johanson, R. (1999). "Higher education in the Philippines." Technical Background Paper No. 3. *ADB-WB Philippine Education for the 21st Century: The 1998 Philippine Education Sector Study.* Manila: Asian Development Bank.

Joint Congressional Committee on Education (JCCE). (1951). *Improving the Philippine Educational System: Report of the Joint Congressional Committee on Education to the Congress.* Manila: Bureau of Printing.

Luz, J.M. (2005). Presentation by DepEd Undersecretary to several audiences in 2005.

Maglen, L. and Manasan, R. (1999). "Education costs and financing in the Philippines." Technical Background Paper No. 2. *ADB-WB Philippine Education for the 21st Century: The 1998 Philippine Education Sector Study.* Manila: Asian Development Bank.

May, G.A. (1984). *Social Engineering in the Philippines: The Aims, Execution, and Impact of American Colonial Policy, 1900–1913.* Quezon City: New Day Publishers.

National Economic and Development Authority (NEDA) (2004). *Medium-Term Philippine Development Plan 2004–2010.* Manila: NEDA.

National Statistics Office (NSO) (2003). *The 2003 Functional Literacy, Education and Mass Media Survey.* Updated January 2006.

——(2006). *Philippines in Figures. Quickstat.* Accessed on May 3, 2006 from www.census.gov.ph /data/ sectordata/ dataedlit.

Orbeta, A. (2003). *Education, Labor Market and Development: A Review of the Trends and Issues in the Philippines for the Past 25 Years.* Perspective Paper Series No. 9. Manila: Philippine Institute for Development Studies.

Presidential Commission to Survey Philippine Education (PCSPE) (1970). "Education for national development: New Patterns, new directions." Unpublished Manuscript.

Schumacher, J.N. (1991). "Higher Education and the Origins of Nationalism," in *The Making of a Nation: Essays on Nineteenth-Century Filipino Nationalism*, pp. 35–43. Quezon City: Ateneo de Manila University Press.

Tan, E. (2001). *The Political Economy of Education Reforms.* Tokyo: Institute of Developing Economies.

Task Force on Higher Education (1995). *Philippine Higher Education in the 21st Century: Strategies for Excellence and Equity.* Manila: Task Force on Higher Education, Commission on Higher Education.

Chapter 13

SCHOOLING IN SINGAPORE

Jason Tan

INTRODUCTION

Singapore is renowned internationally as one of the four Asian tigers, and has made rapid economic progress over the past four decades since attaining political independence in 1965. More recently, it has received international attention because of its students' performance in the Third International Mathematics and Science Study in 1997. With an ethnically diverse population of just over 4 million within a relatively small land area, Singapore represents a case of a country with a governing party that has enjoyed interrupted political power for over 45 years. This government has, since coming to power in 1959, accorded education key priority in terms of serving the needs of economic development and social cohesion. This chapter provides a brief historical description of major trends and developments over the past two centuries, covering British colonial rule and the postcolonial period. Readers will then be introduced to the various levels of education. The chapter then concludes with an overview of the current state of the education system.

HISTORICAL CONTEXT

According to Wilson (1978: 20), there were two factors that significantly affected the formulation of educational policy in Singapore during the period of British colonial settlement from 1819 to 1959. The first factor was the predominant laissez-faire philosophy of leaving educational provision largely in the hands of enterprising individuals, missionary bodies, or private organizations, with occasional government grants. Second, the administration was concerned with the needs of British Malaya as a whole, rather than with the specific needs of Singapore. This resulted in a preoccupation with the perceived needs of the indigenous Malays in a rural setting as opposed to the needs of a cosmopolitan urban society.

Government involvement in education was initially restricted almost entirely to the encouragement of Malay-medium vernacular schools for Malays, with occasional small grants to English-medium schools. A system of grants-in-aid was introduced in 1854 (Doraisamy, 1969: 13). A number of Malay-medium schools were officially funded. The Malays were the only ethnic community in Singapore for whom there was government provision for free elementary schooling (Zahoor, 1969: 106). With one exception, no funding was provided for Chinese-medium schools (Gopinathan, 1976: 68). These schools were entirely community-funded. Likewise, no Tamil-medium schools were sponsored. These institutions survived almost entirely through community support (Gopinathan, 1974: 3). The aid given to schools run by missionary societies was contingent on two conditions. Not only did the schools have to be open to government inspection, they also had to charge fees, no matter how small. After 1874 a third condition was imposed. Public funds could not be used for proselytizing. Also, religious instruction should be given outside of regular school hours and only to those who had requested it (Wong and Gwee, 1980: 6). The support for English-medium education was undertaken in order to meet the demand for English-speaking clerks in the colonial civil service as well as trading houses (Wilson, 1978: 26).

At the beginning of the 20th century, education was far from universal in Singapore. In 1900, only 20,784 of the 45,755 boys between the ages of five and thirteen attended schools of any kind. Female education was confined almost exclusively to Europeans and Eurasians (Wilson, 1978: 27). Secondary education was limited to the English-medium schools, largely run by missionary bodies. The Education Department had taken over the direct administration of two prestigious schools, Raffles Institution and Raffles Girls' School, in 1903. This takeover resulted from the recommendations of a Commission of Enquiry into the system of English-medium education in Singapore (Wilson, 1978; Wong and Gwee, 1980). The situation that prevailed in 1920 could be summarized as follows:

A compartmentalized system of education—education in Christian mission schools, government Malay schools, community and estate run Chinese and Tamil schools; education through the media of English, Chinese, Tamil and Malay with texts from London, Shanghai and Madras, differences in financial assistance, supervision and management— each obviously implanting its own values and tending to emphasize disparate and often opposing goals. The education system . . . strengthened the racial and linguistic differences amongst the population, promoted mutual ignorance and divided the majority Chinese population into two linguistic camps, those educated in English and those educated in Chinese. Further, it had begun to lay the foundations that, even today, characterize the English and the non-English-educated segments of the population. (Gopinathan, 1976: 69)

The years between World War I and World War II continued to be marked by the lack of any clear educational policy. Interest in educational matters among the various colonial Governors varied according to individual temperament and according to the strength of beliefs held by the incumbent Director of Education (Wilson, 1978: 76). Political considerations also played a part in influencing official policy. For instance, the first major attempt to control Chinese-medium schools started in 1920 in the wake of anti-Japanese activities by students from Chinese-medium schools in Singapore. The Registration of Schools Ordinance sought to register schools, teachers, and managers, and to regulate the conduct of schools. It also outlawed all schools that promoted ideas in conflict with the interests of the government. The Ordinance was strengthened by several subsequent legislative amendments in the 1920s and 1930s aimed at controlling the growth of Chinese-medium schools and the spread of political activities in these schools (Doraisamy, 1969: 30–32, 86–89). Another means of control over these community-run schools was the provision, for the first time, of grants-in-aid in 1923. Schools that desired such aid had to submit to official inspections. These various government moves generated a great deal of mutual suspicion and hostility between the colonial administration and the Chinese schools and community. These feelings were to last well past the end of British rule in Singapore, thus making the task of subsequent educational reform much more delicate.

The "first effort in Singapore's history" (Gopinathan, 1974: 7) to design educational policies that were related to clearly defined goals came in the form of the Ten Years Program, which was adopted in 1947. Two of the general principles underlying the policy were the need for education to foster the capacity for self-government and for education to inculcate civic loyalty and responsibility. The Program also outlined plans to provide universal free primary education through one the following languages: English, Malay, Chinese, and Tamil. In addition, all schools should be "regional" rather than racial in order to ensure intermingling in all school activities. Furthermore, the same curriculum should be provided for all races (Colony of Singapore, 1947). This policy was promulgated against the backdrop of increasing recognition by the colonial government that self-government for the colony was on the horizon (Doraisamy, 1969: 49).

In the wake of growing politicization of students in Chinese-medium schools and their involvement in labor unrest, the newly installed Legislative Assembly commissioned an All-Party Committee to study Chinese-medium education in 1955 (Singapore Legislative Assembly, 1956a) The government responded to the Committee Report by issuing a White Paper on Education the following year that endorsed many of the Committee's recommendations (Singapore Legislative Assembly, 1956b). Three major problems facing the government were identified as those of dealing with racial diversity, coping with the increase in the school-age population, and developing a sense of common Malayan loyalty in schools. The White Paper made several important recommendations that were to lay the foundation for subsequent government educational policy. First, all four language streams were to receive equal treatment. Second, all government and government-aided schools were to be treated equally in terms of grants, conditions of service, and salaries. Third, common curricula and syllabuses were to be established for all schools, along with the use of Malayan-centered textbooks. Next, civics was to be taught in all schools from 1957, subject to the availability of teachers' notes. Fifth, bilingual education (that is, English and one of the other three languages) was to be implemented in primary schools and trilingual education in secondary schools.

Following on the heels of the White Paper, the Education Ordinance (later replaced by the Education Act) came into effect in 1957. It included provisions for the registration of schools, managers, and teachers, and provisions governing the role and responsibilities of school management committees (Colony of Singapore, 1957a). Accompanying regulations gave government and government-aided schools equal recurrent funding and stated that staff qualifications and salaries and fees should be the same in both types of schools. Aided schools were also allowed government grants for capital expenditure as long as such expenditures "fit into the Ministry of Education's overall plan for the development of education" (Colony of Singapore, 1957b, Section 79). In addition, the Director of Education was given control over staff recruitment and dismissal in all schools. Also, aided schools were to adhere to standards comparable to those in government schools in terms of physical facilities, student attainment, and student discipline and behavior. Religious instruction was permitted in aided schools provided that parental consent had been obtained and that the time devoted to such instruction was additional to that required for school subjects in government schools. In addition, schools were not to make attendance at religious instruction or religious observance a condition of admission.

Upon coming to power as the first fully elected government in 1959, the People's Action Party (PAP) reaffirmed its commitment to equal treatment for the four language streams (State of Singapore, 1959: 1). The push for building a national education system proceeded with vigor during the early and mid-1960s, especially since education was seen as a key means of providing skilled manpower for industrialization (People's Action Party, 1959: 5; State of Singapore, 1959: 1). First, common syllabuses and attainment standards were designed for all schools (State of Singapore, 1962: 5). There was also a strong emphasis on science and mathematics and technical education (State of Singapore, 1959: 1). Second, students in the various language streams now underwent the same number of years of schooling and sat for common national terminal examinations (Doraisamy, 1969: 75–76; Wong, 1974: 9). Third, bilingualism became compulsory at the primary and secondary levels in 1960 and 1966 respectively. The second language became a compulsory examination subject at the primary and secondary school leaving examinations in 1966 and 1969 respectively (Gopinathan, 1980: 181–182). An attempt to foster cohesion among students in the various language streams was made through the launching in 1959 of the integrated schools program at the primary and secondary levels (State of Singapore, 1959: 3). This program provided for the integration of two or more language streams into one school building under a common principal. It was hoped that cross-stream intermingling could also be fostered through joint participation in sports and other extra-curricular activities.

After Singapore attained full independence in 1965, the government attempted yet another means of instilling a sense of commonality among student by instituting daily flag-raising and lowering ceremonies from 1966 onwards. These ceremonies were accompanied by the singing of the national anthem and the reciting of the loyalty pledge (Republic of Singapore, 1966: 1). A further move toward standardization was the institution of a single system of teacher training for all the four language media in order to ensure parity in teacher qualifications (State of Singapore, 1959: 5–6; Wong, 1974: 9). Furthermore, the Ministry of Education Inspectorate exercised common supervision over all schools (State of Singapore, 1959: 1). In 1983, another major step toward a unified education system occurred when the government announced, in the face of declining enrollments in Chinese-, Malay-, and Tamil-medium schools, that from 1987 onwards the entire education system would operate through the medium of English. This marked the effective end of separate media of instruction in different schools.

The 1960s were also years of tremendous expansion in educational provision. The government undertook massive school building and teacher recruitment programs (Yip et al., 1990: 5–7). Doraisamy (1969: 67) reported that schools were being built at an average rate of one a month for eight years. By 1966 the goal of universal free primary education had been attained for boys and girls alike. Table 13.1 illustrates not only the extent of expansion during this

Table 13.1
Enrollments by Level of Education and Type of School, 1955–1985

	Primary				Secondary and Preuniversity			
Year	Govt	Aided	Private	Total	Govt	Aided	Private	Total
1955	62,149	98,511	15,573	176,233	6,211	19,253	2,457	27,921
	(35.3)	(55.9)	(8.8)	(100.0)	(22.2)	(69.0)	(8.8)	(100.0)
1960	139,452	141,497	3,753	284,702	27,802	28,438	3,004	59,244
	(49.0)	(49.7)	(1.3)	(100.0)	(46.9)	(48.0)	(5.1)	(100.0)
1965	215,073	140,023	1,979	357,075	72,059	39,332	3,345	114,736
	(60.2)	(39.2)	(0.6)	(100.0)	(62.8)	(34.3)	(2.9)	(100.0)
1970	233,692	129,150	676	363,518	103,874	39,816	2,050	145,740
	(64.3)	(35.5)	(0.2)	(100.0)	(71.3)	(27.3)	(1.4)	(100.0)
1975	215,657	112,377	367	328,401	127,651	46,687	1,886	176,224
	(65.7)	(34.2)	(0.1)	(100.0)	(72.4)	(26.5)	(1.1)	(100.0)
1980	219,956	76,565	87	296,608	121,700	46,678	1,938	170,316
	(74.2)	(25.8)	(0.03)	(100.0)	(71.5)	(27.4)	(1.1)	(100.0)
1985	211,855	66,020	185	278,060	137,256	50,763	2,039	190,328
	(76.2)	(23.7)	(0.07)	(100.0)	(72.3)	(26.7)	(1.1)	(100.0)

Note: Figures in brackets indicate percentages.
Sources: Department of Statistics, 1983: 232, 235; Ministry of Education, 1995: 33.

period, but also the dominant role of government educational provision since the 1960s.

Another important point to note is that the PAP adopted a meritocratic ethos in which rewards were to be based on merit and achievement in a competitive education system as well as on individual effort (Gopinathan, 1991: 281). Individuals deemed to have potential were identified for special scholarships in order to join the top ranks of the civil service and uniformed services. The need to nurture such individuals was also prompted by official concern that Singapore's small population meant a correspondingly small talent pool (Lee, 1982). In 1979 the Ministry of Education began an exclusive program at the junior college level (equivalent to years 11 and 12) for students to study humanities subjects such as English literature, history, geography and economics in order to vie for government undergraduate scholarships to Oxford and Cambridge in the United Kingdom.

The 1980s marked the beginning of more initiatives to nurture this talent group of students and the increasing differentiation of students according to academic ability. In early 1979, the Ministry of Education published a controversial report advocating the streaming of students at both primary and secondary levels (Ministry of Education, 1979). The report claimed that Singapore's bilingual policy to date had been unsuccessful in the case of the vast majority of students and that students would be better off with a system of ability-based streaming. The first round of streaming would take place at the end of the third year of primary school and would be based on the results in English language, a second language, and mathematics. Students would be streamed into one of three streams: Normal, Extended and Monolingual, in descending order of ability. The second round of streaming would take place at the end of primary schooling, after which students would be streamed into one of three streams in secondary school: Special, Express and Normal.

Beginning in 1984 the Ministry of Education established a Gifted Education Program at both primary and secondary levels in a select number of schools. This program was targeted at the top 0.5 percent of each age cohort. An Art Elective Program and Music Elective Program were set up in 1984 and 1982 respectively in a small number of secondary schools. These two programs were later extended to a small number of junior colleges as well. There were also elective programs in a few junior colleges in the Chinese, French, German, Japanese (and later Malay) languages.

Yet another move to cater better for the needs of the top layer of the student cohort was the advent of independent schools and autonomous schools. The early 1980s marked the start of a move toward greater decentralization of school administration. In 1982, the then Director of Schools announced that it was "the declared policy" of the Ministry of Education to decentralize educational management from the Ministry headquarters to the schools (Yip, 1982). A major boost to the idea of freeing schools from centralized control was given by the then First Deputy Prime Minister Goh Chok Tong in 1985. He asserted that because of centralized control, prestigious schools had lost some of their individuality and special character. Goh argued for more autonomy within schools, and that principals should have the right to appoint staff, devise school curricula, and choose textbooks, provided that they conformed to national education policies such as bilingualism, moral education, and common examinations. He thought that principals and teachers should be allowed greater flexibility and independence to innovate and experiment with new ideas, thus improving on the present education system.

Goh's sentiment was echoed the following year by Education Minister Tony Tan, who asserted that creativity and innovation in Singapore schools required greater scope for the initiative of principals and teachers. Tan's talk of creativity and innovation echoed the findings of an official Economic Committee set up by the Ministry of Trade and Industry in the wake of the 1985–1986 economic recession. The report had recommended the education of each individual to his or her maximum potential, and the development of creativity and flexible skills in order to maintain Singapore's economic competitiveness in the global economy (Ministry of Trade and Industry, 1986). At the end of 1986, 12 school principals accompanied Tan on a two week tour to study the management of 25 "acknowledged successful schools" in the United States and Britain, and see what lessons could be learnt for Singapore. The principals' report recommended selected schools be given greater autonomy in order that they might stimulate educational innovation. Accepting the recommendations, Tan favored granting independent status to a few well-established schools with capable principals, experienced teachers, strong alumni networks, and responsible governing boards. These schools would be given greater autonomy in staff deployment, salaries, finance, management, student enrollment, and curriculum, and would serve as role models to improve Singapore's education system. Parents, teachers, and students would enjoy a wider variety of schools to choose from. By 1990 four well-established boys' secondary schools had received Education Ministry approval and had turned independent, while continuing to be heavily dependent on Ministry financial aid. In 1993 two girls' secondary schools turned independent as well. Parliament was informed that the independent schools were meant to be developed into "outstanding institutions, to give the most promising and able students an education matching their promise" (*Parliamentary Debates*, 59, January 6, 1992, Col. 18).

Right from the genesis of the idea of independent schools, there had been widespread criticism of the elitist nature of the proposal. There was also concern over the affordability of independent school fees and the possibility that children from poor families would be discouraged from applying. While defending the government's elitist stance unapologetically, top Cabinet Ministers suggested that greater autonomy might be extended to more schools. This suggestion gained ground in the wake of the August 1991 general elections, which saw the PAP returned to power with fewer parliamentary seats. The loss of votes was officially attributed, among other things, to the increasing costs of public services. Goh announced in 1992 that the number of independent schools would be capped at eight for the time being (Goh, 1992). He also announced that some government and government-aided schools would be turned into "autonomous schools" in order to cope with the excess demand for places in independent schools. These schools would be given greater autonomy and more resources to become more like independent schools and to compete effectively with independent schools in providing quality education. Autonomous schools would be able to charge moderately higher fees than other schools, but not as much as independent schools. In early 1994, six secondary schools turned autonomous. To date, 26 secondary schools have become autonomous schools.

The 1990s were marked by further refinements to the streaming system. Streaming was delayed by one year from primary three to primary four. The various streams at both primary and secondary levels were also reorganized and renamed. Another change involved ensuring that students who enrolled in technical institutes would have completed at least four years of secondary schooling. In the early 1990s the Ministry of Education announced ambitious enrollment targets for postsecondary education: 20 percent of each age cohort in local universities, 40 percent in polytechnics and 25 percent in technical institutes. By the end of the decade, a target of 25 percent for local universities had been announced for the year 2010. The number of polytechnics increased from two at the start of the 1990s to five by 2003. Both polytechnic and university enrollments, which had begun increasing dramatically in the mid-1980s, accelerated further in the early and mid-1990s. The number of universities increased from one—the National University of Singapore—in 1990 to three—with the addition of the Nanyang Technological University and the Singapore Management University—by the year 2000. In addition, by the end of the 1990s, two previously privately run fine arts colleges were granted public funding on a par with the polytechnics, while continuing to exist as private institutions.

It was mentioned earlier that the PAP was singlemindedly gearing the education system to serve two major needs: economic development and social cohesion. Barely a decade after the 1986 Economic Committee report had mentioned creativity and innovation, these two attributes were hurtled into national prominence by the then Prime Minister Goh Chok Tong in 1997 when he launched the Thinking Schools, Learning Nation (TSLN) policy initiative. This initiative, which targeted all schools, was aimed at ensuring that all students would leave the school system with a life-long passion for learning as well as with critical and creative thinking skills in order that they might better adapt to the needs of the knowledge-based economy. Part of the TSLN initiative involved massive government investment in the Information Technology Masterplan in order to equip all schools with computers. Another lynchpin of the TSLN initiative was the concept of an ability-driven education (ADE), which was a further refinement of the 1986 Economic Committee report's advocacy of developing each student to his or her maximum potential. An ADE would identify and develop the varied talents and capabilities of each child to the maximum.

By the first years of the 21st century, the differentiation of students into different tracks carried on apace even as attempts were made to soften what was perceived by many as the harsh, no-second-chances nature of the streaming system. In 2002, a Ministry of Education report advocated allowing top-performing secondary students in a few schools to skip the national General Certificate of Education Ordinary Level examinations (commonly taken at the end of four or five years of secondary schooling) and to proceed directly on to preuniversity schooling (Ministry of Education, 2002). The report also recommended the establishment of specialized independent schools to better cater to talent in sports, the arts, and science and mathematics. To date, 11 schools and junior colleges have begun offering what are termed "integrated programmes" that allow students to skip the Ordinary Level examinations. Two specialized independent schools—the Singapore Sports School and the National University of Singapore High School of Mathematics and Science— have begun admitting students, with an Arts School in the works. Yet another recommendation in the 2002 report involved allowing a few privately funded schools to be established, provided that their foreign student enrollments did not exceed 50 percent, and that they adhered to core education policies. Three such schools have since come into being. In a bid to soften criticism about the harsh, segregationist nature of streaming and the limited opportunities for academic advancement provided students in the less prestigious tracks, the Education Ministry made several policy announcements. For instance, primary schools could allow students from the slowest track to attend some classes alongside their peers in faster tracks. Secondary students in the slower tracks were offered greater chances to read subjects normally offered their peers in faster tracks.

The concern with social cohesion and with the global-local tensions engen-dered by increasing economic and cultural globalization found voice in Goh's announcement in 1997 regarding the alleged lack of knowledge of Singapore's recent history among younger Singaporeans. He called for all schools to imple-ment National Education, which aimed at fostering national cohesion through fostering Singaporean identity, pride and self-respect; teaching about Singapore's nation-building successes against the odds; understanding Singapore's unique developmental challenges, constraints and vulnerabilities; instilling core values such as meritocracy and multiracialism, as well as the will to prevail, in order to ensure Singapore's continued success (Lee, 1997). Behind the NE initiative, one can read official concern over the possible economic and social consequences of the global economy leaving certain disadvantaged sections of the population straggling behind their better educated, globally mobile peers. There is also concern that the latter will abandon national loyalties in favor of the myriad economic opportunities that beckon overseas.

LEVELS OF EDUCATION

Preprimary

Preprimary schooling in Singapore is entirely in the hands of the private sector. There are various providers such as religious bodies, for-profit organisations, and the PAP, and the institutions that provide this form of schooling are commonly referred to as kindergartens or as child-care centers. The Education Ministry registers all kindergartens while the Ministry of Community Development, Youth and Sports takes charge of licensing child care centers. Preprimary schooling is not compulsory, and the Education Ministry has on several occasions insisted that it intends to leave preprimary provision in private sector hands. No official figures are available on enrollment, and on the number of children who do not enroll in preprimary schooling. Over the past two decades, many kindergartens and child-care centers have begun to link their daily activities more closely to the perceived literacy needs of the first year of primary school, with children being taught to write in English and one other official language.

Primary

In 2000, the Ministry of Education published a report advocating compulsory schooling in government and government-aided schools for six years. Parents who wish to home-school have to apply for individual exemption and prove their competence to conduct home-schooling. Their children will have to sit for the national Primary School Leaving Examination (PSLE) along with other children in mainstream schools. Likewise, parents who wish to enroll their children in privately run religious schools will have to apply for exemption. The first cohort of children to be affected by the relevant legislation enrolled for primary one in 2003. Figure 13.1 summarizes the flow of students through the Singapore education system.

The six years of primary schooling are nominally free of charge and are highly subsidized by the Education Ministry. There is a standard monthly miscellaneous fee of S$5.50 for Singaporeans and permanent residents. However, schools are allowed to charge up to an extra S$5.50 per month which may be paid for out of students' individual Edusave funds. This fund, which was first established in 1993, distributes official funding to individual accounts of students aged between six and sixteen. It also distributes funds to each primary and secondary school on a per capita basis. These funds may be used for paying additional miscellaneous fees, and for various educational programs conducted by schools.

Students follow a common curriculum for the first four years of their primary schooling. This stage of primary schooling is officially referred to as the Foundation Stage. At the end of the fourth year, schools are allowed to set their own streaming examinations to determine whether students are streamed into the Mainstream or EM3 streams for the remaining two years of primary schooling, which are referred to as the Orientation Stage. EM3 students follow a slower-paced curriculum and sit for a different examination than the PSLE that

Figure 13.1
The Flow of Students Through the Singapore Education System

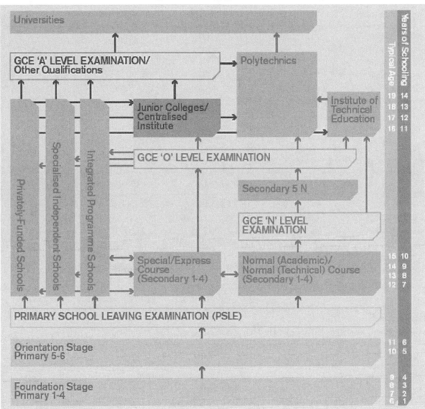

Mainstream students sit for. On average, between 5 and 10 percent (two-thirds of which is male) of each age cohort is streamed into the EM3 stream (Ministry of Education, 2005a). In 2006 the Education Ministry announced that the practice of primary school streaming would be abandoned in favor of subject banding from the year 2008 onwards. Tables 13.2 and 13.3 give information on the number of primary schools, primary school enrollment, and number of primary school teachers. Table 13.4 indicates the major subjects that form the common Ministry-determined curriculum in primary schools.

A Day in the Life of a Primary School Student

"It's going to be another long day ahead for me," thought Lisa, a primary six student, as she pinned her hair neatly together and got ready to put on her school shoes. It was 6.40 A.M., time for her to leave her home and walk to the nearby bus stop to catch a bus to her school. Lisa had been fortunate enough to gain

Table 13.2
Schools by Type and Level (2004)

Type of School	Primary	Secondary	Preuniversity	Total
Government	134	110	12	256
Government-aided	43	20	4	67
Autonomous		24		24
Independent		9	1	10
Total	177	163	17	357

Source: Ministry of Education, 2005a: 3.

Table 13.3
Student Enrollment and Number of Teachers (2004)

	Primary	Secondary	Preuniversity	Total
Student enrollment	296,419	213,534	24,681	534,634
Number of teachers	12,209 (5,169)	11,240 (9,846)	2,267 (2,252)	25,716 (17,876)

Note: Figures in brackets indicate the number with at least a first university degree.
Source: Ministry of Education, 2005a: 3.

Table 13.4
Major Curriculum Subjects in Primary School

Foundation Stage	Orientation Stage
Primary 1 and 2 English language (including health education), mother tongue, mathematics, social studies, art and crafts, civics and moral education, music, physical education *Primary 3 and 4* English language (including health education), mother tongue, mathematics, social studies, art and crafts, civics and moral education, music, physical education, science	*Primary 5 and 6* English language, mother tongue (or higher mother tongue for some students), mathematics, social studies, art and crafts, civics and moral education, music, physical education, science, health education Primary School Leaving Examination Mainstream subjects: English language, mother tongue, mathematics, science, higher mother tongue (for some students) EM3 subjects: foundation English, basic mother tongue, foundation mathematics

Source: Ministry of Education, 2005b.

admission to a coeducational primary school that was a 10-minute bus ride away from her flat. Like over 80 percent of the population, Lisa lived in a public housing estate. Having had an elder sibling enrolled in that school, coupled with her living within 1 km of the school, had accorded her top priority in the first phase of the annual nationwide primary one admission exercise almost six years ago.

She arrived at school in time for the daily morning rituals at 7.20 A.M. during which the entire school would assemble to sing the national anthem as the national flag was raised, and then recite the national pledge. Lessons were scheduled each weekday from 7.30 AM. to 1 P.M. It was only February, but Lisa could already feel the pressure mounting. Only the previous day her principal had assembled all the primary six students in the school auditorium. "You really have to buckle down to some hard work for the rest of this year. If you want to gain admission to Raffles Institution [a top-ranking boys' secondary school] or Raffles Girls' School [a top-ranking girls' secondary school], you need to score at least 260 points [out of a maximum of about 280 points] in your [national] primary school leaving examination [PSLE]. If you don't do well, you'll have to settle for a neighborhood secondary school [a somewhat derogatory term used to refer to a less-than-prestigious secondary school]. Your teachers will be working hard with you too, conducting extra lessons for all of you if they feel you need them. I expect all of you to spend less time on television and computer games and more time on your studies. Our school's examination results for last year were well above the national average and I hope you will help maintain that record. Your teachers and parents want you to do well, and I'm sure you wouldn't want to disappoint them."

After having enjoyed relatively more student-centered lessons during the previous five years of primary schooling, Lisa felt that the teachers were now becoming more teacher-centered instead in their bid to ensure students' examination success during the all-important examinations in October. These examinations were the major means by which students were allocated not only to secondary schools, but also to one of several streams within each school. The amount of homework had increased considerably this year, as had the number of tests. Not only that, the focus seemed to be almost solely on English, Chinese language, mathematics and science, the four subjects that would be tested in the examinations. Other subjects, such as social studies, moral education, art, music and physical education, appeared to be taking a back seat in teachers' priorities, and this invariably influenced most students' attitudes toward the various subjects in the official curriculum. The principal had also cautioned them to reduce their involvement in cocurricular activities so as to pay more attention to their studies.

At times Lisa wished her teachers would not relegate some subjects to secondary importance as she found the incessant examination preparation somewhat exhausting. She also wished she could pursue her active interest in athletics. However, her principal had decided that the school would scale down athletics as a cocurricular activity in favor of basketball, which the school had designated as a "niche" area, or area of strength. Each school had been encouraged by the Education Ministry to select a few "niche" areas that would be eligible for special funding. Lisa's school principal had chosen basketball because the school's basketball team had done well in inter-school competitions for several consecutive years, while the athletics team had yet to prove itself in a similar fashion. However, Lisa felt that this was unfair to students such as herself who had a genuine noncompetitive interest in other sports.

Her parents were as anxious as her teachers that she should do well and gain admission to a prestigious secondary school. Her elder brother had done well in the PSLE the previous year and was now enrolled in Raffles Institution. Lisa's parents were worried that she might not perform as well as her brother had, and were hoping that she might be able to capitalise on her piano skills, which she had acquired through private lessons at home, as an added edge for secondary school admission. The Education Ministry had recently allowed secondary schools the discretion to admit a limited percentage of students based on nonacademic criteria such as artistic, sporting or musical talent.

So anxious were they that they had been hiring private tutors, one for each of the four key examination subjects for the past four years. These tutors showed up once a week at Lisa's flat for an hour each time, and charged fees that accounted for a substantial portion of her parents' income. Not having made it to university themselves, her parents were only too aware of the substantial difference that having a university degree would make to their two children's future job prospects. Their financial investment in tutoring for Lisa was also prompted by their feeling that Lisa's teachers would not be able to afford her individual attention within a class of 40 students. Lisa understood their concern for her academic progress, and knew that most of her schoolmates also engaged private tutors, but felt tired by the heavy demands of school and tutoring. Besides, it seemed that the tutors were also engaging in rather the same sort of repetitive drill-and-practice routine as her teachers were. She hoped that her parents would not continue to insist on private tutoring once she had moved on to secondary school.

At last, the school day had ended. It had seemed endless, with each teacher piling on homework and reminding students not to slacken in their studies. There were three tests—English, mathematics and science—scheduled for the coming week. In addition, her diary indicated piano lessons had been scheduled for 2 P.M. that afternoon, after which the mathematics tutor would be showing up at 4 P.M. Lisa would have time for a quick lunch in the school canteen before taking a bus home. After her mathematics tuition, she would have time for a short nap before dinner at 6.30 P.M. Then she would do at least two hours of homework and another hour of study for the coming tests. "All my hard work will pay off eventually at the end of this year, and my parents will be so proud of me," Lisa told herself in an effort to keep her spirits up.

Secondary

Students' results in the national examinations at the end of Primary 6 determine which stream—Special, Express, Normal (Academic), and Normal (Technical)—they will be streamed into for the four or five years of secondary schooling. The respective percentages for these four streams in the case of the

Secondary 1 cohort in 2004 were 9.3, 53.2, 23.0 and 14.5 (Ministry of Education, 2005a). Not all secondary schools house all the four streams. In fact, a select few schools have only the Special Stream, while a few other select schools have only the Express stream. The majority of secondary schools run the Express, Normal (Academic), and Normal (Technical) streams. Tables 13.2 and 13.3 give information on the number of secondary schools, secondary school enrollment, and number of secondary school teachers.

Special and Express stream students sit for the national General Certificate of Education Ordinary Level examination, which the Education Ministry runs in collaboration with the University of Cambridge Local Examinations Syndicate, at the end of four years. Success in this examination determines admission to pre-university courses, polytechnics (which offer 3-year diplomas), or institutes of technical education (which offer 1- to 2-year technical or vocational courses). Normal (Academic) stream students sit for the General Certificate of Education Normal Level examination at the end of four years, after which the better-performing ones may opt to sit for the Ordinary Level examination after an additional year of study. Normal (Technical) stream students are in general being prepared for enrollment in institutes of technical education. In a small number of schools, students are allowed to skip the Ordinary Level examination and proceed straight on to the national General Certificate of Education Advanced Level examination at the end of six years of secondary schooling. In one of these schools, students are offered the opportunity to sit for the International Baccalaureate diploma instead of the Advanced Level examination.

Schooling is no longer nominally free at the secondary level. Most schools charge Singaporeans and permanent residents a minimum monthly school fee of S$5 and a standard miscellaneous fee of S$8. They are also allowed up to an extra S$8 per month in miscellaneous fees from out of students' Edusave accounts. Autonomous schools are allowed to charge yet another S$3 to S$18 per month, while independent schools' monthly fees ranged between S$125 and S$255 in 2005 (Ministry of Education, 2005b).

As in the case of primary schooling, the Education Ministry prescribes a standard curriculum for all secondary schools to adhere to. The range of subjects tends to broaden at the upper secondary level, and in 2005 the Ministry announced a few new subjects such as Economics and Drama for the Ordinary Level examination. Table 13.5 outlines the major curriculum subjects in secondary school.

Preuniversity

Between 20 and 25 percent of the secondary school cohort proceed to preuniversity courses. These courses last either two years in one of 17 junior colleges, or three years in a centralised institute. Tables 13.2 and 13.3 give information on the number of preuniversity institutions, preuniversity enrollment, and number of preuniversity teachers. These students sit for the national

Table 13.5
Major Curriculum Subjects in Secondary School

Secondary 1 and 2
English language, mother tongue (or higher mother tongue for special stream students), mathematics, science, history, geography, English literature, visual arts, design and technology, home economics, civics and moral education, music, physical education

Secondary 3, 4 and 5
English language, mother tongue (or higher mother tongue for special stream students), mathematics, additional mathematics, biology, chemistry, physics, combined science, combined humanities, history, geography, English literature, Chinese literature, Malay literature, Tamil literature, art and design, music, food and nutrition, computer applications, technical studies, elements of office administration, principles of accounts, design and technology, civics and moral education, physical education

Source: Ministry of Education, 2005b.

Table 13.6
Major Curriculum Subjects in Preuniversity Institutions

3 compulsory subjects
General paper, or knowledge and inquiry
Project work
Mother tongue
Art, biology, chemistry, Chinese language, Chinese language and literature, computing, economics, French, general studies in Chinese, geography, history, history of Chinese literature, Japanese language, English literature, Malay language, Malay language and literature, management of business, mathematics, music, physics, principles of accounting, Tamil language, Tamil language and literature, theatre studies and drama

General Certificate of Education Advanced Level examination conducted jointly by the Education Ministry and the University of Cambridge Local Examinations Syndicate. The monthly school fees charged to Singaporeans and permanent residents continue to be nominal as schooling costs are highly subsidized by the government. They are S$6, with standard monthly miscellaneous fees of S$11. Preuniversity institutions may charge up to S$11 in additional miscellaneous fees each month, and these extra fees may be paid for out of students' individual Edusave accounts.

The preuniversity curriculum is a very academic one and is highly geared toward university preparation. Students generally study a total of seven subjects at different levels of depth. Table 13.6 summarizes the major curriculum subjects available at the preuniversity level.

OVERVIEW OF THE CURRENT EDUCATION SYSTEM

It is apparent from the earlier discussion that the ruling PAP has tried consistently to gear the Singapore education system to serve the twin needs of economic development and social cohesion. To this end, the school system was unified and standardized during the 1960s and 1970s in order to bring together formerly disparate sets of parallel systems. Emphasis was put on common curricula, common school rituals, and on mathematics and science. In line with its elitist philosophy, the PAP put in place special programs for the academic elite. The concern with meeting the twin needs has continued unabated even as the Singapore system received international acclaim for producing top scores in the Third International Mathematics and Science Study in 1997. Not only was the Thinking Schools, Learning Nation launched in a bid to gear students toward meeting the perceived needs of the knowledge-based economy, the National Education initiative was concurrently put in place in a bid to soften some of the possible adverse consequences of globalization.

By many measures, the Singapore education system has achieved success, achieving almost universal attendance for ten years of schooling. Pass rates in national examinations have been steadily rising since the mid-1980s and the proportion of each age cohort proceeding to postsecondary schooling has increased dramatically too over the past two decades. It has been officially acknowledged that much of this success may have been accounted for through intensive drilling and coaching practices by classroom teachers. What has not been officially acknowledged is the possible role played by the widespread phenomenon of private tutoring.

One of the major challenges lying ahead is to change well-entrenched drilling and coaching practices in schools in favor of pedagogical approaches that favor creative and critical thinking instead. Despite almost a decade of the Thinking Schools, Learning Nation initiative, there is evidence that crucial gate-keeping national examinations continue to exert an inhibiting and conservative influence on principals, teachers, parents and students, official talk of creativity and innovation notwithstanding.

Another challenge is how to manage the balance between diversity and uniformity. In spite of official attempts in recent years to promote greater flexibility of academic options and a wider array of school provision, other features of the education landscape push toward uniformity. One of these is the annual publication of performance league tables and the awarding of medals for different areas of school achievement. These measures serve as a powerful, if somewhat indirect, means of ensuring that all schools remain "on track." So crucial are the schools in terms of economic development and social cohesion that the Education Ministry is likely to be unwilling to allow totally unfettered diversity.

Yet another perennial problem is the management of disparities in educational attainment along social class and ethnic lines. There is widespread evidence that minority ethnic groups such as Malays and Indians are under-represented in higher education institutions, despite official attempts to provide financial assistance to various community organizations that are attempting to improve these students' educational attainment. There are no official figures on how many students enter primary school each year not having first attained basic literacy in a school system that begins on the assumption that each child has already attended a preschool. Although the 1990s saw the initiation of compensatory programs such as the Learning Support Program in primary schools to assist such children, there is still evidence that students from less-well-off homes are under-represented in the most prestigious schools.

The Singapore education system has attained a certain amount of regional renown, to the extent that there are regular visits and exchange programs by foreigners keen to study its success or to attend courses in Singapore educational institutions. This success is trumpeted even as officialdom attempts a bold remaking of fundamental ways of teaching and learning. What bears watching is whether the next phase of educational success will in fact prove as spectacularly successful as the previous phase of expansion and consolidation has been.

REFERENCES

Colony of Singapore (1947). *Educational Policy in the Colony of Singapore*. Singapore: Government Printer.

——(1957a). *Education Ordinance (No. 45 of 1957)*. Singapore: Government Printer.

——(1957b). *Government Grant-in-aid Regulations, 1957*. Singapore: Government Printer.

Department of Statistics (1983). *Economic and Social Statistics Singapore 1960–1982*. Singapore: Department of Statistics.

Doraisamy, T.R. (ed.) (1969). *150 Years of Education in Singapore*. Singapore: Teachers' Training College.

Goh, C.T. (1992). *National Day Rally Speech 1992*. Singapore: Ministry of Information and the Arts.

Gopinathan, S. (1974). *Towards a National System of Education in Singapore 1945–1973*. Singapore: Oxford University Press.

——(1976). "Towards a national educational system," in R. Hassan (ed.), *Singapore: Society in transition*, pp. 67–83. Kuala Lumpur: Oxford University Press.

——(1980). "Language policy in education: A Singapore perspective," in E.A. Afendras and E.C.Y. Kuo (eds), *Language and Society in Singapore*, pp. 175–202. Singapore: Singapore University Press.

——(1991). "Education," in E.C.T. Chew and E. Lee (eds), *A History of Singapore*, pp. 268–287. Singapore: Oxford University Press.

Lee, H.L. (1997). *The Launch of National Education*. Accessed on February 8, 2005 from http://www1.moe.edu.sg/ne/KeySpeeches/MAY17–97.html.

Lee, K.Y. (1982). "The search for talent," in S. Jayakumar (ed.), *Our Heritage and Beyond: A Collection of Essays on Singapore, its Past, Present, and Future*, pp. 13–23. Singapore: National Trades Union Congress.

Ministry of Education (1979). *Report on the Ministry of Education 1978*. Singapore: Ministry of Education.

——(1995). *Education Statistics Digest 1995*. Singapore: Ministry of Education.

——(2002). *Report of Junior College/Upper Secondary Education Review Committee*. Singapore: Ministry of Education.

——(2005a). *Education Statistics Digest 2004*. Singapore: Ministry of Education.

——(2005b). *Overview*. Accessed on October 22, 2005 from http://www1.moe.edu.sg.

Ministry of Trade and Industry (1986). *Report of the Economic Committee. The Singapore Economy: New Directions*. Singapore: Ministry of Trade and Industry.

Parliamentary Debates Singapore (1992). Official Report No. 59, Col. 18. Singapore: Government Printers.

People's Action Party (1959). *The Tasks Ahead: PAP's Five-year Plan 1959–1964. Part 2*. Singapore: Petir.

Republic of Singapore (1966). *Ministry of Education Annual Report 1966*. Singapore: Government Printer.

Singapore Legislative Assembly (1956a). *Report of the All-Party Committee of the Singapore Legislative Assembly on Chinese Education*. Singapore: Government Printer.

——(1956b). *White Paper on Education Policy* (Sessional Paper No. Cmd. 15 of 1956). Singapore: Government Printer.

State of Singapore (1959). *Ministry of Education Annual Report 1959*. Singapore: Government Printer.

——(1962). *Ministry of Education Annual Report 1962*. Singapore: Government Printer.

Wilson, H.E. (1978). *Social Engineering in Singapore: Educational Policies and Social Change 1819–1972*. Singapore: Singapore University Press.

Wong, F.H.K. and Gwee, Y.H. (1980). *Official Reports on Education: Straits Settlements and the Federated Malay States, 1870–1939*. Singapore: Pan Pacific Book Distributors.

Wong, R.H.K. (1974). *Educational Innovation in Singapore* (Experiments and Innovations in Education No. 9). Paris: The Unesco Press.

Yip, J.S.K. (1982). "The role of the principal in a decentralised system of education management." Paper presented at principals' seminar on principalship in a decentralised system of education management, Singapore, November.

Yip, J.S.K., Eng, S.P., and Yap, J.Y.C. (1990). "25 years of education reform," in J.S.K. Yip and W.K. Sim (eds), *Evolution of Educational Excellence: 25 Years of Education in the Republic of Singapore*, pp. 1–30. Singapore: Longman.

Zahoor Ahmad bin Haji Fazal Hussain (1969). "Malay education in Singapore," in T.R. Doraisamy (ed.), *150 Years of Education in Singapore*, pp. 100–115. Singapore: Teachers' Training College.

Chapter 14

SCHOOLING IN SOUTH KOREA

Sheena Choi

South Korea's remarkable turnaround from the destruction of colonialism and ashes of the War to an economic miracle has made it an international "poster child" of economic development. The once impoverished agrarian society, liberated from Japanese colonial rule (1910–1945), ravaged by the Korean War (1950–1953), and then ruled by successive autocratic regimes, has become a democratic society with a prosperous economy. Many of these successes have been credited to Korea's educational achievement, which included a conversion from virtual mass illiteracy in 1945 to universal literacy and the highest level of higher educational attainment in the world among the relevant age cohort. The quality of Korean education is regarded highly by the international community—judging from comparative international tests of mathematics and science skills. Korean primary and secondary students score among the highest in the world (Stevenson and Stigler, 1992; U.S. Department of Education cited in Seth, 2002; Park, 2007). While Koreans accomplished monumental economic and educational success, the challenges ahead are also significant. This chapter traces Korean educational achievements and shortcomings through an examination of historical, sociocultural, and political contexts.

OVERVIEW

This chapter is divided into two parts: pre-1945 and post-1945—the year Korea gained independence from the Japanese colonial yoke. Many studies include the Japanese colonial period as a forerunner of the modern era that introduced various modern elements, including an educational system. However, due to the oppressive nature of colonial rule, Koreans were not independent players in their educational future. Thus, these years are integrated into the premodern period here. The pre-1945 era is subdivided into ancient/premodern, early modernization, and Japanese colonial periods. The first section presents an abridged history of Korean education in that era. Due to international politics, Korea since independence (1945) has been divided geographically along the 38th parallel into North Korea (Democratic People's Republic of Korea, DPRK), and South Korea (Republic of Korea, ROK). The division continues as the Demilitarized Zone (DMZ) approximates the 38th parallel after the Korean War. Discussion of the post-1945 period in this chapter focuses exclusively on South Korea.

Seth observed that an emphasis on sequential development characterizes South Korean education (2002). Educational development and reform in modern Korea reflect a political agenda which can be broadly subdivided into four stages. The first stage was the achievement of universal education. Forty years of Japanese colonial rule—five years as a protectorate (1905–1910) and 35 years of direct colonial control (1910–1945)—and the Korean War (1950–1953) left Korea devastated. In this dire situation, the national focus was on universal education to overcome mass illiteracy. Only after the completion of this goal, during the 1960 and 1970s, could the country move into the next stage—expansion of secondary education to meet the human resource need for the developing economy. The booming economy, political turmoil, and illegitimate regime of the 1980s necessitated the administration's concession to public demand for greater higher education opportunities, thus heralding the third stage, expansion of higher education. The fourth stage is signaled by the inauguration of democratic government, 1990s to present, and the recognition of the global economy and its challenges. The rapid expansion from the previous era left poor quality higher education. Criticism led the incoming democratic government to launch successive reform efforts for developing internationally competitive world class higher education. Thus, the second part of this chapter, post-1945, examines the development of primary, secondary, and higher education in the socioeconomic and political context of South Korea.

Premodern Korea: Pre-1945

Ancient/Premodern Era (4th Century through 19th Century)

Formal education in Korea dates back to the Three Kingdom period (around 57 B.C. to A.D. 668). In 372, Koguryo (37 B.C.–A.D. 669) founded the *Taehak* for educating elite class male youths to prepare them for bureaucracy. The *Taehak* is believed to be the second oldest higher educational institution in Asia (Kim, 2000). Study abroad to Tang China was popular among elites from the three Korean kingdoms. The scholarship of some Koreans during this period influenced the neighboring countries of China and Japan. This tradition of higher learning was followed by *Kukhak* during the Unified Silla (668–935), *Kukchagam* during the Koryo Dynasty (918–1392), and *Sungkyunkwan* during the Choson Dynasty (1392–1910) (MOE, 2000). Schools, public libraries, and academic research centers were also built in local areas during the Choson Dynasty.

The independent private schools known as *Sowon* flourished during the Koryo and Choson Dynasties. The *Sowon* of the Choson Dynasty was comparable to a

Table 14.1
Educational Institutions in Ancient and Premodern Korea

Dynasty	Public Institutions		Private Institutions	
	Higher	Middle	Higher/Middle	Lower
Koguryo (37 B.C.–A.D. 669)	Taehak (372)			Kyongdang
Unified Silla (668–918)	Kukhak (682)			
Koryo (918–1392)	Kukchagam (992)	Hakdang Hyanggyo	Shib-I-do (12 Schools)	Sodang
Choson (Yi) Dynasty (1392–1910)	Sungkyunkwan (1398)	Hakdang Hyanggyo	Sowon	Sodang

Notes: * The numbers in parentheses indicate the years of establishment.
** Sungkyunkwan, the exclusive state higher education institution during the Choson Dynasty continues as Sungkyunkwan University.
Source: MOE, 2000.

state higher education institution. *Kyungdang* and *Sodang* offered education for the commoners. The *Sodang* during the Choson Dynasty was expanded into nearly every neighborhood (MOE, 2000). The Choson Dynasty witnessed the flourishing of *Sowon*, which embodied the spirit of scholarly society independent from state control (Choe, 1999; Kim, 2000). Such an extensive spread of schools, relative to that time period, reflects the influence of Confucianism, which attaches great importance to learning (see Table 14.1). In an agrarian society, where entering into government bureaucracy was the only route for social mobility, Confucian statecraft emphasized the governance by scholars—men of talent and virtue (Kim, 2000; Seth, 2002: 9). Studies (Lett, 1998) attribute modern day Koreans' obsession with education to this Confucian tradition.

Early Modernization Period (1880–1905)

Intrusion by foreign powers into Korea toward the end of the 19th century resulted in extensive changes, and the Choson Dynasty began to implement a Western-style educational system. The first group of modern schools included Wonsan Haksa (1883), which was established by wealthy Koreans, especially in major ports, to offer modern and patriotic education; the English School (1883); Yukyong Gongwon (1886–1894), which mirrored the government's desire to advance new ideas; and Paejae hakdang (1885–present) and Ewha Hakdang (1886–present), which were the first of many modern schools founded by American missionary organizations (MOE, 2000; Seth, 2002). Between 1883 and 1908, 12 national schools, 22 private schools, and 31 missionary schools were founded (MOE, 2000: 30).

The impressive growth of private education was an attempt to strengthen the declining nation. Some of the private educational institutions were established by

Western Christian missionaries as part of mission efforts. The indigenous *Han'gul* (Korean alphabet), which had long been pejoratively viewed by Confucian scholars as vulgar script (or female script), was revived during this period and used along with Chinese characters (Schmid, 2002). The use of *Han'gul* was efficient, as it could be easily mastered. More importantly, it emerged as a national symbol. Such efforts, however, were overwhelmed by the Japanese aggression, protectorate status (1905–1910), and finally colonization (1910–1945).

Education under the Japanese (1905–1945)

During Japanese rule, a highly centralized, comprehensive, and modern national education system was established. Development was primarily concentrated on basic education with a paltry expansion in secondary education and severe restriction on tertiary levels. The Educational Ordinance noted that the purpose of the educational system for Koreans was "to give the younger generations of Koreans such moral character and general knowledge as will make them loyal subjects of Japan" (Governor-General of Chosen quoted in Seth, 2002: 20). Recognizing such antagonistic Japanese policies toward Koreans, Seth asserts that "the Japanese came as conquerors, outsiders who ruled over an often hostile Korean population in order to carry out policies that they thought beneficial to Japan" (Seth, 2002: 19).

To secure control over Korea, Japan created an extensive bureaucratic apparatus. The educational system was part of bureaucratic machinery designed to "serve all the needs of the empire" and constituted a "strong, coercive, and exploitative state structure" (Seth, 2002: 19). General colonial educational policy toward Korea is well reflected by Governor-General Terauchi's remark in 1912:

Korea has not yet reached the level of development that demands a high level of education. Koreans should presently be trained as workers, by making a practical education available to them. Schools should educate youngsters with this basic objective in mind so that they may go back home upon graduation and become leaders of their own people. In this type of schooling, practical knowledge should be emphasized. The basic policy of this government will focus on agricultural and vocational schools. I believe the realization of this basic schools or vocational schools, and administrative organizations as well, acted independently and separately from this primary objective, I am afraid smooth rule of Korea cannot be expected in the future. (Takahashi, 1927: 365 cited in Kim, 2000: 25)

The basic educational tenets of the colonial government during the period were:

1. Education is not urgent.
2. All that is needed in the education of Koreans is practical and vocational training, which is better suited to the level of their development.
3. Higher education is superfluous for Koreans.
4. Private schools must be controlled and, if possible, eliminated.
5. Education for the Koreans and that for the Japanese must be different and separate from each other. (Kim, 2000: 25)

Consequently, a conflict developed between Koreans and the Japanese colonial regime over educational policies, and the legacy of Korean bitterness toward their colonial rulers remains.

Two features of colonial educational policy deeply contributed to Korean antagonism and resentment: restriction of access beyond the elementary level and "use of education to indoctrinate Koreans into being loyal subjects of the Japanese empire and later to assimilate them into Japanese culture" (Seth, 2002: 19). The restriction on higher education "led to a pent-up demand for educational access that would burst into the open in South Korea when the Japanese empire collapsed" (ibid.: 19). At the same time, while forced assimilation irritated nationalists, the Japanese colonial example set the pattern for both North and South Korean governments to follow, adopting the use of education as a powerful and centralized political instrument (ibid.: 19).

As a result of restricted expansion of higher education by the colonial government, "in spite of onerous restrictions, private Korean and mission-run schools accounted for half the secondary and most of the higher-level educational institutions in Korea" (Seth, 2002: 21). The only university during the colonial period, Kyungsung (in Japanese Geijo) Imperial University (forbearer of present day Seoul National University, established by Japan in 1922), admitted mostly Japanese expatriates and children of a few high-ranking Korean collaborators. Other higher-level institutions established at the end of the Chosun dynasty and during the early modernization period were reorganized into higher learning institutions of less status or, in some cases, forcibly closed by colonial authority. Nonetheless, some of these surviving schools played indispensable roles in an independent Korea. For example, after independence, Ewha Technical School became Ewha Women's University, a leading women's university in Korea. The Posong Technical School became Korea University; and Yonhui Technical School became Yonsei University, both leading prestigious coeducational universities.

Other legacies of colonial education that influenced South Korea's educational developments are regimentation and centralization. Regimentation promoted orderliness and cleanliness in the nation's schools. While access was limited, high standards and rigor in teacher training, along with traditional Korean respect for teachers, enhanced the teachers' authority in the classroom (Seth, 2002). Administratively, it was a highly centralized, uniform system, in which all schools followed the same curriculum set by the central Education Bureau. A complex system was employed in educational financing. While the separate educational system maintained for Japanese students was heavily subsidized from the state treasury, schools for Koreans relied on many sources of revenue including donations, tuition, and other fees. However, the most important feature that influenced South Korean education was the reliance on competitive entrance examinations, which was at the root of *sihom jiok*, literally "examination hell," that South Koreans encounter presently.

Modern Korea: Post-1945 Educational Development

The period immediately after the liberation of Korea can be characterized as one of rapid change (Seth, 2002: 34). Although Korea became independent from the Japanese colonial yoke, the exhilaration of independence was marred by the partition of the nation along the 38th parallel. American forces in the southern zone set up the United States Military Government in Korea (USAMGIK); and the Soviets occupied the northern zone, both eventually setting up two ideologically antagonistic governments. From this point, the chapter focuses on the educational development of South Korea.

In 1945, when the 35 years of Japanese colonial rule ended, the majority of adult Korans were illiterate. Seth notes that "less than 5 percent of the adult population had more than an elementary school education" (2002: 2). The first stage of educational development (1945–1950s) commenced in this bleak situation. The Korean government focused on building a nationalistic Korean education based on ideals of democracy. The establishment and implementation of compulsory education was the major accomplishment during this period. The second stage (1960s through 1970s), during the Third and Fourth Republic, focused on economic development. Consequently, educational development was intimately linked to production in the labor force that was needed for industrialization. Expansion of middle and high schools were key aspects of this period. An unforeseen side effect of this expansion was the intensified competition for higher education. During the third stage (1980s–1993), South Korea experienced the unparalleled expansion of higher education as a concession by the politically illegitimate Fifth and Sixth Republics. The first popularly elected president, Kim Young-sam's Civilian Government (*mun'min jung'bu*) ushered in the fourth stage. The following administrations of Kim Dae-jung's Popular Government (*kungmin jung'bu*) and Roh Moo-hyun's Participatory Government (*chamyo jungbu*) made internationalization and globalization key aspects of the reform agenda, thus creating internationally competitive world-class education (see Table 14.2).

Another important aspect of Korean educational development is its critical dependence on private initiatives. Such development reduced the financial burden on the government for the provision of education beyond primary education by progressively shifting the responsibility to the private sector. Drawing from MOE statistics as seen in Table 14.3, Seth notes:

Private schools accounted for a third of the middle school and vocational high school enrollment, half that of academic high schools, and about three-quarters of that in higher education. In 1962, 36 of the nation's 48 colleges and universities were private. The relative power of these institutions was accentuated by the fact that they were concentrated in the cities. In 1966, 89 of Seoul's 116 middle schools and 34 of the 50 middle schools in Pusan were private, and they accounted for three-quarters and two-thirds of the corresponding enrollment respectively. Similarly, private academic high schools accounted for three quarters of the high schools and their pupils in Seoul and two-thirds of all high school students in Pusan. Furthermore, nearly 70 percent of all college and university students were concentrated in Seoul, and of these, 90 percent attended private schools. (Seth 2002: 135)

Table 14.2
Postliberation South Korean Educational Development

Stage	Reform Agenda	Achievements
Stage 1 (1945–1950s) USAMGIK (1945–1948); First Republic (1948–1960)	Establishment of nationalistic Korean education and democratic education	Establishment of *Hong'ik In'gan* (Service to humanity) as national educational goal Promulgation of educational law (December 31, 1949) Universal elementary education (December 31, 1949) 6–3–3–4 academic system (1951) Proclamation of elementary, middle, and high school curriculum (1955)
Stage 2 (1960s and 1970s) South Korea Under Park Chung Hee (1961–1979)	Coordinate education to economic development National security and anticommunism as the educational goal	Expansion of technical and science education Containment of Higher education expansion (enrollment allocation system 1965; consolidation of higher education institutions and disciplines 1965; Appointment of presidents for national higher education institutions; Higher education faculty evaluations; Banning of teacher unions; Baccalaureate qualifying exam (December 1961–April 1963) Upgrading of elementary teacher education (from previously high school to junior college level) and establishment of Graduate School for Teacher Education Program. Promulgation of Private School Law (June 26, 1963) Promulgation of National Education Charter (December 5, 1965) First long term educational planning (1972–1986)

		Middle school equalization (abolition of exam) (1969–1971)
		High school equalization (1974–1980)
		Government qualifying exam (1962) (used as basis of higher education admission)
Stage 3 (1980s– 1993) The Fifth Republic (1980–1987); The Sixth Republic (1987–1992)	Coordinate education to economic development National security	Abolition of college entrance exam and replacement with Home School Records System (*naesin*)
		Over the allocation college admission system (30%): "admission over quota, graduation by quota"
		Expansion of higher education
Stage 4 (1993– present) *Mun'min jungbu;* *Kungmin jungbu;* *Cham'yo jungbu*	Democratic education and decentralization Knowledge based society/ global competition	Brain Korea (BK) 21
		Specialization of higher education curriculum
		Diversification of higher education curriculum
		Development of regional higher education institutions
		Restructuring of vocational high schools and technical schools
		Establishment of professional graduate schools (medical, law, divinity schools etc.)
		Support and specialization of regional higher education institutions
		Efficiency and quality control of higher education
		Higher education autonomy and accountability
		Assessment and financial support
		Reform in appointment of president and faculty (national universities)

Table 14.3
School Statistics on Public versus Private in Korea (1999)

Classification	School		
	Total (100%)	National and Public (%)	Private (%)
Kindergarten	8,790	4,351 (49.5)	4,439 (50.5)
Elementary school	5,544	5,468 (98.6)	76 (1.4)
Middle school	2,741	2,057 (75)	684 (25)
Academic high school	1,181	571 (48)	610 (52)
Vocational high school	762	443 (58)	319 (42)
Special school	123	42 (34)	81 (66)
Trade high school	16	—	16 (100)
Air and correspondence high school	41	41 (100)	—
Junior college	161	16 (10)	145 (90)
University of education	11	11 (100)	—
College and university	158	26 (16.5)	132 (83.5)
Air and correspondence university	1	1 (100)	—
Industrial university	19	8 (42)	11 (58)

Source: MOE, 2000: 55.

The First Stage: Realization of Universal Primary Education and Commitment to Nationalistic Korean Education

U.S. Military Occupation Period

When the USAMGIK set out to reorganize and reform Korea, they had very little knowledge about Korea; so the formation and implementation of any policies was chaotic and circumstantial, thus temporary and ineffective. Moreover, the country was in turmoil. Influxes of expatriates were returning from Japan, Manchuria, China, and North Korea, overburdening scarce resources and the fragile infrastructure. Therefore, the primary focus of USAMGIK was to maintain order. Much organization and policy making had to rely on Western, especially American, educated intellectuals for whom the USAMGIK could feel trust (Seki, 1987). Yet, in spite of scarce resources and lack of trained teachers, the educational system began to expand immediately.

With the Cold War escalating, the USAMGIK feared leftist activities. Lack of knowledge about Korea and fear of the political left by the USAMGIK resulted in their using Japanese collaborators whom Koreans despised. Such development sowed the seeds for Korean distrust of the USAMGIK. Yet, this period began with the exuberance of a newly independent nation and set the tone for future educational development. On August 15, 1948, a separate government in the South was organized under the supervision of the U.S. military. Two major objectives were identified by Korean education leaders for educational policy: democratic education and equality of educational opportunity. First, implementation of democratic Korean education (at this historical juncture, democratic

Korean education was an allusion to ultranationalistic education) called for the purging of the remnants of colonial education—of the inflexible, elitist, "fascist, militarist, and totalitarian nature of imperial education" which stripped Koreans of dignity (Abe, 1987; Seki, 1987: 224; Seth, 2002: 35). Second, Koreans wanted equitable and broadly accessible educational opportunity for all, which had been denied to them by the colonial government. After many debates, an education system patterned after that of the United States was adopted which retained the essential feature of a 6–3–3–4 year system (Umakoshi, 1987), the one track system in which students pursued a single curriculum path well into secondary schools (Seth, 2002: 60). At the high school level, students were tracked into academic high school or vocational high school. At the postsecondary level, two or three years of technical colleges paralleled the four year universities and colleges. The curriculum development focused on the Korean ideal of educating "whole persons" as opposed to the U.S. recommendation of technical education. It is noteworthy that much of the instruction was allocated to enrichment subjects such as music, physical education, and art (Abe, 1987). Also, adoption of *Hangul*, the Korean alphabet, quickly diminished mass illiteracy (Inaba, 1987). The following statistics given by the Ministry of Education (MOE) show remarkable expansion of education (see Table 14.4).

With minor modifications over time, this system is still in effect (see Figure 14.1).

Several factors made the American occupation period relatively ineffective in educational reform/reorganization, such as the contingent nature of the American occupation, the shortage of both material and human resources, and political unrest. Despite the American military presence, aid from the U.S. was in short supply. As mentioned earlier, the colonial government's tight control on higher education left Korea dependent on Japanese experts and technicians. Moreover, in the absence of adequate manpower, low-ranking Japanese collaborators were elevated into higher-ranking management positions by the USAMGIK. In addition, although the general public viewed the political left as uncompromising patriots (as opposed to collaborators), the USAMGIK and its

Table 14.4
Expansion of Elementary School Education (1945–1999)

	1945	1960	1970	1980	1990	1999
Schools	2,834	4,496	5,961	6,487	6,335	5,544
Index	100	158	210	229	224	196
Teachers	19,729	61,605	101,095	119,064	136,800	137,577
Index	100	312	512	603	693	697
Students	1,366,685	3,622,685	5,749,301	5,658,002	4,868,520	3,935,537
Index	100	265	420	414	356	288

Note: While the trend is similar, statistics presented by Seth (2002) differ from statistics provided by MOE (2000).
Source: Ministry of Education, Republic of Korea, 2000: 33.

Figure 14.1
School System

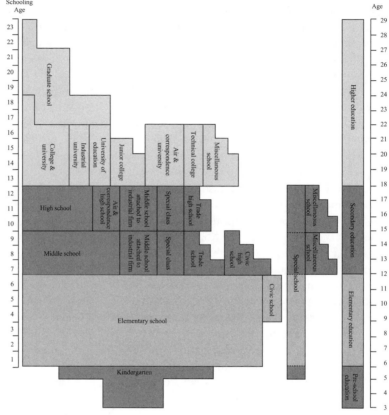

Source: MOE, 2000.

supporters began to suppress all leftists, even moderates and nationalists. The new government, supported by American occupation forces, employed former collaborators who favored the Japanese system and joined the purge of leftists. This sowed the seeds of public distrust toward the American-supported South Korean government. Still, educational policies during the American occupation period laid the groundwork for future democratic reforms.

The First Republic: 1958–1960

Three laws, which were passed in November and promulgated on December 31, 1949, became the basis for South Korean education for the following decades—the Basic Education Law, the Basic School Law, and the Social Education Law. Confronted with a lack of resources, teachers, facilities, and funds, South Korea devoted its limited resources to immediate needs of universal primary education while volunteer organizations focused on literacy education. After the accomplishment of universal education, the Korean government turned to technical education at the secondary level. However, the government's preference for "maintain[ing] a sequential, pyramid structure for the nation's education" (Seth, 2002: 138) often proved ineffective as the government faced the enormous problem of public demand for equal educational opportunity at all levels.

The Korean War (1950–1953) ravaged the country but did not deter Korean educational zeal. At the wartime capital of Pusan, refugees continued their education in makeshift classrooms—tents, bombed buildings, or wherever possible. The classroom and teacher shortages were acute. It was common to see primary classroom sizes of more than 60, and some in cases more than 100 students.

Such efforts were so fruitful that illiteracy declined rapidly. Drawing from the Ministry of Education's report in *Mungyo wolbo* (1959) Inaba notes 78 percent illiteracy among individuals over 12 years old in 1945, the year of independence. In 1948, three years after the use of *Hangul*, illiteracy dropped to 41 percent. In spite of the Korean War (1950–1953) the illiteracy rate declined to 26 percent in 1953. At present, Korea enjoys one of the highest literacy rates in the world.

The effort to establish democratic education was a key element of the "New Education Movement" (NEM = *sae kyoyuk undong* in Korean) and was heavily influenced by American progressive educational ideals. Accordingly, the *sae kyoyuk undong* emphasized democratic ideals of equal opportunity for all and the child-centered and society-centered educational approaches of problem solving skills, self-reliance, and individual responsibility. Furthermore, *sae kyoyuk undong* worked to promote ideas such as independent school boards, decentralization, teacher autonomy from political control, organization of teacher unions, and texts and methods that promote democratic values (Seth, 2002).

Advocates praised the movement as "providing a foundation for the reconstruction of the social order into a progressive cultural identity" (McGinn et al., 1980: 36). The *sae kyoyuk undong* flourished throughout the 1950s but was hijacked during the 1960s by the military regime. Under the military regime, the *sae kyoyuk undong* and its democratic ideals were politically oppressed, as it was incompatible with the regime's goal. It was replaced by education for national security and anticommunism (Kang, 2002). Since the democratic transition in the 1990s, the True Education Movement (*cham kyoyuk*) has called for autonomy of education from political influence, emphasizing democratic education and creative thinking.

By 1999, primary school enrollment rate of the relevant aged population had risen from 64 percent in 1945 to 98.5 percent (MOE, 2000) and this increase was repeated at the middle school level. The initial gender gap, higher enrollment of boys than girls, was closed by the 1960s (Seth, 2002). The problems of overcrowding and a lack of facilities were solved over time. By the early 1980s, a decrease in school-age population and economic prosperity enabled South Korean

Table 14.5
Elementary School Classroom Size (1945–1999)

	1945	1960	1970	1980	1990	1999
Ratio	69.3	58.8	56.9	47.5	35.6	28.6

Source: Based on MOE (2000) statistics.

classrooms to be comparable in teacher–student ratio and facilities to those of developed countries. See Table 14.5 for data on elementary school classroom size for the years 1945–1999.

The Second Stage: Development of Human Resources

Middle School

Secondary education experienced rapid expansion (see Table 14.6). The years between liberation from Japan and the Korean War witnessed fourfold growth. Secondary school enrollment doubled between 1952 and 1960, although the rapid expansion eventually slowed down. An interesting characteristic of Korean education beyond the primary level is its heavy reliance on private initiatives. The government, preoccupied with universal primary education using limited resources, relied considerably on private institutions. According to Seth "[H]alf of all new secondary schools opened at this time were private" (Seth, 2002: 81).

Under the old system, entry into a middle school was based on a competitive entrance examination. This created an extremely hierarchical educational system. Entering an elite middle school was viewed as a way to ensure entering an elite high school, university, and then prestigious occupation. Such a hierarchical system placed great pressure on students to produce excellent examination results. Many parents turned to cram schools known as *hagwon* and private tutoring known as *kwaoi* to gain advantages in competition.

The hierarchical middle school system was criticized for causing many social ills. First, it undermined the physical and mental health of students by driving them into intense preparation for the entrance exam. The South Korean youth in the 1960s were shorter and lighter than their Japanese counterparts, who were traditionally smaller than Koreans (*Korea Times,* 1967). Youth suicide and other misconduct related to examination pressure were often reported on the news. Second, the hierarchical middle school system caused social instability. Thus, after accomplishing universal primary education, the South Korean government carried out the abolition of competitive middle school entrance examinations known as *musheheom jinhak* between 1969 and 1971. Since 1969, there has been free admission to middle school; and all students who opt to enter middle school have been assigned to schools nearest their residence.

The middle school No Entrance Examination policy was successful in many ways. By 1968, 55 percent of primary school graduates were able to advance to middle

Table 14.6
Expansion of Middle School Education (1945–1999)

	1945	1960	1970	1980	1990	1999
Schools	166	1,053	1,608	2,121	2,470	2,741
Index	100	634	968	1,277	1,488	1,651
Teachers	1,186	13,053	31,207	54,858	89,719	93,244
Index	100	1,100	2,631	4,625	7,565	7,862
Students	80,828	528,593	1,318,808	2,471,997	2,275,751	1,896,956
Index	100	654	1,631	3,058	2,815	2,347

Source: Ministry of Education, Republic of Korea, 2000: 34.

school. The numbers steadily increased to 59 percent in 1969, 62 percent in 1970, and during the 1970s middle school attendance became nearly universal (Seth, 2002: 155). According to statistics of the Ministry of Education (2000), 99.9 percent of elementary graduates in 1998 entered middle school. Since 1985, free compulsory middle schools have also been provided in farming and fishing areas (MOE 2000). Since 1995, native speakers have been assigned to middle schools to prepare for the "Age of Internationalization" (MOE, 2000). However, intensified competition for entrance to elite high schools is an unexpected consequence of middle school equalization and the expansion of middle school education.

Since middle and high school equalization, some middle to upper middle class parents began to move to the school district of their preferred school; and residential areas began to form according to the reputation of secondary schools in that area. This is similar to the U.S. phenomenon of quality public schools increasing property values because of middle class suburbanites moving into school districts with good academic reputations. Newspapers during this period often reported cases of illegal transfer of residence records by those who wished to be assigned to "prime" high schools but could not afford to move.

High School

The development of high schools was more contentious than that of middle schools and often left the government and the public at odds with one other. The government, especially since the installation of the military government in the 1960s, planned to strategically coordinate educational development with economic planning. This meant emphasizing technical training at the high school level. However, the increasingly vocal public desired equal access at all levels and favored the academic track leading to higher education.

During the 1960s and 1970s, the Korean public witnessed astonishing educational expansion regardless of their social class background. However, excessive public demand for educational opportunity often clashed with the South Korean government's desire to coordinate educational development with economic planning. The government's emphasis on vocational education linked

Table 14.7
Academic versus Vocational High School Enrollment (1961–1995) (in Thousands)

	1961	1970	1980	1990	1999
Academic high schools	180	315	932	1,490	1,240
Index	100	175	518	828	689
Vocational high schools	102	275	764	810	911
Index	100	270	749	794	893

Source: MOE, Republic of Korea, *Kyoyuk tonggye yonbo* (Statistical yearbook of education, 1971, 1981, 1996 in Seth, 2002: 84).

to economic development conflicted with the public who desired academic high schools leading to university. The absolute number of students opting for the academic track consistently surpassed that of the vocational track (see Table 14.7). Even for those on the technical education track, the public demanded that it be open (not terminal), leaving options for higher education.

The middle school equalization alleviated the high pressure competition for high school. But in reality, the competition for education just moved to the next level of schooling. Abolition of the middle school entrance examination and high school equalization intensified supplementary tutoring by creating a greater pool of potential college aspirants. Drawing from 1988 data, Mark Bray notes "expenditure on private tutoring by the richest 10 percent in a sample of urban households in the Republic of Korea was twelve times that amount spent by the poorest 10 percent of households" (2003: 34). Students also experienced physical and psychological trauma related to the entrance examination:

80 percent of high school students are suffering from various kinds of ailments such as stomach problems, migraine, and astigmatism caused by preparation for examination. Sixty percent of them are suffering from psychological ailments such as a nervous breakdown and anxiety. Besides these ailments, 30 to 40 percent of high school students drink or smoke in order to find relief from stress of study. Further, 20 to 30 percent of students are addicted to some kind of drug. (PCER Report cited in Park, 2000: 167)

While these statistics may be exaggerated, they capture the extraordinary stress in gaining admission to universities and colleges. To relieve this pressure, some chose "education immigration" (*kyoyuk yimin*) to English speaking countries or early study abroad (*joki yuhak*). Also, psychological and financial burdens caused by family separations for education, creating what is known as the *kiroki* [wild goose] family, arose as a social issue and drew national and international attention (Choi, 2004; *Washington Post*, 2005).

The Third Stage: Elite to Universal Higher Education

Higher education institutions in Korea are established in three ways: national institutions which are founded, administered, and financially supported by the national government's Ministry of Education and Human Resources Development; public institutions which are founded, administered, and financially supported by local governments; and private colleges and universities which are founded and administered by individuals or organizations. Higher education institutions in Korea can be categorized into 10 groups: universities, industrial universities, universities of education, junior colleges, Air and Correspondence Universities, cyber colleges and universities, technical colleges, colleges within companies, graduate school colleges, and other miscellaneous institutions. The following Tables 14.8 and 14.9 present the numbers of institution, faculty, and enrollment by types of institution as of 2004.

Korean higher education is highly centralized. All higher education institutions, regardless of their status as national, public, or private, are subject to direct supervision by the Ministry of Education and Human Resource. This includes the establishment of academic departments, student quotas, faculty hiring, credit hours, and degree conferring (MOE, 2000).

Unlike the case of primary education expansion, which the South Korean government promoted as part of the plan for national development, the uncontrolled expansion of higher education was viewed as a great risk to social, economic and political stability. There was a fear that the developing economy would not be able to absorb the large number of university graduates. Concern about unemployment and underemployment of university graduates caused the South Korean government under Park Chung Hee to employ varying measures to restrain the expansion. The first measure was the establishment of a quota system, which failed due to high demand and universities' need for tuition fees. Higher education institutions went far beyond their quota allotment. Among the other methods used to deal with the situation were mergers and departmental closings. In some cases, the government denied foreign aid funds to higher education except for engineering and some other technical fields (*Tonga Ilbo*, 1961 cited in Seth, 2002: 131). The government also attempted to institute a national qualifying examination for baccalaureate degrees in order to screen out incompetent students (Seth, 2002: 133).

While these methods helped to rein in the expansion during the regime of Park Chung Hee, expansion skyrocketed during the regimes of Chun Doo Hwan (who came to power in a military coup d'etat) and Roh Tae Woo (Chun's close associate who was elected president). A booming economy and these administrations' need for political legitimacy led to the expansion of higher education.

As of 2004, 81.3 percent of high school graduates advance into higher education (Kim n.d.) This figure is the highest in the world. Such expansion led Seth (2002) to assert that there are limits of a "strong developmental state," which was often perceived as insulated from public pressure (see Figure 14.2) (Johnson, 1987; Migdal, 1988; Haggard and Moon, 1990).

However, the rapid growth of higher education resulted in several problems. A foremost weakness was that a quantitative expansion was not accompanied by a qualitative development in higher education. Today, the quality of Korean higher education is rated unfavorably compared to other developed nations

Table 14.8
Summary Statistics of Higher Education by Types of Institution

	Institutions	Enrollments	Faculty	Student–Faculty Ratio
University				
National	24	376,413	11,974	31.44
Public	2	20,939	529	39.58
Private	145	1,439,297	34,502	41.72
Subtotal	171	1,836,649	47,005	39.07
University of education				
National	11	23,335	756	30.87
Air and correspondence university				
National	1	290,728	123	2,363.64
Industrial university				
National	8	86,892	1,399	62.11
Private	10	102,143	1,144	89.29
Subtotal	18	189,035	2,543	74.34
Technical college				
Private	1	196	0	
Miscellaneous school				
Undergraduate course	4	1,064	30	35.47
Junior college course	1	89	5	17.80
Sub-total	5	1,153	35	32.94
Cyber college and university				
Undergraduate course	15	36,716	276	133.03
Junior college course	2	2,734	21	130.19
Subtotal	17	39,450	297	132.83
Junior college				
National	7	14,721	374	39.36
Public	8	24,026	357	67.30
Private	143	858,842	11,141	77.09
Subtotal	158	897,589	11,872	75.61
Colleges within companies				
Private	1	62	0	
Graduate school college				
Private	28			
Grand total	411	3,278,197	62,631	39.53

Source: Lee Hyun-Chong (n.d.).

(Bahn, 2003). They are behind "[M]easured in terms of various science and technology development indexes, such as the ratio of research and development (R&D) investment to GNP, the number of researchers, the number of patent rights obtained, and the number of research papers published in international journals" (Kim, 2000b: 258). According to Seok (1999), Korean higher education expansion ranks as one of the highest in the world, while quality improvement scarcely ranks middle in Asia.

Table 14.9
Growth of Higher Education from 1970 to 2004

Year	No. of Institutions	Enrollment	No. of Faculty	Student–faculty Ratio
1970	142	201,436	10,435	19.30
1975	205	238,719	11,416	20.91
1980	343	601,494	20,900	28.78
1985	262	1,277,825	33,895	37.70
1990	270	1,691,681	41,920	40.35
1995	333	2,343,894	58,977	39.74
2000	372	3,363,549	56,903	59.11
2004	411	3,555,115	62,631	56.76

Source: Educational Statistics, KEDI, cited in Lee (n.d.).

Figure 14.2
Entrance Ratio of High School Students to College by Nation

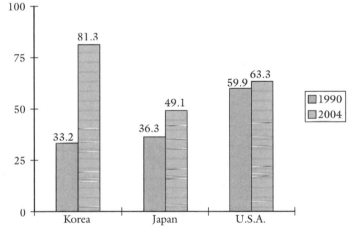

Source: Lee (n.d.).

Korean higher education faces numerous problems. Korean higher education is very homogenous. The rigid central control in all areas of higher education administration caused a lack of diversity and specialty in its curriculum offerings, resulting in a highly hierarchical institutional pecking order that fans the "examination hell" (Park, 2000). Korean higher education also confronts a demographic challenge—the continuing decline of the college-bound population. Recent population projection indicates that the college-bound population (age 18–21) will drop by 29 percent in a 20 year span and will be further reduced to half in another 10 years. It is projected that the college-age population will be reduced from 3,278,000 in 2000 to 2,336,000 in 2020 and will further go down to 1,511,000 in 2030 (Lee, n.d.). This will bring about intense competition among colleges. Above all, there is great public dissatisfaction over the poor quality of higher education. Public criticism centers on higher education being neither responsive to public demands nor competitive in the advent of the "information age" and globalization.

The Fourth Stage: Toward World Class Education

The election of Kim Young-sam (1992–1996), the first civilian president in over 30 years, heralded Korea's democratic transition. By then, Korea had become the world's 11th largest economy and gained entry into the Organization of Economic Cooperation and Development (OECD) (Kim, 2003: 3). A previously war-ravaged, dismal country attained recognition as "an East Asian model of prosperity and democracy" (*New York Times*, 1995). Acknowledging the arrival of the knowledge-based society, the Kim Young-sam government declared globalization (*segyehwa*) as "the most expedient way for Korea to become a world-class, advanced country." Kim viewed globalization as "no longer a matter of choice but one of necessity" (Kim, 2000a: 2). The administration attempted to project a new Korean national identity by "moving away from and beyond inter-Korean competition [and] to the center of the action not only in the Asia-Pacific region but also in the world community" (Kim, 2000b: 244). Kim Dae Jung (1997–2001), who was the first dissident elected to the presidency, envisioned the globalization era as a time in which "intangible knowledge and information [that] will be the driving power for economic development" (*Korea Herald*, 1998 cited in Kim 2000b: 258). These quotes from the two presidents are important in understanding the Korean approach to higher education reform in the globalization era.

In 1995, the Presidential Commission on Education Reform (PCER) put forward a series of proposals for political and financial support to develop a world class education system in Korea (Presidential Commission on Education Reform, 1997). In spring 1999, the Korean government launched a new national education policy, Brain Korea (BK) 21, to enhance the international competitiveness of Korean higher education in the 21st century. BK 21 focused on cultivating highly qualified R&D manpower by concentrating governmental funds on education and research activities at graduate schools. The essence of the BK 21 project is to develop world class graduate schools by boosting research capabilities (Lee, n.d.). The New University for Regional Innovation (NURI) (2004–2008) Project is another initiative to strengthen the capability of regional institutions that are located outside the Seoul metropolitan area (Seoul, Incheon, and Kyunggi-do). The NURI Project is aligned with the national policy of "Balanced Development of the Nation" (Lee, n.d.). The restructuring of higher education initiated in 2004 provides financial support for university mergers. The Study Korea Project, developed in 2004, aims to attract foreign students to Korean colleges and universities.

Some of this higher education reform effort is devoted to creating a knowledge-based society, through the development of "human capital," to compete in a diverse, information based, and increasingly globalized world. Some of the continuing reform agendas considered since the period of the democratically elected Kim Yong-sam presidency (Bahn, 2003) include focusing on principles of equality, democracy, diversity, and autonomy; supporting regional universities; making structural adjustments; reeducating about ranking systems; and upgrading science/engineering education. Kim Dae-jung's Popular Government, *Kungmin jungbu* (1998–2003) and Roh Moo-hyun's Participatory Government, *Chamyo jungbu*, implemented similar educational reform agendas in order to increase global competitiveness and internal efficiency. Kim Dae-jung's BK 21 is an exemplary project drawn to create world-class universities. However, there has been criticism that educational reform is dogmatic and regressive along the lines of neoliberal market ideology, which views education as a consumption good as opposed to a public good. Critics say the government is shifting a greater proportion of educational expenditure to overburdened consumers (parents), amplifying inequality in educational quality and opportunity according to affordability.

CONCLUSION

Schooling in South Korea can be characterized as having sequential development heavily affected by the relentless public pursuit of higher education. Korean education is most impressive at the lower levels and less so at the tertiary level (Seth, 2002: 252). South Korean elementary and secondary students consistently score among the highest in mathematics and science on international tests conducted by various educational organizations, outperforming students from the United States and virtually all developing countries (*Korea News Review*, 1995 cited in Seth 2002: 252). The initial gender gap, higher enrollment of boys than girls, was closed by the 1960s (Seth, 2002). The problems of overcrowding and a lack of facilities were solved over time. By the early 1980s, a decrease in school-age population and economic prosperity enabled South Korean classrooms to be comparable in teacher–student ratio and facilities to those of developed countries. South Korean teachers are well trained and maintain a high level of professionalism. South Koreans also have the lowest rates of dropping out, absenteeism, tardiness, and occurrences of school violence.

In contrast, university education, which became the focus of extreme competition, generally lacks quality when compared to the United States and other developed nations. Recently, this low quality became a focus of educational reform. As the country entered into the information age, the South Korean economy no longer could depend on "borrowed" knowledge and technology. In order to retain its competitive edge in an increasingly globalizing world, production of knowledge (as opposed to acquisition) arose as urgent and crucial items on the educational reform agenda. Therefore, efforts to build world class universities are underway.

South Korean educational development is paradoxical. The government directed and managed educational development with its own political agenda and created a highly centralized hierarchical system vulnerable to pressures from authority. It also

South Korean students taking a recess from physical education class.
Courtsey of Sheena Choi.

ran into conflict with public aspirations for open and equal access at every level. Popular obsession with education created a rapid expansion of the system, which in turn contributed to national development. Yet, this zeal also created problems. The linking of educational credentials with the traditional eminent social status of Confucian gentry/scholars impeded implementation of technical and vocational education, resulting in an oversupply of students in humanities and social sciences. The intense pressure for educational attainment created a competitive entrance examination system, which ultimately became distorted into a test preparation system. This competition placed enormous pressure on students and a financial burden on families, as well as stifled innovative educational reform efforts.

No doubt, its high cost, high pressure, inflexibility, and low quality higher education comprise a troubling side of South Korean education. Naturally, in spite of spectacular educational achievements since its independence in 1945, South Koreans are distressed about the dinosaur system. In search of more educational opportunity, which is often unavailable or inadequate, many students have chosen to study abroad in recent decades. In 1998, about 133,000 students studied abroad, most of them in the United States (*Korea Herald*, 1998).

Yet, the Korean public in general is optimistic about their educational future. According to a Korean Gallup Poll conducted in 2000, most people still feel education is the single most important factor in the country's future and profess a willingness to finance it through high taxation. Furthermore, the public maintains an unwavering faith in academic credentials. Through education, South Koreans achieved one of the most extraordinary transformations in modern history—from a land of illiteracy to one of the most highly schooled in the world; from abject poverty to inclusion in the league of affluent nations.

REFERENCES

Abe, Hiroshi (1987). "U.S. educational policy in Korea," in H. Abe (ed.), *Educational Reform in Korea under the U.S. Military Government (1945–1948)*, pp. 202–213. Seoul: Han'guk Yon'guwon.

Bahn, Sang-Jin (2003). "*Sae Jungbu ei Godung Kyoyuk Gaehyuk Kwaje* [Higher education reform agendas of the new administration]," *The Journal of Educational Administration* 21(1): 169–191.

Bray, Mark (1999). *The Shadow Educational System: Private Tutoring and Its Implication for Planners, Fundamentals of educational Planning*. Paris: UNESCO (International Institute for Educational Planning).

———(2003). *Adverse Effects of Private Supplementary Tutoring: Dimensions, Implications, and Government Responses*. Paris: UNESCO International Institute for Educational Planning.

Choe, Yong-ho (1999). "Private academies and the state in late Choson Korea," in Haboush, JaHyun Kim and Martina Deuchler (eds), *Culture and the State In Late Choson Korea*, pp. 15–45. Cambridge, MA: Harvard University Press.

Choi, Sheena (2004). "Globalization or marketization?: The dilemmas of international schools in S. Korea," *International Journal of Educational Reform*, 13(4): 325–337.

Cummings, Bruce (1981). *The Origins of the Korean War*. Princeton, NJ: Princeton University Press.

Donga Ilbo [Donga Daily News] (1961). December 3.

Eckert, Carter (1996). "Total war, industrialization, and social change in late colonial Korea," in Peter Duus, Ramon H. Myers, and Mark R. Peattie (eds), *The Japanese Wartime Empire, 1931–1945*. Princeton, NJ: Princeton University Press.

Haggard, Stephan and Moon, Chung-in (1990). "Institutions and economic policy: Theory and a Korean case study," *World Politics*, January, 17(2): 210–237.

Inaba, Tsugio (1987). "Development of the language policy under the U.S. military government," in H. Abe (ed.), *Educational Reform in Korea under the U.S. Military Government (1945–1948)*, pp. 230–253. Seoul: Han'guk Yon'guwon.

Johnson, Chalmers (1987). "Political institutions and economic performance: The government business relationship in Japan, South Korea, and Taiwan," in Frederic C. Deyo (ed.), *The Political Economy of the New Asian Industrialism*, pp. 136–164. Ithaca, NY: Cornell University Press.

Kang, Hilde (2001). *Under the Black Umbrella: Voices from Colonial Korea 1910–1945*. Ithaca, NY: Cornell University Press.

Kang, Il Guk (2002). "Haebang yihu chodeng hakgyoei kyoyuk gaehyukkwa bangong kyoyukei chungae kwajung [The reformation movement of the primary schools and the formation of the anti-communist education after 1945]," *Sociology of Education* 12(2): 1–17.

Kim, Hyung Kee (n.d.). Alternative Regional Development Based on Decentralization and Innovation. *6th Global Forum on Reinventing Government*.

Kim, Jongchol (1971). "Impact and problems of the middle school no-examination admission policy," *Korea Journal*, 11: 4–7.

———(2000). "Historical development," in John C. Weidman and Namgi Park (eds), *Higher Education in Korea: Tradition and Adaptation*, pp. 7–54. New York: Falmer Press.

Kim, Jung-gull (1999). "Han'guk kyo'yuk Gaehyuk ui Chungae Kwajung ei Daehan Pyung'ga juk Yon'gu [Studies on Korea's educational reform process]," *The Journal of Educational Administration*, 17(4): 41–70.

Kim, Samuel (2000a). "Korea and globalization (Segyehwa): A framework for analysis," in Samuel Kim (ed.), *Korea's Globalization*, pp. 1–28. Cambridge: Cambridge University Press.

———(2000b). "Korea's Segyehwa drive: Promise versus performance," in Samuel Kim (ed.), *Korea's Globalization*, pp. 242–281. Cambridge: Cambridge University Press.

———(2003). "Korea's democratization in the global-local nexus," in Samuel Kim (ed.), *Korea's Democratization*, pp. 3–44. Cambridge: Cambridge University Press.

Korea Herald (1998). February 26, cited in Kim (2000b).

Korea News Review (1995). January 7, 1995 cited in Seth 2002: 252.

Korea Times (1967). October 29.

Lee, Eun-Jun (2002). "Brain Korea 21: Development-oriented national policy in Korea higher education," *International Higher Education*. Center for International Higher Education, Boston College. Accessed on June 11, 2006 from http://www.bc.edu/bc_org/avp/soe/cihe/newsletter/News19/text16.html.

Lee, Hyun-Chong (n.d.). *Country Report:Korea*. Accessed on June 12, 2006 from http://64.233.167.104/search?q=cache:Vdq_7IxoID0J:www.aparnet.org/documents/8th_session_country_reports/Country_Report-Korea.rtf+New+University+for+Regional+Innovation%E2%80%99(NURI).&hl=en&gl=us&ct=clnk&cd=2.

Lett, Denise Potrzeba (1998). *In Pursuit of Status: The Making of South Korea's "New" Urban Middle Class*. Cambridge, MA: Harvard University Asia Center.

McGinn, Noel F., Snodgrass, Donald, Yung Bong Kim, Shin-bok Kim, and Quee-yong Kim (1980). *Education and Development in Korea*. Cambridge, MA: Harvard University Press.

Migdal, Joel S. (1988). *Strong Societies and Weak States: State–Society Relations and State Capabilities in the Third World*. Princeton, NJ: Princeton University Press.

Ministry of Education (MOE) (2000). *Education in Korea 1999–2000*. Seoul: Ministry of Education.

New York Times (1995). December 26, A14.

Park, Hyunjoon (2007). "Japanese and Korean high schools and students in comparative perspective," Paper presented at the Conference European Forum: Assessing the Quality of Education and its Relationships with Inequality in European and other Modern Societies, June 22–23, 2007, Florence.

Park, Namgi (2000). "The 31 May 1995 higher education reform," in John C. Weidman and Namgi Park (eds) *Higher Education in Korea: Tradition and Adaptation*, pp. 149–176. New York: Falmer Press.

PCER (1997). *Education Reform for New Education System*, Seoul, Korea.

Phuong Ly (2005). A Wrenching Choice, *Washington Post*, January 9.

Reed, Gay Garland (2004). "Multidimensional citizenship, Confucian humanism and the imagined community: South Korea and China," in W.O. Lee, David L. Grossman, Kerry J. Kennedy, and Gregory P. Fairbrother (eds) *Citizenship Education in Asia and the Pacific: Concepts and Issues*, pp. 239–256. Hong Kong: The Comparative Education Research Centre, University of Hong Kong; Kluwer Academic Publishers.

Republic of Korea, Mungyobu [Ministry of Education] (1963). *Mungyo tonggye yoram* [Outline of Educational Statistics], pp. 347–351. Seoul: Mungyobu.

Schmid, Andre (2002). *Korea between Empires 1895–1919*. New York: Columbia University Press.

Seki, Eiko (1987). "Korean endeavors toward the reestablishment of their educational system under the U.S. military government," in H. Abe (ed.), *Educational Reform in Korea Under the U.S. Military Government (1945–1948)*, pp. 214–229. Seoul: Han'guk Yon'guwon.

Seok, Tae-jong (1999). "Kungmin ei Jungbu Daehak Kyoyuk Kaehyuk Sa'up ei Pipanjok Gumto [Critical evaluation of Kungmin government's higher education reform effort]," *Sociology of Education* 9(3): 87–104.

Seth, Michael J. (2002). *Education Fever: Society, Politics, and the Pursuit of Schooling in South Korea*. Honolulu, HI: Center for Korean Studies, University of Hawaii.

Steinberg, David (ed.) (2005). *Korean Attitudes toward the United States:Changing Dynamics*. Armonk, NY: M.E. Sharpe.

Stevenson, Harold W. and Stigler, James W. (1992). *The Learning Gap: Why Our Schools are Falling and What we can Learn from Japanese and Chinese Education*. New York: Summit Books.

Takahashi, Hamakichi (1927). *Chosen kyoiku shi ko* (A Study of Korean Educational History). Keijo (Seoul). Teikoku Chiho Gyosei Gakkai Chosen Honbu.

Umakoshi, Toru (1987). "The implications of U.S. educational assistance in rebuilding Korean education after the independence," in H. Abe (ed.), *Educational Reform in Korea under the U.S. Military Government (1945–1948)*, pp. 243–253. Seoul: Han'guk Yon'guwon.

U.S. Department of Education (1987). *Japanese Education Today*. Washington, DC: Government Printing Office.

Chapter 15

SCHOOLING IN TAIWAN

Chuing Prudence Chou and Ai-Hsin Ho

INTRODUCTION OF TAIWAN

For centuries, Taiwan was referred to especially in the West as Formosa. At present it is officially recognized in Taiwan as the Republic of China, and in mainland China, as a renegade province of the People's Republic of China. Despite this, it is universally renowned for its breathtaking natural scenery and its miraculous economic development earned it the title of an Asian Tigers, one of only four. In the mid-16th century, when their ships passed through the Taiwan Straits, the Portuguese became amazed at the forest-cloaked island, and shouted out, "Ilha Formosa," meaning "Beautiful Island." This marked the first of many encounters between Taiwan and the West. According to the Chinese, Taiwan was called Yizhou or Liuqiu in ancient times and different dynasties set up administrative bodies to exercise jurisdiction over Taiwan from the mid-12th century. The Dutch East India Company occupied Peng-Hu (an off-shore isle of Taiwan) as a trading harbor base for her East Asian business dealings in the 17th century. In 1622, a war broke out between China's Ming Dynasty government and the Dutch troops. As a result, Taiwan was colonized by the Dutch from 1642 to 1662. After 1662, the Dutch were defeated by a former Ming government official, Zheng Chenggong, who used Taiwan as a military foundation against the Qing government. From 1662 to 1683, Taiwan was under the reign of Zheng's family. In Zheng family's 23-year sovereignty, Taiwan once again underwent social reconstruction and economic development. It was once known as the "Taiwanese Kingdom" or the "Kingdom of Formosa" by the English East India Company (National Institute for Compilation and Translation, 1997). After 1683, Taiwan came under the control of the Qing Empire when Zheng was defeated by Chi-Lang, the Qing general. It was the first time that Taiwan was reclaimed officially by the Chinese government. In the mid-19th century, the European countries threatened China in the Opium War of 1840 which led to

China's loss of Hong Kong until 1997. Although the Qing government took a more positive attitude toward Taiwan's development, Taiwan was ceded to Japan under the terms of the Treaty of Shimonoseki after 1895, and remained under Japanese colonization for half a century.

Taiwan was returned to China after 1945 and once again after the defeat of Japan in World War II. Nevertheless, following the Chinese communist party takeover of the Mainland in 1949, Taiwan became a shelter for Mainlanders who supported Nationalist (Kuomingtang, known as the KMT) leader Chiang Kai-Shek (Cooper, 2000). Nearly two million Chinese civilians, government officials and military troops relocated from the mainland to Taiwan.

Over the next five decades (1949–2000), the ruling authorities gradually democratized and incorporated the local Taiwanese within the governing structure. In 2000, Taiwan underwent its first peaceful transfer of power from the Nationalists to the Democratic Progressive Party (DPP). Throughout the period 1980–2005, the island prospered and became one of East Asia's economic "Little Tigers." The dominant political issues across the island remained the question of eventual unification with mainland China, as well as domestic political and economic reform.

Geography, Population, and Economy

Taiwan's total land mass occupies 35,980 sq. km. The population growth rate was estimated at 0.63 percent in 2005, with a GNP in 2004 of NT$463,056 (US$14,032) (Directorate-General of Budget, Accounting and Statistics, Executive Yuan, ROC, 2004). According to J.F. Cooper (2000), Taiwan's population is comprised of four cultural and ethnic groups. They are Taiwanese (Hokkien and Hakka) 84 percent, mainland Chinese 14 percent, aboriginal 2 percent. Each group has its own dialect and cultural perspectives. Taiwan used to adopt the doctrine "Three Principles of the People" invented by her founding father, Dr. Sun-Yat Sen in 1905. Since the 1990s, Taiwan has enjoyed a dynamic capitalist economy with gradually decreasing government control of investment and foreign trade. In keeping with this trend, some large government-owned banks and industrial firms have been incorporated and privatized. Exports have provided the primary impetus for Taiwan's development. The trade surplus has been substantial up to 2004, and foreign reserves were among the world's top 10 in the 1990s. Agriculture contributes less than 2 percent to the GDP, nowadays, in contrast with 32 percent in 1952. Taiwan is also one of the major investors throughout Southeast Asia. The Chinese mainland has overtaken the position formally held by the United States as Taiwan's largest export market. Growing economic ties with the mainland since the 1990s have led to the successful move of much of Taiwan's assembly of parts and equipment for production of export goods to developed countries.

Taiwan Education

In 1922, the American "six-three-three-four" system was implemented in mainland China: six years in elementary school, three in junior high, three in senior high, and four in university. Since the Nationalist government's relocation to Taiwan in 1949, this system has continued.

Since the 1950s, Taiwan encountered political and military uncertainty across the Straits, but between 1957 and 1980, the emphasis shifted to the planning and development of human resources in tandem with the national goal of economic development. Additional challenges to the education system came in response to the forces of economic liberalization and globalization which have transformed Taiwan since the 1980s. Taiwan's educational system entered an era of transition and reform as the nation's industrial structure shifted from a labor-intensive to a capital and technology-intensive base, and political democratization intensified.

A BRIEF HISTORY OF TAIWANESE EDUCATION

Prior to colonization by Japan, there were some forms of primary, secondary, and specialized schools for different purposes. Under the Japanese, a formal education system was established in 1919. Before then, the Japanese government issued the "Taiwanese Education Act" that divided the education system into four categories: general, vocational, specialized, and normal (teacher) education. At the general education or primary level, there were public schools, upper general schools, and girls' high schools. All of these admitted children between the ages of 7 and 13. Students were to learn knowledge and skills for life and basic needs. Not until 1943, was six-year compulsory education implemented. By that time, the enrollment rate for primary school level in Taiwan was 71.3 percent versus 99.6 percent for Japanese children (among the highest in Asia). After World War II, when Taiwan was returned to China, an Act regarding compulsory primary education in Taiwan was issued in 1947. By 1968 compulsory education was extended to 9 years and by 1984, both the primary and secondary education enrollment rates had reached over 99 percent (Directorate-General of Budget, Accounting and Statistics, Executive Yuan, ROC, 2005).

Taiwanese education has been very much influenced by Confucianism. According to Tu (1995, as cited in Zhou, 2000), East Asian societies continue to be very much influenced by Confucian values such as political authoritarianism, family system, examination systems, saving habits, local organization, and human networks (Tu, 1995, as cited in Zhou, 2000). Therefore, education has been regarded as a priority in Confucian culture. Study involves hard work, effort, persistence, cultivation, and rigidity, whereas game playing is considered idling. The learning attitude for most students was expected to be one of diligence coupled with hard work and effort (Zhou, 2000).

As a result, Chinese society in Taiwan, places an emphasis on credentialism and examination systems. The Imperial Examination in ancient China (694–1895), which lasted for more than 1,000 years, had three social functions: First, to diminish the effect of social and family origin on social mobility. Second, to enforce the social control of the ruling class, by selecting intellectuals for the governing class through public examinations. Although the Chinese Imperial

Examination was abolished in 1905, Taiwan is still under the influence of this examination tradition. As a result, these examinations are expected to be fair and allow social upward mobility.

A cooperative research project involving Taiwan, Hong Kong, Singapore, and China (Zhou, 2000) found schools in the Pacific rim to have a common high regard for credentialism. Parents value their children's academic performance highly and are actively involved in school affairs. The school curriculum is highly geared toward school examinations. School accountability is usually judged by examination performance. Consequently, most secondary schools provide examination preparation programs for children after school. There is a common belief that students with better academic achievements will enjoy higher incomes.

The following paragraphs discuss three major educational issues in modern Taiwan education. They are: globalization versus localization, gender stereotyping, and equity of educational opportunity.

Globalization versus Localization

Education system in Taiwan, similar to other education systems in East Asia, has undergone an enormous transformation over the last two decades. Education has become interconnected with trends of globalization and internationalization, development of information communications technology, and a set of political, sociological, economic, and management changes. These changes together produce multifaceted influences on education in Taiwan. In particular, the ideology of globalization and localization acts as one of the driving policy agendas in Taiwan.

The notion of globalization encompasses a plethora of meanings. According to Mok and Lee (2000: 362), globalization is "the processes that are not only confined to an ever growing interconnectedness and interdependency among different countries in the economic sphere but also to tighter interactions and interconnections in social, political and cultural realms." Governments in Taiwan have endeavored to follow the trend of globalization, especially in education.

In the efforts of Taiwanese educational globalization, English instruction was very much emphasized throughout primary and secondary education. In the earlier history of education in Taiwan, English was only instructed in secondary schools as one of the compulsory classes. However, in order to follow the trend of globalization and to connect with the world internationally, Taiwanese government started to push second language instruction into primary schools, targeting fifth and sixth graders in the elementary level in 2001, in order to cultivate their youth to become internationally competitive.

Another significant measure under the influence of globalization is the nine-year spiral curriculum reform in secondary education introduced in 2001. The objective of this curriculum reform program is considered the backbone of the major educational reform during the last decade. Its major goals are to promote cultural learning and international understanding as well as other demanding abilities for the 21st century. In order to achieve educational globalization, related issues and ideas were implemented within secondary curriculum in subjects such as civil and social studies.

The Ministry of Education (MOE) also stressed globalization in higher education. Taiwan followed the world trend of higher education globalization, redirected the aim of education toward market-oriented. Lessening government control and integrating social demand with market forces, Taiwanese education in the 1990s has been influenced by globalization to a great extent. Also, beginning in 2003, MOE started to promote a "World Class Research University" project, proposing to upgrade at least one of the universities in Taiwan to be ranked among the top 100 leading international institutions of higher education within the next 10 years. Universities are required to establish a system of evaluation using methods as the SCI, SSCI, and the EI, or to be in accordance with the standards that meet international recognition for awards, achievements, and contributions within their field of expertise. In 2005, MOE granted NT$50 billion (equals US$1.56 billion) to 12 universities in the following five years to empower their research capacity to reach the world class level.

On the other hand, Taiwan has also strived for localization along with the globalization trend since the 1990s. As Giddens (1994) yielded, globalization concerns localization. The two concepts can be viewed as two sides of the coin that jointly shape the identity of self and the nation. Besides globalization, Taiwan itself has confronted with the demand of education localization within the country. This can be dated back to 1945, when Taiwan was under Japanese ruling. Under Japanese administration (1895–1945), the purpose of Taiwanese education was to assimilate local people into Japanese culture. After the restoration of Taiwan to China in 1945, the urgent mission of the Taiwan authorities was to abolish the effect of Japanese colonialism on Taiwan by setting up a new education system for the advancement of Chinese national identity (Yang, 2001: 204). There was a process of Chinese-oriented education which emphasized education for preserving Chinese culture and the national language, Mandarin. The American "six-three-three-four" system was adopted in Taiwan after World War II. Therefore, in the latter half of the 20th century, Taiwanese education went through a series of nationalism campaigns that drew heavily on Chinese culture and economic rationalism striving for western efficiency and effectiveness.

After 1949, the priority was to strengthen Chinese identity as means of eventually reasserting sovereignty for China over Taiwan. During that period of time, indigenous Taiwanese cultures and languages were banned especially after the "228 (February 28th) incident" in 1947 which involved violent suppression by KMT troops of the Taiwanese people.

Since the late 1980s, Taiwanese society has gone through a period of localization involving the renovation of Chinese identity with Taiwanese heritage and tradition. These trends of indigenization or so-called localization stem from historical complaints against KMT authoritarianism.

During the political transition period of the 1990s, the former president Lee Teng Hui tried to incite a Taiwanese independence movement against China. Since then, education has focused extensively on local issues and Taiwanese identity such as the declaration of calls for the country to be known as Taiwan rather than the Republic of China, the shift of textbook content in elementary and secondary schools from China to Taiwan issues, and the increasing proportion of Taiwanization of the national civil service examination questions.

However, under the above multiple political, social, and cultural influences in education, less attention was drawn to some of the risks and conflicts encompassing with globalization and localization in education. In the case of the language policy in the education system of Taiwan, there has been increasing concern over the decline in Taiwanese primary students' achievements in the Chinese subject area and Mandarin literacy (*Central Daily News*, May 5, 2005). The number of teaching hours that used to be allocated to the Chinese curriculum has been reduced from one-half to one-third across primary and secondary school sectors. Also, localization within Taiwan is a unique and great predicament, unlike the rise of localization of third world countries around the globe, which has been mostly against western oppression. Taiwan is confronting a cultural identity problem (Taiwanese versus Chinese) that could split the country into two. At present, it is most important to participate in process of globalization and internationalization, and at the same time reduce the cultural identity conflicts to its lowest possibility in education as well as in other societal aspects.

Gender Stereotyping

Gender stereotyping is nothing new in Taiwan where the culture and society has placed priority of males over females. In the past, women used to be regarded as second class. Families have traditionally regarded boys as inheritors of the family name and property. Many married couples would try every method to have a son. Families typically invested more resources on boys' education than on girls' education. Nevertheless, this traditional value system has been challenged and criticized by many women's rights advocates.

In the transformation from a traditional to a newly developed society, the Taiwanese government has passed several laws to promote gender equity. In 1997, the MOE in Taiwan initiated a Gender Equity Act which requires each primary and secondary school to conduct at least four hours of gender equity education each semester. It attempts to provide students with better opportunities for gender equity and to eliminate gender stereotyping against women (Tsai and Shavit, 2003).

In terms of educational achievement, the participation of women in Taiwan has increased at all levels of education over the past five decades. Specifically in higher education, Taiwan's female participation increased more than fourfold, from 11 percent in 1951 to 49 percent in 2005 (see Table 15.1).

Table 15.1
Percentage of Female Educational Participation in Taiwan

Type of Education	Year	Percent
Primary education	1950	39
	1971	48
	1994	48
	2005	48
Secondary education	1950	28
	1971	40
	1994	47
	2005	48
Higher education	1951	11
	1971	37
	1994	43
	2005	49

Source: Chou and Chang, 1998: 354.

Equity of Educational Opportunity

Although Boudon (1974) indicated that the high degree of educational development does not necessarily result in an equitable society after World War II, there is always a positive correlation between family background and educational opportunity. According to Blau and Duncan (1967), there is a positive correlation between family background and educational opportunity. In this regard, Taiwan has been considered one of the most equitable societies in terms of her income distribution and educational opportunity. Similar to other Western developed societies, educational opportunity in Taiwan has been correlated with family background and parental occupation.

The Taiwanese examination system from the 1950s to 2000 became one of the major avenues for upward mobility. Parents invested most of their savings in their children's educational activities such as going to cram schools or extra tutoring hours. According to Lin (2001), a major streaming exercise takes place between junior high and senior high school—one that divides students into different academic tracks based on their test results. Entry to different types of senior high schools will have a major impact on students' future careers (Lin, 2001).

In Taiwan, as in other East Asian societies, the higher the parental socioeconomic status, the higher the parental expectations for school success and the greater the family resources for supporting the education of their children (Zhang and Huang, 1997). Unlike in Western societies, where cultural capital seems to count more, in the Taiwanese context, family educational resources and going to cram school make a major difference in patterns of school success. According to Stevenson and Baker (1992), Japanese students will have a better opportunity in university if they receive more cram schooling and students from upper income backgrounds gain more from education. This is also the case in Taiwan (Hwang and Sun, 1996).

According to Hwang (1978), family background did not have a major impact on the joint-university entrance examination in Taiwan, which means the poor and rich enjoy the same educational opportunity to be admitted by the universities according to their examination results. However, scholars such as Chen (1988), Hwang (1990) and Wang (1983) argued that the design of the college entrance examination in Taiwan could be fair only because the educational processes from primary to secondary level have screened out students to a great extent so that those who are successful have very similar family backgrounds. Thus, it is argued that the university entrance examination cannot be a fair system when students' family backgrounds are actually taken into account.

Another area of concern is the educational opportunity for indigenous peoples. Aboriginal peoples comprise 2 percent of the population and their educational opportunities continue to lag behind those of the majority. For example, only 11.03 percent of the indigenous students gain access to higher education whereas 25.70 percent of their majority ethnic group counterparts do so (Council of Indigenous Peoples, Executive Yuan, 2002).

Furthermore, the introduction of market mechanism and deregulation into Taiwanese education reforms since the 1990s have reinforced this trend. As more and more reform programs such as different versions of textbooks and multiple channels of entrance examinations for high school and university have been introduced, the grading competition among schools and families has in turn accelerated. It is argued that Taiwan's old profile as one of the most equitable societies has been altered in the last 10 years. According to the 2001 National Annual Statistics (2002) Taiwanese income discrepancy between the top and bottom 10 percent was 161 times, in contrast to only 39 times one year ago and 19 times in 1991. When comparing the family annual income differences, the gap between the top 20 and bottom 20 percent was 6.39 times in 2003. The number 10 years ago was only 4.97 times, which was interpreted as lesser earnings of the lower-income families compared to 10 years ago. The increasing income inequity has made the dream of upward mobility within one generation less feasible.

AN OVERVIEW OF TAIWAN'S CONTEMPORARY EDUCATION SYSTEM

Background to the Present Education System

Education has been highly valued in Taiwan and a key item on the policy agenda of the ROC after the Kuomintang government's relocation from the mainland to Taiwan in 1949. The promulgation of educational legislation by the central government framed the foundation for the nation's ongoing educational development and achievement. For example, nine-year compulsory education, first initiated in 1968, is a milestone in contemporary Taiwanese education history for its significant impact on the development of the nation's human capital. All levels of education institutions have experienced dramatic growth in student and school numbers since the implementation of the Nine-year Compulsory Education program in the late 1960s. The Education Basic Law (the Law) came into force in 1999 to fully protect people's right to education, and entitled the Government to extend the period for compulsory education from the conventional nine years to twelve years. According to Yang (2001), the Law acts as the cornerstone of fundamental educational innovations in the millennium.

Educational development in Taiwan over the past five decades is briefly represented in the following statistics. The percentage of graduates admitted to the next level of education has increased steadily since 1968. According to the report on "2004 education in the Republic of China" (MOE, 2004a), the percentage of graduates admitted to the next level of education during school year (SY) 1965–1966 was 58.2 percent at the primary school level, 78.5 percent at the junior high school level, and 38.3 percent at the senior high school level (see Table 15.2). The percentage of primary graduates admitted to junior high schools entered a period of phenomenal growth in the beginning of the 1970s. The growth then became steady in the following years. By the year 2004, the average percentage of graduates admitted to the next level of education had reached 99.42 percent at the primary school level, 96.03 percent at the junior high school level, 80.05 percent at the senior high school level, and 67.17 percent at the senior vocational school level (see Table 15.2). Female graduates' enrollment rate has increased since the implementation of nine-year compulsory education. According to the statistics, in 1966, 69.38 percent of male primary school graduates attended junior high schools whereas only 47.42 percent of female students did so. The percentage of primary graduates admitted to junior high school education soon became 88.70 percent of male students and 72.28 percent of female students in 1971, and 99.45 percent of male students and 99.39 percent of female students in 2004.

Since the 1980s, the economy of Taiwan has grown rapidly and the political stability in Taiwan has provided the Government with a safe ground to pursue democratization, pluralism and liberalization in every sociocultural sphere (Yang, 2001). The present education system therefore reflects the social, political, and economic status of Taiwan, and has moved toward a more comprehensive system in the field of education.

In terms of its functions, the education system in Taiwan can be categorized into six major strands, including preschool education, nine-year compulsory education (including primary and junior high education), senior high and vocational schools, higher education, special education, and supplementary and continuing education (see Figure 15.1).

The present education structure supports a minimum period of 22 years of formal study, starting from preschool education to doctoral programs (see Figure 15.2). In particular, basic and intermediate education generally involves two years of preschool education, nine years of compulsory education, which integrates six years of primary education and three years of junior high education, and three years of senior high or senior vocational education. This section discusses the

Table 15.2

Graduates Admitted to Next Level of Education (Unit: Percent)

Year	Elementary School			Junior High School			Senior High School			Vocational School		
	Average	M	F	Average	M	F	Average	M	F	Average	M	F
1950	31.78	35.93	24.91	51.15	56.07	39.38	39.76	—	—	—	—	—
1956	47.75	53.67	38.91	71.39	77.24	58.73	41.94	—	—	—	—	—
1961	53.79	63.02	42.39	78.60	85.87	66.87	44.65	—	—	—	—	—
1966	59.04	69.38	47.42	75.80	77.58	73.20	38.62	—	—	—	—	—
1971	80.85	88.70	72.28	69.62	68.78	70.84	43.47	35.29	56.64	—	—	—
1976	90.41	95.12	85.42	61.57	59.50	64.17	42.39	36.99	49.84	—	—	—
1981	96.77	98.29	95.16	68.11	66.29	70.12	45.39	39.56	52.72	—	—	—
1986	99.04	99.47	98.59	77.13	73.96	80.50	40.98	36.31	46.45	—	—	—
1991	99.28	99.34	99.22	86.09	83.08	89.19	51.94	55.24	48.43	13.68	14.47	13.04
1992	99.54	99.37	99.71	88.32	85.17	91.58	59.15	63.61	54.29	13.71	14.87	12.78
1993	99.53	99.27	99.80	87.78	84.94	90.75	61.32	64.47	58.29	18.03	18.44	17.71
1994	99.83	99.77	99.89	88.49	85.79	91.31	57.38	55.64	59.32	16.22	16.11	16.31
1995	99.75	99.77	99.72	89.17	86.73	91.71	56.58	53.01	60.51	17.84	17.13	18.43
1996	98.89	98.70	99.09	90.70	88.59	92.91	58.88	55.31	62.71	17.71	16.67	18.58
1997	99.18	99.19	99.18	92.02	90.15	93.98	61.95	60.30	63.73	23.32	22.53	23.99
1998	99.60	99.46	99.75	93.94	92.64	95.30	67.43	66.43	68.46	24.74	22.85	26.37
1999	99.89	99.88	99.91	94.73	94.69	94.79	66.64	68.43	64.83	30.49	27.56	33.18
2000	99.79	99.78	99.79	95.31	94.46	96.20	68.74	67.74	69.71	38.43	33.75	42.80
2001	99.15	99.34	98.98	95.97	94.91	97.10	70.73	69.68	71.78	41.82	37.18	46.27
2002	99.70	99.64	99.76	95.48	94.81	96.20	69.01	68.02	70.00	45.73	42.58	48.83
2003	99.44	99.44	99.44	95.74	94.74	96.82	74.85	73.48	76.20	62.63	58.93	66.33
2004	99.42	99.45	99.39	96.03	95.26	96.86	80.05	78.17	81.85	67.17	64.81	69.72

Source: MOE, 2005a, sheet 2.

Figure 15.1
The Education System in Taiwan

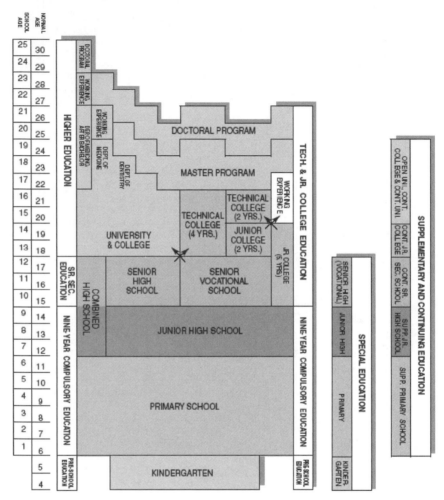

Source: MOE, 2004a: 18.

dominant education system, educational tracks, forms of admission, and related events according to levels, under the following themes: preschool education, nine-year compulsory education, senior high and vocational schools, teacher education, special education, higher education, teacher education, and supplementary and continuing education.

Preschool Education

In Taiwan, preschool education was uncommon in the 1950s. According to the Government Information Office, Republic of China (Taiwan), "Limited

Figure 15.2
The Educational Structure

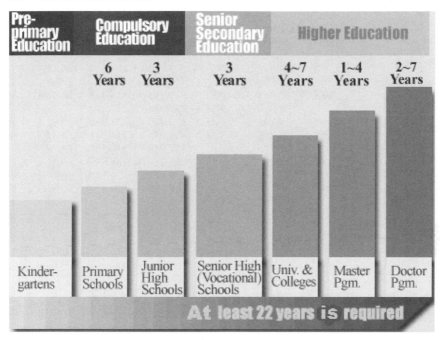

Pre-primary Education	Compulsory Education		Senior Secondary Education	Higher Education		
6 Years	3 Years	3 Years	4~7 Years	1~4 Years	2~7 Years	
Kinder-gartens	Primary Schools	Junior High Schools	Senior High (Vocational) Schools	Univ. & Colleges	Master Pgm.	Doctor Pgm.

At least 22 years is required

Source: MOE, 2004a: 18.

financial resources have kept two-year preschool education an optional part of the educational system" (GIO, 2004). It directly impacted on the enrollment rate of preschool education. The "Preschool Education Act" was promulgated in 1981 to set basic standards for preschools. The Ministry of Education (MOE) has also recognized the need for promoting preschool education and is working on affiliating preschools with existing elementary schools (GIO, 2004). However, the Act did not effectively transform the low coverage of preschool education. In 2001, the enrollment rate of 26.96 percent was still far below the Government's expected rate of 80 percent (GIO, 2004).

In SY 2004, preschool children accounted for only 10.66 per 1,000 population (see Table 15.3). Table 15.3 indicates that, during SY 2004, 10,417 classes in 3,306 kindergartens attracted 240,926 preschool students who were taught by 21,251 teachers. The average ratio of students to teachers was 11.34:1 (240,926:21,251) in 2004 which was a marked improvement over the student–teacher ratio of 40.50:1 in public kindergartens and 30.59:1 in private ones in 1976 (MOE, 2005c).

Private kindergartens comprise a large proportion of preschool education institutions, which are most independently operated, while most public ones

Table 15.3
Summary of Education at All Levels: SY2004

	No. of Schools	No. of Teachers	No. of Classes	No. of Students	No. of Graduates in 2003	No. of Students Per 1.000 Population
Total	8,252	274,837	156,095	5,384,926	1,269,529	238.22
Kindergarten	3,306	21,251	10,417	240,926	—	10.66
Primary School	2,638	103,793	64,000	1,912,791	318,718	84.62
Jr. High School	720	48,845	26,573	957,285	313,549	42.35
Sr. High School	308	33,122	9,569	393,689	124,739	17.42
Sr. Vocational Sch.	164	15,771	8,275	325,996	114,041	14.42
Jr. College	16	1,770	6,210	289,025	110,208	12.79
Uni.& College	142	45,702	22,615	981,169	208,659	43.41
Special School	24	1,687	600	5,921	1,740	0.26
Supplementary Sch.	932	2,803	7,186	248,888	74,406	11.01
Open University	2	93	650	29,236	3,469	1.29

Source: MOE, 2004a: 56.

are affiliated with public primary schools. In SY 2004, 240,926 children attended 3,306 registered kindergartens, among which 1,358 were public schools and 1,948 were private (MOE, 2004b). Private kindergartens were 1.43 times as many as public ones. The large number of private preschool institutions charge higher tuition fees than public ones (up to 10–40 times), and this therefore imposes a heavy financial burden on the parents. Specifically, the Government Information Office, Taiwan, points out the following phenomenon that

Private kindergartens in metropolitan areas usually have fewer problems recruiting students, because most parents want their children to get a head start in the highly competitive educational system. Outside the larger cities, however, private preschool fees are often a burden for average-income families. (GIO 2004, para 10)

In addition, many private preschools offer accelerated courses in various subject areas to meet public demands for academic achievement, often encompassing science, art, physical education and mathematics (Wikipedia, 2005). There has also been a huge growth in the number of English immersion or bilingual preschools to meet parents' expectations of an English immersion learning environment for the younger generation. In Chinese societies such as Taiwan, parents have high expectations on children's intellectual growth and capacity building (Hwang, 2004; Stevenson, 1996, cited in Smith, 1997). However, there is heated debate on whether children in Taiwan should start foreign language learning in early childhood with concerns that this may harm students' abilities in learning their mother tongue (Wikipedia, 2005). Despite these debates, the "English-learning fever"

(Chen, 2004: 8) phenomenon continues to increase at every single level of education in Taiwan.

Nine-Year Compulsory Education

After preschool education, students of six years of age are admitted to elementary schools under the nationwide compulsory education policy. Two years after the implementation of nine-year compulsory education, the junior high vocational program was abolished in 1970. Some of the vocational courses were merged into the junior high curriculum. The implementation of compulsory education does not simply mean extending the length of compulsory education from six years to nine years, but allowing students to acquire more comprehensive education than in the past (Liu, 1981). The MOE also set curriculum standards for elementary and junior high school education in order to ensure effective teaching. The "National Education Act 1979" further stipulates that all school-age children between six and fifteen years old must attend elementary schools and junior high schools. Children with special educational needs, students who spend time in supplementary education, and a small number of students in experimental schools are exempt from this rule (GIO, 2004).

In 1992, the MOE implemented the trial Prolonged National Education Based upon Vocational Education Program that combined junior high school and senior vocational school curricula, and allowed junior high students who do not seek academic career paths to receive relevant occupational training. The program became an extension of the compulsory education system in 1994, and was implemented nationwide in 1996.

Textbooks have traditionally been controlled and published by the central government and served as tools to convey political and social ideologies. Along with the political reform and social protest movements in the 1970s and 1980s, issues of textbooks became a burgeoning topic of debate. Traditional textbooks have been criticized for reinforcing the dominant cultures of the governing party without considering the specific perspectives and voices of different gender, cultural, and ethnic groups. A new textbook publication system was introduced in 1996 to decentralize the textbook market, parallel to the trend for diversification and liberalization in Taiwanese society and education. The new textbook system entitles private companies to publish textbooks and teaching materials after being reviewed, screened and approved by the National Institute for Compilation and Translation (NICT) under the Ministry of Education (MOE). This approach implies that the MOE "is still responsible for setting the standards for the curriculum and overseeing educational quality control" (Pan and Yu, 1999: 80). Since September 2001, schools in Taiwan now implement the "nine-year spiral curriculum" with continuity of courses from year to year, and without sharp divisions between elementary and junior high school education (Li, 2002). This curricular reform is congruent with many developed countries' reform processes of integrating the curricula for compulsory education. The new curriculum incorporates seven main fields of study, and ten major basic skills. The seven study fields are:

1. Language: Languages of Taiwan (Mandarin, Hokkien, Hakka, Aboriginal languages) and English;
2. Health and physical education: Health, physical education, and sex education;
3. Social studies: History, geography, civics, economics, law, and human rights;
4. Arts: Music, visual arts, and performing arts;
5. Mathematics;
6. Science: Biology, physics, chemistry, earth science, environmental science, and life and information sciences; and
7. General activities: Computers, club activities, scouting, outdoor activities, and home economics. (Li, 2002, para 7)

The ten basic skills include:

1. Understand self, and develop one's potential;
2. Appreciation, expression, and creation;
3. Life and career planning; lifelong learning;
4. Expression, communication, and sharing;
5. Respect, compassion, and group cooperation;
6. Cultural learning, international understanding;
7. Planning, organization, and implementation;
8. Use of science, technology, and information;
9. Self-directed exploration and research; and
10. Independent thought and problem solving. (Li, 2002, para 15)

The size of the school and the class is one of the key factors for student learning outcome, and greatly influences the teacher's workload, performance, and interaction with students (Pan and Yu, 1999). Reducing the size of schools and classes and making it manageable has become part of the educational reform agenda. In addition, Table 15.3 indicates that, in SY 2004, 1,912,791 students attended 64,000 classes in 2,638 primary schools in Taiwan among which 318,718 students graduated. The ratio of students to teachers was 18.42:1 (1,912,791:103,793). At the junior high school level, 393,689 students attended 26,573 classes in 720 schools in SY 2004, among which 313,549 students were students who graduated that year. The student–teacher ratio was 19.60:1 (957,285:48,845) that is lower when compared with the ratio of students to teachers, 33.79:1, in 1976. This improvement in student–teacher ratio shows the Government's commitment in reducing the class size, and promoting the quality of compulsory education.

Senior High and Vocational Schools

Upon the completion of compulsory education, junior high school graduates who aim to acquire further education attend senior high and vocational schools. Public or private senior high and vocational schools are categorized into six types: normal senior high, senior vocational, comprehensive, single discipline, and experimental and combined high schools. The most common types of upper secondary institutions are normal and vocational ones. Many junior high graduates prefer senior high schools over vocational ones. Some junior high graduates choose to go into vocational schools which place a heavier emphasis on practical and vocational skills than their counterparts. Some attend five-year junior colleges that cover their high school years and contain the Practical Technical Program. In addition, Pan and Yu (1999) note that not only have new high schools been established, but also a number of junior high schools have been integrated with senior high schools and become six-year full secondary schools. This could have contributed to the difficulty in allocating land for schools. Comprehensive high schools have also been established to meet the demand for more high schools.

Furthermore, the development of senior high and vocational schools has reflected a shift in the need for manpower in Taiwan. Pan and Yu (1999) acknowledge that

In the 1970s, many 2-year junior colleges or 5-year technical ones were established to meet the urgent need for manpower. With the transformation of the economic structure from labor-intensive industries to a capital and technology-intensive ones, public 4-year technical institutes were set up to meet the higher-level need for manpower. (Pan and Yu, 1999: 74)

The demand for skilled manpower has further impacted on the types of upper secondary institutions that were established. The ratio of vocational school students to high school students was set to reach 7:3 by 1981. As Tien (1996) notes, "Under this policy, vocational education became the mainstream of middle education in terms of quantity" (ibid., para 8). From 1971 to 1982, "the number of students admitted into senior high schools gradually declined, while the number of students entering senior vocational schools increased to meet the growing demand for skilled workers in the rapidly growing economy" (GIO, 2004b, para 33). As the demand for high-quality professionals increased, educational policies were reversed by expanding senior high schools. The expansion of senior high schools has outnumbered the students who are admitted to vocational schools. Here the term "senior high school" refers to normal senior high schools and other types of high schools, excluding vocational schools, as mentioned earlier in this section. In particular, the expansion of senior high schools involves integrating the vocational curriculum with the mainstream curricula. This has attracted a large number of students who in the past have to attend traditional vocational schools. Thus, vocational schools have faced difficulties in recruiting students.

Most junior high graduates used to sit for the Joint Public Senior High School (JPSHS) Entrance Examination before they were admitted to senior high schools. The JPSHS was replaced by the Basic Competency Test (the Test) in SY 2001. The Test contents are confined to the subject areas as defined by the nine-year spiral curriculum. Under the Test, candidates can be granted admission "by applying, by meeting requirements and passing the entrance examination of individual schools for special subjects (admission through selection), by being registered and then assigned, or by recommendation" (MOE, 2004a: 20).

In terms of numbers, combining senior high schools, senior vocational schools, and junior colleges, 1,008,710 students attended 24,054 classes in 488 schools in SY 2004 among which were 342,988 students who graduated that year (see Table 15.3). Curriculum guidelines have been set up for senior high and senior vocational schools in the following specialized areas: agriculture, industry, business, maritime studies, marine products, medicine, nursing, home economics, drama, and art. Comprehensive high schools also deliver some proportion of vocational programs in these curricular areas. Textbooks for the senior high level must be reviewed and approved by the NICT according to present curriculum standards.

Special Education

Special education provides students with special needs alternative channels for schooling, and involves at least six years in preschools and together with primary schools, three years in junior high schools, and three years in senior high and senior vocational schools. Specifically, the MOE (2004a: 17) regulates that "Only designated schools are allowed to admit students who are mentally and physically challenged . . . special classes are offered to regular education institutions, including primary, junior, and senior high schools." In other words, some primary and secondary schools integrate special classes on their campuses, whereas there are independent special schools that provide special training for students with special needs. Universities and colleges also allocate resource classes for students who identify as having impairment. In SY 2004, 5,921 students with special needs attended 600 classes in 24 special schools among which were 1,740 students who graduated that year (see Table 15.3).

Higher Education

According to Pan and Yu (1999: 75), "Post-secondary education includes 3 years of junior college or, usually, 4 years of college/university with the exception of departments such as dental and medical science, which take 6 and 7 years respectively." Two-year junior colleges, two-year technical colleges, and four-year technical colleges are designed for graduates to continue with advanced vocational programs. Those who wish to pursue academic career paths will choose university education. Channels for admission to colleges or universities now include "allocation based on test scores of entrance examinations and entry based on selection from personal applications and recommendations by high schools" (MOE, 2004a: 21). For most high school students, the main goal of high school education is to score highly on the MPPCS at the end of their third year in order to attend universities.

The higher education system in Taiwan entered a stage of dramatic growth after the lifting of martial law in 1987. The revision to the University Law in 1994 further changed the higher education system dominated traditionally by the Ministry of Education. The Law also "reduced the power of the Ministry of Education over higher education institutions, and campus operations have become more flexible" (Tsai, 1996, para 2) in appointing presidents, charging tuition fees, offering courses, and recruiting students.

In addition, there has been long-term growth in the number of higher education institutions over the decades. In SY 1987, there were only 107 higher education institutions in Taiwan. The number of higher education institutions has increased dramatically from seven in 1950 to 159 in 2005, among which are 75 universities, 70 colleges, and 14 junior colleges (MOE, 2005d). However, there has been gradual decline in junior college numbers from 76 schools in SY 1976 to 14 in SY 2004 (MOE, 2005b). Vocational school graduates may also participate in the MPPCS before being admitted to four-year universities and colleges. Students of vocational schools usually proceed to four year technical colleges or two-year junior colleges afterward.

The ratio of public to private institutions is 1:1.94 (54:105) (MOE, 2005d). This number indicates that the expansion of higher education in Taiwan can be accounted for mainly by an increasing number of private institutions. However, public higher education institutions are viewed as being more prestigious than private ones. Specifically, the expansion was "accommodated mainly by creating new institutions and by upgrading existing ones, although other strategies, such as splitting, merging, and increasing the size of the existing institutions, were also used in historical sequences" (Tsai and Shavit, 2003: 3). There has also been constant growth in the net enrollment rate of higher education among the 18–21 age group, particularly among female students. According to the MOE,

The net enrollment rate rose from 10.0 percent in 1976 to 38.7 percent in 2000, and the increase was more profound for females than for males. To be more precise, in 1976 the net enrollment rate of males aged 18–21 (11.2 percent) was higher than that of females (8.7 percent), whereas the opposite was true after the mid-1980s. In 2000, the net enrollment rate for women aged 18–21 was 42.1 percent, higher than that for men (35.5 percent) of the same age. (cited in Tsai and Shavit, 2003: 2)

Traditionally, upper secondary graduates used to sit for the traditional "Joint University Entrance Examination" (JUEE) before being admitted to universities and colleges prior to SY 2002. Presently, admission channels to higher education institutions have become more flexible and multidimensional than in the past. Starting SY 2002, JUEE was replaced by a new system, the Multiroute Promotion Program for College-bound Seniors (MPPCS). The new system comprises application, selection by recommendation, or a new version of the JUEE.

At the higher education level, individual students' academic progression or program completion time varies greatly depending upon their personal, academic, or vocational needs and goals. Higher education in Taiwan usually comprises four to seven years of college or university programs, one to four years of master's programs, and two to seven years of doctoral programs that are either run by public or private institutions. Specifically, applicants to master's and doctoral programs must meet specific admission criteria and pass entrance examinations, usually including a written examination and/or an interview, that are administered by individual institutions. A master's or doctoral degree will be conferred by the university only when the student has fully met his or her program requirements, and passed a comprehensive examination. Furthermore, doctoral candidates are obliged to undergo the qualifying evaluation process. Teaching materials for higher educational institutions are either compiled by the MOE or the NICT regulations. However, lecturers have the autonomy to choose teaching materials in specialized fields.

Teacher Education

Normal universities and teachers' colleges traditionally deliver teacher education in Taiwan. They offer mostly four-year teacher education and training programs for student teachers of secondary schools, elementary schools, and kindergartens. Normal universities primarily offer secondary education programs while teachers' colleges primarily prepare teachers for primary schools and kindergartens (MOE, 2004a: 17). In the past two decades, there has been rapid expansion across various levels of education in Taiwan. The demand for quality teacher development is paramount. Under the umbrella of pluralism, the new Teacher Education Act (the Act) was promulgated in 1994 and revised in July 2002 to meet the needs of a more diversified society. The Act entitles qualified higher education institutions to deliver teacher education programs, thus altering the previous monopolistic policy on teacher education (Yang, et al., 2001; Yang, 2003).

The Teacher Education Council, organized by the MOE, accredit and authorizes qualified teacher education programs. Colleges and universities that include the department or college of education, and meet relevant requirements are now entitled to deliver teacher education and training programs in a minimum two-year period. One-year teacher training is available for college and university graduates, whose expertise is other than education and who aim to seek a career path in teaching. In general, student teachers pay the tuition fees of their teacher education programs. However, full or partial financial assistance is available for some students.

The Act plays a crucial role in the development of teacher education and induction in Taiwan, and provides guidelines for formulating regulations and support systems leading to full registration (Ho, 2003). "The Regulations of Induction and Registration for Probationary Teachers in Secondary, Elementary Schools and Kindergartens 1995" entitles the teacher education institutions to select collaboration schools based on their effectiveness and sufficient numbers of qualified teachers who can guide probationary teachers.

The Regulations empower teacher education institutions to guide these schools, and to sign induction collaboration contracts with schools to provide induction programs for probationary teachers. The Regulations also regulate probationary teachers' professional development, the amount of time involved in probationary teaching, participation in educational activities required by schools, and assessments based on the following criteria: morals and integrity; attitudes and spirituality; interpersonal and communication skills; the capability and knowledge of teaching and guiding students; and the performance in professional development programs. However, leadership as a key dimension of teacher qualities in the era of educational reforms (e.g., Silva et al., 2000; Robertson and Strachan, 2001: 320–334; Harris, 2003) is absent in the professional teaching dimensions for teachers of Taiwan. This has directly impacted on teachers' capacity to respond to enormous demands on change and innovations in Taiwanese schools.

In addition, the duration and structure of probationary teaching for student teachers to become fully certified is another area of debate. The 1994 Act mandated that a student teacher who has graduated from the required teacher education program in a teacher education institution has to complete an additional one-year probationary period in order to obtain a teaching qualification. Under the one-year probationary structure, first-year teachers are no longer students, are attached to mentor teachers on the school site, and are responsible for some teaching and administrative duties in schools in negotiation with their mentors.

Nevertheless, most studies on the overall effectiveness of the induction programs for probationary teachers after the implementation of the Act have found numerous problems, including the absence of supportive networks, the shortfall of financial support for probationary teachers, the lack of clarity about their positions or work responsibilities, and the need for professional development programs to provide mentoring skills for mentor teachers (e.g., Lee, 2000; Lin, 2000). Under the Act, a Taiwanese probationary teacher is granted NT$8,000 (equivalent to US$267) per month. In Ho's (2003) study on three New Zealand and three Taiwanese beginning secondary teachers, all the Taiwanese probationary teachers regarded the salary or subsidy level as too low.

Yuang-Ching and Yi-Ping (pseudonyms), two Taiwanese participants, further indicated that many probationary teachers have to take on additional teaching duties after school in order to survive. Ho concluded that the inadequate subsidy has had a negative impact on the probationary teachers' perceptions of their teacher status and their own worth, on other teachers' perceptions of probationary teachers, and on the degree of distrust between probationary teachers and their schools. Criticism toward the probationary teaching structure under the Act led to further amendments to the Act in July 2002.

Under the 2002 Act, the probationary period has been reduced to a half-year period. A teaching assessment at the end of the probationary teaching is additional to the probationary teaching. In other words, student teachers will not become fully registered until they pass the teaching assessment after the half-year probationary teaching period. The new teacher certification system involves two steps. The first stage reviews student teachers' performance over their teacher education programs in common courses, disciplinary courses, and education specialization courses to verify that they have met the standards. After the first stage, student teachers are located in a school to fulfill the half-year internship as a requirement of becoming fully certified. Teacher education institutions and schools collaborate to provide support and mentoring services for student teachers. The second step evaluates student teachers' in-school performance to determine if they can be granted teacher certificates. Qualification requirements for teachers at special or supplementary schools are the same as those for teachers at regular schools. The previous one-year probationary structure still applied to student teachers who had enrolled in their teacher education programs prior to the amendments to the Act in 2002.

In other words, graduates of SY 2005 are entitled to choose their beginning teaching period upon graduation between the old one-year probationary system, and the new half-year probationary structure. It is noteworthy that graduates, who are under the half-year probationary teaching period, need to pay tuition fees. This implies that those teacher candidates retain their role as students, and therefore have limited responsibilities. There has been a lack of empirical studies on the new teacher certification structure in Taiwan.

Supplementary and Continuing Education

Apart from the above education pathways, social education is available to all citizens of Taiwan, including "supplementary and continuing education, education on-air, adult and lifelong learning, national language education, citizen's education, art education, library education, museum education, audio-visual education, family education and guidance in spiritual renewal" (MOE, 2004a: 50). Among these social education programs, supplementary and continuing education programs are more formal than others, and are "designed to supplement regular education, raise education attainment, teach practical skills, and upgrade productivity" (MOE, 2004a: 50). Social education provides out-of-school citizens as well as working youths in Taiwan with an alternative way to acquire basic education, advanced studies, and/or short-term supplementary education. The MOE (2004a) statistics shows that, during SY 2003 to 2004, 1.101 percent of citizens in Taiwan attended 7,186 classes in 932 schools that offers supplementary school programs whereas 650 classes in two open universities attracted 0.129 percent of Taiwanese citizens (see Table 15.3). The development of supplementary and continuing education in Taiwan is part of a growing momentum leading toward a lifelong learning society.

A SCHOOL DAY

Going to secondary schools is one of the most trying periods in a Taiwanese student's life. The reason is though Taiwan has a free nine-year compulsory education, students need to sit for qualifying examinations for admission to senior high schools or vocational high schools, and universities or colleges if they want to continue to the tertiary level. That is the source of the examination pressure within each school.

Unlike many Western counterparts who attend school from 9 A.M. to 3 P.M., Taiwanese secondary students have a much longer school day from 7:30 A.M. to 5:30 P.M. depending on different schools. In most junior high schools, prior to the first period of the class, there is always a period of time for campus cleaning up, and morning-self-study in the homeroom, followed by a morning assembly which altogether lasts from 45 minutes to one hour. Campus cleaning up and morning assemblies are not mandatory for all. Students rotate every other week depending on what year of study the students are in. Senior students busy preparing for the Basic Competency Test are relieved from most of the campus cleaning and assembly duties. The school assembly takes place where students gather—in the assembly hall or the school field (by rotation among different classes) for civic education. Flag-raising ceremonies, principal's talks for daily rules and other routine assignments will be announced at that time. With respect to the morning homeroom self-study time, this period of time allows students to engage in self-reviewing lessons or take quizzes that are required by their teachers.

In junior high schools, each class lasts 45 minutes. There is a lunch break followed by napping time. Students may choose to remain seated and read or study during that time. The philosophy behind this naptime is not only a social tradition in Taiwan but also to refresh students' minds during hot weather. In the afternoon, most schools start from 1:20 till 4:10 P.M. The so-called main-subject courses such as Chinese literature, science, English, and mathematics are arranged usually in the morning session. Then, classes such as civic education, history, geography, integrated activities, music, health and physical education are offered in the later hours of the day. It is believed that the main subjects require clearer minds for better concentration and more effective learning.

Another tidy-up period for the class and the final campus cleaning time lasts about 25 minutes during the afternoon session. Afterwards classes start at 3:25 again till 4:10 P.M. by which time most schools close except for some classes. For example, the senior-year students will remain in the homeroom for extra tutorials in subject areas of English, mathematics, Chinese, science, and so on. Then the seventh period ends around 4:10 P.M. Many schools ask students to attend an extra period for supplemental instruction or quizzes. Students need to pay for this extra hour of instruction. Students can receive extra lecturing for their main subject areas that will, hopefully, enhance their academic performance.

Praise for the students is less common and good behavior is expected from them by the Taiwanese parents (Hwang, 2004). When asked, "What is the most important factor in determining a child's performance in the school?," parents in Taiwan usually respond "effort" rather than "innate ability" whereas American parents mostly cite the latter (Stevenson, 1996, cited in Smith, 1997). It is also the home environment that supports Taiwanese children for academic performance rather than extra curricular activities. In modern Taiwanese society, many young parents are also keen on cultural activities. In addition to their school tasks, many of the students also take language and music classes after school.

Nevertheless, at higher levels of schooling the students are less likely to continue these lessons because of examination pressure.

In the era of education reform after 1994, many parents have become uneasy because of unfamiliarity with many new education initiatives. Consequently, parents pay for extra classes in cram schools or tutoring lessons for their children even after the abolition of junior high school and university entrance examinations. Ironically, the slogan that education reform will relieve children from carrying overloaded school bags has not prevented more and more textbooks and homework for students.

Smith (1997) described the competitive setting of the modern Taiwanese secondary schools as "Academic Darwinism" which implies that only the most able and capable students will move on to higher levels of schooling. In Taiwan, secondary education emphasizes individual competitiveness which requires students to compete aggressively to survive to the next education level.

Researchers like Harold W. Stevenson and his colleagues (the Stevenson group) often mentioned that the academic performances of American children are below their counterparts at the same age level in Japan, Korea, and Taiwan (Stevenson, 1996, cited in Smith, 1997). Unlike many American public schools which are very much concerned with students' security, Taiwanese put extra burden on school teachers and students for academic achievement. According to the Stevenson group, American schools are less effective in classroom management and instruction than those in Taiwan. The average school day is much longer in Taiwan, around 200 days versus Americans' 180 calendar days. School time is also much better used in Taiwan schools. Taiwanese students use a lot more of their school day in academically oriented activities. In addition, discipline problems are not as serious as American schools. In addition, parents play a crucial role in children's attitude toward schooling. Taiwanese mothers are much more likely to be involved in their children's school activities and PTA (parent-teacher association).

The following class schedule is from a southern Taiwanese public junior high school that opens from 7:10 A.M. till 6 P.M. Monday through Friday (see Table 15.4). In the school, although most classes start at 8:10 A.M., students are required to arrive on campus by 7:30 A.M. During each morning, students spend 10 minutes on campus cleaning. Between 7:20 A.M. and 7:50 A.M. students usually stay in their homeroom for self-study in their seats. Teachers need not be present at this time but most are. Between 7:50 A.M. and 8:10 A.M., school assembly takes place in the school field or hall.

After the morning assembly, all classes begin at 8:10 A.M., and go on till 8:55 A.M. Then second period starts from 9:10 A.M. and goes on till 9:55 A.M., the third period lasts from 10:10 A.M. to 10:45 A.M. and then the fourth period from 11:05 A.M. to 11:45 A.M. Lunch time lasts from 11:50 A.M. to 12:30 P.M. After that, students are required to take a nap from 12:30 P.M. to 1:10 P.M.. Some student groups engage in other activities such as daily alert or campus patrolling. The afternoon section, which starts from 1:20 P.M., lasts all the way till 4 P.M.

Table 15.4
Class Schedule

Yen-Ping Year 7 Class 1 Schedule

Period	Class Period	Mon	Tue	Wed	Thu	Fri
7:10–7:20	Clean campus					
7:20–7:50	Morning homeroom					
7:50–8:10	Morning meeting					
1	8:10–8:55	Chinese	Science	English	Geography	Chinese
2	9:10–9:55	Chinese	Chinese	Science	Chinese	Art Performance
3	10:10–10:55	Science	English	Mathematics	English	Mathematics
4	11:05–11:50	Mathematics	Health and P.E.	Integrated and Activities	Mathematics	Art
11:50–12:30	Lunch break					
12:30–13:10	Nap time					
5	13:20–14:05	School meeting	Civics	Chinese reading	History	English conversation
6	14:15–15:00	Class meeting	Integrated and activities	Music	English composition	Science
15:00–15:25	Clean campus					
7	15:25–16:10	Clubs	Integrated and activities	Health and P.E.	English composition	Health and P.E.
8	16:20–17:05	English	Mathematics	Chinese	Science	English reading

Source: Yen Ping Junior high school, 2003, para 5.

Cram School

Most junior high students leave school after 5 P.M. Some of them go home for dinner and others continue their study at "cram schools." These cram schools are examination-oriented private institutes which focus on drills and practices. Some students also choose English conversation lessons or science laboratory experiment classes. Parents have to pay approximately NT$2,640 (US$80) per subject per month. If one student takes three subjects at the cram school, the fees may run up to NT$7,920 (US$240) per month. This is a great burden for an average family in Taiwan.

A 15-year-old girl, Amy (see the attached photo on page 370), who just graduated from junior high school, mentioned in an interview that she used to fill in numerous examination practice sheets although these were not necessarily relevant to their daily learning. Amy accepted this reality as a natural course of learning at her secondary school.

On the other hand, there is not much homework at Amy's former school. Instead, the daily examinations replace homework. It is more likely that most students in her school are asked to prepare for the quizzes on the next day than do their homework.

Every new entrant to junior high school is required to take an IQ test and mathematics ability assessment. These test results serve as a foundation for normal distribution of class grouping. In the past decades, the MOE has been enforcing restrictions on ability-grouping in secondary schools in order to eliminate any discrimination against different ability groups. Presently all junior secondary schools need to comply with this policy. However, the reality is that some schools continue to engage in ability-grouping practices. For example, teachers of the subject areas may divide students into different ability groups for instruction and learning. It depends very much on individual teacher autonomy in the classroom. If a teacher is not competent enough, this streaming will result in unequal resource allocation among different ability-groups. Most teachers will teach a class in successive years from year 7 to year 9. Teachers from compulsory levels enjoy tax-free salary and social respect.

Amy's former school is located in downtown Taipei. Amy considers herself lucky enough not to spend too much time playing video games or watching TV due to her busy daily school schedule. She wears glasses like most of her classmates. She started developing myopia around grade 5. She does not enjoy leisure reading. She prefers chatting with her classmates on campus, playing around with friends from whom she gains recognition and inspiration for learning. Her father also provides her with pocket money though she is not keen to spend money except for lunch, bus fare, and so on. She mentioned once: "I don't need much money to spend because I'm always at school or in the cram school and my parents will provide anything I need. So I don't really spend money on my own." Even her mobile phone and the internet fee are paid by her parents. She is quite obedient to her parents. She has a mobile phone for the sake of communication with her parents, especially her father. Her life is very simple, mostly surrounded by school, classmates, parents, brothers, and sisters. Unlike her classmates who spend a lot of time on MSN chat with friends, Amy only checks her e-mail once in a while and completes her homework with the help of Internet searches. In her mind, her best friends are those who can study hard and get high grades, and also know how to have a good time.

When asked "What if you were a junior high student again?" Amy replied, "I would adjust my learning habits and make the best use of my time rather than idling." Amy is determined to specialize in tourism or hotel management and this is partly a result of her mediocre grades in the Basic Competency Test. Amy laughed when being asked about her future plans. She said, "I'm very fond of playing. So the best way for me is to earn a living in the future by joining the recreation business, such as working as a staff in the hotel, in the airline company or in a restaurant."

Regarding her daily schedule, she usually goes to bed around 11 P.M. and gets up around 6:30 A.M. She plays video games once in a while for relaxation as well as watches TV. In so doing, she does not have special interests except for killing time or joining her family activities. Amy seldom engages herself in sporting activities (typical of most Taiwanese students) although she takes two physical education classes (equals 90 minutes per week) for playing basketball, ping-pong, and other sporting activities on campus.

Survey Results on Secondary Students, Parents and Schools

According to the "Taiwan Education Panel Survey (TEPS)," junior high students spend more time with their parents every day than do senior high or college students. In addition, junior high students spend more time with their mothers than fathers. Nearly 58 percent reported spending four hours per day with their mother compared with 36 percent with their father. Compared with the groups which spend less than one hour with their parents, the more time they spend with parents, the better parent-child relationships they have (TEPS, 2005a).

Another TEPS indicates that 84.4 percent of junior high school students regard schools as a happy place, especially when the classroom climate is positive, and teachers are dedicated to teaching. In other studies, peer groups also have an influential impact on secondary students' socialization. There is a positive relationship between peer atmosphere and their positive feelings about the school. According to the TEPS, the more a student studies with his or her classmates, the more fulfilled the student feels (TEPS, 2005b).

If the teacher has an encouraging and positive attitude toward students, and assigns students more learning tasks or homework, the student will feel more positive toward teachers. If teachers are indifferent, students will regard schools as an unhappy place. After all, students are concerned about their learning atmosphere in the school. The more learning activities in the school, the more satisfied the students will experience. Campus security is another source of students' happiness in the school. A supportive and secure campus environment will provide students with a better place to study in Taiwan (TEPS, 2005b).

Picture of Amy (Yi-Shan) Chen at the age of 15 when she was in 9th grade. Courtesy of Mr. Hsun-hui Chen, 2004.

The experience of Amy does not necessarily represent the rest of secondary student population in Taiwan. However, it indicates how school practices, and competition within conventional Taiwanese schools reflect reform dilemmas.

DISCUSSIONS AND CONCLUSION

Taiwan is a Confucian society that highly values education. The modern education system also retains vestiges of Japanese colonial influence. The present Taiwanese education system supports a period of 16 years of formal education. In particular, a nine-year compulsory education introduced in 1968 emphasizes individual students' competitiveness in order to proceed to the next higher level in the education system. The education system has undergone a number of controversial reform programs and policy practices, and it proceeds to the goal of becoming more diversified, democratised, pluralized, and liberalized.

The education system has been successful in terms of key indicators such as student enrollment rates, percentages of graduates admitted to next levels of education, and students' high scores in international mathematics and science tests, such as International Mathematical Olympiad (IMO), Programme for International Student Assessment (PISA), American Invitational Mathematics Examination (AIME), and Trends in International Mathematics and Science Study (TIMSS).

However, achievement in quantitative terms is insufficient to determine the overall effectiveness of Taiwan education. Education in Taiwan has been criticized for "placing excessive pressure on students and eschewing creativity in favor of rote memorization" (Wikipedia, 2005, para 1). Furthermore, Pan and Yu pointed out that "the normal development of individuals has been distorted, and schools have become preparation institutions for high schools and colleges" (Pan and Yu, 1999). In order to address these issues, people in Taiwan therefore began to engage in civic organizations to facilitate educational reform activities, as did the academics, and the Ministry of Education. Change and transformation has become the main characteristics of educational development in Taiwan.

Since late 1990s, educational reform in Taiwan encompasses a mixture of ideas and multidimensional demands of a robust education system. Since the 1980s, an international trend of free-market economy and deregulation has emerged to change the education environment around the world. The education systems in New Zealand, Australia, United Kingdom, United States, Argentina, Mexico, and other Latin American countries, are identified as experiencing a similar reform approach under the influence of "neo-liberalism" ideology (Chou, 2005). As the literature suggests, reform activities in the field of education have mainly dealt with "deregulation, equality of educational opportunity, opening teacher education programs, reformation of the school system, reducing school size and class size, multiple ways of recruiting students, opening the textbook market" (Pan and Yu, 1999: 77–80). Other education reform areas include curriculum reforms for economic globalization, and emphasis on information and communication technology and English as transnational skills (Law, 2004: 507–11). Reforms are also struggling to strike a balance between internationalization and localization (Yang, 2001).

In 2002, the Ministry of Education implemented the project entitled "e-Generation Human Capacity-Building," which is part of a comprehensive six-year national development plan entitled "Embracing challenges of 2008." This reform effort is consistent with the above educational reform movements toward a dynamic and socially responsive education system. In particular, it aims to foster creativity and the capacity of the young citizens of Taiwan to be internationally competitive in the knowledge-based economy. The highlights of the project include fostering an international environment, enhancing the ability to master foreign languages, promoting e-learning and education in culture, arts, sports and civility, and advocating lifelong learning (MOE, 2002b). As such, educational reforms in Taiwan have embraced many reform ideas, theories, actions, experiments, and influences throughout the years.

Chou (2003) categorizes many controversial issues regarding Taiwanese primary and secondary educational reforms launched by the government during 1987–2003 into the following four stages. First, the "break-out stage" (1987–1988) incorporated various external and internal environmental factors resulting in a series of nationwide education changes.

Second, the "developing stage" (1989–1993) began when legislators passed many education bills and acts to ensure that the reform policies were implemented throughout the country.

Third, the "maturing stage" (1994–1998) involved the formation of the Committee on Education Reform (1996–1998) under the Executive Yuan that drew many representatives from all walks of life to design the themes and frameworks of educational reforms. The appointment of the Nobel Prize winner in Chemistry, Dr. Yuan-Tseh Lee, from the University of California at Berkeley as the head of the Committee was remarkable at this stage. The framework for educational reform activities was proposed in 1996 involved the following agenda (see Figure 15.3). The agenda covered parents' right of choice, protection of learners' right, autonomy of teaching profession, educational deregulation, internationalization, science and technology-orientation, pluralism, democratization, humanization, educational modernization, building lifelong learning society, upgrading educational quality, open grading channels, and a policy of "no child left behind."

In 1998, the Twelve Education Reform Mandates, which were allocated a special budget of NT$150,000,000,000 (equivalent to US$5 billion) to be accomplished in five years, were approved by the Executive Yuan and Legislative Yuan. According to Yang (2001), these revolutionary mandates were key to "leaving greater leverage for unprecedented education changes in Taiwan" (Yang, 2001: 8) in the following 12 areas. They are:

1. Revamping national education projects, K–12.
2. Fostering preschool and kindergarten education programs.
3. Renovating teacher education and in-service training programs.
4. Promoting impeccable diversified vocational education.
5. Pursuing excellence in higher education and its development.
6. Advocating lifelong learning projects.
7. Strengthening educational programs designed for the handicapped.
8. Invigorating educational programs for the native Taiwanese (aboriginals).
9. Expanding access to colleges and universities.
10. Creating a new system integrating teaching, guidance, and counseling.
11. Increasing the educational budget for the enhancement of educational research.
12. Accelerating the promotion of family value/ethics through parental education.

Finally, the "reform controversial stage" (1999–present) has been characterized by numerous negative public opinions against educational reform programs. Chou (2003) and Hwang (2003) identify some of the problematic reform areas, including:

1. the replacement of seven Ministers of Education between 1987 and 2003, which resulted in discontinuity and conflicts between various reform policies;
2. the lack of small-scale pilot or trial studies on the reform practices;
3. lack of in-service teacher training;
4. miscommunication and misinformation among schools, parents, and the government; and
5. increasing gaps between the urban versus the rural, and the rich versus the poor have also aroused great concerns in the country.

Yang (2001: 15) also argues that some of these problems are rooted in ideological conflicts behind education reform measures, the imbalance between competition and social justice, and the tussle for power among the private sector, parents,

Figure 15.3
The Framework for Education Reform, 1996

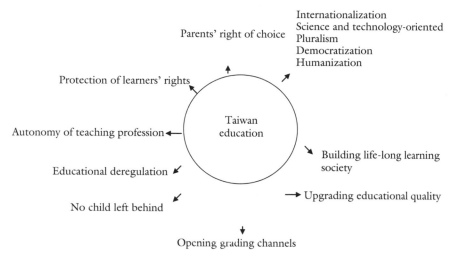

Internationalization
Science and technology-oriented
Parents' right of choice   Pluralism
Democratization
Humanization

Protection of learners' rights

Taiwan
education

Autonomy of teaching profession

Building life-long learning
society

Educational deregulation

Upgrading educational quality

No child left behind

Opening grading channels

Source: Chou, 2003.

schools and government. Other problems are connected to the lack of new norms to maintain educational excellence, the shortfall of educational budgets, the crisis of teacher professionalism, and the lack of recognition of the school as the center for change (Pan and Yu, 1999: 81–82).

In conclusion, education in Taiwan has been used as one of the most influential avenues for national building and economic development. Based on the influences of Japanese educational practices and ideals during the colonization period, Chinese culture, and Confucian traditions from Mainland China, Taiwanese schools have experienced dramatic increases in enrollments. However, the pressure for credentialism and for examinations has remained constant through the 20th century. Many educational innovations have been launched to deal with examination systems, curricular contents and instruction, and to reduce government ideological control. In so doing, teachers will have more flexibility for self-governance and autonomy to accelerate students' creativity and thinking skills for the 21st century. Nevertheless, the increasing discrepancies between income distribution and resources between urban and rural areas, the dilemma between the pursuit of education quality versus quantity, and the balance between localization and internationalization have created numerous challenges and foreseeable risks for the people of Taiwan.

What will happen in 2020 if Taiwan continues to maintain the *status quo*? What will happen to the next generation of Taiwan after a series of nationwide education reforms? What are the follow-ups and outcomes? Who benefits and who suffers as a result of reform activities? These yet to be answered questions are similar for education systems in many countries around the world. As Taiwan actively participates in global events, how Taiwan learns from her education experiences in the reform era deserves more attention.

REFERENCES

Blau, P. M. and Duncan, O. D. (1967). *The American Occupation Structure*. New York: Wiley.

Boudon, Raymond (1974). *Education, Opportunity, and Social Inequality*. New York: John Wiley and Sons.

Central Daily News (2005). "KMT worries students' low achievements in Chinese language," May 5. Accessed on May 18, 2005 from http://72.14.203.104/search? q=cache:5ARKvFw4AUgJ:www.cdn.com.tw/live/2006/05/05/text/950505e1. htm+%E5%9C%8B%E8%AA%9E%E6%96%87%E6%88%90%E5%B0%B1%E4%BD% 8E&hl=zh-TW&ct=clnk&cd=10.

Central Intelligence Agency, USA (2005). The World Factbook. Accessed on June 4, 2007 from http://www.cia.gov/cia/publications/factbook/index.html.

Chen, J.K. (1988). "The change and distribution of educational opportunities," *China Forum Magazine*, No. 366.

Chen, Shu-Chin (2004). "English is a blight on young kids," *Taipei Times*, February 17, E5.

Chou, Chuing P. (2003). *The Great Experiment of Taiwanese Education (1987–2003)*. Taipei: Psychological Publishing.

——(2005). "The influence of neoliberalism on higher education—New Zealand Model," *Journal of Education Research* (136): 148–158.

Chou, Zhu-Ying and Chang, Chia-I (1998). "Gender differences in Taiwan's academic–Implications for the PRC," in Michael Agelasto and Bob Adamson (eds), *Higher Education in Post-Mao China*, pp. 345–357. Hong Kong: Hong Kong University Press.

Cooper, J.F. (2000). *Historical Dictionary of Taiwan*, 2nd edn. Lanham, MD: Scarecrow Press.

Dai, Tian-Zhao (1996). *International Political History of Taiwan*. Taipei: Qian-wei Press.

Directorate-General of Budget, Accounting and Statistics (2004). Taiwan GNP Statistic. Taipei, Taiwan: Executive Yuan. Accessed on July 27, 2006 from http:// www.dgbas.gov.tw/public/data/dgbas03/bs4/table.xls#a234.

——(2005). Student Enrollment Rate at the Primary and Secondary Education Levels. Taipei, Taiwan: Executive Yuan. Accessed on July 27, 2006 from http://www. stat.gov.tw/public/data/dgbas03/bs7/yearbook/ch4/4–6–1&7.xls#a29.

Educational Statistics of Indigenous People (2002). Executive Yuan, Taiwan.

Giddens, A. (1994). *Beyond Left and Right: The Future of Radical Politics*. Cambridge, UK: Polity Press.

Government Information Office (2004). *Mainstream Education*. Accessed on June 2, 2007 from http://www.gio.gov.tw/ct.asp?xItem=19027&ctNode=2598&mp=807.

——(2005a). Taiwan Year Book 2004: Education 2004. Taipei, Taiwan: Government Information Office. Accessed on August 18, 2005 from http://www.gio.gov.tw/ taiwan-website/5-gp/yearbook/P269.htm.

——(2005b). A Brief Introduction to Taiwan: Education 2004. Taipei, Taiwan: Government Information Office. Accessed on August 18, 2005 from http://www. gio.gov.tw/taiwan-website/5-gp/brief/info04_15.html.

——(2005c). Taiwan's Educational Development and Present Situation. Taipei, Taiwan: Government Information Office. Accessed on July 27, 2006 from http://www. gio.gov.tw/info/taiwan-story/education/edown/3-1.htm.

Guo, Yi-Ling (2003). "Two worlds in Taiwan," *Business Weekly*, 800: 80–86.

Harris, Alma (2003). "Teacher leadership as distributed leadership: Heresy, fantasy or possibility?" *School Leadership and Management*, 23(3): 313–324.

Ho, Ai-Hsin (2003). "Exploring New Zealand and Taiwanese beginning secondary teachers' perceptions of leadership," Masters Dissertation, University of Waikato, Hamilton, New Zealand.

Hong, Zuway-R, McCarthy, Patricia, and Lawrenz, Frances (2003). "An investigation of the gender stereotyped thinking of Taiwanese secondary school boys and girls," *Sex Roles: a Journal of Research*, 48(11–12), 495–504.

Huang, Kun-Hui (1978). Comparison and Analysis of the Family and Socioeconomic Status (SES) of the Candidates and Enrollees of the University and College Entrance Examination in Taiwan. Taiwan: Center for Educational Research, National Taiwan Normal University, Taiwan.

Hwang, Guang-Guo (2004). "Life goals and role responsibilities in Confucian societies," *Indigenous Psychological Research in Chinese Societies*, 22: 121–193.

Hwang, K.H. (1978). "A comparative analysis on family backgrounds between college entrance examinees and the successful ones in Taiwan," *Bulletin of Graduate Institute of Education*, National Taiwan Normal University, Vol. 20: 148–203.

Hwang, Kwang-Kuo (2003). *What's Wrong with Taiwanese Education Reform?* Taipei, Taiwan: INK Publishing.

Hwang, Y.J. (1990). "Taiwanese unequal educational opportunities." *Thoughts and Words: Journal of the Humanities and Social Science*, 28(1): 93–125.

Law, Wing-Wah (2004). "Translating globalization and democratization into local policy: Educational reform in Hong Kong and Taiwan," *International Review of Education*, 50(5–6): 497–524.

Lee, C.F. (2000). "The study of the internship of probationary teachers for primary and secondary education in current Taiwan," *Education Research and Information*, 8(5): 1–14.

Li, Laura (2002). "Quiet revolution in the classroom: The Nine-year integrated curriculum 2002," *Sinorama Magazine* (02/2002)16–25. Accessed on August 18, 2005 from http://www.sinorama.com.tw/en/search/show_issue.php3?id=2002 29102016E.TXT&query=Quiet%20revolution%20in%20the%20classroom&page= 1&row=1&total=1&scope=2&type=all&sort=desc&MaxResults=10.

Lin, S.R. (2000). "Factors related to pre-service teachers' professional development," *Educational Review*, 16: 73–103.

Ling, Da-Sen (2001). "The effect of family educational resources on tracking and educational status attainment," *The National Cheng-Chi University Journal of Sociology*, 31: 45–75.

Liu, Jeng (1981). *The Future of Chinese Education*. Taipei, Taiwan: Jia-Yi Publisher.

Matras, Judah (1990). *Social Inequality, Stratification, and Mobility*. Taipei: Gui-guan Press.

Ministry of Education (MOE) (2002a). The Current Educational System. Taipei, Taiwan: Ministry of Education. Accessed on August 1, 2005 from http://140.111.1. 192/statistics/multi/current-e.htm.

——(2002b). Embracing Challenges of 2008: E-Generation Human Capacity-building. Taipei, Taiwan: Ministry of Education. Accessed on August 18, 2005 from http://140.111.1.22/english/home_ministry.htm.

Ministry of Education (MOE) (2004a). Education in the Republic of China. Taipei, Taiwan: Department of Statistics, Ministry of Education.
——(2004b). Summary of Education at All Levels. Taipei, Taiwan: Ministry of Education. Accessed on August 18, 2005 from http://140.111.1.22/english/en05/other/yr04.htm.
——(2005a). Education Situation. Taipei, Taiwan: Ministry of Education. Accessed on August 18, 2005 from http://140.111.1.22/english/en05/2005/c1.htm.
——(2005b). Educational Development. Taipei, Taiwan: Ministry of Education. Accessed on August 18, 2005 from http://140.111.1.22/english/en05/2005/c2.htm.
——(2005c). Quality of Education. Taipei, Taiwan: Ministry of Education. Accessed on August 18, 2005 from http://140.111.1.22/english/en05/2005/c4.htm.
——(2005d). Summary of Universities, Colleges and Junior Colleges. Taipei, Taiwan: Ministry of Education. Accessed on September 15, 2005 from http://www.edu.tw/EDU_WEB/EDU_MGT/STATISTICS/EDU7220001/data/serial/u.htm?UNITID=139&CATEGORYID=260&FILEID=130551&open.
Mok, K.-H. and Lee, H.-H. (2000). Globalization ore re-colonization: Higher education reforms in Hong Kong. *Higher Education Policy*, 13: 361–377.
National Institute of Compilation and Translation (1997). Junior High School Textbook: *Understanding Taiwan (History)*, Trial Version. Taipei, Taiwan: National Institute of Compilation and Translation.
Pan, Hui-Ling, and Yu, Chien (1999). "Educational reforms with their impacts on school effectiveness and school improvement in Taiwan, R.O.C," *School Effectiveness and School Improvement*, 10(1): 72–85.
Report on the Survey of Family Income and Expenditure in Taiwan Area (2002). Directorate-General of Budget, Accounting and Statistics, Executive Yuan, ROC (Taiwan) Accessed on June 4, 2007 from http://www129.tpg.gov.tw/mbas/income.htm.
Robertson, Jan and Strachan, Jane (2001). "Teachers taking leadership," in C. McGee and D. Fraser (eds), *The Professional Practice of Teaching*, pp. 320–334. Palmerston North, NZ: The Dunmore Press.
Silva, D.Y., Gimbert, B., and Nolan, J. (2000). "Sliding the doors: Looking and unlocking possibilities for teacher leadership," *Teacher College Record*, 102(4): 779–804.
Smith, Douglas C. (1997). *Middle Education in the Middle Kingdom: The Chinese Junior High School in Modern Taiwan*. Westport, CT: Greenwood Press.
Stevenson, David Lee and Baker, David P. (1992). "Shadow education and allocation in formal schooling," *American Journal of Sociology*, 97(6): 1639–1657.
Stevenson, H.W. and Stigler, J.W (1992). *The Learning Gap: Why Our Schools Are Failing and What We Can Learn from Japanese and Chinese Education*. New York: Simon & Schuster.
Sun, C.S. and Hwang, Y.J. (1997). "The social structure of Taiwan," in Publication series on Taiwanese society in the 1990s. Taipei: Academia Sinica, Institute of Sociology.
Taiwan Education Panel Survey (TEPS) (2005a). "Comparison of parental time at the high school level," E-paper 34, June 24. Accessed on July 26, 2006 from http://www.teps.sinica.edu.tw/TEPSNews/TEPS~News_034.pdf.
——(2005b). "The relationship between junior high school students' happiness and campus environments," E-paper 33, June 11. Accessed on June 2, 2007 from http://www.teps.sinica.edu.tw/TEPSNews/TEPS~News_033.pdf.

Tien, Flora F. (1996). "How education drove Taiwan's economic development," Economic Reform Today: Market Solutions to Social Issues 4, Accessed on August 18, 2005 from http://www.cipe.org/printerfriendly/printpage.php.

Tsai, Ching-Hwa (1996). "The deregulation of higher education in Taiwan," International Higher Education, 4. Accessed on August 18, 2005 from http://www.bc.edu/bc_org/avp/soe/cihe/newsletter/News04/textcy3.html.

Tsai, Shu-Ling and Shavit,Yossi (2003). "Higher education in Taiwan: Expansion and inequality of educational opportunity," Paper prepared for presentation at the International Sociology Association RC28 Research Committee on Social Stratification and Mobility's New York Meeting, August 22–24, 2003.

Tu, Wei-ming (ed.) (1994). *The Living Tree: The Changing Meaning of Being Chinese Today*. Stanford, CA: Stanford University Press.

Wang, Da-Xiu (1983). "Critiques on equal educational opportunity at the university level in Taiwan," *Thought and Words: Journal of the Humanities and Social Science*, 2(21), 165–178.

Wang, Feng-Yan (2004). "Confucian thinking in traditional moral education: Key ideas and fundamental features," *Journal of Moral Education*, 33: 429.

Wikipedia (2005). "Education in the Republic of China," in Wikipedia, The Free Encyclopedia. Accessed on July 26, 2005 from http://en.wikipedia.org/w/index.php?title=Education_in_the_Republic_of_China&oldid=60313528.

Yang, Shen-Keng (2001). "Dilemmas of education reform in Taiwan: Internationalization or localization?" Paper presented at the Annual Meeting of the Comparative and International Education Society, March 13–17, Washington DC, USA.

——(2003). "From colonization to professionalization: Historical construction of teacher professionalism in Taiwan," National Taiwan Normal University, Taiwan. Accessed on August 2, 2005 from http://www.ntnu.edu.tw/teach/ISCHE%202003_FullText_Prof.%20Yang.htm.

Yang, Shen-Keng, Wu, Ming-Chin, and Shan, Peter Wen-Jing (2001). "The historical development and current issues of teacher education in Taiwan," Paper presented at the 46th International Council of Education for Teachers, July 23–27, in Santiago, Chile.

Yen Ping Junior High School (2003). "Our class schedule," Accessed on August 1, 2005 from http://www.ypjh.tn.edu.tw/award/apec2003/apec2003_2/default.htm.

Zhang, De-Shui (1992). *Excitement! The History of Taiwan*. Taipei: Qian-wei Press.

Zhang, Shan-Nan and Huang, Yi-Zhi (1997). "The causal relationship of ethnicity and academic achievement," Paper prepared for presentation at the International Conference for Educational Research on Education of Minority Groups, Han, and Aboriginal People. National Taitung University of Education, Taitung, Taiwan.

Zhou, Yu-Wen (2000). "Confucianism and competition of education," Paper presented at International Conference for a Study on the Competition of Education in Confucian Asia for Center for Educational Research, March 26, National Taiwan Normal University, Taipei, Taiwan.

Chapter 16

SCHOOLING IN THAILAND

Paitoon Sinlarat

THE HISTORY OF THAI EDUCATION:
A CONSTANTLY MOVING PICTURE

Historically in Thai society, schools were not the only source of education. Learning centers took the form of houses, temples, and the palace. All of these places provided a response to the demands of a traditional society and followed the same form of its essential characteristics. As centers of the community, houses and temples were combined together as towns—the ordinary communities. In addition, the Palace was the city—the central community of the state with temples as coordinating agents. Education in this period corresponded to the demand of each community. The towns would teach occupational skills and the temples would teach ethics and the academic subjects.

At the beginning of the 20th century, schools became a significant source of education. Towns changed into modern cities in an attempt to re-create Western styles. Cities were the centers of trade and transportation while the towns served as places from which goods were distributed from the cities to the communities. This followed the style of the colonial system that included an industrial center and satellite towns. Even though Thailand was one of the very few countries in Southeast Asia that was never colonized, it did bear some resemblance to a colony, especially in terms of its methods of development and evolving form of intellect.

When schools were first established in Thailand the people, at first, become rather displeased and uncertain about it. Many feared that it would become a channel for the state to draft the young people into the army. After some time, however, the school became the main institution for education and source of learning in the country. As a result, schools were firmly established in Thailand.

At the initial stage of organized education schools taught a similar curriculum for the purpose of creating a united Thai people. Once students graduated from schools, they would know, think, and perform their duties in the same way, almost like products from a factory. Ideas, differences, and self-identity were not

Figure 16.1
The Change of Thai Education from Tradition to Present Time

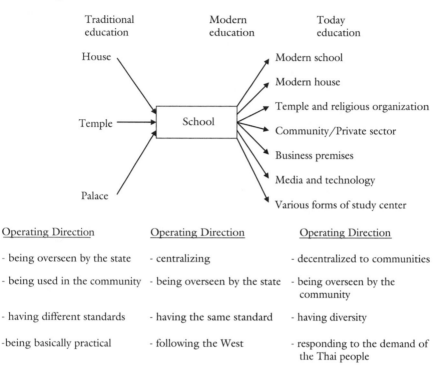

Traditional education	Modern education	Today education

House

Temple → School

Palace

Modern school

Modern house

Temple and religious organization

Community/Private sector

Business premises

Media and technology

Various forms of study center

Operating Direction	Operating Direction	Operating Direction
- being overseen by the state	- centralizing	- decentralized to communities
- being used in the community	- being overseen by the state	- being overseen by the community
- having different standards	- having the same standard	- having diversity
-being basically practical	- following the West	- responding to the demand of the Thai people

emphasized and it was only much later that they attempted to promote these more sought-after qualities. Dramatic changes finally occurred from 1932 to the period after World War II, when the schools promoted creative thinking, distinctiveness, and personal progress.

Much later on, with further technological development Thais experienced a rapid spread of it to each individual, house, temple, agency, and organization. They became further linked into common channels for access to new sources of knowledge. Schools were able to serve as a bridge to modern education for the Thai people. At this point, schools were not the only place for education. Many places such as houses, hospitals, and factories could provide education to people. The change of Thai education from tradition to present time can be framed as follows as given in Figure 16.1.

Traditional Education: Responding to Classes and Communities (1283–1871)

Traditional education in Thai history began in the Sukhothai Period and continued until the drastic improvement and change of the country in the reign of King Chulalongkorn (King Rama V).

The political, economic, and social characteristics of this period were those of the ancient times. The king was the owner of his subjects' lives and the owner of the country, and he ruled it together with the nobles. The majority of the people were serfs and slaves (slavery was abolished during the reign of King Rama V) under the rule and the supervision of the king and the aristocrats. Economically and socially it was a self-sufficient economy. Most people farmed in the villages and the temples were the center of village life. The city was the center of the country; the king and the aristocrats ruled the country with safety and peacefulness as their goal (Raphiphat, 1975). Once again, at this time there were three sources of education, the houses, the temples, and the palace.

Houses

The home schools of the Thai people were similar to the home schooling in any society. They taught trades that would provide living, codes of conduct to be part of society, and moral education and ethics to create good people. The teachers were parents or senior relatives taught things based upon experiences. The things they taught were the occupations for their own living and mostly they stayed within the family or were handed down. Teaching was conducted in the form of apprenticeship, with theories and practices in parallel. Life lessons, ethics and virtues were simultaneously taught.

Temples

Temples provided another source of education for the general public, namely the serfs and the slaves. The temples would teach religious and academic knowledge together with moral education and ethics. One drawback was that the temples taught only boys, leaving the girls out of a chance to study. The teachers were the monks who were mostly drawn from the local people. These teachers demonstrated through practice how to acquire wisdom by oneself. Temple-based education was divided into many levels, starting from the 1st to the 3rd level of the dharma scholar through to the 9th level of Pali studies graduate. This education was based on the Buddhist religious system and its training, not traditional school system (Anuman Rajadhon, 1972).

The Palace

The palace was set up as residence of the king, members of royal family, nobles in government service, philosophers, and royal scholars. Since these were some of best scholars in the land the palace was the center of education, government, public administration, and most of the professions in the fields of arts, literature, and crafts. It was the center of management for the whole country and society alike. Furthermore, this system of education simultaneously taught morality and ethics. Like other sources of education, these teachers as courtiers had skillful specializations in particular areas. Their teachings and further study emphasized demonstration, or the following of and practicing of given examples until the newly learned skills could be applied.

In traditional education, the knowledge learned was useful in the daily lives of the citizenry. Teaching aimed principally at real application and the communities would oversee this education by themselves. The model and the standard varied according to each household and community.

In the past, teaching and learning in the previously mentioned three institutions held local society together. These institutions allowed for the linkage of teaching and the learning of moral education and ethics with Buddhism. The things that were taught and learned were directly in line with what the communities wanted and as the people of these respective communities managed the system themselves the teaching focused mainly on practical uses.

Education Institution/ Main Task	Teacher	Common substance	Common method
Houses/occupations	Parents	Moral education and ethics	Demonstration and practice
Temples/beliefs	Monks	Moral education and ethics	Providing examples/ following examples
The palace/ Government	King/ noblemen	Moral education and ethics	Watching/practicing/ following examples

Therefore, the Thai traditional education had characteristics that corresponded directly to a self-sufficient society with the temples being the center of moral education and ethics, the household offering career training, and the palace responsible for overseeing the peacefulness, order, and progress of the country. Nevertheless, the limitations of this traditional form of education were very real.

Limitations

First, traditional education gave little importance to the improvement and development of advanced technology. Rather, it gave importance to local, domestic technology and to the development of the mind, feelings and attitudes. Education was to emphasize thought and the spirit and values of each district. Much of the studying focused on the study of religious ideas and beliefs. In the temples, monks initiated this aspect of education in favor of emphasizing technological innovation as happened in the West.

Second, each individualized district provided education. For instance, the village provided the community specified education that included home schools and what to teach and learn. Teaching reflected a parochial bias and thus limited its extension and diversity.

Third, teaching was not clearly divided between occupational training, moral education, or the learning for academic knowledge. As an example, the sword training at Buddhai Sawan School included the sword dance, various fighting techniques, morality training, and the code of lifestyle. What was lacking was the development of the scientific principles and theory to complement other aspects of the educational system.

Fourth, there was an attempt to use an education model in order to limit thinking through the creation of religious idealism. As another example, Trai Phum Phra Ruang, the classic Thai literature, would teach people to believe in Nirvana therefore limiting the amount of thinking in other directions. Trai Phum Phra Ruang did not totally aim at religious teaching but also at political peacefulness.

Fifth, education was socially stratified so that class and status would determine, for the most part, what kind of education was received and what rewards attached to it.

What were the results of this kind of education? An obvious result was that it produced a social model highly emphasizing the ideals of the spirit but forgoing material production knowledge. Even when materials were produced, the main purpose was to enhance the spirit. Good examples of this are the building of temples and the creation of literary works and other types of art. Each district was responsible for the educational movements in its own sphere and as a result usually determined its own sources of education.

Receiving the School System: Factory Model in Education (1871–1932)

Although Thailand was never a European colony in the Colonial Period it still was influenced through ideas and operations that concerned a country's development. As Thailand moved in the direction of capitalistic industrial production and developing more modern cities, there was a need to develop new characteristics in society to response to such form of development. To support this, schooling was established and expanded beginning with the first stage of modern schooling in 1871. In 1932 once the rule of the country changed from an absolute monarchy toward democracy, the concept of a school system was no longer a new concept. The school system of Thailand in that period followed a kind of factory model as happened in other colonial countries. This meant that graduates were now more disciplined and responsible; worked according to regulations and orders and did not give much consideration to creative thinking, differences, diversity, changes, and self-identity.

In the face of Western threats to local culture, the Thai king wanted to further unify the nation. To do this he worked toward making his people know and understand a common set of elements so that they could communicate with each other, live out their lives in a similar style, learn modern knowledge and be ready to serve the nation. As a consequence the school system came into existence (Moonsin, 1969).

Early on, many of the main schools had a Christian flavor and were run by the missionaries. In this era, in 1871, Thailand established its first royal school in the Royal Palace. In the same year the Royal English School was established (Committee on the History of the Ministry of Education, 1964).

The students in both schools consisted mainly of members of the royal family and aristocrats. The state provided for the teachers and paid their salaries. In the Thai Language School, teachers taught Thai, calculation, and government tradition while the English Language School put more emphasis on the English language that was being taught by foreign teachers. In 1981, the Royal Pages School was also established.

In 1884, King Rama V established the first school for the people at Wat Mahunpharam. This was a precedent for many public schools which were established at various temples. The development of education in Thailand was furthered with the Department of Education being established in 1887. The main purpose was to supervise education in the country. Later, schools expanded widely.

1871	*Establishing the Thai Language Royal School*
1874	Establishing the English Language Royal School
	Establishing Kunsattri Wang Lang School
1881	Establishing the Royal Pages School
1882	Establishing the Royal Survey School
1884	*Establishing the school for the public*
	Establishing 14 schools
	Administering the final examination of the Thai language
1887	Establishing the Department of Education
1889	Establishing the School of Medicine
1890	Establishing the Ministry of Education
1892	*Establishing Teachers Training School*
1898	Establishing the National Education Project 1898
	Publishing royal textbooks for public use
1910	Establishing the Civil Servant School
1916	*Establishing Chulalongkorn University*
1918	Issuing the Private School Act
1921	Issuing the Primary Education Act
1930	Canceling the local education tax
1932	*Changing the government system*

Education in this age was distinguished by the establishment and the expansion of schools in various levels all over the country together and a system being set up to supervise the process.

Because traditional education was to be found in the Thai home, temples, and at the palace, it had specific characteristics and contents. In a situation when the country wanted the Thai people to have new characteristics, it had to adapt to provide new things to learn. In order to do this in an all-consuming nationalistic way, the expansion of schooling was important. At the beginning, Thailand tried to use temples as schools and monks as the teachers of modern subjects but in the later period schools were specifically established and teachers training institutions of the state produced teachers.

Basic Education

In this period, the distinctive purpose of education at both the primary and secondary education levels was to provide the Thai people with a common knowledge and understanding to better communicate with one another and live together peacefully in the society. It is for this reason that the contents of the system emphasized language communication, particularly the national language. It also emphasized academic knowledge including: history, geography, and science to better understand the modern world and enter the Civil Service. Examples of the three levels of the curriculums in this period are given in Tables 16.1, 16.2, and 16.3 (Witsathawet, n.d.).

Table 16.1
Primary School Curriculum, 1981

	Number of Study Hours Per Week		
Subject	1st Year	2nd Year	3rd Year
Ethics	1.00	1.30	1.30
Thai	10.45	10.00	9.00
Calculation	6.00	6.00	6.45
Chronicle geography	2.15	2.15	2.00
Science	1.30	1.30	2.00
Drawing	2.00	2.00	2.00
Craft	1.00	1.00	1.00
Cultivation	—	1.00	2.00
Trade	—	1.00	2.00
Gymnastics	2.30	2.45	2.45
	27.00	27.00	27–28

Table 16.2
Secondary School Curriculum, 1913

	Number of Study Hours Per Week		
Subject	1st Year	2nd Year	3rd Year
Ethics	1.00	1.00	1.00
Thai and English	10.45	10.45	10.45
Calculation	5.00	5.00	5.00
Chronicle geography	2.15	2.15	2.15
Drawing	2.00	2.00	2.00
Science	2.00	2.00	2.00
Scouting	2.00	2.00	2.00
	25.00	25.00	25.00

Table 16.3
Primary School Curriculum, 1928

Subject	Number of Study Hours Per Week		
	1st Year	2nd Year	3rd Year
Ethics	1.00	1.00	1.00
Thai	5.00	5.00	4.00
Foreign languages	9.00	13.00	7.00
	one language	two languages	one language
Geography and history	3.00	3.00	—
Mathematics	6.00	2.00	7.00
Science	2.00	2.00	7.00
	one kind	one kind	three kinds
Physical education	1.00	1.00	1.00
	27.00	27.00	27.00

Although the curriculum models were changed in later years the basic principle never changed much. An emphasis was still put on contents. In addition to the contents having Thai and English, new academic knowledge, especially mathematics, geography, and science were taught. The goal was for Thai people to keep up with changes and to adhere to changes occurring in the modern world of the industrial age. This was the goal despite the fact that they were on the receiving side of it as consumers rather than as producers (Department of Curriculum and Instruction Development, 1970).

Furthermore, such academic content was the same nationwide. Schools in the North, the South or the Northeast used the same curriculum with the same goal to create a nationalized Thai society through uniform education. This new curriculum was delivered in local areas by school teachers who were usually state personnel or civil servants trained by the central administration, particularly in teacher training schools, and posted to schools all over the country.

The teaching–learning process corresponded to the process of modern nation building. Naturally this affected the learning process in a way that much of the "new" knowledge communicated in the local schools was not always familiar or relevant to local rural society. This led to an instructional format that consisted of telling and learning by heart—the teachers taught and the students memorized. School examinations focused on the quantity rather than the quality of learning (Witsathawet, n.d.).

Higher Education

In basic form the education system at the higher education level was not much different from that of the primary and secondary levels. However, many of the teachers were not Thais. This was the case particularly in the fields of science and technology, as well as in the schools of agriculture, surveying, forestry, and railroads; the principal teachers were not Thais but foreigners.

With respect to the student population, most were children of government officials. Children of agricultural families, for example, rarely had a chance to study at the higher education level.

For various academic disciplines and curriculum there were two groups of subjects. The first group of subjects concerned techniques linked to the country's development process with the goal to keep up with the developed countries. The subjects in this group were related to the new plans for agriculture, surveying, irrigation, forestry, engineering (especially regarding railroads), medicine and nursing. These subjects required the introduction of new knowledge and techniques that were still lacking in Thai society. For that reason a foreign body of knowledge was heavily relied upon.

The second group of subjects were those concerning the country's administration and management. This extended the study of Thai traditional knowledge into the country's management and administration for such new areas in military education, police education, as well as law and public administration (Sinlarat, 2003).

The school models mentioned earlier at the primary, secondary, or higher education levels had the same characteristic emphasized in the education provided by the state's central administration. The state set forth a single curriculum model and the result was that it resembled a factory model. The products of this education system, as exemplified in the graduates had nearly uniform characteristics. There were expected to be good citizens for the country, to obey the wise elder Thai people, and to work according to the existing state plan. The success of schools with the factory-model characteristics made Thais who learnt similar things, thought in a similar manner, were able to communicate with one another and the country had unity.

Limitations

Nevertheless, several limitations existed in this education model.

First, King Rama V established public schools that were not under local jurisdiction. Initially this met with resistance in some quarters as not everyone accepted that education ought to come from one source, namely, the school. This meant that anyone who did not enter school or did not graduate was to be considered inferior. This situation was in contrast with the countryside, where often people who studied in school were alienated from their own community.

Second, in the past, education was the responsibility of the district. For instance, the countrymen tried to have good monks in the village so as to ensure that the village had good education. However, in the period under discussion, education was drawn into the central administration, and the central administration supervised it through schools. Specific curriculums were offered, and these curriculums were created by the central administration. This system required that there must be inspectors to supervise teaching so that it would be conducted in this direction; therefore, there were inspectors, teachers, and various representatives of the capital.

Third, although the total image of Thai society is that of the homogeneous society, in reality Thais are composed of many groups of local and expatriates. Each of these groups have their own thoughts, beliefs, and cultures, especially Chinese-Thais in the capital and the Muslims in the South who had strong cultural roots. When central government tried to provide the same education all over the country for political and administrative purposes (Education, 1982), this immensely disturbed local cultures and led to protests and disputes from minority groups including Chinese (Watson, 1980), and could be one of the reasons for the problems in the southern part of Thailand.

Fourth, education linked with government. In those days, it was desirable to have a unified government so for that reason governors were created through education. The Civil Service School was established to produce governors and later on this became Chulalongkorn University. In the beginning, the persons selected to study in this school had to be children of aristocrats. They were taught government methodology and after completion of the program, they were required to serve as the royal pages for the purpose of understanding the king's benevolence. After the king's power was lessened or terminated according to the Constitution, the interior civil servants' governing powers were enhanced.

Fifth, education was not only for the government and for the operation of the country but it also was linked to the central administration. At this time, there was the school of law, the Civil Servant School, teacher training school, and the military training school. The management of these schools was centralized in the capital city. Education was drawn into the central administration and it served to supervise all circles. The content of teaching centered on lifestyle learning as well as content centered on the reading and writing style of the city people. As a result the students increased their understanding of the culture of the city people.

Sixth, the things that were taught and learned were mainly based on academic knowledge from abroad. The knowledge in the palace, the profound knowledge taught in the Civil Service School, the teacher training school, philosophy, psychology, law, and governing methods were all derived from the West. Only the things that were perceived as having practical benefits were chosen, for instance, Western governing philosophies were not adopted. Also, teaching continued to be conducted in a traditional manner. Significantly, integration as done in the past was replaced by separation. For example, in teaching moral education, the duties of the citizens and academic knowledge were separated. Theories and practices were also taught separately because they were a product of school already at this point. In school, theories were taught separately. There were fewer schools that taught practical information or trades.

Seventh, the result of these changes was that people increasingly felt that education was the duty of the school. Parents could not provide their children education, and the children began to feel that their parents were foolish and old-fashioned. At first, the parents did not feel it, but later they admitted that they were really foolish and encouraged the children to study at higher levels in order to enter the palace and become high-ranking officials. What had been traditionally taught and learned were the things that existed in life, the mind and the society. The things which the society talked about were replaced by science that was the knowledge of the capital. This knowledge distinguished the real things that the children saw from the life in their old schools. Therefore, when the children received higher education, they went to the capital; and once they graduated, they would not return home.

Eighth, some of the values that followed from the West emerged and were consequently emulated. When children were gradually drawn out of the districts and provinces, the results were the city values increased. Cities became more developed. In comparison, one effect of colonialism was the construction of big cities like Saigon and Kuala Lumpur in Southeast Asia. These were created as the ports for loading and unloading resources that were taken from the local country. The other effect was less teaching of culture, customs, religion, and beliefs as the interest focused more on academic knowledge. In the high-level institutions the interest focused only on increasing technological knowledge and cultural knowledge waned. There was more focus on Western techniques regarding railroads, transportation, and telegrams. In those days, the influence of colonialism had existed for a long time and as more Western goods came in, teaching and learning accepted the value system of the developed West more. Soon as more students graduated this combination led to Thais in the capital to adopt more Western culture.

As a result, the total picture that became clear when the educational system had been in place like this for a long time was a change in social values. In the modern system the change that took place was that the people who were outside the cities and were in the provinces came to be considered inferior in this new system and started to feel less educated than the city people. The more gifted small town and provincial children had to study in the capital and become government officials; those who stayed home traditionally earned traditional living and little by little began to accept the city values and the education that it involved. When the number of schools increased the education standard curriculums developed. This resulted in education becoming more and more diverse, especially those who had lived abroad and absorbed Western values, adding new values to teaching. This led many to criticize the educational system as aristocratic. In fact about 50–60 percent of the bachelor's degree holders were the children of merchants while only 8 percent were from farmer backgrounds. Those who could study were rich. The country people who came to the city for studies were brought up to follow the value system of the people of Bangkok.

The Beginning of Democracy: Liberty and Freedom in Education (1932–1999)

When the People's Party seized power and changed the country's government from the absolute monarchy to the constitutional monarchy, they encouraged education in Thailand to be more expansive, to give equal opportunities to more people, and to be more democratic. They also encouraged education to be beneficial to the society as a whole. This concept was greatly supported in the period after World War II when the influence of an American liberal education played a more significant role. The remarkable changes in the education of this period were:

1. Emphasizing on promoting democracy among students
2. Emphasizing on all aspects of students' growth
3. Emphasizing on expanding opportunity, equality and diversity
4. Emphasizing on occupations and cooperation with the community
5. Emphasizing on standards and quality.

When the People's Party began to develop education, they announced the policy stating that the Government would make the "citizens know the democratic ruling system and live appropriately in the Constitution Age." After World War II, there was an emphasis on education in order to promote democracy with the goal to resist against the communism that was emerging and growing during the postwar period (Phisanbut, 1969).

The expansion of opportunity became increasingly more noticeable and after World War II, and compulsory education was expanded to seven years. It was then that students were encouraged to study as much as they could according to affordability and ability. Education for women was also expanded widely.

After the change in government, education put more emphasis on occupations. The Government gave more support to vocational education, and after World War II they stressed education for the economic development of the country.

The development of every aspect of student growth was more clearly seen in the period after the change in government. An emphasis was put on intellectual education, ethics, and physical education. After World War II, the focus was still on the development of all aspects of the students with an emphasis on manual education. Following the change an attempt to supervise the standard and quality changed to a stress on the extensive improvement of curriculum and teaching. After World War II assistance and collaboration from foreign countries had become the significant motivation to support the improvement of the quality and standard of Thai education.

We can see the picture of the change in education as follows.

1932	*Changing government to democracy*
	Establishing the Education Council
	Proposing the new education plan
1933	Establishing Thammasat and Politics University
1935	Making amendments to Chulalongkorn University Act to make it a legal entity
	Making amendments to the Primary Education Act
1936	Announcing to use the National Education Plan 1936 with emphasis on the rights, the duties and the citizenship—three elements of education and vocational education
1940	Establishing the Division of Adult Education

1945	Establishing the Teachers Council of Thailand
1948	Establishing the Division of Overseas Education
1949	*Waiving tuition fees in public schools*
1951	Revising the National Education Plan
	Upgrading municipal schools
	Chachoengsao Education Promotion Project
1952	Providing welfare education
1952–1962	Cooperating with the United States
1954	Establishing Center for Adult Training, Ubon Ratchathani
	The Colombo Plan
1959	Establishing the National Education Commission
1960	Making a new education and curriculum development plan
1961	Implementing the National Economic and Social Development plan
1961–1996	Developing according to the National Economic and Social Development Plan
1965	Rural Teachers Training Project
1967–1971	Receiving assistance from the World Bank
1973	Demonstration of students and the people
1974	Education reform for life and society
1987	Developing the country in the direction of the newly industrialized countries
1994	Receiving the influence of globalization

The characteristics and the roles of school differed from the previous period. During the past period similar characteristics and the same model were both distinct and emphasized but diversity was scarce. On the other hand, in this period, we see a variety of education models and children were encouraged to fulfill their potential while the provision of teaching becomes more diversified.

Basic Education

The National Education Plans in 1936 and 1960 were similarly written. It was education that depended on the students' personal circumstances and aimed at making them good citizens who could work to do something deemed useful for the nation. In 1936, all aspects of education, namely intellectual education, ethics, and physical education were emphasized. Apart from those three aspects, manual education was also added in 1960. In 1978, the curriculum was again revised but the original principle maintained that children would grow in all aspects, live well in the society, and have a variety of alternatives.

The purpose of the primary education curriculum was clearly stated, "The primary education curriculum aims at encouraging the development of children to live as good citizens of the nation in the democratic system, and at training and bringing them up with 4 major qualifications as follows.

1. The intention concerning their prosperity
2. The intention concerning human relations

3. The intention concerning the ability to earn their living
4. The intention concerning the responsibility and duties of citizens.

The contents of the primary education curriculum were composed of eight categories, namely Thai, social studies, mathematics, physical education, arts, and science. Apart from the main substances, there were also things that were used in daily life, and the major emphasis was on being the good citizens of the society.

Furthermore, at the primary education level, careers were emphasized more, especially in manual education that more electives were offered for students to choose throughout their three years of senior primary education. Examples of these electives are: agriculture, home economics, drawing, carpentry, and masonry; the other categories could be studied in just one year.

In junior secondary education, the concept of liberty and freedom was clearly reflected. The students should learn according to their aptitude and interest and had more freedom in their educational growth. Electives were diverse, and the curriculum also included vocational education with the goal for the learners to study according to their aptitude and interest, to acquire sufficient knowledge and skills for their careers, or to have the necessary basic knowledge for further internship or studies. The study time of junior secondary education was not less than five days; 30 hours per week for the general education field; 35 hours per week for the vocational education field; and 18 hours for the subjects that both fields studied together.

Senior secondary education also had the same characteristic. All students had to study general education system that was comprised of Thai, English, social studies, mathematics and algebra for 12 hours per week; and study the subjects in their fields of general education, science, or arts for 18 hours. There was also the vocational field to choose as in the following study timetable as given in Table 16.4.

Teachers and the teaching learning process tremendously changed from the previous education systems. It was in this age that the teachers had a broader outlook and a variety of concepts and experiences because they had obtained new knowledge and training. More than ever Thai teachers who studied and were trained abroad for the purpose of coming back to jointly teach the Thai teachers with foreign specialists. Also, there were a great number of documents and textbooks. The concept of teaching psychology for teaching, particularly from the assistance by the United States in the USOM Project, assistance from the United Kingdom and Australia in the Colombo Plan, and assistance from international organizations such as UNESCO resulted in a teaching model that taught the children to develop themselves in every aspect, including the intellect, the body, society, and the mind. It also put an emphasis on more liberty and freedom. The concept of education in this period was highly developed and became diverse as well (Sinlarat, 1983).

Higher Education

Higher education would distinctly reflect liberalism in education. After a successful coup in 1932, the People's Party made amendments to the

Table 16.4
Number of Hours Per Week

Subject Category	General Education Field — Science Department		General Education Field — Arts Department		General Education Field — General Education Department			Vocational Education Field	
	Common Compulsory Subject	Specific Compulsory Subject	Common Compulsory Subject	Specific Compulsory Subject	Common Compulsory Subject	Specific Compulsory Subject	Specific Elective	Common Compulsory Subject	Specific Compulsory Subject
Thai									
Thai A	3	—	3	—	3	—	—	3	—
Thai B	—	—	—	2	—	—	2	—	—
English									
English A	4	—	4	—	4	—	4	4	—
English B	—	2	—	2	—	—	2	—	—
English C	—	—	—	2	—	—	2	—	—
Social studies									
Social studies A	3	—	3	—	3	—	—	3	—
Social studies B	—	—	—	2	—	—	2	—	—
Science									
General science	—	—	—	4	—	4	—	—	—
Physics chemistry	—	8	—	—	—	4	—	—	—
Biology	—	—	—	—	—	—	—	—	—
Laboratory	—	2	—	—	—	—	—	—	—
Mathematics									
Mathematics A	2	—	2	—	2	—	—	2	—
Mathematics B	—	4	—	4	—	—	4	—	—
The Second foreign language	—	—	—	4	—	—	4	—	—
Arts or handicraft	—	2	—	2	—	2	4	—	—
Commerce	—	—	—	—	—	—	4	—	—
Secretarial course	—	—	—	—	—	—	4	—	—
Career	—	—	—	—	—	—	4 or 8	—	18 or 23
Sub Total	12	18	12	18	12	6	12	12	18 or 23
Grand Total	30		30		30			30 or 35	18 or 23

Chulalongkorn University Act in order to liberate the university by giving the University Council the power to manage the university by themselves. In addition they established Thammasat and Political Science University with the goal to create new academics and politicians to supervise and manage the nation. Following that there was the establishment of universities to develop occupations, such as agriculture, medicine, and the arts. Universities were also established in the provinces.

The curriculum of higher education was also greatly improved once the country started to offer a curriculum that offered general education subjects. This enabled the students to undergo specific disciplines in order to study other subjects outside their disciplines and to allow for broad social knowledge. Meanwhile, a provision gave children the liberty and freedom to fully grow according to their potential with a credit-based system. Teaching and learning turned more toward the use of self-study method together with prepared lectures (Sinlarat, 2005).

In this period, teachers themselves were growing in diversity. Foreign teachers from both Europe and America assisted in the teaching but the number of Thai teachers graduating from abroad increased. The disciplines that they taught were promoted and apart from the new public administration discipline, were the subjects concerning national development, such as administration, economics, and business administration.

The other group of subjects that experienced tremendous growth was the group of science subjects (Thipayathasana, 1982). Each year a number of new subjects were added and offered, as seen from the study report given in Table 16.5.

Table 16.5
Number of Subjects Illustrated in the Teaching Timetable Book of Faculty of Science, Chulalongkorn University

Department	Number of Subjects Offered in the Academic Year			
	1959–1960	1964–1965	1972–1973	1979–1980
Botany	25	27	37	49
Chemical technology	18	44	54	28
Chemistry	53	33	55	67
Geology	32	23	41	27
Mathematics	77	29	35	51
Physics	52	26	31	51
Biology	27	31	30	54
General Science	—	15	37	64
Bio-chemistry	—	—	18	19
Marine science	—	—	29	27
Materials science	—	—	42	49
Micro-biology	—	—	—	22
Electives that are not science	17	16	31	Plenty 518*

Note: * Excluding electives.

Limitations

Looking at educational trends in this period, the following points may be discerned.

First, education had been used for career and economic development from the time when a government change of power with Field Marshal Sarit in 1958. The industrial foundation was consequently established and loans were now available. The government sector provided specialists and purchased more supplies for studies, the schools and universities. Accordingly, education was focused to be in line with the economic system. As the education plan was drawn, there was greater promotion of vocational education and universities were given more support in the areas of engineering, agricultural, and medical technologies while social sciences were underrepresented and lacked governmental support.

Second, in teaching, new technology was increasingly required in order to keep up with development. Engineering taught us how to disassemble, fix and make machines work, but it did not really teach us how to produce them. In social sciences, we learned the theories of social sciences and sociology, but in a manner devoid of local context. Universities taught like this; teacher training colleges taught like this; and teachers in the rural areas also taught like this. Accordingly, the kind of education that stressed the values of the city enhanced the capitalist development of the country. Thus, the countryside also accepted the capital development movement as the model for developing the mountain dwellers in the same system. This allowed them to adhere to the system in order to increase their productivity so that to promote the economy through increased income and more purchasing power.

Third, education did not teach what the good life was. It is obvious that education was a planned social movement and tool of capitalism. As an example, today education has been planned to match economic aspirations but this does not always turn out as expected. People were encouraged to study but when there were a large number of graduates in similar programs, there was no work for them. The development system depended on the capitalist system and the results were that Thailand could not set its own development path. This lead to a direction that linked national development too closely tied to that of the West.

Information and Communication Technology (ICT): Schools Are Not Monopoly Institutions Any More (1999–Present)

Because of the growth in the use of ICT, especially the Internet system, schools could not monopolize education any more. Ordinary people could learn from various places by way of surfing the net, and they could get any kind of information, anywhere, anytime. Unfortunately, many schools were not in a condition to keep pace with this change, and were in fact, out of date. Some of the home school systems were even more obsolete than temples, factories, hospitals, or museums. In addition to this some schools maintained the same traditional characteristics that they had since their establishment in the 18th or 19th centuries. They were still stuck in the "factory model" that taught students the same and left graduates with the same characteristics all over the country. They used the same curriculum nationwide and used the same kind of teachers for teaching and the results were that educational system was once again out of date, centralized, and discordant with the district. The problem was that the system could not compete with other countries.

Accordingly, the idea to develop or reform education emerged again amidst the stream of information that came together with the growth and expansion of the ICT in the age of the borderless world.

The starting point of this new development was in 1994 when the Royal Institute of Thailand had translated the world globalization into the Thai language as "Lokapivatna" which means spreading around the world. During this period, various universities extensively studied and tried to understand globalization and education and proposed that education be provided in order to keep pace with the globalization system quickly (Sinlarat, 2005) and widely as can be seen from the following activities concerning globalization:

January 14, 1994	Education in the Information Age: Chulalongkorn University
June 29, 1994	Education in Globalization Age: Surat Thani Province
October 27, 1994	Education in Globalization Age: Kasikorn Bank
December 17, 1995	Thai Education and Globalization: Ministry of Education
February 11–12, 1995	Education in Globalization Age: Sethabut Girl School
March 10, 1995	Education and Globalization: Chulalongkorn University
October 18, 1996	Education Strategies and Globalization Age: Queen Sirikit National Center
September 12,1996	Education Technology in Globalization Age: Chulalongkorn University

The Seminars concerning education and globalization mentioned in the aforesaid list are only some examples. In fact, these were a large number of meetings that were not quoted, and during 1994–1996 there were also a lot of articles on education and globalization (Sinlarat, 2005) that well reflected the influences of globalization in Thai education system and schools. The topics discussed in various meeting included "Being Complete Man," "Students as the Center," "Keeping up with Technology," "Power Decentralization," "People's Participation," "Business-oriented Management," and so on.

Resulting from these activities and good reason, in 1999 there was another drastic reform in the educational system by which the National Education Act was issued as the first education law in Thailand. This Act reflected the major changes to move toward and global learning environment, as follows:

1. Purpose	From enhancing the learners to work in the government	Being the complete human beings
2. Teaching contents	From urban/ foreign contents	Contents including districts/ communities
3. Teaching method	From teachers as the center	Students as the center
4. Education institutions	From schools only	Home/communities/work places and so on
5. Professional standard	From the responsibility of the administrators	The responsibility of the administrators and professional organizations
6. Administrative pattern	From the decision by individuals	Decision by committees
7. Management	From the supervision of the government service	The supervision of the communities
8. Supervision	From the central supervision	The district and school supervision
9. Quality control	From internal control	External control

The meaning of all these changes was that the Thai people would move toward a system that offered an education without entering schools. They could learn from the various study centers that the Education Act has provided, including study places provided by the informal education units, persons, households, communities, community bodies, local administration organizations, private organizations, professional organizations, institutions, religions, business premises, hospitals, medical institutions, welfare units, and other social institutions (Office of the National Education Commission, 1999). Each unit has a freedom to provide education in their own direction with their own investment, and the standard is overseen by the central agency.

The concept of the National Education Act together with the concept of education in the direction of globalization led to the concept of providing education in accordance with the new age in three main directions, namely Modernizing Thai People, Commercializing Education System, and McDonaldizing the School.

Modernizing Thai People

The concept of education in the direction of globalization on the principle basis of the National Education Act and the influence of the international business is to push the people to be modern and keep abreast of the world and changes by encouraging them to study English and computer usage, to establish international relationships, to emphasize on living freely like westerners, on individualism, modernism and on the full consumption in accordance with each person's interest, the power of advertising, and the drive of business and trade. Education does not need to be in public schools any more. Anybody who wants to have any knowledge will go to a place that specializes in it, such as a music institute, an art institute, a language institute, and so on.

Commercializing Education System

Putting emphasis on freedom, liberty, individualism, decentralization of power to the private sector in the districts to oversee education by themselves and on raising the funds from the communities in combination with the process of business that stresses on competitions and the private sector, schools and universities have to seek more income. Consequently, income generation has become the major issue for education institutions in this age that basically hold on to marketing.

McDonaldizing the School

The worldwide system of McDonald food shop is the system that makes McDonald food anywhere in the world have the same characteristics and lack the local identity, flexibility, and diversity. The system of education is also operated in the same way. Schools all over the country and in the whole world must be run in the same direction by the concept of standardization that holds fast to the same standard and principles, so the schools lack the outstanding feature of each institution.

Limitations

The operation of education in line with globalization made Thai education much more modern as previously stated, but it also caused an impact on the Thai education and society in many aspects as follows:

1. The promotion of modernism and the Western free and liberal life style made the youth and the Thai people in general have the consumerist characteristics. The value of the Thai people is to buy, eat, and use imported products as much as possible. Consequently, this led to the rising value of imitation, especially the imitation of advertisements, so there were not many analytical thinking, creation, and pressure to bring about the products.
2. Education has become the learners' investment and a part of the expensive goods. A large number of education institutions organized projects to generate more income. The public goods that all the youth should have received turned to be the thing that could be bought, so the people who have a small income lost the opportunity to study.
3. The "student and teacher" value of education in the direction of the Thai society began to fade away and became the "customer and seller" value. The teacher will be the service supplier who must take care and satisfy the student who has the status of the customer in the business and trade system.
4. Education was more intensively used for economy. Education should be more utilized. Education led to more economic benefits. Education and economy must respond more

to each other. Education must lead to more economic growth. Education will lead to more knowledge-based economy.

5. Dependence on foreign academic knowledge increased tremendously because the academic and business growth at the international level went on rapidly and expansively in line with the knowledge-based economy. While knowledge is rarely created in the country, it is unavoidable to depend on the foreign academic knowledge, and this will continuously increase in accordance with the academic growth of the West.

Changing the education system into a business-oriented one made education become an expensive merchandise. This led to the problems in consumerism in education as mentioned. The academic gap had become wider. It also changed the consciousness of Thai teachers and students. The professional relationship, the sacrifice, and the sympathy between teachers and students turned to be the benefits. These problems led to wide discussions on reversing globalization in Thai education. The following main directions have been introduced: "critical-izing" Thai people, who have critical thinking; decommercializing Thai educa-tion system, to make them more humane; and Tom Yam Gung-izing Thai schools, which are more individualized and variable (Sinlarat, 2006).

The Way Out for Schools: The Fertile Field

As mentioned earlier, even though there were many endeavors in this century to establish knowledge centers to replace schools, these centers are not in the position to completely replace the stable and fixed system. The roles of school still exist but how they will continue to exist and which model should be used are issues that merit further discussion.

The limitation of the Thai education model that critics were unanimous about was the fact that the country has a rigid model for schools that was too static and it affected the learners' lives. Schools must be a specific place that offers freedom and creative thinking. With the system now the students have to totally adapt, adjust, and fit themselves within the school system. The schools are like a dry field that makes the students become withered, dry, undersized. We can see the typical lifestyle in the following daily routine of a Thai student at almost every levels, as follows:

The Daily Routine of the Thai Students

Monday to Friday

6:00	get out of bed
6:30	breakfast
7:00	go to school
8:00	National Anthem
8:30–12:00	class
12:00	lunch
13:00–15:30	class
15:30–16:30	game
16:30–18:30	Special Class

19:00–22:00   homework/internet/phone
22:00   go to bed

Saturday and Sunday
7:00   get out of bed
7:30   breakfast
8:00–12:00   Special Class
12:00   lunch
13:00   home
afternoon   free

It can be seen from this that the typical life of the Thai students in the Thai schools overly focuses on studying and homework so much that the students' lives are not fully developed and lack sufficient personal autonomy.

In the Thai society, there is a saying that the fertile rice seedling will grow in the fertile field. This means that if we have good quality rice grain, it will fully grow in the fertile field, and the rice seedling will grow to be the fertile ear of rice that is valuable to the farmers and the Thai society.

The best option for the future of the Thai school system to become the rice field that is full of rice grains. One could say that the students have already fallen to the field and they will fully grow according to their own potential, and will have their own identities in order to progress with dignity and to take forward the values of Thai society. Schools cannot afford to be stagnant and averse to this change, otherwise the educational system with remain an arid field that produces undersized rice plants.

Students paying homage to teachers. Courtesy of Paitoon Sinlarat, Ph.D.

REFERENCES

Anuman Rajadhon, Phya (1972). *The Study of the Thai Customs and the Thai Life in Former Times*. Bangkok: Khlang Witthaya Printing Press (in Thai).

Committee on History of the Ministry of Education (1964). *History of the Ministry of Education 1891–1964*. Bangkok: Kurusapa Printing House (in Thai).

Department of Curriculum and Instruction Development (1970). *Background of the General Education Curriculum*. Bangkok: Ministry of Education (in Thai).

Ministry of Education (1982). *Two Hundred Years of Thai Education*. Bangkok: Ministry of Education (in Thai).

Moonsin, Wutthichai (1969). *The Management Policy of the Thai Education in the Reign of King Chulalongkorn*. Bangkok: Prasarnmit College of Education (in Thai).

Office of the National Education Commission (1999). *The National Education Act 1999*. Bangkok: ONEC.

Phisanbut, Duangduan (1969). *Brief Content of the History of the Thai Education Subject*. Bangkok: Faculty of Education, Chulalongkorn University (in Thai).

Raphiphat, Akin, M.R. (1975). *The Thai Society at the Early Rattanakosin Period 1782–1873*. Bangkok: Phikkhanet Printing Center (in Thai).

Sinlarat, Paitoon (1983). *The Thai Education System in Three Decades*. Bangkok: Faculty of Education, Chulalongkorn University (in Thai).

———(2003). *The Programs Opened at the Higher Education Level: The Development in 200 Years of Rattanakosin (1782–1982)*. Bangkok: Textbook and Academic Document Center, Faculty of Education, Chulalongkorn University (in Thai).

———(2005). *Thai Universities after World War II: Adjustment for the Modern Society*. Bangkok: Chulalongkorn University Press (in Thai).

———(2006). *Reversing Globalization in Thailand: New Directions for Edcuation Reform*. Bangkok: Higher Education Program, Chulalongkorn University (in Thai).

Thipayathasana, Pairor (1982). *The Evolution of Scientific Dissemination in Thailand*. Bangkok: Chulalongkorn University (in Thai).

Watson, Keith (1980). *Educational Development in Thailand*. Hong Kong: Heineman.

Witsathawet, Wit (n.d.). *The Thai Education Philosophy (1868–1932)*. Bangkok: Office of the National Education Commission (in Thai).

Chapter 17

SCHOOLING IN TIMOR LESTE

J.A. Berlie

INTRODUCTION

The Encyclopedia Britannica 2005 defines "education" as "the action or process of educating or of being educated, a stage of such a process; and also the knowledge and development resulting from an educational process." In new countries it is crucial to try to upgrade the education, a powerful tool to reduce poverty.

This chapter looks at the history, the three levels of education and the current evolution of the education of the newest country, north of Darwin, the Democratic Republic of East Timor, which became independent on May 20, 2002. Education is an extremely sensitive sector of the new country which between 1942 and 1999 suffered a long military and political stress. The stress is still vivid in the memory of all the Timorese. World War II, the end of the Salazar regime in 1974, and 24 years of Indonesian occupation, constitute unique trials and tribulations for this very courageous people. This situation compelled the Timorese to resist and finally they successfully became independent, finding a way to have their own system. This happy end is not yet concretized concerning "the knowledge and development" of the educational process. Education is a central point to develop a tool to make a people, who suffered so much, happier and wealthier.

HISTORICAL CONTEXT

East Timor (Timor Leste in Portuguese) was a former Portuguese colony at the extreme end of an empire during some 500 years. Its education in Portuguese was mostly in the hands of the Catholic Church. Many representative members of the Timorese elite, including the President Xanana Gusmão and the Prime Minister Mari Alakatiri, were educated under this system. The Interior Minister, Ana Maria Pessoa, had the chance to be educated at the Liceo created only at the end of the Portuguese domination (a Portuguese Secondary School of the Government which was redeveloped in 2001). The education of women was often forgotten on the Island before the 21st century. The Portuguese, after moving their colonial government to Dili in 1769, tried to promote indirectly Tetum language, spoken in Dili, Suai, and Viqueque, and largely influenced this language; particularly in the capital, a modern Portuguese vocabulary was directly assimilated. However, the Western colonizer did nothing to promote Tetum education; Portuguese remained the only language taught in schools. Portuguese remained the sole medium of education between the 16th century and 1975. Contrary to West Timor, a former Dutch colony, where the Bible was translated into Meto language, nothing was done which was likely to promote Tetum language. The Bible in Portuguese was considered sufficient for an underdeveloped colony with only 30 percent of the local population converted to Catholicism and relying on sandalwood and later on coffee plantations. So in Atambua, Western Indonesia, the local language of Dili is simply called "Portuguese Tetum" (*Tetum Porto*). The monarchic Portuguese State and later the Portuguese Republic were only interested to promote Catholic education. The period after World War II, was marked by total stagnation of education under the Japanese occupation (1942–1945), and was also characterized by ambiguity because the Portuguese governor remained in the capital Dili during the whole period.

Under the Indonesian occupation (December 7, 1975–September 27, 1999) education was developed in Indonesian. For the first time in the history of East Timor, a university was established in Dili.

The United Nations tried to help the Timorese after the Santa Cruz massacre on November 12, 1991, and at the end of August 1999, a successful Timorese referendum was promoted by the Indonesian President Habibie strongly advised by the American President Bill Clinton. The East Timorese courageously massively voted for independence. On September 20, 1999, a military operation led by Australia under a UN mandate entered East Timor. It was the beginning of a stalemate in education between September 1999 and March 2000 (see photo of the first class in Dili), all the schools and the University of Dili were closed and many houses and buildings were burned by militiamen.

In 2000, Portugal understood its crucial role in the education linked to its colonial duty; first, the IPOR (Portuguese Institute in the East) was in charge of developing the teaching of Portuguese language under the UN mandate and the Director posted in Macau came to Dili. But soon Portugal discovered that it was a colossal work and decided to commit the Ministry of Education. Various delegations came to Timor to solve this question; in January 2002, Portugal's Minister of Education, Julio Pédrosa, met in Dili the UN Administrator, Sergio de Mello (1948–2004), and the Chief Minister Mari Alkatiri. Under the United Nations Transitional Administration in East Timor (UNTAET) with the help of Portugal and Brazil, and the diligence of the Administrator de Mello, education restarted in Portuguese with a priority for Tetum language. This necessary preeminence of Tetum sometimes created incomprehension in regions such as the extreme east of the country where the local Fataluku and Indonesian languages were mostly spoken.

Education is the key for the world's newest nation state, the heart of nation building, and the best opportunity for development and modernization. Even with around 50 percent of East Timor spending on education and healthcare, the adult literacy (linked to poverty and insecurity during so many years) is low and does not reach 60 percent. For women above 15 of age, this percentage is even lower. In particular, it is estimated by Bonner of Caritas Australia East Timorese that two-third of adult women have never attended any kind of school. The Salesian Brothers with their great experience in teaching, and organizations such as Australia Global Education Centre in Adelaide, are doing their best to improve the present rather low level of education.

LEVELS OF EDUCATION (PRIMARY, SECONDARY, AND TERTIARY EDUCATION)

Portuguese and Indonesian Legacies

Before looking at the level of education it seems necessary to explain the complex linguistic problem of the new country.

Each ethnic group in Timor is called according to the language spoken, except groups such as the Atoni (meaning "man" in their own language), Meto speakers in Oecussi, and West Timor. There are more than 14 languages and many dialects in the new country. In Atauro Island three dialects are currently spoken: Makili, Rahesuk (Adabe), and Makadede. Galole spoken in Manatuto is close to these dialects of this island called Pulau Kambing by the Indonesians. All these languages are Austronesian (formerly Malayo-Polynesian) except three non-Austronesian or Western Papuan languages: Bunak, Fataluco (including Lovaia in Tutuala), and Makasai (including Maklere). These Timorese languages are spoken in different districts as follows:

1. Tetum is spoken in Dili, Batugade (Batugadé), Suai (Tetum Terik), and Viqueque but also in Atambua, West Timor
2. Mambai (Mambae) is used in Aileu (North dialect), (Samé) and Ainaro
3. Fataluco, or Fataluku, is spoken in Lautem (Lautenu is one of the four dialects) and Los Palos (Lospala in Fataluco)
4. Meto (incorrectly called Vaikenu, Baikenu, or Dawan) in Oecussi
5. Tokodede (Tokode or simply Tokod) in Liquica and Maubara
6. Makasai (Makasae) in Baucau (Maklere is probably related)
7. Galole (Galoli) in Manatuto
8. Bunak in Bobonaro
9. Ema, Emak, or Kemak in Kailaku
10. Idate (Idaté, Idalaka) in Laclubar
11. Kairui in Aitalo (Kawaimina?)
12. Nauete (Nauoti) (Hull classifies it with Kawaimina)
13. Midik (Midiki) (Kawaimina?)
14. Naumik (part of Nauete for Hull or Lere?)

Tetum, the national language, is divided into Tetum Prasa around Dili (the national language *stricto sensu*) and Tetum Terik in Suai, Viqueque and Atambua,

Wehali (West Timor). Tetum is classified in the Austronesian family of languages (formerly called Malayo-Polynesian) but with a heavy Portuguese substratum and also "Melanesian" and Western Papuan borrowings. This high diversity of languages and cultures is the nightmare of the education ministry of East Timor which evidently has to follow the laws and the Constitution which states that "the State shall promote education and vocational training for the youth" (Section 19).

Indonesia during 24 years bypassed this linguistic complexity and promoted only the Indonesian language which has the great advantage of being grammatically simple. Its sister language, Malay, was a *lingua franca* before and after the arrival of the first Europeans (Portuguese and British) from Malacca to Timor. In a pure theoretical question which does not touch politics and the repressive military occupation, the new education system—thanks to the structure and simplicity of the Bahasa Indonesia, the national language of the Republic of Indonesia—was in a certain way favorable to East Timor and a good opportunity to acquire an education for many young leaders such as Armando da Silva, a deputy and president of the Liberal Party. For the first time a university was opened in Dili, once capital of an Indonesian Province.

After being imposed to study Portuguese, the Timorese people were obliged to switch to Indonesian between 1976 and 1999, and in 2000 the young and educated graduates in Indonesian had often problems to speak Portuguese if their parents were not really fluent in the language of their European colonizer. The UNTAET followed the line of the present Constitution which favors Portuguese and Tetum, the two official languages of the country. It was very difficult to find competent teachers, as those having a teaching training had been taught in Indonesian. Very few Timorese refugees in Australia and Portugal had a basic pedagogical training. At present, except the Catholic Church which has its own system, there is not yet a Teachers' University in East Timor. At all the levels of education—primary, secondary and tertiary—there is a critical shortage of staff in this sector according to Caritas, Mercy corps and many other institutions. In remote parts of the country, such as in the Island of Atauro and the enclave of Oecussi, the author's fieldwork confirms this crucial fact of the lack of teachers. Excellent teachers are essential for a country with 50 percent of the population under the age of 15 (some 400,000 children and youths).

Primary Education

There are at present some 3,500 primary schools in the country attended by some 150,000 students or 96 percent of the population in the schooling age (BETA electronic information). I cannot scientifically confirm these rather optimistic statistics. To upgrade the education it is necessary to improve "the action and process of educating" and for that the highest level of education of the teachers is fundamental. Many Timorese teachers at primary level have only senior secondary education. Education is particularly vulnerable in rural and remote areas. Competent teachers do not want to teach in the countryside.

In Oecussi there is at present a unique teacher really competent in Portuguese, Inacio da Costa, a son of a competent Timorese traditional head of the region (*Liurai*) João Hermenegildo da Costa who died in the 1990s.

In rural areas, and in remote parts of the country, the attendance of many classes is low, which fact is confirmed by a UNESCO educator posted in Dili. Many parents are not always motivated and do not understand the importance of a good education for their children. Is it because they have too many problems to solve to improve their basic standard of living? Is it also because there is a lack of motivation of the teachers, a consequence of their low salaries?

Secondary Education

Around 27,000 students attend 114 secondary schools in East Timor, so the gap between the number of primary school students and teenagers is huge. However it seems that the percentage of enrolled students and their motivation to attend their class is hopefully higher. This comparative study of attendance demonstrates that in fact few students are able to join a secondary level of education but many of those enrolled like to go to school. It is surprising, considering the will of many parents in the Asia-Pacific Region to have children joining secondary and tertiary levels of education, to find according to a UNICEF report (2005) that many parents in East Timor do not view education as a worthwhile investment. The crucial point of poverty may probably give a first answer to this question of upgrading education.

Australia and the United States have certainly the will to develop English language in the new country and the youth also like very much to study this international language of communication. The departure of the majority of the UN staff does not favor evidently the teaching of English all over the country which requires a huge financial and technical investment and which does not fit the Timorese Constitution approved by the Constituent Assembly on March 22, 2002: "Tetum and Portuguese shall be the official languages" (Section 13).

Concerning secondary and tertiary education, the role of Portugal is essential, but the former colonial power needs currently the constant support of the European Union to develop education in East Timor, and the cooperation of Brazil continues to be central. In 2002, 300 East Timorese students went to Portugal to study. At present there are a few Timorese students enrolled at the Law Faculty of Macau University.

The teaching of Portuguese is slow. The author helped the Crystal Foundation in 2000–2002 to have the useful assistance of the Portuguese Mission (now an Embassy) to send competent and experienced Portuguese teachers to teach Portuguese to Timorese graduated teachers who had to transfer their competence in Indonesian to become Portuguese teachers in the school of this foundation which had some 2,000 students. It was not an easy task, not only for the experienced Portuguese teachers of teachers, but also for the Timorese teachers of that school. This question could be also addressed at all the three levels of education including the tertiary level.

Tertiary Education

Young Timorese clamor to go to university, but there is no sufficient international financial support for the State to promote such a move. Around 16,000 students attend one of the 53 high schools. The most prestigious is the National University (*Universidade Nacional de Timor Leste*) in Dili under the supervision of a linguist Benjamin Araujo Corte Real, a descendant of a well-known Liurai family of Ainaro.

The Democratic Republic of East Timor also wants its own system which is at present only a dream in tertiary education because it needs competence, time, will, and money.

David Hicks of New York University stayed in the island many months, starting in the 1960s. For the third time, in 2005, as a professor, under a one-year American Fulbright Scholarship he came to help the Timorese and to teach Anthropology. He was obliged to teach in Tetum to a very limited number of postgraduates. Concerning Timor, this competent and highly knowledgeable scholar evidently masters Tetum less well than English, and also, through his mother tongue, could really develop the teaching ability of many students and university lecturers. Is it possible for East Timor planners in education to correct the fact that many competent non-Timorese scholars are freely willing to improve the teaching ability and competence of Timorese professors and teachers under the financial resources of their own overseas universities? Brazil has recently implemented a program to improve the level of University staffs and selected 47 candidates among some 17,000 candidates.

Before looking at the daily life of a student, the question of professional schools (in particular in agriculture, construction industry, computer training) and vocational schools has to be addressed in passing. The Minister of Agriculture, Forestry and Fisheries, Estanislau da Silva, who completed his university education in Australia, got his main backing in education in one of the only two Catholic Agriculture Schools in the eastern part of the country.

DAILY LIFE OF A TIMORESE STUDENT

João, the 11-year-old adoptive son of a Timorese businessman called Benjamin to protect his identity, is a rather lucky and intelligent young boy of Dili who is really an ideal companion for his divorced father. João knows many things including politics, an unknown topic even for most of his high-class classmates. He is a student in his last year of primary school at one of the most prestigious school of East Timor, the Portuguese School of the capital. The lady director is a classmate of the Prime Minister Alkatiri, so she explained kindly to the author that in fact it is not difficult to have a meeting concerning education with the General Secretary of the ruling Fretilin Party. For me, it is a currently a taboo topic for many reasons, even if, before 2006, I had the great privilege to meet the minister of education and his deputy several times.

After taking a rather early lunch, around 11:30 (generally "Portuguese" lunch is taken at a much later time), at 12:30 Benjamin drives his son to the school.

There is no convenient transport facility in the residential suburb where Benjamin and his son live. Most of the students walk, sometimes hours in remote places, to reach their school.

Every day, at 1 P.M. João starts his class. There are many holidays in the new country, and most of the schools are closed on Saturdays and Sundays.

João attends various classes. Portuguese language is evidently a priority in his school. I was particularly impressed by the high capacity of a mathematics female teacher who is also teaching methodology, and important topics for upgrading the capacity of each student.

All teachers at this school are fully graduated. They willingly want to help the Timorese. This elite school successfully fulfils one of the government objectives, the implementation of Portuguese in the level of primary education and will in some years probably reach the preuniversity level. Each year a new upper class is open. João will probably be able to get his Portuguese School Leaving Certificate in his own school, enabling him to study in Portugal.

At 6 P.M. the school closes. João returns home where he conscientiously does his homework under the diligent supervision of his father. Many parents are poor and have no time and capacity to supervise the education of their children; their level of education is often low. How could they improve the education of their children with a low level of education themselves?

At 8 P.M. and sometimes later, João takes his dinner with his adoptive father; they speak in Portuguese. The female servant and the family of the door-keeper use Tetum that the boy also masters. João studies English at school and speaks it rather correctly, so compared to other young Timorese students he is lucky. After watching TV and during the meals he exchanges ideas with his father who feels lonely after his divorce and loss of fortune. This does not undermine the fact that João is a privileged young Timorese. Around 10 P.M. he goes to bed and in the morning he gets up around 7 A.M. After his breakfast he continues his homework.

CURRENT EVOLUTION OF THE EDUCATION IN THE NEW COUNTRY

There is a great global interest on East Timor education among in particular, the donor countries, the United Nations, the World Bank, UNICEF, UNESCO, and many NGOs. Is it enough? What about a new Teachers College in Dili?

Numerous problems cannot be addressed in a short chapter, but the peaceful demonstration that occurred in the capital in 2005 gives some light to understand the complex linked questions of education and development, key elements in state-building.

A Peaceful Demonstration: April–May 2005

In the 19th century Macau ruled the province of Portuguese Timor and the Catholic Church had already an essential role as confirmed by numerous interviews of the author between 1995 and 2004, with Teixeira (1974) who wrote one hundred books on Macau and Timor, and Padre Francisco Fernandes (1936–2005), a national hero of Timor Leste. It was far from enough to help the Timorese to reach development in education and this was one of the reasons that led to many rebellions. Smythe's book on East Timor politics and religion (2004) carries concrete lessons concerning the challenges of the Catholic Church in the 20th century. In a former Portuguese colony where in the Census of 1971, only 25 percent of the population was Catholic, no present and future Timorese government could ignore the essential role of the Church in a country badly handicapped by the low level of education (*Decolonization*, 1976). We are in a new millennium and the opposition between Fretilin, the ruling party, and the Church is a crucial education issue in a new State where more than 90 percent of the people are Catholic. The publication of a pastoral note on February 25, 2005 (Ricardo, 2005), marked the beginning of the confrontation between the Church and the Government concerning religious education. This question goes further than religious education. The current structures of the country are not strong enough yet and State building is still in its infancy even if the Constitution gives a coherent framework to a slow development of the education system. The prime minister Ramos-Horta (now elected president) and the bishops did their best to solve this crisis between July 2006 and the elections in 2007. There is separation between church and state but "the State shall recognize and respect the different religious denominations, which are free in their organization and in the exercise of their own activities, to take place in due observance of the Constitution and the law . . . different religious denominations that contribute to the well-being of the people of East Timor" (Constitution Part I-12.1).

Finally concerning education the problem of languages will not be solved between 2007 and 2012; Portuguese, an official language with Tetum, will remain the sole language of secondary and tertiary education. Portugal, the European Union, and Brazil are not rich enough to upgrade drastically the education in the faraway independent East Timor. Tetum, the national language needs many years to be upgraded. As an example, it took more than 30 years to upgrade Tagalog in the Philippines and English is still the main language of education. The Timorese youths want Indonesian and English to be implemented as languages of education, but the political elite wants only Tetum and Portuguese.

The pattern of social movement in East Timor is modern and can be interpreted as a struggle against social inequalities. Fretilin, and its bureaucracy and its bureaucracy did not manage to solve this problem and consequently lost the presidential election—Ramos-Horta, an independent candidate was finally elected president. Mobilization is also fueled by alienated people such as veterans without pensions (there is a similar situation in Guinea Bissau, a former Portuguese colony with similar types of unrest). The May 2005 demonstration organized by the Church was partly instigated by a proposal passed on November 19, 2004 by the Ministry of Education and approved by the Council of Ministers of the government. The teaching of religion was suddenly considered optional in order "to respect liberty of belief" in a country where around 96 percent of the population is Catholic. This program was implemented in January 2005 in 32 experimental public schools in 13 districts. Two bishops declared: (1) The state receives the power from the people. Religion constitutes an important human heritage. (2) Dropping out of the religious dimension from the state was unacceptable. (3) The state's "budget arithmetic" and the life of the nation should be balanced properly. (4) Why is Portuguese an important subject in the school curriculum and not religion? Religion must be considered on the same level as other courses.

During a symposium on religious education in April 2005, the Minister of Education, Dr Armindo Maia, maintained his proposition "to make religion an optional subject in schools." On April 11, that same year, the Minister of Foreign Affairs, José Ramos-Horta, deemed the position of the Church on religious instruction as an "unwanted interference in state plans." On April 27, 2005, Prime Minister Dr Mari Alkatiri stated that "The world is made up of changes, a static world does not develop . . . The decision to end compulsory religious classes in state schools was made by the cabinet (any such change would have to be made by the cabinet)."

Between April 19 and May 9, 2005, the center of Dili was paralyzed by peaceful demonstrations which were well-controlled by the Timorese police, but for only one incident when two Portuguese were attacked by the mob.

The consequences of these events were as follows. This long demonstration showed the strength of the Catholic Church in East Timor. An ambiguous compromise was eventually agreed upon. Parents can sign a form to authorize their children not to attend religious courses.

For the Prime Minister Mari Alkatiri, this demonstration was a "war of religion to transform a legitimate decision" taken by the Legislative Assembly to introduce a modification of the educational curriculum (*Jornal Nacional Diário*, Dili, May 2005). For Bishops Dom Ricardo and Basilio the modifications planned by the government jeopardized the teaching of religion and morality. The legendary figure, Xanana Gusmão, tried to deliver a speech to the demonstrators on May 9, 2005, but the crowd refused to listen to him. The bishops finally managed to cool down the mob. Since the events of December 4, 2002, this was the first example when the public popularity of the most admired Timorese leader appeared to wane. Interestingly, just as in December 2002, the donors' conference was held two days later. As it started on April 28, 2005, this demonstration occurred at a strategic moment.

This political confrontation highlighted the progress of the police in handling demonstrations peacefully; however, a recent rash of thefts of computers, cameras, mobile telephones, and valuables in private houses in Dili points to new types of criminal activity in the capital. Outside the capital, the National Police in Bobonaro subdistrict have stopped patrolling in the summer due to lack of equipment such as vehicles. More importantly, on April 18, 2005, a police officer, Thomas da Costa, was killed in Lautem, and Kera Sakti, a member of a martial group was stabbed to death in Comoro, Dili. In July 2005, in response to this type of violence, President Xanana asked the karate associations, Kera Sakti, Korka, and Setia Hati, to cease attacks disturbing the security of the country and political peace and order of the State. Peace is a key political issue for a new nation.

It remains to be seen if the new party of L7 and other commanders of the Falintil (*União da Resistência* renamed Undertim) can build a real partnership with the Catholic Church. Bishop Ricardo confirmed his commitment to the people of Timor and expressed his viewpoint on the last sociopolitical crisis during an interview. He did not comment, however, that he might possibly back this new party. The World Bank, the United Nations, donors, and the government of East Timor have all ranked poverty high on their agendas for change, but the people want concrete actions not just media-oriented humanitarian discourses. The Bishop of Dili will continue to play a significant role in East Timor's social affairs as confirmed when he managed to supply food to the hungry in faraway southeastern districts in January 2005. In July 2005, understanding the importance of this sociopolitical issue, the government decided to take action. Minister of Agriculture Estanislau da Silva in a report delivered in July 2005, stated that 139 villages suffered food shortages. Atauro Island was mentioned. Agencies such as Oxfam tried to solve this urgent need. The Fretilin party did its best in April and May 2007 to import rice from Vietnam and send it to all districts before the presidential elections, but the people voted for Ramos-Horta (elected president on May 20, 2007) against the president of the Fretilin, Lu Olo.

The Amu (Bishop) combines theology with a genuine concern for the poor. His fluency in Portuguese and Tetum and his good knowledge of the people of Timor pale in comparison with the intellectuality of Dom Basilio do Nascimento. The English language is not significant for the Timorese except for a few young people in Dili and the educated elite. The international community according to the BBC in its program on Sunday, June 26, 2005, was particularly concerned by the Church/Fretilin confrontation. Sixty five percent of the Timorese converted from animism to Christianity in the 1980s and are still very poor. Catholicism is of central importance, and there is no sign of decline in the Church's ability to mobilize. This power is often praised by Portugal, which partly explains the official visit of the Prime Minister, who went to find support in Portugal in May 2005.

Fretilin and some foreign embassies in Dili blame the Church for the long mass mobilization in April–May 2005. More than a hundred truckloads of demonstrators came to the capital during three turbulent weeks. Five trucks full of protesters came twice from Ainaro to Dili. From Los Palos and Baucau 50 trucks in a row drove to the capital. Only in Suai and Maliana did it seem that the police had the strength to block such a movement of protestors headed from their own rural district to Dili. Bishop Ricardo considered the police intervention in these two districts as "anti-constitutional and against human rights."

According to a keen observer of Timorese society who analyzed this demonstration, it looked like ancient *Jacquerie* coming by waves from the countryside to the center of power, but this scholar never expected such a peaceful uprising, which was contrary to the report of violent demonstrations made by some high-ranking foreign officials. With the mid-2005 withdrawal of the last Australian contingent of the UN Peacekeeping Force (PKF), the only safeguarding principle for East Timor from external threat but also in emergencies from internal disturbances is partly balanced by the noninterference policy among ASEAN members. Timorese Defense and Police constitute in fact a limited dissuasive force. Furthermore, the Defense Force was never classified as an antisubversive army and using it as an additional police force was rarely considered even in December 2004.

To conclude the discussion of this 2005 sociopolitical movement, it is worth noting that Bishop Belo's political note written in Mozambique, and printed in a local newspaper and calling for a quick end to the April–May demonstration was torn away by a demonstrator before his astonished companions.

A month after they began, these events were almost forgotten. This sort of peaceful demonstration constitutes an excellent model for the future because religion could create great trouble in the present global world. Prime Minister Mari Alkatiri and his government will probably try to ease the political tension with tact and diplomacy. His recently restructured government includes 52 ministers, vice-ministers, secretaries of state, and governors. PM Alkatiri named his new cabinet on July 28, 2005. To ease tensions between the Church and government, a vice-minister of the Department of Education, Rosária Corte-Real, was designated to assist the Minister of Education, Armindo Maia.

Shops in the center of Dili were closed in April–May for the first time since the events following the 1999 Referendum. The economic activity of an important part of the city was paralyzed during that April–May period. For the East Timor economy, already weak, such a long shutdown had a negative impact.

The country has recently undertaken considerable effort to promote tourism, which could become a financial resource for the economy, but this goal, already launched unsuccessfully by the United Nations is still far off and upgrading the education system will certainly help. The *New York Times* has noticed the country's interest in tourism as a potential source of development monies; however, achieving harmony between the government and the Church continues to be an essential factor in stabilizing Timorese society and upgrading the education system.

CONCLUSION

For East Timor, strengthening of public institutions of education and local capacity of the teachers remains critical. The idea to create a high standard Teachers College is an essential point. The question of professional schools (in particular in agriculture, construction industry, computer training) and vocational schools has also to be addressed by the Government of East Timor and the Donors.

A cooperation of all sorts of institutions, including the Catholic Church (at present around 95 percent of the East Timorese are Catholic), which has a teaching history of 500 years in the region, being the main former educational institution

The Minister of Education, Armindo Maia (center), trying to convince a
mob of youths who wanted to invade his ministry at Dili in June 2006.
Courtesy of J.A. Berlie.

at the extreme end of Portugal's empire. Portugal needs the constant support of
the European Union to develop education in East Timor, and the cooperation of
Brazil continues to be essential to improve Timor's ability to develop its own
system. There is a shortage of staff in this educational sector. Education is
particularly vulnerable in rural and remote areas where teachers do not want to go.

The great interest of the United Nations, the World Bank, UNICEF,
UNESCO, and many NGOs concerning education in the newest country is a
necessary but not sufficient condition of success.

REFERENCES

Caritas Australia (n.d.). Annual report 03/04, accessed on February 22, 2007 from
    www.caritas.org.au/education/easttimor.
Decolonization in East Timor (1976). N.p.: The Department of Foreign Affairs, Republic
    of Indonesia, August.
The Encyclopedia Brittanica 2005 (2005).
Hicks, David (1976). *Eastern Timorese Society. Tetum Ghosts and Kin: Fieldwork in an
    Indonesian Community*, reprinted 2004. Palo Alto, CA: Mayfield.
Ricardo da Silva, Alberto and Basilio do Nascimento (2005). "Nota Pastoral: Dos Bispos
    Católicos de Timor-Leste sobre o Ensino da Religião nas Escolas Públicas (Pastoral
    note: Two Catholic bishops on the teaching of religion in public schools)," in
    Jornal Nacional Semanário, February 25, 4–5.
Smythe, Patrick A. (2004) *"The Heavy Blow"—The Catholic Church and the East Timor
    Issue.* Munster: Lit Verlag.
Teixeira, Manuel (1974). (1913–2004). *Macau e a sua Diocese: Missóes de Timor* (Macau
    and its Diocese. Catholic Mission in Timor), p. 593. Macau: Missão do Padroado.
UNICEF (2005). Report accessed on April 18, 2005 from www.unicef.com.au/mediaCentre.

Chapter 18

SCHOOLING IN VIETNAM

Jonathan D. London

What is the relation between schooling, state formation, and processes of state transformation associated with the erosion of state socialism and its replacement with new institutional forms? Such a question, while historical and sociological in nature, is not merely of academic interest. For in any society, processes of state formation and transformation play a crucial role in determining the qualities, costs, and distributions of formal schooling and, in so doing, profoundly affect patterns of social change within and beyond the sphere of education.

Questions about schooling and the state are particularly interesting with respect to contemporary Vietnam, where a communist party that rose to power on the basis of anticolonial struggle and socialist revolution, and which pursued development on the basis of state socialism for 35 years, now presides over a rapidly growing market economy that is increasingly enmeshed with the institutions and processes of global capitalism.

In this chapter I examine formal schooling in contemporary Vietnam from an historical perspective and in relation to the formation and transformation of Vietnam's state. I focus my attention on primary and secondary schooling and explain their development in relation to continuity and change in Vietnam's political and economic institutions. I am particularly interested in explaining the principles and institutions governing access to formal schooling under the rule of the Communist Party of Vietnam (CPV), which has held power in the north of Vietnam since the early 1950s and the whole of Vietnam since 1975. I am especially interested in theorizing patterns of institutionalized inequality in Vietnam's education system under the CPV.

The perspective I adopt in this chapter is a political sociological one. It appreciates the practical contributions schooling makes to skills-formation, economic growth, and the promotion of social welfare. It also, however, views formal schooling as part of a larger human resource complex, which the state designs and uses to secure vital state imperatives.[1] These imperatives include the need to promote economic accumulation and social welfare, but also the need to maintain social order and to promote subjective legitimacy and consent.

This is not a reductionist perspective. The social forces governing the selection, conduct, and institutionalized outcomes of education policies are extremely complex and historically contingent. Viewed most broadly, they are determined through the mutually constitutive and competitive relationship between state and society. State–society relations are mutually constitutive in that the state is a socially constituted product of broader social relations, functions to govern and shape social life, but in so doing is continuously subject to society's influences and limits. State–society relations are competitive, in that they involve struggles over the control and use of valued resources. Ultimately, state–society relations determine the content of state policies, the manner in which state policies, once decided upon, are actually carried out and the institutionalized outcomes of those policies. But explaining these processes and the mechanisms involved requires more concrete historical analysis.

States craft and implement education policies, but they do so in established institutional contexts that shape and limit state power. The premise of this chapter is that to explain continuity and change in the principles and institutions governing education and formal schooling in Vietnam requires an analysis of processes of state formation and transformation in relation to continuity and change in that country's political and economic institutions.

Correspondingly, the discussion is organized in three sections. In the first section I examine the development of formal schooling in Vietnam up until the late 1980s. In it, I show how the expansion of formal schooling in Vietnam during the 1950s, 1960s, and 1970s went hand in hand with processes of state formation. In Vietnam, state formation involved the imposition of a revolutionary state socialist institutional template that was designed to regulate all aspects of society. Under state socialism, the formal principles governing education and schooling were quasi-universalist, in that they were designed to eventually ensure access to formal K–12 education as a right of citizenship, but actually promoted and reproduced inequalities characteristic of other state-socialist societies. Of course, process of state formation and educational development in Vietnam also took place in the context of national partition, international and civil war, and an overwhelming scarcity of resources. I examine patterns of schooling under Vietnamese state socialism and explain how war and the poor performance of state socialist economic institutions limited the ability of the state to achieve its universalist goals. I also explain how the erosion of state socialist economic institutions over the course of the 1980s undermined state goals and generated large gaps between the formal principles and institutions governing formal schooling and the actual institutionalized outcomes of education policies.

The second section examines developments in Vietnam's education system in the market reform era and since 1989 in particular. Vietnam's transition to a market economy involved fundamental changes in the country's economic institutions, but also in the principles and institutions governing education and access to schooling. I show that, in many respects, developments in Vietnam's education system since 1989 have been encouraging: economic growth has permitted continuous increases in education spending and enrollments have risen continuously at all levels, both absolutely and in proportion to the population. As I demonstrate, however, the development of Vietnam's education system, though viewed as a "success story" by the CPV and international development organizations, has also generated new tensions and contradictions between the CPV's professed ideologies and the actual institutionalized features of education and schooling. Of specific concern are emerging inequalities in the education system, which are in large part the product of state policies and their unintended consequences.

In the final section, I reflect on recent developments in the education sector from the perspective of inequality, social class, and the state. I argue that the changing class configuration of Vietnam is an outgrowth of specific accumulation strategies pursued by the state. These emerging class inequalities have propelled income inequality, which tend to reinforce institutionalized inequalities in formal schooling. To conclude that the CPV has completely abandoned redistributive principles is clearly inaccurate, however. Over the last 10 years, the CPV has sought to address emerging inequalities of access to schooling by way of safety-nets programs. I examine these initiatives and assess their efficacy.

When CPV rose to power in the 1940s and 1950s, it formed a new state and instituted specific formal institutional arrangements to govern politics, the economy, and education. Gradually, due to war and the poor performance of state socialist economic institutions, functional incompatibilities emerged between state education goals and the actual performance of the state socialist institutions on which education and schooling depended. The crisis of state socialism that Vietnam experienced in the late 1980s required the CPV to fix its political rule to new strategies of economic accumulation. The transition to a market economy involved the development of a new "education regime," under which the state provides a floor of basic educational services, while education beyond this basic floor is contingent on out-of-pocket payments by households.

Overall, Vietnam's transition to a market economy and the growth associated with it has benefited the country and its education system in numerous ways. It has also, however, injected pernicious market principles into the shell of nominally public schools. This, in turn, has generated institutionalized inequalities whose durability and intensification over nearly two decades raises fresh questions about the interests and indeed the class character of the CPV and its avowedly socialist state.

FORMAL SCHOOLING UNTIL 1989:
THE RISE AND DEMISE OF UNIVERSALISM

To understand education and schooling in contemporary Vietnam requires an appreciation of its historical antecedents. I discuss these historical antecedents first by way of an overview of formal schooling in the long period leading up to the CPV's rise of power. The main focus of this section, however, is the development of schooling under Vietnamese state socialism, a period running from the early 1950s in the north, and from 1975 on a national scale, up until the late 1980s, when core institutions of state socialism and state socialist education policy unraveled in a fiscal crisis.

Historical Antecedents: Idealized Cultural Values vs. Historical Patterns

Vietnam has a Confucian cultural heritage. Formal education, learning, and academic and intellectual achievement have been regarded for thousands of years to be among the noblest human pursuits. The actual social history of formal education and schooling in Vietnam is another matter. Until very recently, formal schooling in Vietnam was an opportunity for a privileged few. In what follows, I provide a brief historical overview of the principles and institutions governing formal schooling during Vietnam's long period of dynastic feudalism and during the subsequent period of French colonialism. Macrohistorical antecedents are not my primary concern, and are therefore discussed in the briefest possible terms. Be that as it may, an appreciation of these historical antecedents permits a fuller understanding of formal schooling in the contemporary context.

Education and formal schooling are closely linked to Vietnam's Confucian heritage. Education has and continues to be viewed not simply or even primarily as a means for personal pursuits, but also requisite for the inculcation of wisdom and rectitude. However, through centuries of dynastic rule and feudalistic class relations, formal education remained beyond the reach of all but a tiny minority. Vietnam's rich Confucian heritage must not be confused with "education for all." While village schools were an important institution in dynastic-feudal Vietnam, such schools never approximated a coherent formal system of schooling.

Opportunity structures within Vietnam's education system have a longstanding relation to the country's political institutions. As Alexander Woodside (2006) has recently pointed out, the competitive examination system that existed in Vietnam and funneled qualified subjects into its mandarinate amounted to a "meritocratic" and formally rational system of bureaucratic recruitment and preceded the development of similar arrangements in Europe by several centuries.[2]

French colonialism altered but did not radically transform Vietnam's education system, as the goals of formal schooling under French colonialism ran subordinate to the interests of colonial domination and exploitation. Despite the establishment of new primary schools in some areas, the operation of informal or autonomous schools was generally prohibited. Formal schooling remained the privilege of a relatively small minority, while the content of the education served the interests of empire. Schools provided training tailored to the needs and functions of the colonial bureaucracy. As late as the 1940s, Vietnam featured only three high schools, in Hà Nội, Huế, and Sai Gòn.

Although the development of formal education under French colonialism was limited, formal education played an important role in determining opportunity structures under the French colonial regime. Positions in that colonial bureaucracy were limited, however. Some Vietnamese who failed to gain such positions grew increasingly disaffected and traveled overseas for training and to develop the anti-colonial movement. One such individual was Nguyen Ai Quoc, who later took the name Ho Chi Minh.

Vietnam went through a period of lively intellectual debate and increasing political ferment during the 19th and early 20th centuries.[3] For the anticolonial-ists and broader segments of Vietnam's population, education and schooling were perceived as clear instances of colonial oppression. Calls to expand education and schooling were rallying cries from the very beginning of the anticolonial and proindependence struggles. While the Workers Party (later renamed as the CPV), established in 1929, was certainly not the first to integrate education and school-ing into its political platform, it consistently linked the country's colonial exploita-tion to the French authorities' restrictive education policies. The party criticized the French denial of education to Vietnam's masses, calling it a deliberate strategy of promoting ignorance (*ngu dân*), and therefore dependence and submission.

For the centuries of social history that preceded the rise of the CPV, the principles and institutions governing education in Vietnam produced conditions under which education, though accorded great respect, was available to a small minority of the population. French colonialism transformed Vietnam, but limited the growth of its education system at a time when Vietnamese were beginning to recognize the necessity of mass education. The revolutionary politics of the Workers Party recognized this from the beginning, and when it declared independence in 1945, it had ambitious ideas about the future of education and formal schooling in Vietnam.

Revolutionary Ruptures and the Principles and Practices of Socialist Universalism

The rise of the CPV in the 1940s owed to an alliance between a small cosmopolitan and radicalized intelligentsia on the one hand, and peasants and proletarians mobilized under the banner of self-determination and emancipation on the other. This class alliance, infused with nationalist and Leninist ideologies, created the conditions for the defeat of the French and, after 1954, the devel-opment of an independent state, the Democratic Republic of Vietnam (DRV).

The DRV was a bureaucratic-authoritarian and revolutionary state founded on the principles of social justice, coercive-collectivist economic organization, and quasi-egalitarian social welfare institutions that promised universal access to state-funded social services as rights of citizenship. Crucially, the development of the DRV involved the establishment and imposition of a new template of formal institutions. This template included political and administrative institutions, eco-nomic institutions, and new fiscal arrangements. After 1975, the CPV extended this institutional template to the southern half of the country.

The development of formal schooling in Vietnam during the 1950s, 1960s, and 1970s thus coincided with this process of extensive state formation under the CPV's leadership. This was a period characterized by revolutionary politics, rapid institutional change, war and large-scale wartime social mobilizations. Viewed historically, however, the 1950s and 1960s represented a particularly radical turning point in the history for formal schooling in Vietnam, as the CPV promoted formal schooling on a mass scale.

As I illustrate, however, the development of state socialism in Vietnam as in other socialist states did not go according to plan. The formal institutions of state socialism generated new class tensions and new contradictions, and these were visible in the institutionalized outcomes of education policies. After the war, Vietnam experienced extensive developments in that the geographic coverage of the system expanded rapidly, while sharp limitations remained on the quality of schooling, due in large part to the severe economic constraints the country faced during the period.

The Political Economy of State Socialism in Vietnam

The state socialist development model the CPV pursued until the late 1980s was designed to achieve rapid industrialization. By promoting a dual economy where agriculture would feed industry, the strategy was designed to avoid the perceived traps of dependent capitalist development. Although the collectivization of agriculture showed promising results in the early stages, the full implementation of the Vietnamese state socialist development strategy was retarded and distorted by ever-pressing military and strategic demands. The poor performance of state socialist economic institutions combined with systemic flaws of central planning and a prevailing poverty of resources undermined the aims of state socialism.

Politically, state socialism rested on bureaucratic-authoritarian control. In principle, this was "democratic centralism," whereby the state machinery would work as a conveyor belt to bring the masses' concerns to the political center. In effect, the political institutions of state socialism were designed to control and govern all facets of social life, from politics and the economy to culture.[4] In times of war, this system proved useful for the purposes of mass mobilization and to reinforce the political authority of the CPV. In wartime northern Vietnam, the CPV did indeed gain broad popular support as it was viewed as the champion of national self-determination and a more just social order. After the war, in southern Vietnam, political support for the Party was more fragile. As we will see, this hampered efforts to implement state socialism in the postwar context.[5]

In the economic sphere, the state socialist regime's most important components were the coercive collectivization of all economic activity and the subordination of those activities to the institutions of central planning. In so doing, the state sought to boost production in all spheres, accumulate surplus savings from agriculture, and use these savings to invest in heavy industry and infrastructure, to lower the wage and food bills of state officials and urban workers, and to finance the provision of social services, such as public health and education. There was, however, a clear dualism in the system, as agriculture and with it rural populations' livelihoods were subordinate to the development of industry and the material interests of state officials and workers in cities. In rural areas, agricultural collectives were expected to finance the operation of social services, including education, whereas in urban areas funds for education were transferred to localities from the central budget.

The economic outcomes of Vietnamese state socialism were correspondingly uneven. The collectivization of agriculture provided economic security to scores of previously landless peasants and boosted agricultural production in northern Vietnam in the late 1950s and 1960s. But, over the long haul, both agricultural and industrial policies failed to produce the promised outcomes. Decades of war were massively destructive and inevitably contributed to Vietnam's poverty, and the political and economic blockade imposed on Vietnam for 15 years by China and the United States only made matters worse. But poorly integrated and poorly performing state socialist economic institutions were, in and of themselves, a great contributor to Vietnam's continued poverty in the 1980s.[6]

In essence, the state socialist regime was a *dualist* regime that subordinated and exploited the agrarian population for the advancement of industrialization.[7] Though inspired by principles of egalitarianism, state socialism promoted its own form of inequality and unequal citizenship. The functioning of the Vietnam's political and economic institutions ensured party members and state managers privileged access to scarce resources. Before 1975 in the north, and after 1975 in the south, Vietnamese with "suspect" class backgrounds or affiliations were routinely subject to political, economic, and social exclusion and were denied equal treatment. Clearly, the CPV's political and economic policies achieved significant redistribution of land and capital in what had been a vastly inegalitarian society. Yet, to view the CPV as a timeless champion of social equality—the starting point for many contemporary analyses—is to vastly oversimplify the party's mixed record.

Formal Principles and Institutions of Education under State Socialism

That the formation of Vietnam's mass education developed as quickly as it did in the context of a war of national independence and amid severe poverty and scarcity is a testament to the determination and mobilizational capacities of the Communist leadership and the sheer enthusiasm for education of Vietnam's population. The expansion of formal education in Vietnam in the 1950s and 1960s was indeed undertaken with revolutionary fervor. Education policies during this period appeared to embody the class interests of the newly forming and broad based revolutionary state. That these "objective" class interests contained their own internal contradictions became apparent with the development of state socialism.

Under the CPV, Vietnam completed a transition from centuries of exclusionary, elitist educational institutions to a mass education system designed to improve literacy and eventually create a foundation for socialist development. During this period, the scale of formal schooling in Vietnam experienced remarkable growth.

Under dynastic feudalism and French colonial domination, formal schooling in Vietnam was accessible only to a tiny minority. By contrast, the CPV promoted mass education, and eventually made access to K–12 education a right of citizenship.[8] In the 1940s and 1950s, the CPV pursued mass education largely through literacy campaigns.[9] In the 1950s, the new DRV state undertook concerted efforts to build a comprehensive formal education system in northern Vietnam. This was a massive task that required the recruitment and training of hundreds and thousands of teachers and the development of new administrative institutions. The distinctiveness of mass education in Vietnam under state socialism lay in the formal principles and institutions governing education finance.

During the period of state socialism, the state (formally) assumed all costs of education provision. As indicated, in rural areas schools were funded on the basis of resources from local economic units (principally agricultural collectives) and transfers from the central budget (mostly for infrastructure and, less so, to supplement teachers' wages). In urban areas, schools were financed by transfers from the local and central budgets. As such, schools in rural areas had a greater dependence on the performance of local economic institutions.

Another important formal principle governing education under state socialism was its high degree of centralized organization. In theory, if not in practice, the Ministry of Education (later the Ministry of Education and Training) established all budgetary, administrative, and pedagogical norms.[10] In Vietnam today, institutions of governance in the education sector have grown increasingly decentralized, a consequential difference to which I will return later in this chapter.

Institutionalized Outcomes: Patterns of Formal Schooling under State Socialism

Viewed in terms of enrollments, the history of formal schooling in Vietnam under state socialism followed a trajectory of rapid expansion during the 1950s and 1960s, slow growth and postwar expansion in the 1970s, and stagnation and crisis in the mid- to late-1980s.

During the late 1940s and 1950s, the CPV expanded the scale of formal schooling, building on the pre-existing patchwork of informal village schools and the smaller number of colonial schools. By 1957, the number of primary school students in northern Vietnam *alone* was three times the number of primary students in the entire country in 1939. In 1939, only 2 percent of primary school students advanced to higher educational levels. By 1957, this figure had risen to 13 percent (Pham, 1999: 51). Massive dislocations that accompanied the onset of U.S. bombing in northern Vietnam in 1965 did not throw the education system into turmoil. On the contrary, the urgency associated with the war effort created conditions for more effective mass mobilization and the scale of formal schooling actually expanded.[11] Urban schools destroyed by U.S. bombs were rebuilt in the countryside, where they were less vulnerable to attack.[12] Between

1965 and 1975, gross enrollments in northern Vietnam saw increases at all levels, as did staffing levels (MOET, 1995a: 7–8).

After 1975, under the banner of the new and unified Socialist Republic of Vietnam, the CPV implemented education policies that aimed to ensure access to K–12 education for all Vietnamese and to expand the country's higher education in the service of socialist industrialization. According to official statistics, Vietnam continued to achieve important gains in terms of accessibility to formal schooling.[13] By the mid-1980s, education indicators were comparable to countries with income levels 10 times that of Vietnam's.

As impressive as these statistics appeared, official statistics on ebbs and flows in enrollment figures leave much concealed and are inadequate metrics for grasping the realities of schooling during the state socialist period. State statistics and official documents did not call attention to prevailing inequalities in the spatial distribution of education provision across regions, the limited scope and quality of schooling, or access to education among different population segments. Of course, spatially uneven development is a feature of social life in any society. My point is simply to note differences between the ideals underpinning education policies and those policies' actual institutionalized outcomes.

Three points warrant particular emphasis. First, the combined effects of wars, prolonged economic isolation, and the poor performance of state socialist economic institutions severely constrained the scope and quality of formal schooling. In most rural areas, going to school consisted of three hours of studies in dirt-floored thatched huts. Second, while education policies were progressive in principle—and were indeed more egalitarian than policies pursued in many other societies, they also promoted and reinforced inequality by conferring greater access to better services for urban dwellers over rural ones and, even more pronouncedly, to those with party ties.[14] Finally, after 1975, significant segments of southern Vietnam faced exclusionary practices on the basis of their families' past political allegiances. There is an abundance of anecdotal evidence that families and entire villages with past ties to the Republic of Vietnam regime were denied access to schooling.

From a class perspective, the education system that developed under the state socialist regime displayed clear cleavages, both with respect to the question of access to educational opportunities and to the quality of formal education. It subordinated the countryside to the city while creating privileged strata of state functionaries. Within this broad structural relation, a class hierarchy existed in which members of the nomenclature and state-affiliated populations enjoyed relatively privileged access to educational opportunities. Urban residents had comparatively good access to schooling, while rural populations enjoyed considerably less. Ethnic minority groups, comprising some 15 percent of the population, experienced varying degrees of exclusion due to their settlement in remote areas, as well as linguistic differences and the paltry amount of state resources committed to their education compared to their needs. Finally, in the post-American War context, Vietnam exhibited a political underclass of those with historical ties to the fallen Republic of Vietnam, and who were systematically denied educational opportunities beyond a certain level.

Formal Schooling and the Demise of State Socialist Universalism

Indicators of progress regarding the extension of formal schooling during the mid-1980s masked the fragility of the state socialist economic institutions on which formal schooling. During the late 1980s, the institutional arrangements responsible for financing education in Vietnam gradually disintegrated as the planned economy unraveled.[15] The results were devastating. Between 1980 and 1990, Vietnam registered only a minor increase in its gross enrollment, even though the country gained millions more school-age children. By end of the decade, dropout rates soared, particularly at the secondary level of education. The causes and consequences of these developments are discussed later.

Vietnam's transition to a market economy was a 10-year process of institutional decay whereby the core institutions of state socialism gradually lost their force, threatening the coherence of the economy and the survival of the state. After 1975, war-damage, international isolation, and a severe poverty of resources undermined the viability of state socialist developmentalism. But the mechanism that unraveled the state socialist economy lay at the microfoundations of the economy where, in all sectors, there were economic producers' grassroots deviates from the dictates of central planning.[16]

In principle, all economic actors in a planned economy, from agricultural producers to state-owned industrial enterprises, produce to boost economic accumulation and advance the political and economic causes of the state. Yet, by the 1980s, responding to conditions of extreme poverty and to incentives in a poorly integrated economy, economic producers (including state-owned enterprises) adopted increasingly brazen survival strategies that contravened formal state procedures and rules. The central government sought to contain these "spontaneous" reforms by introducing successive rounds of top-down reforms designed to control, limit, and steer change processes that were already occurring.

Economic reforms toward the late 1980s, such as output-contracts in agriculture and new trade laws for state-owned enterprises, boosted economic outputs by allowing economic producers to engage in market exchange. These post hoc reforms improved economic incentives. But this limited liberalization also had the effect of diverting economic resources from the central budget, and thus undercut the financial bases of state functions, including education. Politically, the gradual disintegration of the planned economy and its fiscal institutions weakened the powers of the central state vis-à-vis the localities and compromised the central state's fiscal integrity, resulting in a prolonged fiscal crisis that ended only with the abandonment of core state socialist institutions.

Locally, the disintegration of state socialist economic institutions meant the demise of collectivist arrangements set in place to finance formal schooling. This would prove especially damaging to schooling in rural areas. As the 1980s wore on, the gradual dissolution of agricultural collectives gathered pace. The already paltry amount of local resources available for schooling declined precipitously.

In economic terms and with respect to living standards, the shift to household production in agriculture and the expansion of markets provided direct and immediate relief. For education and other public services, there would be no short-term relief. With the hyperinflation and evaporating state budgets of the late 1980s, national and local investments in education fell sharply in real terms. Education sector workers faced declining wages from an already low base. In many, especially rural, areas, teachers went for months without compensation, and teachers across the country expanded their economic activities outside of the school. Across the country, the quality of education deteriorated as the flow of resources into the education system dwindled. Morale among teachers also declined and many left teaching altogether in search of a living wage.

Under state socialism, the CPV-led state realized many important gains in education and did so in the face of overwhelming challenges. But by 1989, Vietnam's 35-year experiment with state socialism came to an unexpected conclusion. The withering of state socialist economic institutions necessitated a reworking of the financial and fiscal basis of formal schooling. In 1989, the CPV took its first step away from the universalist principles that had guided education policies since the 1950s, when the (rubber-stamp) National Assembly met in a special session to pass a constitutional amendment permitting the state to charge school fees. Whether sharp declines in enrollment at the time predated or were exacerbated by the introduction of fees is the subject of some debate. What is clear is that enrollment rates fell sharply while dropout rates soared. Between 1989 and 1991, dropouts increased dramatically by up to 80 percent in secondary schools in some areas, while nationally, new enrollments declined sharply and would not reach 1985 levels until the mid-1990s.

STATE TRANSFORMATION AND SCHOOLING UNDER
A MARKET-LENINIST REGIME

Since the end of the 1980s Vietnam has developed a market-Leninist welfare regime that, alongside its bureaucratic-authoritarian political institutions, exhibits the economic institutions of a state-dominated market economy. In the sphere of social policy, this welfare market regime offers a basic floor of social services but demands large-scale out-of-pocket payments from service users. With images of Marx and Lenin adorning school teachers' offices but access to education on a pay-as-you go basis, the CPV's ideology, its policies, and their outcomes are a strange and often contradictory amalgam of Leninist and neoliberal principles.

Clearly, Vietnam's rapid growth has permitted increases in the scale and accessibility of formal schooling. But economic growth has been accompanied by fundamental changes in the principles and institutions governing education and other formerly nominally public services. Understanding the scope, significance, and limits of the improvements in formal schooling since the early 1990s requires an appreciation of Vietnam's political and economic institutions during this period, continuity and chance in the formal principles governing education, and outcomes of these policies nationally and at the grassroots.

Political and Economic Institutions of Market Leninism

Vietnam's transition to a more market-oriented economy has entailed important changes in its economic institutions and less dramatic, though still significant, changes in its political and administrative institutions. Politically, however, Vietnam's experience contradicts the conventional liberal assumption that the transition from central planning to a market economy entails a decline in the political and economic power of the state, and the central government in particular. In Vietnam, the state has used the expansion of the economy (and especially foreign trade) to strengthen its revenue base. Though the fiscal crisis of the middle and late 1980s did test the CPV's political command, the command of the Party today is arguably stronger than ever.

Substantively, however, it is changes in the economy that have been most consequential for schooling. Over the course of the 1990s, Vietnam developed an economy comprised of a combination of household-based agriculture, state oligopolies in industry and trade, and a lively small-scale services sector. State-owned enterprises remain the most important players in the domestic economy, and they have partnered with foreign investors to produce for both the domestic and foreign markets.

Spatially, industrialization has been concentrated in and around Ho Chi Minh City and Ha Noi, boosting local revenues of provinces and municipal authorities in those areas. While there have been quite significant transfers of economic resources from wealthy provinces to the central government for redistribution, provinces with high revenues enjoy residual claimancy status in that they have been entitled to retain control over revenues in excess of central state targets (World Bank, 1996a; Socialist Republic of Vietnam and World Bank, 2005).[17] The essential spatial duality of Vietnam's economy has remained: the country has seen high growth in a few provinces, but quite slow growth in many others. In poor areas of the country, growth in household earnings has lagged far behind and economic change has transpired at a much slower pace, and local authorities rely heavily on the central budget for the lion's share of their revenue. The agglomeration of economic activities, facilitated by patterns of state investment, has contributed to the generation, reproduction, and intensification of regional inequalities, which are visible in the education sector, as we will see.

Formal Principles and Institutions of Education under Market Leninism

The collapse of state socialism required Vietnam's state to reconstitute state-society relations on the basis of new economic institutions. It occasioned a reconstitution of the social contract. Prior to 1989, mass education policies in Vietnam had sought to ensure access to K–12 education as a right of citizenship. Since 1989, and especially since the early 1990s, the thrust of Vietnam's mass education policies has been to provide a basic floor of education services through a free primary school education, while promoting a "cost-sharing" regime at most other levels of schooling, effectively shifting the financial burden of education provision from the state onto individual households. In the 1992 constitution, access to K–12 education was no longer described as a right of citizenship.

In terms of principles, perhaps the most important change is associated with the party line on *socialization*. Socialization (*xã hội hóa*) is an oddity, lying somewhere between an institutionalized rhetorical refrain and official doctrine. Its starting point is the assertion that, in the "post-subsidy period" (*hậu thời kỳ bao cấp*), the state cannot provide for all needs and therefore the state must encourage and create conditions for "all segments of society" to contribute to the provision of education. Socialization, then, sounds a note of communalism. Through some discussions with Party members in Hanoi, I have come to believe there is some substance to socialization, after having initially dismissed it as privatization by another name. Of course, not everyone in Vietnam is a Hanoi policy intellectual and "socialization" is interpreted and acted upon by different individuals and organizations in different ways. Indeed, while socialization is often discussed as a bottom-up and top-down strategy for mobilizing societal resources, its basic effect in education has been to shift an increasing share of the costs of schooling onto households. In this sense, socialization in Vietnam carries a meaning precisely opposite of the term's most widely understood meaning in "the West," where socialization refers to a process whereby the state assumes financial responsibility for certain services.

Two practical effects of socialization are particularly noteworthy. First, since 1989, fees for schooling have expanded continuously so that an average household can expect to pay five or six different types of school fees, in addition to other expenses discussed later.[18] As a result, tuition fees have become a significant expenditure for households.[19] A second important effect of socialization is the state's decision to permit and promote "semi-public" and "non-state" (i.e., private) provision of non-primary education and to promote a new and rather odd type of student—the "semi-public student." These components of socialization reduce financial burdens on the state while increasing burdens on certain households. Resolution 90 of the National Assembly, which was adopted in 1993, introduced a full set of rules permitting the foundation of nonstate school forms, including semipublic (*ban cong*) schools, semipublic classes within public schools, and people-founded (*dan lap*) private schools.[20] Semipublic schools and classes are partially subsidized through the state budget, but students have to pay three to four times more than public students. In practice, this is a blueprint for a two-tiered dualist education system.

Institutionalized Outcomes: Patterns of Schooling under Market Leninism

Vietnam's economic growth over the last two decades has permitted continuous expansion in the scale and scope of schooling. Rapid economic growth has enabled continuous growth in total spending (i.e., state and nonstate) on education, including substantial investments in infrastructure and establishment of schools in previously underserved areas. As a result, Vietnam is approaching universal provision of primary education, something striven for but not achieved under state socialism, when it was a significantly poorer country. Gross and net enrollments in primary schools, and lower and upper secondary schools have increased dramatically since the early 1990s. Vietnamese today enjoy wider access to formal schooling than at any time in the country's history.

With a single-minded focus on qualitative indicators of progress, one misses some of the most important problems, tensions, and contradictions in Vietnam's education system. These include unevenness in the accessibility and quality of education across regions and population segments, inequalities within the education system owing to state policies and their intended and unintended effects, and the general movement toward an education system in which opportunities are increasingly contingent on households' ability to mount increasingly large out-of-pocket expenditures. Some of these problems can be observed in data on enrollment and patterns of education finance. What aggregated data fail to capture are the actually institutionalized features, or the "institutionalized rules," governing schooling at the grassroots.

Enrollments

After declining in the late 1980s and early 1990s, school enrollment in Vietnam has since expanded continuously at all levels. The most rapid expansions occurred during the mid-1990s, but the upward trend has continued since, with especially notable improvements at the lower secondary level. Upper secondary education has grown at a slower pace, partly, as we shall see, because it involves significant household expenses.

Between 1994 and 2003, net primary school enrollment increased from 91.4 to 97.5 percent. Dropout rates at the primary level have declined markedly.[21] Enrollment gains are significantly due, in part, to investments in infrastructure, such as the construction of new classrooms and schoolhouses, as well as roads, bridges, and improvements in transport, all of which have made schools more accessible in spatial terms. Triple-shift schools—where classes were offered three times a day due to space constraints—have been virtually eliminated (World Bank, 2004). Large gaps that previously existed in enrollment rates between rural and urban areas have declined at the primary and lower secondary levels.

There remain problems with respect to primary schooling. The poorest segments of society have not been effectively integrated. According to the World Bank (2004), almost half the 10 percent of children not attending primary school came from ethnic minority groups. In 1998, 82 percent of children from the lowest expenditure quintile of the population were enrolled in primary schools, compared to 96 percent for the wealthiest quintile (General Statistics Office, 1999). While all segments of Vietnam's population experienced gains in enrollment during the 1990s, over 50 percent of all children not in school came from the poorest fifth of the population (World Bank, 2004: 14).

The most dramatic gains in enrollment have occurred at the lower secondary level. Between 1990 and 1998, gross lower secondary enrollment nearly doubled, from 2.7 million to 5 million (Poverty Working Group, 1999: 9), while net enrollment rates increased from 57.6 percent in 1998 to 80.6 percent in 2003 (SRV and World Bank, 2005: 10). Vietnam's government aims to achieve universal access to lower secondary education by 2010 and to eliminate all fees for this level of schooling. Enrollment in upper secondary education has shown similarly rapid increases. The growth of enrollment in upper secondary schools has risen from roughly 700,000 in 1991 to two million in 1999, with net enrollment increasing from 25.7 percent in 1998 to 36.6 percent in 2002. Notably, Vietnam has not experienced large gaps in enrollment among boys and girls, although gaps increase at higher levels. The government has been targeting a nationwide net enrollment rate of 80 percent by 2005 and 90 percent by 2010 for lower secondary education (SRV and World Bank, 2005).

While secondary enrollment in Vietnam has grown significantly over the last 15 years, the country's secondary schools exhibit significant and, in some senses, intensifying social inequalities. This is evident in the different rates with which enrollment figures have risen across regions and social groups and in inequalities between ethnic groups and between boys and girls. According to Vietnam's most recent household living standards survey (General Statistics Office, 2003), the gross enrollment rate for lower secondary education was just 53.8 percent for the poorest income group, compared to 85.8 percent for the richest group, while for upper secondary education the corresponding figures were 17.1 percent and 67 percent, respectively. While the net enrollment rate for lower secondary education was almost 80 percent for ethnic Vietnamese (or *Kinh*), it was just 48 percent for ethnic minorities. Between 1993 and 1998, the gap in enrollment figures between the richest and poorest quintiles of the population fell for the 6–10 and 11–14 age groups, but rose for the 15–17 age group. In 1998, 15- to 17-year-old students from the wealthiest quintile were some 61 times more likely to be enrolled in school than those from the poorest quintile (General Statistics Office, 1999). There is also a persisting and, in some respects, widening gap in the scale, scope, and quality of schooling across regions. This owes in large part to the inability of poor provinces, districts, and schools to mobilize funds, a problem whose dimensions become clearer through an analysis of patterns of education finance.

Paying for Schooling

The most distinctive differences between the principles and institutions of the state socialist and market-Leninist regimes concern education finance. Vietnam's rapid economic growth has expanded the overall amount of resources available for investment in education and the country has seen increases in education spending by the state, households, and international donors.[22] However, increases in the scale of investments have been accompanied by a shifting of the burden of education finance from the state onto households. Some analysts have argued that the state's emphasis on achieving universal provision of primary education has improved the "progressiveness" of education provision for the simple reason that poorer households in Vietnam tend, on average, to have more children (see World Bank, 2004). The changing responsibility for education finance has introduced new problems, however. Specifically, the increased responsibility of households has fuelled the development and reproduction of inequalities of access to secondary education and upper secondary education in particular.

Since the early 1990s, annual state expenditure on education has increased continuously, both in absolute terms and as a share of GDP.[23] By 2002, state expenditure on education (and training together) amounted to 4.4 percent of GDP.[24] The government's increasing capital expenditure in education, which nearly doubled between 1990 and 2002 (SRV and World Bank, 2005), has allowed for the extension of education services to previously underserved areas. In recent years, the government has also undertaken two rounds of long-awaited pay increases for teachers, who had been among the lowest paid in the region (in relative terms). Still, Vietnam's state spends less on education than many other countries in the region.[25]

One of the most important recent changes in Vietnam's education system has been the decentralization of education administration, and this may have a profound effect on schooling in the years to come. Currently, transfers from the central budget to provinces for education are set every three years, based on the projected population size, the school-age population, and other considerations such as the socio-economic status of the province. At the same time, education authorities at the provincial and district levels exercise an increasing degree of discretion in allocation of funds and setting of fees. In 2006, Decree 43 of the government granted all public service providers increased discretion over their financial operations and encouraged providers to adopt a "business model" of management to increase revenues and reduce their dependence on the state budget. The impacts of this decree in the education sector have not yet been subjected to systematic research. In theory, central norms are supposed to prevent provinces and districts from adopting onerous policies as there are various inspectorates and Party cells within the education sector. Actual practices may be expected to diverge, though.

Already, Vietnam's households invest a sizeable portion of their incomes in their children's schooling. The increased average household earnings that Vietnam experienced during the 1990s were reflected in expenditure data on education. Although inflation in Vietnam between 1993 and 1998 was a cumulative 44.6 percent, household expenditure on primary, lower secondary, and upper secondary education during the same period increased by 70, 65, and 70 percent, respectively.[26] Annual household expenditure on education rose by 14 percent between 1998 and 2002 (General Statistics Office, 2003). According to estimates, household expenditure now accounts for over 50 percent of all spending on education. However, household expenditure on education varies sharply between urban and rural areas, and across seven different geographical regions.[27] Household expenditure on education was, on average, three times greater in urban areas than rural ones, while the wealthiest quintile of the population spent more than six times that of the poorest (ibid.). Hence, economic growth and improved household earnings have led to increased education expenditure, but these expenditure levels reflect the uneven spatial distribution of economic growth and growing inequalities in household income.

Fees are one cause of rising household expenditures on schooling. Although the state charges lower fees for education in rural areas (and especially in poor regions), fees in both urban and rural areas have increased over time. Moreover, fees increase as students advance through the grades of mass education, meaning that poorer households in urban and rural areas are confronted with increased costs over time, making the incentive to stay in school questionable for many households as their children proceed up the school ladder. As indicated, fees are several times greater for students attending semipublic or people-founded schools. Although these categories represented less than 1 percent of all primary education and just 5 percent for lower secondary education, 32 percent of upper secondary students were enrolled in semipublic schools by 2003, and the numbers are growing (MOET, 2005).[28] (During fieldwork in Quang Nam province in 2000, I found that semipublic students in public schools paid five times the tuition of public students.) In addition to tuition, local (i.e., district and commune) authorities also collect annual construction "contributions," compulsory payments that are earmarked for school upkeep and renovation. Nontuition costs can be more onerous for poorer households and, thus, the cost of education can remain burdensome even when fees are exempted or reduced. In essence, then, formal fees and other government cost-recovery schemes represent an important but limited portion of total household expenditures on education.

Outside of rising enrollments and increased overall spending on mass education, one of the most important, though typically underreported,[29] dimensions of change in Vietnam's mass education system has been the rapid growth of an informal education economy known as "extra study" (*hoc them*), which operates within, outside, and on the borders of the state's formal school system. It is difficult to detect the presence or significance of this informal economy from standard education statistics or reports from international aid organizations. However, extra study is pervasive and, in practical terms, can be as important as the formal school system itself. Any Vietnamese parent will agree.

Extra study sessions are "cram" sessions in two senses. They are intended to help students pass exams by providing them with additional lesson time. They also typically (though not always) operate in cramped quarters. A clue for any visitor to a Vietnamese community is the tangle of 20 to 40 bicycles outside an otherwise ordinary house. Peer inside, and one will find the same students from the local school. "School" is in session again.

How did this state of affairs come to pass? Under state socialism, the scale of private tutoring in Vietnam was negligible. During the lean years of the 1980s, and especially at the end of the 1980s, in the context of fiscal crisis, teachers struggled to ensure a livelihood in teaching. Throughout the 1990s, growth in teachers' wages lagged behind contemporaneous growth in household earnings, particularly in urban areas.[30] To supplement their wages, and increasingly as a main source of income, teachers began offering extra study sessions after school, before school, on the weekends, and during the summer recess, almost always with tacit knowledge or explicit approval from state administrators, and sometimes within nominally public school systems. On the demand side, competitive examinations and the real and perceived improvements in the economic returns of education have prompted households to invest progressively more in extra study.

While there is a great demand for extra study and many teachers benefit from its existence, its practice is in many important respects contrary to the state's socialist rhetoric. Basically, wealthier households are more able to afford extra study and thus, students from wealthier households enjoy an advantage over their poorer classmates in competitive examinations. Extra study privileges students in urban areas, in particular, where households have more disposable income. In relatively wealthy urban households (especially in Ho Chi Minh City and Ha Noi), it is not uncommon to pay hundreds in U.S. dollars per year on extra study.[31] Likewise, teachers in urban areas benefit from extra study more than their rural counterparts. In 2000, one high school teacher in Da Nang indicated he earned US$1,000 a month from his extra teaching as compared to US$40 a month from his salary at the time.[32] In poor rural areas, we might expect that low household incomes would have limited the growth of extra study. Still, by the late 1990s, most rural area school systems also featured a parallel informal economy. In some rural areas, expenditures on extra study can be a household's largest expenditure item, after food and fuel. Seventy percent of in-school youth in Vietnam between the ages of 14 and 21 report going to a private tutor (Ministry of Health et al., 2005).

In some respects, extra study in Vietnam is comparable to experiences in other Asian countries included in this volume. But three features of extra study in Vietnam distinguish it from other countries. First, it is occurring in the context of a much poorer society—the majority of households in Vietnam must weigh the advantages of expenditure on extra study versus expenditure on basic subsistence needs. Second, there is an element of conflict of interest—if not institutionalized corruption—as Vietnam's students face pressure to take extra study courses from their own public school teachers.[33] Those who do not enroll in (and pay for) extra classes stand a much poorer chance of doing well in public schools and competitive entrance examinations. Finally, the importance of these "supplemental" lessons sometimes surpasses that of the formal curriculum.[34] The result is not only inequality between rich and poor households, but a pervasive sense of inequality, even as overall school participation rates are improving in objective terms. It is notable that in the recently released *Survey Assessment of*

Vietnam's Youth, 44.1 percent of youth not attending school cited financial reasons, while 25 percent of those who dropped out of school reportedly did so for financial reasons (Ministry of Health et al., 2005).

STATE, SOCIAL CLASS, AND THE FUTURE OF EDUCATIONAL INEQUALITIES IN VIETNAM

In this section, I reflect on the historical development of educational inequalities in Vietnam through the lenses of state and social class in order first to make sense of present efforts by the CPV to contain educational inequalities and second to assess the future prospects of schooling in light of existing inequalities.

I begin by theorizing the relation between social class, the state, and formal education in Vietnam in light of the foregoing historical analysis. I argue that class alliance between cosmopolitan intellectuals and peasants that formed the foundation for the socialist state has given rise to a contradictory class configuration in contemporary Vietnam. These contradictions are expressed in state policies, including the specific strategies of economic accumulation pursued by the state and education policies that have shifted the costs of nominally public services onto households. I also argue that intensifying inequalities in Vietnam have threatened the credibility of the CPV's legitimacy, but that the CPV has responded to these threats with a series of safety-net policies designed to ensure access to social services among the very poor and certain political constituencies. I assess the performance of these safety-nets programs with respect to schooling.

The State, Social Class, and Schooling under Market Leninism

To clarify the significance and relation between state, class, and formal schooling in Vietnam requires a baseline understanding of the nature and significance of social class and its relation to the state and schooling. This is easier said than done, as there are wide disagreements as to the meaning and significance of social class, whether and how social classes shape states interests and capacities, and whether and how states are shaped by social classes. Even if these debates are indeed insoluble, I believe it is both possible and useful to conceptualize social class in general terms and to identify its significance with respect to the development of formal schooling. I believe this exercise can be especially helpful for the purposes of this chapter.

For present purposes I proceed with a simplified conception of social class that draws on the work of classical and contemporary social theorists.[35] This formulation understands social classes as more or less distinctive and stable social groupings that are socially constituted through competitive struggles over access to and control of valued resources. Dominant classes, which derive their power from their control over valued resources, use this power to derive net benefits through repeated transactions with other social classes. In the absence of redistributive mechanisms, class relations conform to what Erik Wright (2000: 1563) has referred to as the "inverse interdependent welfare principle," which obtains when the welfare gains of a dominant class are inversely related to the deprivation of another. Finally, dominant social classes and their constituent members use their positions of power to reproduce and reinforce class divisions.

A Marxist perspective on social class and the state views the latter as an instrument of class power. One need not accept all the assumptions of Marx's theory of history, but still accept the idea that social classes do shape state interests, and state interests shape social class. The broad contours of these dynamics in the Vietnamese context have been spelled out in earlier sections. But a more explicit formulation is needed to address a question posed at the outset: do institutionalized inequalities in Vietnam reflect the CPV state's class character?

Numerous social theorists have commented on a commonly observed and paradoxical outcome of state socialism. Namely, that in an effort to abolish feudal, capitalist, or colonial relations of class domination, the institutions of state socialism generated and reproduced new class hierarchies, under which state officials and urban populations were privileged over the rural masses and a politicized class of extractors pursued economic accumulation and self-maximization. Inequalities emerged under state socialism as consequences of both the structural properties of state socialist models of economic accumulation and the rent-seeking practices that took place at the microfoundations of the economy. As we have observed, the formation of a socialist state and the development of its attendant political and economic institutions promoted such cleavages in Vietnam. These inequalities were reflected in and reproduced through the state socialist education system. In the previous sections, we observed how a combination of spatially uneven economic growth and state policies affected institutionalized inequalities in the education sector in the post state-socialist period.

But how do changes in the state and in structures of inequality and social class associated with the transition to a market economy affect education policies and their outcomes? What kind of state is the CPV-led Socialist Republic of Vietnam today? And how, in turn, might institutionalized patterns of formal schooling in a post state-socialist context affect social class and inequality more broadly?

International experience suggests the exit paths that countries take from state socialism toward new social institutional arrangements can profoundly affect the development of and relations between social classes, the state, and schooling, as well as the costs, qualities, and distributions of formal education. In the wake of state-socialism's dissolution, Vietnam's political leaders harnessed to its authoritarian political system strategies of economic accumulation that would ensure state dominance in both the political and economic spheres. These strategies of accumulation have promoted certain patterns of inequality and, I argue, the development of a new and more differentiated class configuration.

International scholars and development agencies have given abundant attention to poverty reduction in Vietnam. Much has been made, too, about relatively low inequalities *within* rural areas, suggesting that Vietnam's development has been relatively "equitable." While rising inequality has been noted, the magnitude of emerging inequalities has not been commonly appreciated. Figure 18.1

Figure 18.1
Household Income in Vietnam, 1996–2004

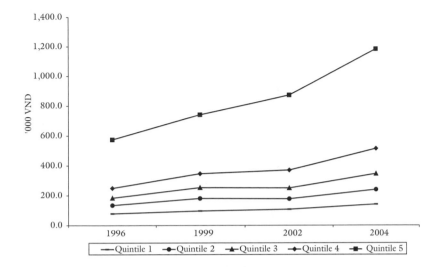

Note: Data in current prices.
Source: General Statistics office, various years.

presents data on income across five expenditure quintiles from 1996 to 2004, the latter being the most recent year for which data are available.

As the data above suggest, income inequalities in Vietnam are surging. But I also believe Vietnam is experiencing the emergence of a new class configuration. The exact contours of this class configuration I can only tentatively state.

Specifically, I believe Vietnam displays a class configuration consisting of eight distinctive classes. In descending order of power, income, assets, and economic opportunities, these include the state business class, the emerging petty bourgeois class, a composite middle class that is constituent of skilled wage labor, state workers, and rich peasants, the middle peasant class distinguished by their relatively stable income stream from agriculture and sideline activities, the urban poor, low-skilled economic migrants, poor and near poor peasants, and economically excluded ethnic minorities.

As formal schooling in Vietnam has become increasingly subject to market principles, households in the lower ranks of this hierarchy have confronted increasing financial obstacles to academic achievement. I have already presented data in previous sections illustrating the difficulties poor households confront in meeting increasing expenses for education and schooling. Gauging the implications of these inequalities for the development of human capital and social mobility will require further study.

In the meantime, what do rising inequalities, including institutionalized inequalities in formal schooling, say about the goals and interests of Vietnam's state? On the one hand, it is clear that the commodification of formal schooling contradicts prominent streams in the CPV's ideology, even as other ideological streams couch commodification in terms of "socialization." Ethnographic research I have conducted in Vietnamese communities across regions reveals a widely shared sense of angst over the costs involved in education. Given the idiosyncratic if not dogmatic rhetoric generated by Vietnam's state, it is no surprise that the continuous flow of socialist rhetoric amid rising inequalities leads one to dismiss outright the content of such rhetoric. However, the idea that the CPV has totally abandoned the principles of socialism is to go too far. Indeed, the CPV is well aware that its legitimacy rests on its ability to credibly portray itself as a defender of social justice. To this end, the CPV has, over the last decade, introduced a range of safety-nets programs designed to ensure access to formal schooling to the country's poor. I describe these programs and assess their effectiveness and limitations, in the following section.

Efforts to Reduce Educational Inequalities and Their Outcomes

The CPV has always professed a commitment to providing equitable access to education and has maintained this pledge even in the context of markets. Since the mid-1990s, the CPV has voiced its intent to improve the welfare of the poorest members of society,[36] especially those in poor, remote, and "difficult" regions (including ethnic minority groups), and those with recognized contributions to the "revolution" and national "liberation." To this end, for the last decade the state has implemented a set of well-publicized national antipoverty programs explicitly designed to ameliorate widening socioeconomic disparities, including those in education. The government's Hunger Eradication and Poverty Reduction (HEPR) policy and Poverty Reduction Program 135 have been particularly prominent in this regard, and it is worth examining the scope and outcomes of these programs. Do these programs represent an effective socialist response to inequality?

The HEPR program's components include expanding access to land and credit among the poor, as well as securing for the poor free access to basic education and health services. It is extraordinarily complex as it involves means-testing millions of households.[37] Program 135, by contrast, is a grant program designed for the country's poorest communes and has typically been used to achieve infrastructure improvements. The education provisions of the HEPR program aim to eradicate illiteracy by exempting or reducing school fees and contributions for designated poor households, and to provide books and grant scholarships to the rural poor in order to make it possible for them to attend upper secondary and higher education institutions in towns and cities. In 2001, funding for HEPR and Program 135 amounted to 0.5 percent of GDP. Funding has increased in recent years, though Program 135 enjoys twice the funding of HEPR.[38] At current levels, an estimated 12–20 percent of poor households in Vietnam receive some education benefits through HEPR, and roughly 12 percent of these recipients indicated that they would not have sent their children for schooling had they not received tuition exemptions.[39]

However, these programs have numerous practical limitations. First, it is widely recognized that these seemingly complementary programs are not well-coordinated, that there is a lack of transparency and no consistent norms for how provinces distribute funds via the HEPR, and that there have been incidences of misappropriation of funds and political favoritism in allocation of funds (Ministry of Labour, War Invalids and Social Affairs, 1999). Second, HEPR's education provisions only reach a fraction of the poor—roughly one-fourth of the poorest quintile and a fifth of the second poorest quintile of the population received full exemptions (SRV and World Bank, 2005: 14). Importantly, the HEPR program "allows" local officials to categorize only a certain number of households as poor, regardless of whether the number of households falling below the (quite low) state-set poverty line is getting bigger. To be officially poor, households require the official stamp of local authorities and, in general, the process is subject to the arbitrary discussion of local officials. Finally, while fee exemptions eliminate one component of the costs of education services, poor households almost invariably lack the means to pay for other costs (e.g., food, transport, informal payments, etc.), let alone that required to participate in the informal economies that so often dictate access to quality education. Despite consistent state claims that these programs effectively protect the poor, they have important limitations. Unless the scale of these programs is dramatically expanded, they cannot be understood as a truly socialist alternative.

CONCLUSION

Vietnam is a country with a rich Confucian heritage. But Confucian respect for education ought not to be confused with egalitarian or universalist principles regarding access to schooling. For most of Vietnam's history, formal schooling has been the privilege of a small minority. When the Communist Party of Vietnam rose to power in the 1940s and 1950s and consolidated that power nationally in 1975, it set in place a truly revolutionary education system, one that was designed eventually to ensure universal access to K–12 schooling as a right of citizenship. This was also a system designed to furnish the newly independent state with generations of a "new socialist man," equipped with all the virtues, knowledge, and skills necessary to "build socialism." Quintessentially, it was a system subordinate to the social, political, economic, and cultural agendas of the CPV, a party whose legitimacy rested on its claim as the sole legitimate defender of Vietnam's independence and its sole legitimate champion of social justice.

During the 1950s and 1960s, and in the south after 1975, Vietnam's system of formal schooling at the primary and secondary levels developed extensively, alongside the formation of a socialist state and the imposition by that state of a uniform formal template of political and economic institutions across Vietnam's territory. Access was to be based on the principles of state-socialist universalism, whose institutions actually promoted and reproduced social hierarchies and inequalities between state and society, town and country, and cadre and peasant. Official statistics that suggested Vietnam's education was out-performing that of countries 10 times as wealthy, however impressive in some regards, masked threadbare conditions in the provision of schooling and sharp inequalities mentioned earlier. Still, that the development of schooling in Vietnam took place under conditions of war and economic scarcity is a testament to the mobilizational capacities of Vietnam's CPV, its state, and the society at large.

Over the course of the 1980s, Vietnam's poorly performing and embargoed economy sustained relentless fiscal shocks, before spiraling downward in a fiscal crisis of the state. By the middle of the decade, the state was struggling to sustain its basic functions. By late 1989, when Vietnam's government approved school fees for the first time, enrollments had already begun to drop precipitously at all educational levels, as quality and morale declined and teachers sought second and third jobs to sustain themselves.

Fiscal crises frequently entail a fundamental rethinking if not an actually reworking of established principles and institutions. In Vietnam, the fiscal crisis of the late 1980s hastened the abandonment of core principles and institutions of state socialism, including those that governed schooling.

Since 1989, Vietnam has had one of the fastest growing economies in the world. Overall, access to education has improved at all levels. Paradoxically, while there is greater access to formal education in Vietnam today than at any time in the country's history, education has become increasingly commodified, generating institutionalized inequalities both within and outside the sphere of education. These institutionalized inequalities stand in clear contradiction to the professed aims of the CPV and their continued existence and development raises questions about the long term goals of the CPV, if not the class character of the Party state.

Upper Secondary School Qhang Norm Province. Courtesy of Jonathan London.

In this chapter, I have sought to explain the principles and institutions governing schooling in Vietnam in relation to continuity and change in the country's political and economic institutions. I illustrated how the CPV's quasi-universalistic education policies under state socialism gradually degenerated and were ultimately replaced by policies that shifted an increasing share of the costs of education from the state onto households.

I believe that the institutionalized inequalities within Vietnam's education system, and in particular its system of formal schooling reflect and are being exacerbated by a newly emerging class configuration. This class configuration is a product of accumulation strategies undertaken by a Market-Leninist regime under which a state business elite and a growing urban-based petty bourgeoisie have thrived on market opportunities. In Vietnam's system of formal schooling, education at the basic level is accessible to all. But educational opportunities beyond that level are much more difficult to grasp for those toward the bottom of the country's developing class hierarchy. As inequalities in Vietnam's education system become further institutionalized, we might expect they will perpetuate and exacerbate rather than ameliorate present class cleavages. Whether and how the CPV responds to these trends will tell us a lot about the nature of the CPV and its unique brand of market Leninism.

NOTES

1. The term "human resource complex" is used by David Harvey (1982).

2. Alexander Woodside. *Lost Modernities: China, Vietnam, Korea, and the Hazards of World History* (The Edwin O. Reischauer Lectures, 2001). Cambridge: Harvard University Press. 2006, p. 142.

3. For a particularly stimulating account of intellectual currents during the later phases of French colonialism, see Marr (1981).

4. The integrated political and administrative grid the CPV used to manage society under state socialism remains largely intact today. For more on Vietnam's politico-administrative hierarchies, see Porter (1993), Phong and Beresford (1998), and Kerkvliet (2005).

5. In the postwar south, the party's efforts to implement land reforms met with myriad forms of resistance (Ngo, 1991; White, 1986). As Benedict Kerkvliet (2005) has recently shown, even in northern Vietnam of the 1960s, the state's efforts at coercive collectivization met various forms of resistance.

6. See Beresford (1989a, 1989b, 1997); Fforde (1999); Fforde and deVylder (1996).

7. Specifically, agricultural producers had to sell their produce at artificially low prices, to the detriment of household welfare, local revenue, and the quantity and quality of services in rural areas (Vo, 1990).

8. The 1982 constitution stipulated that all citizens had a right to K–12 education.

9. For more on this, see Pham (1999: 51) and London (2003).

10. Local spending on education was supposed to follow a series of centrally determined budgetary norms and formulae and, in principle, was tailored to the conditions and needs of urban and rural areas.

11. According to anecdotal evidence, boys drafted into the army were often awarded upper secondary school diplomas after one year of education.

12. See Ministry of National Defense (1990).

13. For example, between 1975 and 1980, gross enrollments in primary, lower secondary, and upper secondary education increased by 19 percent, 25 percent, and 28 percent, respectively (General Statistics Office, 2001), while between 1981 and 1990, the number of primary school teachers in Vietnam increased by some 20 percent, including an increase of 35 percent in the southern part of the country (MOET, 1992: p. 40).

14. Ethnic minority groups account for roughly 15 percent of the population and, with the exception of the wealthier Chinese, were far less likely to have access to education due to their settlement in remote and neglected regions, cultural barriers, and other reasons.

15. The continuing poor performance of Vietnam's economy was compounded by the country's political and economic isolation under the US-Sino embargo.

16. This account draws largely on the work of Adam Fforde (1999) and Melanie Beresford (1997).

17. Sepehri (2004) provides a useful summary of research on user fees in Vietnam's education and health sectors.

18. When first introduced in 1989, school fees were set at the cash equivalent of 4 kg and 7 kg of rice per month for lower and upper secondary students, respectively. By 1993, the state eliminated school fees at the primary level, but increased fees for lower and upper secondary education.

19. Survey data on household education expenditure reveal that by 1996–1997, school fees accounted for 46.1 percent and 61.7 percent of yearly education expenditures per lower and upper secondary student, respectively (General Statistics Office, 1999). Other education expenditure includes spending on books, transport, as well as after school "extra study" (discussed in the next section).

20. The semi-public status is for students who perform below a certain level in lower and upper secondary school entrance examinations. People-founded schools are, by contrast, financially autonomous from the state education budget but are subject to state curriculum requirements, and are typically more expensive. Both semi-public and people-founded forms are permitted at all levels of education except the primary level.

21. By 1998, roughly 66 percent of children of primary school age were actually completing their primary level education (United Nations, 1999). This figure had increased to 83 percent by 2002, though to just 76 percent according to the World Bank (2004).

22. International organizations include bilateral donors and multilateral development agencies, as well as non-governmental organizations. Together, they represent a significant source of education finance, with the development agencies intimately involved in shaping education policy. The role of international organizations in Vietnam's education is to be discussed elsewhere due to space consideration.

23. Today, education expenditures represent roughly 17 percent of the national budget ("Labour and education issues put on Prime Minister's table today," *Thanh Nien*, July 12, 2004).

24. London (2004) specifies the functional distribution of state education expenditures.

25. Whereas Vietnam's education budget has just recently eclipsed the 3 percent of GDP mark, the corresponding figure is 4.2 percent in the Philippines, 5.4 percent in Thailand, and 6.7 percent in Malaysia (ADB data cited in "Lao dong va giao duc [Labour and education]," *Lao Dong*, September 20, 2004).

26. According to the Ministry of Finance, inflation for the years 1994, 1995, 1996, 1997, and 1998 ran at 14.7 percent, 12.4 percent, 4.5 percent, 3.8 percent, and 9.2 percent, respectively.

27. Vietnam's seven geographical regions include the two richest regions—the southeast (including Ho Chi Minh City) and Red River Delta (including Ha Noi and Hai Phong)—and five other geographical regions.

28. By 2003, some 58 percent of kindergarten students were enrolled in non-state schools (MOET, 2005).

29. In recent years the volume of scholarly and policy literature on Vietnam's education system has increased dramatically. Prior to the 1990s, data on education were typically unreliable and in any case uninformative about actual conditions in the education sector. Today, the situation is vastly improved, particularly with the publications of *Vietnam Households Living Standards Survey* (VNLSS). Still, despite the improvement in the quality and availability of data, many facets of Vietnam's education system remain beyond the grasp of conventional measures. One of the most glaring examples in this regard is the sprawling informal economy that has grown up within, outside, and on the borders of the (nominally) public education system.

30. A 1996 World Bank study found that primary and secondary school teachers in Vietnam were paid significantly lower wages than in other Asian countries, if wages were measured in relation to GDP per capita (World Bank, 1996b). Although there have been recent increases in pay and administrative decentralization measures allow local authorities to raise teachers' pay, it is unclear how these developments have affected the overall standing of teachers' wages in Vietnam.

31. According to the 1998 Vietnam Living Standards Survey, extra study expenses, on average, comprised roughly 18 percent of household education expenditures for lower secondary students and 28 percent for upper secondary students. These figures are misleading. First, there is considerable evidence that extra study has increased since 1998. Second, average expenditures on tutoring do not take into consideration the wide disparities in expenditure on extra study between rich and poor. During my own research in 2000 in central Vietnam's Quang Nam province, it was observed that many rural households expended VND100,000 per month on extra study for secondary school students, as compared to VND17,000 for school fees.

32. Notes from personal communication with an upper secondary teacher in Da Nang in May 2000.

33. There is much anecdotal evidence supporting this claim, though no systematic survey has been conducted. In recent years, some provinces have instituted rules where teachers may not have their own students in the extra study classes.

34. This is more eloquently captured in Vietnamese as "*hoc them la chinh va hoc chinh la phu*," as one Vietnamese put it (http://diendan.edu.net.vn/PrintPost.aspx?PostID=17353).

35. The theorists I have in mind are Marx and Weber, as more recent theorists such as Charles Tilly (1997) and Erik Wright (1997). These theorists' formulations of social class differ, but they each provide useful insights and share sufficient fundamental similarities as to permit a useful if simplified synthetic conception of social class.

36. The seventh Party Congress in 1991 explicitly recognized the problem of education and health access for the poor (UN Development Program-Deutsche Gesellschaft für Technische Zusammenarbeit, 1999).

37. It took the government two years to specify the institutional arrangements for its implementation. To conduct this means testing, by the end of 1998, the state established HEPR boards in 6,958 communes (out of 7,518 at the time) and local authorities commenced poverty-mapping efforts using the government's criteria to identify poor households in each commune.

38. For the first three years of the HEPR, for example, the Ministry of Education and Training committed, on average, an amount equal only to roughly 2 percent of the education budget.

39. Although the HEPR scheme was designed to incorporate democratic participation at the grassroots level, the implementation of the programs is frequently top-down (Vietnam Consultative Group, 2004, pp. 27 & 30).

REFERENCES

Beresford, M. (1989a). "Vietnam: Socialist agriculture in transition," *Journal of Contemporary Asia*, 20(4): 466–486.

——(1989b). *National Development and Reunification in Vietnam*. London: Macmillan.

——(1997). "Vietnam: The transition from central planning," in G. Rodan, K. Hewison, and R. Robison (eds), *The Political Economy of Southeast Asia*, pp. 179–204. Oxford: Oxford University Press.

Davis, P.R. (2001). "Rethinking the welfare regime approach," *Global Social Policy*, 1(1): 79–107.

Esping-Andersen, G. (1990). *Three Worlds of Welfare Capitalism*. Cambridge, UK: Polity Press.

——(1999). *Social Foundations of Post-Industrial Economies*. Oxford: Oxford University Press.

Fforde, A. (1999). "The Institutions of the transition from central planning," in C. Barlow (ed.), *Institutions and Economic Change in Southeast Asia: The Context of Development From the 1960s to the 1990s*, pp. 118–132. Cheltenham: Edward Elgar.

Fforde, A. and deVylder, S. (1996). *From Plan to Market: The Economic Transition in Vietnam*. Boulder, CO: Westview Press.

General Statistics Office (1999). *Vietnam Households Living Standards Survey, 1997–1998*. Hanoi, Vietnam: Statistical Publishing House.

——(2001). *So lieu dan so va Kinh te xa hoi, 1975–2000* [Population and Socioeconomic Data, 1975–2000]. Hanoi, Vietnam: Statistical Publishing House.

——(2003). *Vietnam Households Living Standards Survey, 2001–2002*. Hanoi, Vietnam: Statistical Publishing House.

——(2005). *Vietnam Households Living Standards Survey, 2004*. Hanoi, Vietnam: Statistical Publishing House.

Gough, I. (1999). "Welfare regimes: On adapting the framework to developing countries." Unpublished manuscript, University of Bath, UK.

Harvey, David (1982). *The Limits to Capital*. Oxford: Blackwell.

Kerkvliet, B.J.T. (2005). *The Power of Everyday Politics: How Vietnamese Peasants Transformed National Policy*. Ithaca, NY: Cornell University Press.

London, J.D. (2003). "Vietnam's mass education and health systems: A regimes perspective," *American Asian Review*, 21(2): 125–170.

——(2004). "Social provision and the transformation of the socialist state: Mass education and health provision in Vietnam's market transition." Ph.D. dissertation, Madison, WI: University of Wisconsin-Madison.

Marr, D. (1981). *Vietnamese Tradition on Trial, 1920–1945*. Berkeley, CA: University of California Press.

Ministry of Education and Training of Vietnam (1992). *Statistical Data of Education and Training, 1981–1990*. Hanoi, Vietnam: Ministry of Education and Training of Vietnam.

——(1995a). "So lieu thong ke giao duc va dao tao, 1945–1995 [Statistical data of education and training, 1945–1995]." Unpublished statistical brief.

——(1995b). "Statistical data of general education: School year 1995–1996." Unpublished statistical brief.

——(2000). "Bao cao: Chuyen de giao duc [Report on education]." Unpublished brief.

——(2005). "So lieu thong ke giao duc [Statistical education data]." Accessed on May 20, 2005 from http://edu.net.vn/data/thongke/.

Ministry of Health, General Statistics Office, United Nations Children's Fund, and World Health Organization (2005). *Survey Assessment of Vietnamese Youth*. Hanoi, Vietnam: Ministry of Health.

Ministry of Labour, War Invalids and Social Affairs (1999). "Tinh hinh thuc hien chuong trinh xoa doi giam ngheo cac tinh khu vuv mien trung va tay nguyen 6 thang dau nam 1999 [The situation of implementing the hunger eradication and poverty reduction programs in the central region and central highlands in the first six months of 1999]." Unpublished report.

Ministry of National Defense (1990). *Khang chien chong my cuu nuoc* [The Uprising to Defeat America and Save the Country]. Hanoi, Vietnam: Nha Xuat Ban Su That Vietnam.

Ngo, V.H. (1991). "Post-war Vietnam: Political economy," in D. Allen and N.V. Long (eds), *Coming to Terms: Indochina, the United States, and the War*, pp. 65–88. Boulder, CO: Westview Press.

Nguyen, N.N. (2002). "Trends in the education sector from 1993 to 1998." World Bank Policy Research Working Paper No. 2891, September. Washington, DC: World Bank.

Nguyen, T.C. (1997). "*Van de giao duc va dao tao trong nen Kinh te chuyen doi Vietnam* [The problem of education and training in Vietnam's transitional economy]," *Phat Trien Kinh Te*, 861: 28–31.

Nguyen, V.C. (1997). "Looking for the future: Work versus education." Unpublished paper, Amsterdam School for Social Science Research, Centre for Asian Studies, Netherlands.

Pham, M.H. (1999). *Giao duc Vietnam: Truoc nguong cua they ky XXI* [Vietnam's Education System on the Threshold of the 21st Century]. Hanoi, Vietnam: Nha Xuat Ban Chinh Tri Quoc Gia.

Phong, D. and Beresford, M. (1998). *Authority Relations and Economic Decision-Making in Vietnam: An Historical Perspective*. Copenhagen, Denmark: Nordic Institute of Asian Studies.

Porter, G. (1993). *Vietnam: The Politics of Bureaucratic Socialism*. Ithaca, NY: Cornell University Press.

Poverty Working Group (1999). *Attacking Poverty: Vietnam Development Report, 2000*. Washington, DC: World Bank.

Sepheri, A. (2004). "User fees, financial autonomy, and access to social services in Vietnam." Unpublished working paper.

Socialist Republic of Vietnam (SRV) and World Bank (2005). *Managing Public Expenditure for Poverty Reduction and Growth: Public Expenditure Review and Integrated Fiduciary Assessment*. Hanoi, Vietnam: Financial Publishing House.

Tilly, C. (1998). *Durable Inequality*. Berkeley and Los Angeles, CA: University of California Press.

United Nations (1999). *Looking Ahead: A Common Country Assessment*. Hanoi, Viet Nam: United Nations.

United Nations and Ministry of Labour, War Invalids, and Social Affairs (1999). *Dich vu xa hoi co ban o Vietnam* [Basic Social Services in Vietnam]. Hanoi, Vietnam: United Nations.

United Nations Development Program–Deutsche Gesellschaft für Technische Zusammenarbeit (1999). "First forum on the national target programme on hunger eradication and poverty reduction." Unpublished paper.

Vietnam Consultative Group (2004). "Governance: Vietnam development report 2005." Joint Donor Report to the Consultative Group Meeting, December. Hanoi, Vietnam: Vietnam Consultative Group.

Vo, N.T. (1990). *Vietnam's Economic Policy since 1975.* Singapore: Institute of Southeast Asian Studies.

Vo, T.S., Truong, T.K.N., Doan, T.H., and Nguyen, T.T. (2001). "School enrollments and dropouts," in D. Haughton, J. Haughton, and P. Nguyen (eds), *Living Standards during an Economic Boom*, pp. 157–170. Hanoi, Vietnam: United Nations Development Program and Statistical Publishing House.

White, C. P. (1986). "Everyday Resistance, Socialist Revolution and Rural Development: the Vietnamese Case," *Journal of Peasant Studies*, 13(2): 49–63.

Woodside, A. (2006). *Lost Modernities: China, Vietnam, Korea, and the Hazards of World History.* Cambridge, MA: Harvard University Press.

World Bank (1996a). "Vietnam: Fiscal decentralization and the delivery of rural services," Report No. 15745-VN. October. Washington, DC: World Bank, East Asia and Pacific Division, Country Department I, Country Operations Division.

——(1996b). *Vietnam Education Finance Sector Study.* Washington, DC: World Bank, East Asia Pacific Region, Human Resources Operations Division.

——(2004). "Global poverty down by half since 1981 but progress uneven as economic growth eludes many countries." Accessed on May 20, 2005 from http://www.worldbank.org.vn/news/press46_01.htm.

Wright, E.O. (1997). *Class Counts: Comparative Studies in Class Analysis.* Cambridge: Cambridge University Press.

——(2000). "Class, exploitation, and economic rents: Reflections on Sørensen's 'Sounder Basis,'" *American Journal of Sociology*, 105(6): 1559–71.

BIBLIOGRAPHY

Abe, Hiroshi (1987). "U.S. educational policy in Korea," in H. Abe (ed.), *Educational Reform in Korea under the U.S. Military Government (1945–1948)*, pp. 202–213. Seoul: Han'guk Yon'guwon.

Altbach, P.G. (1981). "The university as center and periphery," *Teachers College Record*, 82(4): 601–621.

——(1997). *Comparative Higher Education: Knowledge, the University, and Development*. Boston, MA: Centre for International Higher Education.

——(2004). *Asian Universities: Historical Perspectives and Contemporary Challenges*. Baltimore, MD: Johns Hopkins University Press.

Altbach, P.G. and Selvaratnam, V. (1989). *From Dependence to Autonomy: The Development of Asian Universities*. Amsterdam: Kluwer Academic Publishers.

Altbach, P G. and Umakoshi, Toru (2004). *Asian Universities: Historical Perspectives and Contemporary Challenges*. Baltimore, MD: Johns Hopkins University Press.

Amano, I. (1986). *Koto Kyoiku no Nipponteki Kozo* (Japanese Structure of Higher Education). Tokyo: Tamagawa University Press.

Amos, K., Keiner, E., Proske, M., and Olaf-Radtke, F. (2002). "Globalisation: Autonomy of education under siege? Shifting boundaries between politics, economy and education," *European Educational Research Journal*, 1(2): 193–213.

Arimoto, A. (1984). "Gendai shakaito kyoiku byori (Modern society and educational pathology)," in M. Shinbori and S. Tuganezawa (eds), *Environment of Education and Pathology*, pp. 35–67. Tokyo: Daiichi Houki Publishing Co.

——(ed.) (2003). *Daigaku no Curriculum Kaikaku* (Academic Curriculum Reforms). Tokyo: Tamagawa University Press.

——(2005). "Structure and functions of financing higher education in Asia," *Higher Education in the World 2006—The Financing of Universities* (GUNI Series on the Social Commitment of Universities), pp. 176–187. Houndmill, Basingstoke, Hampshire, and New York: Palgrave Macmillan.

Asian Development Bank (2004). *Education Reforms in Countries in Transition: Policies and Processes*. Six Country Case Studies Commissioned by the Asian Development

Bank in Azerbaijan, Kazakhstan, Kyrgyz Republic, Mongolia, Tajikistan, and Uzbekistan. Manila, Philippines. Accessed on July 27, 2006 from http://www.adb.org/Education/educ-reforms-countries.pdf.

Ayres, David (2000). *Anatomy of a Crisis: Education, Development, and the State in Cambodia, 1953–1998.* Honolulu, HI: University of Hawai'i Press.

Badamsambuu, Khishigbayar (2006). "The external influences on the development of Mongolian higher education system." Unpublished Ph.D. Dissertation, Graduate School for International Development and Cooperation, Hiroshima University, Japan (March).

Bahn, Sang-Jin (2003). "Sae jungbu ei godung kyoyuk gaehyuk kwaje [Higher education reform agendas of the new administration]," *The Journal of Educational Administration,* 21(1): 169–191.

Bailey, P.J. (1990). *Reform the People: Changing Attitudes towards Popular Education in Early Twentieth-century China.* Edinburgh: Edinburgh University Press.

Baki, Aminuddin and Chang, P. (1959). *Report of the Education Commission Brunei.* Brunei Darussalam: Brunei Government Press.

Batbaatar, M., Bold, Ts., Marshall, J., Oyuntsetseg, D., Tamir, Ch., and Tumenast, G. (2005). *Children on the Move: Rural-Urban Migration and Access to Education in Mongolia.* CHIP Report No. 17. London: Childhood Poverty Research and Policy Centre (CHIP), Save the Children (U.K.).

Bazaco, E. (1953). *History of Education in the Philippines,* 2nd rev. edn. Manila: University of Santo Tomas Press.

Berman, E.H. (1992). "Donor agencies and the Third World educational development: 1945–1985," in R.F. Arnove, P.G. Altbach, and Gail Kelly (eds.), *Emergent Issues in Education: Comparative Perspectives,* pp. 57–74. New York: SUNNY Press.

Bilodeau, Charles (1955). "Compulsory education in Cambodia," in Charles Bilodeau, Somlith Pathammavong, and Lê Quang Hông (eds.), *Compulsory Education in Cambodia, Laos and Viet-Nam,* pp. 9–67. Paris: United Nations Educational, Scientific, and Cultural Organization (UNESCO).

Bjork, C. (2004). "Decentralisation in education, institutional culture and teacher autonomy in Indonesia," *International Review of Education,* 50(3): 245–263.

Bjork, Christopher (2006). *Educational Decentralization: Asian Experiences and Conceptual Contributions.* Netherlands: Springer Press.

Board of Education (1997). *Report on Review of 9-year Compulsory Education* (Revised Version). Hong Kong: Government Printer.

Board of Educational Survey Created under Acts 3162 and 3196 of the Philippine Legislature (BES) (1925). *A Survey of the Educational System of the Philippine Islands.* Manila: Bureau of Printing.

Borthwick, S. (1983). *Education and Social Change in China: The Beginnings of the Modern Era.* Stanford, CA: Hoover Institution Press.

Bray, Mark (1999). *The Shadow Educational System: Private Tutoring and its Implication for Planners, Fundamentals of Educational Planning.* Paris: UNESCO International Institute for Educational Planning.

——(2003). *Adverse Effects of Private Supplementary Tutoring: Dimensions, Implications, and Government Responses.* Paris: UNESCO International Institute for Educational Planning.

Bredenberg, Kurt, Somanee, Lon, and Sopheap, Ma (2003). *Gender and Education in Cambodia: Historical Trends and the Way Forward.* Phnom Penh: Oxfam.

Brown, David (1994). *The State and Ethnic Politics in Southeast Asia.* London: Routledge and Kegan Paul.

Buchori, M. and Malik, A. (2004). "The evolution of higher education in Indonesia," in P. Altbach and T. Umakoshi (eds), *Asian Universities: Historical Perspectives and Contemporary Challenges,* pp. 249–277. Baltimore, MD: Johns Hopkins University Press.

Buresh, S.A. (2002). "Pesantren-based development: Islam, education, and economic development in Indonesia." Ph.D. Dissertation, University of Virginia.

Cai, Y.Q. (2006). "Zhongguo you'er jiaoyu fazhan zhuangkuang (The Situation of China's Preschool Education)," in Yang Dongbing (ed.), *Jiaoyu lanpishu: 2005 nian zhongguo jiaoyu fazhan baogao* (Blue Book of Education: The Development Report on China's Education, 2005), pp. 94–108. Beijing: Shehui kexue wenxian chu ban she

Caillods, François, Göttelmann-Duret, Gabrielle, and Lewin, Keith (1996). *Science Education and Development: Planning and Policy Issues at Secondary Level.* Paris: International Institute for Education Planning.

Cao, Tai Sheng (1997). "Xianggang Jiaoyu Zhidushi Yanjiu, 1840–1997 (The history of Hong Kong education system, 1840–1997)," *Huadong Shifan Daxue Xuebao Jiaoyu Kexueban (East China Normal University Journal, Educational Sciences),* 2: 1–15.

CARE and Ministry of Education, Youth, and Sport (1998). *Survey on Girls' Education in Cambodia.* Phnom Penh: CARE and Australian Agency for International Development.

CEC (Central Educational Council) (2002). *Kyoyou Kyoiku no Kaizen* (Improvement of General Education). Tokyo: Central Education Council.

——(2005). *University Teachers Organization.* Tokyo: Central Education Council.

Chandler, David (1992). *A History of Cambodia,* 2nd edn. Boulder, CO: Westview Press.

Chang Cheng-Li (1963) "Merit and money," in Johanna M. Menzel (ed.), *The Chinese Civil Service: Careers Open to Talent,* pp. 22–27. Boston, MA: D.C. Heath Co.

Chapman, D. and Austin, A. (eds) (2002). *Higher Education in the Developing World: Changing Contexts and Institutional Responses.* Westport, CT: Greenwood Press.

Chen, Y.K. (1999). "Shi lun gaodeng jiaoyu de bongping yu xiaolu wenti (The issue of equality and efficiency in higher education)," in Chen Xuefei (ed.), *Zhongguo gaodeng jiaoyu yanjiu 50 nian (Higher Education Research in China for 50 Years),* pp. 788–790. Beijing: Jiaoyu kexue chu ban she.

Cheng, Kai Ming (1996). "Efficiency, equity and quality in higher education in a time of expansion," in M.K. Nyaw and S.M. Li (eds), *The Other Hong Kong Report 1996,* pp. 409–418. Hong Kong: Chinese University Press.

Cho, M.C. and Zang, H. (2002). "North Korea's education policy and system, and external cooperation with international organizations," *Journal of Asia-Pacific Affairs,* 3(2): 73–111.

Choe, Yong-ho (1999). "Private academies and the state in late Choson Korea," in Haboush, JaHyun Kim and Martina Deuchler (eds), *Culture and the State In Late Choson Korea,* pp. 15–45. Cambridge, MA, London: Harvard University Press.

Choi, Sheena (2004). "Globalization or marketization?: The dilemmas of international schools in S. Korea," *International Journal of Educational Reform,* 13(4): 325–337.

Chong, N.C. (1979). "An examination of dysfunctional roles and problems of education in national unity and development with special reference to Brunei Darussalam." Unpublished M.Ed. Thesis, University of Hull.

Chou, Chuing P. (2003). *The Great Experiment of Taiwanese Education (1987–2003)*. Taipei: Psychological Publishing.

Chou, Zhu-Ying and Chang, Chia-I. (1998). "Gender differences in Taiwan's academic—Implications for the PRC," in Michael Agelasto and Bob Adamson (eds), *Higher Education in Post-Mao China*, pp. 345–357. Hong Kong: Hong Kong University Press.

Chung, Chak and Ming Yan Ngan (2002). "From 'Rooftop' to 'Millennium': The development of primary schools in Hong Kong since 1945," *New Horizons in Education*, 46: 24–32.

Clarke, Paul, West, Mel, and Ainscow, Mel (2005). *Using an Established School Improvement Programme to Build Capacity at School and System Level: The Hong Kong IQEA Programme*. Accessed on February 2, 2006 from http://www.aare.edu.au/05pap/cla05195.pdf.

Clayton, Thomas (1995). "Restriction or resistance? French colonial educational development in Cambodia," *Education Policy Analysis Archives*, 3(19). Accessed on June 23, 2004 from http://epaa.asu.edu/epaa/v3n19.html.

——(1998). "Building the New Cambodia: Educational destruction and construction under the Khmer Rouge, 1975–1979," *History of Education Quarterly*, 38: 1–16.

——(2000). *Education and the Politics of Language: Hegemony and Pragmatism in Cambodia, 1979–1989*. Hong Kong: Comparative Education Research Center, University of Hong Kong.

Cleverley, J.F. (1991). *The Schooling of China: Tradition and Modernity in Chinese Education*, 2nd edn. Sydney: Allen & Unwin.

Cookson, Peter, Sadovnik, Alan, and Semel, Susan (1992). *The International Handbook of Educational Reform*. Westport, CT: Greenwood Press.

Cummings, W.K. (1979). "Expansion, examination fever, and equality," in W.K. Cummings, K. Kitamura, and M. Nagai (eds), *Changes in the Japanese University: A Comparative Perspective*, pp. 83–106. New York: Praeger.

Cummings, William K. (2003). *The Institutions of Education: A Comparative Study of Education Development in the Six Core Nations*. Oxford: Symposium Books.

Cummings, William K. and Altbach, Philip G. (1997). *The Challenge of East Asian Education: Implications for America*. Albany, NY: State University of New York.

Curriculum Development Council (1996). *Guidelines on Civic Education in Schools*. Hong Kong: Government Printer.

——(2001). *Learning to Learn: The Way Forward in Curriculum Development*. Hong Kong: Printing Department.

Dang Ba Lam (1997). "Vietnam," in G. Postiglione (ed.), *Asian Higher Education*, pp. 359–372. Westport, CT: Greenwood Press.

del Rosario, Mercedes, Donrov, B., Bayarsaihan, B., Tsetsegee, B., Batmonkh, D., Sengedorj, T., Tseveen, Ts., and Delger, E. (2005). *The Mongolian Drop out Study*. Ulaanbaatar: Mongolian Education Alliance.

Department of Islamic Education (1996). *Pendidikan Ugama Di Negara Brunei Darussalam* (Islamic Religious Education in Brunei Darussalam). Brunei Darussalam: Government Printing Department.

——(1998). *Laporan 10 Tahun 1986 Hingga 1995 Jabatan Pengajaian Islam* (The 10 Year Report: 1986 to 1995 Department of Islamic Education). Brunei Darussalam: Government Printing Department.

Department of Islamic Studies (1996). *Sejarah Persekolahan Ugama Bersistem Di Brunei* (The History of Systematic Religious Education in Brunei). Brunei Darussalam: Ministry of Religious Affairs.

Dhofier, Z. (1999). *The Pesantren Tradition: The Role of the Kyai in the Maintenance of Traditional Islam in Java.* Tempe, AZ: Arizona State University, Program for Southeast Asian Studies.

Ding, G. (2001). "Nationalization and internationalization: Two turning points in China's education in the twentieth century," in Glen Peterson, Ruth Hayhoe, and Yongling Lu (eds.), *Education, Culture, and Identity in Twentieth-century China,* pp. 161–186. Hong Kong: Hong Kong University Press.

Doraisamy, T.R. (ed.) (1969). *150 years of Education in Singapore.* Singapore: Teachers' Training College.

Dore, D. (Translated by H. Matsui) (1970). *Edojidai no Kyoiku* (Education in Edo Era). Tokyo: Iwanami Publishing Co.

——(1978). *Gakureki Shakai—Atarashii Bunmeibyou* (Degree-o-cratic Society: Diploma Disease). Tokyo: Asahi Shinbunsha.

DPRK Ministry of Education and DPRK National Commission for UNESCO (2003). *Democratic People's Republic of Korea National Plan of Action on Education for All.* Accessed on February 22, 2004 from http://portal.unesco.org/education/en/ ev.php-URL_ID=30256&URL_DO=DO_TOPIC&URL_SECTION=201.html.

Duflo, E. (2001). "Schooling and labour market consequences of school construction in Indonesia: Evidence from an unusual policy experiment," *The American Economic Review* 91(4): 795–813.

Duggan, Stephen (1996). "Education, teacher training and prospects for economic recovery in Cambodia," *Comparative Education,* 32: 361–375.

Dumlao-Valisno, Mona (2001). "A note on the economic crisis and higher education in the Philippines," in *Impact of the Economic Crisis on Higher Education in East Asia.* pp. 147–155. Paris: UNESCO (IIEP).

Duncan, W. (2000). "Basic education in Indonesia: A partnership in crisis," in Y. Wang (ed.), *Partnerships in the Social Sector: Issues and Country Experiences in Asia and the South Pacific,* pp. 144–167. Tokyo: Asian Development Bank.

Duvieusart, Baudouin and Ughetto, R. (1973). *République Khmère: Projet de Restructuration du Système d'Education.* Paris: UNESCO.

Education Commission (1984). *Education Commission Report No. 1.* Hong Kong: Government Printer.

——(1986). *Education Commission Report No. 2.* Hong Kong: Government Printer.

——(1990). *Education Commission Report No. 4: The Curriculum and Behavioural Problems in Schools.* Hong Kong: Government Printer.

——(2005). *Review of Medium of Instruction for Secondary Schools and Secondary School Places Allocation.* Hong Kong: Government Logistics Department.

Education Department (1981). *General Guidelines on Moral Education in Schools.* Hong Kong: Government Printer.

Education Department Curriculum Development Committee (1985). *Guidelines on Civic Education in Schools.* Hong Kong: Government Printer.

Evans, Stephen (2000). "Hong Kong's new English language policy in education," *World Englishes*, 19(2): 185–204.

Fairbank, John K., Reischauer, Edwin O., and Craig, Albert M. (1989). *East Asia: Traditions and Transformations*. Boston, MA: Houghton Mifflin.

Fergusson, Lee and Le Masson, Gildas (1997). "A culture under siege: Post-colonial higher education and teacher education in Cambodia from 1953 to 1979," *History of Education*, 26: 91–112.

Fiske, Edward (1995). *Using Both Hands: Women and Education in Cambodia*. Manila: Asian Development Bank.

Fung, Alex C.W., Pefianco, Erlinda C., and Teather, David B. (2000). "Challenges in the new millenium," *Journal of Southeast Asian Education*, 1(1). Bangkok: SEAMO.

Galasso, Elisabetta (1990). *Education in Cambodia: Notes and Suggestions*. Phnom Penh: Redd Barna.

Gonzalez, E. (1997). "Philippines," in Gerard A. Postiglione and Grace C.L. Mak (eds), *Asian Higher Education: An International Handbook and Reference Guide*, pp. 265–284. Westport, CT: Greenwood Press.

Gopinathan, S. (1974). *Towards a National System of Education in Singapore 1945–1973*. Singapore: Oxford University Press.

——(1976). "Towards a national educational system," in R. Hassan (ed.), *Singapore: Society in Transition*, pp. 67–83. Kuala Lumpur: Oxford University Press.

——(1980). "Language policy in education: A Singapore perspective," in E.A. Afendras and E.C.Y. Kuo (eds), *Language and Society in Singapore*, pp. 175–202. Singapore: Singapore University Press.

——(1991). "Education," in E.C.T. Chew and E. Lee (eds), *A History of Singapore*, pp. 268–287. Singapore: Oxford University Press.

Government Information Office (2005). *Taiwan's Educational Development and Present Situation*. Taipei, Taiwan: Government Information Office. Accessed on July 27, 2006 from http://www.gio.gov.tw/info/taiwan-story/education/edown/3-1.htm.

Government of Mongolia (1993). *Mongolia Human Resource Development and Education Reform Project: Sector Review*. Prepared for the Government of Mongolia by the Ministry of Science and Education; the Academy for Educational Development; the School of Education, University of Pittsburgh; and Dan Educ Consulting (contributing author).

——(1994). *Mongolia Education and Human Resource Master Plan*. Prepared for the Government of Mongolia by the Ministry of Science and Education and the Academy for Educational Development.

Gu, M.Y. (2001). *Education in China and Abroad: Perspectives from a Lifetime in Comparative Education*. Hong Kong: Comparative Education Research Centre, University of Hong Kong.

Gu, N. (2005). "Jianguo yilai nuxing jiaoyu de chengguo,wenti ji duice (Achievement, problems and suggested measures of female education after the foundation of PRC)," *Dangdai zhongguo shi yanjiu (Contemporary China History Studies)*, 1(6): 56–64.

Guthrie, Doug (2006). *China and Globalization: The Social, Economic and Political Transformation of Chinese Society*. New York: Routledge.

Gyallay-Pap, Peter (1989). "Reclaiming a shattered past: Education for the displaced Khmer in Thailand," *Journal of Refugee Studies*, 2: 257–275.

Han, Man-Gil, Yun, Jong-Hyeok, Lee, Jeoung-Kyu (2001). *"Pukhan Kyoyuk ŭi Hyeonsilgwa Byeonhwa* [Analysis of the Realities and Changes of North Korean Education]." Monograph, Korean Educational Development Institute (KEDI), Seoul, Korea, pp 57–89.

Hannum, E. (2003). "Poverty and basic education in rural China: Villages, households, and girls' and boys' enrollment," *Comparative Education Review*, 47(2): 141–159.

Hao, K.M. (1998). *Zhongguo jiao yu ti zhi gai ge 20 nian* (Reforms of China's Educational System during the past 20 years). Zhengzhou: Zhongzhou gu ji chu ban she.

Hawkins, J.N. and Su, Z.X. (2003). "Asian education," in Robert F. Arnove and Carlos Alberto Torres (eds), *Comparative Education: The Dialectic of the Global and the Local*, 2nd edn., pp. 338–356. Lanham, MD: Rowman & Littlefield.

Hayhoe, Ruth (1992) *Education and Modernization: The Chinese Experience*. New York: Pergammon Press.

——(1996). *China's Universities, 1895–1995: A Century of Cultural Conflict*. Hong Kong: The Comparative Education Research Center, the University of Hong Kong.

He, Z. and Geng, J. (2006). "The opportunities and challenges of vocational education," in Yang Dongbing (ed.), *Jiaoyu lanpishu: 2005 nian zhongguo jiaoyu fazhan baoguo* (Blue Book of Education: The Development of Report of China's Education, 2005), pp. 109–122. Beijing: Shehui kexue wenxian chu ban she.

Henders, Susan J. (ed.) (2004). *Democratization and Identity: Regimes and Ethnicity in East and Southeast Asia*. Lanham, MD: Lexington Press.

Hernandez, I.C. (2006). "An evaluation of the integrated core curriculum and its implementation in selected schools of San Juan, Metro Manila." Unpublished Manuscript. Manila: University of Asia and the Pacific.

Ho, Ai-Hsin (2003). "Exploring New Zealand and Taiwanese beginning secondary teachers' perceptions of leadership." Masters Dissertation, University of Waikato, Hamilton, New Zealand.

Hong, Zuway-R., McCarthy, Patricia, and Lawrenz, Frances (2003). "An investigation of the gender stereotyped thinking of Taiwanese secondary school boys and girls," *Sex Roles: A Journal of Research*, 48(11–12): 495–504.

Hong Kong Government (1964). *Education Policy*. Hong Kong: Government Printer.

——(1965). *Education Policy*. Hong Kong: Government Printer.

——(1974). *Secondary Education in Hong Kong over the Next Decade*. Hong Kong: Government Printer.

——(1978). *The Development of Senior Secondary and Tertiary Education*. Hong Kong: Government Printer.

Hong Kong Government Secretariat (1981). *The Hong Kong Education System*. Hong Kong: Government Printer.

Hu, G.W. (2005). "Reforms of basic English-language education in China: An overview," *International Journal of Educational Reform*, 14(2): 140–165.

Huang, F. (2006). "Internationalization of curricula in higher education institutions in comparative perspectives: Case Studies of China, Japan and the Netherlands," *Higher Education*, 51(4): 521–539.

Huang, Kun-Hui (1978). "Comparison and analysis of the family and socioeconomic status (SES) of the candidates and enrollees of the University and College Entrance Examination in Taiwan," *Periodical of Graduate Institute of Education*, vol. 20, pp. 143–319. Taiwan: Center for Educational Research, National Taiwan Normal University, Taiwan.

Hwang, Chung-kyu (1990). *Pukhan kyoyuk ŭi Jomyeong* [Spotlight on North Korean Education]. Seoul: Bobmunsa.

Hwang, Kwang-Kuo (2003). *What's Wrong with Taiwanese Education Reform?* Taipei, Taiwan: INK Publishing.

Im, Eric Iksoon and Mansourov, Alexandre Y. (2001). "Contemporary general and vocational education in the Democratic People's Republic of Korea," in Lee-Jay Cho and Eric Iksoon Im (eds), *North Korean Labor and Its Prospects*. Northeast Asia Economic Forum, pp. 81–112. Honolulu, Hawaii: East-West Center.

Inoue, H. (1977). *Nippon no Kyoiku Shiso* (Educational Ideology of Japan). Tokyo: Fukumura Publishing Co.

Isidro, A. and Ramos, M. (1973). *Private Colleges and Universities in the Philippines*. Quezon City: Alemar-Phoenix Publishing House, Inc.

Jin, Y.L. (2000). *Jin dai Zhongguo da xue yan jiu: 1895–1949* (Study on University in Modern China: 1895–1949). Beijing: Zhong yang wen xian chu ban she.

Johanson, R. (1999). "Higher education in the Philippines." Technical Background Paper No. 3, in *ADB-WB Philippine Education for the 21st Century. The 1998 Philippine Education Sector Study*. Manila: Asian Development Bank.

Johnson, J.M. (1993). *Human Resources for Science and Technology: The Asian Region (Surveys of Science Resources Series, Special Report, NSF 93-303)*. Washington, DC: National Science Foundation.

Johnson, Robert Keith (1998). "Language and education in Hong Kong," in M.C. Pennington (ed.), *Language in Hong Kong at Century's End*, pp. 265–276. Hong Kong: Hong Kong University Press.

Joint Congressional Committee on Education (JCCE) (1951). *Improving the Philippine Educational System: Report of the Joint Congressional Committee on Education to the Congress*. Manila: Bureau of Printing.

Jones, G. and Hagul, P. (2001). "Schooling in Indonesia: Crisis-related and longer-term issues," *Bulletin of Indonesian Economic Studies*, 37(2): 207–231.

Kalab, Milada (1976). "Monastic education, social mobility, and village structure in Cambodia," in Craig Calhoun and Francis Ianni (eds), *The Anthropological Study of Education*, pp. 61–74. The Hague: Mouton Publishers.

Kang, Il Guk (2002). "Haebang yihu chodeng hakgyoei kyoyuk gaehyukkwa bangong kyoyukei chungae kwajung [The reformation movement of the primary schools and the formation of the anti-communist education after 1945]," *Sociology of Education*, 12(2): 1–17.

Kerckhoff, Alan (2001). "Educational stratification in comparative perspective," *Sociology of Education*, Extra Issue. Sociology at the Dawn of the 21st Century, 3–18.

Kewin, K. and Xu, H. (1989). "Rethinking revolution: Reflections on China's 1985 educational reforms," *Comparative Education*, 25(1): 7–17.

Kim, Chang-ho (1990). *Choson kyoyuksa* [*History of North Korean Education*]. Pyongyang: Social Science Publishing.

Kim, Dong-kyu (1990). *Pukhan ŭi kyoyukhak* [Pedagogy of North Korea]. Seoul: Mun Maek Sa.

Kim, Hyong-chan (1990). *Pukhan ŭi kyoyuk* [North Korean Education]. Seoul: Ulyoumunhwasa.

Kim, Il Sung (1977). *Theses on Socialist Education*. Pyongyang, Korea: Foreign Languages Press.

Kim, Jongchol (2000). "Historical development," in John C. Weidman and Namgi Park (eds), *Higher Education in Korea: Tradition and Adaptation*, pp. 7–54. New York: Falmer Press.

Kim, Jung-gull (1999). "Han'guk kyo'yuk Gaehyuk ui Chungae Kwajung ei Daehan Pyung'ga juk Yon'gu [Studies on Korea's educational reform process]," *The Journal of Educational Administration*, 17(4): 41–70.

Kim, Ransoo and Yong Sop Ahn (1993). "Higher education in South and North Korea," *Higher Education Policy*, 6(2): 29–36.

Komolmas, Prathip M. (1998). "Thailand: New trends in higher education toward the 21st Century," in *New Trends in Higher Education: Market Mechanisms in Higher Education Toward the 21st Century*, pp. 111–125. Jakarta: The Association of Southeast Asian Institutions of Higher Education.

Kwong, J.L. (1997). "The reemergence of private schools in Socialist China," *Comparative Education Review*, 41(3): 244–259.

Lao People's Revolutionary Party (1979). *Politbureau's Resolutions regarding Education Tasks of the New Revolutionary Era*. Vientiane: Ministry of Education, Sports and Culture.

Lavely, W., Xiao, Z.Y., Li, B.H., and Freedman, R. (1990). "The rise of female education in China: National and regional patterns," *The China Quarterly*, 121 (March): 61–93.

Law, Wing-Wah (2004). "Globalization and citizenship education in Hong Kong and Taiwan," *Comparative Education Review*, 48(3): 253–273.

——(2004). "Translating globalization and democratization into local policy: Educational reform in Hong Kong and Taiwan," *International Review of Education*, 50(5–6): 497–524.

Lê, Thao and Shi, Li (2006). *Chinese-background Students' Learning Approaches*, AARE, Adelaide November, 27. Accessed on April 20, 2007 from http://www.aare.edu.au/06pap/le06370.pdf.

Lee, C.F. (2000). "The study of the internship of probationary teachers for primary and secondary education in current Taiwan," *Education Research and Information*, 8(5): 1–14.

Lee, Eun-Jun (2002). *Brain Korea 21: Development-Oriented National Policy in Korea Higher Education*. International Higher Education. Boston: Center for International Higher Education, Boston College. Accessed on June 11, 2006 from http://www.bc.edu/bc_org/avp/soe/cihe/newsletter/News19/text16.html.

Lee, Molly Nyet Ngo, Yoong, Suan, Loo, Seng Piew, Zon, Khadijah, Ghazali, Munirah, and Lim, Chap Sam (1996). *Students' Orientations towards Science and Mathematics: Why are Enrolments Falling?* Penang, Malaysia: Universiti Sains Malaysia.

Lee, T.H.C. (1985). *Government Education and the Examinations in Sung China*. Hong Kong: Chinese University Press.

Lee, Wing On (2004). "Citizenship education in Hong Kong: Development and challenges," in W.O. Lee, D.L. Grossman, K.J. Kennedy, and G.P. Fairbrother (eds), *Citizenship Education in Asia and the Pacific: Concepts and Issues*, pp. 59–80. Hong Kong: Comparative Education Research Centre, University of Hong Kong.

Legge, James (Translated) (1970). *The Four Books; Confucian Analects*, Chapter XXXVIII, Taipei: Culture Book Company, p. 357.

Leung, Sai Wing (1995). "Depoliticization and trivialization of civic education in secondary schools: Institutional constraints on promoting civic education in transitional Hong Kong," in P.K. Siu and T.K. Tam (eds), *Quality in Education: Insights from Different Perspectives*, pp. 283–312. Hong Kong: Educational Research Association.

Li, Cheng (ed.) (2005). *Bridging Minds across the Pacific: U.S.–China Educational Exchanges, 1978–2003.* New York: Lexington Books.

Li, G.J. and Wang, B.Z. (2000). *Zhongguo jiao yu zhi du tong shi* (General History of China's Educational System). Jinan Shi: Shandong jiao yu chu ban she.

Li, H. and Rao, N. (2005). "Curricular and instructional influences on early literacy attainment: Evidence from Beijing, Hong Kong and Singapore," *International Journal of Early Years Education*, 13(3): 235–253.

Lin, J. (1993). *Education in Post-Mao China.* Westport, CT: Praeger.

Ling, Da-Sen (2001). "The effect of family educational resources on tracking and educational status attainment," *The National Cheng-Chi University Journal of Sociology*, 31: 45–75.

Liu, J. and Carpenter, M. (2005). "Trends and issues of women's education in China," *The Clearing House*, 78(6): 277–281.

Liu, Jeng (1981). *TheFuture of Chinese Education.* Taipei, Taiwan: Jia-Yi Publisher.

Liu, N.C. and Liu, L. (2005). "University rankings in China," *Higher Education in Europe*, 30(2): 217–226.

Liu, P. and Qi, C.X. (2005). "Reform in the curriculum of basic education in the People's Republic of China: Pedagogy, application, and learners," *International Journal of Educational Reform*, 14(1): 35–44.

Liu, S.J. and Maxey, S. (2005). "Are Dewey's educational ideas involved in China's education once again?" *International Journal of Educational Reform*, 14(2): 162–177.

Liu, Y.K. (1998). "Educational utilitarianism: Where goes higher education?" in Michael Agelasto and Bob Adamson (eds), *Higher Education in Post-Mao China*, pp. 121–140. Hong Kong: Hong Kong University Press.

Llewellyn, John (1982). *A Perspective on Education in Hong Kong.* Hong Kong: Government Printer.

Lockhart, Bruce (2001). "Education in Laos in historical perspective." Unpublished paper, National University of Singapore.

Lofstedt, J.I. (1980). *Chinese Educational Policy: Changes and Contradictions, 1949–79.* Stockholm: Almqvist & Wiksell.

Loh, Fook Seng (1970). "The nineteenth century British approach to Malay education," *Jurnal Pendidekan*, 1(1).

Lu, H.J. (1983). *Zhongguo jin shi de jiao yu fa zhan, 1800–1949 (Educational Development in Modern China: 1800–1949).* Hong Kong: Hua feng shu ju.

Lukens-Bull, R.A. (1997). "A peaceful jihad: Javanese Islamic education and religious identity construction." Ph.D. Dissertation, Arizona State University.

Mackerras, Colin (1994). *China's Minorities: Integration and Modernization in the 20th Century.* Hong Kong: Oxford University Press.

——(1995). *China's Minority Cultures: Identities and Integration since 1912.* New York: Longman and St. Martin's Press.

Maglen, L. and Manasan, R. (1999). "Education costs and financing in the Philippines," Technical Background Paper No.2, in *ADB-WB Philippine Education for the 21st Century. The 1998 Philippine Education Sector Study.* Manila.

Malaya (1951a). *Report of the Committee on Malay Education.* Kuala Lumpur: Government Press.

——(1951b). *Report on the Barnes Report on Malay Education and the Fenn-Wu Report on Chinese Education.* Kuala Lumpur: Government Press.

——(1956). *Report of the Education Committee, 1956.* Kuala Lumpur: Government Press.

——(1960). *Report of the Education Review Committee, 1960.* Kuala Lumpur: Government Press.

Mansourov, Alexandre Y. (2001). "Evolution of education and continuing training in the DPRK since the 1950s," in Lee-Jay Cho and Eric Iksoon Im (eds), *North Korean Labor and Its Prospects.* Northeast Asia Economic Forum, pp. 47–79. Honolulu, Hawaii: East-West Center.

McArthur, M.S.H. (1987). *Report on Brunei in 1904.* Ohio University Monograph in International Studies. S.E. Asian series No. 74, Athens, OH: Ohio University.

McCloud, Donald G. (1995). *Southeast Asia: Tradition and Modernity in the Contemporary World,* Boulder, CO: Westview.

McElroy, S.C. (2001). "Forging a new role for women: Zhili first women's normal school and the growth of women's education in China, 1901–21," in Glen Peterson, Ruth Hayhoe, and Yongling Lu (eds), *Education, Culture, and Identity in Twentieth-century China,* pp. 348–374. Hong Kong: Hong Kong University Press.

McGinn, Noel F., Snodgrass, Donald, Yung Bong Kim, Shin-bok Kim, and Quee-yong Kim (1980). *Education and Development in Korea.* Cambridge: Harvard University Press.

MECS (Ministry of Education, Culture and Science) (2001). *Foundation of the Education Sector in Mongolia and its Development in 80 Years.* Ulaanbaatar, Mongolia.

——(2005). *EFA Assessment of Mongolia.* Ulaanbaatar, Mongolia (November).

Meyer, John (2001). "Reflections: The worldwide commitment to educational equality," *Sociology of Education,* Extra Issue. Sociology at the Dawn of the 21st Century, 154–158.

Min, Weifang (2004). "Chinese higher education: The legacy of the past and the context of the future," in Philip G. Altbach (ed.), *Asian Universities: Historical Perspectives and Contemporary Challenges,* pp. 53–83. Baltimore, MD: Johns Hopkins Press.

Ministère de l'Education (1990). *Bulletin de Statistiques de l'Education de l'Etat du Cambodge.* Phnom Penh: Ministère de l'Education.

Ministry of Education (1979). *Report on the Ministry of Education 1978.* Singapore: Ministry of Education.

——(1982). *Two Hundred Years of Thai Education.* Bangkok: Ministry of Education (in Thai).

——(1990). *Education: State of Cambodia.* Phnom Penh: Ministry of Education.

——(2000). *Education in Korea 1999–2000.* Seoul: Ministry of Education.

——(2002). *Report of junior college/upper secondary education review committee.* Singapore: Ministry of Education.

——(2002). *The current educational system.* Taipei, Taiwan: Ministry of Education. Accessed on August 1, 2005 from http://140.111.1.192/statistics/multi/current-e.htm.

——(2002). *Embracing challenges of 2008: E-Generation human capacity-building.* Taipei, Taiwan: Ministry of Education. Accessed on August 18, 2005 from http://140.111.1.22/english/home_ministry.htm.

——(2004). *The Development of Education: National Report of the Democratic People's Republic of Korea.* Pyong-yang: Ministry of Education, DPRK.

Ministry of Education (2004). *Education in the Republic of China*. Taipei, Taiwan: Department of Statistics, Ministry of Education.

——(2004). *Summary of education at all levels*. Taipei, Taiwan: Ministry of Education. Accessed on August 18, 2005 from http://140.111.1.22/english/en05/other/ yr04.htm.

——(2005). *Educational development*. Taipei, Taiwan: Ministry of Education. Accessed on August 18, 2005 from http://140.111.1.22/english/en05/2005/c2.htm.

Ministry of Education, Malaysia (2001). *Pembangunan pendidikan 2001–2010: Perancangan bersepadu penjana kecemerlangan pendidikan* (Education Development Plan 2001–2010: Generating Educational Excellence through Collaborative Planning). Malaysia: Ministry of Education.

Ministry of Education, Youth, and Sport (2001). *Education Sector Support Program 2001–2005*. Phnom Penh: Ministry of Education, Youth, and Sport.

——(2001). *Education Strategic Plan 2001–2005*. Phnom Penh: Ministry of Education, Youth, and Sport.

——(2002). *Education Sector Support Program 2002–2006*. Phnom Penh: Ministry of Education, Youth, and Sport.

——(2002). *The Five-Year Gender Mainstreaming Strategy 2002–2006: From Commitment to Action*. Phnom Penh: Ministry of Education, Youth, and Sport.

Mok, K.H. (1997). "Marketization or quasi-marketization: Educational development in post-Mao China," *International Review of Education*, 43(5–6): 1–21.

——(1999). "Education and the market place in Hong Kong and Mainland China," *Higher Education*, 37(2): 133–158.

——(2004). *Centralization and Decentralization: Educational Reform and Changing Governance Chinese Societies*, edited by Mak Ka-Ho, pp. 157–172. Hong Kong: Comparative Education Research Centre and Kluwer Press.

——(2005). "Globalization and educational restructuring: University merging and changing governance in China," *Higher Education*, 50(1): 57–88.

——(2006). *Education Reform and Education Policy in East Asia*. London: Routledge.

Moonsin, Wutthichai (1969). *The Management Policy of the Thai Education in the Reign of King Chulalongkorn*. Bangkok: Prasarnmit College of Education (in Thai).

Morris, Paul and Sweeting, Anthony (eds) (1995). *Education and Development in East Asia*. New York: Garland Press.

MOSTEC (Ministry of Science, Technology, Education and Culture), Government of Mongolia (1999). *Mongolia Education Sector Strategy 2000–2005*. Ulaanbaatar, Mongolia: MOSTEC.

Mustapa, Kassim (1989). "Preferential policy in higher education in Malaysia: A case study of Malay graduates at the University of Science Malaysia." Ph.D. Dissertation, University of Wisconsin.

Nash, M.J. (1994). "Tigers in the lab: Asian-born, US-trained researchers are headed home to challenge the technological supremacy of the West," *Time* (International Edition), November 21, pp. 48–49.

National Education Inspection Group (Guojia jiaoyu dudaotuan) (2005). "You'er jiaoyu dudao jiancha gongbao (The report of inspection on childhood education)," in Yang Dongbing (ed.), *Jiaoyu lanpishu: 2005 nian zhongguo jiaoyu fazhan baogao* (Blue Book of Education: The Development Report on China's Education, 2005), pp. 291–294. Beijing: Shehui kexue wenxian chu ban she.

Népote, Jacques (1979). "Education et Développement dans le Cambodge Moderne," *Mondes en Développement*, 28: 767–792.

Nielson, H.D. (2003). "Reforms to teacher education in Indonesia: Does more mean better?" in E.R. Beauchamp (ed.), *Comparative Education Reader*, pp. 391–410. New York: Routledge Falmer.

Nilan, P. (2003). "Teachers' work and schooling in Bali," *International Review of Education*, 49(6): 563–584.

Oey-Gardiner, M. (2000). "Schooling in a decentralized Indonesia: New approaches to access and decision making," *Bulletin of Indonesian Economic Studies* 36(3): 127–134.

Orbeta, A. (2003). *Education, Labor Market and Development: A Review of the Trends and Issues in the Philippines for the Past 25 Years*. Perspective Paper Series No. 9. Manila: Philippine Institute for Development Studies.

Pak, Jane (2004). "Socio-political influences on educational goals in North Korea: An analysis of Kim Il Sung and Kim Jong Il's works on education (1946–1986)." Unpublished Monograph, International Educational Administration and Policy Analysis, School of Education, Stanford University.

Pan, Hui-Ling and Yu, Chien (1999). "Educational reforms with their impacts on school effectiveness and school improvement in Taiwan, R.O.C.," *School Effectiveness and School Improvement*, 10(1): 72–85.

Pang, Y.H. and Richey, D. (2007). "Preschool education in China and the United States: A personal perspective," *Early Child Development and Care*, 177(1), 1–13.

Park, Kyung-Jae (2005). "Policies and strategies to meet the challenges of internationalization of higher education." Paper read at the Third Regional Follow-up Committee for the 1998 World Conference on Higher Education in Asia and the Pacific, Seoul, Korea, July 5, 2005.

Park, Namgi (2000). "The 31 May 1995 higher education reform," in John C. Weidman and Namgi Park (eds), *Higher Education in Korea: Tradition and Adaptation*. New York: Falmer Press.

Pepper, S. (1990). *China's Education Reform in the 1980s: Policies, Issues and Historical Perspective*. Berkeley, CA: Institute of East Asian Studies, University of California.

——(1996). *Radicalism and Education Reform in 20th-Century China: The Search for an Ideal Development Model*. New York: Cambridge University Press.

Peterson, G., Hayhoe, R., and Lu, Y.L. (eds) (2001). *Education, Culture, and Identity in Twentieth-century China*. Hong Kong: Hong Kong University Press.

Pham, Minh Hac (1988). *Vietnam's Education: The Current Position and Future Prospects*. Hanoi: Gioi Publishers.

Postiglione, Gerard A. (ed.) (1991). *Education and Society in Hong Kong: Toward One Country and Two Systems*. New York: M.E. Sharpe.

——(1999). *China's National Minority Education: Culture, Schooling and Development*. New York: Falmer Press.

——(1999–2000). "Introduction: State schooling and ethnicity in China," in G. Postiglione (ed.), *China's National Minority Education: Culture, Schooling and Development*, pp. 3–20. New York: Falmer Press.

——(2000). "National minority regions: Studying school discontinuation," in Judith Liu, H.A. Ross and D.P. Kelly (eds), *The Ethnographic Eye: Interpretive Studies of Education In China*, pp. 51–72. New York: Falmer Press.

——(2005). "Higher education in China: Perils and promises for a new century," *Harvard China Review*, Spring: 138–143.

Postiglione, Gerard A. (ed.) (2006). *Education and Social Change in China: Inequality in a Market Economy*. Armonk, NY: M.E. Sharpe.

——(2006). "Finance and governance in Southeast Asian higher education," *Higher Education in the World, 2006: The Financing of Universities*, pp. 187–192. New York: Palgrave.

——(in press). "Ethnicity and the role of education as a mechanism for national unity in China," in Santosh Saha (ed.), *The Politics of Ethnicity and National Identity*. New York: Macmillan/Palgrave.

Postiglione, Gerard A. and Lee Wing On (1995). *Social Change and Educational Development: Mainland China, Taiwan and Hong Kong*. Hong Kong: Centre of Asian Studies.

Postiglione, Gerard A. and Mak, G.C.L. (1997). *Asian Higher Education*. Westport, CT: Greenwood Press.

Postiglione, Gerard A. and Tang, J.T.H. (eds.) (1997). *Hong Kong's Reunion with China: The Global Dimensions*. New York: M.E. Sharpe.

Presidential Commission on Education Reform (PCER) (1997). *Education Reform for New Education System*. Seoul, Korea: PCER.

President Kim Il Sung and Development of Education in Korea (1992). Pyongyang: Kyowon Sinmun.

Price, R.F. (1979). *Education in Modern China*, 2nd edn. London: Routledge and Kegan Paul.

Purwadi, A. and S. Muljoatmodjo (2000). "Education in Indonesia: Coping with challenges in the third millennium," *Journal of Southeast Asian Education*, 1(1): 79–102.

Rachman, H.A. (1997). "The pesantren architects and their socio-religious teachings." Ph.D. Dissertation, University of California, Los Angeles.

Rahman, A. (1997). "Social class, school structure, and schooling outcomes in Indonesia." Ph.D. Dissertation, Florida State University.

Rao, N., Cheng, K.M., and Narain, K. (2003). "Primary schooling in China and India: Understanding how sociocontextual factors moderate the role of the state," in Mark Bray (ed.), *Comparative Education: Continuing Traditions, New Challenges, and New Paradigms*, pp. 153–176. Dordrecht: Kluwer Academic Publishers.

Reed, Gay Garland (1997). "Globalisation and education: The case of North Korea," *Compare*, 27(2): 167–178.

——(2004). "Multidimensional citizenship, Confucian humanism and the imagined community: South Korea and China," in W.O. Lee, David L.Grossman, Kerry J. Kennedy, and Gregory P. Fairbrother (eds.), *Citizenship Education in Asia and the Pacific: Concepts and Issues*, pp. 239–256. Hong Kong: Comparative Education Research Centre, The University of Hong Kong; Kluwer Academic Publishers.

Reed, Gay Garland and Choi, Sheena (2001). "Confucian legacy, global future: Values education policy in South Korea," in William Cummings, Maria Teresa Tatto and John Hawkins (eds), *Values Education for Dynamic Societies: Individualism or Collectivism*, pp. 175–190. Hong Kong: University of Hong Kong Press.

Reed, Gay Garland and Chung, Bong Gun (1997). "North Korea," in Gerard Postiglione and Grace Mak (eds), *Asian Higher Education: An International Handbook and Reference Guide*, pp. 231–244. Westport, CT: Greenwood Press.

Reiff, Hans (1980). *Educational Emergency Assistance and Rehabilitation in Kampuchea.* Bangkok: United Nations Educational, Scientific, and Cultural Organization (UNESCO).

Rhee, Dong-gun and Choi, Su-il (1979). *Juche Ideology in the Ideological amd Methodological Foundation of Socialist Education.* Pyongyang: Science Encyclopedia Publishing.

Rohlen, T.P. (1983). *Japan's High Schools.* Berkeley and Los Angeles, CA: University of California Press.

——(1995). "Building character," in T.P. Rohlen and G.K. LeTendre (eds), *Teaching and Learning in Japan*, pp. 50–74. Cambridge: Cambridge University Press.

Rosen, Stanley (2004). Beida Reforms, a special issue of the journal *Chinese Education and Society*, 37(6), November–December, New York: M.E. Sharpe.

Ross, H. (2001). "Historical memory, community service, hope: Reclaiming the social purposes of education for the Shanghai McTyeire School for girls," in Glen Peterson, Ruth Hayhoe, and Yongling Lu (eds), *Education, Culture, and Identity in Twentieth-century China*, pp. 375–402. Hong Kong: Hong Kong University Press.

Royal Government of Cambodia (1994). *Basic Education Investment Plan 1995–2000.* Phnom Penh: Royal Government of Cambodia.

——(2003). *Education for All National Plan 2003–2015.* Phnom Penh: Royal Government of Cambodia.

Ruzzi, Betsy Brown (2005). *International Education Tests: An Overview, New Commission on the Skills for the American Work Force.* National Center on Education and Economy (April). Accessed on January 22, 2007 from http://www.skillscommission.org/pdf/Staff%20Papers/International%20Tests.pdf.

Sahara, Ahmad (2000). *Education for all (Malaysian country report).* United Nations: UNESCO.

SarDesai, D.R. (1994). *Southeast Asia: Past and Present*, 3rd edn. Boulder, CO: Westview Press.

Sautman, B. (1999). "Expanding access to higher education for China's national minorities: Policies of preferential admissions," in Gerard A. Postiglione (ed.), *China's National Minority Education Culture, Schooling, and Development*, pp. 173–210. New York; London: Falmer Press.

Schneewind, S. (2006). *Community Schools and the State in Ming China.* Stanford, CA: Stanford University Press.

Schumacher, J.N. (1991). "Higher education and the origins of nationalism," in J.N. Schumacher (ed.), *The Making of a Nation: Essays on Nineteenth-Century Filipino Nationalism*, pp. 35–43. Quezon City: Ateneo de Manila University Press.

Seki, Eiko (1987). "Korean endeavors toward the reestablishment of their educational system under the U.S. Military Government," in H. Abe (ed.), *Educational Reform in Korea Under the U.S. Military Government (1945–1948)*, pp. 214–229. Seoul: Han'guk Yon'guwon.

Seok, Tae-jong (1999). "Kungmin ei Jungbu Daehak Kyoyuk Kaehyuk Sa'up ei Pipanjok Gumto [Critical evaluation of Kungmin Government's higher education reform effort]," *Sociology of Education*, 9(3): 87–104.

Seth, Michael J. (2002). *Education Fever: Society, Politics and the Pursuit of Schooling.* Honolulu, HI: University of Hawaii Press and Center for Korean Studies, University of Hawaii.

Shils, E. (1972). "Metropolis and province in the intellectual community," in E. Shils (ed.), *The Intellectuals and the Powers and other Essays*, pp. 355–371. Chicago, IL: University of Chicago Press.

Singapore Legislative Assembly (1956). *Report of the All-Party Committee of the Singapore Legislative Assembly on Chinese Education*. Singapore: Government Printer.

——(1956). *White Paper on Education Policy* (Sessional Paper No. Cmd. 15 of 1956). Singapore: Government Printer.

Sinlarat, Paitoon (1983). *The Thai Education System in Three Decades*. Bangkok: Faculty of Education, Chulalongkorn University (in Thai).

——(2003). *The Programs Opened at the Higher Education Level: The Development in 200 Years of Rattanakosin (1782–1982)*. Bangkok: Textbook and Academic Document Center, Faculty of Education, Chulalongkorn University (in Thai).

——(2004). "Thai universities: Past, present, and future," in P.G. Altbach (ed.), *Asian Universities: Historical Perspectives and Contemporary Challenges*, pp. 201–220. Baltimore, MD: John's Hopkins University Press.

——(2005). *Thai Universities after World War II: Adjustment for the Modern Society*. Bangkok: Chulalongkorn University Press (in Thai).

——(2006). *Reversing Globalization in Thailand: New Directions for Edcuation Reform*. Bangkok: Higher Education Program, Chulalongkorn University (in Thai).

Sirozi, M. (2004). "Secular-religious debates on the Indonesian National Education System: Colonial legacy and a search for national identity in education," *Intercultural Education*, 15(2): 123–137.

Siti Zahara, Sulaiman (1975). "MARA Junior Science College: Students selection and its implication for educational development in Malaya." Ph.D. Dissertation, University of Cornell.

Smith, Douglas C. (1997). *Middle Education in the Middle Kingdom: The Chinese Junior High School in Modern Taiwan*. Westport, CT: Greenwood Press.

Steiner-Khamsi, Gita and Stolpe, Ines (2006). *Educational Import: Local Encounters with Global Forces in Mongolia*. New York: Palgrave Macmillan.

Suárez-Orozco, Marcelo M. and Qin-Hilliard, Desirée Baolian (eds) (2004). *Globalization: Culture and Education in the New Millennium*. Berkeley, CA: University of California Press.

Sweeting, A.E. (1990). *Education in Hong Kong: Pre 1841 to 1941*. Hong Kong: Hong Kong University Press.

——(2004). *Education in Hong Kong: 1941–2001*. Hong Kong: Hong Kong University Press.

Takeuchi, K. (2003). "Gakusei to Daigaku Kaikaku (Student and university reform)," in A. Arimoto and S. Yamamoto (ed.), *Daigaku Kaikaku no Genzai* (University Reform Today), pp. 119–138. Tokyo: Toshindo Publishing Co.

Tan, E. (2001). *The Political Economy of Education Reforms*. Tokyo: Institute of Developing Economies.

Tan, J. (2004). "Singapore: Small nation, big plans," in P.G. Altbach (ed.), *Asian Universities: Historical Perspectives and Contemporary Challenges*, pp. 175–200. Baltimore, MD: John's Hopkins University Press.

Tan, Jee-Peng and Mingat, Alain (1992). *Education in Asia: A Comparative Study of Cost and Financing*. Washington: The World Bank.

Tang, Feng L. (2006). "The child as an active learner: Views, practices, and barriers in Chinese early childhood education," *Childhood Education*, 82(6): 342–346.

Teng, T. (1994). "China, People's Republic of: System of education," in Torsten Husen and T. Neville Postlethwaite (eds), *The International Encyclopedia of Education*, 2nd edn., pp. 750–755. Oxford: Pergamon.

Thomas, R. Murray and Postlethwaite, Neville (eds) (1983). *Schooling in East Asia: Forces of Change*, London: Pergamon.

Tian, Z.P. (2004). *Zhong wai jiao yu jiao liu shi* (Sino-foreign Educational Exchange History). Guangzhou Shi: Guangdong jiao yu chu ban she.

Ting, Joseph S.P. (1993). "Preface," in S.K. Yau, K.L. Leung, and S.L. Chow (eds), *Xianggan Jiaoyu Fazhan: Bainian Shuren* (Education in Hong Kong: Past and Present), pp. 8–11. Hong Kong: Urban Council.

Tomoda, Y. (1988). "Politics and moral education in Japan," in W.K. Cummings, S. Gopinathan, and Y. Tomoda (eds), *The Revival of Values Education in Asia and the West*, pp.75–91. New York: Pergamon Press.

Tsai, Ching-Hwa (1996). "The deregulation of higher education in Taiwan." *International Higher Education*, 4. Accessed on August 18, 2005 from http://www.bc.edu/bc_org/avp/soe/cihe/newsletter/News04/textcy3.html.

Tse, Kwan Choi (2005). "Quality education in Hong Kong: The anomalies of managerialism and marketization," in L.S. Ho, P. Morris and Y.P. Chung (eds), *Education Reform and the Quest for Excellence: The Hong Kong Story*, pp. 99–123. Hong Kong: Hong Kong University Press.

Tsui, Amy B.M. (2004). "Medium of instruction in Hong Kong: One country, two systems, whose language?" in J.W. Tollefson and A.B.M. Tsui (eds), *Medium of Instruction Policies: Which Agenda? Whose Agenda?*, pp. 97–116. Mahwah, NJ.: L. Erlbaum Publishers.

Tu Wei-Ming (ed.) (1996). *Confucian Traditions in East Asian Modernity: Moral Education and Economic Culture in Japan and the Four Mini-Dragons*. Cambridge, MA: Harvard University Press.

Umakoshi, Toru (1987). "The implications of U.S. educational assistance in rebuilding Korean education after the independence," in H. Abe (ed.), *Educational Reform in Korea Under the U.S. Military Government (1945–1948)*, pp. 243–253. Seoul: Han'guk Yon'guwon.

UNESCO (2004). UNESCO Institute for Statistics. Accessed on January 12, 2007 from http://www.uis.unesco.org/profiles/EN/EDU/countryProfile_en.aspx?code=40313.

Upex, S.G. (2000). "An outline of some of the sources for research into the development of education within Brunei Darussalam," in M. Clements, H. Tairab, and K. Wong (eds), *Science, Mathematics and Technical Education in the 20th and 21st centuries*, pp. 356–364. Gadong: Universiti Brunei Darussalam.

Upton, J.L. (1999). "Development of modern Tibetan language education in the PRC," in Gerard A. Postiglione (ed.), *China's National Minority Education Culture, Schooling, and Development*, pp. 281–340. New York, London: Falmer Press.

USDOE (1999). "Highlights from TIMMS, overview and key findings across grade levels," *The Third International Mathematics and Science Study*, National Center for Education Statistics, Office of Educational Research and Improvement, U.S. Department of Education, NCES 1999-081. Accessed on February 4, 2007 from http://nces.ed.gov/pubs99/1999081.pdf.

USDOE (2007). *International Comparisons in Education: Trends in International Mathematics and Science Study*. Washington, DC: National Center for Education Science, National Center for Educational Statistics, U.S. Department of Education.

Van Der Kroef, J.M. (1955). "Higher education in Indonesia," *The Journal of Higher Education*, 26(7): 366–377.

Varghese, N.V. (2001). *Impact of the Economic Crisis on Higher Education in East Asia*. Paris: UNESCO (IIEP).

Vaughan, J. (1993). "Early childhood education in China," *Childhood Education*, 69(4): 196–200.

Velasco, Esther (2001). *Why are Girls not in School? Perception, Realities and Contradictions in Changing Cambodia*. Phnom Penh: United Nations Children's Fund (UNICEF) and Swedish International Development Cooperation Agency.

——(2004). "Ensuring gender equity in education for all: Is Cambodia on track?" *Prospects*, 34: 37–51.

Wang, B.Z., Guo, Q.J., Liu, D.H., He, X.X., and Gao, Q. (1985). *Jian ming Zhongguo jiao yu shi* (A Brief History of Education in China). Beijing: Beijing shi fan da xue chu ban she.

Wang, Da-Xiu (1983). "Critiques on equal educational opportunity at the university level in Taiwan," *Thought and Words: Journal of the Humanities and Social Science*, 2(21): 165–178.

Watkins, David A. and Biggs, John B. (eds) (1996). *The Chinese Learner: Cultural, Psychological, and Contextual Influences*. Hong Kong: Hong Kong University Press.

——(2001). *Teaching the Chinese Learner: Psychological and Pedagogical Perspectives*. Hong Kong: Hong Kong University Press.

Watson, James (2004). "Globalization in Asia: Anthropological perspectives," in Marcelo M. Suárez-Orozco and Desirée Baolian Qin-Hilliard (eds), *Globalization: Culture and Education in the New Millennium*, pp. 141–172. Berkeley, CA: University of California Press.

Watson, Keith (1980). *Educational Development in Thailand*. Hong Kong: Heinemann.

Weidman, John C. (2001). "Developing the Mongolia education sector strategy 2000–2005: Reflections of a consultant for the Asian Development Bank," *Current Issues in Comparative Education* [Online], 3(2), May 1. Accessed on May 29, 2007 from http://www.tc.columbia.edu/cice/Archives/3.2/32weidman.pdf.

Weidman, John C. and Bat-Erdene, Regsurengiin (2002). "Higher education and the state in Mongolia: Dilemmas of democratic transition," in David W. Chapman and Ann E. Austin (eds), *Higher Education in the Developing World: Changing Contexts and Institutional Responses*, pp. 129–148. Westport, CT: Greenwood Press.

Weidman, John C., Chapman, David W., Cohen, Marc, and Lelei, Macrina C. (2004). "Access to education in five newly independent states of Central Asia and Mongolia: A regional agenda," in Stephen P. Heyneman and Alan J. DeYoung (eds), *Challenges for Education in Central Asia*, pp. 181–197. Greenwich, CT: Information Age Publishing.

White, M. (1987). *The Japanese Educational Change: A Commitment to Children*. New York: Free Press.

——(1993). *The Material Child: Coming of Age in Japan and America*. New York: Free Press.

Williams, G., Liu, S.S., and Shi, Q. (1997). "Marketization of higher education in the People's Republic of China," *Higher Education Policy*, 10(2): 151–157.

Williams, R. (1999). "Planning for economic diversification in Brunei: Can schools help?" *Studies in Education*, 4: 39–51.

Wilson, H.E. (1978). *Social Engineering in Singapore: Educational Policies and Social Change 1819–1972*. Singapore: Singapore University Press.

Wong, F.H.K. and Gwee, Y.H. (1980). *Official Reports on Education: Straits Settlements and the Federated Malay States, 1870–1939*. Singapore: Pan Pacific Book Distributors.

Wong, Ho Wing (ed.) (1993). *Xianggang Jiaoyu Shouce* (Hong Kong Education Handbook), rev. edn. Hong Kong: Commercial Press.

Wong, Ho Wing and King On Ho (1996). *Jinri Xianggang Jiaoyu* (Education Hong Kong Today). Guangzhou: Guangdong Education Press.

Wong, Kam Cheung (1995). "School management initiative in Hong Kong—The devolution of power to schools, real or rhetoric?" in K.C. Wong and K.M. Cheng (eds), *Educational Leadership and Change: An International Perspective*, pp. 141–154. Hong Kong: Hong Kong University Press.

Wong, R.H.K. (1974). *Educational Innovation in Singapore* (Experiments and Innovations in Education No. 9). Paris: The Unesco Press.

World Bank (1996). Preparation of an Implementation Plan for Human Resources Training and Capacity Building: Lao People's Democratic Republic, April (Vientiane: World Bank).

——(1998). *Education in Indonesia: From Crisis to Recovery* (Report No. 18651-IND). Washington, DC: World Bank.

Xue, L.R. and Shi, T.J. (2001). "Inequality in Chinese Education," *Journal of Contemporary China*, 10(26): 107–124.

Yang, D.P. (ed.) (2006). *Jiaoyu lanpishu: 2005 nian zhongguo jiaoyu fazhan baogao* (Blue Book of Education: The Development Report on China's Education, 2005). Beijing: Shehui kexue wenxian chu ban she.

Yang, J.Y. (2003). *Zhongguo dalu gaodeng jiaoyu zhi yanjiu* (The Study of China Higher Education). Taibei Shi: Gao deng jiao yu wen hua shi ye you xian gong si.

Yang, Key P. and Chee, Chang-boh (1963). "The North Korean educational system: 1945 to the present," in Robert Scalapino (ed.), *North Korea Today*, pp. 125–140. New York: Praeger.

Yang, Rui (2007). "China's soft power projection in higher education," *International Higher Education*, (46): 24.

Yau, Siu Kam, Leung, Kit Ling and Chow, Siu Lun (1993). *Xianggan Jiaoyu Fazhan: Bainian Shuren* (Education in Hong Kong: Past and Present). Hong Kong: Urban Council.

Yin, Q. and White, G. (2002). "The 'Marketisation' of Chinese higher education: A critical assessment," in F.N. Pieke (ed.), *People's Republic of China*, Vol. I, pp. 409–429. Aldershot, England/Burlington, VT: Ashgate.

Yip, J.S.K., Eng, S.P., and Yap, J.Y.C. (1990). "25 years of education reform," in J.S.K. Yip and W.K. Sim (eds.), *Evolution of Educational Excellence: 25 Years of Education in the Republic of Singapore*, pp. 1–30. Singapore: Longman.

Yonezawa, A. and Muta, H. (2001). "Financing junior secondary education in decentralized administrative structures: The Indonesian example," *Journal of International Cooperation in Education*, 4(2): 109–124.

Yong, B. (1995). "Teacher trainees' motives for entering into a teaching career in Brunei Darussalam," *Teaching and Teacher Education*, 11: 275–280.

Zahoor, Ahmad bin Haji Fazal Hussain (1969). "Malay education in Singapore," in T.R. Doraisamy (ed.), *150 Years of Education in Singapore*, pp. 100–115. Singapore: Teachers' Training College.

Zhang, Hui Zhen and Qiang, Sheng Kong (2005). *Cong Shiyiwan Dao Sanqian: Lunxian Shiqi Xianggang Jiaoyu Koushu Lishi* (From 110000 to 3000: Oral History on Hong Kong's Education under the Japanese Occupation). Hong Kong: Oxford University Press.

Zhang, Shan-Nan and Huang, Yi-Zhi (1997). "The causal relationship of ethnicity and academic achievement." Paper prepared for presentation at the International Conference for Educational Research on Education of Minority Groups, Han, and Aboriginal People. National Taitung University of Education, Taitung, Taiwan.

Zhang, T.D. and Zhao, M.X. (2006). "Universalizing nine-year compulsory education for poverty reduction in rural China," *Review of Education*, 52: 261–286.

Zheng, Y. (2001). The status of Confucianism in modern Chinese educry *China* (pp. 193–216). Hong Kong: Hong Kong University Press.

Zhong, N.S. and Hayhoe, R. (2001). "University autonomy in twentieth-century China," in Glen Peterson, Ruth Hayhoe, and Yongling Lu (eds), *Education, Culture, and Identity in Twentieth-century China*, pp. 265–296. Hong Kong: Hong Kong University Press.

Zhou, H.Y. and Chen, Q.B. (2003). "Zhongguo dalu yu Taiwan daxue gongshi jiaoyu kecheng de bijiao (A comparison of general education in universities between Mainland China and Taiwan)," in Koo Ding Yee, Ramsey, Wu Siu Wai, Li Siu Pang, and Titus (eds), *Jiao yu fa zhan yu ke cheng ge xin* (Education Development and Curriculum Innovations), pp. 46–58. Xianggang: Gang Ao er tong jiao yu guo ji xie hui.

Zhou, H.Y. and Shen, G.C. (2006). "Nongcun mianfei yiwu jiaoyu de tuijin (The promotion of free compulsory education in rural areas)," in Yang Dongbing (ed.), *Jiaoyu lanpishu: 2005 nian zhongguo jiaoyu fazhan baogao* (Blue Book of Education: The Development Report on China's Education, 2005), pp. 48–57. Beijing: Shehui kexue wenxian chu ban she.

Zhou, J.Y. (2006). "Zouxiang junheng fazhan de yiwu jiaoyu (Strive to balanced development of compulsory education)," in Yang Dongbing (ed.), *Jiaoyu lanpishu: 2005 nian zhongguo jiaoyu fazhan baogao* (Blue Book of Education: The Development Report on China's Education, 2005), pp. 58–71. Beijing: Shehui kexue wenxian chu ban she.

INDEX

ABOUT THE EDITORS AND CONTRIBUTORS

EDITORS

GERARD A. POSTIGLIONE is Professor and Head, Division of Policy, Administration and Social Sciences at the Faculty of Education of the University of Hong Kong. His research focuses on the social and cultural underpinnings of reform and development in China and East Asia. He was a researcher/consultant for projects of the Academy of Educational Development, Asian Development Bank, Carnegie Foundation for the Advancement of Teaching, Department for International Development, Institute of International Education, International Development Research Center, United Nations Development Program, and he was also a senior consultant to the Ford Foundation/Beijing. Postiglione is co-editor of the journal *Chinese Education and Society*, and was Director of Centre of Research on Education in China of the University of Hong Kong from 2000–2005. He has appeared on CNN and CCTV, and has been quoted in publications such as *The New York Times, International Herald Tribune, Business Week and Newsweek*, and writes for the Hong Kong English and Chinese language press. Among his other books are: *Asian Higher Education, Education and Social Change in China, China's National Minority Education*, and *Hong Kong's Reunion with China*. He is general editor of four book series: *Emerging Perspectives on Education in China, Education in China: Reform and Diversity, Hong Kong Becoming China*, and *Hong Kong Culture and Society*.

JASON TAN completed his Masters in Education in education and national development at the University of Hong Kong and his doctoral studies in comparative education at the State University of New York at Buffalo. He is currently associate professor in policy and leadership studies at the National Institute of Education in Singapore. Jason is an international editorial board member of several international journals, including *Asia Pacific Journal of Education, Journal of Studies in International Education* and *Globalisation, Societies and Education*. His most recent publications include *Globalization and Marketization of Education: A Comparative Analysis of Hong Kong and Singapore* and *Shaping Singapore's Future: Thinking Schools, Learning Nation*.

CONTRIBUTORS

AKIRA ARIMOTO is Director and Professor of the Research Institute for Higher Education, Graduate School of Education, Hiroshima University, Hiroshima, Japan. He got his Ph.D. in Education from the same university. He is an international expert in comparative and sociological study on academic reform, academic profession, academic productivity, and academic. He was recently a visiting professor at Research Institute for Faculty Development, Niigata University, Japan, and Research Institute for Higher Education, Xiamen University, China. Professor Arimoto is also President of Japanese Association of Higher Education Research (JAHER) and Chair of the Regional Scientific Committee for Asia and the Pacific and member of the Global Scientific Committee.

ERIKA BAT-ERDENE is currently an undergraduate student at the Ritsumeikan Asia Pacific University in Japan majoring in management. After attending school in Mongolia, she completed her last three years of secondary school at Taylor Alderdice High School in Pittsburgh, PA. This provided her with a unique opportunity to reflect on her schooling in the largest city in Mongolia as compared with her experience in a high school in a mid-sized American city.

REGSUREN BAT-ERDENE is Director of the Department of Higher and Vocational Education in the Ministry of Education, Culture and Science of Mongolia. Since the early 1990s, he has served in a variety of positions in Mongolian education, including State Secretary in the Ministry of Science, Technology, Education and Culture. He earned both a masters and a doctorate in higher education management from the University of Pittsburgh. He is the author of several articles and chapters on education in Mongolia.

J.A. BERLIE, an anthropologist, is a specialist dealing in Southeast Asia and China. He joined the Centre of Asian Studies, Hong Kong University in 1991. Many articles on education appeared in particular in the book he edited in 1999, entitled *Macao 2000*. He has carried out more than two years of research in East Timor. His main present interest is on Islam (*Islam in China*, 2004). Two books on East Timor politics and elections in Chinese societies is forthcoming in 2007, along with an article on Islamic education and another manuscript entitled *Myanmar's Muslims*.

SHEENA CHOI is an associate professor at Indiana University—Purdue University Fort Wayne, Fort Wayne, Indiana. As a comparative and international education specialist, her research interests include educational reforms with a focus on South Korea. Currently, she is studying higher education reforms, internationalization of higher education, and the New Universities of Regional Innovations (NURI) in South Korea. Her publications include a book, *Gender, Ethnicity, and Market Forces on Educational Choices: Ethnic Chinese in Korea* and various essays and articles, including "Globalization or Marketization?: The Dilemmas of International Schools in S. Korea" and "Citizenship, Education, and Identity Formation: Comparative Study of Ethnic Chinese in ROK and Koreans in PRC," both published in the *International Journal of Educational Reform.*

CHUING PRUDENCE CHOU was a visiting scholar at the Fairbank Center, Harvard University, on a Fulbright Fellowship, 2006–2007. She received a Ph.D. in Comparative and International Education from the University of California, Los Angeles, and is a professor in the Department of Education at National Cheng-Chi University, Taipei, Taiwan. Chou has worked in the fields of comparative higher education, special issues on education reform, and gender studies. She has written and edited numerous books, articles, reports, and papers in Chinese and English. Her teaching efforts focus on comparative education, special education issues in the People's Republic of China, gender equity education, and other special topics pertaining to higher education. She has also served as an education reform advocate since late 1990s. In addition, she plays an active role in critiquing/reviewing Taiwanese education reform of the 1990s and has published a book entitled *The Great Experiment of Taiwanese Education: 1987–2003*, a well-known and widely cited publication in Taiwan. She has been visiting professor at the University of Auckland (New Zealand), the University of Toronto and the University of British Columbia (Canada), Beijing Normal University and an Honorary Professor at the South Normal University in China. During her stay at the Fairbank Center, she conducted research within the broad context of American doctoral training of the younger generation of China specialists and attempted to see how these experts interpret the role/impact of their U.S.-based doctoral training on their later lives—both personally and socially. Chou has conducted interviews with individuals who have worked on China studies in China, Taiwan, and the United States.

RITA OSWALD CHRISTANO completed her MA in International Education from George Washington University, with a focus on educational reform in developing countries. Her research interests include the role and function of Islamic education in Indonesia as well as the effects of decentralization on Indonesia's education system. Prior to completing her graduate studies, Rita was employed as a middle school teacher in Chicago, IL.

THOMAS CLAYTON is Associate Professor of English and Linguistics at the University of Kentucky, where he teaches classes in applied linguistics and directs the Master of Arts in English with a Concentration in Teaching English as a

Second Language Program. In 1991, Clayton established the first U.S. university educational program in postwar Cambodia, the English Language Training Center for the State University of New York at Buffalo at the Cambodia Development Resource Institute. In 2000, he taught at the Faculty of Law and Economics in Phnom Penh as the first-ever Fulbright scholar to Cambodia. Professor Clayton has published more than two dozen articles on language and educational policy issues, often in the Cambodian context, in books and journals such as the *Comparative Education Review, the History of Education Quarterly, the International Journal of Educational Development, Language Policy, Language Problems and Language Planning,* and *South East Asia Research.* Clayton's first book, *Education and the Politics of Language: Hegemony and Pragmatism in Cambodia, 1979–1989* (2000), examines language and education in Cambodia during the Vietnamese occupation.

WILLIAM K. CUMMINGS is a Professor of International Education and International Affairs of The George Washington University. Dr. Cummings has been involved in development work for over 25 years, including long-term residence in Ethiopia, India, Indonesia, Japan, and Singapore, and short-term consultancies in over 15 countries in Asia, the Middle-East, Africa, Latin America, and Eastern Europe. His assignments have focused on evaluation and monitoring, policy analysis, sector assessment, management analysis (including strategies for enhancing decentralization and privatization), and teacher training. Along with applied work, Dr. Cummings has written extensively on the challenges of development and on models that describe successful development strategies. He has authored or edited over 100 articles and 20 books or monographs on education and development including *Policy-making for Education Reform in Developing Countries: Contexts and Processes,* with James H. Williams (2005); *Education and Equality in Japan; Values Education for Dynamic Societies* (2002) and *The Institutions of Education* (Symposium Books 2003). Dr. Cummings is past president of the Comparative and International Education Society.

PAUL DUMOL is Vice President for Academic Affairs of the University of Asia and the Pacific (UAP), Philippines, where he is an associate professor of the Department of History. He has a doctorate in Medieval Studies with specialization in philosophy from the University of Toronto, Canada. His book on Dante Alighieri's theory of the imagination was published by Peter Lang (1998). Before joining UAP, he worked for Southridge School, a grade school and high school, of which he was first Associate Director for Academic Formation and later Executive Director. He was Acting Dean of the School of Education of UAP from 1999 to 2002. He is also a playwright who writes in Tagalog. He was one of 100 Filipinos who received the Centennial Honors for the Arts from the Cultural Center of the Philippines on the occasion of the Centennial of Philippine Independence (1999).

MANYNOOCH FAMING is a candidate for the Ph.D. in anthropology at the University of Hong Kong. She is currently completing a dissertation on ethnic minority education in Laos, entitled *National Integration: Education for Ethnic Minorities of the Lao PDR*.

AI-HSIN HO completed her conjoint BA degree in Education and Business Administration at the National Chengchi University, Taiwan. During her undergraduate studies, she had worked for three years as a research assistant to Professor Chuing Chou at the Chengchi University. After working as a project manager in a business consultant corporation upon graduation, she completed her M.Ed. Leadership (Master of Educational Leadership) with first class honors at the University of Waikato in New Zealand. She is currently a doctoral candidate in the Doctor of Education programme at the University of Waikato. She has been teaching assistant and tutor at the masters level in the School of Education since 2004. Her research interests include educational leadership, beginning teachers, comparative studies, and internationalization in higher education. She is completing her doctoral thesis exploring international or cross-cultural partnerships between New Zealand and some Asian countries. She has maintained enormous research interest in the great Chinese context although she has chosen New Zealand as her second home.

YOON-YOUNG KIM is a Ph.D. candidate in the Department of Anthropology at the University of Hawai'i. She wrote an M.A. thesis in the Department of Cultural Anthropology at Hanyang University, Korea in 2002, entitled, "School Life and Identity of North Korean Refugees in South Korea." Her research interests surround the issues of cultural adaptation, refugee studies, diaspora and immigration, and multi ethnic education, with particular focus on North Korean refugees' transition from socialism to capitalism in the Republic of Korea. She continually has conducted research on the development of educational adaptation program for North Korean refugees in the Republic of Korea.

WING-WAH LAW is Associate Professor in the Faculty of Education, The University of Hong Kong. His research interests include education and development; globalization and education reforms; higher education; citizenship education; values education and curriculum; and education in Chinese societies including Mainland China, Hong Kong and Taiwan.

JONATHAN D. LONDON is Assistant Professor of Sociology in the Division of Sociology, School for Social Sciences and Humanities, Nanyang Technological University, in Singapore. He worked in Viet Nam between 1997 and 2000 and now travels there regularly. London received his Ph.D. in Sociology from the University of Wisconsin-Madison.

SENG PIEW LOO was an Associate Professor at the School of Educational Studies, Universiti Sains Malaysia. Currently Loo is a faculty member of the

Sultan Hassanal Bolkiah Institute of Education, Universiti Brunei Darussalam. He has written articles on comparative education, culture and science, and comparative philosophy of science in leading journals such as the *International Journal of Science Education, Science and Education*, and *Studies in Science Education*. He is the winner of the 2006 International Association of Universities/Palgrave Essay Prize in Higher Education Policy Research. The essay, "The Two Cultures of Science: On Language-Culture Incommensurability Concerning 'Nature' and 'Observation,' " was published in Volume 20, Number 1 of *Higher Education Policy* in 2007.

MARIA MANZON is a doctoral student in comparative education at the Faculty of Education of the University of Hong Kong. She is a member of the management committee of the Comparative Education Research Centre (CERC) at the University of Hong Kong and had collaborated in various projects of the World Council of Comparative Education Societies (WCCES). She initially studied in the Philippines and in Italy, and then graduated with distinction from the MEd programme in Comparative Education at the University of Hong Kong. Her thesis "Building Alliances: Schools, Parents and Communities in Hong Kong and Singapore" was published in 2004. Her publications and research interests focus on comparative education, sociology of knowledge, and on home-school partnerships.

GAY GARLAND REED is an Associate Professor in the Department of Educational Foundations at the University of Hawai'i. She received her M.Ed. (1987) & Ph.D. (1991) in Social Foundations of Education from the University of Virginia. Besides the United States, she has also taught in China, Korea, the United Arab Emirates, Iran, and American Samoa. Currently she teaches courses in Multicultural Education, Social and Cultural Contexts of Education and Foundations of Education at the graduate and undergraduate levels. Her research and publications focus on moral/political education in China, Korea and the United States, multicultural education, identity construction, globalization and education, and the intersection of cultural values and education.

PAITOON SINLARAT is Associate Professor at Chulalongkorn University and formerly Dean of the Faculty of Education at that University. He received his B.Ed. and M.Ed. degrees in Education from Chulalongkorn University in Thailand. He earned his Ph.D. from the University of Pittsburgh. He has conducted research mostly on history and philosophy of Thai education. His recent publications include *Creative and Productive Education and Higher Education in Thailand: Critical Perspectives*.

KENG CHAN SOPHEAK received her Ph.D. in international development studies from Nagoya University. She currently teaches in the Master of Development Studies Program at the Royal University of Phnom Penh, in Cambodia.

ANTONIO TORRALBA is an Associate Professor in Education and is Arts and Sciences dean of the University of Asia and the Pacific, Philippines. He finished his Doctor of Philosophy in Philosophy, with specialization in Pedagogy, *sobresaliente*, at the Universidad de Navarra in Pamplona, Spain (1977). He has founded several schools and education entities and has taught in all levels of education, from grade school to graduate school. He serves as consultant for the Philippine Department of Education, the Commission on Higher Education (CHED), and the Technical Education and Skills Development Authority (TESDA), and local governments in teacher and curriculum development and the organization of national and international congresses, conferences, and research projects in education.

STEPHEN G. UPEX was born in England and completed his first degree at London University and then moved to Nottingham where he wrote a Ph.D. on medieval agricultural history. He taught for several years in schools and colleges before moving to become a university lecturer. He worked at the University of Brunei Darussalam for ten years where he developed an interest in South East Asian affairs and traveled extensively through much of the region dealt with in this book. He has written widely on educational and geographical topics in Asia as well as publishing many articles on aspects of the archaeology and landscape history of Britain. His book on early settlement and agriculture in England is due to be published in early 2007. Dr. Upex now lives in Britain where he is a freelance archaeologist and writer.

JOHN C. WEIDMAN is Professor of Higher Education and of Sociology as well as Director, Institute of International Studies in Education (IISE), at the University of Pittsburgh. He has held the UNESCO Chair of Higher Education Research at Maseno University College in Kenya and been a Fulbright Scholar and Visiting Professor of the Sociology of Education at the University of Augsburg in Germany. He has been working on Asian Development Bank projects in Mongolia since 1993, including assisting with all three education master plans and the establishment of the national agency for higher education accreditation. He has written extensively on education in Mongolia.

ZHENZHOU ZHAO is currently teaching at the School of education, Beijing Normal University. Her research interests include social development in education, civic and moral education, and ethnic and women's studies. She received a bachelors degree from the Beijing Normal University and a Ph.D. from the University of Hong Kong. Her Ph.D. dissertation is on ethnic minority education in the PRC, entitled " 'Am I Privileged?': Ethnic Mongol Students and Cultural Recognition in Chinese Universities." Her English publications include *Cultural Representation and China's University Media: An Analysis of Discourse on Ethnic Minorities* (2006), *Ethnic Identity at University: Mongolian Students in Beijing* (2005), and *Children, Gender, and Language Teaching Materials* (2002).